1 MONTH OF
FREE
READING

at

www.ForgottenBooks.com

By purchasing this book you are eligible for one month membership to ForgottenBooks.com, giving you unlimited access to our entire collection of over 1,000,000 titles via our web site and mobile apps.

To claim your free month visit: www.forgottenbooks.com/free84125

* Offer is valid for 45 days from date of purchase. Terms and conditions apply.

ISBN 978-0-267-81199-1
PIBN 10084125

This book is a reproduction of an important historical work. Forgotten Books uses state-of-the-art technology to digitally reconstruct the work, preserving the original format whilst repairing imperfections present in the aged copy. In rare cases, an imperfection in the original, such as a blemish or missing page, may be replicated in our edition. We do, however, repair the vast majority of imperfections successfully; any imperfections that remain are intentionally left to preserve the state of such historical works.

Forgotten Books is a registered trademark of FB &c Ltd.
Copyright © 2018 FB &c Ltd.
FB &c Ltd, Dalton House, 60 Windsor Avenue, London, SW19 2RR.
Company number 08720141. Registered in England and Wales.

For support please visit www.forgottenbooks.com

Captain Cook's

Voyages Round the World

WITH

AN INTRODUCTORY LIFE

BY

M. B. SYNGE

THOMAS NELSON AND SONS
London, Edinburgh, and New York

1897

G
420
C62 S80
1897

PREFACE.

THE following Three Voyages of Captain Cook are taken direct from the folio volumes of his own journals, and but slightly abridged. By kind permission of Messrs. Elliot Stock, we have made use of Captain Cook's journal during his first voyage round the world, made in H.M. barque *Endeavour*, 1768-71—a literal transcription of the original MSS., edited by Captain W. J. L. Wharton, R.N., F.R.S., Hydrographer of the Admiralty, published in 1893.

This has greatly added to the value of the present edition, and we would acknowledge with thanks the generosity of Messrs. Elliot Stock.

CONTENTS.

LIFE OF CAPTAIN COOK..i

First Voyage.

CHAPTER I.
PASSAGE FROM PLYMOUTH TO MADEIRA, AND FROM MADEIRA TO RIO DE JANEIRO—THE PASSAGE FROM RIO DE JANEIRO TO THE ENTRANCE OF THE STRAIT OF LE MAIRE 11

CHAPTER II.
EXPEDITION IN SEARCH OF PLANTS—PASSAGE THROUGH THE STRAIT OF LE MAIRE—SEQUEL OF THE PASSAGE FROM CAPE HORN TO THE NEWLY-DISCOVERED ISLANDS IN THE SOUTH SEAS 20

CHAPTÉR III.
ARRIVAL OF THE "ENDEAVOUR" AT OTAHEITE OR KING GEORGE THE THIRD'S ISLAND 31

CHAPTER IV.
OBSERVATION OF THE TRANSIT OF VENUS—TRANSACTIONS AND INCIDENTS AT OTAHEITE—CIRCUMNAVIGATION OF THE ISLAND—MR. BANKS'S EXPEDITION—DISAPPEARANCE OF TWO MEN.. 43

CHAPTER V.
DESCRIPTION OF THE ISLAND—ITS PEOPLE, HABITS, AND CUSTOMS—VISITS TO HUÁHEINÉ, ULIETEA (RAIATEA), OTAHA (TAHAA), BOLABOLA—DEPARTURE FROM THE SOCIETY ISLANDS FOR NEW ZEALAND 56

CHAPTER VI.
PASSAGE FROM SOCIETY ISLES TO NEW ZEALAND—INCIDENTS WHICH HAPPENED WHILE THE SHIP LAY IN POVERTY BAY—DEPARTURE FROM POVERTY BAY.. 72

CHAPTER VII.
THE RANGE FROM POVERTY BAY TO CAPE TURNAGAIN, AND BACK TO TOLAGO, WITH SOME ACCOUNT OF THE PEOPLE AND THE COUNTRY........................ 84

CONTENTS.

CHAPTER VIII.
FROM MERCURY BAY TO THE BAY OF ISLANDS—EXPEDITION UP THE RIVER THAMES—INTERVIEWS WITH THE NATIVES—RANGE FROM THE BAY OF ISLANDS ROUND NORTH CAPE TO QUEEN CHARLOTTE'S SOUND.................. 98

CHAPTER IX.
TRANSACTIONS IN QUEEN CHARLOTTE'S SOUND—PASSAGE THROUGH COOK'S STRAIT AND BACK TO CAPE TURNAGAIN—FROM CAPE TURNAGAIN SOUTHWARD, ROUND CAPE SOUTH, AND BACK TO THE WESTERN ENTRANCE OF COOK'S STRAIT .... .109

CHAPTER X.
A GENERAL ACCOUNT OF NEW ZEALAND—PASSAGE FROM NEW ZEALAND TO BOTANY BAY ON THE EAST COAST OF NEW HOLLAND (NEW SOUTH WALES)—AN ACCOUNT OF BOTANY BAY. 119

CHAPTER XI.
RANGE FROM BOTANY BAY TO TRINITY BAY, WITH A FURTHER ACCOUNT OF THE COUNTRY, ETC.—DANGEROUS SITUATION OF THE SHIP IN HER COURSE FROM TRINITY BAY TO ENDEAVOUR RIVER—APPEARANCE OF SCURVY........130

CHAPTER XII.
TRANSACTIONS WHILE THE SHIP WAS REFITTING IN ENDEAVOUR RIVER.............144

CHAPTER XIII.
THE SHIP IN DANGER OFF THE BARRIER REEFS—PASSAGE FROM PROVIDENTIAL CHANNEL TO ENDEAVOUR STRAITS 157

CHAPTER XIV.
DEPARTURE FROM NEW SOUTH WALES—DESCRIPTION OF THE COUNTRY, PEOPLE, ETC.—PASSAGE FROM NEW SOUTH WALES TO NEW GUINEA—PASSAGE FROM NEW GUINEA TO THE ISLAND OF SAVU 165

CHAPTER XV.
THE RUN FROM THE ISLAND OF SAVU TO BATAVIA—TRANSACTIONS AT BATAVIA WHILE THE SHIP WAS REFITTING..178

CHAPTER XVI.
SOME ACCOUNT OF BATAVIA—PASSAGE FROM BATAVIA TO THE CAPE OF GOOD HOPE—PRINCE'S ISLAND—CAPE OF GOOD HOPE AND ST. HELENA—RETURN OF THE SHIP TO ENGLAND...................................... 186

Second Voyage.

CHAPTER XVII.
PASSAGE FROM DEPTFORD TO THE CAPE OF GOOD HOPE, WITH AN ACCOUNT OF SEVERAL INCIDENTS THAT HAPPENED BY THE WAY AND TRANSACTIONS THERE... 193

CONTENTS.

CHAPTER XVIII.

DEPARTURE FROM THE CAPE OF GOOD HOPE IN SEARCH OF A SOUTHERN CONTINENT—SEPARATION OF THE TWO SHIPS—ARRIVAL OF THE "RESOLUTION" IN DUSKY BAY..................198

CHAPTER XIX.

TRANSACTIONS IN DUSKY BAY..................203

CHAPTER XX.

PASSAGE FROM DUSKY BAY TO QUEEN CHARLOTTE'S SOUND, WITH AN ACCOUNT OF SOME WATER-SPOUTS, AND OF OUR JOINING THE "ADVENTURE"—CAPTAIN FURNEAUX'S NARRATIVE..................216

CHAPTER XXI.

TRANSACTIONS IN QUEEN CHARLOTTE'S SOUND, WITH SOME REMARKS ON THE INHABITANTS—ROUTE FROM NEW ZEALAND TO OTAHEITE..................223

CHAPTER XXII.

THE ARRIVAL OF THE SHIPS AT OTAHEITE, WITH AN ACCOUNT OF THE CRITICAL SITUATION THEY WERE IN, AND OF SEVERAL INCIDENTS THAT HAPPENED WHILE THEY LAY IN OAITI-PIHA BAY—AN ACCOUNT OF SEVERAL VISITS TO AND FROM OTOO, OF GOATS BEING LEFT ON THE ISLAND, AND MANY OTHER PARTICULARS WHICH HAPPENED WHILE THE SHIPS LAY IN MATAVAI BAY..234

CHAPTER XXIII.

AN ACCOUNT OF THE RECEPTION WE MET WITH AT HUAHEINE, WITH THE INCIDENTS THAT HAPPENED WHILE THE SHIPS LAY THERE, AND OF OMAI, ONE OF THE NATIVES, COMING AWAY IN THE "ADVENTURE"—ARRIVAL AT AND DEPARTURE OF THE SHIPS FROM ULIETEA, WITH AN ACCOUNT OF WHAT HAPPENED THERE, AND OF OEDIDEE, ONE OF THE NATIVES, COMING AWAY IN THE "RESOLUTION."..................241

CHAPTER XXIV.

PASSAGE FROM ULIETEA TO THE FRIENDLY ISLANDS, WITH AN ACCOUNT OF THE DISCOVERY OF HERVEY'S ISLAND AND THE INCIDENTS THAT HAPPENED AT MIDDLEBURG—THE ARRIVAL OF THE SHIPS AT AMSTERDAM; A DESCRIPTION OF A PLACE OF WORSHIP, AND AN ACCOUNT OF THE INCIDENTS WHICH HAPPENED WHILE THEY REMAINED AT THAT ISLAND—A DESCRIPTION OF THE ISLANDS, THEIR PRODUCE, ETC...................247

CHAPTER XXV.

PASSAGE FROM AMSTERDAM TO QUEEN CHARLOTTE'S SOUND, WITH AN ACCOUNT OF AN INTERVIEW WITH THE INHABITANTS, AND THE FINAL SEPARATION OF THE TWO SHIPS—TRANSACTIONS IN QUEEN CHARLOTTE'S SOUND, WITH AN ACCOUNT OF THE INHABITANTS BEING CANNIBALS, AND VARIOUS OTHER INCIDENTS—DEPARTURE FROM THE SOUND, AND OUR ENDEAVOURS TO FIND THE "ADVENTURE," WITH SOME DESCRIPTION OF THE COAST..................258

CHAPTER XXVI.

ROUTE OF THE SHIP FROM NEW ZEALAND IN SEARCH OF A CONTINENT, WITH AN ACCOUNT OF VARIOUS OBSTRUCTIONS MET WITH FROM THE ICE, AND THE METHODS PURSUED TO EXPLORE THE SOUTHERN PACIFIC OCEAN—PASSAGE TO EASTER ISLAND AND TRANSACTIONS THERE—PASSAGE FROM EASTER ISLAND TO THE MARQUESAS ISLANDS—DEPARTURE FROM THE MARQUESAS..................266

CHAPTER XXVII.

PREPARATIONS TO LEAVE THE ISLAND—THE ARRIVAL OF THE SHIP AT THE ISLAND OF HUAHEINE, WITH AN ACCOUNT OF SEVERAL INCIDENTS WHICH HAPPENED WHILE SHE LAY THERE—ARRIVAL AT ULIETEA...............276

CHAPTER XXVIII.

PASSAGE FROM ULIETEA TO NEW ZEALAND—DISCOVERY OF HOWE ISLAND, PALMERSTON ISLAND, SAVAGE ISLAND—RECEPTION AT ANNAMOOKA—THE PASSAGE FROM THE FRIENDLY ISLES TO THE NEW HEBRIDES—DISCOVERY OF TURTLE ISLAND AND THE ISLAND OF MALLICOLLO—ARRIVAL OF THE SHIP AT TANNA—RECEPTION..................281

CHAPTER XXIX.

DEPARTURE FROM TANNA—SOME ACCOUNTS OF ITS INHABITANTS—DISCOVERY OF NEW CALEDONIA, AND INCIDENTS THAT HAPPENED WHILE THE SHIP LAY IN BALADE—THE ISLE OF PINES—DEPARTURE FOR NEW ZEALAND.............289

CHAPTER XXX.

PASSAGE FROM NEW CALEDONIA TO NEW ZEALAND, WITH AN ACCOUNT OF THE DISCOVERY OF NORFOLK ISLAND, AND THE INCIDENTS THAT HAPPENED WHILE THE SHIP LAY AT QUEEN CHARLOTTE'S SOUND—FROM NEW ZEALAND TO TIERRA DEL FUEGO—TRANSACTIONS IN CHRISTMAS SOUND—RANGE FROM CHRISTMAS SOUND, ROUND CAPE HORN, THROUGH STRAIT LE MAIRE, AND ROUND STATEN LAND..................296

CHAPTER XXXI.

DISCOVERY OF THE ISLE OF GEORGIA—PROCEEDINGS AFTER LEAVING THE ISLE OF GEORGIA, AND AN ACCOUNT OF THE DISCOVERY OF SANDWICH LAND; WITH SOME REASONS FOR THERE BEING LAND ABOUT THE SOUTH POLE—AN ACCOUNT OF OUR PROCEEDINGS TILL OUR ARRIVAL AT THE CAPE OF GOOD HOPE..................304

CHAPTER XXXII.

CAPTAIN FURNEAUX'S NARRATIVE OF HIS PROCEEDINGS IN THE "ADVENTURE," INCLUDING LIEUTENANT BURNEY'S REPORT CONCERNING THE BOAT'S CREW WHO WERE MURDERED BY THE INHABITANTS OF QUEEN CHARLOTTE'S SOUND..................312

CHAPTER XXXIII.

TRANSACTIONS AT THE CAPE OF GOOD HOPE—ARRIVAL OF THE SHIP AT ST. HELENA—PASSAGE FROM ST. HELENA TO THE WESTERN ISLANDS, WITH AN ACCOUNT OF THE ISLAND OF ASCENSION AND FERNANDO NORONHA—ARRIVAL AT THE ISLAND OF FAYAL—THE RETURN OF THE "RESOLUTION" TO ENGLAND...320

Third Voyage.

CHAPTER XXXIV.
PREPARATION FOR THE VOYAGE—OMAI'S BEHAVIOUR ON EMBARKING—INSTRUCTIONS TO CAPTAIN COOK—DEPARTURE OF THE "RESOLUTION".........327

CHAPTER XXXV.
ARRIVAL OF THE "RESOLUTION" AT TENERIFFE—DEPARTURE FROM TENERIFFE—DANGER OF THE SHIP NEAR BONAVISTA—ARRIVAL AT THE CAPE OF GOOD HOPE—THE TWO SHIPS LEAVE THE CAPE OF GOOD HOPE—ARRIVAL IN CHRISTMAS HARBOUR—PASSAGE TO VAN DIEMEN'S LAND—FROM VAN DIEMEN'S LAND TO NEW ZEALAND—TRANSACTIONS WITH THE NATIVES......335

CHAPTER XXXVI.
PROSECUTION OF THE VOYAGE—AN ISLAND CALLED MANGEEA DISCOVERED—THE DISCOVERY OF AN ISLAND CALLED WATEEOO—MR. ANDERSON'S NARRATIVE—OTAKOOTAIA VISITED—HERVEY'S ISLAND FOUND TO BE INHABITED—PALMERSTON'S ISLAND TOUCHED AT—REFRESHMENTS OBTAINED—ARRIVAL AT THE FRIENDLY ISLANDS.........346

CHAPTER XXXVII.
ARRIVAL AT ANNAMOOKA—TRANSACTIONS THERE—ARRIVAL OF THE SHIPS AT HAPAEE, AND FRIENDLY RECEPTION—ENTERTAINMENTS—POULAHO, KING OF THE FRIENDLY ISLES—RETURN TO ANNAMOOKA—ARRIVAL AT TONGATABU.........356

CHAPTER XXXVIII.
FRIENDLY RECEPTION AT TONGATABU—ENTERTAINMENT GIVEN BY MAREEWAGEE—ECLIPSE OF THE SUN—ACCOUNT OF THE ISLAND—DEPARTURE FROM TONGATABU—ARRIVAL AT EOOA—ACCOUNT OF THAT ISLAND—ACCOUNT OF THE FRIENDLY ISLES.........368

CHAPTER XXXIX.
THE ISLAND TOOBOUAI DISCOVERED—ARRIVAL IN OHEITEPEHA BAY AT OTAHEITE—OMAI'S RECEPTION—INTERVIEW WITH OTOO, KING OF THE ISLAND—HUMAN SACRIFICE—OTOO'S PRESENT TO THE KING OF GREAT BRITAIN—DEPARTURE FROM OTAHEITE.........380

CHAPTER XL.
ARRIVAL AT EIMEO—ARRIVAL AT HUAHEINE—COUNCIL OF CHIEFS—OMAI'S ESTABLISHMENT IN THE ISLAND AGREED TO—A HOUSE BUILT FOR HIM—ARRIVAL AT ULIETEA—ARRIVAL AT BOLABOLA.........392

CHAPTER XLI.
PROGRESS OF THE VOYAGE AFTER LEAVING THE SOCIETY ISLANDS—CHRISTMAS ISLAND DISCOVERED—ACCOUNT OF THE ISLAND—DISCOVERY OF THE SANDWICH ISLANDS—SOME ACCOUNT OF ATOOI.........407

xiv   CONTENTS.

CHAPTER XLII.
PROSECUTION OF THE VOYAGE—ARRIVAL ON THE COAST OF AMERICA—THE SHIPS ENTER ST. GEORGE'S SOUND, OR NOOTKA—TRANSACTIONS WITH THE NATIVES—SOME ACCOUNT OF NOOTKA AND ITS INHABITANTS. 424

CHAPTER XLIII.
THE SHIPS LEAVE NOOTKA SOUND—TRANSACTIONS IN PRINCE WILLIAM'S SOUND—PROGRESS ALONG THE COAST—DISCOVERY OF COOK'S RIVER................. 439

CHAPTER XLIV.
PROGRESS NORTHWARD AFTER LEAVING OONALASHKA—DEATH OF MR. ANDERSON, THE SURGEON—THE COUNTRY OF THE TSCHUTSKI—THE SHIPS CROSS THE STRAIT TO THE COAST OF AMERICA—SITUATION OF ICY CAPE—SEA-HORSES—THE SEA BLOCKED UP WITH ICE—CAPE NORTH 453

CHAPTER XLV.
RETURN FROM CAPE NORTH ALONG THE COAST OF ASIA—THE TSCHUTSKI—BAY OF ST. LAWRENCE—NORTON SOUND—ACCOUNT OF THE SETTLEMENT AT OONALASHKA—DEPARTURE FROM OONALASHKA—ARRIVAL AT OWHYHEE, ONE OF THE SANDWICH ISLANDS 463

CHAPTER XLVI.
DESCRIPTION OF KARAKAKOOA BAY—VAST CONCOURSE OF NATIVES—VISIT FROM KOAH—THE MÓRAI AT KAKOOA DESCRIBED—CEREMONIES AT THE LANDING OF CAPTAIN COOK—RECEPTION OF CAPTAIN COOK—ARRIVAL OF TERREEOBOO, KING OF THE ISLAND—VISIT FROM THE KING—RETURNED BY CAPTAIN COOK 480

CHAPTER XLVII.
FURTHER TRANSACTIONS WITH THE NATIVES—THEIR HOSPITALITY—DEATH OF ONE OF OUR SEAMEN—THE WOODWORK AND IMAGES ON THE MORAI PURCHASED—MAGNIFICENT PRESENTS OF TERREEOBOO TO CAPTAIN COOK—THE SHIPS LEAVE THE ISLAND—THE "RESOLUTION" DAMAGED IN A GALE AND OBLIGED TO RETURN 492

CHAPTER XLVIII.
SUSPICIOUS BEHAVIOUR OF THE NATIVES ON OUR RETURN TO KARAKAKOOA BAY—THEFT ON BOARD THE "DISCOVERY"—THE PINNACE ATTACKED—THE CUTTER OF THE "DISCOVERY" STOLEN—MEASURES TAKEN BY CAPTAIN COOK FOR ITS RECOVERY—NEWS ARRIVES OF ONE OF THE CHIEFS BEING KILLED BY OUR PEOPLE—FERMENT ON THIS OCCASION—ONE OF THE NATIVES THREATENS CAPTAIN COOK, AND IS SHOT BY HIM—GENERAL ATTACK BY THE NATIVES—DEATH OF CAPTAIN COOK 503

LIST OF ILLUSTRATIONS.

PORTRAIT OF CAPTAIN COOK,	*Frontispiece.*
MAP OF POLYNESIA,	31
THE TRANSIT OF VENUS,	45
NATIVE HOUSE, OTAHEITE,	60
MAP OF NEW ZEALAND,	74
NEW ZEALANDER,	121
WAR CANOE, NEW ZEALAND,	122
MAP OF AUSTRALIA,	124
AUSTRALIAN LANDSCAPE WITH KANGAROOS,	148
WHITE GUM TREE, AUSTRALIA,	166
TABLE BAY, CAPE OF GOOD HOPE,	189
AMONG THE ICE ISLANDS,	200
DANCING WOMAN, OTAHEITE,	240
DOUBLE CANOE OF TONGATABU,	254
WOMAN OF EASTER ISLAND,	271
STATUES ON EASTER ISLAND,	271
MAP OF THE NEW HEBRIDES, ETC.,	290
SCENE IN NEW CALEDONIA,	292
COAST OF VAN DIEMEN'S LAND,	338
SCENE IN ATOOI, SANDWICH ISLANDS,	411
SURF-SWIMMING, SANDWICH ISLANDS,	419
MAN OF NOOTKA SOUND,	432
WOMAN OF NOOTKA SOUND,	433
MAN OF PRINCE WILLIAM'S SOUND,	442
WOMAN OF PRINCE WILLIAM'S SOUND,	442
MOWEE, SANDWICH ISLANDS,	472
DEATH OF CAPTAIN COOK,	509

LIFE OF CAPTAIN COOK.
1728-1779.

JAMES COOK was born in the little village of Marton, on the edge of the Cleveland Hills, on October 27, 1728. His father, James Cook, was in the humble station of a "servant in husbandry." He married a woman of the same rank with himself, whose Christian name was Grace. Both of them were noted in their neighbourhood for their honesty, sobriety, and diligence. "The mud house in which Captain Cook drew his first breath" no longer exists, and the only relic of his childhood is a pump called "Captain Cook's pump," constructed, it is said, by his father. The first rudiments of young Cook's education were received by him at Marton, where he was taught to read by Dame Walker, the schoolmistress of the village.

When he was eight years old, his father, "in consequence of the character he had obtained for industry, frugality, and skill in husbandry," had a little promotion bestowed on him, and he removed with his family to the village of Great Ayton, some five miles from Marton. Here James was put to a day-school, where he was instructed in "writing, and in a few of the first rules of arithmetic." Before he was thirteen years of age, he was bound an apprentice to one Sanderson, a shopkeeper at Staithes, a considerable fishing village some nine miles north of Whitby.

No more unsuitable employment could have been found for the boy. To go to sea was the object of his life; and his passion for it must have been strengthened by the situation of the village in which he was placed, and the conversation of those amongst whom he was chiefly known.

Apprentices slept under the counter in those days, and James

Cook was no exception. In the mornings he swept out and arranged the shop, ate his breakfast—which consisted of a "hunch of bread, a lump of fat bacon, and a mug of small ale"—and all day long fetched, carried, and waited on his master. When his hours of work were over he would listen to the fishermen's yarns of the sea. He soon knew all about the men who fished all night for herrings, of those who had gone to the Arctic seas in whalers and had met with perils among the ice, of those who had been pressed into King George's service, fought His Majesty's battles, and returned with backs bearing marks of the captain's discipline. He knew about the clumsy boats that went to sea, too clumsy to answer their helm; of the foul water to drink, salt junk to eat; of the sufferings from scurvy and brutality of commanders; but notwithstanding all this, a great longing seized the boy to go to sea.

At last a time came when shop work became intolerable to him. He tied up his few belongings—one shirt and a jack-knife—in his only handkerchief, and one July morning, at daybreak, he stole out of the shop, passed down the narrow street, and started off to walk the nine miles to Whitby.

His master woke at six, found the shop shutters still closed, the shop unswept, and crept to the corner for the stick which daily admonished his apprentice; but the boy was gone, the blanket thrown back, the sacking on which he lay crumpled up. He never inquired where he had gone. All his apprentices ran away to sea sooner or later: James Cook was not likely to prove an exception.

Arrived at Whitby, James Cook was taken as ship's boy on board the *Freelove*, a collier belonging to the brothers Walker. The period following this is dark and obscure; all details of his life between 1742 and 1755 are lost. We do not know what voyages he made, or between which ports he traded. Only one thing is certain—in these thirteen years Cook learned thoroughly the duties of a sailor. He learned to endure the utmost hardships of the sea: constant fighting with North Sea gales, bad food, and fierce encounters with storm and danger, taught him to treat with indifference the hardships he endured later, enabled him to persevere when others were ready to give up.

On this collier vessel he seems to have served till 1755, when he had already risen to the position of mate.

War breaking out between England and France in this year, and there consequently being a great demand for sailors, James Cook entered His Majesty's service as an "able seaman," and was at once sent on board the *Eagle*, bound for North America. Captain Hugh Palliser, who succeeded to the command of the *Eagle* in October, marked the young sailor as one full of promise; and by his interest Cook was, at the age of thirty, given command of the *Mercury*, with orders to join the English fleet then engaged in the siege of Quebec.

The *Mercury* went to North America, where she joined the fleet which, with the land forces under General Wolfe, was engaged in the siege of Quebec. During that siege a difficult and dangerous service had to be performed. This was to take the soundings in the channel of the river St. Lawrence directly in the front of the French fortified camp, in order to enable the admiral to place ships against the enemy's batteries, and to cover our army in a general attack which Wolfe intended to make on the camp.

Cook was chosen for this service, and he performed it, we are told, "in the most complete manner." He was employed during the night-time for several nights together. At length he was discovered by the enemy, who collected a great number of Indians and canoes in a wood near the water-side for the purpose of surrounding him and cutting him off. On this occasion he had a very narrow escape. He was obliged to run for it, and pushed on shore near the guard of the English hospital. Some of the Indians entered at the stern of the boat as Cook leaped out at the bow; and the boat, which was a barge belonging to one of the ships of war, was carried away in triumph. However, he presented the admiral with a correct and complete draft of the channel and soundings, though he had hardly ever used a pencil and knew nothing of drawing. "But such was his capacity," says his old biographer, "that he speedily made himself master of every object to which he applied his attention."

He was immediately employed in making a survey of the intricate channels of the river St. Lawrence below Quebec; and again he was so successful that his chart of the river was published with soundings and directions for sailing. "And," adds his biographer proudly, "of the accuracy and utility of this chart it is sufficient to say that it hath never since been found necessary to publish any other."

How Cook obtained all the knowledge he did there is no record to show; but there is no other case of a sailor boy of humble birth starting in the lowest place, being promoted to the rank of "master" in the king's navy at the age of thirty, and moreover selected for a piece of work needing considerable experience.

He was at this time over six feet high. His face was remarkable for its patience, resolution, and perseverance; his eyes were quick and piercing, with large bushy eyebrows; his face was long and thin; his hair was rolled back and tied behind in a "pigtail," after the fashion of his time. Possessed of a strong constitution, he was capable of enduring the severest hardships. He could eat the coarsest food. He desired no better fare than he served to his men. With them he would "labour hard till sunset;" with them he would "sleep on a stony beach," or struggle with frozen ropes.

On the 22nd of September 1759 Cook was appointed master of the *Northumberland* man-of-war, bearing the admiral's flag. Wintering at Halifax, he set himself to learn Euclid, astronomy, and other branches of science. The *Northumberland* returned to England in 1762. About Christmas the same year Cook married Elizabeth Batts, "an amiable and deserving woman, who was justly entitled to enjoy his tenderest regard and affection." Four months later, he was called on to make marine surveys about Newfoundland. A schooner, the *Grenville*, was placed under his command, and he spent four years in making out charts, which were so admirable in execution that they have not yet been wholly superseded by the surveys of modern times. Whilst there, too, he wrote a short paper, "An Observation of the Eclipse of the Sun at the Island of Newfoundland, August 5, 1766, with the Longitude of the Place of Observation deduced from it."

And this was the work of one who, twenty-five years before, had tied a shirt and a jack-knife up in his handkerchief, and run away to sea to take his place as cabin-boy on board a collier ship!

And his life was yet before him.

Cook returned to England in 1767 to find a keen interest

awakening in men's minds with regard to the great unknown Pacific Ocean. True, the century had produced explorers and navigators : the names of Anson, Byron, Willis, Carteret stand out in connection with hitherto unknown islands and unexplored continents. But navigation at this time was fraught with dangers undreamed of now, and one by one the ships returned, their crews dying from the scourge of the sailor's life, scurvy. Each voyage tells its own story—limited water, contrary winds, inability to get fresh food, and consequent outbreak of scurvy, put an end to each expedition in turn.

James Cook too had to buy his experience.

In 1768 a new expedition was planned to the Pacific Ocean, and Cook, raised to the rank of lieutenant, was singled out for the command. He was also to observe the approaching transit of Venus over the sun's disc from the island of Otaheite the following year. Allowed to choose his own ship, he returned to his old friends at Whitby and selected the *Endeavour*, a strong, stoutly-built collier of 370 tons, designed perhaps more for safety in bad weather than for speed. With a crew of ninety-four men, and provisions for ten months, the *Endeavour* sailed from Plymouth Sound on August 26, 1768.

Precautions against scurvy had not been forgotten. Sour krout, a quantity of malt to be made into wort, mustard, vinegar, wheat, orange and lemon juices, portable soup, etc., were on board. Cold bathing was not only encouraged, but enforced by example. Wild celery and other wild herbs were eaten whenever an opportunity occurred of getting them.

So the ship passed Cape Horn, her crew well, and sailed into the South Pacific Ocean in January 1769, arriving at Otaheite three months later. Having there observed the transit of Venus, Cook discovered and visited the Society Isles. In October he " fell in " with the east coast of New Zealand, which he continued to explore for six months, proving it to consist of two large islands, and to form no part of the great southern continent. The health of his crew allowed him to make good use of his time, instead of hurrying on, as his predecessors had been forced to do. In March 1770, he sailed for the coast of Australia, following it northward for nearly two thousand miles. When near the northern end, the ship grounded on a coral reef near the land. "Cook's seamanship was, however, equal to the occasion." Again and again his calmness and dexterity saved him and his ship. Passing between the northern extremity of Australia and New Guinea, he proved them to be entirely separate, and not united as the early maps represented.

So far all had gone well. The *Endeavour* was on her homeward track when disease and death overtook the little crew. Cook's biographer tells the story. "As the *Endeavour* proceeded on her voyage to the Cape of Good Hope, the seeds of disease appeared with the most threatening symptoms, and reduced our navigators to a very melancholy situation. The ship was, in fact, nothing better than a hospital, in which those who could go about were not sufficient for a due attendance upon those who were sick. The lieutenant ordered all the parts of the vessel between the decks to be washed with vinegar. But the malady had taken too deep root to be speedily eradicated. Mr. Banks was reduced so low that for some time there was no hope of his life; and so fatal was the disease to many others, that almost every night a dead body was committed to the sea. There were buried in the course of six weeks the natural-history painter, the astronomer, the boatswain, the carpenter and his mate, two midshipmen, the old jolly sailmaker and his assistant, the ship's cook, the corporal of the marines, two of the carpenter's crew, and nine seamen."

The *Endeavour* arrived in England on July 2, 1771, after three years' absence.

But one great problem was filling the mind of Lieutenant Cook. He had mastered the difficulties and dangers of navigation in unknown seas: he had not mastered the problem of feeding his crew to prevent the appearance of scurvy.

Accordingly, when he was appointed to command the *Resolution*, in November 1771, "to complete the discovery of the Southern Hemisphere," his whole attention was turned to this one subjcet. And so successful was he in victualling the ships, and in redoubling his precautions as to cleanliness, that the result was a clean bill of health after a voyage of three years of unsurpassed hardship and exposure.

The *Resolution*, 462 tons, together with the *Adventure*, under the command of Captain Furneaux, left England, July 13, 1772. Leaving the Cape at the end of November, Cook sailed to the south till fields of ice drove him northwards. Having sailed over eleven thousand miles without seeing land, he anchored in Dusky Bay on March 26, 1773. Having refreshed his crew in New Zealand, and spent three months at Otaheite, he sailed south, and was soon battling with ice again. Still his crew was free from scurvy, a silent proof of the unwearying supervision the commander exercised over his men. Again stopped by ice, Cook left the southern latitudes and sailed north. A few days at Easter Island, on to the Marquesas, and once more the *Resolution* sailed into Matavai Bay, Otaheite, to be welcomed as usual with general friendliness and affection.

On May 15, 1774, they sailed for Huaheine, and discovered Palmerston Island, Savage Island, the Sandwich Islands, New Caledonia, and Staten Island, on his way once more to seek for the supposed southern continent. But he did not find it. He found the island of Georgia, covered in the middle of the Antarctic summer with snow and ice. But no refreshment was possible in these ice-bound regions; the sails and riggings of the ship were so much worn that "something was giving way every hour," and the provisions of the vessel were in such a state of decay that they offered but little nourishment, so reluctantly Cook decided to turn home again.

Thus, having completely circumnavigated the globe near the Antarctic circle, the *Resolution* arrived at Spithead, July 30, 1775, having been absent three years eighteen days, in which time, and under all the changes of climate, he had lost but four men, and only one of them by sickness. Only a year's rest, mostly spent with his wife and children in a modest suburb, and Captain Cook was off again, this time to explore the much-disputed North-West Passage.

On July 11, 1776, the little *Resolution*, with the *Discovery* in company, started with her usual complement of men and officers, and the following January found Captain Cook anchoring in Adventure Bay, Van Diemen's Land. After spending some weeks at the Friendly Isles, the Society Isles, and the Sandwich Islands, Cook sailed north, up the west coast of North America, until stopped by ice. Unable to find a northern passage, and the season being far advanced, he returned to the Sandwich Islands to refresh his crew before sailing to the north in the spring. At Hawaii he was murdered on February 14, 1779. The last chapter in Cook's life is tragic, and until recent years has remained unexplained. But the explanation is interesting.

It would appear that long ago there lived one Lono or Rono, a swine-god. After killing his wife he became insane, and after boxing and wrestling with every man he met, he had sailed away in a canoe, prophesying, "I will return again, on an island with trees, hogs, and dogs." He was looked on as a god by the natives, and temples were erected in his honour.

When Cook arrived at Hawaii, it was the day after a great battle, in which the king of Hawaii had been victorious. The victors made no doubt that Lono had come in person to sanction their victory. And in their minds Lono was Cook. When Cook landed he was received with adoration: the crowds, which flocked in their thousands, prostrated themselves before him; the priests attended him with mysterious ceremony. But of the cause Cook was in total ignorance. To him this adoration was inexplicable. He blindly did what was evidently required of him, and the ships sailed away, to the evident relief of the people. But the *Resolution* sprang her foremast in a gale, and Cook returned for repairs. All was changed. No crowd of canoes, no adoration, no enthusiasm; the old power was gone.

It was eight o'clock on Sunday morning. One of the *Discovery's* cutters had been stolen, and Cook went on shore to take and detain the king on board his ship till the missing boat was restored. Meanwhile, unintentionally, a chief had been killed.

"It is war; they have killed a chief," cried the ignorant natives. Confusion followed. The English sailors, fearing for their captain, began to fire without orders. Cook was moving towards the shore, when he was stabbed in the back with a dagger. He fell with his face to the water, dead.

Thus, at the age of fifty-one, died one of the greatest navigators the world has seen: great not only as a navigator, but as a man who had opened the way for further navigation, by discovering how to keep off disease, and so enable ships to keep at sea without endangering the lives of the crews.

The man's life had been a hard one. The secret of his success was that indomitable perseverance and determination that never gave up till the object in view was attained, however great the suffering it entailed. It is difficult to extract much of personal interest from the great folio volumes of Cook's journals: the captain preserves an ominous silence with regard to his own feelings; his likes and dislikes are never alluded to. He was capable of great endurance, disdainful of comfort or luxuries, satisfied to fulfil his duty at any cost. He commanded unbounded respect from those serving under him. His long service in the stormy waters of the German Ocean; the rough and coarse food on which he had lived as a boy; his close contact with rough, uneducated sailors, "whose wants, whose vices, and whose virtues" he knew better than any other officer of his time—these had enabled him to endure and to command. When the men complain of the "salted junk" and the "rotten sea-biscuit," and the *Resolution* is hung with icicles on rigging and mast—when grey albatrosses and blue petrels are the only signs of life to enliven the monotonous days—the captain, "his face set southwards," steers on through the ice-bound seas, thinking not of hunger and monotony, but of "how soon he can break through that wall of ice and learn what is beyond."

To fulfil all that was required of him, to exert himself unweariedly in the service of his country—these were the objects he set before him to fulfil. And surely in these he did not fail.

ROUND THE WORLD.

First Voyage.

CHAPTER I.

PASSAGE FROM PLYMOUTH TO MADEIRA, AND FROM MADEIRA TO RIO DE JANEIRO —THE PASSAGE FROM RIO DE JANEIRO TO THE ENTRANCE OF THE STRAIT OF LE MAIRE.

HAVING received my commission, which was dated the 25th of May 1768, I went on board on the 27th, hoisted the pennant, and took charge of the ship, which then lay in the basin in Deptford yard. She was fitted for sea with all expedition; and stores and provisions being taken on board, sailed down the river on the 30th of July, and on the 13th of August anchored in Plymouth Sound.

1768.
May.

August.

While we lay here waiting for a wind, the articles of war and the Act of Parliament were read to the ship's company, who were paid two months' wages in advance, and told that they were to expect no additional pay for the performance of the voyage.

On Friday the 26th of August, the wind becoming fair, we got under sail, and put to sea. On the 31st we saw several of the birds which the sailors call Mother Carey's chickens, and which they suppose to be the forerunners of a storm; and on the next day we had a very hard gale, which brought us under our courses, washed overboard a small boat belonging to the boatswain, and drowned three or four dozen of our poultry, which we regretted still more.

Sept.

On the 12th we discovered the islands of Porto Santo and Madeira, and on the next day anchored in Funchal Road, and moored with the stream-anchor; but, in the night, the bend of the hawser of the stream-anchor slipped, owing to the negligence of the person who had been employed to make it fast. In the morning the anchor was heaved up into the boat, and carried out to the southward; but in heaving it again, Mr. Weir, the master's mate, was carried overboard by the buoy-rope, and went to the bottom with the anchor. The people in the ship saw the accident, and got the anchor up with all possible expedition. It was, however, too late; the body came up entangled in the buoy-rope, but it was dead.

On Thursday the 15th we had squalls of wind from the land, with rain most part of these twenty-four hours. I received on board fresh beef and greens for the ship's company, and sent on shore all our casks for wine and water.

On Friday the 16th I punished Henry Stevens, seaman, and Thomas Dunster, marine, with twelve lashes each, for refusing to take their allowance of fresh beef. I also issued to the whole ship's company twenty pounds of onions per man.

The refreshments to be had here are water, wine, fruit of several sorts, onions in plenty, and some sweetmeats; fresh meat and poultry are not to be had without leave from the governor, and the payment of a very high price.

We took in 270 lbs. of fresh beef, and a live bullock charged at 613 lbs., 3,032 gallons of water, and ten tuns of wine; and in the night between Sunday the 18th and Monday the 19th of September we set sail in prosecution of our voyage.

On Friday the 23rd we saw the Peak of Teneriffe bearing W. by S. $\frac{1}{2}$ S. The height of this mountain, from which I took a new departure, has been determined by Dr. Heberden, who has been upon it, to be 15,396 feet, which is but 148 yards less than three miles, reckoning the mile at 1760 yards. Its appearance at sunset was very striking; when the sun was below the horizon, and the rest of the island appeared of a deep black, the mountain still reflected his rays, and glowed with a warmth of colour which no painting can express. There is no eruption of visible fire from it, but a heat issues from the chinks near the top, too strong to be borne by the hand when it is held near them.

On Saturday the 24th we had a fresh breeze and clear weather. I take this to be the NE. trade we have now got into. I now served wine to the ship's company, the beer being all expended but two casks, which I intend to keep some time longer, as the whole has proved very good to the last cask.

At 6 a.m. on the 30th we saw the island of Bonavista (one of the Cape de Verd Islands). We ranged the east side of this island at the distance of three or four miles from the shore, until we were obliged to haul off to avoid a ledge of rocks which stretched out SW. by W. from the body.

On the 1st of October, in lat. 14° 6′ N. and long. 22° 10′ W., we found the variation by a very good azimuth to be 10° 37′ W., and the next morning it appeared to be 10°. This day we found the ship five miles ahead of the log, and the next day seven. On the 3rd, hoisted out the boat to discover whether there was a current, and found one to the eastward, at the rate of three-quarters of a mile an hour.

During our course from Teneriffe to Bonavista we saw great numbers of flying-fish, which from the cabin windows appear beautiful beyond imagination, their sides having the colour and brightness of burnished silver; when they are seen from the deck they do not appear to so much advantage, because their backs are of a dark colour. We also took a shark, which proved to be the *Squalus carcharias* of Linnæus.

Having lost the trade-wind on the 3rd, in lat. 12° 14′ and long. 22° 10′, the wind became somewhat variable, and we had light airs and calms by turns.

On the 25th we crossed the line, and the next day, when it was no longer doubted that we were to the southward of the line, the ceremony on this occasion practised by all nations was not omitted. Every one that could not prove upon the sea chart that he had before crossed the line was either to pay a bottle of rum or be ducked in the sea, which former case was the fate of by far the greatest part on board; and as several of the men chose to be ducked, and the weather was favourable for that purpose, this ceremony was performed over about twenty or thirty, to the no small diversion of the rest.

I now determined to put into Rio de Janeiro in preference to any other port in Brazil or Falkland Islands, for at this place I knew we could recruit our stock of provisions, several articles of which I found we should in time be in want of, and at the same time procure live-stock and refreshment for the people; and from the reception former ships had met with here, I doubted not but we should be well received.

Nov. On the 8th, at daybreak, we saw the coast of Brazil, and about ten o'clock we brought to, and spoke with a fishing-boat. The people on board told us that the land which we saw lay to the southward of Santo Espirito, but belonged to the captainship of that place. It appears high and mountainous.

We stood off and on along the shore till the 12th, and successively saw a remarkable hill near Santo Espirito, then Cape St. Thomas, and then an island just without Cape Frio, which in some maps is called the island of Frio, and which being high, with a hollow in the middle, has the appearance of two islands when seen at a distance. On this day we stood along the shore for Rio de Janeiro, and at nine the next morning made sail for the harbour. I then sent Mr. Hicks, my first lieutenant, before us in the pinnace, up to the city, to acquaint the governor that we put in there to procure water and refreshments, and to desire the assistance of a pilot to bring us into proper anchoring-ground. I continued to stand up the river till five o'clock in the evening, expecting the return of my lieutenant; and just as I was about to anchor above the island of Cobras, which lies before the city, the pinnace came back without him, having on board a Portuguese officer, but no pilot. The people in the boat told me that my lieutenant was detained by the viceroy till I should go on shore. We came immediately to an anchor; and, almost at the same time, a ten-oared boat, full of soldiers, came up and kept rowing round the ship, without exchanging a word. In less than a quarter of an hour, another boat came with several of the viceroy's officers, who asked whence we came, what was our cargo, the number of men and guns on board, the object of our voyage, and several other questions, which we directly and truly answered. They then told me, as a kind of apology for detaining my lieutenant and putting an officer on board my pinnace, that it was the invariable custom of the place to detain the first officer who came on shore from any ship on her arrival, till a boat from the viceroy had visited her, and to suffer no boat to go either from or to a ship, while she lay there, without having a soldier on board. They said that I might go on shore when I pleased; but wished that every other person might remain on board till the paper which they should draw up had been delivered to the viceroy, promising that, immediately upon their return, the lieutenant should be sent on board.

This promise was performed; and on the next morning, the 14th, I went on shore, and obtained leave of the viceroy to purchase provisions and refreshments for the ship, provided I would employ one of their own people as a factor, but not otherwise. I made some objections to this, but he insisted upon it as the custom of the place. I objected also against the putting a soldier into the boat every time she went between the ship and the shore; but he told me that this was done by the express orders of his court, with which he could in no case dispense. I then requested that the gentlemen whom I had on board might reside on shore during our stay, and that Mr. Banks might go up the country to gather plants; but this he absolutely refused. I judged from his extreme caution and the severity of these restrictions that be suspected we were come to trade; I therefore took some pains to convince him of the contrary. I told him that we were bound to the southward, by the order of His Britannic Majesty, to observe a transit of the planet Venus over the sun. Of the transit of Venus he could form no other conception than that it was the passing of the North Star through the South Pole.

On the 15th I received on board fresh beef and greens for the ship's company, with which they were served every day during our stay here.

For three days past I have remonstrated to the viceroy and his officers against his putting a guard into my boat, thinking I could not answer to the Admiralty for tamely submitting to such a custom, which, when practised in its full force, must bring disgrace to the British flag. On the other hand, I was loth to enter into disputes, seeing how much I was like to be delayed and embarrassed in getting the supplies I wanted; for it was with much difficulty that I obtained leave for one of my people to attend the market to buy necessaries for my table, and to assist the agent to buy the things for the ship. Having gained this point, and settled everything with the agent in regard to what was wanting for the ship,

I resolved, rather than be made a prisoner in my own boat, not to go any more ashore unless I could do it without having a soldier put into the boat, as had hitherto been done; and thinking that the viceroy might lie under some mistake which on proper application might be cleared up, I therefore drew up a memorial stating the whole case, and sent to the viceroy this afternoon; and thus a paper war commenced between me and His Excellency, wherein I had no other advantage than the racking his invention to find reasons for treating us in the manner he did, for he never would relax the least from any one point.

On Friday the 18th I received an answer to my memorial, wherein he tells me, amongst other things, that if I think it hard submitting to the customs of this port, I may leave it when I please; this did not suit my purpose at present, but I resolved to make my stay as short as possible. I must own that the memorial of the viceroy's was well drawn up and very much to the purpose, which is more than I can say of any of the subsequent ones.

On Wednesday the 30th I punished Robert Anderson, seaman, and William Judge, marine, with twelve lashes each, the former for leaving his duty ashore and attempting to desert from the ship, and the latter for using abusive language to the officer of the watch; and John Reading, boatswain's mate, with twelve lashes for not doing his duty in punishing the above two men. Sent ashore to the viceroy for a pilot to carry us to sea, who sent one on board together with a large boat, which I did not want; but it is the custom in this port for the pilots to have such a boat to attend upon the ship they pilot out, and for which you must pay ten shillings per day, besides the pilot's fee, which is seven pounds four shillings sterling.

Dec. On the 1st we received on board a large quantity of fresh beef, greens, and yams for the ship's company. At nine o'clock next day we weighed, and came to sail, and turned down the bay. Peter Flower, seaman, fell overboard, and before any assistance could be given him was drowned; in his room we got a Portuguese.

On Wednesday the 7th, with a gentle breeze at SE., we weighed and towed out of the bay, discharging the pilot and his boat.

A breeze of wind springing up easterly, made sail out to sea, and sent a boat to one of the islands lying before the bay to cut brooms, a thing we were not permitted to do while we lay in the harbour; the guard boat, which had constantly attended all the time we lay in the bay and harbour, did not leave us until the pilot was discharged. It is remarkable that, during the last three or four days of our staying in this harbour, the air was loaded with butterflies. They were chiefly of one sort, but in such numbers that thousands were in view in every direction, and the greatest part of them above our mast-head.

Upon the whole, Rio de Janeiro is a very good place for ships to put in at wanting refreshment; the harbour is safe and commodious, and provisions, except wheaten bread and flour, may be easily procured. As a succedaneum for bread, there are yams and cassada in plenty; beef, both fresh and jerked, may be bought at about twopence farthing a pound, though it is very lean. The people here jerk their beef by taking out the bones, cutting it into large but thin slices, then curing it with salt, and drying it in the shade; it eats very well, and, if kept dry, will remain good a long time at sea. Mutton is scarcely to be procured, and hogs and poultry are dear; of garden stuff and fruit there is abundance, of which, however, none can be preserved at sea but the pumpkin; rum, sugar, and molasses, all excellent in their kind, may be had at a reasonable price; tobacco also is cheap, but it is not good. Here is a yard for building shipping, and a small hulk to heave down by, for, as the tide never rises above six or seven feet, there is no other way of coming at a ship's bottom.

When the boat which had been sent on shore returned, we hoisted her on board and stood out to sea.

Nothing remarkable happened till the 30th, except that we prepared for the bad weather which we were shortly to expect by bending a new suit of sails. But on this day we caught a great number of insects. Some of them were on the wing, but the greater part were on the water, and many of these alive and of such sort as cannot fly far, and yet at this time we could not be less than thirty leagues from the land.

On the 3rd of January, being in lat. 47° 17′ S. and long. 61° 29′ 45″ W., we were all looking out for Pepys' Island, and for some time an appearance was seen in the east which so much resembled land that we bore away for it; and it was more than two hours and a half before we were convinced that it was nothing but what sailors call a fogbank.

The people now beginning to complain of cold, each of them received what is called a Magellanic jacket and a pair of trousers. The jacket is made of a thick woollen stuff, called *fearnought*, which is provided by the government. We saw, from time to time, a great number of penguins, albatrosses, and sheerwaters, seals, whales, and porpoises; and on the 11th, having passed Falkland's Islands, we discovered the coast of Tierra del Fuego, at the distance of about four leagues, extending from the W. to SE. by S. We had here five and thirty fathoms; the ground was soft. As we ranged along the shore to the SE. at the distance of two or three leagues, we perceived smoke in several places, which was made by the natives, probably as a signal, for they did not continue it after we had passed by.

This day we discovered that the ship had got near a degree of longitude to the westward of the log, which, in this latitude, is thirty-five minutes of a degree on the equator; probably there is a small current setting to the westward, which may be caused by the westerly current coming round Cape Horn and through the Strait of Le Maire and the indraught of the Strait of Magellan.

Having continued to range the coast, on the 14th we entered the Strait of Le Maire; but the tide turning against us, drove us out with great violence, and raised such a sea off Cape St. Diego that the waves had exactly the same appearance as they would have had if they had broke over a ledge of rocks; and when the ship was in this torrent she frequently pitched so that the bowsprit was under water. About noon we got under the land between Cape St. Diego and Cape St. Vincent, where I intended to have anchored; but finding the ground everywhere hard and rocky, and shallowing from thirty to twelve fathoms, I sent the master to examine a little cove which lay at a small distance to the eastward of Cape St. Vincent. When he returned he reported that there was anchorage in four fathoms and a good bottom close to the eastward of the first bluff point on the east of Cape St. Vincent, at the very entrance of the cove, to which I gave the name of Vincent's Bay.

ARRIVAL AT THE STRAIT OF LE MAIRE.

At 2 p.m. on the 16th we anchored in the Bay of Success. Having hoisted out the boats and moored with the stream-anchor, I went ashore to look for a watering place and to speak with the natives, who were assembled on the beach at the head of the bay to the number of thirty or forty. They were so far from being afraid or surprised at our coming amongst them, that three of them came on board without the least hesitation. They are something above the middle size, of a dark copper colour, with long black hair; they paint their bodies in streaks, mostly red and black. Their clothing consists wholly in a guanaco skin or that of a seal, in the same form as it came from the animal's back.

Their huts are made like a beehive, and open on one side where they have their fires; they are made of small sticks and covered with branches of trees, long grass, etc., in such a manner that they are proof against neither wind, hail, rain, nor snow—a sufficient proof that these people must be a very hardy race. They live chiefly on shellfish, such as mussels, which they gather from off the rocks along the sea-shore, and this seems to be the work of the women. Their arms are bows and arrows neatly made. Their arrows are bearded, some with glass and others with fine flint; several pieces of the former we saw amongst them with other European things, such as rings, buttons, cloth, canvas, etc., which I think proves that they must sometimes travel to the northward, as we know of no ship that has been in these parts for many years. Besides, they were not at all surprised at our firearms; on the contrary, they seemed to know the use of them, by making signs to us to fire at seals or birds that might come in the way.

They have no boats that we saw, or anything to go upon the water with; their number does not exceed fifty or sixty, young and old, and there are fewer women than men. They are extremely fond of any red thing, and seemed to set more value on beads than anything we could give them. In this consists their whole pride; few, either men or women, are without a necklace or string of beads made of small shells or bones about their necks. They would not taste any strong liquor, neither did they seem fond of our provisions. In a word, they are perhaps as miserable a set of people as are this day upon the earth.

CHAPTER II.

EXPEDITION IN SEARCH OF PLANTS—PASSAGE THROUGH THE STRAIT OF LE MAIRE —SEQUEL OF THE PASSAGE FROM CAPE HORN TO THE NEWLY-DISCOVERED ISLANDS IN THE SOUTH SEAS.

1769. January. ON the 16th, early in the morning, Mr. Banks and Dr. Solander, with their attendants and servants, and two seamen to assist in carrying the baggage, accompanied by Mr. Monkhouse, the surgeon, and Mr. Green, the astronomer, set out from the ship, with a view to penetrate as far as they could into the country, and return at night. The hills, when viewed at a distance, seemed to be partly a wood, partly a plain, and above them a bare rock. Mr. Banks hoped to get through the wood, and made no doubt but that beyond it he should, in a country which no botanist had ever yet visited, find alpine plants which would abundantly compensate his labour. They entered the wood at a small sandy beach, a little to the westward of the watering place, and continued to ascend the hill, through the pathless wilderness, till three o'clock, before they got a near view of the places which they intended to visit. Soon after they reached what they had taken for a plain; but, to their great disappointment, found it a swamp covered with low bushes of birch, about three feet high, interwoven with each other, and so stubborn that they could not be bent out of the way; it was therefore necessary to lift the leg over them, which, at every step, was buried ankle deep in the soil. To aggravate the pain and difficulty of such travelling, the weather, which hitherto had been very fine, much like one of our bright days in May, became gloomy and cold; with sudden blasts of a most piercing wind, accompanied with snow. They pushed forward, however, in good spirits, notwithstanding their fatigue, hoping the worst of the way was past; but when they had got about two-thirds over this woody swamp, Mr. Buchan was unhappily seized with a fit. This made it necessary for the whole company to halt, and as it was impossible that he should go any farther, a fire was kindled, and those who were most fatigued were left behind to take care of him. The others pushed on, and in a short time reached the summit. As botanists, their expectations were here abundantly gratified.

The cold was now become more severe and the snow blasts more frequent; the day also was so far spent that it was found impossible to get back to the ship before the next morning. To pass the night upon such a mountain, in such a climate, was not only comfortless, but dreadful. It was proposed that they should push through the swamp, which seemed to be more than half a mile over, into the shelter of the wood, and there build their wigwam and make a fire; this, as their way was all down hill, it seemed easy to accomplish. Their whole company assembled at the rendezvous, and, though pinched with the cold, were in health and spirits, Mr. Buchan himself having recovered his strength in a much greater degree than could have been expected.

It was now near eight o'clock in the evening, but still good daylight, and they set forward for the nearest valley, Mr. Banks himself undertaking to bring up the rear, and see that no straggler was left behind. This may, perhaps, be thought a superfluous caution, but it will soon appear to be otherwise. Dr. Solander, who had more than once crossed the mountains which divide Sweden from Norway, well knew that extreme cold, especially when joined with fatigue, produces a torpor and sleepiness that are almost irresistible; he therefore conjured the company to keep moving, whatever pain it might cost them, and whatever relief they might be promised by an inclination to rest.

"Whoever sits down," says he, "will sleep; and whoever sleeps will wake no more." Thus, at once admonished and alarmed, they set forward; but while they were still upon the naked rock, and before they had got among the bushes, the cold became suddenly so intense as to produce the effects that had been most dreaded. Dr. Solander himself was the first who found the inclination, against which he had warned others, irresistible, and insisted upon being suffered to lie down. Mr. Banks entreated and remonstrated in vain : down he lay upon the ground, though it was covered with snow; and it was with great difficulty that his friend kept him from sleeping. Richmond also, one of the black servants, began to linger, having suffered from the cold in the same manner as the doctor. Mr. Banks therefore sent five of the company, among whom was Mr. Buchan, forward to get a fire ready at the first convenient place they could find, and himself, with four others, remained with the doctor and Richmond, whom, partly by persuasion and entreaty, and partly by force, they brought on ; but when they had got through the greatest part of the birch and swamp they both declared they could go no farther.

Mr. Banks had recourse again to entreaty and expostulation, but they produced no effect. When Richmond was told that if he did not go on he would in a short time be frozen to death, he answered that he desired nothing but to lie down and die : the doctor did not so explicitly renounce his life ; he said he was willing to go on, but that he must first take some sleep, though he had before told the company that to sleep was to perish. Mr. Banks and the rest found it impossible to carry them, and, there being no remedy, they were both suffered to sit down, being partly supported by the bushes, and in a few minutes they fell into a profound sleep. Soon after, some of the people who had been sent forward returned with the welcome news that a fire was kindled about a quarter of a mile farther on the way. Mr. Banks then endeavoured to wake Dr. Solander, and happily succeeded ; but, though he had not slept five minutes, he had almost lost the use of his limbs, and the muscles were so shrunk that his shoes fell from his feet. He consented to go forward with such assistance as could be given him, but no attempts to relieve poor Richmond were successful.

It being found impossible to make him stir, after some time had been lost in the attempt, Mr. Banks left his other black servant and a seaman, who seemed to have suffered least by the cold, to look after him, promising that as soon as two others should be sufficiently warmed they should be relieved. Mr. Banks, with much difficulty, at length got the doctor to the fire, and soon after sent two of the people who had been refreshed, in hopes that, with the assistance of those who had been left behind, they would be able to bring Richmond, even though it should still be found impossible to wake him. In about half an hour, however, they had the mortification to see these men return alone: they said they could neither find Richmond nor those who had been left with him, and that, though they had shouted many times, no voice had replied. This was matter of equal surprise and concern, particularly to Mr. Banks, who, while he was wondering how it could happen, missed a bottle of rum, the company's whole stock, which they now concluded to be in the knapsack of one of the absentees.

Another fall of snow came on and continued incessantly for two hours, so that all hope of seeing them again, at least alive, was given up; but about twelve o'clock, to the great joy of those at the fire, a shouting was heard at some distance. Mr. Banks immediately went out, and found the seaman with just strength enough left to stagger along and call out for assistance. Mr. Banks proceeded in search of the other two, whom he soon after found. Richmond was upon his legs, but unable to put one before the other; his companion was lying upon the ground, as insensible as a stone.

All hands were now called from the fire, and an attempt was made to carry them to it; but this, notwithstanding the united efforts of the whole company, was found to be impossible. The night was extremely dark, the snow was now very deep, and, under these additional disadvantages, they found it very difficult to make way through the bushes and the bog for themselves, all of them getting many falls in the attempt. The only alternative was to make a fire upon the spot; but the snow which had fallen, and was still falling, besides what was every moment shaken in flakes from the trees, rendered it equally impracticable to kindle one there, and to bring any part of that which had been kindled in the wood thither. They were therefore reduced to the sad necessity of leaving the unhappy wretches to their fate, having first made them a bed of boughs from the trees, and spread a covering of the same kind over them to a considerable height.

Having now been exposed to the cold and the snow near an hour and a half, some of the rest began to lose their sensibility; and one Briscoe, another of Mr. Banks's servants, was so ill that it was thought he must die before he could be got to the fire.

At the fire, however, at length they arrived; and passed the night in a situation which, however dreadful in itself, was rendered more afflicting by the remembrance of what was past, and the uncertainty of what was to come. Of twelve, the number that set out together in health and spirits, two were supposed to be already dead; a third was so ill that it was very doubtful whether he would be able to go forward in the morning; and a fourth, Mr. Buchan, was in danger of a return of his fits, by fresh fatigue after so uncomfortable a night. They were distant from the ship a long day's journey, through pathless woods. They were wholly destitute of provisions, except a vulture, which they happened to shoot while they were out, and which, if equally divided, would not afford each of them half a meal.

When the morning dawned, they saw nothing round them, as far as the eye could reach, but snow, which seemed to lie as thick upon the trees as upon the ground; and the blasts returned so frequently and with such violence, that they found it impossible for them to set out.

After having suffered the misery and terror of this situation till six o'clock in the morning, they conceived some hope of deliverance by discovering the place of the sun through the clouds, which had become thinner and begun to break away. Their first care was to see whether the poor wretches whom they had been obliged to leave among the bushes were yet alive. Three of the company were despatched for that purpose, and very soon afterwards returned with the melancholy news that they were dead.

Notwithstanding the flattering appearance of the sky, the snow still continued to fall so thick that they could not venture out upon their journey to the ship; but about eight o'clock a small regular breeze sprung up, which, with the prevailing influence of the sun, at length cleared the air; and they soon after, with great joy, saw the snow falling in large flakes from the trees, a certain sign of an approaching thaw. *T*hey now examined more critically the state of their invalids. Briscoe was still very ill, but said that he thought himself able to walk; and Mr. Buchan was much better than either he or his friends had any reason to expect. *T*hey were now, however, pressed by the calls of hunger, to which, after long fasting, every consideration of future good or evil immediately gives way. Before they set forward, therefore, it was unanimously agreed that they should eat their vulture. The bird was accordingly skinned, and, it being thought best to divide it before it was fit to be eaten, it was cut into ten portions, and every man cooked his own as he thought fit. After this repast, which furnished each of them with about three mouthfuls, they prepared to set out; but it was ten o'clock before the snow was sufficiently gone off to render a march practicable. After a walk of about three hours, they were very agreeably surprised to find themselves upon the beach, and much nearer to the ship than they had any reason to expect. Upon reviewing their track from the vessel, they perceived that, instead of ascending the hill in a line, so as to penetrate into the country, they had made almost a circle round it. When they came on board they congratulated each other upon their safety, with a joy that no man can feel who has not been exposed to equal danger; and as I had suffered great anxiety at their not returning in the evening of the day on which they set out, I was not wholly without my share.

On the 18th and 19th we were delayed in getting on board our wood and water by the great surf that always will be upon the shore when the wind blows hard from the southward. This evening the surf abated, and at 2 a.m. I sent the people on shore to wood and water and cut brooms, all of which we completed this day. In this service we lost our small kedge-anchor, it having been laid off the watering place to ride the longboat by; and the gale had broke away the hawser and buoy-rope, and perhaps buried the anchor in the sand, for notwithstanding our utmost endeavours, we were not able to hook it. I now took up the stream-anchor and made ready for sailing. At 2 a.m. on the 21st we weighed and made sail out of the bay, and continued our course through the strait.

Almost all writers who have mentioned the island of Tierra del Fuego describe it as destitute of wood, and covered with snow. In the winter it may possibly be covered with snow, and those who saw it at that season might perhaps be easily deceived, by its appearance, into an opinion that it was destitute of wood. Lord Anson was there in the beginning of March, which answers to our September; and we were there the beginning of January, which answers to our July, which may account for the difference of his description of it from ours. We fell in with it about twenty-one leagues to the westward of the Strait of Le Maire, and from the time that we first saw it, trees were plainly to be distinguished with our glasses; and as we came nearer, though here and there we discovered patches of snow, the sides of the hills and the sea-coast appeared to be covered with a beautiful verdure. The hills are lofty, but not mountainous, though the summits of them are quite naked. The soil in the valleys is rich, and of a considerable depth; and at the foot of almost every hill there is a brook, the water of which has a reddish hue, like that which runs through our turf bogs in England; but it is by no means ill tasted, and upon the whole proved to be the best that we took in during our voyage. We ranged the coast to the strait, and had soundings all the way from forty to twenty fathoms, upon a gravelly and sandy bottom. The most remarkable land on Tierra del Fuego is a hill, in the form of a sugar-loaf, which stands on the west side not far from the sea; and the three hills, called the Three Brothers, about nine miles to the westward of Cape St. Diego, the low point that forms the north entrance of the Strait of Le Maire. The entrance of the strait should not be attempted but with a fair wind and moderate weather, and upon the very beginning of the tide of flood, which happens here, at the full and change of the moon, about one or two o'clock. It is also best to keep as near to the Tierra del Fuego shore as the winds will admit. By attending to these particulars, a ship may be got quite through the strait. Between Strait Le Maire and Cape Horn we found a current setting, generally very strong, to the NE., when we were in with the shore, but lost it when we were at the distance of fifteen or twenty leagues.

January. On the 26th we took our departure from Cape Horn, which lies in lat. 55° 53′ S., long. 68° 13′ W. The farthest southern latitude that we made was 60° 10′. Our longitude was then 74° 30′ W.; and we found the variation of the compass, by the mean of eighteen azimuths, to be 27° 9′ E. As the weather was frequently calm, Mr. Banks went out in a small boat to shoot birds, among which were some albatrosses and sheerwaters. The albatrosses were observed to be larger than those which had been taken northward of the strait. One of them measured ten feet two inches from the tip of one wing to that of the other, when they were extended. The sheerwater, on the contrary, is less, and darker coloured on the back. The albatrosses we skinned, and having soaked them in salt water till the morning, we parboiled them; then throwing away the liquor, stewed them in a very little fresh water till they were tender, and had them served up with savoury sauce. Thus dressed, the dish was universally commended, and we ate of it very heartily even when there was fresh pork upon the table.

We now began to have strong gales and heavy seas, with irregular intervals of calm and fine weather.

We had been thirty-three days in doubling Cape Horn or the land of Tierra del Fuego, without being brought once under our close-reefed topsails since we left Strait Le Maire, a circumstance that perhaps never happened before to any ship in those seas so much dreaded for hard gales of wind; in so much that the doubling of Cape Horn is thought by some to be a mighty thing, and others to this day prefer the Straits of Magellan. As I have never been in those straits, I can only form my judgment on a careful comparison of the different ships' journals that have passed them, and those that have sailed round Cape Horn, particularly the *Dolphin's* last two voyages and this of ours, being made at the same season of the year, when one may reasonably expect the same winds to prevail. The *Dolphin* in her last voyage was three months in getting through the straits, not reckoning the time she lay in Port Famine; and I am firmly persuaded from the winds we have had, that had we come by that passage we should not have been in these seas, besides the fatiguing of our people, the damage we must have done to our anchors, cables, sails, and rigging, none of which have suffered in our passage round Cape Horn.

On the 1st we were in lat. 38° 44' S. and long. 110° 33' W., both by observation and by the log. This agreement, after a run of 660 leagues, was thought to be very extraordinary, and is a demonstration that after we left the land of Cape Horn we had no current that affected the ship. It renders it also highly probable that we had been near no land of any

March.

considerable extent; for currents are always found when land is not remote, and sometimes, particularly on the east side of the continent in the North Sea, when land has been distant 100 leagues.

The albatrosses now began to leave us, and after the 8th there was not one to be seen. We continued our course till the 24th, when some of the people who were upon the watch in the night reported that they saw a log of wood pass by the ship. It was a general opinion that there was land to windward.

At 5 p.m. on the 26th saw some seaweed pass the ship, and at seven William Greenslade, marine, either by accident or design, went overboard and was drowned. The following circumstances make it appear as though it was done designedly. He had been sentinel at the steerage door between twelve and four o'clock, when he had taken part of a seal-skin put under his charge, and which was found upon him. The other marines thought themselves hurt by one of their party committing a crime of this nature. He was a raw young fellow, and this very probably made him resolve upon committing this rash action; for the sergeant, not being willing that it should pass over unknown to me, was about seven o'clock going to bring him aft and have it inquired into, when he gave him the slip between decks, and was seen to go upon the forecastle, and from that time was seen no more. I was neither made acquainted with the theft nor the circumstances attending it until the man was gone.

April. At 10.30 a.m. on the 1st saw land bearing south, distance three or four leagues. Hauled up for it, and soon found it to be an island of about two leagues in circuit, and of an oval form, with a lagoon in the middle, from which I named it Lagoon Island. The border of land circumscribing this lagoon is in many places very low and narrow, particularly on the south side, where it is mostly a beach or reef of rocks. It is the same on the north side in three places, and these disjoin the firm land and make it appear like so many islands covered with wood. On the west end of the island is a large tree which looks like a large tower, and about the middle of the island are two cocoa-nut trees that appear above all the other wood, which as we approached the island looked very much like a flag. We approached the north side of this island within a mile, and found no bottom with 130 fathoms of line, nor did there appear to be anchorage about it. We saw several of the inhabitants, the most of them men, and these marched along the shore abreast of the ships with long clubs in their hands as though they meant to oppose our landing. They were all naked, and were of a dark copper colour with long black hair; but upon our leaving the island some of them were seen to put on a covering, and one or two we saw in the skirts of the wood were clothed in white : these we supposed to be women.

At 2.30 p.m. on the 7th we got up with the east end of the land seen yesterday at noon, and which proved to be an assemblage of islands joined together by reef, and extending themselves NW. by N. and SE. by S. in eight or nine leagues, and of various breadths; but there appeared to be a total separation in the middle by a channel of half a mile broad, and on this account they are called the two groups.

We ranged along the SW. side of these islands, and hauled into a bay which lies to the NW. of the southernmost point of them, and where there appeared to be anchorage, and the sea was smooth, and not much surf on the shore; but we found no ground with 100 fathoms three-quarters of a mile from the shore, and nearer we did not go. Here several of the inhabitants assembled together with their canoes, with a design, as we thought, to come off to us, as they hauled one of them over the reef seemingly for that purpose; but after waiting near half an hour, and they not attempting to come, we bore away and made sail, and presently the canoe put off after us; but, as we did not stop, they soon went back again. They were in all respects like those we had seen on Lagoon Island, and armed with clubs and long pikes like them.

On the 7th we discovered another island, which we judged to be about four miles in circumference. The land lay very low, and there was a piece of water in the middle of it. There seemed to be some wood upon it, and it looked green and pleasant; but we saw neither cocoa trees nor inhabitants. It abounded, however, with birds, and we therefore gave it the name of Bird Island.

On the 10th, having had a tempestuous night with thunder

and rain, the weather was hazy till about nine o'clock in the morning, when it cleared up, and we saw the island to which Captain Wallis, who first discovered it, gave the name of Osnaburgh Island, called by the natives *Maitea*, bearing NW. by W., distant about five leagues. It is a high round island, not above a league in circuit. In some parts it is covered with trees, and in others a naked rock. In this direction it looked like a high-crowned hat; but when it bears north, the top of it has more the appearance of the roof of a house.

MAP OF POLYNESIA.

Page 31.

CHAPTER III.

ARRIVAL OF THE "ENDEAVOUR" AT OTAHEITE OR KING GEORGE THE THIRD'S ISLAND.

ABOUT one o'clock, on Monday the 10th of April, 1769. some of the people who were looking out for the April island to which we were bound said they saw land ahead, in that part of the horizon where it was expected to appear; but it was so faint that whether there was land in sight or not remained a matter of dispute till sunset. The next morning, however, at six o'clock, we were convinced that those who said they had discovered land were not mistaken. It appeared to be very high and mountainous, and we knew it to be the same that Captain Wallis had called King George the Third's Island.

We were delayed in our approach to it by light airs and calms, so that in the morning of the 12th we were but little nearer than we had been the night before; but about seven a breeze sprung up, and before eleven several canoes were seen making towards the ship. There were but few of them, however, that would come near; and the people in those that did, could not be persuaded to come on board. In every canoe there were young plantains, and branches of a tree which the Indians call *e'midho*. These, as we afterwards learned, were brought as tokens of peace and amity; and the people in one of the canoes handed them up the ship's side, making signals at the same time with great earnestness, which we did not immediately understand. At length we guessed that they wished these symbols should be placed in some conspicuous part of the ship. We therefore immediately stuck them among the rigging, at which they expressed the greatest satisfaction. We then purchased their cargoes, consisting of cocoa-nuts and various kinds of fruit, which after our long voyage were very acceptable.

At 5 a.m. I made sail for Matavai Bay, and at seven anchored in thirteen fathoms. At this time we had but very few men upon the sick list, and these had but slight complaints. The ship's company had in general been very healthy, owing in a great measure to the sour krout, portable soup, and malt. The first two were served to the people, the one on beef days, and the other on banyan days. Wort was made of the malt, and at the discretion of the surgeon given to every man that had the least symptoms of scurvy upon him. By this means, and the care and vigilance of Mr. Monkhouse, the surgeon, this disease was prevented from getting a footing in the ship. The sour krout the men at first would not eat, until I put it in practice—a method I never once knew to fail with seamen—and this was to have some of it dressed every day for the cabin table, and permitted all the officers, without exception, to make use of it, and left it to the option of the men either to take as much as they pleased or none at all. But this practice was not continued above a week before I found it necessary to put every one on board to an allowance; for such are the tempers and disposition of seamen in general, that whatever you give them out of the common way—although it be ever so much for their good—it will not go down, and you will hear nothing but murmurings against the man that first invented it; but the moment they see their superiors set a value upon it, it becomes the finest stuff in the world, and the inventor an honest fellow.

As our stay here was not likely to be very short, and as it was necessary that the merchandise which we had brought for traffic with the natives should not diminish in its value—which it would certainly have done if every person had been left at liberty to give what he pleased for such things as he should purchase, at the same time that confusion and quarrels must necessarily have arisen from there being no standard at market—I drew up the following rules, and ordered that they should be punctually observed :—

"Rules to be observed by every person in or belonging to His Majesty's bark the 'Endeavour,' for the better establishing a regular and uniform trade for provision, etc., with the inhabitants of George's Island.

"I. To endeavour, by every fair means, to cultivate a friendship with the natives; and to treat them with all imaginable humanity.

"II. A proper person, or persons, will be appointed to trade with the natives for all manner of provisions, fruit, and other productions of the earth; and no officer or seaman, or other person belonging to the ship, excepting such as are so appointed, shall trade or offer to trade for any sort of provision, fruit, or other productions of the earth, unless they have leave so to do.

"III. Every person employed on shore, on any duty whatsoever, is strictly to attend to the same; and if by any neglect he loseth any of his arms, or working tools, or suffers them to be stolen, the full value thereof will be charged against his pay, according to the custom of the navy in such cases, and he shall receive such further punishment as the nature of the offence may deserve.

"IV. The same penalty will be inflicted on every person who is found to embezzle, trade, or offer to trade with any of the ship's stores of what nature soever.

"V. No sort of iron or any sort of cloth or other useful or necessary articles are to be given in exchange for anything but provisions.   J. C."

As soon as the ship was properly secured I went on shore, accompanied by Mr. Banks and the other gentlemen, with a party of men under arms. We took along with us Owhaa, who took us to the place where the *Dolphin* watered, and made signs to us as well as we could understand that we might occupy that ground, but it happened not to be fit for our purpose. No one of the natives made the least opposition at our landing, but came to us with all imaginable marks of friendship and submission. We afterwards made a circuit through the woods, and then came on board. We did not find the inhabitants to be numerous, and we imagined that several of them had fled from their habitations upon our arrival in the bay.

On Friday the 14th we had a great many canoes about the ship; the most of them came from the westward, and brought nothing with them but a few cocoa-nuts, etc. Two that appeared to be chiefs we had on board, together with several others, for it was a hard matter to keep them out of the ship, as they climb like monkeys. But it was still harder to keep them from stealing everything that came within their reach; in this they are prodigious experts. I made each of these two chiefs a present of a hatchet, things that they seem mostly to value. As soon as we had partly got clear of these people, I took two boats and went to the westward, all the gentlemen being along with me. My design was to see if there was not a more commodious harbour, and to try the disposition of the natives, having along with us the two chiefs above mentioned.

The first place we landed at was in Great Canoe Harbour (so called by Captain Wallis). Here the natives flocked about us in great numbers, and in as friendly a manner as we could wish, only that they showed a great inclination to pick our pockets. We were conducted to a chief, whom for distinction's sake we called Hercules. After staying a short time with him, and distributing a few presents about us, we proceeded farther, and came to a chief whom I shall call Lycurgus. This man entertained us with broiled fish, cocoa-nuts, etc., with great hospitality, and all the time took great care to tell us to take care of our pockets, as a great number of people had crowded about us. Notwithstanding the care we took, Dr. Solander and Dr. Monkhouse had each of them their pockets picked, the one of his spyglass and the other of his snuff-box.

On the next morning, Saturday the 15th, several of the chiefs whom we had seen the day before came on board, and brought with them hogs, bread-fruit, and other refreshments, for which we gave them hatchets and linen, and such things as seemed to be most acceptable.

On Sunday the 16th we worked the ship nearer the shore, and moored her in such a manner as to command all the shore of the NE. part of the bay, but more particularly the place where we intended to erect a fort. I punished Richard Hutchins, seaman, with twelve lashes for disobeying commands. Several of the natives came down to the shore of the bay, but not one of them came off to the ship during the whole day. In the evening I went on shore with only a boat's crew and some of the gentlemen. The natives gathered about us to the number of about thirty or forty, and brought us cocoa-nuts, etc., and seemed as friendly as ever.

On Monday, 17th, at two o'clock, departed this life Mr. Alex. Buchan, landscape draftsman to Mr. Banks, a gentleman well skilled in his profession, and one that will be greatly missed in the course of this voyage. He had more than once been brought to the very point of death, and was at one time subject to fits, of one of which he was taken on Saturday morning. This brought on his former disorder, which put a period to his life. Mr. Banks thought it was not advisable to inter the body ashore in a place where we were utter strangers to the custom of the natives on such occasions. It was therefore sent out to sea and committed to that element with all the decency the circumstance of the place would admit of. This morning several of the chiefs from the westward made us a visit. They brought with them emblems of peace, which are young plantain trees. These they put on board the ship before they would venture themselves. They brought us a present of two hogs (an article we find here very scarce) and some bread-fruit; for these they had hatchets and other things. In the afternoon we set up one of the ship's tents ashore, and Mr. Green and myself stayed there the night to observe an eclipse of Jupiter's first satellite, which we were hindered from seeing by clouds.

On Tuesday the 18th we had cloudy weather with some showers of rain. This morning I took as many people out of the ship as could possibly be spared, and set about erecting a fort. Some were employed in throwing up intrenchments, while others were cutting fascines, pickets, etc. The natives were so far from hindering us that several of them assisted in bringing the pickets and fascines out of the woods, and seemed quite unconcerned at what we were about. The wood we made use of for this occasion we purchased of them, and we cut no tree down before we had first obtained their consent. By this time all the ship's sails were unbent and the armourer's forge set up to repair the ironwork, etc. I served fresh pork to the ship's company to-day for the first time. This is like to be a very scarce article with us, but as to bread-fruit, cocoa-nuts, and plantains, the natives supply us with as much as we can manage.

The next morning our friend Tubourai Tamaide made Mr. Banks a visit at the tent, and brought with him not only his wife and family, but the roof of a house, and several materials for setting it up, with furniture and implements of various kinds, intending, as we understood him, to take up his residence in our neighbourhood. This instance of his confidence and good-will gave us great pleasure, and we determined to strengthen his attachment to us by every means in our power.

Tubourai Tamaide was our constant guest, imitating our manners even to the using of a knife and fork, which he did very handily.

On the 27th, Tubourai Tamaide, with a friend who ate with a voracity that I never saw before, and the three women that usually attended him, whose names were Terapo, Tirao, and Omië, dined at the fort. In the evening they took their leave, and set out for the house which Tubourai Tamaide had set up in the skirts of the wood; but in less than a quarter of an hour he returned in great emotion, and hastily seizing Mr. Banks's arm, made signs that he should follow him. Mr. Banks immediately complied, and they soon came up to a place where they found the ship's butcher with a reaping-hook in his hand. Here the chief stopped, and, in a transport of rage which rendered his signs scarcely intelligible, intimated that the butcher had threatened, or attempted, to cut his wife's throat with the reaping-hook. Mr. Banks then signified to him that if he could fully explain the offence the man should be punished. Upon this he became more calm, and made Mr. Banks understand that the offender, having taken a fancy to a stone hatchet which lay in his house, had offered to purchase it of his wife for a nail; that she having refused to part with it upon any terms, he had catched it up, and throwing down the nail, threatened to cut her throat if she made any resistance. To prove this charge the hatchet and the nail were produced, and the butcher had so little to say in his defence that there was not the least reason to doubt of its truth.

Mr. Banks having reported this matter to me, I took an opportunity, when the chief and his women, with other Indians, were on board the ship, to call up the butcher; and after a recapitulation of the charge and the proof, I gave orders that he should be pun-

1769.] THE SUPPOSED QUEEN OF THE ISLAND. 37

ished, as well to prevent other offences of the same kind, as to acquit Mr. Banks of his promise. The Indians saw him stripped and tied up to the rigging with a fixed attention, waiting in silent suspense for the event; but as soon as the first stroke was given they interfered with great agitation, earnestly entreating that the rest of the punishment might be remitted. To this, however, for many reasons, I could not consent; and when they found that they could not prevail by their intercession, they gave vent to their pity by tears.

Their tears indeed, like those of children, were always ready to express any passion that was strongly excited, and like those of children, they also appeared to be forgotten as soon as shed.

Canoes were continually coming in during all this forenoon, and the tents at the fort were crowded with people of both sexes from different parts of the island. I was myself busy on board the ship; but Mr. Molineux, our master, who was one of those that made the last voyage in the *Dolphin*, went on shore.

As soon as he entered Mr. Banks's tent he fixed his eyes upon one of the women, who was sitting there with great composure among the rest, and immediately declared her to be the person who at that time was supposed to be queen of the island; she also at the same time acknowledging him to be one of the strangers whom she had seen before. The attention of all present was now diverted from every other object, and wholly engaged in considering a person who had made so distinguished a figure in the accounts that had been given of this island by its first discoverers; and we soon learned that her name was Oberea. She seemed to be about forty years of age, and was not only tall, but of a large make. Her skin was white, and there was an uncommon intelligence and sensibility in her eyes. She appeared to have been handsome when she was young, but at this time little more than memorials of her beauty were left.

As soon as her quality was known, an offer was made to conduct her to the ship. Of this she readily accepted, and came on board with two men and several women, who seemed to be all of her family. I received her with such marks of distinction as I thought would gratify her most, and was not sparing of my presents, among which this august personage seemed particularly delighted with a child's doll. After some time spent on board, I attended her back to the shore, and as soon as we landed, she presented me with a hog and several bunches of plantains, which she caused to be carried from her canoes up to the fort in a kind of procession, of which she and myself brought up the rear. In our way to the fort we met Tootaha, who, though not king, appeared to be at this time invested with the sovereign authority. He seemed not to be well pleased with the distinction that was showed to the lady, and became so jealous when she produced her doll, that to propitiate him it was thought proper to compliment him with another. At this time he thought fit to prefer a doll to a hatchet; but this preference only arose from a childish jealousy, which could not be soothed but by a gift of exactly the same kind with that which had been presented to Oberea.

On the 29th, Mr. Banks paid a visit to Tubourai Tamaide, and was grieved and surprised to find him and his family in a melancholy mood, and most of them in tears. When he reported this circumstance to the officers at the fort, they recollected that Owhaa had foretold that in four days we should fire our great guns, and as this was the eve of the third day, the situation in which Tubourai Tamaide and his family had been found alarmed them. The sentries therefore were doubled at the fort and the gentlemen slept under arms.

We continued our vigilance the next day, though we had no particular reason to think it necessary; but about ten o'clock in the morning Tomio came running to the tents with a mixture of grief and fear in her countenance, and taking Mr. Banks, to whom they applied in every emergency and distress, by the arm, intimated that Tubourai Tamaide was dying, in consequence of something which our people had given him to eat, and that he must instantly go with her to his house. Mr. Banks set out without delay, and found his Indian friend leaning his head against a post, in an attitude of the utmost languor and despondency. The people about him intimated that he had been vomiting, and brought out a leaf folded up with great care, which they said contained some of the poison by the deleterious effects of which he was now dying. Mr. Banks hastily opened the leaf, and upon examining its contents found them to be no other than a chew of tobacco, which the chief had begged of some of our people, and which they had indiscreetly given him. He had observed that they kept it long in the mouth, and being desirous of doing the same, he had chewed it to powder, and swallowed the spittle. During the examination of the leaf and its contents, he looked up at Mr. Banks with the most piteous aspect, and intimated that he had but a very short time to live. Mr. Banks, however, being now master of his disease, directed him to drink plentifully of cocoa-nut milk, which in a short time put an end to his sickness and apprehensions, and he spent the day at the fort with that uncommon flow of cheerfulness and good-humour which is always produced by a sudden and unexpected relief from pain either of body or mind.

On Tuesday, 2nd, about 9 o'clock, when Mr. Green and I went to set up the quadrant, it was not to be found. May. It had never been taken out of the packing-case (which was about eighteen inches square) since it came from Mr. Bird, the maker; and the whole was pretty heavy, so that it was a matter of astonishment to us all how it could be taken away, as a sentinel stood the whole night within five yards of the door of the tent where it was put, together with several other instruments; but none of them were missing but this. However, it was not long before we got information that one of the natives had taken it away and carried it to the eastward. Immediately a resolution was taken to detain all the large canoes that were in the bay, and to seize upon Tootaha and some others of the principal people, and keep them in custody until the quadrant was produced; but this last we did not think proper immediately to put in execution, as we had only Oberea in our power, and the detaining of her by force would have alarmed all the rest. In the meantime Mr. Banks (who is always very alert upon all occasions wherein the natives are concerned) and Mr. Green went into the woods to inquire of Tubourai Tamaide which way and where the quadrant was gone. I very soon was informed that these three were gone to the eastward in quest of it, and some time after I followed myself with a small party of men; but before I went away I gave orders that if Tootaha came either to the ship or the fort he was not to be detained, for I found he had no hand in taking away the quadrant, and that there was almost a certainty of getting it again. I met Mr. Banks and Mr. Green about four miles from the fort returning with the quadrant. This was about sunset, and we all got back to the fort about eight o'clock, where I found Tootaha in custody, and a number of the natives crowding about the gate of the fort. My going into the woods with a party of armed men so alarmed the natives that in the evening they began to move off with their effects, and a double canoe putting off from the bottom of the bay was observed by the ship, and a boat sent after her.

In this canoe happened to be Tootaha, and as soon as our boat came up with her, he and all the people that were in the canoe jumped overboard. And he only was taken up and brought on board the ship, together with the canoe; the rest were permitted to swim to the shore. From the ship Tootaha was sent to the fort, where Mr. Hicks thought proper to detain him until I returned. The scene between Tubourai Tamaide and Tootaha, when the former came into the fort and found the latter in custody, was really moving. They wept over each other for some time. As for Tootaha, he was so far prepossessed with the thought that he was to be killed, that he could not be made sensible to the contrary till he was carried out of the fort to the people, many of whom expressed their joy by embracing him; and, after all, he would not go away until he had given us two hogs, notwithstanding we did all in our power to hinder him, for it is very certain that the treatment he had met with from us did not merit such a reward. However, we had it in our power to make him a present of equal value whenever we pleased.

On the 9th, Oberea, the *Dolphin's* queen, made us a visit for the first time since the quadrant was stolen. She introduced herself with a small pig, for which she had a hatchet; and as soon as she got it she lugged out a broken axe, and several pieces of old iron. These, I believe, she must have had from the *Dolphin*. The axe she wanted to be mended, and axes made of the old iron. I obliged her in the first, but excused myself in the latter. Since the natives had seen the forge at work they have frequently brought pieces of iron to be made into one sort of tool or other, which hath generally been done whenever it did not hinder our own work, being willing to oblige them in everything in my power. These pieces of old iron the natives must have got from the *Dolphin*, as we know of no other ship being here; and very probably some from us, for there is no species of theft they will not commit to get this article, and I may say the same of the common seamen when in these parts.

On the 10th, I put some seeds of melons and other plants into a spot of ground which had been turned up for the purpose. They had all been sealed up, by the person of whom they were bought, in small bottles with rosin; but none of them came up except mustard. Even the cucumbers and melons failed, and Mr. Banks is of opinion that they were spoiled by the total exclusion of fresh air.

This day we learned the Indian name of the island, which is Otaheite, and by that name I shall hereafter distinguish it. But, after great pains taken, we found it utterly impossible to teach the Indians to pronounce our names. We had therefore new names, consisting of such sounds as they produced in the attempt. They called me *Toote;* Mr. Hicks, *Hete;* Molineux they renounced in absolute despair, and called the master *Boba*, from his Christian name Robert; Mr. Gore was *Toarro;* Dr. Solander, *Torano;* and Mr. Banks, *Tapane;* Mr. Green, *Eteree;* Mr. Parkinson, *Patini;* Mr. Sporing, *Polini;* Petersgill, *Petrodero;* and in this manner they had now formed names for almost every man in the ship: in some, however, it was not easy to find any traces of the original.

On the 14th, which was Sunday, I directed that divine service should be performed at the fort. We were desirous that some of the principal Indians should be present, but when the hour came most of them were returned home. Mr. Banks, however, crossed the river, and brought back Tubourai Tamaide and his wife Tomio, hoping that it would give occasion to some inquiries on their part, and some instruction on ours. Having seated them, he placed himself between them, and during the whole service they very attentively observed his behaviour, and very exactly imitated it, standing, sitting, or kneeling as they saw him do. They were conscious that we were employed about something serious and important, as appeared by their calling to the Indians without the fort to be silent; yet when the service was over, neither of them asked any questions, nor would they attend to any attempt that was made to explain what had been done.

As our longboat had appeared to be leaky, I thought it necessary to examine her bottom, and, to my great surprise, found it so much eaten by the worms, that it was necessary to give her a new one. No such accident had happened to the *Dolphin's* boats, as I was informed by the officers on board, and therefore it was a misfortune that I did not expect. I feared that the pinnace also might be nearly in the same condition; but upon examining her, I had the satisfaction to find that not a worm had touched her, though she was built of the same wood, and had been as much in the water. The reason of this difference I imagine to be, that the longboat was paid with varnish of pine, and the pinnace painted with white-lead and oil. The bottoms of all boats, therefore, which are sent into this country should be painted like that of the pinnace, and the ships should be supplied with a good stock, in order to give them a new coating when it should be found necessary.

Having received repeated messages from Tootaha that, if we would pay him a visit, he would acknowledge the favour by a present of four hogs, I sent Mr. Hicks, my first lieutenant, to try if he could not procure the hogs upon easier terms, with orders to show him every civility in his power. Mr. Hicks found that he was removed from Apparra to a place five miles farther to the westward. He was received with great cordiality; one hog was immediately produced, and he was told that the other three, which were at some distance, should be brought in the morning. Mr. Hicks readily consented to stay; but the morning came without the hogs, and, it not being convenient to stay longer, he returned in the evening with the one that he had got.

CHAPTER IV.

OBSERVATION OF THE TRANSIT OF VENUS—TRANSACTIONS AND INCIDENTS AT OTAHEITE—CIRCUMNAVIGATION OF THE ISLAND—MR. BANKS'S EXPEDITION —DISAPPEARANCE OF TWO MEN.

ON the 27th, myself, Mr. Banks, and Dr. Solander set out in the pinnace to pay Tootaha a visit, who had moved from Apparra to the SW. part of the island. What induced us to make him this visit was a message we had received from him some days ago, importing that if we would go to him he would give us several hogs. We had no great faith in this, yet we were resolved to try, and set out accordingly. It was night before we reached the place where he was, and as we had left the boat about half-way behind us, we were obliged to take up our quarters with him for the night. The chief received us in a friendly manner, and a pig was ordered to be killed and dressed for supper; but we saved his life for the present, thinking it would do us more service in another place, and we supped on fruit and what else we could get. Here was, along with the chief, Obarea and many more that we knew. They all seemed to be travellers like ourselves, for neither the canoes they had along with them nor the houses where they were were sufficient to contain the one-half of them. We were in all six of us, and, after supper, began to look out for lodgings. Mr. Banks went to one place, Dr. Solander to another, while I and the other three went to a third. We all of us took as much care of the little we had about us as possible, knowing very well what sort of people we were among; yet, notwithstanding all the care we took, before twelve o'clock most of us had lost something or other. For my own part I had my stockings taken from under my head, and yet I am certain that I was not asleep the whole time. Obarea took charge of Mr. Banks's things, and yet they were stolen from her, as she pretended. Tootaha was acquainted

1769.
May.

with what had happened, I believe by Obarea herself, and both he and she made some stir about it; but this was all mere show, and ended in nothing. A little time after this Tootaha came to the hut where I and those that were with me lay, and entertained us with a concert of music, consisting of three drums, four flutes, and singing. This lasted about an hour, and then they retired. The music and singing was so much of a piece that I was very glad when it was over. We stayed with them till near noon the next day in hopes of getting some of our things again, and likewise some hogs; but we were obliged at last to come away with the one we had saved out of the fire last night, and a promise from Tootaha that he would come to the ship in a day or two with more, and bring with him the things that are lost, a promise we had no reason to expect he would fulfil. Thus ended our visit, and we got to the fort late in the evening.

As we were returning to the boat, however, we were entertained with a sight that in some measure compensated for our fatigue and disappointment. In our way we came to one of the few places where access to the island is not guarded by a reef, and consequently a high surf breaks upon the shore. A more dreadful one indeed I had seldom seen: it was impossible for any European boat to have lived in it; and if the best swimmer in Europe had, by any accident, been exposed to its fury, I am confident that he would not have been able to preserve himself from drowning, especially as the shore was covered with pebbles and large stones; yet in the midst of these breakers were ten or twelve Indians swimming for their amusement. Whenever a surf broke near them, they dived under it, and, to all appearance with infinite facility, rose again on the other side.

As the day of observation now approached, I determined, in consequence of some hints which had been given me by Lord Morton, to send out two parties to observe the transit from other situations; hoping that if we should fail at Otaheite, they might have better success. We were therefore now busily employed in preparing our instruments, and instructing such gentlemen in the use of them as I intended to send out.

On Thursday the 1st of June, the Saturday following being the day of the transit, I dispatched Mr. Gore in the longboat to

Transit of ♀ Sat. June 3ʳᵈ 1769.

Time by the Clock
Morning
H . ʹ .. ʺ
9 . 21 . 50 — The first visible appearance of ♀ on the ☉ʹˢ Limb. Very faint as in Fig. 1.   Fig 1.

— 39 . 20 — First Internal Contact or the outer Limb of ♀ seem'd to coincide with that of the ☉ and appear'd as in Fig. 2.   Fig 2.

— 40 . 20   A small Thread of light seen below the Penumbra, as in Fig. 3 —   Fig 3.

Evening

(The part of the N.S. wanting)

the Limb of Venus and the Penumbra was hardly to be distinguished from each other and the precise time that the Penumbra left the sun could not be observ'd to a great degree of certainty, at least not by me

The Penumbra was Visible during the whole Transit and appear'd to be equal to ⅛ part of Venus's Semidiameter

Jam⁵ Cook

THE TRANSIT OF VENUS.

Imao, with Mr. Monkhouse and Mr. Sporing, a gentleman belonging to Mr. Banks, Mr. Green having furnished them with proper instruments. Mr. Banks himself thought fit to go upon this expedition, and several natives, particularly Tubourai Tamaide and Tomio, were also of the party. Very early on the Friday morning I sent Mr. Hicks, with Mr. Clerk and Mr. Petersgill, the master's mates, and Mr. Saunders, one of the midshipmen, in the pinnace to the eastward, with orders to fix on some convenient spot, at a distance from our principal observatory, where they also might employ the instruments with which they had been furnished for the same purpose.

The day proved as favourable to our purpose as we could wish. Not a cloud was to be seen the whole day, and the air was perfectly clear, so that we had every advantage we could desire in observing the whole of the passage of the planet Venus over the sun's disc. We very distinctly saw an atmosphere or dusky shade round the body of the planet, which very much disturbed the times of the contact, particularly the two internal ones. Mr. Green's telescope and mine were of the same magnifying power, but that of the doctor was greater than ours. It was nearly calm the whole day, and the thermometer exposed to the sun about the middle of the day rose to a degree of heat we have not before met with.

On Sunday the 4th, I punished Archibald Wolf with two dozen lashes for theft, having broken into one of the storerooms and stolen from thence a large quantity of spike-nails. Some ten of them were found upon him. The same evening, the gentlemen that were sent to observe the transit of Venus returned with success. Those that were sent to York Island were well received by the natives.

On the 5th, we kept His Majesty's birthday; for though it is the 4th, we were unwilling to celebrate it during the absence of the two parties who had been sent out to observe the transit. We had several of the Indian chiefs at our entertainment, who drank His Majesty's health by the name of Kihiargo, which was the nearest imitation they could produce of King George.

On the 12th, complaint being made to me by some of the natives that two of the seamen had taken from them several bows and arrows and some strings of plaited hair, I examined the matter, and finding the charge well supported, I punished each of the criminals with two dozen lashes.

Their bows and arrows have not been mentioned before, nor were they often brought down to the fort. This day, however, Tubourai Tamaide brought down his, in consequence of a challenge which he had received from Mr. Gore. The chief supposed it was to try who could send the arrow farthest; Mr. Gore, who best could hit a mark: and as Mr. Gore did not value himself upon shooting to a great distance, nor the chief upon hitting a mark, there was no trial of skill between them. Tubourai Tamaide, however, to show us what he could do, drew his bow, and sent an arrow, none of which are feathered, two hundred and seventy-four yards, which is something more than a seventh, and something less than a sixth part of a mile. Their manner of shooting is somewhat singular; they kneel down, and the moment the arrow is discharged drop the bow.

On Wednesday the 14th, between two and four o'clock in the morning, one of the natives stole out of the fort an iron rake made use of for the oven. It happened to be set up against the wall, and by that means was visible from the outside, and had been seen by them in the evening, as a man had been seen lurking about the fort some hours before the thing was missed. I was informed by some others of the natives that he watched an opportunity when the sentinel's back was turned; he hooked it with a long crooked stick, and hauled it over the wall. When I came to be informed of this theft in the morning, I resolved to recover it by some means or other, and accordingly went and took possession of all the canoes of any value I could meet with, and brought them into the river behind the fort to the number of twenty-two, and told the natives then present (most of them being the owners of the canoes) that unless the principal things they had stolen from us were restored, I would burn them every one—not that I ever intended to put this in execution. And yet I was very much displeased with them, as they were daily committing, or attempting to commit, one theft or other, when at the same time —contrary to the opinion of everybody—I would not suffer them to be fired upon, for this would have been putting it in the power of the sentinels to have fired upon them upon the slightest occasions, as I had before experienced. And I have a great objection to firing with powder amongst people who know not the difference, for by this they would learn to despise firearms and think their own arms superior, and if ever such an opinion prevailed they would certainly attack you, the event of which might prove as unfavourable to you as to them. About noon the rake was restored us, when they wanted to have their canoes again; but now, as I had them in my possession, I was resolved to try if they would not redeem them by restoring what they had stolen from us before. The principal things which we had lost were a marine musket, a pair of pistols belonging to Mr. Banks, a sword belonging to one of the petty officers, and a water-cask, with some other articles not worth mentioning. Some said that these things were not in the island, others that Tootaha had them, and those of Tootaha's friends laid the whole to Obarea; and I believe the whole was between these two persons.

Thursday, 15th, we employed in overhauling all the sea provisions, and stowing such as we found in a state of decay to hand, in order to be first expended; but having the people divided between the ship and the shore, this work, as well as refitting the ship, goes on but slowly.

Another accident also about this time was, notwithstanding all our caution, very near embroiling us with the Indians. I sent the boat on shore with an officer to get ballast for the ship, and not immediately finding stones convenient for the purpose, he began to pull down some part of an enclosure where they deposited the bones of their dead. This the Indians violently opposed, and a messenger came down to the tents to acquaint the officers that they would not suffer it. Mr. Banks immediately repaired to the place, and an amicable end was soon put to the dispute by sending the boat's crew to the river, where stones enough were to be gathered without a possibility of giving offence. It is very remarkable that these Indians appeared to be much more jealous of what was done to the dead than the living. This was the only measure in which they ventured to oppose us, and the only insult that was offered to any individual among us was upon a similar occasion. Mr. Monkhouse happening one day to pull a flower from a tree which grew in one of their sepulchral enclosures, an Indian, whose jealousy had probably been upon the watch, came suddenly behind him and struck him. Mr. Monkhouse laid hold of him, but he was instantly rescued by two more, who took hold of Mr. Monkhouse's hair, and forced him to quit his hold of their companion, and then ran away without offering him any further violence.

In the morning Obarea brought her canoe, with everything she had, to the gate of the fort; after which we could not help admiring her for her courage and the confidence she seemed to place in us, and thought that we could do no less than to receive her into favour, and accept the present she had brought us, which consisted of a hog, a dog, some bread-fruit, and plantains.

We refused to accept of the dog, as being an animal we had no use for, at which she seemed a little surprised, and told us it was very good eating; and we very soon had an opportunity to find that it was so, for Mr. Banks having bought a basket of fruit in which was the thigh of a dog ready dressed, of this several of us tasted, and found that it was meat not to be despised, and therefore took Obarea's dog and had him immediately dressed by some of the natives in the following manner :—They first made a hole in the ground about a foot deep, in which they made a fire and heated some small stones. While this was doing the dog was strangled and the hair got off by laying him frequently on the fire, and as clean as if it had been scalded off with hot water. His entrails were taken out, and the whole washed clean; and as soon as the stones and hole were sufficiently heated, the fire was put out and part of the stones were left in the bottom of the hole. Upon these stones were laid green leaves, and upon them the dog, together with the entrails; these were likewise covered with leaves, and over them hot stones, and then the hole was close covered with mould. After he had lain here about four hours, the oven (for so I must call it) was opened and the dog taken out, whole and well done; and it was the opinion of every one who tasted it that they never ate sweeter meat, therefore we resolved for the future never to despise dog's flesh. It is in this manner that the natives dress and bake all their victuals that require it—flesh, fish, and fruit.

On Monday, 26th, very early in the morning, I set out in the pinnace, accompanied by Mr. Banks, with an intent to make the circuit of the island in order to examine and draw a sketch of the coast and harbours thereof. We took our route to the eastward, and this night reached the isthmus, which is a low neck of land running across the island, which divides it into two districts or governments wholly independent of each other, as we were informed. The first thing we saw which struck our attention in this day's route was a small pig that had not been roasted above a day or two, laid upon one of their altars near to a place where lay the body or bones of a dead person. This pig must have been put there as an offering to their god, but on what account we know not.

Soon after we had examined this place, we took boat, and asked one, Tituboalo, to go with us to the other side of the bay; but he refused, and advised us not to go, for he said the country there was inhabited by people who were not subject to Tootaha, and who would kill both him and us. Upon receiving this intelligence, we did not, as may be imagined, relinquish our enterprise; but we immediately loaded our pieces with ball. This was so well understood by Tituboalo as a precaution which rendered us formidable, that he now consented to be of our party.

Having rowed till it was dark, we reached a low neck of land, or isthmus, at the bottom of the bay that divides the island into two peninsulas, each of which is a district or government wholly independent of the other. From Port-Royal, where the ship was at anchor, the coast trends E. by S. and ESE. ten miles, then S. by E. and S. eleven miles to the isthmus. In the first direction, the shore is in general open to the sea; but in the last, it is covered by reefs of rocks which form several good harbours, with safe anchorage in sixteen, eighteen, twenty, and twenty-four fathoms of water, with other conveniences. As we had not yet got into our enemy's country, we determined to sleep on shore. We landed, and though we found but few houses, we saw several double canoes whose owners were well known to us, and who provided us with supper and lodging.

It was late last night before we reached the isthmus, and all the observation I could make this morning was that it appeared to be a marshy flat of about two miles in extent, across which the natives haul their canoes, partly by land and partly by water. From the isthmus the land trends east-southerly near three leagues, to the south-east point of the great bay which lies before the isthmus. On the west side of this point is a bay called Ohitepepa, which is in many respects similar to Royal Bay, and is situated in every bit as fertile and populous a part of the island. There are other places formed by the reefs that lie along the shore between this and the isthmus where shipping can lie in perfect security.

In a long house in this neighbourhood we saw what was altogether new to us. At one end of it, fastened to a semicircular board, hung fifteen human jawbones. They appeared to be fresh, and there was not one of them that wanted a single tooth. A sight so extraordinary strongly excited our curiosity, and we made many inquiries about it, but at this time could get no information, for the people either could not, or would not, understand us.

The next district in which we landed was the last in Tiarrabou, and governed by a chief whose name we understood to be Omoe. Omoe was building a house, and being therefore very desirous of procuring a hatchet, he would have been glad to have purchased one with anything that he had in his possession. It happened, however, rather unfortunately for him and us, that we had not one hatchet left in the boat. We offered to trade with nails, but he would not part with anything in exchange for them. We therefore re-embarked, and put off our boat; but the chief, being unwilling to relinquish all hope of obtaining something from us that would be of use to him, embarked in a canoe with his wife Whanno-ouda, and followed us. After some time, we took them into the boat; and when we had rowed about a league, they desired we would put ashore. We immediately complied with his request, and found some of his people who had brought down a very large hog. We were as unwilling to lose the hog as the chief was to part with us, and it was indeed worth the best axe we had in the ship. We therefore hit upon an expedient, and told him that if he would bring his hog to the fort at Matavai—the Indian name for Port Royal Bay—he should have a large axe, and a nail into the bargain, for his trouble. To this proposal, after having consulted with his wife, he agreed, and gave us a large piece of his country cloth as a pledge that he would perform his agreement, which, however, he never did.

At this place we saw a very singular curiosity. It was the

figure of a man, constructed of basket-work, rudely made, but not ill designed; it was something more than seven feet high, and rather too bulky in proportion to its height. The wicker skeleton was completely covered with feathers, which were white where the skin was to appear, and black in the parts which it is their custom to paint or stain, and upon the head, where there was to be a representation of hair. Upon the head also were four protuberances, three in front and one behind, which we should have called horns, but which the Indians dignified with the name of *Tate Ete*— little men. The image was called Manioe, and was said to be the only one of the kind in Otaheite. They attempted to give us an explanation of its use and design, but we had not then acquired enough of their language to understand them. We learned, however, afterwards that it was a representation of Manwe, one of their eatuas, or gods of the second class.

After having thus gratified our curiosity we returned to our quarters, where we passed the night in perfect security and quiet. By the next evening we arrived at Atahourou, the residence of our friend Tootaha, where, the last time we passed the night under his protection, we had been obliged to leave the best part of our clothes behind us. This adventure, however, seemed now to be forgotten on both sides. Our friends received us with great pleasure, and gave us a good supper and a good lodging, where we suffered neither loss nor disturbance.

The next day, Saturday, July the 1st, we got back to our fort at Matavai, having found the circuit of the island, including both peninsulas, to be about thirty leagues. Upon our complaining of the want of bread-fruit, we were told that the produce of the last season was nearly exhausted, and that what was seen sprouting upon the trees would not be fit to use in less than three months; this accounted for our having been able to procure so little of it in our route.

*T*he natives live now on sour paste which is made from bread-fruit, and some bread-fruit and plantains that they get from the mountains where the season is later, and on a nut not unlike a chestnut, which are now in perfection; but all these articles are at present very scarce, and therefore it is no wonder that the natives have not supplied us with these things of late. Upon my return to the ship I found that the provisions had been all examined, and the water got on board, amounting to sixty-five tuns. I now determined to get everything off from the shore, and leave the place as soon as possible. The getting the several articles on board, and scraping and paying the ship's side, took us up the following week without anything remarkable happening.

On Sunday, July 9, some time in the middle watch, Clement Webb and Samuel Gibson, both marines and young men, found means to get away from the fort (which was now no hard matter to do), and in the morning were not to be found. As it was known to everybody that all hands were to go on board on the Monday morning, and that the ship would sail in a day or two, there was reason to think that these two men intended to stay behind. However, I was willing to stay one day to see if they would return before I took any step to find them.

On Monday morning the 10th, the marines, to my great concern, not being returned, an inquiry was made after them of the Indians, who frankly told us that they did not intend to return, and had taken refuge in the mountains, where it was impossible for our people to find them. They were then requested to assist in the search, and after some deliberation, two of them undertook to conduct such persons as I should think proper to send after them to the place of their retreat. As they were known to be without arms, I thought two would be sufficient, and accordingly dispatched a petty officer and the corporal of the marines, with the Indian guides, to fetch them back. As the recovery of these men was a matter of great importance, as I had no time to lose, and as the Indians spoke doubtfully of their return, telling us that they had each of them taken a wife and were become inhabitants of the country, it was intimated to several of the chiefs who were in the fort with their women, among whom were Tubourai *T*amaide, Tomio, and Oberea, that they would not be permitted to leave it till our deserters were brought back. This precaution I thought the more necessary, as, by concealing them a few days, they might compel me to go without them; and I had the pleasure to observe that they received the intimation with very little signs either of fear or discontent, assuring me that my people should be secured and sent back as soon as possible. While this was doing at the fort, I sent Mr. Hicks in the pinnace to fetch Tootaha on board the ship, which he did, without alarming either him or his people. If the Indian guides proved faithful and in earnest, I had reason to expect the return of my people with the deserters before evening. Being disappointed, my suspicions increased; and night coming on, I thought it was not safe to let the people whom I had detained as hostages continue at the fort, and I therefore ordered Tubourai Tamaide, Oberea, and others to be taken on board the ship. This spread a general alarm, and several of them, especially the women, expressed their apprehensions with great emotion and many tears when they were put into the boat.

About nine o'clock Webb was brought back by some of the natives, who declared that Gibson and the petty officer and corporal would be detained till Tootaha should be set at liberty. Immediately upon getting this information I dispatched Mr. Hicks away in the longboat with a strong party of men to rescue them; but before he went, Tootaha and the other chiefs were made to understand that they must send some of their people with Mr. Hicks to show him the place where our men were, and at the same time to send orders for their immediate release, for if any harm came to the men, they (the chiefs) would suffer for it; and I believe at this time they wished as much to see the men return in safety as I did, for the guides conducted Mr. Hicks to the place before daylight, and he recovered the men without the least opposition, and returned with them about seven o'clock in the morning of Tuesday, 11th. I then told the chiefs that there remained nothing more to be done to regain their liberty but to deliver up the arms the people had taken from the petty officer and corporal, and these were brought on board in less than half an hour, and then I sent them all on shore.

Among the natives who were almost constantly with us was Tupia. He had been the first minister of Oberea, when she was in the height of her power. He was also the chief tahowa, or priest, of the island; consequently well acquainted with the religion of the country, as well with respect to its ceremonies as principles. He had also great experience and knowledge in navigation, and was particularly acquainted with the number and situation of the neighbouring islands. This man had often expressed a desire to go with us, and on the 12th, in the morning, having with the other natives left us the day before, he came on board with a boy about thirteen years of age, his servant, and urged us to let him proceed with us on our voyage. To have such a person on board was certainly desirable for many reasons; by learning his language, and teaching him ours, we should be able to acquire a much better knowledge of the customs, policy, and religion of the people than our short stay among them could give us. I therefore gladly agreed to receive them on board. As we were prevented from sailing to-day, by having found it necessary to make new stocks to our small and best bower-anchors, the old ones having been totally destroyed by the worms, Tupia said he would go once more on shore, and make a signal for the boat to fetch him off in the evening. He went accordingly, and took with him a miniature picture of Mr. Banks's to show his friends, and several little things to give them as parting presents.

On the next morning, Thursday the 13th of July, the ship was very early crowded with our friends, and surrounded by a multitude of canoes, which were filled with the natives of an inferior class. Between eleven and twelve we weighed anchor, and as soon as the ship was under sail the Indians on board took their leave, and wept, with a decent and silent sorrow, in which there was something very striking and tender. The people in the canoes, on the contrary, seemed to vie with each other in the loudness of their lamentations, which we considered rather as affectation than grief. Tupia sustained himself in this scene with a firmness and resolution truly admirable. He wept, indeed; but the effort that he made to conceal his tears concurred with them to do him honour. He sent his last present, a shirt, by Otheothea to Potomai, and then went with Mr. Banks to the mast-head, waving to the canoes as long as they continued in sight.

Thus we took leave of Otaheite and its inhabitants after a stay of just three months. For much the greater part of the time we lived together in the most cordial friendship. The accidental differences which now and then happened could not be more sincerely regretted on their part than they were on ours. The principal causes were such as necessarily resulted from our situation and circumstances, from our not being able perfectly to understand each other, and from the disposition of the inhabitants to theft, which we could not at all times bear with or prevent.

For the first two months we were at this island the natives supplied us with as much bread-fruit, cocoa-nuts, etc., as we could well dispense with, and now and then a few hogs, but of these hardly sufficient to give the ship's company one and sometimes two fresh meals a week. As to fowls, I did not see above three dozen upon the whole island, and fish they seldom would part with; but during the last month we got little refreshment of any sort. The detaining of their canoes broke off trade at that time, and it never after was begun again with any spirit. However, it was not wholly owing to this, but to a scarcity. The season for bread-fruit was wholly over, and what other fruits they had were hardly sufficient for themselves; at least, they did not care to part with them. All sorts of fruits we purchased with beads and nails, not less than forty a penny, for a nail under that size was of no value; but we could not get a hog above ten or twelve pounds weight for anything less than a hatchet—not but that they set great value upon spike-nails, but as this was an article many in the ship are provided with, the women soon found a much easier way at coming at them than by bringing provisions. Our traffic with this people was carried on with as much order as in the best-regulated market in Europe. It was managed ashore chiefly by Mr. Banks, who took uncommon pains to procure from the natives every kind of refreshment that was to be got. Axes, hatchets, spikes, large nails, looking-glasses, knives, and beads are all highly valued by this people, and nothing more is wanting to traffic with them for everything they have to dispose of. They are likewise very fond of fine linen cloth, both white and printed; but an axe worth half a crown will fetch more than a piece of cloth worth twenty shillings.

CHAPTER V.

DESCRIPTION OF THE ISLAND—ITS PEOPLE, HABITS, AND CUSTOMS—VISITS TO HUAHEINE, ULIETEA (RAIATEA), OTAHA (TAHAA), BOLABOLA—DEPARTURE FROM THE SOCIETY ISLANDS FOR NEW ZEALAND.

1769.
July.

THE produce of this island is bread-fruit, cocoa-nuts, bananas of thirteen sorts, the best we had ever eaten; plantains, a fruit not unlike an apple, which, when ripe, is very pleasant; sweet potatoes, yams, cocoas, a kind of *arum;* a fruit known here by the name of *jambu*, and reckoned most delicions; sugar-cane, which the inhabitants eat raw; a root of the salop kind, called by the inhabitants *pea;* a plant called *ethee*, of which the root only is eaten; a fruit that grows in a pod, like that of a large kidney-bean, which, when it is roasted, eats very much like a chestnut, by the natives called *ahee;* a tree called *wharra*—called in the East Indies *pandanes*—which produces fruit something like the pine-apple; a shrub called *nono;* the *morinda*, which also produces fruit; a species of fern, of which the root is eaten, and sometimes the leaves; and a plant called *theve*, of which the root also is eaten: but the fruits of the *nono*, the fern, and the *theve* are eaten only by the inferior people, and in times of scarcity. Not only fish, but almost everything that comes out of the sea, is eaten and esteemed by these people; shellfish, lobsters, crabs, and even sea insects, and what is commonly called blubbers of many kinds, conduce to their support.

For tame animals they have hogs, fowls, and dogs—the latter of which we learned to eat from them, and few were there of us but what allowed that a South Sea dog was next to an English lamb. One thing in their favour is that they live entirely upon vegetables; probably our dogs would not eat half so well. Little can be said in favour of their fowls, but their pork is most excellent.

They have no beasts of prey of any sort, and wild fowls are scarce and confined to a few species. When any of the chiefs kill a hog, it seems to be almost equally divided among all his dependants, and as these are generally very numerous, it is but a little that comes to each person's share, so that their chief food is vegetables, and of these they eat a large quantity.

Cookery seems to have been but little studied here. They have only two methods of applying fire—broiling and baking, as we called it. The method by which this is done I have before described, and I am of opinion that victuals dressed this way are more juicy and more equally done than by any of our methods, large fish in particular, bread-fruit, bananas. Plantains cooked this way eat like boiled potatoes, and were much used by us by way of bread whenever we could get them. Of bread-fruit they make two or three dishes by beating it with a stone pestle till it makes a paste, mixing water or cocoa-nut liquor, or both, with it, and adding ripe plantains, bananas, sour paste, etc.

This last is made from bread-fruit in the following manner. This fruit, from what I can find, remains in season only eight or nine months in the year, and as it is the chief support of the inhabitants, a reserve of food must be made for those months when they are without it. To do this the fruit is gathered when upon the point of ripening; after the rind is scraped off it is laid in heaps and covered close with leaves, where it undergoes a fermentation and becomes soft and disagreeably sweet. The core is taken out, and the rest of the fruit thrown into a hole dug for that purpose, the sides and bottom of which are neatly laid with grass. The whole is covered with leaves and heavy stones laid upon them. Here it undergoes a second fermentation and becomes sourish, in which condition, they say, it will keep good ten or twelve months. As they want to use it they make it into balls, which they wrap up in leaves and bake in the same manner as they do the fruit from the tree. It is then ready for eating, either hot or cold, and hath a sour and disagreeable taste. In this last state it will keep good a month or six weeks. It is called by them *mahai*, and they seldom make a meal without some of it, one way or another. To this plain diet salt water is the universal sauce. Hardly any one sits down to a meal without a cocoa-nut shell full of it standing by them, into which they dip most of what they eat, especially fish, drinking at intervals large sops of it out of their hands, so that a man may use half a pint at a meal.

With respect to their persons, the men in general are tall, strong limbed, and well shaped. One of the tallest we saw measured six feet three inches and a half. The superior women are in every respect as large as Europeans, but the inferior sort are in general small, owing possibly to their early amours, which they are more addicted to than their superiors. They are of various colours: those of the inferior sort, who are obliged to be much exposed to the sun and air, are of a very dark brown; the superiors again, who spend most of their time in their houses under shelter, are not browner than people who are born or reside long in the West Indies; nay, some of the women are almost as fair as Europeans. Their hair is almost universally black, thick, and strong; this the women wear short cropped round their ears. The men, on the other hand, wear it different ways; the better sort let it grow long, sometimes tying it up on the top of their heads, or letting it hang loose over their shoulders.

They have all fine white teeth, and, for the most part, short flat noses and thick lips; yet their features are agreeable and their gait graceful, and their behaviour to strangers and to each other is open, affable, and courteous, and, from all I could see, free from treachery, only that they are thieves to a man; and would steal everything that came in their way, and that with such dexterity as would shame the most noted pickpocket in Europe. They are very cleanly people both in their persons and diet, always washing their hands and mouth immediately before and after their meals, and wash or bathe themselves in fresh water three times a day, morning, noon, and night.

The only disagreeable thing about them is the oil with which they anoint their heads, *monoe*, as they call it. This is made of cocoa-nut oil in which some sweet herbs or flowers are infused. The oil is generally very rancid, which makes the wearer of it smell not very agreeable. Another custom they have that is disagreeable to Europeans is eating lice, a pretty good stock of which they generally carry about them. However, this custom is not universal, for I seldom saw it done but among children and common people, and I am persuaded that, had they the means, they would keep themselves as free from lice as we do; but the want of combs in a hot climate makes this hardly possible.

Both sexes paint their bodies, *tattow*, as it is called in their language. This is done by inlaying the colour of black under their skins, in such a manner as to be indelible. Some have ill-designed figures of men, birds, or dogs; the women generally have this figure Z simply on every joint of their fingers and toes. Their clothing is either of cloth or matting of several different sorts. The dress of both men and women is much the same. A piece of cloth or matting wrapped two or three times round their waist hangs down below their knees, both behind and before, like a petticoat. Through another piece, about two, or two and a half yards long, with a hole in the middle, they put their heads. This hangs over their shoulders, down behind and before, and is tied round their waist with a long piece of thin cloth, and, being open at the sides, gives liberty to their arms. This is the common dress of all ranks of people, and there are few without such an one, except the children, who go quite naked, the boys until they are six or seven years of age, and the girls until three or four.

Both sexes sometimes shade their faces from the sun with little bonnets made of cocoa-nut leaves. Some have them of fine matting, but this is less common. They sometimes wear turbans, but their chief head-dress is what they call *tomou*, which is human hair plaited scarce thicker than common thread. Of this I can safely affirm that I have seen pieces near a mile in length worked upon one end without a knot. These are made and worn only by the women, five or six such pieces of which they will sometimes wind round their heads, the effect of which, if done with taste, is very becoming. They have earrings by way of ornament, but wear them only at one ear. These are made of shells, stones, berries, red peas, and some small pearls which they wear three tied together; but our beads, buttons, etc., very soon supplied their places.

The houses or dwellings of these people are admirably calculated for the continual warmth of the climate. They do not build them in towns or villages, but separate each from the other, and always in the woods, and are without walls; so that the air, cooled by the shade of the trees, has free access in whatever direction it happens to blow. No country can boast of more delightful walks than this. The whole plains where the natives reside are covered with groves of bread-fruit and cocoa-nut trees, without underwood, and intersected in all directions by the paths which go from house to house, so that nothing can be more grateful in a climate where the sun hath so powerful an influence. The houses are generally built in form of an oblong square. The roofs are supported by three rows of pillars or posts, and neatly covered with thatch made of palm-leaves. A middle-sized house is about twenty-four feet by twelve, extreme height about eight or nine, and height of the eaves three and a half or four. The floors are covered some inches deep with hay, upon which, here and there, lie mats for the convenience of sitting down; few houses have more than one stool, which is only used by the master of the family.

Their canoes are built all of them very narrow, and some of the largest are sixty or seventy feet long. These consist of several pieces: the bottom is round and made of large logs hollowed out to the thickness of about three inches, and may consist of three or four pieces; the sides are of plank of nearly the same thickness, and are built nearly perpendicular, rounding in a little towards the gunwale. The pieces on which they are built are well fitted, and fastened or sewed together with strong plaiting, something in the same manner as old china, wooden bowls, etc., are mended. The greatest breadth is at the after part, which is generally about eighteen or twenty inches, and the fore part about one-third narrower. The height from the bottom to the gunwale seldom exceeds two and a half or three feet. They build them with high, curved sterns, which are generally ornamented with carved work; the head or fore part curves little or nothing. The smaller canoes are built after the same plan, some out of one, two, or more trees, according to their size or the use they are for. In order to prevent them from oversetting when in the water, all those that go single, both great and small, have what is called outriggers, which are pieces of wood fastened to the gunwale and projecting out on one side about six, eight, or ten feet, according to the size of the boat. At the end is fastened in a parallel direction to the canoe a long log of wood simply—or some have it shaped in the form of a small boat, but this is not common; this

NATIV

OTAHEITE.

Page 60.

lies in the water and balances the boat. Those that are for sailing have outriggers only on the other side, abreast of the mast; these serve to fasten the shrouds to, and are of use in trimming the boat when it blows fresh. The sailing proes have some one, and some two masts. The sails are of matting, and are made narrow at the head and square at the foot, something like a shoulder-of-mutton sail, such as are generally used in man-of-war barges, etc.

Having described their canoes, I shall next describe their arms with which they attack their enemies, both by sea and land. These are clubs, spears or lances, slings and stones which they throw by hand. The clubs are made of a hard wood, and are about eight or nine feet long. The one half is made flattish with two edges, and the other half is round and not thicker than to be easily grasped by the hand. The lances are of various lengths, some from twelve to twenty or thirty feet, and are generally armed at the small end with the stings of sting-rays, which make them very dangerous weapons. Although these people have bows and arrows—and those none of the worst—we are told that they never use them in their wars, which doubtless is very extraordinary, and not easily accounted for. They have very curious breastplates, made of small wickers, pieces of matting, etc., and neatly covered with sharks' teeth, pearl-oyster shells, birds' feathers, and dogs' hair. Thus much for their arms, etc.

The island is divided into two districts or kingdoms, which are frequently at war with each other, as happened about twelve months ago, and each of these is again divided into smaller districts, *whennuas* as they call them. Over each of the kingdoms is an *eare dehi*, or head, whom we call a king, and in the *whennuas* are *eares*, or chiefs. The king's power seems to be but very little. He may be reverenced as a father, but he is neither feared nor respected as a monarch, and the same may be said of the other chiefs. However, they have a pre-eminence over the rest of the people, who pay them a kind of a voluntary obedience. Upon the whole, these people seem to enjoy liberty in its fullest extent. Every man seems to be the sole judge of his own actions, and to know no punishment but death, and this, perhaps, is never inflicted but upon a public enemy. There are three ranks of men and women : first, the *eares*, or chiefs ; second, the *manahoonas*, or middling sort ; and, lastly, the *toutous*, which comprehend all the lower class, and are by far the most numerous. These seem to live in some sort dependent on the *eares*, who, together with the *manahoonas*, own most, if not all the land. This is hereditary in their families, and the moment the heir is born he succeeds the father both in title and estate; at least to the name, for it is most likely that the latter must have the power during his son or daughter's minority.

Having given the best account I can of the manners and customs of these people, it will be expected that I should give some account of their religion, which is a thing I have learned so little of that I hardly dare to touch upon it, and should have passed it over in silence, were it not my duty as well as inclination to insert in this journal all the knowledge I may obtain of a people who for many centuries have been shut up from almost every other part of the world.

They believe that there is one supreme god, whom they call *Tane*. From him sprung a number of inferior deities, *eatuas* as they call them : these they think preside over them and intermeddle in their affairs. To these they offer oblations such as hogs, dogs, fish, fruit, etc., and invoke them on some particular occasions, as in time of real or apparent danger, the setting out of a long voyage, sicknesses, etc. ; but the ceremony made use of on these occasions I know not. The *mories*, which we at first thought were burying places, are wholly built for places of worship and for the performing of religious ceremonies in. The viands are laid upon altars erected eight or twelve feet high by stout posts, and the table of the altar on which the viands lie is generally made of palm leaves ; they are not always in the *mories*, but very often at some distance from them. Their *mories*, as well as the tombs of the dead, they seem to hold sacred, and the women never enter the former, whatever they may do the latter. The viands laid near the tombs of the dead are not for the deceased, but as an offering to the *eatua* made upon that occasion, who, if not, would destroy the body and not accept the soul ; for they believe in a future state of rewards and punishments, but what their ideas are of it I know not.

They compute time by the moon, which they call *malama*, reckoning thirty days to each moon, during two of which they say the moon is *mattee*, that is, dead, and this is at the time of the new moon, when she cannot be seen. The day they divide into smaller portions, not less than two hours. Their computation is by units, tens, and scores, up to ten score, or two hundred, etc. In counting they generally take hold on their fingers one by one, shifting from one hand to the other until they come to the number they want to express; but if it be a high number, instead of their fingers, they use pieces of leaves, etc.

In conversation one with another they frequently join signs to their words, in which they are so expressive that a stranger will very soon comprehend their meaning by their actions.

Having now done with the people, I must once more return to the island before I quit it altogether, which, notwithstanding nature hath been so very bountiful to it, does not produce any one thing of intrinsic value or that can be converted into an article of trade; so that the value of the discovery consists wholly in the refreshments it will always afford to shipping passing through those seas, and in this it may be greatly improved by transporting hither horned cattle, etc. Pumpkins have got quite a footing here, the seeds of which, most probably, were brought here by the Spaniards. We sowed the seeds of water and musk melons, which grew up and throve very fast. We also gave these seeds and the seeds of pine apples to several of the natives, and it cannot be doubted that they will thrive here and will be a great addition to the fruits they already have. Upon our first arrival we sowed all sorts of English garden seeds and grain, but not a single thing came up except mustard salad; but this, I know, was not owing either to the soil or climate, but to the badness of the seeds, which were spoiled by the length of the passage.

Although this island lies within the Tropic of Capricorn, yet the heat is not troublesome, nor do the winds blow constantly from the east, but are subject to variations, frequently blowing a fresh gale from the south-west quarter for two or three days together, but very seldom from the north-west. Whenever these variable winds happen, they are always accompanied with a swell from the SW.

or WSW., and the same thing happens whenever it is calm and the atmosphere at the same time loaded with clouds—sure indication that the winds are variable or westerly out at sea, for clear weather generally attends the settled trade.

After parting with our friends, we made an easy sail, with gentle breezes and clear weather, and were informed by Tupia that four of the neighbouring islands, which he distinguished by the names of Huaheine, Ulietea, Otaha, and Bolabola, lay at the distance of between one and two days' sail from Otaheite, and that hogs, fowls, and other refreshments, with which we had of late been but sparingly supplied, were there to be procured in great plenty; but having discovered from the hills of Otaheite an island lying to the northward, which he called Tethuroa, I determined first to stand that way, to take a nearer view of it. It lies N. ½ W. distant eight leagues from the northern extremity of Otaheite, upon which we had observed the transit, and to which we had, for that reason, given the name of Point Venus. We found it to be a small, low island, and were told by Tupia that it had no settled inhabitants, but was occasionally visited by the inhabitants of Otaheite, who sometimes went thither for a few days to fish; we therefore determined to spend no more time in a further examination of it, but to go in search of Huaheine and Ulietea, which he described to be well peopled, and as large as Otaheite.

On the 16th, being close in with the north-west part of the island of Huaheine, we sounded, but had no ground with eighty fathoms.

Some of the natives came off to the ship, but they were very shy of coming near until they discovered Tupia; but after that they came on board without hesitation. Among those who came on board was the king of the island. He had not been long on board before I was given to understand that his name was Oree, and he proposed, as a mark of amity, that we should exchange names. To this I readily consented; and he was Cookee—for so he pronounced my name—and I was Oree for the rest of the time we were together. We found these people to be very nearly the same with those of Otaheite, in person, dress, language, and every other circumstance, except, if *T*upia might be believed, that they would not steal.

Soon after dinner we came to an anchor in a small but excellent harbour on the west side of the island, which the natives call Owharre, in eighteen fathoms water, clear ground, and secure from all winds. I went immediately ashore, accompanied by Mr. Banks, Dr. Solander, Mr. Monkhouse, Tupia, King Cookee, and some other of the natives who had been on board ever since the morning.

Tupia at once sat down before a great number of the natives that were collected together in a large shed or house, the rest of us, by his own desire, standing behind; he then began a long speech or prayer, which lasted near a quarter of an hour, and in the course of this speech presented to the people two handkerchiefs, a black silk neckcloth, some beads, and two very small bunches of feathers. These things he had before provided for that purpose. At the same time two chiefs spoke on the other side in answer to Tupia, as I suppose, in behalf of the people, and presented us with some young plantain plants, and two small bunches of feathers. These were by Tupia ordered to be carried on board the ship. After the peace was thus concluded and ratified, every one was at liberty to go where he pleased, and the first thing Tupia did was to go and pay his oblations at one of the mories. This seemed to be a common ceremony with this people, and I suppose always performed upon landing on each other's territories in a peaceable manner. It further appeared that the things which Tupia gave away were for the god of this people, as they gave us a hog and some cocoa-nuts for our God, and thus they have certainly drawn us in to commit sacrilege, for the hog hath already received sentence of death, and is to be dissected to-morrow.

We had commenced a kind of trade with the natives, but it went on slowly; for when anything was offered, not one of them would take it upon his own judgment, but collected the opinions of twenty or thirty people, which could not be done without great loss of time. We got, however, eleven pigs, and determined to try for more the next day.

The next day we brought out some hatchets, for which we hoped we should have had no occasion upon an island which no European had ever visited before. These procured us three very large hogs; and as we proposed to sail in the afternoon, King Oree and several others came on board to take their leave. To the king I gave a small plate of pewter, on which was stamped this inscription, "His Britannic Majesty's Ship *Endeavour*, Lieutenant Cook Commander, 16th July 1769, Huaheine." I gave him also some medals or counters, resembling the coin of England, struck in the year 1761, with some other presents; and he promised that with none of these, particularly the plate, he would ever part. I thought it as lasting a testimony of our having first discovered this island as any we could leave behind; and having dismissed our visitors well satisfied, and in great good-humour, we set sail about half an hour after two in the afternoon.

We now made sail for the island of Ulietea, which lies SW. by W., distant seven or eight leagues from Huaheine, and at half an hour after six in the evening we were within three leagues of the shore, on the eastern side. We stood off and on all night, and when the day broke the next morning, we stood in for the shore. We soon after discovered an opening in the reef which lies before the island, within which Tupia told us there was a good harbour. I did not, however, implicitly take his word, but sent the master out in the pinnace to examine it. He soon made the signal for the ship to follow; we accordingly stood in, and anchored in two and twenty fathoms, with soft ground.

The natives soon came off to us in two canoes, each of which brought a woman and a pig. The woman we supposed was a mark of confidence, and the pig was a present. We received both with proper acknowledgments, and complimented each of the ladies with a spike-nail and some beads, much to their satisfaction. We were told by Tupia, who had always expressed much fear of the men of Bolabola, that they had made a conquest of this island, and that, if we remained here, they would certainly come down to-morrow and fight us.

The principal refreshments we have got here consist in plantains, cocoa-nuts, some yams, and a few hogs and fowls. This side of the island is neither populous nor rich in produce, if compared to George's Island, or even Huaheine: however, there is no want of refreshments for a ship that may put in here and stay but a short time; and wood and water may be got everywhere, though the latter is not very convenient to come at.

On the 26th we were again at sea, without having received any interruption from the hostile inhabitants of Bolabola, whom, notwithstanding the fears of Tupia, we intended to visit. At four o'clock in the afternoon of the 25th, we were within a league of Otaha, which bore N. 77 W. To the northward of the south end of that island, on the east side of it, and something more than a mile from the shore, lie two small islands, called Toahoutu and Whennuaia; between which, Tupia says, there is a channel into a very good harbour.

Between five and six in the evening of the 26th, as I was standing to the northward, I discovered a small low island, lying N. by W. or NNW., distant four or five leagues from Bolabola. We were told by Tupia that the name of this island is Tubai; that it produces nothing but cocoa-nuts, and is inhabited only by three families, though it is visited by the inhabitants of the neighbouring islands, who resort thither to catch fish, with which the coast abounds.

I made sail to the northward, and at eight o'clock in the morning of the 29th, we were close under the Peak of Bolabola, which was high, rude, and craggy. As the island was altogether inaccessible in this part, and we found it impossible to weather it, we tacked and stood off, then tacked again, and after many trips did not weather the south end of it till twelve o'clock at night. At eight o'clock the next morning we discovered an island, which bore from us N. 63 W., distant about eight leagues; at the same time the Peak of Bolabola bore N. ½ E., distant three or four leagues. This island Tupia called Maurua, and said that it was small, wholly surrounded by a reef, and without any harbour for shipping, but inhabited, and bearing the same produce as the neighbouring islands. The middle of it rises in a high round hill, that may be seen at the distance of ten leagues.

On the 1st of August we found ourselves nearly the length of the south end of Ulietea, and to windward of some harbours that lay on the west side of this island. Into one of them I intended to go with the ship, in order to stop a leak in the powder room, which could not be easily done at sea, and to take in more ballast, as I found her too light to carry sail upon a wind.

August.

A great many natives came off to us both last night and this morning, and brought with them hogs, fowls, plantains, etc., which they parted with at a very easy rate.

On *T*hursday the 3rd I went ashore to look for a place to get stones for ballast, and a watering place, both of which I found very convenient; and in the morning sent an officer ashore to superintend the getting off the ballast and water, and I went in the pinnace to the northward to survey that part of the island, accompanied by Mr. Banks and Dr. Solander, while the carpenters were employed on board stopping the leaks of the powder room and foresail room.

On Friday the 4th it was calm, hot, and sultry. In our route to the northward this afternoon we were entertained at one place with music and dancing. The music consisted of three drums, and the dancing was mostly performed by two young women and one man, and this seemed to be their profession. The dress of the women was such as we had not seen before: it was neat, decent, and well chosen, and in many respects not much unlike a European dress; only their arms, necks, and shoulders were bare, and their head-dress was the *tomow* stuck with flowers. They made very little use of their feet and legs in dancing, but one part or another of their bodies was in continual motion and in various postures, as standing, sitting, and upon their hands and knees. Their arms, hands, and fingers they moved with great agility and in a very extraordinary manner, and although they were very exact in observing the same motion in all their movements, yet neither their music nor dancing was at all calculated to please a European.

Being desirous to see King Opoony, we made a party this afternoon, and I went ashore for that purpose, carrying along with us a small present. Upon our landing he did not receive us sitting, as all the other chiefs had hitherto done, or in any manner of form; this we attributed to his stupidity. However, he gave me a hog in return for the present I made him, and this was paying us full as great a compliment. Before we took our leave we let him know that we should go to Otaha in the morning in our boats, and would be glad to have him along with us, and he accordingly promised to accompany us thither. Accordingly, very early in the morning, I set out with both pinnace and longboat for Otaha, and some of the gentlemen along with me; and in our way called upon Opoony, who was in his canoe ready to set out. As soon as we landed on Otaha, I made him a present of an axe; this I thought would induce him to encourage his subjects to bring us such provisions as we wanted, but I believe we had already got all they intended us, for after staying with him until noon, we were obliged to go away without getting any one thing.

After leaving Opoony we proceeded towards the north point of the island, and in our way picked up half a dozen hogs, as many fowls, and some plantains and yams; and I had an opportunity to view and draw a sketch of the harbour which lies on this side of the island, and which was the only thing that induced me to make this excursion. After it was dark we met with the longboat, which I had in the morning dispatched to another part of the island; and we now made the best of our way to the ship, and got on board about ten at night. The carpenter having finished stopping the leaks about the powder room and sail room, I now intend to sail as soon as ever the wind will permit us to get out of the harbour.

At 11 a.m. on the 9th a breeze of wind sprung up at E., which carried us out of the harbour, and as soon as the boats were hoisted in made sail to the southward. Since we have been about these islands we have expended but little of our sea provisions, and have at this last place been very plentifully supplied with hogs, fowls, plantains, and yams, which will be of very great use to us in case we should not discover any lands in our route to the southward, the way I now intend to steer.

To these six islands, Ulietea, Otaha, Bolabola, Huaheine, Tubai, and Maurua, as they lie contiguous to each other, I gave the name of Society Islands, but did not think it proper to distinguish them separately by any other names than those by which they were known to the natives.

The produce of these islands, and manners and customs of the natives, are much the same as at King George's Island, only as the bread-fruit tree is here in not such plenty, the natives, to supply that deficiency, plant and cultivate a greater quantity of plantains and yams of several sorts, and these they have in the greatest perfection.

The inhabitants are rather of a fairer colour than the generality of the natives of George's Island, but more especially the women, who are much fairer and handsomer; and the men are not so much addicted to thieving, and are more open and free in their behaviour.

The only difference we could see in their religion was in the houses of their gods, which were very different from those we saw on George's Island. Those here were made about the size and shape of a coffin open at one end; they are laid upon a number of small wooden arches, which are framed and fastened together like the roof of a house, and these are generally supported about three or four feet above the ground by posts. Over the box is a small roof or shade made of palm thatch; in this box are deposited the oblations to the gods, such as pieces of cloth, human bone, etc., and these places they hold sacred, and some are placed in their mories, and some not. They have a custom of preserving the skulls and under jaw-bones of the dead, but whether of their friends or enemies I cannot pretend to say.

Several of the skulls, we observed, were broken, and it is very probable that the owners of them had been killed in battle, as some of their weapons are well calculated for breaking of heads; and from what we could learn, it is a custom with them to cut out the lower jaw of their enemies, but I believe not before they are killed, and these they keep as trophies, and sometimes hang up in their houses.

The chief or king of Bolabola hath of late years usurped the sovereignty of the other two, and the Bolabola men at this time possess great part of the lands on Ulietea and Otaha that they have taken from the natives. The lands adjoining to the harbours of Oraotanue belonged to Tupia, the person we have on board, who is a native of Ulietea. These people are very ingenious in building their canoes, and seem to take much care of them, having large shades or houses to put them in, built for the purpose; and in these houses they likewise build and repair them, and in this they show a great deal of ingenuity, far more than one could expect.

In these canoes—*pahies* as they call them—from all the accounts we can learn, these people sail in those seas from island to island for several hundred leagues, the sun serving them for a compass by day, and the moon and stars by night. When this comes to be proved, we shall be no longer at a loss to know how the islands lying in those seas came to be peopled; for if the inhabitants of Ulietea have been at islands lying two or three hundred leagues to the westward of them, it cannot be doubted that the inhabitants of those western islands may have been at others as far to westward of them, and so we may trace them from island to island quite to the East Indies.

Tupia tells us that during the months of November, December, and January westerly winds, with rain, prevail; and as the inhabitants of the islands know very well how to make the proper use of the winds, no difficulty will arise in trading or sailing from island to island, even though they lie in an east and west direction.

CHAPTER VI.

PASSAGE FROM SOCIETY ISLES TO NEW ZEALAND—INCIDENTS WHICH HAPPENED WHILE THE SHIP LAY IN POVERTY BAY—DEPARTURE FROM POVERTY BAY.

1769.
August. WE sailed again on the 15th, and steered southward. The farthest island to the southward that Tupia has been at, or knows anything of, lies but two days' sail from Ohetiroa, and is called *Moutou*, but he says that his father once told him that there were islands to the southward of it; but we cannot find that he either knows or ever heard of a continent or large tract of land. I have no reason to doubt Tupia's information on these islands, for when we left Ulietea and steered to the southward he told us that if we would keep a little more to the east (which the wind would not permit us to do) we should see Manua, but as we then steered we should see Ohetiroa, which happened accordingly. If we meet with the islands to the southward he speaks of, it is well; but if not, I shall spend no more time searching for them, being now fully resolved to stand directly to the southward in search of a continent. As we advanced to the southward, into cold weather and a troubled sea, the hogs we got at Ulietea began to die apace. They cannot endure the least cold, nor will they eat anything but vegetables, so that they are not at all to be depended upon at sea. The fowls also have a complaint general among them which affects their heads, so that they continue holding them down betwixt their legs until they die; this, at least, was the fate of most of ours. This is necessary to be known to those who come such voyages as these, lest they place too much dependence on the live-stock they get at the islands.

On Friday the 25th we celebrated the anniversary of our leaving England by taking a Cheshire cheese from a locker, where it had been carefully treasured up for this occasion, and tapping a cask of porter, which proved to be very good and in excellent order. On the 28th one of the sailors got so drunk that the next morning he died. We thought at first that he could not have come honestly by the liquor, but we afterwards learned that the boatswain, whose mate he was, had in mere good nature given him part of a bottle of rum.

On the 30th we saw the comet. At one o'clock in the morning it was a little above the horizon in the east; at about half an hour after four it passed the meridian, and its tail subtended an angle of forty-two degrees.

On Saturday, 2nd, we had very strong gales, with heavy squalls of wind, hail, and rain. At 4 p.m., being in the latitude of 40° 22′ S., and having not the least visible signs of land, we wore, and brought to under the foresail, and reefed the mainsail, and handed it. I did intend to have stood to the southward if the winds had been moderate, so long as they continued westerly, notwithstanding we had no prospect of meeting with land, rather than stand back to the northward on the same track as we came; but as the weather was so very tempestuous I laid aside this design, and thought it more advisable to stand to the northward into better weather, lest we should receive such damage in our sails and rigging as might hinder the further prosecution of the voyage. Some albatrosses, pintado birds, and doves about the ship, and a bird larger than a duck, his plumage of a dark brown, with a yellow beak. We saw some of these birds in our passage to the northward, after doubling Cape Horn. At noon the weather was more moderate, but we had a great sea from the WSW.

Sept.

On Sunday, October 1st, we saw an immense number of birds, the most of them were doves; saw likewise a seal asleep upon the water, which we at first took for a crooked billet. These creatures, as they lie upon the water, hold their fins up in a very odd manner, and very different from any I have seen before. We generally reckon that seals never go out of soundings or far from land; but the few we have seen in this sea are certainly an exception to that rule. However, one would think that we were not far from some land, from the pieces of rock weed we see daily

October.

floating upon the water. To-day we took up a small piece of stick, but to all appearance it had been a long time at sea.

At 2 p.m. on Saturday, 7th, we saw land * from the mast-head bearing WSW., which we stood directly for, and could but just see it from the deck by sunset.

At 5 p.m. next day, seeing the opening of a bay that appeared to run pretty far inland, hauled our wind and stood in for it; but as soon as night came on we kept plying on and off until daylight, when we found ourselves to leeward of the bay, the wind being at north. By noon we fetched in with the SW. point, but not being able to weather it, we tacked and stood off. We saw in the bay several canoes, people upon the shore, and some houses in the country. The land on the sea-coast is high, with steep cliffs, and back inland are very high mountains. The face of the country is of a hilly surface, and appears to be clothed with wood and verdure.

About four o'clock in the afternoon we anchored on the northwest side of the bay, before the entrance of a small river, in ten fathoms water, with a fine sandy bottom, and at about half a league from the shore. The sides of the bay are white cliffs of a great height; the middle is low land, with hills gradually rising behind, one towering above another, and terminating in the chain of mountains which appeared to be far inland.

In the evening I went on shore, accompanied by Mr. Banks and Dr. Solander, with the pinnace and yawl and a party of men. We landed abreast of the ship, on the east side of the river, which was here about forty yards broad; but seeing some natives on the west side whom I wished to speak with, and finding the river not fordable, I ordered the yawl in to carry us over, and left the pinnace at the entrance. When we came near the place where the people were assembled, they all ran away; however, we landed, and leaving four boys to take care of the yawl, we walked up to some huts which were about two or three hundred yards from the water side. When we had got some distance from the boat, four men, armed with long lances, rushed out of the woods, and running up to attack the boat, would certainly have cut her off, if the people in the pinnace had not discovered them, and called to the

* The North Island of New Zealand.

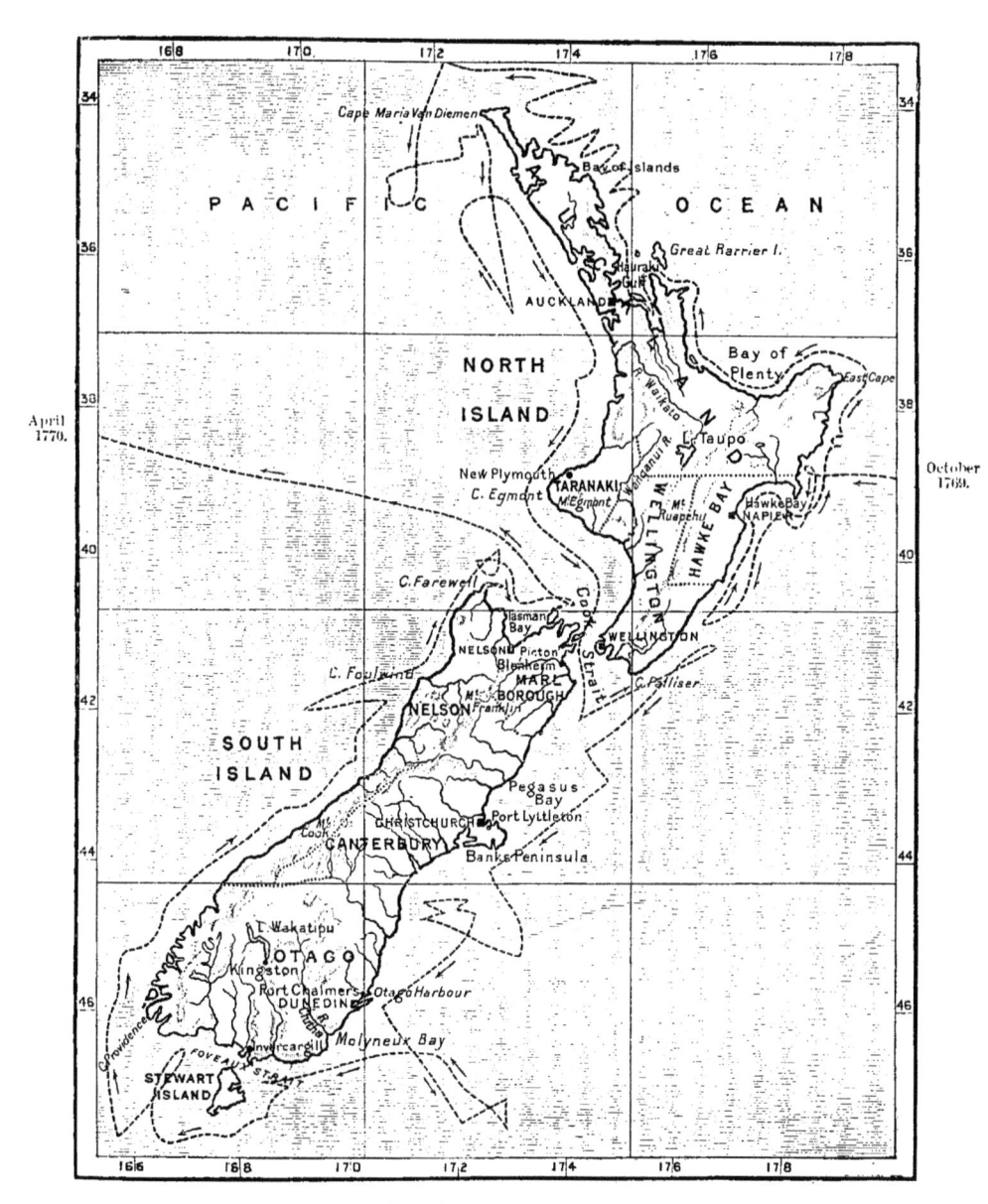

MAP OF NEW ZEALAND.

Page 74.

boys to drop down the stream. The boys instantly obeyed; but being closely pursued by the Indians, the cockswain of the pinnace, who had the charge of the boats, fired a musket over their heads. At this they stopped and looked round them, but in a few minutes renewed the pursuit, brandishing their lances in a threatening manner. The cockswain then fired a second musket over their heads, but of this they took no notice; and one of them lifting up his spear to dart it at the boat, another piece was fired, which shot him dead. When he fell, the other three stood motionless for some minutes, as if petrified with astonishment; as soon as they recovered, they went back, dragging after them the dead body, which, however, they soon left, that it might not encumber their flight.

Upon our hearing the report of the muskets we immediately repaired to the boats, and after viewing the dead body we returned on board. In the morning, seeing a number of the natives at the same place where we saw them last night, I went on shore with the boats, manned and armed, and landed on the opposite side of the river. Mr. Banks, Dr. Solander, and myself only landed at first, and went to the side of the river, the natives being got together on the opposite side. We called to them in the George's Island language, but they answered us by flourishing their weapons over their heads and dancing, as we supposed, the war dance; upon this we retired until the marines were landed and drawn up about two hundred yards behind us. We went again to the river side, having Tupia, Mr. Green, and Dr. Monkhouse along with us. Tupia spoke to them in his own language, and it was an agreeable surprise to us to find that they perfectly understood him. After some little conversation had passed, one of them swam over to us, and after him twenty or thirty more; these last brought their arms, which the first man did not. We made them every one presents, but this did not satisfy them; they wanted everything we had about us, particularly our arms, and made several attempts to snatch them out of our hands. Tupia told us several times, as soon as they came over, to take care of ourselves, for they were not our friends; and this we very soon found, for one of them snatched Mr. Green's hanger from him and would not give it up. This encouraged the rest to be more insolent; and seeing others coming over to join them, I ordered the man who had taken the hanger to be fired at, which was accordingly done, and wounded in such a manner that he died soon after. Upon the first fire, which was only two muskets, the others retired to a rock which lay nearly in the middle of the river; but on seeing the man fall they returned, probably to carry him off or his arms, the last of which they accomplished, and this we could not prevent unless we had run our bayonets into them, for upon their returning from off the rock we had discharged our pieces, which were loaded with small shot, and wounded three more; but these got over the river, and were carried off by the others, who now thought proper to retire. Finding nothing was to be done with the people on this side, and the water in the river being salt, I embarked with an intent to row round the head of the bay in search of fresh water, and, if possible, to surprise some of the natives and to take them on board, and by good treatment and presents endeavour to gain their friendship with this view.

On Tuesday the 10th I rowed round the head of the bay, but, to my great regret, I found no place where I could land, a dangerous surf everywhere beating upon the shore; but I saw two canoes coming in from the sea, one under sail and the other worked with paddles. I thought this a favourable opportunity to get some of the people into my possession without mischief, as those in the canoe were probably fishermen, and without arms, and I had three boats full of men. I therefore disposed the boats so as most effectually to intercept them in their way to the shore. The people in the canoe that was paddled perceived us so soon that, by making to the nearest land with their utmost strength, they escaped us. The other sailed on till she was in the midst of us, without discerning what we were; but the moment she discovered us, the people on board struck their sail and took to their paddles, which they plied so briskly that she outran the boat. They were, however, within hearing, and Tupia called out to them to come alongside, and promised for us that they should come to no hurt: they chose, however, rather to trust to their paddles than our promises, and continued to make from us with all their power. I then ordered a musket to be fired over their heads, as the least exceptionable expedient to accomplish my design, hoping it would either make them surrender or leap into the water. Upon the discharge of the piece they ceased paddling, and all of them, being seven in number, began to strip, as we imagined to jump overboard; but it happened otherwise. They immediately formed a resolution not to fly, but to fight; and when the boat came up they began the attack with their paddles, and with stones and other offensive weapons that were in the boat, so vigorously that we were obliged to fire upon them in our own defence. Four were unhappily killed, and the other three, who were boys, the eldest about nineteen and the youngest about eleven, instantly leaped into the water. The eldest swam with great vigour and resisted the attempts of our people to take him into the boat by every effort that he could make; he was, however, at last overpowered, and the other two were taken up with less difficulty.

As soon as the poor wretches whom we had taken out of the water were in the boat, they squatted down, expecting, no doubt, instantly to be put to death. We made haste to convince them to the contrary by every method in our power; we furnished them with clothes, and gave them every other testimony of kindness that could remove their fears. Before we reached the ship, their suspicions and fears being wholly removed, they appeared to be not only reconciled to their situation, but in high spirits, and upon being offered some bread when they came on board, they devoured it with a voracious appetite. They answered and asked many questions with great appearance of pleasure and curiosity; and when our dinner came, they expressed an inclination to taste everything that they saw. They seemed best pleased with the salt pork, though we had other provisions upon the table. At sunset they ate another meal with great eagerness, each devouring a large quantity of bread and drinking above a quart of water. We then made them beds upon the lockers, and they went to sleep with great seeming content. In the night, however, the tumult of their minds having subsided and given way to reflection, they sighed often and loud. Tupia, who was always upon the watch to comfort them, got up, and by soothing and encouragement made them not only easy but cheerful. Their cheerfulness was encouraged so that they sung a song with a degree of taste that surprised us; the tune was solemn and slow, like those of our psalms, containing many notes and semitones. Their countenances were intelligent and expressive, and the middlemost, who seemed to be about fifteen, had an openness in his aspect and an ease in his deportment which were very striking. We found that the two eldest were brothers, and that their names were Taahourange and Koikerange; the name of the youngest was Maragovete. As we were returning to the ship, after having taken these boys into the boat, we picked up a large piece of pumice stone floating upon the water—a sure sign that there either is or has been a volcano in this neighbourhood.

In the morning they seemed to be cheerful, and ate another enormous meal. We adorned them with bracelets, anklets, and necklaces, after their own fashion; and the boat being hoisted out, they were told that we were going to set them ashore. This produced a transport of joy; but upon perceiving that we made towards our first landing place near the river, their countenances changed, and they entreated with great earnestness that they might not be set ashore at that place, because they said it was inhabited by their enemies, who would kill them and eat them.

Upon our landing with the boys and crossing the river, they seemed at first to be unwilling to leave us; but at length, with some tears, they took their leave.

After we had advanced about a mile we heard that a large body of the Indians was in sight, and advancing at a great rate. Upon receiving this intelligence we drew together, and resolved to make the best of our way to the boats. We had scarcely begun to put this into execution when the three Indian boys started suddenly from some bushes where they had concealed themselves, and again claimed our protection. We readily received them, and repairing to the beach as the clearest place, we walked briskly towards the boats. The Indians were in two bodies; one ran along the bank which had been quitted by the marines, the other fetched a compass by the swamp, so that we could not see them. When they perceived that we had formed into one body, they slackened their pace, but still followed us in a gentle walk. That they slackened their pace was for us, as well as for them, a fortunate circumstance; for when we came to the side of the river where we expected to find the boats that were to carry us over to the wooders, we found the pinnace at least a mile from her station, having been sent to pick up a bird which had been shot by the officer on shore; and the little boat was obliged to make three trips before we could all get over to the rest of the party. As soon as we were drawn up on the other side, the Indians came down, not in a body as we expected, but by two or three at a time, all armed; and in a short time their number increased to about two hundred. As we now despaired of making peace with them, seeing that the dread of our small-arms did not keep them at a distance, and that the ship was too far off to reach the place with a shot, we resolved to re-embark, lest our stay should embroil us in another quarrel, and cost more of the Indians their lives. We therefore advanced towards the pinnace, which was now returning, when one of the boys suddenly cried out that his uncle was among the people who had marched down to us, and desired us to stay and talk with them. We complied, and a parley immediately commenced between them and Tupia, during which the boys held up everything that we had given them as tokens of our kindness and liberality. At last one of the men, uncle of one of the boys, swam over to us, bringing in his hand a green branch, which we supposed, as well here as at Otaheite, to be an emblem of peace. We received his branch by the hands of Tupia, and made him many presents; we also invited him to go on board the ship, but he declined. We therefore left him, and expected that his nephew and the two other young Indians would have stayed with him; but to our great surprise, they chose rather to go with us.

After dinner, I directed Tupia to ask the boys if they had now any objection to going ashore where we had left their uncle. They said they had not; and the boat being ordered, they went into it with great alacrity. When the boat, in which I had sent two midshipmen, came to land, they went willingly ashore; but soon after she put off they returned to the rocks, and wading into the water, earnestly entreated to be taken on board again; but the people in the boat, having positive orders to leave them, could not comply. We were very attentive to what happened on shore; and keeping a constant watch with our glasses, we saw a man pass the river upon another raft, and fetch them to a place where forty or fifty of the natives were assembled, who closed round them, and continued in the same place till sunset. Upon looking again, when we saw them in motion, we could plainly distinguish our three prisoners, who separated themselves from the rest, came down to the beach, and having waved their hands three times towards the ship, ran nimbly back and joined their companions, who walked leisurely away towards that part which the boys had pointed to as their dwelling-place. We had therefore the greatest reason to believe that no mischief would happen to them, especially as we perceived that they went off in the clothes we had given them.

After it was dark, loud voices were heard on shore in the bottom of the bay as usual, of which we could never learn the meaning.

At 6 a.m. we weighed and stood out of the bay, which I have named Poverty Bay, because it afforded us no one thing we wanted (lat. 38° 42' S., long. 181° 36' W.). It is in the form of a horse-shoe, and is known by an island lying close under the north-east point. The two points which form the entrance are high, with steep white cliffs, and lay a league and a half or two leagues from each other. The depth of water in this bay is from twelve to six and five fathoms, a sandy bottom and good anchorage, but you lie open to the winds between the S. and E. Boats can go in and out of the river above mentioned at any time of tide in fine weather; but there is a bar at the entrance, on which the sea sometimes runs so high that no boat can either get in or out, which happened while we lay here. However, I believe that boats can generally land on the north-east side of the river. The shore of this bay, from a little within each entrance, is a low, flat sand; but this is only a narrow slip, for the face of the country appears with a variety of hills and valleys, all clothed with woods and verdure, and to all appearance well inhabited, especially in the valleys leading up from the bay, where we daily saw smoke at a great distance inland; and far back in the country are very high mountains. At noon the south-west point of Poverty Bay, which I have named Young Nick's Head (after the boy who first saw this land), bore N. by W., distance three or four leagues, being at this time about three miles from the shore, and had twenty-five fathoms water, the mainland extending from NE. by N. to S. My intention is to follow the direction of the coast to the southward as far as the latitude of 40° or 41°, and then to return to the northward in case we meet with nothing to encourage us to proceed farther.

In the afternoon we lay becalmed, which the people on shore perceiving, several canoes put off, and came within less than a quarter of a mile of the vessel, but could not be persuaded to come nearer, though Tupia exerted all the powers of his lungs and his eloquence upon the occasion, shouting, and promising that they should not be hurt. Another canoe was now seen coming from Poverty Bay, with only four people on board, one of whom we well remembered to have seen in our first interview upon the rock. This canoe, without stopping or taking the least notice of the others, came directly alongside of the ship, and with very little persuasion we got the Indians on board. Their example was soon followed by the rest, and we had about us seven canoes, and about fifty men. We made them all presents with a liberal hand; notwithstanding which, they were so desirous to have more of our commodities, that they sold us everything they had, even the clothes from their backs, and the paddles from their boats.

When these people had recovered from the first impressions of fear—which, notwithstanding their resolution in coming on board, had manifestly thrown them into some confusion—we inquired after our poor boys. The man who first came on board immediately answered that they were unhurt and at home; adding that he had been induced to venture on board by the account which they had given him of the kindness with which they had been treated, and the wonders that were in the ship.

A light breeze springing up soon after it was dark, we steered along the shore under an easy sail till midnight, and then brought to, soon after which it fell calm. We were now some leagues distant from the place where the canoes had left us; and at daybreak, when the Indians perceived it, they were seized with consternation and terror, and lamented their situation in loud complaints, with gestures of despair and many tears. Tupia with great difficulty pacified them; and about seven o'clock in the morning, a light breeze springing up, we continued to stand southwest along the shore. Fortunately for our poor Indians, two canoes came off about this time, and made towards the ship. They stopped, however, at a little distance, and seemed unwilling to trust themselves nearer. Our Indians were greatly agitated in this state of uncertainty, and urged their fellows to come alongside of the ship both by their voice and gestures with the utmost eagerness and impatience. Tupia interpreted what they said, and we were much surprised to find that, among other arguments, they assured the people in the canoes we did not eat men. We now began seriously to believe that this horrid custom prevailed among them; for what the boys had said we considered as a mere hyperbolical expression of their fear. One of the canoes at length ventured to come under the ship's side; and an old man came on board, who seemed to be a chief, from the finery of his garment, and the superiority of his weapon, which was a patoo-patoo, made of bone that, as he said, had belonged to a whale. He stayed on board but a short time, and when he went away he took with him our guests, very much to the satisfaction both of them and us.

On Wednesday the 11th we passed a point which, on account of its figure, I called Cape Table. This point lies seven leagues to the southward of Poverty Bay. It is of a considerable height, and appears to be quite flat at the top.

At noon a small island, which was the southernmost land in sight, appeared at the distance of about three miles. This island, which the natives call Teahowray, I named the island of Portland, from its very great resemblance to Portland in the English Channel.

In the evening we stood in for a place that had the appearance of an opening, but found no harbour. We therefore stood out again, and were soon followed by a large canoe, with eighteen or twenty men, all armed, who, though they could not reach us, shouted defiance, and brandished their weapons with many gestures of menace and insult.

In the morning we had a view of the mountains inland, upon which the snow was still lying. The country near the shore was low and unfit for culture, but in one place we perceived a patch of something yellow, which had greatly the appearance of a cornfield, yet was probably nothing more than some dead flags, which are not uncommon in swampy places. At some distance we saw groves of trees, which appeared high and tapering; and being not above two leagues from the great bay in which we had been coasting for the two last days, I hoisted out the pinnace and longboat to search for fresh water. But just as they were about to put off, we saw several boats full of people coming from the shore, and therefore I did not think it safe for them to leave the ship. About ten o'clock, five of these boats having drawn together as if to hold a consultation, made towards the ship, having on board between eighty and ninety men; and four more followed at some distance, as if to sustain the attack. When the first five came within about a hundred yards of the ship, they began to sing their war song, and brandishing their pikes, prepared for an engagement. We had now no time to lose, for if we could not prevent the attack, we should come under the unhappy necessity of using our firearms against them, which we were very desirous to avoid. Tupia was therefore ordered to acquaint them that we had weapons which, like thunder, would destroy them in a moment; and they soon paddled away with all their might.

The land near the shore is of a moderate height, with white cliffs and sandy beaches. Inland are several pretty high mountains, and the whole face of the country appears with a very hilly surface, and for the most part covered with snow; but between them and the sea the land is clothed with wood.

CHAPTER VII.

THE RANGE FROM POVERTY BAY TO CAPE TURNAGAIN, AND BACK TO TOLAGO,
WITH SOME ACCOUNT OF THE PEOPLE AND THE COUNTRY.

1769.
October.
AT 8 a.m. on the 15th, being abreast of the south-west point of the bay, some fishing-boats came off to us, and sold us some stinking fish. However, it was such as they had, and we were glad to enter into traffic with them upon any terms. These people behaved at first very well, until a large armed boat, wherein were twenty-two men, came alongside. We soon saw that this boat had nothing for traffic, yet, as they came boldly alongside, we gave them two or three pieces of cloth, articles they seemed the most fond of. One man in this boat had on him a black skin, something like a bear-skin, which I was desirous of having, that I might be a better judge what sort of an animal the first owner was. I offered him for it a piece of red cloth, which he seemed to jump at by immediately putting off the skin and holding it up to us; but he would not part with it until he had the cloth in his possession, and after that not at all, but put off the boat and went away, and with him all the rest. But in a very short time they returned again, and one of the fishing-boats came alongside and offered us some more fish. The Indian boy, Tiata, Tupia's servant, being over the side, they seized hold of him, pulled him into the boat, and endeavoured to carry him off. This obliged us to fire upon them, which gave the boy an opportunity to jump overboard. We brought the ship to, lowered a boat into the water, and took him up unhurt. Two or three paid for this daring attempt with the loss of their lives, and many more would have suffered had it not been for fear of killing the boy. This affair occasioned my giving this point of land the name of Cape Kidnappers. It is remarkable on account of two white rocks in form of haystacks

standing very near it. On each side of the cape are tolerably high white, steep cliffs, lat. 39° 43' S., long. 182° 24' W. It lies SW. by W., distant thirteen leagues from the island of Portland. Between them is a large bay wherein we have been for these three days past. This bay I have named Hawke's Bay in honour of Sir Edward, First Lord of the Admiralty. We found in it from twenty-four to eight and seven fathoms, everywhere good anchoring.

In the afternoon we had a fresh breeze at west, and during the night variable light airs and calms. In the morning a gentle breeze sprang up between the NW. and NE., and having till now stood to the southward without seeing any probability of meeting with a harbour, and the country manifestly altering for the worse, I thought that standing farther in that direction would be attended with no advantage, but on the contrary would be a loss of time that might be employed with a better prospect of success in examining the coast to the northward. About one, therefore, in the afternoon I tacked and stood north, with a fresh breeze at west. The high bluff head, with yellowish cliffs, which we were abreast of at noon, I called Cape Turnagain, because here we turned back. It lies in lat. 40° 34' S., long. 182° 55' W., distant eighteen leagues SSW. and SSW.½W. from Cape Kidnapper. The land between them is of a very unequal height. In some places it is lofty next the sea, with white cliffs; in others low, with sandy beaches. The face of the country is not so well clothed with wood as it is about Hawke's Bay, but looks more like our high downs in England. It is, however, to all appearance well inhabited, for as we stood along the shore we saw several villages, not only in the valleys, but on the tops and sides of the hills, and smoke in many other places. The ridge of mountains which has been mentioned before extends to the southward farther than we could see, and was then everywhere chequered with snow. At night we saw two fires inland, so very large that we concluded they must have been made to clear the land for tillage; but, however that be, they are a demonstration that the part of the country where they appeared is inhabited.

Soon after we tacked, a boat or canoe came off from the shore, wherein were five people. They came on board without showing the least signs of fear, and insisted upon staying with us the whole night. Indeed, there was no getting them away without turning them out of the ship by force, and that I did not care to do; but, to prevent them playing us any trick, I hoisted their canoe up alongside. Two appeared to be chiefs, and the other three their servants. One of the chiefs seemed to be of a free, open, and gentle disposition. They both took great notice of everything they saw, and were very thankful for what was given them. The two chiefs would neither eat nor drink with us, but the other three ate whatever was offered them. Notwithstanding that these people had heard of the treatment the others had met with who had been on board before, yet it appeared a little strange that they should place so much confidence in us as to put themselves wholly in our power whether we would or not, especially as the others we had met with in this bay had upon every occasion behaved in quite a different manner. At eleven, brought to until daylight (the night being dark and rainy), then made sail. At 7 a.m. brought to under Cape Table, and sent away the Indian canoe. At this time some others were putting off from the shore; but we did not wait their coming, but made sail to the northward. 3 p.m., passed by a remarkable head, which I called Gable-end Foreland, on account of the very great resemblance the white cliff at the very point has to the gable-end of a house. It is made still more remarkable by a spired rock standing a little distance from it. It lies from Cape Table N. 24 E., distant about twelve leagues. The shore between them forms a bay, within which lies Poverty Bay, at the distance of four leagues from the headland and eight from the cape. At this place three canoes came off to us, and one man came on board. We gave him some trifles, and he soon returned to his boat, which, with all the rest, dropped astern.

In the morning I made sail inshore, in order to look into two bays which appeared about two leagues to the northward of the foreland. The southernmost I could not fetch, but I anchored in the other about eleven o'clock.

Into this bay we were invited by the people on board many canoes, who pointed to a place where they said there was plenty of fresh water. I did not find so good a shelter from the sea as I expected; but the natives who came about us appearing to be of a friendly disposition, I was determined to try whether I could not get some knowledge of the country here before I proceeded farther to the northward.

In one of the canoes that came about us as soon as we anchored we saw two men who by their habits appeared to be chiefs. One of them was dressed in a jacket which was ornamented, after their manner, with dog's skin. The jacket of the other was almost covered with small tufts of red feathers. These men I invited on board, and they entered the ship with very little hesitation. I gave each of them about four yards of linen and a spike-nail. With the linen they were much pleased, but seemed to set no value upon the nail. We perceived that they knew what had happened in Poverty Bay, and we had therefore no reason to doubt that they would behave peaceably. However, for further security, Tupia was ordered to tell them for what purpose we came thither, and to assure them that we would offer them no injury if they offered none to us. In the meantime those who remained in the canoes traded with our people very fairly for what they happened to have with them. The chiefs, who were old men, stayed with us till we had dined, and about two o'clock I put off with the boats, manned and armed, in order to go on shore in search of water, and the two chiefs went into the boat with me. The afternoon was tempestuous, with much rain, and the surf everywhere ran so high that although we rowed almost round the bay, we found no place where we could land. I determined, therefore, to return to the ship, which being intimated to the chiefs, they called to the people on shore, and ordered a canoe to be sent off for themselves. This was accordingly done, and they left us, promising to come on board again in the morning, and bring us some fish and sweet potatoes.

In the evening, the weather having become fair and moderate, the boats were again ordered out, and I landed, accompanied by Mr. Banks and Dr. Solander. We were received with great expressions of friendship by the natives, who behaved with a scrupulous attention not to give offence. In particular, they took care not to appear in great bodies. One family, or the inhabitants of two or three houses only, were generally placed together, to the number of fifteen or twenty, consisting of men, women, and children. These little companies sat upon the ground, not advancing towards us, but inviting us to them by a kind of beckon, moving one hand towards the breast. We made them several little presents, and in our walk round the bay found two small streams of fresh water. This convenience and the friendly behaviour of the people determined me to stay some time at least. The women were plain, and made themselves more so by painting their faces with red ochre and oil, which, being generally fresh and wet upon their cheeks and foreheads, was easily transferred to the noses of those who thought fit to salute them; and that they were not wholly averse to such familiarity, the noses of several of our people strongly testified.

The faces of the men were not so generally painted, yet we saw one whose whole body, and even his garments, were rubbed over with dry ochre, of which he kept a piece constantly in his hand, and was every minute renewing the decoration in one part or another where he supposed it was become deficient. In personal delicacy they were not equal to our friends at Otaheite, for the coldness of the climate did not invite them so often to bathe.

As I found it exceedingly difficult to get water on board on account of the surf, I determined to stay no longer at this place. On the next morning, therefore, about five o'clock, I weighed anchor and put to sea.

This bay, which is called by the natives Tegadoo, lies in the latitude of 38° 10' S., but as it has nothing to recommend it, a description of it is unnecessary.

From this bay I intended to stand on to the northward, but the wind being right against me, I could make no way. While I was beating about to windward, some of the natives came on board, and told me that in a bay which lay a little to the southward, being the same that I could not fetch the day I put into Tegadoo, there was excellent water, where the boats might land without a surf. I thought it better, therefore, to put into this bay, where I might complete my water and form further connections with the Indians, than to keep the sea. With this view, I bore up for it, and sent in two boats, manned and armed, to examine the watering place. The report of the Indians being confirmed, I came to an anchor about one o'clock in eleven fathoms water, with a fine sandy bottom, the north point of the bay N. by E., and the south point SE. The watering place, which was in a small cove a little within the south point of the bay, bore S. by E., distant about a mile. Many canoes came immediately off from the shore, and all traded very honestly for Otaheite cloth and glass bottles, of which they were immoderately fond.

In the afternoon of the 23rd, as soon as the ship was moored, I went on shore to examine the watering place, accompanied by Mr. Banks and Dr. Solander. The boat landed in the cove without the least surf. The water was excellent and conveniently situated, there was plenty of wood close to high-water mark, and the disposition of the people was in every respect such as we could wish.

Having, with Mr. Green, taken several observations of the sun and moon, the mean result of them gave 180° 47' W. longitude; but as all the observations made before exceeded these, I have laid down the coast from the mean of the whole. At noon I took the sun's meridian altitude with an astronomical quadrant, which was set up at the watering place, and found the latitude to be 38° 22' 24".

On the 24th, early in the morning, I sent Lieutenant Gore on shore to superintend the cutting of wood and filling of water, with a sufficient number of men for both purposes, and all the marines as a guard.

Next day was employed wooding, cutting, and making of brooms, there being a shrub here very fit for that purpose; and as I intended to sail in the morning, some hands were employed picking celery to take to sea with us. This is found here in great plenty, and I have caused it to be boiled with portable soup and oatmeal every morning for the people's breakfast; and this I design to continue as long as it will last, or any is to be got, as I look upon it to be very wholesome and a great anti-scorbutic.

This bay is called by the natives Tolago. It is moderately large, and has from seven to thirteen fathoms, with a clean, sandy bottom and good anchorage, and is sheltered from all winds except the north-east. It lies in lat. 38° 22' S., and four leagues and a half to the north of Gable-end Foreland. On the south point lies a small but high island, so near the main as not to be distinguished from it. Close to the north end of the island, at the entrance into the bay, are two high rocks. One is round like a corn-stack, but the other is long, and perforated in several places, so that the openings appear like the arches of a bridge. Within these rocks is the cove where we cut wood and filled our water-casks. Off the north point of the bay is a pretty high rocky island, and about a mile without it are some rocks and breakers.

During our stay in this bay we had every day more or less traffic with the natives, they bringing us fish, and now and then a few sweet potatoes and several trifles which we deemed curiosities. For these we gave them cloth, beads, nails, etc. The cloth we got at King George's Island and Ulietea they valued more than anything we could give them; and as every one in the ship was provided with some of this sort of cloth, I suffered everybody to purchase whatever they pleased without limitation, for by this means I knew that the natives would not only sell but get a good price for everything they brought. This I thought would induce them to bring to market whatever the country afforded, and I have great reason to think that they did, yet it amounted to no more than what is above mentioned. We saw no four-footed animals, either tame or wild, or signs of any, except dogs and rats, and these were very scarce, especially the latter. The flesh of the former they eat, and ornament their clothing with their skins.

We found in the woods trees of above twenty different sorts. Specimens of each I took on board, as all of them were unknown to any of us. The tree which we cut for firing was something like maple, and yielded a whitish gum. There was another sort of a deep yellow, which we imagined might prove useful in dyeing. We likewise found one cabbage-tree, which we cut down for the sake of the cabbage. The country abounds with a great number of plants, and the woods with as great a variety of beautiful birds, many of them unknown to us. The soil of both the hills and valleys is light and sandy, and very proper for producing all kinds of roots, but we saw only sweet potatoes and yams among them. These they plant in little round hills, and have plantations of them containing several acres neatly laid out and kept in good order, and many of them are fenced in with low paling which can only serve for ornament.

On Monday the 30th, about half an hour after one o'clock, having made sail again to the northward for about ten hours with a light breeze, I hauled round a small island which lay east one mile from the north-east point of the land. From this place I found the land trend away NW. by W. and WNW. as far as I could see, this point being the easternmost land on the whole coast. I gave it the name of East Cape, and I called the island that lies off it East Island. It is of a small circuit, high and round, and appears white and barren. The cape is high, with white cliffs, and lies in lat. 37° 42′ 30″ S. and long. 181° W. The land from Tolago Bay to East Cape is of a moderate but unequal height, forming several small bays, in which are sandy beaches. Of the inland country we could not see much, the weather being cloudy and hazy. The soundings were from twenty to thirty fathoms at the distance of about a league from the shore. After we had rounded the cape, we saw in our run along the shore a great number of villages and much cultivated land. The country in general appeared more fertile than before, and was low near the sea, but hilly within. At six in the evening, being four leagues to the westward of East Cape, we passed a bay, which was first discovered by Lieutenant Hicks, and which therefore I called Hicks' Bay. At eight in the evening, being eight leagues to the westward of the cape, and three or four miles from the shore, I shortened sail and brought to for the night, having at this time a fresh gale at SSE. and squally; but it soon became moderate, and at two in the morning we made sail again to the SW. as the land now trended, and at eight o'clock in the morning saw land, which made like an island, bearing west, the south-westernmost part of the main bearing south-west.

At nine, five canoes came off to us, in one of which were upwards of forty men, all armed with pikes, etc. From this and other circumstances it fully appeared that they came with no friendly intentions, and I at this time being very busy, and having no inclination to stay upon deck to watch their motions, I ordered a grape shot to be fired a little wide of them. This made them pull off a little, and then they got together either to consult what to do or to look about them. Upon this I ordered a round shot to be fired over their heads, which frightened them to that degree that I believe they did not think themselves safe until they got ashore. This occasioned our calling the point of land off which this happened Cape Runaway. In this day's run we found that the land which made like an island in the morning, bearing west, was so, and we gave it the name of White Island.

Nov.
At daybreak on the 1st of November we counted no less than five and forty canoes that were coming from the shore towards the ship. Seven of them came up with us, and after some conversation with Tupia, sold us some lobsters and mussels, and two conger eels. These people traded pretty fairly; but when they were gone, some others came from another place, who began also to trade fairly; but after some time they took what was handed down to them, without making any return. One of them who had done so, upon being threatened, began to laugh, and with many marks of derision set us at defiance, at the same time putting off the canoe from the ship. A musket was then fired over his head, which brought him back in a more serious mood, and trade went on with great regularity. At length, when the cabin and gun-room had got as much as they wanted, the men were allowed to come to the gangway and trade for themselves. Unhappily, the same care was not taken to prevent frauds as had been taken before, so that the Indians, finding that they could cheat with impunity, grew insolent again, and proceeded to take greater liberties.

One of the canoes, having sold everything on board, pulled forward, and the people that were in her seeing some linen hanging over the ship's side to dry, one of them, without any ceremony, untied it, and put it up in his bundle. He was immediately called to, and required to return it; instead of which, he let his canoe drop astern, and laughed at us. A musket was fired over his head, which did not put a stop to his mirth; another was then fired at him with small shot, which struck him upon the back. He shrunk a little when the shot hit him, but did not regard it more than one of our men would have done the stroke of a rattan: he continned with great composure to pack up the linen that he had stolen. All the canoes now dropped astern about a hundred yards, and all set up their song of defiance, which they continued till the ship was distant from them about four hundred yards.

About two in the afternoon, we saw a pretty high island bearing west from us.

We learned from Tupia that the people in the canoe called the island which we were under Mowtohora. It is but of a small circuit, though high, and lies six miles from the main; on the south side is anchorage in fourteen fathoms water. Upon the mainland SW. by W. of this island, and apparently at no great distance from the sea, is a high round mountain, which I called Mount Edgecumbe; it stands in the middle of a large plain, and is therefore the more conspicuous; lat. 37° 59', long. 193° 7'.

In standing westward, we suddenly shoaled our water from seventeen to ten fathoms; and knowing that we were not far from the small islands and rocks which we had seen before dark, and which I intended to have passed before I brought to for the night, I thought it more prudent to tack, and spend the night under Mowtohora, where I knew there was no danger. It was indeed happy for us that we did so; for in the morning, after we had made sail to the westward, we discovered ahead of us several rocks, some of which were level with the surface of the water, and some below it: they lay NNE. from Mount Edgecumbe, one league and a half distant from the island Mowtohora, and about nine miles from the main. We passed between these rocks and the main, having from ten to seven fathoms water.

This morning, many canoes and much people were seen along the shore. Several of the canoes followed us, but none of them could reach us, except one with a sail, which proved to be the same that had pelted us the night before. The people on board again entered into conversation with Tupia; but we expected another volley of their ammunition, which was not indeed dangerous to anything but the cabin windows. They continued abreast of the ship about an hour, and behaved very peaceably.

At two on the 3rd we passed a small high island lying four miles from a high round head on the main; from this head the land trends NW. as far as we could see, and appeared to be very rugged and hilly. The weather being very hazy, and the wind blowing fresh on shore, we hauled off close upon a wind for the weathermost island in sight. Under this island we spent the night, having a fresh gale at NE., and hazy weather with rain; this island I have called the Mayor. The cluster of islands and rocks just mentioned we named the Court of Aldermen; they lay in the compass of about half a league every way, and five leagues from the main, between which and them lay other islands. The most of them are barren rocks, and of these there is a very great variety; some of them are of as small a compass as the monument in London, and spire up to a much greater height.

As far as we had yet coasted this country from Cape Turnagain, the people acknowledged one chief, whom they called Teratu, and to whose residence they pointed, in a direction that we thought to be very far inland, but afterwards found to be otherwise.

About one o'clock three canoes came off to us from the main, with one and twenty men on board. The construction of these vessels appeared to be more simple than that of any we had seen, they being nothing more than trunks of a single tree hollowed by fire, without any convenience or ornament. The people on board were almost naked, and appeared to be of a browner complexion; yet naked and despicable as they were, they sung their song of defiance, and seemed to denounce against us inevitable destruction. They remained, however, some time out of stones' throw, and then venturing nearer, with less appearance of hostility, one of our men went to the ship's side, and was about to hand them a rope. This courtesy, however, they thought fit to return by throwing a lance at him, which having missed him, they immediately threw another into the ship; upon this a musket was fired over them, which at once sent them away.

In the morning, at daybreak, no less than twelve canoes came against us, with about one hundred and fifty men, all armed with pikes, lances, and stones. As they could do nothing till they came very near the ship, Tupia was ordered to expostulate with them, and if possible divert them from their purpose. During the conversation they appeared to be sometimes friendly and sometimes otherwise. At length, however, they began to trade, and we offered to purchase their weapons, which some of them consented to sell. They sold two very fairly, but having received what had been agreed upon for the purchase of a third, they refused to send it up, but offered it for a second price. A second was sent down, but the weapon was still detained, and a demand made for a third. This being refused with some expressions of displeasure and resentment, the offender, with many ludicrous tokens of contempt and defiance, paddled his canoe off a few yards from the ship. As I intended to continue in this place five or six days, in order to make an observation of the transit of Mercury, it was absolutely necessary, in order to prevent future mischief, to show these people that we were not to be treated ill with impunity; some small shot were therefore fired at the thief, and a musket ball through the bottom of his boat. Upon this it was paddled to about one hundred yards' distance, and to our great surprise the people in the other canoes took not the least notice of their wounded companion, though he bled very much, but returned to the ship, and continued to trade with the most perfect indifference and unconcern.

In the morning the natives came off again to the ship, but their behaviour was very different from what it was yesterday morning, and the little traffic we had with them was carried on very fair and friendly. Two came on board the ship—to each I gave a piece of English cloth and some spike-nails. After the natives were gone I went with the pinnace and longboat into the river to haul the seine, and sent the master to sound the bay and dredge for fish in the yawl. We hauled the seine in several places in the river, but caught only a few mullet, with which we returned on board about noon.

Monday, 6th.—Moderate breezes at NNW., and hazy weather with rain in the night. I went to another part of the bay to haul the seine, but met with as little success as before; and the master did not get above half a bucketful of shells with the dredge. The natives brought to the ship, and sold to our people, small cockles, clams, and mussels, enough for all hands. These are found in great plenty upon the sand-banks of the river. In the morning I sent the longboat to trawl in the bay, and one officer with the marines and a party of men to cut wood and haul the seine, but neither the seine nor the trawl met with any success; but the natives in some measure made up for this by bringing several baskets of dried or ready-dressed fish. Although it was none of the best, I ordered it all to be bought up, in order to encourage them to trade. I found here a great quantity of celery, which is boiled every day for the ship's company as usual.

On the 9th, at daybreak, a great number of canoes came on board, loaded with mackerel of two sorts, one exactly the same with those caught in England, and the other somewhat different. We imagined the people had taken a large shoal, and brought us an overplus which they could not consume; for they sold them at a very low rate. They were, however, very welcome to us. At eight o'clock, the ship had more fish on board than all her people could eat in three days; and before night, the quantity was so much increased, that every man who could get salt cured as many as would last him a month.

After an early breakfast, I went ashore, with Mr. Green and proper instruments, to observe the transit of Mercury, Mr. Banks and Dr. Solander being of the party. The weather had for some time been very thick, with much rain, but this day was so favourable that not a cloud intervened during the whole transit.

About noon, we were alarmed by the firing of a great gun from the ship. Mr. Gore, my second lieutenant, was at this time commanding officer on board, and the account that he gave was this. When the natives first came alongside they began to sell our people some of their arms, and one man offered to sell a *haāhow*, that is a square piece of cloth. Lieutenant Gore sent into the canoe a piece of cloth which the man had agreed to take in exchange for his, but as soon as he had got Mr. Gore's cloth in his possession he would not part with his own, but put off the canoe from alongside, and then shook his paddles at the people in the ship. Upon this, Mr. Gore fired a musket at them, and, from what I can learn, killed the man who took the cloth; after this they soon went away. I have here inserted the account of this affair just as I had it from Mr. Gore, but I must own it did not meet with my approbation, because I thought the punishment a little too severe for the crime, and we had now been long enough acquainted with these people to know how to chastise trifling faults like this without taking away their lives.

Between seven and eight o'clock p.m., I returned on board from out the river, having been about four or five miles up it, and could have gone much farther had the weather been favourable. I landed on the east side and went upon the hills, from whence I saw—or at least I thought I saw—the head of the river. It here branched into several channels, and formed a number of very low flat islands, all covered with a sort of mangrove tree, and several places of the shores on both sides the river were covered with the same sort of wood. The sand-banks were well stored with cockles and clams, and in many places were rock-oysters. Here is likewise pretty plenty of wild fowl, such as shags, ducks, curlews, and a black bird about as big as a crow, with a long, sharp bill of a colour between red and yellow; we also saw fish in the river, but of what sort I know not. The country, especially on the east side, is barren, and for the most part destitute of wood, or any other signs of fertility; but the face of the country on the other side looked much better, and is in many places covered with wood. We met with some of the natives, but saw not the least signs of cultivation, either here or in any other part about the bay.

After taking a slight view of the country, and loading both the boats with celery, which we found in great plenty near the beach, we returned from our excursion, and about five o'clock in the evening got on board the ship.

To the bay which we had now left I gave the name of Mercury Bay, on account of the observation which we had made there of the transit of that planet over the sun. This place is very convenient both for wooding and watering, and in the river there is an immense quantity of oysters and other shellfish: I have for this reason given it the name of Oyster River. But for a ship that wants to stay here any time, the best and safest place is in the river at the head of the bay, which, from the number of mangrove trees about it, I have called Mangrove River.

Before we left the bay, we cut upon one of the trees near the watering place the ship's name, and that of the commander, with the date of the year and month when we went there; and after displaying the English colours, I took a formal possession of it in the name of His Britannic Majesty King George the Third.

CHAPTER VIII.

FROM MERCURY BAY TO THE BAY OF ISLANDS—EXPEDITION UP THE RIVER THAMES—INTERVIEWS WITH THE NATIVES—RANGE FROM THE BAY OF ISLANDS ROUND NORTH CAPE TO QUEEN CHARLOTTE'S SOUND.

1769.
Nov.

I CONTINUED plying to windward two days to get under the land, and on the 18th, about seven in the morning, we were abreast of a very conspicuous promontory, being then in lat. 36° 26', and in the direction of N. 48 W. from the north head of Mercury Bay or Point Mercury, which was distant nine leagues. Upon this point stood many people, who seemed to take little notice of us, but talked together with great earnestness. In about half an hour several canoes put off from different places and came towards the ship; upon which the people on the point also launched a canoe, and about twenty of them came in her up with the others. When two of these canoes, in which there might be about sixty men, came near enough to make themselves heard, they sung their war song; but seeing that we took little notice of it, they threw a few stones at us, and then rowed off towards the shore. We hoped that we had now done with them; but in a short time they returned, as if with a fixed resolution to provoke us into a battle, animating themselves by their song as they had done before. *T*upia, without any directions from us, went to the poop and began to expostulate. He told them that we had weapons which would destroy them in a moment, and that if they ventured to attack us we should be obliged to use them. Upon this they flourished their weapons, and cried out in their language: "Come on shore, and we will kill you all."

"Well," said *T*upia, "but why should you molest us while we are at sea? As we do not wish to fight, we shall not accept your challenge to come on shore; and here there is no pretence for a quarrel, the sea being no more your property than the ship."

This eloquence of Tupia, though it greatly surprised us, having given him no hints for the arguments he used, had no effect upon our enemies, who very soon renewed their battery. A musket was then fired through one of their boats, and they immediately fell astern and left us.

Accordingly at daylight in the morning I set out with the pinnace and longboat, accompanied by Mr. Banks, Dr. Solander, and Tupia. We found the inlet end in a river, about nine miles above the ship, into which we entered with the first of the flood, and before we had gone three miles up it, found the water quite fresh. We saw a number of natives, and landed at one of their villages, the inhabitants of which received us with open arms. We made but a short stay with them, but proceeded up the river until near noon, when finding the face of the country to continue pretty much the same, and no alteration in the course or stream of the river, or the least probability of seeing the end of it, we landed on the west side, in order to take a view of the lofty trees which adorn its banks, being at this time twelve or fourteen miles within the entrance, and here the tide of flood runs as strong as it does in the river Thames below bridge.

Tuesday, 21st.—After landing as above mentioned, we had not gone a hundred yards into the woods before we found a tree that girthed nineteen feet eight inches, six feet above the ground; and having a quadrant with me, I found its length from the root to the first branch to be eighty-nine feet. It was as straight as an arrow, and tapered but very little in proportion to its length, so that I judged that there were 356 solid feet of timber in this tree, clear of the branches. We saw many others of the same sort, several of which were taller than the one we measured, and all of them very stout. There were likewise many other sorts of very stout timber trees, all of them wholly unknown to any of us. We brought away a few specimens, and at three o'clock we embarked, in order to return (but not before we had named this river the Thames, on account of its bearing some resemblance to that river in England) on board with the very first of the ebb. In our return down the river, the inhabitants of the village where we landed in going, seeing that we returned by another channel, put off in their canoes, and met us and trafficked with us in the most friendly manner imaginable, until they had disposed of the few trifles they had. The tide of ebb just carried us out of the narrow part of the river into the sea-reach, as I may call it, where meeting with the flood and a strong breeze at NNW., obliged us to come to a grapnel, and we did not reach the ship until seven o'clock in the morning. Intending to get under sail at high water, the longboat was sent to take up the kedge anchor, but it blew so strong that she could not reach the buoy, and the gale increasing soon obliged us to veer away more cable and strike topgallant yards.

On the 23rd, the wind being contrary, we kept plying down the river, and at seven in the evening got without the north-west point of the islands lying on the west side of it. The weather being bad, night coming on, and having land on every side of us, I thought it most advisable to tack, and stretch in under the point, where we anchored in nineteen fathoms. At five in the morning of the 24th we weighed, and made sail to the NW. under our courses and double-reefed topsails, the wind being at SW. by W. and WSW., a strong gale and squally. As the gale would not permit us to come near the land, we had but a slight and distant view of it from the time when we got under sail till noon, during a run of twelve leagues; but we never once lost sight of it. At this time our latitude, by observation, was 36° 15′ 20″. We were not above two miles from a point of land on the main, and three leagues and a half from a very high island, which bore NE. by E. In this situation we had twenty-six fathoms water. The farthest point on the main that we could see bore NW., but we could perceive several small islands lying to the north of that direction. The point of land of which we were now abreast, and which I called Point Rodney, is the north-west extremity of the river Thames—for under that name I comprehend the deep bay which terminates in the fresh-water stream; and the north-east extremity is the promontory which we passed when we entered it, and which I called Cape Colville, in honour of the Right Honourable Lord Colville.

Cape Colville lies in lat. 36° 26′, long. 194° 27′. It rises directly from the sea to a considerable height, and is remarkable for a lofty rock, which stands to the pitch of the point, and may be distinguished at a very great distance.

The natives residing about this river do not appear to be very numerous, considering the great extent of country. At least not many came off to the ship at one time; and as we were but little ashore ourselves, we could not so well judge of their numbers. They are as strong, well-made, active people as any we have seen yet, and all of them paint their bodies with red ochre and oil from head to foot—a thing that we have not seen before. Their canoes are large, well built, and ornamented with carved work in general as well as most we have seen.

We kept standing along shore to the NW., having the mainland on the one side and islands on the other. At half-past seven p.m. we anchored in a bay in fourteen fathoms, sandy bottom. We had no sooner come to an anchor than we caught between ninety and one hundred bream (a fish so called). This occasioned my giving this place the name of Bream Bay. The bay is everywhere pretty broad, and between three and four leagues deep; at the bottom of it there appears to be a fresh-water river. The north head of the bay, called Bream Head, is high land, and remarkable on account of several peaked rocks ranged in order upon the top of it. This bay may likewise be known by some small islands lying before it called the Hen and Chickens, one of which is pretty high, and terminates at top in two peaks. The land between Point Rodney and Bream Head, which is ten leagues, is low and wooded in turfs, and between the sea and the firm land are white sand-banks. We saw no inhabitants, but saw fires in the night, a proof that the country is not uninhabited. At daylight we left the bay and directed our course along shore to the northward, having a gentle breeze at S. by W. and clear weather. At noon we saw some small islands, to which I gave the name of the Poor Knights.

The country appeared low, but well covered with wood. We saw some straggling houses, three or four fortified towns, and near them a large quantity of cultivated land.

In the evening, seven large canoes came off to us, with about two hundred men. Some of them came on board, and said that they had heard of us. To two of them, who appeared to be chiefs, I gave presents. But when these were gone out of the ship, the others became exceedingly troublesome. Some of those in the canoes began to trade, and, according to their custom, to cheat, by refusing to deliver what had been bought, after they had received the price. Among these was one who had received an old pair of black breeches, which, upon a few small shot being fired at him, he threw into the sea. All the boats soon after paddled off to some distance, and when they thought they were out of reach they began to defy us, by singing their song and brandishing their weapons. We thought it advisable to intimidate them, as well for their sakes as our own, and therefore fired first some small arms and then round shot over their heads. The last put them in a terrible fright, though they received no damage, except by overheating themselves in paddling away, which they did with astonishing expedition.

At noon the mainland extended from S. by E. to NW. by W., a remarkable point of land bearing W., distant four or five miles. At three we passed it; and I gave it the name of Cape Brett, in honour of Sir Percy. The land of this cape is considerably higher than any part of the adjacent coast. At the point of it is a high round hillock, and NE. by N., at the distance of about a mile, is a small high island or rock, which, like several that have already been described, was perforated quite through, so as to appear like the arch of a bridge. This cape, or at least some part of it, is by the natives called Motugogogo, and it lies in lat. 35° 10′ 30″ S., long. 185° 25′ W. On the west side of it is a large and pretty deep bay, lying in SW. by W., in which there appeared to be several small islands. The point that forms the north-west entrance lies W. ¼ N. at the distance of three or four leagues from Cape Brett, and I distinguished it by the name of Point Pococke.

On the south-west side of this bay we saw several villages, situated both on islands and on the mainland, from whence came off to us several large canoes full of people; but, like those that had been alongside before, would not enter into a friendly traffic with us, but would cheat whenever they had an opportunity. The people in these canoes made a very good appearance, being all stout, well-made men, having their hair—which was black— combed up and tied upon the crown of their heads, and there stuck with white feathers. In each of the canoes were two or three chiefs, and the habits of these were rather superior to any we had yet seen. The cloth they wore was of the best sort, and covered on the outside with dog-skins, put on in such a manner as to look agreeable enough to the eye. Few of these people were tattooed or marked in the face, like those we have seen farther to the south. In the course of this day—that is, this afternoon and yesterday forenoon—we reckoned that we had not less than four or five hundred of the natives alongside and on board the ship, and in that time did not range above six or eight leagues off the sea-coast—a strong proof that this part of the country must be well inhabited. At 8 a.m. we were within a mile of groups of islands lying close under the mainland, distance twenty-two miles from Cape Brett. Here we lay for nearly two hours, having little or no wind. During this time several canoes came off to the ship, and two or three of them sold us some fish—cavalles, as they are called, which occasioned my giving the islands the same name. After this some others began to pelt us with stones, and would not desist at the firing of two musket balls through one of their boats. At last I was obliged to pepper two or three fellows with small shot, after which they retired; and the wind coming at NW., we stood off to sea.

Having taken a view of the bay, and loaded both boats with celery, which we found here in great plenty, we returned on board, and at 4 a.m. hove up the anchor in order to put to sea, with a light breeze at E.; but it soon falling calm, obliged us to come to again; and about eight or nine o'clock, seeing no probability of our getting to sea, I sent the master to sound the harbour. But before this, I ordered Matthew Cox, Henry Stevens, and Eman Farreyra to be punished with a dozen lashes each for leaving their duty when ashore last night, and digging up potatoes out of one of the plantations. The first of the three I remitted back to confinement, because he insisted that there was no harm in what he had done. All this forenoon had abundance of the natives about the ship and some few on board. We trafficked with them for a few trifles, in which they dealt very fair and friendly.

At 3 p.m., the boats having returned from sounding, I went with them over to the south side of the harbour and landed upon the main, accompanied by Mr. Banks and Dr. Solander. We met with nothing new or remarkable. The place where we landed was in a small sandy cove, where there are two small streams of fresh water, and plenty of wood for fuel. Here were likewise several little plantations planted with potatoes and yams. The soil and natural produce of the country were much the same as what we have hitherto met with. The face of the country appeared green and pleasant, and the soil seemed to be pretty rich and proper for cultivation. The land is everywhere about this bay of a moderate height, but full of small hills and valleys, and not much encumbered with wood. We met with about half a dozen cloth plants, being those of which the inhabitants of the islands lying within the tropics make their finest cloth. This plant must be very scarce among them, as the cloth made from it is only worn in small pieces by way of ornaments at their ears, and even this we have seen but very seldom. Their knowing the use of this sort of cloth doth in some measure account for the extraordinary fondness they have showed for it above every other thing we had to give them. Even a sheet of white paper is of more value than so much English cloth of any sort whatever; but as we have been at few places where I have not given away more or less of the latter, it is more than probable that they will soon learn to set a value upon it, and likewise upon iron, a thing not one of them knows the use of or sets the least value upon. But were European commodities in ever such esteem amongst them, they have no one thing of equal value to give in return, at least that we have seen.

At three o'clock on the 5th December we returned on board, and after dinner visited another part of the bay, but met with nothing new. By the evening all our empty casks were filled with water, and we had at the same time got on board a large quantity of celery, which is found here in great plenty. This I still caused to be boiled every morning with oatmeal and portable soup for the ship's company's breakfast.

This bay lies on the west side of Cape Brett, and I named it the Bay of Islands, from the great number of islands which line its shores, and form several harbours equally safe and commodious, where there is room and depth for any number of shipping. That in which we lay is on the south-west side of the south-westernmost island, called Matuaro, on the south-east side of the bay.

On the 9th, daylight brought us pretty well in with the land, seven leagues to the westward of the Cavalle Isles, and where lies a deep bay running in SW. by W. and WSW., the bottom of which we could but just see, and there the land appeared to be low and level, two points forming the entrance. This bay I have named Doubtless Bay. The wind not permitting us to look into this bay, we steered for the westernmost land we had in sight.

While we lay becalmed, several canoes came off to us; but the people having heard of our guns, it was not without great difficulty that they were persuaded to come under our stern. After having bought some of their cloths, as well as their fish, we began to make inquiries concerning their country, and learned, by the help of Tupia, that, at the distance of three days' rowing in their canoes, at a place called Moore-whennua, the land would take a short turn to the southward, and from thence extend no more to the west. This place we concluded to be the land discovered by Tasman, which he called Cape Maria van Diemen; and finding these people so intelligent, we inquired further if they knew of any country besides their own. They answered that they never had visited any other, but that their ancestors had told them that to the NW. by N. or NNW. there was a country of great extent, called Ulimaroa, to which some people had sailed in a very large canoe; that only part of them returned, and reported that after a passage of a month they had seen a country where the people ate hogs.

Early in the morning we stood in with the land, seven leagues to the westward of Doubtless Bay, the bottom of which is not far distant from the bottom of another large bay, which the shore forms at this place, being separated only by a low neck of land, which juts out into a peninsula that I have called Knuckle Point. About the middle of this bay, which we called Sandy Bay, is a high mountain, standing upon a distant shore, to which I gave the name of Mount Camel. The latitude here is 34° 51' S., and longitude 186° 50'. We had twenty-four and twenty-five fathoms water, with a good bottom; but there seems to be nothing in this bay that can induce a ship to put into it, for the land about it is utterly barren and desolate, and, except Mount Camel, the situation is low. The soil appears to be nothing but white sand, thrown up in low irregular hills and narrow ridges, lying parallel with the shore. But barren and desolate as this place is, it is not without inhabitants; we saw one village on the west side of Mount Camel, and another on the east side. We saw also five canoes full of people, who pulled after the ship, but could not come up with us.

On the 16th, at six in the morning, we saw land from the mast-head bearing SSW.; and at noon it bore S. by W., distant fourteen leagues. While we were standing in for the shore we sounded several times, but had no ground with ninety fathoms. At eight we tacked in one hundred and eight fathoms, at about three or four miles from the shore, which was the same point of land that we had to the NW. before we were blown off. At noon it bore SW., distant about three miles; Mount Camel bore S. by E., distant about eleven leagues, and the westernmost land in sight bore S. 75 W.; the latitude by observation was 34° 20′ S. At four o'clock we tacked and stood inshore, in doing which we met with a strong rippling, and the ship fell fast to leeward, which we imputed to a current setting east. At eight we tacked and stood off till eight the next morning, when we tacked and stood in, being about ten leagues from the land. At noon the point of land which we were near the day before bore SSW., distant five leagues. The wind still continued at west, and at seven o'clock we tacked in thirty-five fathoms, when the point of land which has been mentioned before bore NW. by N., distant four or five miles; so that we had not gained one inch to windward the last twenty-four hours, which confirmed our opinion that there was a current to the eastward. The point of land I called North Cape, it being the northern extremity of this country. It forms the north point of Sandy Bay, and is a peninsula jutting out NE. about two miles, and terminating in a bluff head that is flat at the top. The isthmus which joins this head to the mainland is very low, and for that reason the land of the cape, from several situations, has the appearance of an island.

At 7 p.m. on the 24th we saw land from the mast-head which proved to be a small island, which we took to be the Three Kings discovered by *T*asman.

At four o'clock in the morning the wind freshened, and at nine blew a storm, so that we were obliged to bring the ship to under her mainsail. Our course made good between noon this day and yesterday was SSW. ½ W., distance eleven miles. The Three Kings bore N. 27 E., distant seventy-seven miles. The gale continued all this day and till two the next morning, when it fell, and began to veer to the southward and SW., where it fixed about four, when we made sail and steered east in for the land, under the foresail and mainsail; but the wind then rising, and by eight o'clock being increased to a hurricane, with a prodigious sea, we were obliged to take in the mainsail. We then wore the ship, and brought her to with her head to the north-west. At noon the gale was somewhat abated, but we had still heavy squalls.

At six we saw the land, bearing NE., distant about six leagues, which we judged to be Cape Maria van Diemen, and which corresponded with the account that had been given of it by the Indians. At midnight we wore and stood to the SE.

I cannot help thinking it will appear a little strange that at this season of the year we should be three weeks in getting ten leagues to the westward and five weeks in getting fifty leagues, for so long it is since we passed Cape Brett; but it will hardly be credited that in the midst of summer and in the latitude of 35° S. such a gale of wind as we have had could have happened, which for its strength and continuance was such as I hardly was ever in before. Fortunately at this time we were a good distance from land, otherwise it would have proved fatal to us.

1770.
Jan. 1.

At this time we tacked and stood to the NW. At noon we were between three and four leagues from the land, and in the latitude of 36° 31' and longitude 185° 50' W. Cape Maria van Diemen bore distant forty-four and a half leagues. From this I form my judgment of the direction of this coast, which must be nearly a straight shore. In about latitude 35° 45' is some high land adjoining the sea; to the southward of that the land is of a moderate height, and wears a most desolate and inhospitable aspect. Nothing is to be seen but long sand-hills, with hardly any green thing upon them, and the great sea which the prevailing westerly winds impel upon the shore must render this a very dangerous coast. This I am so fully sensible of, that were we once clear of it I am determined not to come so near again, if I can possibly avoid it, unless we have a very favourable wind indeed.

At nine, on the 10th, we were abreast of a point which rises with an easy ascent from the sea to a considerable height. This point, which lies in latitude 37° 43', I named Woody Head. About eleven miles from this head, in the direction of SW. ¼ W., lies a very small island, upon which we saw a great number of gannets, and which we therefore called Gannet Island. At noon, a high craggy point bore ENE., distant about a league and a half, to which I gave the name of Albatross Point. It lies in lat. 38° 4' S., long. 184° 42' W., and is distant seven leagues in the direction of S. 17 W. from Woody Head. On the north side of this point the shore forms a bay, in which there appears to be anchorage and shelter for shipping.

At noon, on the 12th, had the winds very variable, with dark, cloudy weather, attended with excessive heavy showers of rain. At this time we were about three leagues from the shore, which lies under a peaked mountain. This peak we did not see, it being hid in the clouds, but judged it to bear about SSE. ; and some very remarkable peaked islands, lying under the shore, bore distant three or four leagues.

At seven o'clock next day I sounded and had forty-two fathoms water, being distant from the shore between two and three leagues, and the peaked mountain, as near as I could judge, bore E. After it was dark saw a fire upon the shore, a sure sign that the country is inhabited. In the night we had some thunder, lightning, and rain ; at 5 a.m. we saw for a few minutes the top of the peaked mountain above the clouds, bearing NE. It is of a prodigious height, and its top is covered with everlasting snow. I have named it Mount Egmont, in honour of the Earl of Egmont. This mountain seems to have a pretty large base, and to rise with a gradual ascent to the peak ; and what makes it more conspicuous is its being situated near the sea, and in the midst of a flat country, which afforded a very good aspect, being clothed with woods and verdure.

Between the mainland and Cape Egmont is a very broad and deep bay, and here the land is of a considerable height, distinguished by hills and valleys, and the shore seems to form several bays, into one of which I intend to go with the ship in order to careen her (she being very foul), and to repair some few defects, recruit our stock of wood, water, etc.

CHAPTER IX.

TRANSACTIONS IN QUEEN CHARLOTTE'S SOUND—PASSAGE THROUGH COOK'S STRAIT AND BACK TO CAPE TURNAGAIN—FROM CAPE TURNAGAIN SOUTHWARD, ROUND CAPE SOUTH, AND BACK TO THE WESTERN ENTRANCE OF COOK'S STRAIT.

1770.
Jan.

AT two o'clock on the 16th we anchored in a very snug cove,* which is on the NW. side of the bay facing the SW. end of the island, in eleven fathoms; soft ground, and moored with the stream anchor. By this time several of the natives had come off to the ship in their canoes, and after heaving a few stones at us and having some conversation with Tupia, some of them ventured on board, where they made but a very short stay before they went into their canoes again, and soon after left us altogether. I then went ashore in the bottom of the cove, accompanied by most of the gentlemen on board. We found a fine stream of excellent water, and as to wood, the land is here one entire forest. Having the seine with us, we made a few hauls, and caught 300 lbs. weight of different sorts of fish, which were equally distributed to the ship's company.

Several of the natives visited us this morning, and brought with them some stinking fish, which, however, I ordered to be bought up to encourage them in this kind of traffic. But trade at this time seemed not to be their object; they were more inclinable to quarrel; and as the ship was upon the careen, I thought they might give us some trouble, and perhaps hurt some of our people that were in the boats alongside. For this reason I fired some small shot at one of the first offenders. This made them keep at a proper distance while they stayed, and it was not long before they all went away. These people declared to us this morning that they never either saw or heard of

* Ship Cove.

a ship like ours being upon this coast before. From this it appears that they have no tradition among them of Tasman being here, for I believe Murderer's Bay, the place where he anchored, not to be far from this place; but this cannot be it from the latitude.

Soon after we landed we met with two or three of the natives, who not long before must have been regaling themselves upon human flesh, for I got from one of them the bone of the forearm of a man or woman which was quite fresh, and the flesh had been but lately picked off, which they told us they had eaten. They gave us to understand that but a few days before they had taken, killed, and eaten a boat's crew of their enemies, or strangers, for I believe they look upon all strangers as enemies. There was not one of us that had the least doubt that these people were cannibals; but the finding this bone with part of the sinews fresh upon it was a stronger proof than any we had yet met with. And in order to be fully satisfied of the truth of what they had told us, we told one of them that it was not the bone of a man, but that of a dog; but he, with great fervency, took hold of his forearm and told us again that it was that bone, and to convince us that he had eaten the flesh, he took hold of the flesh of his own arm with his teeth and made signs of eating. This morning we careened, scrubbed, and paid the starboard side of the ship. While this was doing, some of the natives came alongside, seemingly only to look at us. Mr. Banks got from one of them a bone of the forearm, much in the same state as the one before mentioned; and to show us that they ate the flesh, they bit and gnawed the bone, and drew it through their mouths, showing by signs that it had afforded a delicious repast.

In the forenoon a small canoe came off from the Indian village to the ship, and among those that were in it was the old man who had first come on board at our arrival in the bay. As soon as it came alongside, Tupia renewed the conversation that had passed the day before concerning their practice of eating human flesh, during which they repeated what they had told us already. "But," said Tupia, "where are the heads? Do you eat them too?"

"Of the heads," said the old man, "we eat only the brains; and the next time I come I will bring some of them to convince you that what we have told you is truth."

After some further conversation between these people and

Tupia, they told him that they expected their enemies to come very shortly, to revenge the death of the seven men whom they had killed and eaten.

On the 24th we went to visit our friends, at the *hippah* or village on the point of the island near the ship's station, who had come off to us on our first arrival in the bay. They received us with the utmost confidence and civility, showing us every part of their habitations, which were commodious and neat. The island or rock on which this town is situated is divided from the main by a breach or fissure so narrow that a man might almost leap from one to the other; the sides of it are everywhere so steep as to render the artificial fortification of these people almost unnecessary. There was, however, one slight palisade, and one small fighting-stage, towards that part of the rock where access was least difficult.

The people here brought us out several human bones, the flesh of which they had eaten, and offered them for sale; for the curiosity of those among us who had purchased them as memorials of the horrid practice—which many, notwithstanding the reports of travellers, have professed not to believe—had rendered them a kind of article of trade.

The carpenter having prepared two posts to be left as memorials of our having visited this place, I ordered them to be inscribed with the ship's name, and the year and month. One of them I set up at the watering place, hoisting the Union flag upon the top of it, and the other I carried over to the island that lies nearest to the sea, called by the natives Motuara. I went first to the village or hippah, accompanied by Mr. Monkhouse and *T*upia, where I met with our old man, and told him and several others, by means of Tupia, that we were come to set up a mark upon the island, in order to show to any other ship which should happen to come thither that we had been there before. To this they readily consented, and promised that they never would pull it down. I then gave something to every one present, and to the old man I gave a silver threepence, dated 1736, and some spike-nails, with the king's broad arrow cut deep upon them—things which I thought most likely to remain long among them. I then took the post to the highest part of the island, and after fixing it firmly in the ground,

I hoisted upon it the Union flag, and honoured this inlet with the name of Queen Charlotte's Sound, at the same time taking formal possession of this and the adjacent country in the name and for the use of His Majesty King George the *T*hird. We then drank a bottle of wine to Her Majesty's health, and gave the bottle to the old man, who had attended us up the hill, and who was mightily delighted with his present.

While the post was setting up, we inquired of the old man concerning the passage into the eastern sea, the existence of which he confirmed; and then asked him about the land to the SW. of the strait where we were then situated. This land, he said, consisted of two whennuas or islands, which might be circumnavigated in a few days, and which he called Tovy Poenammoo. The literal translation of this word is "the water of green talc;" and probably, if we had understood him better, we should have found that Tovy Poenammoo was the name of some particular place where they got the green talc or stone of which they make their ornaments and tools, and not a general name for the whole southern district. He said there was also a third whennua on the east side of the strait, the circumnavigation of which would take up many moons. This he called Eaheinomauwe; and to the land on the borders of the strait he gave the name of *T*erawite. Having set up our post and procured this intelligence, we returned on board the ship, and brought the old man with us, who was attended by his canoe, in which, after dinner, he returned home.

On the 31st, having completed our wooding and filled all our water-casks, I sent out two parties, one to cut and make brooms and another to catch fish. In the evening we had a strong gale from the NW., with such a heavy rain that our little wild musicians on shore suspended their song, which till now we had constantly heard during the night, with a pleasure which it was impossible to lose without regret.

February. On the 1st the gale increased to a storm, with heavy gusts from the high land, one of which broke the hawser that we had fastened to the shore, and obliged us to let go another anchor. *T*owards midnight the gale became more moderate, but the rain continued with such violence that the brook which had supplied us with water overflowed its banks, and carried away ten small casks which had been left there full of water; and notwithstanding we searched the whole cove, we could never recover one of them.

On the 6th, about six o'clock in the morning, a light breeze sprung up at north, and we again got under sail; but the wind proving variable, we reached no farther than just without Motuara. In the afternoon, however, a more steady gale at N. by W. set us clear of the sound.

As soon as we got out of the sound, I stood over to the eastward, in order to get the strait well open before the tide of ebb came on. At seven in the evening the two small islands which lie off Cape Koamaroo, the south-east head of Queen Charlotte's Sound, bore east, distant about four miles. At this time it was nearly calm, and the tide of ebb setting out, we were in a very short time carried by the rapidity of the stream close upon one of the islands, which was a rock rising almost perpendicularly out of the sea. We perceived our danger increase every moment, and had but one expedient to prevent our being dashed to pieces, the success of which a few minutes would determine. We were now within little more than a cable's length of the rock, and had more than seventy-five fathoms water; but upon dropping an anchor and veering about one hundred and fifty fathoms of cable, the ship was happily brought up. This, however, would not have saved us if the tide, which set S. by E., had not, upon meeting with the island, changed its direction to SE. and carried us beyond the first point.

About nine leagues N. from Cape Terawite, under the same shore, is a high remarkable island that may be distinctly seen from Queen Charlotte's Sound, from which it lies seven leagues. I have called it Entry Isle, and it was taken notice of when we first passed it on Sunday, 14th of last month. On the east side of Cape Terawite the land trends away SE. by E. about eight leagues, where it ends in a point, and is the southernmost land on Eaheinomauwe, which I have named Cape Palliser in honour of my worthy friend Captain Palliser.

At this time we were about three leagues from the shore, and abreast of a deep bay or inlet, to which I gave the name of Cloudy

Bay, and at the bottom of which there appeared low land covered with tall trees.

At three o'clock in the afternoon we were abreast of the southernmost point of land that we had seen at noon, which I called Cape Campbell.

On the 8th, three canoes came up to the ship with between thirty and forty people on board, who had been pulling after us with great labour and perseverance for some time. They appeared to be more cleanly and a better class than any we had met with since we left the Bay of Islands, and their canoes were also distinguished by the same ornaments which we had seen upon the northerly part of the coast. They came on board with very little invitation, and their behaviour was courteous and friendly. Upon receiving presents from us they made us presents in return, which had not been done by any of the natives that we had seen before. We soon perceived that our guests had heard of us, for as soon as they came on board they asked for *whow*, the name by which nails were known among the people with whom we had trafficked; but though they had heard of nails, it was plain they had seen none, for when nails were given them they asked Tupia what they were. The term *whow*, indeed, conveyed to them the idea not of their quality, but only of their use; for it is the same by which they distinguish a tool, commonly made of bone, which they use both as an auger and a chisel. However, their knowing that we had *whow* to sell was a proof that their connections extended as far north as Cape Kidnappers, which was distant no less than forty-five leagues, for that was the southernmost place on this side the coast where we had had any traffic with the natives. After a short time they went away, much gratified with the presents we had made them.

On the 9th, at eleven o'clock a.m., we saw Cape Turnagain, distant seven leagues. I then called the officers upon deck and asked them if they were now satisfied that this land was an island, to which they answered in the affirmative, and we hauled our wind to the eastward.

At daybreak on the 16th we discovered land bearing S. by W., and seemingly detached from the coast we were on. This island, which I named after Mr. Banks, lies about five leagues from the coast of Tovy Poenammoo.

At sunset on the 22nd, the weather, which had been hazy, clearing up, we saw a mountain which rose in a high peak bearing NW. by N.; and at the same time we saw the land more distinctly than before, extending from N. to SW. by S., which, at some distance within the coast, had a lofty and mountainous appearance. We soon found that the accounts which had been given us by the Indians in Queen Charlotte's Sound of the land to the southward were not true, for they had told us that it might be circumnavigated in four days.

On the 9th, at four in the morning, we had sixty fathoms water; and at daylight we discovered under our bow a ledge of rocks, extending from S. by W. to W. by S., upon which the sea broke very high. They were not more than three-quarters of a mile distant, yet we had five and forty fathoms water. As the wind was at NW. we could not now weather them, and as I was unwilling to run to leeward, I tacked and made a trip to the eastward; the wind, however, soon after coming to the northward, enabled us to get clear of all. Our soundings, while we were passing within the ledge, were from thirty-five to forty-seven fathoms, with a rocky bottom.

March.

This ledge lies SE. six leagues from the southernmost part of the land, and SE. by E. from some remarkable hills which stand near the shore. About three leagues to the northward of it there is another ledge, which lies full three leagues from the shore, and on which the sea broke in a dreadful surf. As we passed these rocks to the north in the night, and discovered the others under our bow at break of day, it is manifest that our danger was imminent, and our escape critical in the highest degree. From the situation of these rocks, so well adapted to catch unwary strangers, I called them the Traps. This land is of a moderate height, and has a very barren aspect—not a tree to be seen upon it, only a few small shrubs. There were several white patches, on which the sun's rays reflected very strongly, which I take to be a kind of marble such as we have seen in many places of this country, particularly to the northward.

On Saturday, 10th, we stood close upon a wind to the westward. At sunset we saw the southernmost point of land, which I afterwards named South Cape. We stood away NNE. close upon a wind, without seeing any land, till two the next morning, when we discovered an island bearing NW. by N., distant about five leagues. About two hours afterwards we saw land ahead, upon which we tacked and stood off till six, when we stood in to take a nearer view of it. At eleven we were within three leagues of it, but the wind seeming to incline upon the shore, I tacked and stood off to the southward. This island I named after Dr. Solander, and called it Solander's Island. The shore of the main lies nearest E. by S. and W. by N., and forms a large open bay, in which there is no appearance of any harbour or shelter for shipping against SW. and southerly winds. The surface of the country is broken into craggy hills of a great height, on the summits of which are several patches of snow.

On Wednesday, 14th, we had a fresh gale from the southward, attended with squalls. At two it cleared up over the land, which appeared high and mountainous. At half-past three double-reefed the topsails, and hauled in for a bay wherein there appeared to be good anchorage, and into which I had thought of going with the ship. But after standing in an hour we found the distance too great to run before dark, and it blew too hard to attempt it in the night, or even to keep to windward; for these reasons we gave it up, and bore away along shore. This bay I have named Dusky Bay. It is about three or four miles broad at the entrance, and seems to be fully as deep. In it are several islands, behind which there must be shelter from all winds, provided there is a sufficient depth of water. The N. point of this bay is very remarkable, there being off it five high-peaked rocks, standing up like the four fingers and thumb of a man's hand, on which account I have named it Point Five Fingers. The land of this point is further remarkable by being the only level land near it, and extends near two leagues to the northward. It is pretty high, wholly covered with wood, and hath very much the appearance of an island by its aspect being so very different from the land behind it, which is nothing but barren rocky mountains. At sunset the southernmost land in sight bore due S., distant five or six leagues; and as this is the westernmost point of land upon the whole coast, I have called it West Cape. The land of this cape seems to be of a moderate height next the sea, and hath nothing remarkable about it that we could see, except a very white cliff two or three leagues to the southward of it. At seven o'clock brought the ship to under the foresail, with her head off shore, having a fresh gale at S. by E. At midnight it moderated, and we wore and lay her head inshore until 4 a.m., then made sail, and steered along shore. A little before noon we passed a little narrow opening in the land, where there appeared to be a very snug harbour, formed by an island. Inland, behind this opening, were mountains, the summits of which were covered with snow that seemed to have fallen lately; and this is not to be wondered at, for we have found it very cold for these two days past.

Having now nearly run down the whole of this NW. coast of Tovy Poenammoo, it is time I should describe the face of the country as it hath at different times appeared to us. I have mentioned then that the land seen was rugged and mountainous; and there is great reason to believe that the same ridge of mountains extends nearly the whole length of the island.

There is a space of about six or eight leagues of the sea-coast unexplored, but the mountains inland were visible enough. The land near the shore about Cape West is rather low, and riseth with a gradual ascent up to the foot of the mountains, and appears to be mostly covered with wood. From Point Five Fingers down to the latitude of 44° 20′, there is a narrow ridge of hills rising directly from the sea, which are clothed with wood; close behind these hills lies the ridge of mountains, which are of a prodigious height, and appear to consist of nothing but barren rocks, covered in many places with large patches of snow, which perhaps have lain there since the creation. No country upon earth can appear with a more rugged and barren aspect than this doth; from the sea, for as far inland as the eye can reach, nothing is to be seen but the summits of these rocky mountains, which seem to lie so near one another as not to admit any valleys between them. The country between them and the sea consists of woody hills and valleys of various extent, both for height and depth, and hath much the appearance of fertility.

Many of the valleys are large, low, and flat, and appeared to be wholly covered with wood; but it is very probable that great part of the land is taken up in lakes, ponds, etc., as is very common in such-like places. From the last-mentioned latitude to Cape Farewell, afterwards so called, the land is not distinguished by anything remarkable; it rises into hills directly from the sea, and is covered with wood. While we were upon this part of the coast the weather was foggy, in so much that we could see but a very little way inland; however, we sometimes saw the summits of the mountains above the fog and clouds, which plainly showed that the inland parts were high and mountainous, and gave me great reason to think that there is a continued chain of mountains from the one end of the island to the other. I resolved therefore to quit the country and return home by such a ronte as might be of most advantage to the service; and upon this subject took the opinion of my officers. I had myself a strong desire to return by Cape Horn, because that would have enabled me finally to determine whether there is or is not a southern continent; but against this it was a sufficient objection that we must have kept in a high southern latitude in the very depth of winter, with a vessel which was not thought sufficient for the undertaking. And the same reason was urged against our proceeding directly for the Cape of Good Hope, with still more force, because no discovery of moment could be hoped for in that route.

It was therefore resolved that we should return by the East Indies, and that with this view we should, upon leaving the coast, steer westward, till we should fall in with the east coast of New Holland, and then follow the direction of that coast to the northward, till we should arrive at its northern extremity; but if that should be found impracticable, it was further resolved that we should endeavour to fall in with the land or islands said to have been discovered by Quiros.

Before I quit this land altogether I shall give a short general description of the country, its inhabitants, their manners, customs, etc.; in which it is necessary to observe that many things are founded only on conjecture, for we were too short a time in any one place to learn much of their interior policy, and therefore could only draw conclusions from what we saw at different times.

CHAPTER X.

A GENERAL ACCOUNT OF NEW ZEALAND—PASSAGE FROM NEW ZEALAND TO BOTANY BAY ON THE EAST COAST OF NEW HOLLAND (NEW SOUTH WALES)—AN ACCOUNT OF BOTANY BAY.

1770. March.

NEW ZEALAND was first discovered by Abel Jansen Tasman, a Dutch navigator whose name has been several times mentioned in this narrative, on the 13th of December in the year 1642. He traversed the eastern coast from latitude 34° to 43°, and entered the strait which divides the two islands, and in the chart is called Cook's Strait; but being attacked by the natives soon after he came to an anchor in the place to which he gave the name of Murderers' Bay, he never went on shore. He gave the country the name of Staaten Land, or the land of the states, in honour of the States-General, and it is now generally distinguished in our maps and charts by the name of New Zealand. As the whole of this country, except that part of the coast which was seen by Tasman from on board his ship, has from his time to the voyage of the *Endeavour* remained altogether unknown, it has by many been supposed to be part of a southern continent. It is, however, now known to consist of two large islands divided from each other by a strait or passage, which is about four or five leagues broad.

The northernmost of these islands is called by the natives Eaheinomauwe, and the southernmost Tovy or *T*avai Poenammoo.

Tovy Poenammoo is for the most part a mountainous, and to all appearance a barren country; and the people whom we saw in Queen Charlotte's Sound, those that came off to us under the snowy mountains, and the fires to the west of Cape Saunders, were all the inhabitants and signs of inhabitants that we discovered upon the whole island.

Eaheinomauwe has a much better appearance. It is indeed

not only hilly, but mountainous; yet even the hills and mountains are covered with wood, and every valley has a rivulet of water. The soil in these valleys and in the plains, of which there are many that are not overgrown with wood, is in general light but fertile; and in the opinion of Mr. Banks and Dr. Solander, as well as of every other gentleman on board, every kind of European grain, plants, and fruit would flourish here in the utmost luxuriance. From the vegetables that we found here, there is reason to conclude that the winters are milder than those in England, and we found the summer not hotter, though it was more equally warm; so that if this country should be settled by people from Europe, they would, with a little industry, be very soon supplied not only with the necessaries but the luxuries of life in great abundance.

In this country there are no quadrupeds but dogs and rats—at least we saw no other—and the rats are so scarce that many of us never saw them. The dogs live with the people, who breed them for no other purpose than to eat them. There might indeed be quadrupeds that we did not see, but this is not probable, because the chief pride of the natives, with respect to their dress, is in the skins and hair of such animals as they have, and we never saw the skin of any animal about them but those of dogs and birds.

For this scarcity of animals upon the land, the sea, however, makes an abundant recompense; every creek swarming with fish, which are not only wholesome, but equally delicious with those of Europe. The ship seldom anchored in any station, or with a light gale passed any place, that did not afford us enough with hook and line to serve the whole ship's company, especially to the southward.

Should it ever become an object of settling this country, the best place for the first fixing of a colony would be either in the river Thames or the Bay of Islands; for at either of these places they would have the advantage of a good harbour, and by means of the former an easy communication would be had, and settlements might be extended into the inland parts of the country. For a very little trouble and expense small vessels might be built in the river proper for the navigation thereof. It is too much for me to assert how little water a vessel ought to draw to navigate this river, even so far up as I was in the boat. This depends entirely upon the depth of water that is upon the bar or flat that lay before

NEW ZEALANDER.
Page 121.

WAR CANOE, NEW ZEALAND.
Page 122.

the narrow part of the river, which I had not an opportunity of making myself acquainted with; but I am of opinion that a vessel that draws not above ten or twelve feet may do it with ease. So far as I have been able to judge of the genius of these people, it does not appear to me to be at all difficult for strangers to form a settlement in this country. They seem to be too much divided among themselves to unite in opposing; by which means, and kind and gentle usage, the colonists would be able to form strong parties among them.

The natives of this country are a strong, raw-boned, well-made, active people, rather above than under the common size, especially the men. They are of a very dark-brown colour, with black hair, thin black beards, and white teeth; and such as do not disfigure their faces by tattooing, etc., have in general very good features. The men generally wear their hair long, combed up and tied upon the crown of their heads. Some of the women wear it long and loose upon their shoulders, old women especially; others again wear it cropped short. Their combs are made some of bones and others of wood; they sometimes wear them as an ornament stuck upright in their hair. Both sexes paint their faces and bodies at times more or less with red ochre mixed with fish oil.

Their common clothing is very much like square thrumbed mats that are made of rope yarns, to lay at the doors or passages into houses to clean one's shoes upon. These they tie round their necks, and they are generally large enough to cover the body as low as the knee. They are made with very little preparation of the broad grass-plant before mentioned. Beside the thrumbed mats, as I call them, they have other much finer clothing, made of the same plant after it is bleached and prepared in such a manner that it is as white and almost as soft as flax, but much stronger. Of this they make pieces of cloth about five feet long and four broad. These are woven some pieces close and others very open; the former are as stout as the strongest sail-cloth, and not unlike it, and yet it is all worked or made by hand with no other instrument than a needle or bodkin. To one end of every piece is generally worked a very neat border of different colours of four or six inches broad, and they very often trim them with pieces of dog-skin or birds' feathers. These pieces of cloth they wear as they do the other, tying one end round their necks with a piece of string, to one end of which is fixed a needle or bodkin made of bone, by means of which they can easily fasten, or put the string through any part of the cloth. They sometimes wear pieces of this kind of cloth round their middles, as well as over their shoulders.

Both men and women wear ornaments at their ears and about their necks. These are made of stone, bone, shells, etc., and are variously shaped; and some I have seen wearing human teeth and finger nails. The men, when they are dressed, generally wear two or three long white feathers stuck upright in their hair, and at Queen Charlotte's Sound many wore round caps made of black feathers.

Whenever we were visited by any number of them that had never heard or seen anything of us before, they generally came off in the largest canoe they had, some of which will carry sixty, eighty, or one hundred people. They always brought their best clothes along with them, which they put on as soon as they came near the ship. In each canoe was generally an old man, in some two or three. These used always to direct the others, were better clothed, and generally carried a halberd or battle-axe in their hands, or some such like thing that distinguished them from the others. As soon as they came within about a stone's throw of the ship they would there lie, and call out, "Haromoi harenta a patoo ago!" that is, "Come here, come ashore with us, and we will kill you with our patapatoos!" and at the same time would shake them at us. At times they would dance the war dance; and other times they would trade with and talk to us, and answer such questions as were put to them with all the calmness imaginable, and then again begin the war dance, shaking their paddles, patoo-patoos, etc., and make strange contortions at the same time. As soon as they had worked themselves up to a proper pitch they would begin to attack us with stones and darts, and oblige us, whether we would or not, to fire upon them. Musketry they never regarded unless they felt the effect; but great guns they did, because they threw stones farther than they could comprehend. After they found that our arms were so much superior to theirs, and that we took no advantage of that superiority, and a little time had been given them to reflect upon it, they ever after were our very good friends;

and we never had an instance of their attempting to surprise or cut off any of our people when they were ashore. Opportunity for so doing they must have had at one time or another.

It is hard to account for what we have everywhere been told of their eating their enemies killed in battle, which they most certainly do. Circumstances enough we have seen to convince us of the truth of this. Tupia, who holds this custom in great aversion, hath very often argued with them against it, but they have always as strenuously supported it, and never would own that it was wrong. It is reasonable to suppose that men with whom this custom is found, seldom, if ever, give quarter to those they overcome in battle; and if so, they must fight desperately to the very last. A strong proof of this supposition we had from the people of Queen Charlotte's Sound, who told us that, but a few days before we arrived, they had killed and eaten a whole boat's crew. Surely a single boat's crew, or at least a part of them, when they found themselves beset and overpowered by numbers, would have surrendered themselves prisoners, were such their practice. The heads of these unfortunate people they preserved as trophies.

With respect to religion, I believe these people trouble themselves very little about it. They, however, believe that there is one supreme god, whom they call Tawney, and likewise a number of other inferior deities; but whether or not they worship or pray to either one or the other we know not with any degree of certainty. It is reasonable to suppose that they do, and I believe it; yet I never saw the least action or thing among them that tended to prove it.

Having sailed from Cape Farewell, which lies in lat. 40° 33′ S., long. 186° W., on Saturday the 31st of March 1770, we steered westward, with a fresh gale at NNE., and at noon on the 2nd of April our latitude, by observation, was 40°, our longitude from Cape Farewell 2° 31′ W.

On the 19th, at 5 a.m., we saw land. We continued standing westward, with the wind at SSW., till eight, when we made all the sail we could, and bore away along the shore NE. for the easternmost land in sight, being at this time in lat. 37° 58′ S., and long. 210° 39′ W. The southernmost point of land in

April.

sight, which bore from us W. ¼ S., I judged to lie in lat. 38°, long. 211° 7', and gave it the name of Point Hicks, because Mr Hicks, the first lieutenant, was the first who discovered it. To the southward of this point no land was to be seen, though it was very clear in that quarter, and by our longitude, compared with that of Tasman—not as it is laid down in the printed charts, but in the extracts from Tasman's journal, published by Rembrantse—the body of Van Diemen's Land ought to have borne due south. And, indeed, from the sudden falling of the sea after the wind abated, I had reason to think it did; yet as I did not see it, and as I found this coast trend NE. and SW. or rather more to the eastward, I cannot determine whether it joins to Van Diemen's Land or not.

At six in the evening on the 20th we shortened sail and brought to for the night. The northernmost land in sight was a small island lying close to a point on the main. This point I called Cape Howe.

At four in the morning we made sail again, at the distance of about five leagues from the land, and at six we were abreast of a high mountain, lying near the shore, which, on account of its figure, I called Mount Dromedary. Under this mountain the shore forms a point, to which I gave the name of Point Dromedary, and over it there is a peaked hillock. After this we steered along shore, having a gentle breeze at SW., and were so near the shore as to distinguish several people upon the sea beach. They appeared to be of a very dark or black colour, but whether this was the real colour of their skins or the clothes they might have on, I know not. A remarkable peaked hill lay inland, the top of which looked like a pigeon-house, and occasioned my giving it that name. A small low island lay close under the shore. When we first discovered this island in the morning I was in hopes, from its appearance, that we should have found shelter for the ship behind it; but when we came to approach it near I did not think that there was even security for a boat to land. But this, I believe, I should have attempted had not the wind come on shore, after which I did not think it safe to send a boat from the ship, as we had a large hollow sea from the SE. rolling in upon the land, which beat everywhere very high upon the shore; and this we have had ever since we came upon the coast. The land near the sea-coast still continues of a moderate height, forming alternately rocky

MAP OF AUSTRALIA.

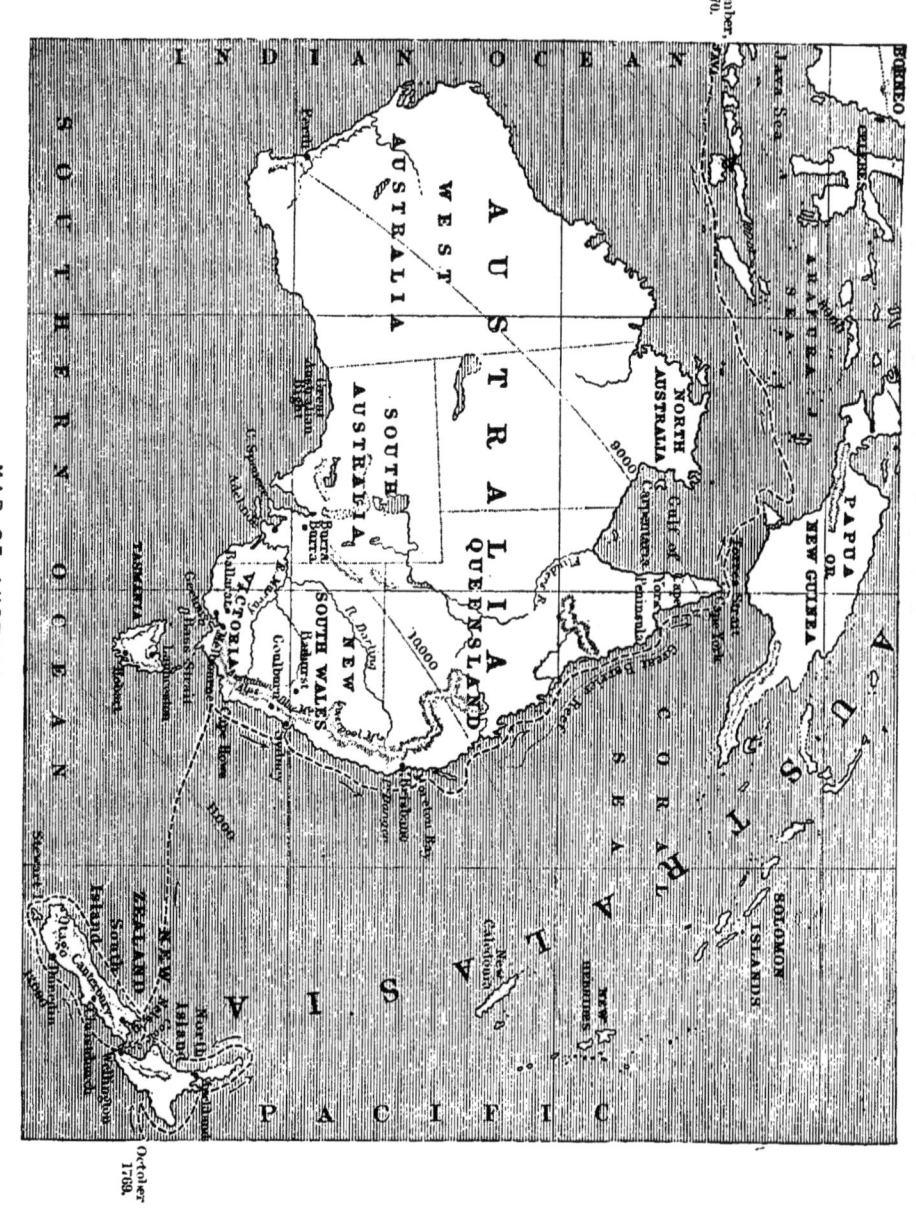

points and sandy beaches; but inland, between Mount Dromedary and the Pigeon-House, are several pretty high mountains, two only of which we saw, but which were covered with trees, and these lay inland behind the Pigeon-House, and are remarkably flat atop, with steep rocky cliffs all round them. As far as we could see, the trees in this country have all the appearance of being stout and lofty.

On the 25th, at three in the morning, we made sail again to the northward, having the advantage of a fresh gale at SW. At noon we were about three or four leagues from the shore, and in lat. 34° 22′ S., long. 208° 36′ W. In the course of this day's run from the preceding noon, which was forty-five miles north-east, we saw smoke in several places near the beach. About two leagues to the northward of Cape George, the shore seemed to form a bay, which promised shelter from the north-east winds; but as the wind was with us, it was not in my power to look into it without beating up, which would have cost me more time than I was willing to spare. The north point of this bay, on account of its figure, I named Long Nose. Its latitude is 35° 6′, and about eight leagues north of it there lies a point, which, from the colour of the land about it, I called Red Point.

On the 28th I hoisted out the pinnace and yawl to attempt a landing; but the pinnace proved to be so leaky that I was obliged to hoist her in again. I embarked in the yawl, and we pulled for that part of the shore where some Indians appeared.

The Indians sat down upon the rocks, and seemed to wait for our landing; but to our great regret, when we came within about a quarter of a mile, they ran away into the woods. We determined, however, to go ashore, and endeavour to procure an interview; but in this we were again disappointed, for we found so great a surf beating upon every part of the beach, that landing with our little boat was altogether impracticable. We were therefore obliged to be content with gazing at such objects as presented themselves from the water. The canoes, upon a near view, seemed very much to resemble those of the smaller sort at New Zealand. We observed that among the trees on shore, which were not very large, there was no underwood, and could distinguish that many of them were of the palm kind, and some of them cabbage trees. After many a wistful look we were obliged to return, with our curiosity rather excited than satisfied, and about five in the evening got on board the ship. About this time it fell calm, and our situation was by no means agreeable. We were now not more than a mile and a half from the shore, and within some breakers, which lay to the southward; but happily a light breeze came off the land, and carried us out of danger. With this breeze we stood to the northward, and at daybreak we discovered a bay which seemed to be well sheltered from all winds, and into which, therefore, I determined to go with the ship.

We continued to stand into the bay, and early in the afternoon anchored under the south shore, about two miles within the entrance, in six fathoms water, the south point bearing SE., and the north point E. As we came in we saw, on both points of the bay, a few huts and several of the natives—men, women, and children. Under the south head we saw four small canoes, with each one man on board, who were very busily employed in striking fish with a long pike or spear. They ventured almost into the surf, and were so intent upon what they were doing, that, although the ship passed within a quarter of a mile of them, they scarcely turned their eyes towards her; possibly being deafened by the surf, and their attention wholly fixed upon their business or sport, they neither saw nor heard her go past them.

The place where the ship had anchored was abreast of a small village consisting of about six or eight houses; and while we were preparing to hoist out the boat, we saw an old woman, followed by three children, come out of the wood. She was loaded with firewood, and each of the children had also its little burden. When she came to the houses, three more children, younger than the others, came out to meet her. She often looked at the ship, but expressed neither fear nor surprise. In a short time she kindled a fire, and the four canoes came in from fishing. The men landed, and having hauled up their boats, began to dress their dinner, to all appearance wholly unconcerned about us, though we were within half a mile of them. We thought it remarkable that of all the people we had yet seen, not one had the least appearance of clothing.

Soon they called to us in a very loud tone, and in a harsh dissonant language, of which neither we nor Tupia understood a single word. They brandished their weapons, and seemed resolved

THEIR HOSTILE ATTITUDE.

to defend their coast to the uttermost, though they were but two and we were forty. I could not but admire their courage; and being very unwilling that hostilities should commence with such inequality of force between us, I ordered the boat to lie upon her oars. We then parleyed by signs for about a quarter of an hour; and to bespeak their goodwill, I threw them nails, beads, and other trifles, which they took up and seemed to be well pleased with. I then made signs that I wanted water, and, by all the means that I could devise, endeavoured to convince them that we would do them no harm. They now waved to us, and I was willing to interpret it as an invitation; but upon our putting the boat in, they came again to oppose us. One appeared to be a youth about nineteen or twenty, and the other a man of middle age. As I had now no other resource I fired a musket between them. Upon the report, the youngest dropped a bundle of lances upon the rock; but recollecting himself in an instant, he snatched them up again with great haste. A stone was then thrown at us, upon which I ordered a musket to be fired with small shot, which struck the eldest upon the legs, and he immediately ran to one of the houses, which was distant about a hundred yards. I now hoped that our contest was over, and we immediately landed; but we had scarcely left the boat when he returned, and we then perceived that he had left the rock only to fetch a shield or target for his defence. As soon as he came up, he threw a lance at us, and his comrade another. They fell where we stood thickest, but happily hurt nobody. A third musket with small shot was then fired at them, upon which one of them threw another lance, and both immediately ran away.

Early the next morning the body of Forby Sutherland, one of our seamen, who died the evening before, was buried near the watering place; and from this incident I called the south point of this bay Sutherland Point. This day we resolved to make an excursion into the country. Mr. Banks, Dr. Solander, myself, and seven others, properly accoutred for the expedition, set out, and repaired first to the huts near the watering place, whither some of the natives continued every day to resort; and though the little presents which we had left there before had not yet been taken away, we left others of somewhat more value,

May.

consisting of cloth, looking-glasses, combs, and beads, and then went up into the country. We found the soil to be either swamp or light sand, and the face of the country finely diversified by wood and lawn. The trees are tall, straight, and without underwood, standing at such a distance from each other that the whole country, at least where the swamps do not render it incapable of cultivation, might be cultivated without cutting down one of them. Between the trees the ground is covered with grass, of which there is great abundance, growing in tufts about as big as can well be grasped in the hand, which stand very close to each other. We saw many houses of the inhabitants, and places where they had slept upon the grass without any shelter; but we saw only one of the people, who, the moment he discovered us, ran away. At all these places we left presents, hoping that at length they might produce confidence and goodwill. We had a transient and imperfect view of a quadruped about as big as a rabbit. Mr. Banks's greyhound, which was with us, got sight of it, and would probably have caught it; but the moment he set off he lamed himself against a stump which lay concealed in the long grass.

We found the face of the country much the same as I have before described, but the land much richer, for instead of sand I found in many places a deep black soil, which we thought was capable of producing any kind of grain. At present it produceth, besides timber, as fine meadow as ever was seen. However, we found it not all like this: some few places were very rocky; but this, I believe, to be uncommon. The stone is sandy and very proper for building, etc.

The great quantity of plants which Mr. Banks and Dr. Solander collected in this place induced me to give it the name of Botany Bay. It is situated in lat. 34° S., long. 208° 37' W. It is capacious, safe, and convenient, and may be known by the land on the sea-coast, which is nearly level and of a moderate height; in general higher than it is farther inland, with steep rocky cliffs next the sea, which have the appearance of a long island lying close under the shore.

The country is woody, low, and flat as far as we could see, and I believe that the soil is in general sandy. In the wood are a variety of very beautiful birds, such as cockatoos, lorikeets, parrots, etc., and crows exactly like those we have in England. Water-fowl is no less plentiful about the head of the harbour, where there are large flats of sand and mud, on which they seek their food; the most of these were unknown to us, one sort especially, which was black and white, and as large as a goose, but most like a pelican. On the sand and mud-banks are oysters, mussels, cockles, etc., which I believe are the chief support of the inhabitants, who go into shoal water with their little canoes and pick them out of the sand and mud with their hands, and sometimes roast and eat them in the canoe, having often a fire for that purpose, as I suppose, for I know no other it can be for.

The natives do not appear to be numerous, neither do they seem to live in large bodies, but dispersed in small parties along by the water side. Those I saw were about as tall as Europeans, of a very dark-brown colour, but not black, nor had they woolly, frizzled hair, but black and lank like ours. No sort of clothing or ornaments were ever seen by any of us upon any one of them, or in or about any of their huts; from which I conclude that they never wear any. Some that we saw had their faces and bodies painted with a sort of white paint or pigment.

Although I have said that shellfish is their chief support, yet they catch other sorts of fish, some of which we found roasting on the fire the first time we landed. Sting rays, I believe, they do not eat, because I never saw the least remains of one near any of their huts or fireplaces. However, we could know but very little of their customs, as we never were able to form any connections with them. They had not so much as touched the things we had left in their huts on purpose for them to take away. During our stay in this harbour I caused the English colours to be displayed ashore every day, and an inscription to be cut out upon one of the trees near the watering place, setting forth the ship's name, date, etc.

CHAPTER XI.

RANGE FROM BOTANY BAY TO TRINITY BAY, WITH A FURTHER ACCOUNT OF THE COUNTRY, ETC.—DANGEROUS SITUATION OF THE SHIP IN HER COURSE FROM TRINITY BAY TO ENDEAVOUR RIVER—APPEARANCE OF SCURVY.

1770. May.

AT daybreak on Sunday the 6th of May 1770, we set sail from Botany Bay, with a light breeze at NW., which soon after coming to the southward, we steered along the shore NNE., and at noon our latitude, by observation, was 33° 50' S. At this time we were between two and three miles distant from the land, and abreast of a bay or harbour in which there appeared to be good anchorage, and which I called Port Jackson. This harbour lies three leagues to the northward of Botany Bay. The variation, by several azimuths, appeared to be 8° E. At sunset, the northernmost land in sight bore N. 26 E., and some broken land that seemed to form a bay bore N. 40 W., distant four leagues. This bay, which lies in lat. 33° 42', I called Broken Bay.

The northernmost land in sight on the 27th bore N. 19 E., and some lands which projected in three bluff points, and which, for that reason, I called Cape Three Points. At four in the afternoon we passed, at a distance of about a mile, a low rocky point, which I called Point Stephens, on the north side of which is an inlet, which I called Port Stephens.

At eight on the 11th we were abreast of a high point of land, which made in two hillocks. This point I called Cape Hawke. During our run along the shore, in the afternoon, we saw smoke in several places at a little distance from the beach, and upon the top of a hill, which was the first we had seen upon elevated ground since our arrival upon the coast. At sunset we had twenty-three fathoms, at the distance of a league and a half from the shore. The northernmost land then bore N. 13 E.; and three hills, remarkably large and high, were lying contiguous to each other, and not far from the beach, NNW. As these hills bore some resemblance to each other, we called them the Three Brothers.

On the 13th we saw a point or headland, on which were fires that caused a great quantity of smoke, which occasioned my giving it the name of Smoky Cape. It is moderately high land. Over the pitch of the point is a round hillock; within it two others, much higher and larger, and within them very low land.

As we advanced to the northward from Botany Bay, the land gradually increased in height, so that in this latitude it may be called a hilly country. Between this latitude and the bay it exhibits a pleasing variety of ridges, hills, valleys, and plains, all clothed with wood, of the same appearance with that which has been particularly described. The land near the shore is in general low and sandy, except the points, which are rocky, and over many of them are high hills, which, at their first rising out of the water, have the appearance of islands.

At daylight on the 16th we were surprised by finding ourselves farther to the southward than we were in the evening, and yet it had blown strong all night southerly. We now saw the breakers again within us, which we passed at a distance of about one league. Their situation may always be found by a peaked mountain which bears SW. by W. from them, and on their account I have named it Mount Warning. The land is high and hilly about it, but it is conspicuous enough to be distinguished from everything else. The point off which these shoals lay I have named Point Danger. To the northward of it the land, which is low, trends NW. by N.; but we soon found that it did not keep that direction long before it turned again to the northward. We pursued our course along the shore till between four and five in the afternoon, when we discovered breakers on our larboard bow, on the north side of a point to which I gave the name of Point Lookout. The shore forms a wide, open bay, which I called Moreton's Bay. The breakers lie between three and four miles from Point Lookout; and at this time we had a great sea from the southward, which broke upon them very high.

At noon on the 19th we were about four miles from the land, with only thirteen fathoms. Our latitude was 25° 4′, and the northernmost land in sight bore N. 21 W., distant eight miles. At one o'clock, being still four miles distant from the shore, but having seventeen fathoms water, we passed a black bluff head, or point of land, upon which a great number of the natives were assembled, and which therefore I called Indian Head. It lies in latitude 25° 3'. About four miles N. by W. of this head is another very like it. This point I named Sandy Cape, from two very large patches of white sand which lay upon it. It is sufficiently high to be seen at the distance of twelve leagues, in clear weather, and lies in latitude 24° 45'.

Last night, some time in the middle watch, a very extraordinary affair happened to Mr. Orton, my clerk. He having been drinking in the evening, some malicious person or persons in the ship took advantage of his being drunk, and cut all the clothes from off his back. Not being satisfied with this, they sometime after went into his cabin and cut off a part of both his ears as he lay asleep in his bed. The person whom he suspected to have done this was Mr. Magra, one of the midshipmen; but this did not appear to me. Upon inquiry, however, as I had been told that Magra had once or twice before this in their drunken frolics cut off his clothes, and had been heard to say that if it was not for the law he would murder him—these things considered, induced me to think that Magra was not altogether innocent. I therefore, for the present, dismissed him the quarter-deck, and suspended him from doing any duty in the ship, he being one of those gentlemen frequently found on board king's ships that can very well be spared. Besides it was necessary in me to show my immediate resentment against the person on whom the suspicion fell, lest they should not have stopped here. With respect to Mr. Orton, he is a man not without faults; yet from all the inquiry I could make, it evidently appeared to me that, so far from deserving such treatment, he had not designed injuring any person in the ship; so that I do—and shall always—look upon him as an injured man. Some reasons, however, might be given why this misfortune came upon him, in which he himself was in some measure to blame; but as this is only conjecture, and would tend to fix it upon some people in the ship whom I would fain believe could hardly be guilty of such an action, I shall say nothing about it, unless I shall hereafter discover the offenders, which I shall take every method in my power to do; for I look upon such proceedings as highly dangerous in such voyages as this, and the greatest insult that could be offered to my authority in this ship, as I have always been ready to hear and redress every complaint that has been made against any person in the ship.

On the 22nd, at six in the morning, we weighed, with a gentle breeze from the southward, and steered NW. ¼ W., edging in for the land till we got within two miles of it, with water from seven to eleven fathoms. We then steered NNW. as the land lay, and at noon our latitude was 24° 19′. We continued in the same course, at the same distance, with from twelve fathoms to seven, till five in the evening, when we were abreast of the south point of a large open bay, in which I intended to anchor. During this course we discovered with our glasses that the land was covered with palm-nut trees, which we had not seen from the time of our leaving the islands within the tropics. We also saw two men walking along the shore, who did not condescend to take the least notice of us. In the evening, having hauled close upon a wind and made two or three trips, we anchored about eight o'clock in five fathoms, with a fine sandy bottom. The south point of the bay bore E. ¾ S., distant two miles; the north point NW. ¼ N., and about the same distance from the shore.

In the morning I went ashore with a party of men in order to examine the country, accompanied by Mr. Banks and the other gentlemen; we landed a little within the south point of the bay, where there is a channel leading into a large lagoon. The first thing that I did was to sound and examine the channel, in which I found three fathoms, until I got about a mile up it, where I met with a shoal, whereon was little more than one fathom; being over this, I had three fathoms again. The entrance into this channel lies close to the south point of this bay, being formed on the east by the shore, and on the west by a large spit of sand; it is about a quarter of a mile broad. Here is room for a few ships to lie very secure, and a small stream of fresh water. After this I made a little excursion into the woods, while some hands made three or four hauls with the seine, but caught not above a dozen very small fish. By this time the flood was made, and I embarked in the boats in order to row up the lagoon; but in this I was hindered by meeting everywhere with shoal water. As yet we had seen no people, but saw a great deal of smoke up and on the west side of the lagoon, which was all too far off for us to go by land, excepting one. This we went to, and found ten small fires in a very small compass, and some cockle shells lying by them; but the people were gone. On the windward or south side of one of the fires was stuck up a little bark about a foot and a half high, and some few pieces lay about in other places. These we concluded were all the covering they had in the night; and many of them, I firmly believe, have not this, but, naked as they are, sleep in the open air. Tupia, who was with us, observed that they were *taata enos*—that is, bad or poor people. The country is visibly worse than at the last place we were at. The soil is dry and sandy, and the woods are free from underwoods of every kind. Here are of the same sort of trees as we found in Botany Harbour, with a few other sorts.

Upon the shore we saw a species of the bustard, one of which we shot; it was as large as a turkey, and weighed seventeen pounds and a half. We all agreed that this was the best bird we had eaten since we left England; and in honour of it we called this inlet Bustard Bay. The sea seemed to abound with fish; but, unhappily, we tore our seine all to pieces at the first haul. Upon the mud-banks, under the mangroves, we found innumerable oysters of various kinds; among others the hammer-oyster, and a large proportion of small pearl-oysters. If in deeper water there is equal plenty of such oysters at their full growth, a pearl fishery might certainly be established here to very great advantage.

At five in the morning we made sail, and at daylight the northernmost point of the main bore N. 70 W. Soon after we saw more land, making like islands, and bearing NW. by N. At nine we were abreast of the point, at the distance of one mile, with fourteen fathoms water. This point I found to lie directly under the tropic of Capricorn, and for that reason I called it Cape Capricorn. Its longitude is 208° 58′ W. It is of a considerable height, looks white and barren, and may be known by some islands which lie to the NW. of it, and some small rocks at the distance of about a league SE.

At noon on the 27th we were about two leagues distant from the main, and by observation in lat. 22° 53′ S. The northernmost point of land in sight now bore NNW., distant ten miles. To this point I gave the name of Cape Manifold, from the number of high hills which appeared over it. It lies in lat. 22° 43′ S., and distant about seventeen leagues from Cape Capricorn, in the direction of N. 26 W. Between these capes the shore forms a large bay, which I called Keppel Bay; and I also distinguished the islands by the name of Keppel's Islands. In this bay there is good anchorage; but what refreshments it may afford I know not. We caught no fish, though we were at anchor; but probably there is fresh water in several places, as both the islands and the main are inhabited. We saw smoke and fires upon the main, and upon the islands we saw people.

At nine o'clock on the 28th we were abreast of the point, which I named Cape Townshend. At six next day we anchored in ten fathoms, sandy bottom, about two miles from the mainland, having still a number of islands in sight a long way without us. At 5 a.m. I sent away the master with two boats to sound the entrance of an inlet, into which I intended to go with the ship to wait a few days until the moon increased, and in the meantime to examine the country. By such time as we had got the ship under sail the boats made the signal for anchorage, upon which we stood in with the ship, and anchored in five fathoms, about a league within the entrance of the inlet, which we judged to be a river running a good way inland, as I observed the tides to flow and ebb something considerable. I had some thoughts of laying the ship ashore to clean her bottom. With this view both the master and I went to look for a convenient place for that purpose, and at the same time to look for fresh water, not one drop of which we could find, but met with several places where a ship might be laid ashore with safety.

This inlet I have named Thirsty Sound, by reason we could find no fresh water. I have already observed that here is no fresh water, nor could we procure refreshment of any other kind. We saw two turtles, but we were not able to take either of them. Neither did we catch either fish or wild fowl, except a few small land birds. We saw, indeed, the same sorts of water-fowl as in Botany Bay, but they were so shy that we could not get a shot at them. As I had not therefore a single inducement to stay longer in this place, I weighed anchor at six o'clock in the morning of the 31st and put to sea.

June. At eight on the 3rd we discovered low land, quite across what we took for an opening between the main and the islands, which proved to be a bay about five or six leagues deep. Upon this we hauled our wind to the eastward round the northernmost point of the bay, which bore from us at this time NE. by N., distance four leagues. From this point we found the mainland trend away N. by W. $\frac{1}{2}$ W., and a strait or passage between it and a large island or islands lying in a parallel direction with the coast. This passage we stood into, having the tide of ebb in our favour. At noon we were just within the entrance. This point I have named Cape Conway, and the bay, Repulse Bay, which is formed by two capes.

At six o'clock in the evening of the 4th we were nearly the length of the north end of the passage, with an open sea between the two points. As this passage was discovered on Whitsunday, I called it Whitsunday's Passage; and I called the islands that form it Cumberland Islands, in honour of his royal highness the duke. We kept under an easy sail, with the lead going all night, being at the distance of about three leagues from the shore, and having from twenty-one to twenty-three fathoms water. At daybreak we were abreast of the point which had been the farthest in sight to the north-west the evening before, which I named Cape Gloucester. It is a lofty promontory, and may be known by an island which lies out at sea N. by W. $\frac{1}{2}$ W. at the distance of five or six leagues from it, and which I called Holborne Isle. There are also islands lying under the land between Holborne Isle and Whitsunday's Passage. On the west side of Cape Gloucester the land trends away SW. and SSW. and forms a deep bay, the bottom of which I could but just see from the mast-head. It is very low, and a continuation of the low land which we had seen at the bottom of Repulse Bay. This bay I called Edgcumbe Bay.

We continued to steer WNW. as the land lay, with twelve or fourteen fathoms water, till noon on the 6th, when our latitude by observation was 19° 1' S., and we had the mouth of a bay all open, extending from S. ½ E. to SW. ½ S., distant two leagues.

This bay, which I named Cleveland Bay, appeared to be about five or six miles in extent every way. The east point I named Cape Cleveland, and the west, which had the appearance of an island, Magnetical Isle, as we perceived that the compass did not traverse well when we were near it. They are both high, and so is the mainland within them, the whole forming a surface the most rugged, rocky, and barren of any we had seen upon the coast. It was not, however, without inhabitants, for we saw smoke in several parts of the bottom of the bay.

On the 5th we saw several large smokes upon the main, some people, canoes, and, as we thought, cocoa-nut trees upon one of the islands; and as a few of these nuts would have been very acceptable to us at this time, I sent Lieutenant Hicks ashore, with whom went Mr. Banks and Dr. Solander, to see what was to be got. In the meantime we kept standing in for the island with the ship. At seven they returned on board, having met with nothing worth observing. The trees we saw were a small kind of cabbage palms. They heard some of the natives as they were putting off from the shore, but saw none. After the boat was hoisted in we stood away N. by W. for the northernmost land we had in sight, which we were abreast of at three o'clock in the morning, having passed all the islands three or four hours before. This point I have named Point Hillock, on account of its figure. The land of this point is tolerably high, and may be known by a round hillock or rock that appears to be detached from the point, but I believe it joins to it. Between this cape and Cape Cleveland the shore forms a large bay, which I named Halifax Bay. Before it lay the groups of islands before mentioned, and some others nearer the shore. These islands shelter the bay in a manner from all winds, in which is good anchorage. The land near the shore in the bottom of the bay is very low and woody; but a little way back in the country is a continued ridge of high land, which appeared to be barren and rocky. Having passed Point Hillock, we continued standing to the NNW. as the land trended, having the advantage of a light moon. At 6 a.m. we were abreast of a point of land which I named Cape Sandwich; it may be known not only by the high, craggy land over it, but by a small island which lies E. one mile from it, and some others about two leagues to the northward of it. From Cape Sandwich the land trends W., and afterwards N., and forms a fine large bay, which I called Rockingham Bay. It is well sheltered, and affords good anchorage at least so it appeared to me; for, having met with so little encouragement by going ashore, I would not wait to land or examine it further, but continued to range along shore to the northward for a parcel of small islands lying off the northern point of the bay, and finding a channel of a mile broad between the three outermost and those nearer the shore, we pushed through.

At six o'clock in the morning of the 10th we were abreast of some small islands, which we called Frankland's Isles, and which lie about two leagues distant from the mainland. The most distant point in sight to the northward bore N. by W. $\frac{1}{2}$ W., and we thought it was part of the main, but afterwards found it to be an island of considerable height, and about four miles in circuit. Between this island and a point on the main from which it is distant about two miles, I passed with the ship. At noon we were in the middle of the channel, and by observation in the latitude of 16° 57′ S., with twenty fathoms water. The point on the main, of which we were now abreast, I called Cape Grafton. Its latitude is 16° 57′ S. and longitude 214° 6′ W., and the land here, as well as the whole coast for about twenty leagues to the southward, is high, has a rocky surface, and is thinly covered with wood. During the night we had seen several fires, and about noon some people. Having hauled round Cape Grafton, we found the land trend away NW. by W., and three miles to the westward of the cape we found a bay, in which we anchored about two miles from the shore, in four fathoms water with an oozy bottom. The east point of the bay bore S. 74 E., the west point S. 83 W., and a low, green, woody island, which lies in the offing, N. 35 E. This island, which lies N. by E. $\frac{1}{2}$ E., distant three or four leagues from Cape Grafton, is called in the chart Green Island. The shore between Cape Grafton and the northern point forms a large but not very deep bay, which I named Trinity Bay, after the day on which it was discovered.

Hitherto we had safely navigated this dangerous coast, where the sea in all parts conceals shoals that suddenly project from the shore, and rocks that rise abruptly like a pyramid from the bottom, for an extent of two and twenty degrees of latitude, more than 1,300 miles; and therefore hitherto none of the names which distinguish the several parts of the country that we saw are memorials of distress. But here we became acquainted with misfortune, and we therefore called the point which we had just seen farthest to the northward Cape Tribulation. We had the advantage of a fine breeze and a clear moonlight night, and in standing off from six till near nine o'clock we deepened our water from fourteen to twenty-one fathoms; but while we were at supper it suddenly shoaled, and we fell into twelve, ten, and eight fathoms within the space of a few minutes. I immediately ordered everybody to their station, and all was ready to put about and come to an anchor; but meeting at the next cast of the lead with deep water again, we concluded that we had gone over the tail of the shoals which we had seen at sunset, and that all danger was past. Before ten we had twenty and one-and-twenty fathoms, and this depth continuing, the gentlemen left the deck in great tranquillity, and went to bed. But a few minutes before eleven the water shallowed at once from twenty to seventeen fathoms, and before the lead could be cast again the ship struck, and remained immovable, except by the heaving of the surge, that beat her against the crags of the rock upon which she lay. In a few moments everybody was upon the deck, with countenances which sufficiently expressed the horrors of our situation. We had stood off the shore three hours and a half, with a pleasant breeze, and therefore knew that we could not be very near it; and we had too much reason to conclude that we were upon a rock of coral, which is more fatal than any other, because the points of it are sharp, and every part of the surface so rough as to grind away whatever is rubbed against it, even with the gentlest motion.

Immediately upon this we took in all our sails, hoisted out the boats and sounded round the ship, and found that we had got upon the south-east edge of a reef of coral rocks, having in some places round the ship three and four fathoms water, and in other places not quite as many feet, and about a ship's length from us on the starboard side were eight, ten, and twelve fathoms. As soon as the longboat was out, we struck yards and topmast, and carried out the stream anchor on our starboard bow, got the coasting anchor and cable into the boat, and were going to carry it out in the same way; but upon my sounding the second time round the ship I found the most water astern, and therefore had this anchor carried out upon the starboard quarter, and hove upon it a very great strain, which was to no purpose, the ship being quite fast; upon which we went to work to lighten her as fast as possible, which seemed to be the only means we had left to get her off. As we went ashore about the top of high water, we not only started water, but threw overboard our guns, iron and stone ballast, casks, hoop staves, oil jars, decayed·stores, etc.

All this time the ship made little or no water. At 11 a.m., being high water as we thought, we tried to heave her off without success, she not being afloat by a foot or more, notwithstanding by this time we had thrown overboard forty or fifty tons weight. As this was not found sufficient, we continued to lighten her by every method we could think of. As the tide fell, the ship began to make water as much as two pumps could free. At noon she lay with three or four streaks heel to starboard.

On Tuesday the 12th we had little wind, fine weather, and a smooth sea, which gave us an opportunity to carry out the two bower anchors, one on the starboard quarter and the other right astern, and to get blocks and tackles upon the cables.

By this time it was 5 p.m. The tide, we observed, now began to rise, and the leak increased upon us, which obliged us to set the third pump to work, as we should have done the fourth also, but could not make it work. At nine the ship righted, and the leak gained upon the pumps considerably. This was an alarming and, I may say, terrible circumstance, and threatened immediate destruction to us. However, I resolved to risk all, and heave her off in case it was practical, and accordingly turned as many hands to the capstan and windlass as could be spared from the pumps; and about twenty minutes past ten o'clock the ship floated, and we hove her into deep water, having at this time three feet nine inches water in the hold. This done, I sent the longboat to take up the stream anchor; got the anchor, but lost the cable among the rocks. After this turned all hands to the pumps, the leak increasing upon us.

A mistake soon after happened, which for the first time caused fear to approach upon every man in the ship. The man that attended the well took the depth of water above the ceiling; he being relieved by another who did not know in what manner the former had sounded, took the depth of water from the outside plank, the difference being sixteen or eighteen inches, and made it appear that the leak had gained this upon the pumps in a short time. This mistake was no sooner cleared up than it acted upon every man like a charm; they redoubled their vigour, insomuch that before eight o'clock in the morning they gained considerably upon the leak. At eleven we got under sail, and stood in for the land.

It is much easier to conceive than to describe the satisfaction felt by everybody on this occasion. But a few minutes before, our utmost wishes were to get hold of some place upon the main to run the ship ashore, where out of her materials we might build a vessel to carry us to the East Indies. No sooner were we made sensible that the outward application to the ship's bottom had taken effect, than the field of every man's hopes enlarged, so that we thought of nothing but ranging along shore in search of a harbour, where we could repair the damages we had sustained.

In justice and gratitude to the ship's company, I must say that no men ever behaved better than they have done on this occasion. Animated by the behaviour of every gentleman on board, every man seemed to have a just sense of the danger we were in, and exerted himself to the very utmost. The ledge of rocks, or shoal, we have been upon lies in the latitude of 15° 45', and about six or seven leagues from the mainland. But this is not the only shoal that lay upon this part of the coast, especially to the northward, and one which we saw to the southward, the tail of which we passed over when we had the uneven soundings two hours before we struck. A part of this shoal is always above water, and looks to be white sand. Part of the one we were upon was dry at low water, and in that place consists of sand and stones, but everywhere else coral rocks.

While we lay at anchor for the night we found that the ship

made about fifteen inches water an hour, from which no immediate danger was to be apprehended; and at six o'clock in the morning we weighed and stood to the NW., still edging in for the land with a gentle breeze at SSE. At nine we passed close without two small islands that lie in latitude 15° 41' S. and about four leagues from the main. To reach these islands had, in the height of our distress, been the object of our hope, or perhaps rather of our wishes, and therefore I called them Hope Islands.

At three o'clock we saw an opening that had the appearance of a harbour, and stood off and on while the boats examined it; but they soon found that there was not depth of water in it sufficient for the ship. The pinnace was still out with one of the mates, but at nine o'clock on the 13th she returned, and reported that they had found a good harbour about two leagues to leeward. In consequence of this information we, at 6 a.m., weighed and ran down to it, first sending two boats ahead to lie upon the shoals that lay in our way; and notwithstanding this precaution we were once in three fathoms with the ship. Having passed these shoals, the boats were sent to lie in the channel leading into the harbour. By this time it began to blow insomuch that the ship would not work, having missed stays twice; and being entangled among shoals, I was afraid of being driven to leeward before the boats could place themselves, and therefore anchored in four fathoms about a mile from the shore, and then made the signal for the boats to come on board, after which I went myself and buoyed the channel, which I found very narrow, and the harbour much smaller than I had been told, but very convenient for our purpose. In the night, as it blew too fresh to break the ship loose to run into the harbour, we got down the topgallant yards, unbent the mainsail and some of the small sails, got down the foretop-gallant mast, and the jib-boom and sprit-sail yard in, intending to lighten the ship forward as much as possible, in order to lay her ashore to come at the leak.

The scurvy now began to make its appearance among us, with many formidable symptoms. Our poor Indian, Tupia, who had some time before complained that his gums were sore and swelled, and who had taken plentifully of our lemon juice by the surgeon's direction, had now livid spots upon his legs, and other indubitable testimonies that the disease had made a rapid progress, notwithstanding all our remedies, among which the bark had been liberally administered. Mr. Green, our astronomer, was also declining; and these, among other circumstances, embittered the delay which prevented our going ashore.

In the morning of the 17th, though the wind was still fresh, we ventured to weigh and push in for the harbour, but in doing this we twice ran the ship aground. The first time she went off without any trouble, but the second time she stuck fast. We now got down the foreyard, foretopmasts, and booms, and taking them overboard made a raft of them alongside of the ship. The tide was happily rising, and about one o'clock in the afternoon she floated. We soon warped her into the harbour, and having moored her alongside of a steep beach to the south, we got the anchors, cables, and all the hawsers on shore before night.

CHAPTER XII.

TRANSACTIONS WHILE THE SHIP WAS REFITTING IN ENDEAVOUR RIVER.

1770.
June.
IN the morning of Monday the 18th, a stage was made from the ship to the shore, which was so bold that she floated at twenty feet distance. Two tents were also set up, one for the sick and the other for stores and provisions, which were landed in the course of the day. We also landed all the empty water-casks and part of the stores. As soon as the tent for the sick was got ready for their reception, they were sent ashore to the number of eight or nine, and the boat was despatched to haul the seine, in hopes of procuring some fish for their refreshment, but she returned without success. In the meantime I climbed one of the highest hills among those that overlooked the harbour, which afforded by no means a comfortable prospect. The low land near the river is wholly overrun with mangroves, among which the salt water flows every tide, and the high land appeared to be everywhere stony and barren. In the meantime Mr. Banks had also taken a walk up the country, and met with the frames of several old Indian houses, and places where they had dressed shell-fish, but they seemed not to have been frequented for some months. Tupia, who had employed himself in angling, and lived entirely upon what he caught, recovered in a surprising degree, but Mr. Green still continued to be extremely ill.

The next morning we went early to work, and by four o'clock in the afternoon had got out all the coals, cast the moorings loose, and warped the ship a little higher up the harbour to a place which I thought most convenient for laying her ashore in order to stop the leak. Her draught of water forward was now seven feet nine inches, and abaft thirteen feet six inches. At eight o'clock, it being high water, I hauled her bow close ashore, but kept her stern afloat, because I was afraid of neaping her. It was, however, necessary to lay the whole of her as near the ground as possible.

At two o'clock in the morning of the 22nd the tide left her, and gave us an opportunity to examine the leak, which we found to be at her floor heads, a little before the starboard fore-chains. In this place the rocks had made their way through four planks, and even into the timbers; three more planks were much damaged, and the appearance of these breaches was very extraordinary. There was not a splinter to be seen, but all was as smooth as if the whole had been cut away by an instrument. The timbers in this place were happily very close, and if they had not, it would have been absolutely impossible to have saved the ship.

But after all, her preservation depended upon a circumstance still more remarkable. Indeed, one of the holes, which was big enough to have sunk us, if we had had eight pumps instead of four, and been able to keep them incessantly going, was in great measure plugged up by a fragment of the rock, which, after having made the wound, was left sticking in it, so that the water which at first had gained upon our pumps was what came in at the interstices between the stone and the edges of the hole that received it.

Early on the 24th the carpenters began to repair the sheathing under the larboard bow, where we found two planks cut about half through; and in the meantime I sent a party of men, under the direction of Mr. Gore, in search of refreshments for the sick. This party returned about noon with a few palm cabbages and a bunch or two of wild plantain. The plantains were the smallest I had ever seen, and the pulp, though it was well tasted, was full of small stones. As I was walking this morning at a little distance from the ship I saw myself one of the animals[*] which had been so often described. It was of a light mouse colour, and in size and shape very much resembling a greyhound. It had a long tail also, which it carried like a greyhound, and I should have taken it for a wild dog, if, instead of running, it had not leaped like a hare or deer. Its legs were said to be very slender, and the print of its foot to be like that of a goat; but where I saw it the grass

(561)   * Kangaroo.   10

was so high that the legs were concealed, and the ground was too hard to receive the track. Mr. Banks also had an imperfect view of this animal, and was of opinion that its species was hitherto unknown.

The 25th was employed in filling water and overhauling the rigging, and at low water the carpenters finished the repairs under the larboard bow, and every other place which the tide would permit them to come at. Some casks were then lashed under her bows to facilitate her floating, and at night, when it was high water, we endeavoured to heave her off, but without success, for some of the casks that were lashed to her gave way.

The morning of the 26th was employed in getting more casks ready for the same purpose, and in the afternoon we lashed no less than eight and thirty under the ship's bottom, but to our great mortification these also proved ineffectual, and we found ourselves reduced to the necessity of waiting till the next spring-tide.

In some of our excursions we found some wild yams or cocos growing in the swampy grounds, and this afternoon I sent a party of men to gather some. The tops we found made good greens, and ate exceedingly well when boiled, but the roots were so bad that few besides myself could eat them.

Mr. Gore reported that he had this day seen two animals like dogs of a straw colour, that they ran like a hare, and were about the same size. In the afternoon the people returned from hauling the seine, with still better success than before, for I was now able to distribute two pounds and a half to each man. The greens that had been gathered I ordered to be boiled among the peas, and they made an excellent mess, which, with two copious supplies of fish, afforded us unspeakable refreshment.

July. The next day, July the 1st, being Sunday, everybody had liberty to go ashore, except one from each mess, who were again sent out with the seine. The seine was again equally successful, and the people who went up the country gave an account of having seen several animals, though none of them were to be caught.

To-day at noon the thermometer in the shade rose to 87°, which is higher than it hath been on any day before in this place. In the morning four of the natives came down to the sandy point on the north side of the harbour, having along with them a small wooden canoe with outriggers, in which they seemed to be employed striking fish, etc. Some were for going over in a boat to them, but this I would not suffer, but let them alone without seeming to take any notice of them. At length two of them came in the canoe so near the ship as to take some things we threw them. After this they went away, and brought over the other two, and came again alongside, nearer than they had done before, and took such trifles as we gave them.

After this they landed close to the ship, and all four went ashore, carrying their arms with them. But Tupia soon prevailed upon them to lay down their arms and come and sit down by him; after which most of us went to them, made them again some presents, and stayed by them until dinner time, when we made them understand that we were going to eat, and asked them by signals to go with us; but this they declined, and as soon as we left them they went away in their canoe.

One of these men was something above the middle age, the other three were young; none of them were above five and a half feet high, and all their limbs proportionately small. They were wholly naked, their skins the colour of wood soot, and this seemed to be their natural colour. Their hair was black, lank, and cropped short, and neither woolly nor frizzled. Nor did they want any of their fore-teeth, as Dampier has mentioned those did he saw on the western side of this country.

Some part of their bodies had been painted with red, and one of them had his upper lip and breast painted with streaks of white, which he called *carbanda*. Their features were far from being disagreeable, their voices were soft and tunable, and they could easily repeat any word after us, but neither we nor Tupia could understand one word they said.

On the 14th two of the Indians came on board, but after a short stay went along the shore, and applied themselves with great diligence to the striking of fish. Mr. Gore, who went out this day with his gun, had the good fortune to kill one of the animals which had been so much the subject of our speculation. In form it is most like the jerboa, which it also resembles in its motion, as has been observed already, but it greatly differs in size, the jerboa not being larger than a common rat, and this animal when full grown being as big as a sheep. This individual was a young one, much under its full growth, weighing only thirty-eight pounds. The head, neck, and shoulders are very small in proportion to the other parts of the body; the tail is nearly as long as the body, thick near the rump, and tapering towards the end. The fore-legs of this individual were only eight inches long, and the hind-legs two and twenty. Its progress is by successive leaps or hops, of a great length, in an erect posture. The fore-legs are kept bent close to the breast, and seemed to be of use only for digging. The skin is covered with a short fur, of a dark mouse or grey colour, excepting the head and ears, which bear a slight resemblance to those of a hare. This animal is called by the natives *kangaroo.*

The next day our kangaroo was dressed for dinner, and proved most excellent meat. We might now indeed be said to fare sumptuously every day, for we had turtle in great plenty, and we all agreed that they were much better than any we had tasted in England, which we imputed to their being eaten fresh from the sea, before their natural fat had been wasted.

About eight we were visited by several of the natives, who now became more familiar than ever. Soon after this Mr. Banks and I went over to the south side of the river, and travelled six or eight miles along shore to the northward, where we ascended a high hill, from whence I had an extensive view of the sea-coast. It afforded us a melancholy prospect of the difficulties we are to encounter, for in whatever direction we looked it was covered with shoals as far as the eye could see. After this we returned to the ship without meeting with anything remarkable, and found several of the natives on board. At this time we had twelve tortoise or turtle upon our decks, which they took more notice of than anything else in the ship, as I was told by the officers, but their curiosity was satisfied before I got on board, and they went away soon after.

On the 19th we were visited by ten or eleven of the natives. The most of them came from the other side of the harbour, where we saw six or seven more, the most of them women, and, like the men, quite naked. Those that came on board were very desirous of having some of our turtles, and took the liberty to haul two of

AUSTRALIAN LANDSCAPE WITH KANGAROOS.

Page 148.

them to the gangway to put over the side. Being disappointed in this, they grew a little troublesome, and were for throwing everything overboard they could lay their hands upon. As we had no victuals dressed at this time, I offered them some bread to eat, which they rejected with scorn, as I believe they would have done anything else excepting turtle. Soon after this they all went ashore, Mr. Banks, myself, and five or six of our people being there at the same time. Immediately upon their landing, one of them took a handful of dry grass and lighted it at a fire we had ashore, and before we well knew what he was going about he made a large circuit round about us, and set fire to the grass in his way, and in an instant the whole place was in flames. Luckily at this time we had hardly anything ashore besides the forge and a sow with a litter of young pigs, one of which was scorched to death in the fire. As soon as they had done this they all went to a place where some of our people were washing, and where all our nets and a good deal of linen were laid out to dry. Here with the greatest obstinacy they again set fire to the grass, which I and some others who were present could not prevent, until I was obliged to fire a musket load of small shot at one of the ringleaders, which sent them off. As we were apprised of this last attempt of theirs, we got the fire out before it got head, but the first spread like wildfire in the woods and grass. Notwithstanding my firing, in which one must have been a little hurt, because we saw a few drops of blood on some of the linen he had gone over, they did not go far from us, for we soon after heard their voices in the woods, upon which Mr. Banks and I and three or four more went to look for them, and very soon met them coming toward us. As they had each four or five darts, and not knowing their intention, we seized upon six or seven of the first darts we met with. This alarmed them so much that they all made off, and soon after set the woods on fire about a mile and a half or two miles from us.

Early in the morning of the 23rd I sent some people into the country to gather a supply of greens; and one of them having straggled from the rest, suddenly fell in with four Indians, three men and a boy, whom he did not see till, by turning short in the wood, he found himself among them. They had kindled a fire, and were broiling a bird of some kind and part of a kangaroo, the remainder of which, and a cockatoo, hung at a little distance upon a tree. The man, being unarmed, was at first greatly terrified, but he had the presence of mind not to run away, judging, very rightly, that he was most likely to incur danger by appearing to apprehend it; on the contrary, he went and sat down by them, and with an air of cheerfulness and good humour offered them his knife, the only thing he had about him which he thought would be acceptable to them. They received it, and having handed it from one to the other, they gave it him again. He then made an offer to leave them, but this they seemed not disposed to permit; still, however, he dissembled his fears, and sat down again. They considered him with great attention and curiosity, particularly his clothes, and then felt his hands and face, and satisfied themselves that his body was of the same texture with their own. They treated him with the greatest civility; and having kept him about half an hour, they made signs that he might depart. He did not wait for a second dismissal; but when he left them, not taking the direct way to the ship, they came from their fire and directed him, so that they well knew whence he came.

August. On the 1st of August the carpenter examined the pumps, and, to our great mortification, found them all in a state of decay, owing, as he said, to the saps having been left in the wood. One of them was so rotten as, when hoisted up, to drop to pieces, and the rest were little better; so that our chief trust was now in the soundness of our vessel, which happily did not admit more than one inch of water in an hour.

At six o'clock in the morning of Friday the 3rd we made another unsuccessful attempt to warp the ship out of the harbour; but at five o'clock in the morning of the 4th our efforts had a better effect, and about seven we got once more under sail, with a light air from the land, which soon died away, and was followed by the sea-breezes from SE. by S., with which we stood off to sea E. by N., having the pinnace ahead, which was ordered to keep sounding continually.

I shall now give a short description of the harbour or river we have been in, which I named, after the ship, Endeavour River. It is only a small bar, harbour, or creek, which runs winding three or four leagues inland, at the head of which is a small fresh-water brook, as I was told, for I was not so high myself; but there is not water for shipping above a mile within the bar, and this is on the north side, where the bank is so steep for nearly a quarter of a mile that ships may lie afloat at low water so near the shore as to reach it with a stage, and is extremely convenient for heaving a ship down. And this is all the river hath to recommend it, especially for large shipping. Besides, this part of the coast is barricaded with shoals, as to make this harbour more difficult of access; the safest way I know of to come at it is from the south, keeping the mainland close on board all the way.

The refreshments we got here were chiefly turtle; but as we had to go five leagues out to sea for them, and had much blowing weather, we were not overstocked with this article. However, what with these and the fish we caught with the seine we had not much reason to complain, considering the country we were in. Whatever refreshment we got that would bear a division I caused to be equally divided among the whole company, generally by weight; the meanest person in the ship had an equal share with myself or any one on board, and this method every commander of a ship on such a voyage as this ought ever to observe. We found in several places, on the sandy beaches and sand-hills near the sea, purslain and beans, which grow on a creeping kind of a vine. The first we found very good when boiled, and the latter not to be despised; they were at first very serviceable to the sick; but the best greens we found here were the tarro, or coco tops, called in the West Indies Indian kale, which grow in most boggy places. These eat as well as, or better than, spinach. The roots, for want of being transplanted and properly cultivated, were not good, yet we could have dispensed with that could we have got them in any tolerable plenty; but having a good way to go for them, it took up too much time and too many hands to gather both root and branch. The few cabbage palms we found here were in general small, and yielded so little cabbage that they were not worth the looking at.

Besides the kangaroo and the opossum, that have been already mentioned, and a kind of polecat, there are wolves upon this part of the coast—if we were not deceived by the tracks upon the ground—and several species of serpents; some of the serpents are venomous, and some harmless. There are no tame animals here except dogs, and of these we saw but two or three, which frequently came about the tents to pick up the scraps and bones that happened to lie scattered near them. There does not indeed seem to be many of any animal except the kangaroo; we scarcely saw any other above once, but this we met with almost every time we went into the woods.

Of land fowls we saw crows, kites, hawks, cockatoos of two sorts (one white and the other black), a very beautiful kind of lorikeet, some parrots, pigeons of two or three sorts, and several small birds not known in Europe. The water fowls are herons, whistling ducks (which perch, and, I believe, roost upon trees), wild geese, curlews, and a few others, but these do not abound. The face of the country, which has been occasionally mentioned before, is agreeably diversified by hill and valley, lawn and wood. The soil of the hills is hard, dry, and stony, yet it produces coarse grass besides wood. The soil of the plains and valleys is in some places sand, and in some clay; in some, also, it is rocky and stony, like the hills. In general, however, it is well clothed, and has at least the appearance of fertility. The whole country, both hill and valley, wood and plain, abounds with ant-hills, some of which are six or eight feet high, and twice as much in circumference. The trees here are not of many sorts; the gum tree, which we found on the southern part of the coast, is the most common, but here it is not so large. On each side of the river, through its whole course, there are mangroves in great numbers, which in some places extend a mile within the coast. The country is in all parts well watered, there being several fine rivulets at a small distance from each other, but none in the place where we lay—at least not during the time we were there, which was the dry season; we were, however, well supplied with water by springs, which were not far off.

In the morning of the 6th we had a strong gale, so that, instead of weighing, we were obliged to veer away more cable and strike our topgallant yards. At low water, myself, with several of the officers, kept a lookout at the mast-head, to see if any passage could be discovered between the shoals; but nothing was in view except breakers extending from the S. round by the E., as far as NW., and out to sea beyond the reach of our sight. These breakers, however, did not appear to be caused by one continued shoal, but by several, which lay detached from each other. On that which lay farthest to the eastward the sea broke very high, which made me think it was the outermost, for upon many of these within the breakers were inconsiderable, and from about half-ebb to half-flood they were not to be seen at all, which makes sailing among them still more dangerous, especially as the shoals here consist principally of coral rocks, which are as steep as a wall. Upon some of them, however, and generally at the north end, there are patches of sand, which are covered only at high water, and which are to be discerned at some distance. Being now convinced that there was no passage to sea but through the labyrinth formed by these shoals, I was altogether at a loss which way to steer, when the weather should permit us to get under sail. It was the master's opinion that we should beat back the way we came; but this would have been an endless labour, as the wind blew strongly from that quarter almost without intermission. On the other hand, if no passage can be found to the northward, we shall have to come back at last.

On the 10th we judged ourselves to be clear of all danger, having, as we thought, a clear, open sea before us; but this we soon found otherwise, and for that reason I called a headland, two leagues from us, Cape Flattery. It is a high promontory; from this cape the mainland trends away NW. We steered along the shore NW. by W. till one o'clock, for what we thought the open channel, when the petty officer at the mast-head cried out that he saw land ahead, extending quite round to the islands that lay without us, and a large reef between us and them. Upon this I ran up to the mast-head myself, from whence I very plainly saw the reef, which was now so far to windward that we could not weather it; but the land ahead, which he had supposed to be the main, appeared to me to be only a cluster of small islands. As soon as I got down from the mast-head, the master and some others went up, who all insisted that the land ahead was not islands, but the main; and to make their report still more alarming, they said that they saw breakers all round us. In this dilemma we hauled upon a wind in for the land, and made the signal for the boat that was sounding ahead to come on board, but as she was far to leeward, we were obliged to edge away to take her up; and soon after we came to an anchor, under a point of the main, in somewhat less than five fathoms, and at about the distance of a mile from the shore. Cape Flattery now bore SE., distant three leagues and a half. As soon as the ship was at anchor, I went ashore upon the point, which is high, and afforded me a good view of the sea-coast, trending away NW. by W. eight or ten leagues, which, the weather not being very clear, was as far as I could see. Nine or ten small low islands and some shoals appeared off the coast. I saw also some large shoals between the main and the three high islands, without which I was clearly of opinion there were more islands, and not any part of the main. Except the point I was now upon, which I called Point Lookout, and Cape Flattery, the mainland to the northward of Cape Bedford is low, and chequered with white sand and green bushes for ten or twelve miles inland. On the north part of the reef, to the leeward, there is a low sandy island with trees upon it; and upon the reef which we passed over we saw several turtle. We chased one or two, but having little time to spare, and the wind blowing fresh, we did not take any.

About one o'clock we reached the island, and immediately ascended the highest hill, with a mixture of hope and fear, proportioned to the importance of our business and the uncertainty of the event. When I looked round, I discovered a reef of rocks lying between two and three leagues without the islands, and extending in a line NW. and SE. farther than I could see, upon which the sea broke in a dreadful surf. This, however, made me think that there were no shoals beyond them, and I conceived hopes of getting without these, as I perceived several breaks or openings in the reef, and deep water between that and the islands. I continued upon this hill till sunset, but the weather was so hazy during the whole time that I came down much disappointed. After reflecting upon what I had seen, and comparing the intelligence I had gained with what I expected, I determined to stay upon the island all night, hoping that the morning might be clearer and afford me a more distinct and comprehensive view. We therefore took up our lodging under the shelter of a bush which grew upon the beach; and at three in the morning, having sent the pinnace with one of the mates whom I had brought out with me to sound between the island and the reefs, and examine what appeared to be a channel through them, I climbed the hill a second time, but to my great disappointment found the weather much more hazy than it had been the day before. As we saw no animals upon this place but lizards, I called it Lizard Island.

At two in the afternoon, there being no hope of clear weather, we set out from Lizard Island to return to the ship, and in our way landed upon the low sandy island with trees upon it which we had remarked in our going out. Upon this island we saw an incredible number of birds, chiefly sea-fowl. We found also the nest of an eagle with young ones, which we killed, and the nest of some other bird, we knew not what, of a most enormous size. It was built with sticks upon the ground, and was no less than six and twenty feet in circumference, and two feet eight inches high. We found also that this place had been visited by the Indians, probably to eat turtle, many of which we saw upon the island, and a great number of their shells, piled one upon another in different places.

To this spot we gave the name of Eagle Island, and after leaving it, we steered SW. directly for the ship, sounding all the way; and we had never less than eight fathoms, nor more than fourteen, the same depth of water that I had found between this and Lizard Island.

After well considering both what I had seen myself and the report of the master's, I found by experience that by keeping in with the mainland we should be in continued danger, besides the risk we should run of being locked in with shoals and reefs by not finding a passage out to leeward. In case we persevered in keeping the shore on board, an accident of this kind, or any other that might happen to the ship, would infallibly lose our passage to the East Indies this season, and might prove the ruin of both ourselves and the voyage, as we have now little more than three months' provisions on board, and that at short allowance. Wherefore, after consulting with the officers, I resolved to weigh in the morning, and endeavour to quit the coast altogether until such time as I found I could approach it with less danger.

With this view we got under sail at daylight in the morning, and stood out NE. for the NW. end of Lizard Island, having Eagle Island to windward of us, and having the pinnace ahead sounding; and here we found a good channel, wherein we had from nine to fourteen fathoms. We now took the pinnace in tow, knowing that there were no dangers until we got out to the reefs.

Our change of situation was now visible in every countenance, for it was most sensibly felt in every breast. We had been little less than three months entangled among shoals and rocks that every moment threatened us with destruction; frequently passing our nights at anchor within hearing of the surge that broke over them, sometimes driving towards them even while our anchors were out, and knowing that if by any accident, to which an almost continual tempest exposed us, they should not hold, we must in a few minutes inevitably perish. But now, after having sailed no less than three hundred and sixty leagues, without once having a man out of the chains heaving the lead, even for a minute, which perhaps never happened to any other vessel, we found ourselves in an open sea with deep water, and enjoyed a flow of spirits which was equally owing to our late dangers and our present security. Yet the very waves, which by their swell convinced us that we had no rocks or shoals to fear, convinced us also that we could not safely put the same confidence in our vessel as before she had struck; for the blows she received from them so widened her leaks that she admitted no less than nine inches water in an hour, which, considering the state of our pumps and the navigation that was still before us, would have been a subject of more serious consideration to people whose danger had not so lately been so much more imminent.

CHAPTER XIII.

THE SHIP IN DANGER OFF THE BARRIER REEFS—PASSAGE FROM PROVIDENTIAL CHANNEL TO ENDEAVOUR STRAITS.

THE passage or channel through which we passed into the open sea beyond the reef lies in lat. 14° 32′ S., and may always be known by the three high islands within it, which I have called the Islands of Direction, because by these a stranger may find a safe passage through the reef quite to the main. As soon as we were without the reef, we brought to, and having hoisted in the boats, we stood off and on upon a wind all night. At six next evening we shortened sail and brought the ship to, with her head to the NE.; and at six in the morning made sail and steered west, in order to get within sight of land, that I might be sure not to overshoot the passage, if a passage there was, between this land and New Guinea.

1770.
August.

The large hollow sea we have now got into acquaints us with a circumstance we did not before know, which is that the ship hath received more damage than we were aware of, or could perceive when in smooth water; for now she makes as much water as one pump will free, kept constantly at work. However, this was looked upon as trifling to the danger we had lately made an escape from. A little after noon saw the land from the masthead bearing WSW., making high; at two saw more land to the NW. of the former, making in hills like islands; but we took it to be a continuation of the mainland. An hour after this we saw a reef, between us and the land, extending away to the southward, and, as we thought, terminating here to the northward abreast of us; but this was only an opening, for soon after we saw it extend away to the northward as far as we could distinguish anything. Upon this we hauled close upon a wind, which was now at ESE., with all the sail we could set. We had hardly trimmed our sails before the wind came to E. by N., which made our weathering the reef very doubtful, the northern point of which in sight at sunset still bore from us N. by W., distant about two leagues. However, this being the best tack to clear it, we kept standing to the northward, with all the sail we could set till midnight; when, being afraid of standing too far in this direction, we tacked and stood to the southward, our run from sunset to this time being six leagues N. and N. by E. When we had stood about two miles SSE. it fell calm. We had sounded several times during the night, but had no bottom with one hundred and forty fathoms, neither had we any ground now with the same length of line; yet, about four in the morning, we plainly heard the roaring of the surf, and at break of day saw it foaming to a vast height, at not more than a mile's distance. Our distress now returned upon us with double force; the waves which rolled in upon the reef carried us towards it very fast. We could reach no ground with an anchor, and had not a breath of wind for the sail. In this dreadful situation, no resource was left us but the boats; and to aggravate our misfortune the pinnace was under repair. The longboat and yawl, however, were put into the water, and sent ahead to tow, which, by the help of our sweeps abaft, got the ship's head round to the northward; which, if it could not prevent our destruction, might at least delay it. But it was six o'clock before this was effected, and we were not then a hundred yards from the rock, upon which the same billow which washed the side of the ship broke to a tremendous height the very next time it rose; so that between us and destruction there was only a dreary valley, no wider than the base of one wave, and even now the sea under us was unfathomable—at least no bottom was to be found with a hundred and twenty fathoms. During this scene of distress, the carpenter had found means to patch up the pinnace; so that she was hoisted out, and sent ahead, in aid of the other boats, to tow. But all our efforts would have been ineffectual, if, just at this crisis of our fate, a light air of wind had not sprung up, so light, that at any other time we should not have observed it, but which was enough to turn the scale in our favour, and, in conjunction with the assistance which was afforded us by the boats, to give the ship a perceptible motion obliquely from the reef. Our hopes now revived; but in less than ten minutes it was again a dead calm, and the ship was again driven towards the breakers, which were not now two hundred yards distant. The same light breeze, however, returned before we had lost all the ground it had enabled us to gain, and lasted about ten minutes more. During this time we discovered a small opening in the reef, at about the distance of a quarter of a mile. I immediately sent one of the mates to examine it, who reported that its breadth was not more than the length of the ship, but that within it there was smooth water. This discovery seemed to render our escape possible, and that was all, by pushing the ship through the opening, which was immediately attempted. It was uncertain indeed whether we could reach it; but if we should succeed thus far, we made no doubt of being able to get through. In this, however, we were disappointed, for having reached it by the joint assistance of our boats and the breeze, we found that in the meantime it had become high water, and to our great surprise we met the tide of ebb rushing out of it like a mill-stream. We gained, however, some advantage, though in a manner directly contrary to our expectations: we found it impossible to go through the opening, but the stream that prevented us carried us out about a quarter of a mile. It was too narrow for us to keep in it longer; yet this tide of ebb so much assisted the boats that by noon we had got an offing of near two miles. Yet we could hardly flatter ourselves with hopes of getting clear, even if a breeze should spring up, as we were by this time embayed by the reef, and the ship, in spite of our endeavours, driving before the sea into the bight. The ebb had been in our favour, and we had reason to suppose the flood which was now made would be against us. The only hope we had was another opening we saw about a mile to the westward of us, which I sent Lieutenant Hicks in the small boat to examine.

On Friday the 17th, while Mr. Hicks was examining the opening, we struggled hard with the flood, sometimes gaining a little and at other times losing. At two o'clock Mr. Hicks returned with a favourable account of the opening. It was immediately resolved to try to secure the ship in it. Narrow and dangerous as it was, it seemed to be the only means we had of saving her, as well as ourselves. A light breeze soon after sprung up at ENE., with which, the help of our boats, and a flood-tide, we soon entered the opening, and were hurried through in a short time by a rapid tide like a mill-race, which kept us from driving against either side, though the channel was not more than a quarter of a mile broad, having two boats ahead of us sounding. Our depth of water was from thirty to seven fathoms; very irregular soundings and foul ground until we had got quite within the reef, where we anchored in nineteen fathoms, a coral and shelly bottom. The channel we came in by, which I have named Providential Channel, bore ENE., distant ten or twelve miles, being about eight or nine leagues from the mainland.

It is but a few days ago that I rejoiced at having got without the reef; but that joy was nothing when compared to what I now felt at being safe at an anchor within it. Such are the vicissitudes attending this kind of service, and which must always attend an unknown navigation where one steers wholly in the dark without any manner of guide whatever. Were it not for the pleasure which naturally results to a man from his being the first discoverer, even were it nothing more than land or shoals, this kind of service would be insupportable, especially in far-distant parts like this, short of provisions and almost every other necessary. People will hardly admit of an excuse for a man leaving a coast unexplored he has once discovered. If dangers are his excuse, he is then charged with timorousness and want of perseverance, and at once pronounced to be the most unfit man in the world to be employed as a discoverer. If, on the other hand, he boldly encounters all the dangers and obstacles he meets with, and is unfortunate enough not to succeed, he is then charged with temerity and perhaps want of conduct. The former of these aspersions, I am confident, can never be laid to my charge; and if I am fortunate to surmount all the dangers we meet with, the latter will never be brought in question, although I must own that I have engaged more among the islands and shoals upon this coast than perhaps in prudence I ought to have done with a single ship, and every other thing considered. But if I had not, I should not have been able to give any better account of the one half of it than if I had never seen it. At best, I should not have been able to say whether it was mainland or islands; and as to its produce, that we should have been totally ignorant of, as being inseparable with the other; and in this case it would have been far more satisfaction to me never to have discovered it. But it is time I should have done with this subject, which at best is but disagreeable, and which I was led into on reflecting on our late dangers.

At six o'clock on the 18th we got under sail and stood away to the NW. A little before noon, we passed a low sandy island, which we left on our starboard side, at the distance of two miles. Between us and the main were several shoals, besides the main or outermost reef, which we could see from the mast-head.

At half an hour after six, we anchored in thirteen fathoms. The northernmost of the small islands seen at noon bore W. $\frac{1}{2}$ S., distant three miles. These islands are distinguished in the chart by the name of Forbes' Islands, and lie about five leagues from the main, which here forms a high point that we called Bolt Head, from which the land trends more westerly, and is in that direction all low and sandy; to the southward it is high and hilly, even near the sea.

The mainland within the islands forms a point which I called Cape Grenville. It lies in lat. 11° 58', long. 217° 38'; and between it and Bolt Head is a bay which I called Temple Bay. At the distance of nine leagues from Cape Grenville, in the direction of E. $\frac{1}{2}$ N., lie some high islands, which I called Sir Charles Hardy's Isles; and those which lie off the cape, I called Cockburn's Isles.

At four o'clock p.m. we discovered some low islands and rocks bearing WNW. These islands, from the number of birds that I saw upon them, I called Bird Islands.

Early next morning we made sail again, and steered NNW. by compass for the northernmost land in sight. The point of the main, which is the northern promontory of this country, I have named York Cape, in honour of his late Royal Highness the Duke of York. The land over and to the southward of this last point is rather low and very flat, as far inland as the eye could reach, and looks barren. To the southward of the cape, the shore forms a large open bay, which I called Newcastle Bay, wherein are some small, low islands and shoals, and the land all about it is very low, flat, and sandy. The land on the northern part of the cape is rather more hilly, and the shore forms some small bays, wherein there appeared to be good anchorage, and the valleys appeared to be tolerably well clothed with wood. At four o'clock we anchored about a mile and a half or two miles within the entrance in six and a half fathoms, clear ground, distance from the islands on each side of us one mile, the mainland extending away to the SW. Between these two points we could see no land, so that we were in great hopes that we had at last found out a passage into the Indian seas; but in order to be better informed I landed with a party of men, accompanied by Mr. Banks and Dr. Solander, upon the islands which lie at the SE. point of the passage. Before and after we anchored, we saw a number of people upon this island, armed in the same manner as all the others we have seen, except one man, who had a bow and a bundle of arrows—the first we have seen upon this coast. From the appearance of the people, we expected they would have opposed our landing; but as we approached the shore they all made off, and left us in peaceable possession of as much of the island as served our purpose.

After landing, I went up on the highest hill, which, however, was of no great height, yet no less than twice or thrice the height of the ship's mast-heads. From this hill no land could be seen between the SW. and WSW., so that I had no doubt of finding a channel through. The land to the NW. of it consisted of a great number of islands of various extent and different heights, ranged one behind another, as far to the northward and westward as I could see, which could not be less than thirteen leagues. As I was now about to quit the eastern coast of New Holland, which I had coasted from lat. 38° to this place, and which I am confident no European had ever seen before, I once more hoisted English colours, and though I had already taken possession of several particular parts, I now took possession of the whole eastern coast, from lat. 38° to this place, lat. 10½° S., in right of His Majesty King George the Third, by the name of New South Wales, with all the bays, harbours, rivers, and islands situated upon it. We then fired three volleys of small arms, which were answered by the same number from the ship. Having performed this ceremony upon the island, which we called Possession Island, we re-embarked in our boat, but a rapid ebb tide setting NE. made our return to the vessel very difficult and tedious. From the time of our last coming among the shoals, we constantly found a moderate tide, the flood setting to the NW. and the ebb to the SE. At this place it is high water at the full and change of the moon, about one or two o'clock, and the water rises and falls perpendicularly about twelve feet. We saw smoke rising in many places from the adjacent lands and islands, as we had done upon every part of the coast, after our last return to it through the reef.

We continued at anchor all night, and between seven and eight o'clock in the morning we saw three or four of the natives upon the beach gathering shellfish. We discovered, by the help of our glasses, that they were women.

At noon, Possession Island bore N. 53 E., distant four leagues. The western extremity of the mainland in sight appeared to be extremely low; the south-west point of the largest island on the north-west side of the passage was distant eight miles, and this point I called Cape Cornwall. Some low lands lie about the middle of the passage, which I called Wallis's Isles.

On the 23rd a small island came in sight. Here we came to an anchor. Mr. Banks and I landed upon it, and found it to be mostly a barren rock frequented by birds, such as boobies, a few of which we shot, and occasioned my giving it the name of Booby Island. I made but very short stay at this island before I returned to the ship. In the meantime the wind had got to the SW., and although it blew but very faint, yet it was accompanied with a swell from the same quarter. This, together with other concurring circumstances, left me no room to doubt that we had got to the westward of Carpentaria, or the northern extremity of New Holland, and had now an open sea to the westward; which gave me no small satisfaction, not only because the danger and fatigues of the voyage were drawing near to an end, but by being able to prove that New Holland and New Guinea are two separate lands or islands, which until this day hath been a doubtful point with geographers.

The north-east entrance of this passage, or strait, lies in the lat. of 10° 39' S., and in the long. of 218° 36' W. It is formed by the main or the northern extremity of New Holland on the SE., and by a congeries of islands, which I called the Prince of Wales's Islands, to the NW., and it is probable that these islands extend quite to New Guinea. They differ very much both in height and circuit, and many of them seemed to be well clothed with herbage and wood. Upon most, if not all of them, we saw smoke, and therefore there can be no doubt of their being inhabited. It is also probable that among them there are at least as good passages as that we came through, perhaps better, though better would not need to be desired if the access to it from the eastward were less dangerous. That a less dangerous access may be discovered I think there is little reason to doubt, and to find it, little more seems to be necessary than to determine how far the principal or outer reef, which bounds the shoals to the eastward, extends towards the north; which I would not have left to future navigators if I had been less harassed by danger and fatigue, and had had a ship in better condition for the purpose.

To this channel, or passage, I have given the name of the ship, and called it Endeavour Strait.

CHAPTER XIV.

DEPARTURE FROM NEW SOUTH WALES—DESCRIPTION OF THE COUNTRY, PEOPLE, ETC.—PASSAGE FROM NEW SOUTH WALES TO NEW GUINEA—PASSAGE FROM NEW GUINEA TO THE ISLAND OF SAVU.

OF this country, its products, and its people, many particulars have already been related in the course of the narrative, being so interwoven with the events as not to admit of a separation. I shall now give a more full and circumstantial description of each, in which, if some things should happen to be repeated, the greater part will be found new.

1770.
August.

New Holland, or, as I have now called the eastern coast, New South Wales, is of a larger extent than any other country in the known world that does not bear the name of a continent. The length of coast along which we sailed, reduced to a straight line, is no less than twenty-seven degrees of latitude, amounting to near 2,000 miles, so that its square surface must be much more than equal to all Europe. To the southward of 33° or 34°, the land in general is low and level; farther northward it is hilly, but in no part can be called mountainous; and the hills and mountains, taken together, make but a small part of the surface in comparison with the valleys and plains. It is, upon the whole, rather barren than fertile; yet the rising ground is chequered by woods and lawns, and the plains and valleys are in many places covered with herbage. The soil, however, is frequently sandy; and many of the lawns, or savannas, are rocky and barren, especially to the northward, where, in the best spots, vegetation was less vigorous than in the southern part of the country; the trees were not so tall, nor was the herbage so rich. The grass, in general, is high, but thin; and the trees, where they are largest, are seldom less than forty feet asunder; nor is the country inland, as far as we could examine it, better clothed than the sea-coast. The banks of the bays are covered with mangroves to the distance of a mile within the beach, under which the soil is a rank mud, that is always overflowed by a spring tide. Farther in the country we sometimes met with a bog upon which the grass was very thick and luxuriant, and sometimes with a valley that was clothed with underwood. The soil in some parts seemed to be capable of improvement, but the far greater part is such as can admit of no cultivation. The coast, at least that part of it which lies to the northward of 25° S., abounds with fine bays and harbours, where vessels may lie in perfect security from all winds.

If we may judge by the appearance of the country while we were there, which was in the very height of the dry season, it is well watered. We found innumerable small brooks and springs, but no great rivers. These brooks, however, probably become large in the rainy season. Thirsty Sound was the only place where fresh water was not to be procured for the ship, and even there one or two small pools were found in the woods, though the face of the country was everywhere intersected by salt creeks and mangrove land.

The woods do not produce any great variety of trees; there are only two or three sorts that can be called timber. The largest is the gum-tree, which grows all over the country. The wood of this tree is too hard and ponderous for most common uses. The tree which resembles our pines I saw nowhere in perfection but in Botany Bay. This wood, as I have before observed, is something of the same nature as American live oak—in short, most of the large trees in this country are of a hard and ponderous nature, and could not be applied to many purposes. Here are several sorts of the palm kind, mangrove, and several other sorts of small trees and shrubs quite unknown to me, besides a very great number of plants hitherto unknown; but these things are wholly out of my way to describe, nor will this be of any loss, since not only plants, but everything that can be of use to the learned world, will be very accurately described by Mr. Banks and Dr. Solander. The land naturally produces hardly anything fit for man to eat, and the natives know nothing of cultivation. There are, indeed, growing wild in the wood a few sorts of fruit (the

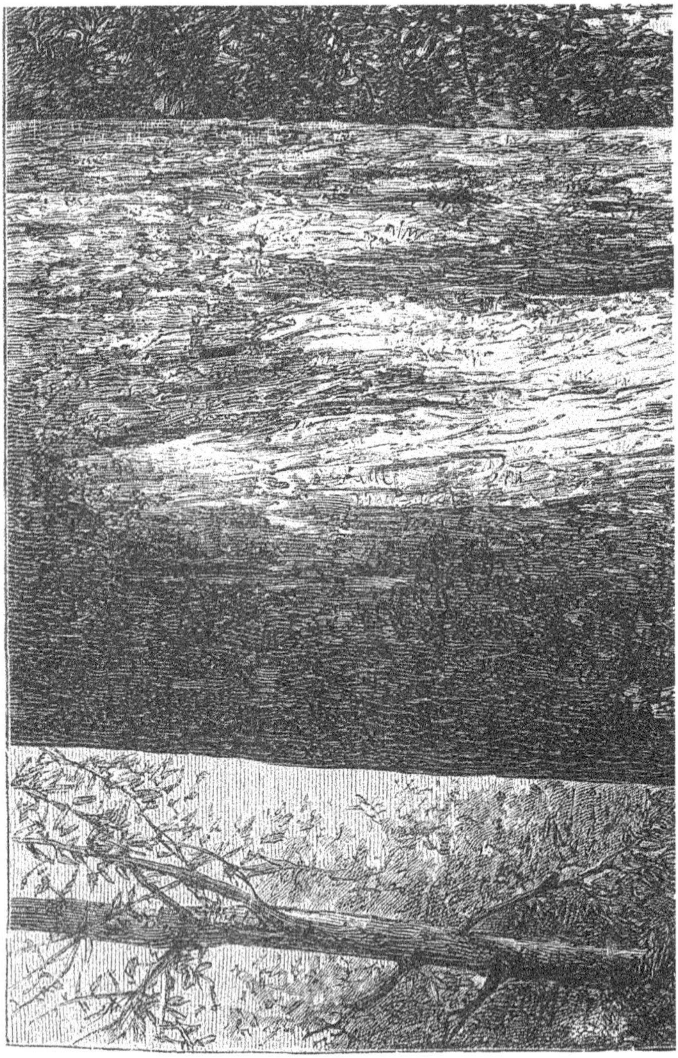

WHITE GUM TREE, AUSTRALIA. *Page 166.*

most of them unknown to us), which when ripe do not eat amiss, one sort especially, which we called apples, being about the size of a crab-apple. It is black and pulpy when ripe, and tastes like a damson; it hath a large hard stone or kernel, and grows on trees or shrubs.

In the northern parts of the country, as about Endeavour River, and probably in many other places, the boggy or watery lands produce taro or cocos, which, when properly cultivated, are very good roots, without which they are hardly eatable. The tops, however, make very good greens.

Land animals are scarce, so far as we know confined to a very few species; all that we saw I have before mentioned. The sort which is in the greatest plenty is the kangaroo or kanguru, so called by the natives. We saw a good many of them about Endeavour River, but killed only three, which we found very good eating. Here are likewise lizards, snakes, scorpions, centipedes, etc., but not in any plenty. Tame animals they have none but dogs, and of these we saw but one, and therefore they must be very scarce; probably they eat them faster than they breed them. We should not have seen this one had he not made us frequent visits while we lay in Endeavour River.

The land fowls are bustards, eagles, hawks, crows, such as we have in England; cockatoos of two sorts, white and brown; very beautiful birds of the parrot kind, such as lorikeets, etc.; pigeons, doves, quails, and several sorts of smaller birds. The sea and water fowls are herons, boobies, noddies, gulls, curlews, ducks, pelicans, etc.; and when Mr. Banks and Mr. Gore were in the country, at the head of Endeavour River, they saw and heard in the night great numbers of geese. The sea is indifferently well stocked with fish, of various sorts, such as sharks, dogfish, rockfish, mullets, breams, cavallies, mackerel, old wives, leather jackets, five fingers, sting rays, whip rays, etc., all excellent in their kind. The shellfish are, oysters of three or four sorts—namely, rock-oysters and mangrove-oysters (which are small), pearl-oysters and mud-oysters (these last are the best and largest I ever saw), cockles and clams of several sorts (many of those that are found upon the reefs are of a prodigious size), crayfish, crabs, mussels, and a variety of other sorts. Here are also upon the shoals and reefs great numbers of the finest green turtle in the world; and in the river and salt creeks are some alligators.

The natives of this country are of a middle stature, straight bodied and slender limbed; their skins the colour of wood soot; their hair mostly black, some lank and others curled—they all wear it cropped short; their beards, which are generally black, they likewise crop short, or singe off. Their features are far from being disagreeable, and their voices are soft and tunable.

They wear as ornaments necklaces made of shells; bracelets or hoops about their arms, made mostly of hair twisted, and made like a cord-hoop—these they wear tight about the upper parts of their arms; and some have girdles made in the same manner. The men wear a bone, about three or four inches long and a finger thick, run through the bridge of their nose. They likewise have holes in their ears for ear-rings, but we never saw them wear any.

Neither are all the other ornaments worn in common, for we have seen as many without as with them. Some of these we saw on Possession Island wore breastplates, which we supposed were made of mother-of-pearl shells. Many of them paint their bodies and faces with a sort of white paste or pigment.

They appeared to have no fixed habitations, for we saw nothing like a town or village in the whole country. Their houses—if houses they may be called—seem to be formed with less art and industry than any we had seen, except the wretched hovels at Tierra del Fuego, and in some respects they are inferior even to them.

At Botany Bay, where they were best, they were just high enough for a man to sit upright in, but not large enough for him to extend himself in his whole length in any direction. They are built with pliable rods about as thick as a man's finger, in the form of an oven, by sticking the two ends into the ground, and then covering them with palm leaves and broad pieces of bark. The door is nothing but a large hole at one end, opposite to which the fire is made, as we perceived by the ashes. Under these houses, or sheds, they sleep, coiled up with their heels to their head; and in this position one of them will hold three or four persons. As we advanced northward, and the climate became warmer, we found these sheds still more slight. They were built, like the others, of twigs, and covered with bark; but none of them were more than four feet deep, and one side was entirely open. The close side was always opposed to the course of the prevailing wind, and opposite to the open side was the fire, probably more as a defence from the mosquitoes than the cold. Under these hovels it is probable that they thrust only their heads and the upper part of their bodies, extending their feet towards the fire. They were set up occasionally by a wandering horde in any place that would furnish them for a time with subsistence, and left behind them when, after it was exhausted, they went away; but in places where they remained only for a night or two, they slept without any shelter except the bushes or grass, which is here near two feet high. We observed, however, that though the sleeping huts which we found upon the main were always turned from the prevailing wind, those upon the islands were turned towards it, which seems to be a proof that they have a mild season here, during which the sea is calm.

Their canoes are as mean as can be conceived, especially to the southward, where all we saw were made of one piece of the bark of trees about twelve or fourteen feet long, drawn or tied together at one end. As I have before made mention, these canoes will not carry above two people—in general there is never more than one in them; but, bad as they are, they do very well for the purpose they apply them to, better than if they were larger, for as they draw but little water they go in them upon the mud-banks, and pick up shell fish, etc., without going out of the canoe. The few canoes we saw to the northward were made out of a log of wood hollowed out, about fourteen feet long and very narrow, with outriggers; these will carry four people. During our whole stay in Endeavour River we saw but one canoe, and had great reason to think that the few people that resided about that place had no more; this one served them to cross the river and to go a-fishing in, etc. They attend the shoals and flats every day at low water, to gather shellfish, or whatever they can find to eat, and have each a little bag to put what they get in; this bag is made of network. They have not the least knowledge of iron or any other metal that we know of. Their working tools must be made of stone, bone, and shells.

Bad and mean as their canoes are, they at certain seasons of the year, so far as we know, go in them to the most distant islands which lie upon the coast, for we never landed upon one but we saw signs of people having been there before. We were surprised to find houses, etc., upon Lizard Island, which lies five leagues from the nearest part of the main, a distance we before thought they could not have gone in their canoes.

The coast of this country—at least so much of it as lies to the northward of 25° of latitude—abounds with a great number of fine bays and harbours, which are sheltered from all winds; but the country itself, so far as we know, doth not produce any one thing that can become an article in trade to invite Europeans to fix a settlement upon it. However, this eastern side is not that barren and miserable country that Dampier and others have described the western side to be. We are to consider that we see this country in the pure state of nature. The industry of man has had nothing to do with any part of it; and yet we find all such things as nature hath bestowed upon it in a flourishing state. In this extensive country it can never be doubted that most sorts of grain, fruit, roots, etc., of every kind would flourish were they once brought hither, planted, and cultivated by the hands of industry; and here is provender for more cattle, at all seasons of the year, than can ever be brought into the country. When one considers the proximity of this country with New Guinea, New Britain, and several other islands which produce cocoa-nuts and many other fruits proper to the support of man, it seems strange that they should not long ago have been transplanted here.

From what I have said of the natives of New Holland they may appear to some to be the most wretched people upon earth; but in reality they are far happier than we Europeans, being wholly unacquainted not only with the superfluous but with the necessary conveniences so much sought after in Europe. They are happy in not knowing the use of them. They live in a tranquillity which is not disturbed by the inequality of condition. The earth and sea of their own accord furnish them with all things necessary for life. They covet not magnificent houses, household

ITS CLIMATE.

stuff, etc. They live in a warm and fine climate, and enjoy wholesome air, so that they have very little need of clothing; and this they seem to be fully sensible of, for many to whom we gave cloth, etc., left it carelessly upon the sea beach and in the woods, as a thing they had no manner of use for. In short, they seemed to set no value upon anything we gave them, nor would they ever part with anything of their own for any one article we could offer them. This, in my opinion, argues that they think themselves provided with all the necessaries of life, and that they have no superfluities.

In the afternoon of Thursday, August 23rd, after leaving Booby Island, we steered WNW. On the 25th we had no land in sight; but about two miles to the southward of us lay a large shoal, upon which the sea broke with great violence. Our depth of water, from the time we weighed till now, was nine fathoms, but it soon shallowed to seven fathoms; and at half an hour after one, having run eleven miles between noon and that time, the boat which was ahead made the signal for shoal water. We immediately let go an anchor, and brought the ship up with all the sails standing, for the boat having just been relieved was at but a little distance. Upon looking out from the ship we saw shoal water almost all around us, both wind and tide at the same time setting upon it. The ship was in six fathoms; but upon sounding round her, at the distance of half a cable's length, we found scarcely two. This shoal reached from the east, round by the north and west, as far as the south-west, so that there was no way for us to get clear but that by which we came. This was another hair's-breadth escape, for it was near high water, and there ran a short cockling sea, which must very soon have bulged the ship if she had struck; and if her direction had been half a cable's length more either to the right or left, she must have struck before the signal for the shoal was made. The shoals which, like these, lie a fathom or two under water are the most dangerous of any, for they do not discover themselves till the vessel is just upon them, and then, indeed, the water looks brown, as if it reflected a dark cloud. The sea in many places here is covered with a kind of brown scum, such as sailors generally call spawn. Upon our first seeing it it alarmed us, thinking we were among shoals; but we found the same depth of water where it was as in other places. Neither Mr. Banks nor Dr. Solander could tell what it was, although they had some of it to examine.

Sept. On the 3rd of September, at daybreak, we saw the land extending from N. by E. to SE. at about four leagues' distance; and we then kept standing in for it with a fresh gale at ESE. and E. by S. till nine o'clock, when, being within about three or four miles of it, and in three fathoms water, we brought to. The pinnace being hoisted out, I set off from the ship with the boat's crew, having a mind to land once in this country before we quit it altogether, which I am now determined to do without delay, for I find that it is only spending time to little purpose and carrying us far out of our way staying upon this coast, which is so shallow that we can hardly keep within sight of land.

The land is very low, like every other part of the coast we have seen here. It is thick and luxuriously clothed with woods and verdure, all of which appear green and flourishing. Here were cocoa-nut trees, bread-fruit trees, and plantain trees; but we saw no fruit but on the former, and that was small and green. The other trees, shrubs, plants, etc., were likewise such as is common in the South Sea Islands and in New Holland.

Upon my return to the ship we hoisted in the boat and made sail to the westward, with a design to leave the coast altogether. This, however, was contrary to the inclination and opinion of some of the officers, who would have had me send a party of men ashore to cut down the cocoa-nut trees for the sake of the nuts—a thing that I think no man living could have justified; for as the natives had attacked us for mere landing without taking away one thing, certainly they would have made a vigorous effort to have defended their property, in which case many of them must have been killed, and perhaps some of our own people too, and all this for two or three hundred green cocoa-nuts, which, when we had got them, would have done us little service. Besides, nothing but the utmost necessity would have obliged me to have taken this method to come at refreshments.

It is true I might have gone farther along the coast to the northward and westward until we had found a place where the

NECESSITY OF REPAIRS.

ship could lie so near the shore as to cover the people with her guns when landed; but it is very probable that before we had found such a place we should have been carried so far to the west as to have been obliged to have gone to Batavia by the way of the Moluccas, and on the north side of Java, where we were all utter strangers. This I did not think was so safe a passage as to go to the south of Java and through the Straits of Sunda, the way I propose to myself to go. Besides, as the ship is leaky, we are not yet sure whether or not we shall not be obliged to heave her down to Batavia. In this case it becomes the more necessary that we should make the best of our way to that place.

We made sail, from noon on Monday the 3rd to noon on Tuesday the 4th, standing to the westward, and all the time kept in soundings, having from fourteen to thirty fathoms—not regular, but sometimes more, sometimes less. At sunset on the 9th we saw the appearance of very high land bearing NW. In the morning of the 10th we saw clearly that what had appeared to be land the night before was Timor.

We continued our course, with little variation, till nine o'clock in the morning of the 16th, when we saw the small island called Rotte; and at noon, the island Semau,* lying off the south end of Timor, bore NW. I was strongly importuned by some of my officers to go to the Dutch settlement at Concordia, on this island, for refreshments; but this I refused to comply with, knowing that the Dutch look with a jealous eye upon all Europeans that come among these islands, and our necessities were not so great as to oblige me to put into a place where I might expect to be but indifferently treated.

Being clear of all the islands which are laid down in the maps we had on board, between Timor and Java, we steered a west course till six o'clock the next morning, when we unexpectedly saw an island bearing WSW., and at first I thought we had made a new discovery. We steered directly for it, and by ten o'clock were close in with the north side of it, where we saw houses, cocoa-nut trees, and, to our very agreeable surprise, numerous flocks of sheep. This was a temptation not to be resisted by people in our situation, especially as many of us were in

* Belonging to the Dutch.

a bad state of health, and many still repining at my not having touched at Timor. It was therefore soon determined to attempt a commerce with people who appeared to be so well able to supply our many necessities, and remove at once the sickness and discontent that had got footing among us. The pinnace was hoisted out, and Lieutenant Gore sent to see if there was any convenient place to land, taking with him some trifles as presents to the natives, if any of them should appear. While he was gone we saw from the ship two men on horseback, who seemed to be riding upon the hills for their amusement, and often stopped to look at the ship. By this we knew that the place had been settled by Europeans, and hoped that the many disagreeable circumstances which always attend the first establishment of commerce with savages would be avoided.

As soon as Mr. Gore landed he was met on the beach by several people, both horse and foot, who gave him to understand that there was a bay to leeward where we could anchor, and likewise get refreshments. Upon Mr. Gore's return with this intelligence we bore away for the bay, in which we anchored at seven o'clock in thirty-eight fathoms water, clean sandy bottom. Two hours before we anchored we saw Dutch colours hoisted in a village which stands about a mile inland, and at daylight in the morning the same colours were hoisted on the beach abreast of the ship. By this I was no longer in doubt that here was a Dutch settlement, and accordingly sent Lieutenant Gore on shore to wait upon the governor, or chief person residing there, to acquaint him with the reasons that induced us to touch at this island. Upon Mr. Gore's landing we could perceive that he was received by a guard of the natives, and not Dutch troops, and conducted up to the village where the colours were hoisted last night. Some time after this I received a message from him, acquainting me that he was there with the king of the island, who had told him that he could not supply him with anything without leave from the Dutch governor, who resided at another part of the island, but that he had sent to acquaint him of our arrival and request.

On Wednesday the 19th the Dutch governor and king of this part of the island, with his attendants, came on board with Mr.

Gore, he having left two gentlemen ashore as hostages. We entertained them at dinner in the best manner we could, gave them plenty of good liquor, made them some considerable presents, and at their going away saluted them with nine guns. In return for these favours they made many fair promises that we should be immediately supplied with everything we wanted at the same price the Dutch East India Company had it; and that in the morning buffaloes, hogs, sheep, etc., should be down on the beach for us to look at, and agree upon a price. I was not at all at a loss for interpreters, for both Dr. Solander and Mr. Sporing understood Dutch enough to keep up a conversation with the Dutchman; and several of the natives could speak Portuguese, which language two or three of my people understood.

In the morning of the 19th I went ashore to return the king's visit; but my chief business was to procure some of the buffaloes, sheep, and fowls which we had been told should be driven down to the beach. We were greatly mortified to find that no steps had been taken to fulfil this promise. We told them that we had in the boat goods of various kinds, which we proposed to barter for such refreshments as they would give us in exchange, and desired leave to bring them on shore, which being granted, they were brought ashore accordingly. We then attempted to settle the price of the buffaloes, sheep, hogs, and other commodities which we proposed to purchase, and for which we were to pay in money; but as soon as this was mentioned Mr. Lange left us, telling us that these preliminaries must be settled with the natives. He said, however, that he had received a letter from the governor of Concordia in *T*imor, the purport of which he would communicate to us when he returned.

As the morning was now far advanced, and we were very unwilling to return on board and eat salt provisions, when so many delicacies surrounded us ashore, we petitioned his majesty for liberty to purchase a small hog and some rice, and to employ his subjects to dress them for us. He answered very graciously that if we could eat victuals dressed by his subjects, which he could scarcely suppose, he would do himself the honour of entertaining us. We expressed our gratitude, and immediately sent on board for liquors.

About five o'clock dinner was ready. It was served in six-and-thirty dishes, or rather baskets, containing alternately rice and pork; and three bowls of earthenware, filled with the liquor in which the pork had been boiled. These were ranged upon the floor, and mats laid round them for us to sit upon. We were then conducted by turns to a hole in the floor, near which stood a man with water in a vessel, made of the leaves of the fan-palm, who assisted us in washing our hands. When this was done we placed ourselves round the victuals. We made a most luxurious meal. We thought the pork and rice excellent, and the broth not to be despised; but the spoons, which were made of leaves, were so small that few of us had patience to use them.

We stayed at the king's palace all the afternoon, and at last were obliged to return on board without doing anything further than a promise of having some buffaloes in the morning, which we had now no great reason to rely on. In the morning I went on shore again, and was shown one small buffalo, which they asked five guineas for. I offered three, which the man told me he would gladly take, and sent a message to the king to let him know what I had offered. The messenger soon returned, and let me know that I could not have it under five guineas; and this I refused to give, knowing it was not worth one-fifth part of the money. But this, my refusal, had like to have overset all we had before done, for soon after about a hundred men, some armed with muskets, others with lances, came down to the landing-place. Besides the officer that commanded this party, there came along with them a man who spoke Portuguese, and I believe was born of Portuguese parents. The man is here, as we afterwards understood, as an assistant to the Dutch factor. He delivered to me the king's order, or rather those of the Dutch factor, the purport of which was that we were to stay no longer than this day, pretending that the people would not trade with us because we wanted their provisions for nothing, etc.; whereas the natives showed the greatest inclination imaginable to supply us with whatever they had, and were far more desirous of goods than money, and were, before this man came, selling us fowls and syrup as fast as they could bring these things down. From this and other circumstances we were well assured that this was all the Dutchman's doing, in order to extort from us a sum of money to put into his own pocket. There happened to be an old raja at this time upon the beach, whose interest I had secured in the morning by presenting him with a spyglass. This man I now took by the hand and presented him with an old broadsword. This effectually secured him in our interest, for the moment he got it he began to flourish it over the old Portuguese, and made him and the officer commmanding the party to sit down at his back. Immediately after this, trade was restored again for fowls, etc., with more spirit than ever; but before I could begin a trade for buffaloes, which was what we most wanted, I was obliged to give ten guineas for two, one of which weighed only 160 pounds. After this I bought seven more at a more reasonable price, one of which we lost after he was paid for. I might now have purchased as many as I pleased, for they now drove them down to the water side by herds. Most of the buffaloes that we bought, after our friend the prime minister had procured us a fair market, were sold for a musket apiece; and at this price we might have bought as many as would have freighted our ship.

The refreshments which we procured here consisted of nine buffaloes, six sheep, three hogs, thirty dozen of fowls, a few limes, and some cocoa-nuts; many dozen of eggs, half of which, however, proved to be rotten; a little garlic, and several hundred gallons of palm-syrup.

CHAPTER XV.

THE RUN FROM THE ISLAND OF SAVU TO BATAVIA—TRANSACTIONS AT BATAVIA WHILE THE SHIP WAS REFITTING.

1770.
Sept.
IN the morning of Friday, the 21st of September, we got under sail and stood away to the westward.

We steered NW. all day on the 28th, in order to make the land of Java, and at noon on the 29th our latitude by observation was 9° 31′ S., long. 254° 10′ W.; and in the morning of the 30th I took into my possession the log-book and journals, at least all I could find, of the officers, petty officers, and seamen, and enjoined them secrecy with respect to where they had been.

At seven in the evening, being in the latitude of Java Head, and not seeing any land, I concluded that we were too far to the westward; I therefore hauled up ENE., having before steered N. by E. In the night we had thunder and lightning; and about twelve o'clock, by the light of the flashes, we saw the land bearing east. I then tacked and stood to the SW. till four o'clock in the morning of the 1st of October; and at six, Java Head, or the west end of Java, bore SE. by E., distant five leagues. Soon after we saw Prince's Island, bearing E. ½ S.; and at ten, the island of Krakatoa, bearing NE. Krakatoa is a remarkably high-peaked island, and at noon it bore N. 40 E., distant seven leagues.

October.
At four o'clock in the morning of the 2nd we fetched close in with the coast of Java, in fifteen fathoms; we then stood along the coast, and early in the forenoon I sent the boat ashore to try if she could procure some fruit for Tupia, who was very ill, and some grass for the buffaloes that were still alive. In an hour or two she returned with four cocoa-nuts and a small bunch of plantains, which had been purchased for a shilling, and some herbage for the cattle, which the Indians not only gave us, but assisted our people to cut.

Having made several attempts to sail with a wind that would not stem the current, and as often come to an anchor, a proa came alongside of us in the morning of the 5th, in which was a Dutch officer, who sent me down a printed paper in English, duplicates of which he had in other languages, particularly in French and Dutch, all regularly signed, in the name of the Governor and Council of the Indies, by their secretary. It contained nine questions, very ill expressed, in the following terms :—

"1. To what nation the ship belongs, and its name?

"2. If it comes from Europe, or any other place?

"3. From what place it lastly departed from?

"4. Whereunto designed to go?

"5. What and how many ships of the Dutch Company by departure from the last shore there layed, and their names?

"6. If one or more of these ships in company with this, is departed for this, or any other place?

"7. If during the voyage any particularities is happened or seen?

"8. If not any ships in sea, or the Straits of Sunda, have seen or hailed in, and which?

"9. If any other news worth of attention, at the place from whence the ship lastly departed, or during the voyage, is happened?

"BATAVIA, in the Castle.

"By order of the Governor-General,
and the Counsellors of India,

"J. BRANDER BUNOL, Sec."

At ten o'clock the same morning we weighed, with a light breeze at SW., but did little more than stem the current; and about two o'clock anchored again under Bantam Point, where we lay till nine. A light breeze then springing up at SE., we weighed and stood to the eastward till ten o'clock the next morning, when the current obliged us again to anchor in twenty-two fathoms, Pulababi bearing E. by S. ½ S., distant between three and four miles. Having alternately weighed and anchored several times, till four in the afternoon of the 7th, we then stood to the eastward, with a very faint breeze at NE., and passed Wapping Island, and the first island to the eastward of it; when the wind dying away, we were carried by the current between the first and second of the islands that lie to the eastward of Wapping Island, where we were obliged to anchor in thirty fathoms, being very near a ledge of rocks that run out from one of the islands. At two the next morning we weighed with the land wind at south, and stood out clear of the shoal; but before noon were obliged to come to again in twenty-eight fathoms, near a small island among those that are called the Thousand Islands, which we did not find laid down in any chart. Pulo Pare at this time bore ENE., distance between six and seven miles.

On Wednesday the 10th, according to our reckoning, but by the people here Thursday the 11th, at four o'clock in the afternoon, we anchored in Batavia Road, where we found the *Harcourt* Indiaman from England, two English country ships, thirteen sail of large Dutch ships, and a number of small vessels. As soon as we anchored, I sent Lieutenant Hicks ashore to acquaint the governor of our arrival, and to make an excuse for not saluting; as we could only do it with three guns, I thought it was better let alone.

As soon as the boat was dispatched, the carpenter delivered me an account of the defects of the ship, of which the following is a copy:—

"The defects of His Majesty's bark *Endeavour*, Lieutenant James Cook, Commander.

"The ship very leaky, as she makes from twelve to six inches water an hour, occasioned by her main keel being wounded in many places, and the scarfs of her stern being very open. The false keel gone beyond the midships from forward, and perhaps farther, as I had no opportunity of seeing for the water when hauled ashore for repairing. Wounded on the larboard side under the main channel, where I imagine the greatest leak is, but could not come at it for the water. One pump on the larboard side useless; the others decayed within an inch and a half of the bore. Otherwise masts, yards, boats, and hull, in pretty good condition."

As it was the universal opinion that the ship could not safely proceed to Europe without an examination of her bottom, I determined to apply for leave to heave her down at this place; and as I understood that it would be necessary to make this application in writing, I drew up a request, and the next morning, having got it translated into Dutch, we all went ashore.

We repaired immediately to the house of Mr. Leith, the only Englishman of any credit who is resident at this place. He received us with great politeness, and engaged us to dinner. To this gentleman we applied for instructions how to provide ourselves with lodgings and necessaries while we should stay ashore, and he told us that there was a hotel, or kind of inn, kept by the order of government, where all merchants and strangers were obliged to reside.

At the hotel, therefore, beds were immediately hired, and word was sent that we should sleep there at night.

At five o'clock in the afternoon I was introduced to the governor-general, who received me very courteously. He told me that I should have everything I wanted.

About nine o'clock in the evening we had much rain, with some very heavy claps of thunder; the lightning carried away a Dutch Indiaman's main-mast by the deck, and split it, the main-topmast, and topgallant-mast all to shivers. She had had an iron spindle at the main-topgallant mast-head which had first attracted the lightning. The ship lay about two cable lengths from us, and we were struck at the same time, and in all probability we should have shared the same fate as the Dutchman, had it not been for the electrical chain which we had but just before got up. This carried the lightning or electrical matter over the side clear of the ship. The shock was so great as to shake the whole ship very sensibly. This instance alone is sufficient to recommend these chains to all ships whatever, and that of the Dutchman ought to caution people from having iron spindles at their mast-heads.

The next morning I attended at the council-chamber, and was told that I should have everything I wanted. In the meantime, the gentlemen ashore agreed with the keeper of the hotel for their lodging and board, at the rate of two rix-dollars, or nine shillings sterling, a day for each; and as there were five of them, and they would probably have many visitors from the ship, he agreed to keep them a separate table, upon condition that they should pay one rix-dollar for the dinner of every stranger, and another for his supper and bed, if he should sleep ashore. Under this stipulation they were to be furnished with tea, coffee, punch, pipes and tobacco, for themselves and their friends, as much as they could consume;

they were also to pay half a rupee, or one shilling and threepence, a day for each of their servants.

They soon learned that these rates were more than double the common charges of board and lodging in the town, and their table, though it had the appearance of magnificence, was wretchedly served. Their dinner consisted of one course of fifteen dishes, and their supper of one course of thirteen, but nine or ten of them consisted of bad poultry, variously dressed, and often served up the second, third, and even the fourth time. The same duck having appeared more than once roasted, found his way again to the table as a fricassee, and a fourth time in the form of forced meat. It was not long, however, before they learned that this treatment was only by way of essay, and that it was the invariable custom of the house to supply all strangers, at their first coming, with such fare as could be procured for the least money, and consequently would produce the most gain; that if either through indolence or good-nature they were content, it was continued for the benefit of the host, but that if they complained, it was gradually amended till they were satisfied.

The expenses that would be incurred by repairing and refitting the ship rendered it necessary for me to take up money in this place, which I imagined might be done without difficulty. But I found myself mistaken; for after the most diligent inquiry, I could not find any private person that had ability and inclination to advance the sum that I wanted. In this difficulty I applied to the governor himself, by a written request, in consequence of which the shebander had orders to supply me with what money I should require out of the Company's treasury.

By this time, having been here only nine days, we began to feel the fatal effects of the climate and situation. Tupia, after the flow of spirits which the novelties of the place produced upon his first landing, sunk on a sudden, and grew every day worse and worse. Tayeto was seized with an inflammation upon his lungs, Mr. Banks's two servants became very ill, and himself and Dr. Solander were attacked by fevers. In a few days almost every person both on board and ashore was sick; affected, no doubt, by the low swampy situation of the place, and the numberless dirty canals which intersect the town in all directions. On the 26th I set up the tent for the reception of the ship's company, of whom there was but a small number able to do duty. Poor Tupia, of whose life we now began to despair, and who till this time had continued ashore with Mr. Banks, desired to be removed to the ship, where, he said, he should breathe a freer air than among the numerous houses which obstructed it ashore. On board the ship, however, he could not go, for she was unrigged, and preparing to be laid down at the careening-place; but on the 28th, Mr. Banks went with him to Cooper's Island, or, as it is called here, Kuypor, where she lay, and as he seemed pleased with the spot, a tent was there pitched for him. At this place both the sea breeze and the land breeze blew directly over him, and he expressed great satisfaction in his situation. Mr. Banks, whose humanity kept him two days with this poor Indian, returned to the town on the 30th, and the fits of his intermittent, which was now become a regular tertian, were so violent as to deprive him of his senses while they lasted, and leave him so weak that he was scarcely able to crawl downstairs. At this time, Dr. Solander's disorder also increased, and Mr. Monkhouse, the surgeon, was confined to his bed.

Nov. On the 5th of November, after many delays in consequence of the Dutch ships coming alongside the wharfs to load pepper, the ship was laid down; and the same day, Mr. Monkhouse, our surgeon, a sensible, skilful man, fell the first sacrifice to this fatal country, a loss which was greatly aggravated by our situation. Dr. Solander was just able to attend his funeral, but Mr. Banks was confined to his bed. Our distress was now very great, and the prospect before us discouraging in the highest degree. Our danger was not such as we could surmount by any efforts of our own; courage, skill, and diligence were all equally ineffectual, and death was every day making advances upon us, where we could neither resist nor fly. Malay servants were hired to attend the sick, but they had so little sense either of duty or humanity that they could not be kept within call, and the patient was frequently obliged to get out of bed to seek them. On the 9th we lost our poor Indian boy Tayeto, and Tupia was so much affected that it was doubted whether he would survive till the next day.

In the meantime, the bottom of the ship being examined, it was found to be in worse condition than we apprehended. A great quantity of the sheathing was torn off, and several planks were damaged. Two of them were so worn that they were not above an inch thick, and here the worms had made their way quite into the timbers; yet in this condition she had sailed many hundred leagues where navigation is dangerous. It seemed, however, that we had been preserved only to perish here. Mr. Banks and Dr. Solander were so bad that the physician declared they had no chance for recovery but by removing into the country. A house was therefore hired for them, at the distance of about two miles from the town. While their preparations were making, they received account of the death of *T*upia, who sank at once after the loss of the boy, whom he loved with the tenderness of a parent.

By the 14th, the bottom of the ship was thoroughly repaired, and very much to my satisfaction. It would, indeed, be injustice to the officers and workmen of this yard not to declare that, in my opinion, there is not a marine yard in the world where a ship can be laid down with more convenience, safety, and dispatch, or repaired with more diligence and skill. At this place they heave down by two masts, a method which we do not now practise; it is, however, unquestionably more safe and expeditious to heave down with two masts than one, and he must have a good share of bigotry to old customs, and an equal want of common sense, who will not allow this, after seeing with what facility the Dutch heave down their largest ships at this place.

Mr. Banks and Dr. Solander recovered slowly at their country house, which was not only open to the sea breeze, but situated upon a running stream, which greatly contributed to the circulation of the air. But I was now taken ill myself; Mr. Sporing, and a seaman who had attended Mr. Banks, were also seized with intermittents; and indeed there was not more than ten of the whole ship's company that were able to do duty.

We proceeded, however, in rigging the ship, and getting water and stores aboard. The water we were obliged to procure from Batavia, at the rate of six shillings and eightpence a leager, or one hundred and fifty gallons.

Dec. The wet season now set in, though we had some intervals of fair weather. The frogs in the ditches, which croak ten times louder than any frogs in Europe, gave notice of rain by an incessant noise that was almost intolerable, and the gnats and mosquitoes were now become innumerable.

On the 8th of December, the ship being perfectly refitted, and having taken in most of her water and stores, and received her sick on board, we ran up to Batavia Road and anchored.

In the afternoon of Christmas eve, the 24th, I took leave of the governor, and several of the principal gentlemen of the place with whom I had formed connections, and from whom I received every possible civility and assistance.

In the evening I went on board, accompanied by Mr. Banks and the rest of the gentlemen who had constantly resided on shore, and who, though better, were not yet perfectly recovered.

At six in the morning of the 26th we weighed and set sail, with a light breeze at SW. The *Elgin* Indiaman saluted us with three cheers and thirteen guns, and the garrison with fourteen, both which, with the help of our swivels, we returned; and soon after the sea breeze set in at N. by W., which obliged us to anchor just without the ships in the road.

At this time the number of sick on board amounted to forty, and the rest of the ship's company were in a very feeble condition. Every individual had been sick except the sailmaker, an old man between seventy and eighty years of age, and it is very remarkable that this old man, during our stay at this place, was constantly drunk every day. We had buried seven—the surgeon, three seamen, Mr. Green's servant, Tupia, and Tayeto his boy. All but Tupia fell a sacrifice to the unwholesome, stagnant, putrid air of the country, and he who from his birth had been used to subsist chiefly upon vegetable food, particularly ripe fruit, soon contracted all the disorders that are incident to a sea life, and would probably have sunk under them before we could have completed our voyage, if we had not been obliged to go to Batavia to refit.

CHAPTER XVI.

SOME ACCOUNT OF BATAVIA—PASSAGE FROM BATAVIA TO THE CAPE OF GOOD HOPE—PRINCE'S ISLAND—CAPE OF GOOD HOPE AND ST. HELENA—RETURN OF THE SHIP TO ENGLAND.

1770.
Dec.

BATAVIA is a place that hath been so often visited by Europeans, and so many accounts of it are extant, that any description I could give would seem unnecessary; besides, I have neither abilities nor materials sufficient for such an undertaking, for whoever gives a faithful account of this place must in many things contradict all the authors I have had an opportunity to consult. But this task I shall leave to some abler hand, and only take notice of such things that seem to me necessary for seamen to know.

The city of Batavia is situated on a low flat near the sea, in the bottom of a large bay of the same name, which lies on the north side of Java, about eight leagues from the Straits of Sunda. Most of the streets in the city have canals of water running through them, which unite into one stream about half a mile before they discharge themselves into the sea; this is about 100 feet broad, and is built far enough out into the sea to have at its entrance a sufficient depth of water to admit small craft, luggage boats, etc. The communication between the sea and the city is by this canal alone, and this only in the day; for it is shut up every night by a boom, through which no boats can pass from about six o'clock in the evening to between five and six the next morning. Here stands the custom-house, where all goods, either imported or exported, pay the customary duty; at least, an account is here taken of them, and nothing can pass without a permit, whether it pays duty or not. All kinds of refreshments, naval stores, and sea provisions are to be had here; but there are few articles which do not bear a very high price, especially if you take them of the Company, which you are obliged to do if you want any quantity; that is, of such articles as they monopolize to themselves, which are all manner of naval stores and salted provisions. Fresh water and wood for fuel must be purchased here. Batavia is certainly a place that Europeans need not covet to go to; but if necessity obliges them, they will do well to make their stay as short as possible, otherwise they will soon feel the effects of the unwholesome air, which, I firmly believe, is the death of more Europeans than any other place upon the globe of the same extent. We came in here with as healthy a ship's company as need go to sea, and after a stay of not quite three months left it in the condition of an hospital ship, besides the loss of seven men.

On Thursday, the 27th of December, at six o'clock in the morning, we weighed again and stood out to sea. On the 31st we stood over to the Sumatra shore, and on the morning of New Year's Day, 1771, we stood over for the Java shore.

We continued our course as the wind permitted us till three o'clock in the afternoon of the 5th, when we anchored under the south-east side of Prince's Island in eighteen fathoms, in order to recruit our wood and water, and procure refreshments for the sick, many of whom were now become much worse than they were when we left Batavia. After coming to an anchor I went on shore to look at the watering place and to speak with the natives, some of whom were upon the beach. I found the watering place convenient, and the water to all appearance good, provided proper care is taken in the filling of it. The natives seemed inclined to supply us with turtle, fowls, etc., articles that I intended laying in as great a stock of as possible for the benefit of the sick, and to suffer every one to purchase what they pleased for themselves, as I found these people as easy to traffic with as Europeans. In the morning sent the gunner ashore with some hands to fill water, while others were employed putting the whole to rights, sending on shore empty casks, etc. Served turtle to the ship's company. Yesterday was the only salt-meat day they have had since our arrival at Java, which is now near four months.

From the 7th till Monday 14th we were employed wooding and watering, being frequently interrupted by heavy rains. Having now completed both, we hoisted in the longboat, and made ready to put to sea, having on board a pretty good stock of refreshments, which we purchased of the natives, such as turtle, fowls, fish, two species of deer, one about as big as a small sheep, the other no bigger than a rabbit; both sorts ate very well, but are only for present use, as they seldom lived above twenty-four hours in our possession. We likewise got fruit of several sorts, such as cocoa-nuts, plantains, limes, etc. The trade on our part was carried on chiefly with money (Spanish dollars); the natives set but little value upon anything else. Such of our people as had not this article traded with old shirts, etc., at a great disadvantage.

On the 15th we had variable light airs of wind, with which we could not get under sail until the morning, when we weighed with a light breeze at NE., which was soon succeeded by a calm. In the night died Mr. Charles Green, who was sent out by the Royal Society to observe the transit of Venus. He had long been in a bad state of health, which he took no care to repair, but, on the contrary, lived in such a manner as greatly promoted the disorders he had had long upon him; this brought on the flux, which put a period to his life.

We now made the best of our way for the Cape of Good Hope, but the seeds of disease which we had received at Batavia began to appear with the most threatening symptoms in dysenteries and slow fevers. Lest the water which we had taken in at Prince's Island should have had any share in our sickness, we purified it with lime, and we washed all parts of the ship between decks with vinegar as a remedy against infection. Mr. Banks was among the sick, and for some time there was no hope of his life. We were very soon in a most deplorable situation; the ship was nothing better than an hospital, in which those that were able to go about were too few to attend the sick, who were confined to their hammocks, and we had almost every night a dead body to commit to the sea. In the course of about six weeks we buried Mr. Sporing, a gentleman who was in Mr. Banks's retinue, Mr. Parkinson, his natural history painter, Mr. Green the astronomer, the boatswain, the carpenter and his mate, Mr. Monkhouse the midshipman, who had fothered the ship after she had been stranded on the coast of

TABLE BAY, CAPE OF GOOD HOPE.
Page 189.

New Holland, our old jolly sailmaker and his assistant, the ship's cook, the corporal of the marines, two of the carpenter's crew, a midshipman, and nine seamen; in all three-and-twenty persons, besides the seven that we buried at Batavia.

On Friday, the 15th of March, about ten o'clock in the morning, we anchored off the Cape of Good Hope in seven fathoms with an oozy bottom. The west point of the bay, called the Lion's Tail, bore WNW. and the castle SW., distant about a mile and a half. I immediately waited upon the governor, who told me that I should have everything the country afforded. My first care was to provide a proper place ashore for the sick, which were not a few; and a house was soon found where it was agreed they should be lodged and boarded at the rate of two shillings a head per day.

March.

Our run from Java Head to this place afforded very few subjects of remark that can be of use to future navigators; such as occurred, however, I shall set down. We had left Java Head eleven days before we got the general south-east trade-wind, during which time we did not advance above 5° to the southward, and 3° to the west, having variable light airs, interrupted by calms, with sultry weather and an unwholesome air, occasioned probably by the load of vapours which the eastern trade-wind and westerly monsoons bring into these latitudes, both which blow in these seas at the time of year when we happened to be there. The easterly wind prevails as far as 10° or 12° S., and the westerly as far as 6° or 8°; in the intermediate space the winds are variable and the air, I believe, always unwholesome. It certainly aggravated the diseases which we brought with us from Batavia, and particularly the flux, which was not in the least degree checked by any medicine, so that whoever was seized with it considered himself as a dead man; but we had no sooner got into the trade-wind than we began to feel its salutary effects, though we lost several men after, but they were such as were brought so low and weak that there was hardly a possibility of their recovery, and yet some of them lingered out in a state of suspense a month after, who in all probability would not have lived twenty-four hours before this change happened. Those that were not so far gone remained in the same state for some time, and at last began to recover; some few, however, were seized with the disorder after we got into the trade-wind, but they had it but slightly, and soon got over it. It is worth remarking that of all those who had it in its last stage only one man lived, who is now in a fair way of recovering; and I think Mr. Banks was the only one that was cured at the first attack that had it to a great degree, or indeed at all, before we got into the SE. trade, for it was before that time that his cure was happily effected.

It is to be wished, for the good of all seamen and mankind in general, that some preventive was found out against this disease and put in practice in climates where it is common, for it is impossible to victual and water a ship in those climates but that some one article or another, according to different people's opinions, must have been the means of bringing on the flux. We were inclined to lay it to the water we took in at Prince's Island and the turtle we got there on which we lived for several days. But there seems to be no reason for this when we consider all the ships from Batavia this year suffered from the same disorder as much as we had done, and many of them arrived at this place in a far worse state, and yet not one of the ships took any water in at Prince's Island. The same may be said of the *Harcourt* Indiaman, Captain Paul, which sailed from Batavia, soon after our arrival, directly for the coast of Sumatra. We afterwards heard that she in a very short time lost by sickness above twenty men; indeed, this seems to have been a year of general sickness over most parts of India. The ships from Bengal and Madras bring melancholy accounts of the havoc made there by the united force of sickness and famine.

On Wednesday, the 20th, the *Houghton* Indiaman sailed; she saluted us with eleven guns, which compliment we returned. This ship, during her stay in India, lost by sickness between thirty and forty men, and had at this time a good many down with the scurvy. Other ships suffered in the same proportion. Thus we find that ships which have been little more than twelve months from England have suffered as much or more by sickness than we have done, who have been out near three times as long. Yet their sufferings will hardly, if at all, be mentioned or known in England; when, on the other hand, those of the *Endeavour*, because the voyage is uncommon, will very probably be mentioned in every newspaper, and, what is not unlikely, with many additional hardships we never experienced. For such are the dispositions of men in general in these voyages that they are seldom content with the hardships and dangers which will naturally occur, but they must add others which hardly ever had existence but in their imaginations, by magnifying the most trifling accidents and circumstances to the greatest hardships and insurmountable dangers without the immediate interposition of Providence, as if the whole merit of the voyage consisted in the dangers and hardships they underwent, or that real ones did not happen often enough to give the mind sufficient anxiety. Thus posterity is taught to look upon these voyages as hazardous to the highest degree.

Having lain here to recover the sick, procure stores, and perform several necessary operations upon the ship and rigging, till the 13th of April, I then got all the sick on board, several of whom were still in a dangerous state, and having taken leave of the governor, I unmoored the next morning and got ready to sail. *April.*

On the morning of the 14th we weighed and stood out of the bay, and at five in the evening anchored under Penguin, or Robben Island. We lay here all night, and as I could not sail in the morning for want of wind, I sent a boat to the island for a few trifling articles which we had forgot to take in at the Cape. But as soon as the boat came near the shore, the Dutch hailed her, and warned the people not to land at their peril, bringing down at the same time six men armed with muskets, who paraded upon the beach. The officer who commanded the boat, not thinking it worth while to risk the lives of the people on board for the sake of a few cabbages, which was all we wanted, returned to the ship.

On the 25th, at three o'clock in the afternoon, we weighed, with a light breeze at SE., and put to sea. About an hour afterwards we lost our master, Mr. Robert Molineux, a young man of good parts, but unhappily given up to intemperance, which brought on disorders that put an end to his life.

At 6 a.m. on the 1st we saw the island of St. Helena bearing W., distant eight or nine leagues. At noon we *May.*

anchored in the road, before James's Fort, in twenty-four fathoms water. I found riding here His Majesty's ship *Portland* and *Swallow* sloop and twelve sail of Indiamen. At our first seeing the fleet in this road we took it for granted that it was a war, but in this we were soon agreeably deceived.

St. Helena is situated, as it were, in the middle of the vast Atlantic Ocean, being 400 leagues distant from the coast of Africa, and 600 from that of America. It is the summit of an immense mountain rising out of the sea, which, at a little distance all round it, is of an unfathomable depth, and it is no more than twelve leagues long and six broad.

At one o'clock in the afternoon of the 4th of May we weighed and stood out of the road, in company with the *Portland* man-of-war and twelve sail of Indiamen.

We continued to sail in company with the fleet till the 10th in the morning, when, perceiving that we sailed much heavier than any other ship, and thinking it for that reason probable that the *Portland* would get home before us, I made the signal to speak with her, upon which Captain Elliot himself came on board, and I delivered to him a letter for the Admiralty, with a box containing the common log-books of the ship and the journals of some of the officers. We continued in company, however, till the 23rd in the morning, and then there was not one of the ships in sight. About one o'clock in the afternoon died our first lieutenant, Mr. Hicks, and in the evening we committed his body to the sea with the usual ceremonies. The disease of which he died was a consumption, and as he was not free from it when we sailed from England, it may truly be said that he was dying during the whole voyage, though his decline was very gradual till we came to Batavia.

June. Our rigging and sails were now become so bad that something was giving way every day. We continued our course, however, in safety till the 10th of June, when land, which proved to be the Lizard, was discovered by Nicholas Young, the same boy that first saw New Zealand. On the 11th we ran up the Channel; at six in the morning of the 12th we passed Beachy Head, at noon we were abreast of Dover, and about three came to an anchor in the Downs, and went ashore at Deal, and soon after I landed in order to repair to London.

Second Voyage.

CHAPTER XVII.

PASSAGE FROM DEPTFORD TO THE CAPE OF GOOD HOPE, WITH AN ACCOUNT OF SEVERAL INCIDENTS THAT HAPPENED BY THE WAY AND TRANSACTIONS THERE.

I SAILED from Deptford, April 9, 1772, but got no farther than Woolwich, where I was detained by easterly winds till the 22nd, when the ship fell down to the Long Reach, and the next day was joined by the *Adventure*. Here both ships received on board their powder, guns, gunners' stores, and marines. *1772. April.*

On the 10th of May we left Long Reach with orders to touch at Plymouth; but in plying down the river the *Resolution* was found to be very crank, which made it necessary to put into Sheerness, in order to remove this evil, by making some alterations in her upper works. *May.*

On the 22nd of June the ship was again completed for sea, when I sailed from Sheerness; and on the 3rd of July joined the *Adventure* in Plymouth Sound. The evening before, we met, off the Sound, Lord Sandwich in the *Augusta* yacht (who was on his return from visiting the several dockyards), with the *Glory* frigate and the *Hazard* sloop. We saluted his lordship with seventeen guns; and soon after he and Sir Hugh Palliser gave us the last mark of the very great attention they had paid to this equipment, by coming on board, to satisfy themselves that everything was done to my wish, and that the ship was found to answer to my satisfaction. *July.*

At Plymouth I received my instructions, dated the 25th of June, directing me to take under my command the *Adventure;* to make the best of my way to the island of Madeira, there to take in a supply of wine, and then proceed to the Cape of Good Hope, where I was to refresh the ships' companies, and to take on board such provisions and necessaries as I might stand in need of.

After leaving the Cape of Good Hope, I was to proceed to the southward, and endeavour to fall in with Cape Circumcision, which was said by Monsieur Bouvet to lie in lat. 54° S., and in about 11° 20′ E. long. from Greenwich. If I discovered this cape, I was to satisfy myself whether it was a part of the continent which had so much engaged the attention of geographers and former navigators, or a part of an island. If it proved to be the former, I was to employ myself diligently in exploring as great an extent of it as I could, and to make such notations thereon and observations of every kind as might be useful either to navigation or commerce, or tend to the promotion of natural knowledge.

I was also directed to observe the genius, temper, disposition, and number of the inhabitants, if there were any, and endeavour, by all proper means, to cultivate a friendship and alliance with them; making them presents of such things as they might value, inviting them to traffic, and showing them every kind of civility and regard.

I was to continue to employ myself on this service, and making discoveries either to the eastward or westward, as my situation might render most eligible; keeping in as high a latitude as I could, and prosecuting my discoveries as near to the South Pole as possible, so long as the condition of the ships, the health of their crews, and the state of their provisions would admit of; taking care to reserve as much of the latter as would enable me to reach some known port, where I was to procure a sufficiency to bring me home to England.

But if Cape Circumcision should prove to be part of an island only, or if I should not be able to find the said cape, I was in the first case to make the necessary survey of the island, and then to stand on to the southward, so long as I judged there was a likelihood of falling in with the continent, which I was also to do in the latter case; and then to proceed to the eastward, in further search of the said continent, as well as to make discoveries of such islands as might be situated in that unexplored part of the southern hemisphere, keeping in high latitudes, and prosecuting my discoveries, as above mentioned, as near the pole as possible, until I had circumnavigated the globe; after which I was to proceed to the Cape of Good Hope, and from thence to Spithead.

In the prosecution of these discoveries, whenever the season of the year rendered it unsafe for me to continue in high latitudes, I was to retire to some known place to the northward, to refresh my people and refit the ships, and to return again to the southward as soon as the season of the year would admit of it.

In all unforeseen cases, I was authorized to proceed according to my own discretion; and in case the *Resolution* should be lost or disabled, I was to prosecute the voyage on board the *Adventure*.

I gave a copy of these instructions to Captain Furneaux, with an order directing him to carry them into execution; and, in case he was separated from me, appointed the island of Madeira for the first place of rendezvous, Port Praya in the island of St. Jago for the second, Cape of Good Hope for the third, and New Zealand for the fourth.

On the 10th of July, according to the custom of the navy, the companies of both ships were paid two months' wages in advance; and as a further encouragement for their going this extraordinary voyage, they were also paid the wages due to them to the 28th of the preceding May. This enabled them to provide necessaries for the voyage.

On the 13th, at six o'clock in the morning, I sailed from Plymouth Sound, with the *Adventure* in company; and in the evening of the 29th anchored in Funchal Road, in the island of Madeira. The next morning I saluted the garrison with eleven guns, which compliment was immediately returned.

During our stay at Funchal, which is the capital of the island, the crews of both ships were supplied with fresh beef and onions. Having got on board a supply of water, wine, and other necessaries, we left Madeira on the 1st of August.

On the 4th we passed Palma, one of the Canary Isles. On finding that our stock of water would not last us to the Cape of Good Hope, I anchored in Port Praya in the island of St. Jago, and dispatched an officer to ask leave to water and purchase refreshments, which was granted. We had no sooner got clear of Port Praya than we got a fresh gale at NNE., which blew in squalls, attended by showers of rain.

On the 19th, in the afternoon, one of the carpenter's mates fell overboard, and was drowned. He was over the side, sitting in one of the scuttles, from whence, it was supposed, he had fallen, for he was not seen till the very instant he sank under the ship's stern, when our endeavours to save him were too late. This loss was sensibly felt during the voyage, as he was a sober man and a good workman.

About noon next day the rain poured down upon us, not in drops, but in streams, so that few in the ships escaped a good soaking. We, however, benefited by it, as it gave us an opportunity of filling all our empty water-casks.

On the 27th, spoke with Captain Furneaux, who informed us that one of his petty officers was dead. At this time we had not one sick on board; but I took every necessary precaution by airing and drying the ship with fires made betwixt decks, and by obliging the people to air their bedding, wash and dry their clothes, whenever there was an opportunity.

Sept. On the 8th of September we crossed the line, after which the ceremony of ducking, etc., generally practised on this occasion, was not omitted.

October. At two o'clock in the afternoon of the 29th we made the land of the Cape of Good Hope. We now crowded all the sail we could, thinking to get into the bay before dark. But when we found this could not be accomplished, we shortened sail and spent the night standing off and on. Between eight and nine o'clock the whole sea became at once, as it were, illuminated, or what the seamen call all on fire. The cause of this is not generally known. I therefore had some buckets of water drawn up from alongside the ship, which we found full of an innumerable quantity of small globular insects, about the size of a common pin's head, and quite transparent. We were now well satisfied with the cause of the sea's illumination.

Daylight brought us fair weather; and having stood into Table Bay, with the *Adventure* in company, we anchored in five fathoms water.

My first step after anchoring was to send an officer to wait on the governor to acquaint him with our arrival, and the reasons which induced me to put in there.

I then arranged for supplying the ships with provisions and all other necessaries; while the seamen were employed in overhauling the rigging, and the carpenters in caulking the ships' sides and decks.

Three or four days after us two Dutch Indiamen arrived here from Holland, after a passage of between four and five months, in which one lost, by the scurvy and other putrid diseases, 150 men, and the other 41.

By the healthy condition of the crews of both ships at our arrival, I thought to have made my stay at the Cape very short. But as the bread we wanted was unbaked, and the spirits, which I found scarce, to be collected from different parts of the country, it was the 18th of November before we got everything on board, and the 22nd before we could put to sea.

CHAPTER XVIII.

DEPARTURE FROM THE CAPE OF GOOD HOPE IN SEARCH OF A SOUTHERN CON-
TINENT—SEPARATION OF THE TWO SHIPS—ARRIVAL OF THE "RESOLUTION"
IN DUSKY BAY.

1772.
Nov.

HAVING got clear of the land, I directed my course for Cape Circumcision. On the noon of the 24th we were in the latitude of 35° 25' S., and longitude 29' W. of the Cape, and had abundance of albatrosses about us, several of which were caught with hook and line, and were very well relished by many of the people, notwithstanding they were at this time served with fresh mutton. Judging that we should soon come into cold weather, I ordered slops to be served to such as were in want, and gave to each man the fearnought jacket and trousers allowed them by the Admiralty.

The wind now blew a moderate gale, and increased on the 29th to a storm, which continued, with some few intervals of moderate weather, till the 6th of December. This gale, which was attended with rain and hail, blew at times with such violence that we could carry no sails, by which means we were carried far out of our intended course.

But the greatest misfortune that attended us was the loss of our live-stock, which we had brought from the Cape, and which consisted of sheep, hogs, and geese. Indeed, this sudden transition from warm mild weather to extreme cold and wet made every man in the ship feel its effects. For by this time the mercury in the thermometer had fallen to 38°, whereas at the Cape it was generally at 67° and upwards. I now made some addition to the people's allowance of spirits by giving them a dram whenever I thought it necessary.

Dec.

On Thursday, the 10th, we saw an island of ice to the westward of us. Soon after, the weather becoming hazy,

I called the *Adventure* by signal under my stern, which was no sooner done than the haze increased so much with snow and sleet, that we did not see an island of ice, which we were steering directly for, till we were less than a mile from it. I judged it to be about fifty feet high and half a mile in circuit. It was flat at top, and its sides rose in a perpendicular direction, against which the sea broke exceedingly high.

At noon on the 11th we saw some white birds about the size of pigeons, with blackish bills and feet. I never saw any such before. I believe them to be of the petrel tribe, and natives of these icy seas.

We still had thick, hazy weather, with sleet and snow, so that we were obliged to proceed with great caution on account of the ice islands. Six of them we passed in one day. Such was the force and height of the waves that the sea broke quite over them. This exhibited a view which for a few moments was pleasing to the eye; but when we reflected on the danger, the mind was filled with horror. For were a ship to get against the weather side of one of these islands, when the sea runs high, she would be dashed to pieces in a moment.

Upon our getting to the ice islands, the albatrosses left us. On the other hand, penguins began to make their appearance. On the 13th the wind veered to SW., a fresh gale, with sleet and snow, which froze on our sails and rigging as it fell, so that they were all hung with icicles. Between noon and eight o'clock in the evening, twenty ice islands presented themselves to our view.

We had not run long to the southward before we fell in with the main field of ice extending from SSW. to E. We steered betwixt E. and SSW., hauling into every bay or opening, in hopes of finding a passage to the south. But we found everywhere the ice was closed. The thermometer was from 30° to 34°; but the weather was more sensibly colder than the thermometer seemed to point out, insomuch that the whole crew complained. In order to enable them to support this weather the better, I caused the sleeves of their jackets, which were so short as to expose their arms, to be lengthened with baize, and had a cap made for each man of the same stuff, together with canvas, which proved of great service to them.

1773.
January.
The weather continued thick and hazy, with sleet and snow, which froze on the rigging and ornamented the whole with icicles. In the afternoon of the 2nd we were favoured with a sight of the moon, whose face we had not seen but once since we left the Cape of Good Hope. We did not fail to seize the opportunity to make several observations of the sun and moon.

On the 17th, between eleven and twelve o'clock, we crossed the Antarctic Circle in the longitude of 39° 35′ E. The weather was now tolerably clear, so that we could see several leagues round us. About 4 p.m., as we were steering to the south, we observed the whole sea in a manner covered with ice. In this space, thirty-eight ice islands, great and small, were seen, besides loose ice in abundance, so that we were obliged to luff for one piece and bear up for another; and as we continued to advance to the south, it increased in such a manner that, at three-quarters past six o'clock, we could proceed no farther. This immense field was composed of different kinds of ice, such as high hills, loose or broken pieces packed close together, and what, I think, Greenland men called field-ice. Here we saw many whales playing about the ice, and for two days before had seen several flocks of the brown and white pintadoes, which we named antarctic petrels, because they seemed natives of that region.

After meeting with this ice I did not think it was at all prudent to persevere in getting farther to the south, especially as the summer was already half spent, and it would have taken some time to get round the ice, even supposing it to have been practicable, which, however, is doubtful. I therefore came to a resolution to proceed directly in search of the land lately discovered by the French.

As the wind still continued at ESE., I was obliged to return to the north, over some of the sea I had already made myself acquainted with, and for that reason wished to have avoided. This course we held till the 1st of February; and being in the meridian of the island of Mauritius, we expected to find the land said to be discovered by the French, but seeing not the least signs, we bore away east.

Feb.

On the 8th of February the hazy weather turned to a thick

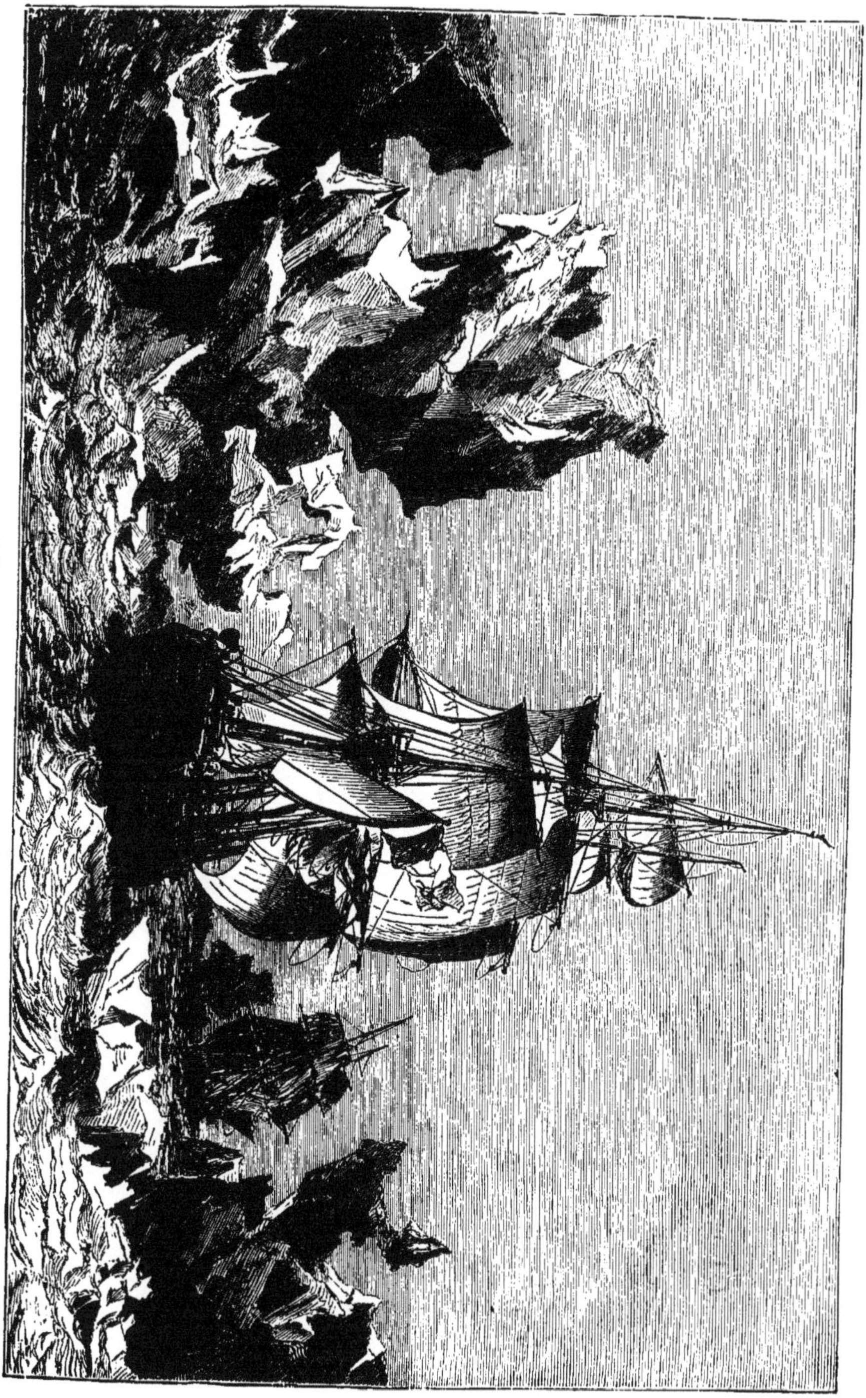

fog. I fired a gun every hour till noon, when I made the signal to tack, and tacked accordingly.

But as neither this signal nor any of the former was answered by the *Adventure*, we had but too much reason to think that a separation had taken place, though we were at a loss to tell how it had been effected. I had directed Captain Furneaux, in case he was separated from me, to cruise three days in the place where he last saw me. I therefore continued making short boards and firing half-hour guns till the 9th in the afternoon, when, the weather having cleared up, we could see several leagues round us, and found that the *Adventure* was not within the limits of our horizon. We were now standing to the westward with a very strong gale at NNW., accompanied with a great sea from the same direction. On the 10th I gave over looking for her, and steered E., with a very fresh gale at WSW.

Between midnight and three o'clock in the morning, lights were seen in the heavens, similar to those in the northern hemisphere known by the name of Aurora Borealis, or Northern Lights; but I never heard of the Aurora Australis being seen before.

On the 28th the height of the thermometer at noon was about 35°, consequently the air was something warmer. While the weather was really *warm*, the gales were not only stronger but more frequent, with almost continual misty, dirty, wet weather. The very animals we had on board felt its effects. A sow having in the morning farrowed nine pigs, every one of them was killed by the cold before four o'clock in the afternoon, notwithstanding all the care we could take of them. From the same cause, myself as well as several of my people had fingers and toes chilblained.

Such is the summer weather we enjoyed.

We prosecuted our course to the east, inclining to the south, till the 17th of March, when being in the lat. of 59° 7' S., long. 146° 53' E., I bore away north-east, and at noon north, having come to a resolution to quit the high southern latitudes and to proceed to New Zealand, to look for the *Adventure* and to refresh my people. I had also some thoughts, and even a desire, to visit the east coast of Van Diemen's Land, in order to satisfy myself if it joined the coast of New South Wales.

March.

On the 19th we saw a seal, and toward noon some penguins

and some rock-weed. In the latitude 54° 4' we also saw a Port Egmont hen. Navigators have generally looked upon all these to be certain signs of the vicinity of land; I cannot, however, support this opinion.

At this time we knew of no land, nor is it even probable that there is any, nearer than New Holland or Van Diemen's Land, from which we were distant 260 leagues. We had at this time several porpoises playing about us, into one of which Mr. Cooper struck a harpoon; but as the ship was running seven knots, it broke its hold, after towing it some minutes and before we could deaden the ship's way.

As the wind, which continued between the north and west, would not permit me to touch at Van Diemen's Land, I shaped my course to New Zealand.

At ten o'clock in the morning of the 25th, the land of New Zealand was seen from the mast-head. As I intended to put into Dusky Bay, or any other port I could find on the southern part of Tavai Poenammoo, we steered in for the land, under all the sail we could carry, having the advantage of a fresh gale at west and tolerably clear weather.

At noon on the 26th we entered Dusky Bay, and anchored in fifty fathoms of water. This was on Friday at three in the afternoon, after having been one hundred and seventeen days at sea, in which time we had sailed 3,660 leagues without having once sight of land.

After such a long continuance at sea, in a high southern latitude, it is but reasonable to think that many of my people must be ill of the scurvy. The contrary, however, happened. Mention hath already been made of sweet wort being given to such as were scorbutic. We did not attribute the general good state of health in the crew wholly to sweet wort, but to the frequent airing and sweetening of the ship by fires, etc. We must also allow portable broth and sour krout to have had some share in it. *T*his last can never be enough recommended. My first care, after the ship was moored, was to send a boat and people a-fishing; in the meantime, some of the gentlemen killed a seal (out of many that were upon a rock), which made us a fresh meal.

CHAPTER XIX.

TRANSACTIONS IN DUSKY BAY.

THE fishing-boat was very successful, returning with fish sufficient for all hands for supper; and in a few hours in the morning caught as many as served for dinner. This gave us certain hopes of being plentifully supplied with this article. Nor did the shores and woods appear less destitute of wild fowl, so that we hoped to enjoy with ease what, in our situation, might be called the luxuries of life.

1773.
March.

This determined me to stay some time in this bay, in order to examine it thoroughly, as no one had ever landed before on any of the southern parts of this country.

We soon began to clear places in the woods, in order to set up the astronomer's observatory, the forge to repair our ironwork, tents for the sailmakers; to land our empty casks, to fill water, and to cut down wood for fuel, all of which were absolutely necessary occupations. We also began to brew beer from the branches or leaves of a tree which much resembles the American black spruce, for I judged that it would make a very wholesome beer, and supply the want of vegetables, which this place did not afford; and the event proved that I was not mistaken.

The few sheep and goats we had left were not likely to fare so well as ourselves, there being no grass here but what was coarse and harsh. It was, however, not so bad but that we expected they would devour it with great greediness, and were the more surprised to find that they would not taste it; nor did they seem over fond of the leaves of more tender plants.

Upon examination, we found their teeth loose, and that many of them had every other symptom of an inveterate sea-scurvy. Out of four ewes and two rams which I brought from the Cape, with an intent to put ashore in this country, I had only been able to preserve one of each; and even these were in so bad a state that it was doubtful if they could recover, notwithstanding all the care possible that had been taken of them.

Some of the officers, on the 28th, went up the bay in a small boat on a shooting party, but discovering inhabitants, they returned to acquaint me therewith, for hitherto we had not seen the least vestige of any. There were seven or eight people. They looked at us for some time, but all the signs of friendship we could make did not prevail on them to come nearer. As we returned from shooting on the 6th of April, the natives discovered themselves again.

April

We should have passed without seeing them, had not one of the men hallooed to us. He stood with his club in his hand upon the point of a rock, and behind him, at the skirts of the wood, stood two women, each of them with a spear. The man could not help discovering great signs of fear when we approached the rock with our boat. He, however, stood firm, nor did he move to take up some things we threw him ashore. At length I landed, went up and embraced him, and presented him with such articles as I had about me, which at once dissipated his fears. Presently we were joined by two women, and spent half an hour in chit chat, little understood on either side, in which the youngest of the two women bore by far the greatest share. This occasioned one of the seamen to say that women did not want tongue in any part of the world.

We presented them with fish and fowl, which we had in our boat, but these they threw into the boat again, giving us to understand that such things they wanted not.

Next morning I paid the natives a visit, carrying with me various articles, which they received with a great deal of indifference, except hatchets and spike-nails; these they most esteemed.

We now saw the whole family. It consisted of the man, his two wives (as we supposed), the young woman before mentioned, a boy about fourteen years old, and three small children. They conducted us to their habitation, which was but a little way within the skirts of the wood, and consisted of two mean huts made of the bark of trees. Their boat, just large enough to transport the whole family from place to place, lay in a small creek near the huts. When we took leave, the chief presented me with a piece of cloth or garment of their own manufacturing, and some other trifles. I at first thought it was meant as a return for the presents I had made him; but he soon undeceived me by expressing a desire for one of our boat-cloaks. I took the hint, and ordered one to be made for him of red baize as soon as I got aboard, where rainy weather detained me the following day.

The 9th being fair weather, we paid the natives another visit, and made known our approach by hallooing to them; but they neither answered us nor met us at the shore as usual. The reason of this we soon saw; for we found them at their habitations, all dressed and dressing in their very best, with their hair combed and oiled, tied up upon the crowns of their head, and stuck with white feathers. Some wore a fillet of feathers round their heads, and all of them had bunches of white feathers stuck in their ears; thus dressed, and all standing, they received us with great courtesy.

I presented the chief with the cloak I had got made for him, with which he seemed so well pleased that he took his patapatoo from his girdle and gave it me.

On the 13th, accompanied by Mr. Forster, I went in the pinnace to survey the isles and rocks which lie in the mouth of the bay. I found a very snug cove sheltered from all winds, which we called Luncheon Cove, because here we dined on crayfish, on the side of a pleasant brook, shaded by the trees from both wind and sun. After dinner we proceeded, by rowing, out to the uttermost isles, where we saw many seals, fourteen of which we killed and brought away with us.

The next morning I went out again to continue the survey. I intended to have landed again on the Seal Isles, but there ran such a high sea that I could not come near them. With some difficulty we rowed out to sea and round the SW. point of Anchor Isle.

It happened very fortunately that chance directed me to take this course, in which we found the sportsmen's boat adrift, and laid hold of her the very moment she would have been dashed against the rocks. I was not long at a loss to guess how she came there, nor was I under any apprehensions for the gentlemen that had been in her; and after refreshing ourselves with such as we had to eat and drink, and securing the boat in a small creek, we proceeded to the place where we supposed them to be. We found them upon a small isle in Goose Cove, where, as it was low water, we could not come with our boat until the return of the tide. As this did not happen till three o'clock in the morning, we landed on a naked beach, not knowing where to find a better place, and after some time, having got a fire and broiled some fish, we made a hearty supper, having for sauce a good appetite.

This done, we lay down to sleep, having a stony beach for a bed and the canopy of heaven for a covering.

When we at last arrived at the creek, we found there an immense number of blue petrels, some on the wing, others in the woods, in holes in the ground, under the roots of trees, and in the crevices of rocks, where there was no getting them, and where we supposed their young were deposited. The noise they made was like the croaking of many frogs. After restoring their boat to the sportsmen, we all proceeded for the ship, which we reached by seven o'clock in the morning, not a little fatigued with our expedition.

On the morning of the 15th I continued my survey of the north-west side of the bay. In the doing of this I picked up about a score of wild fowl, and caught fish sufficient to serve the whole party. Reaching the place where we intended to lodge for the night, a little before dark, I found the other gentlemen out duck-shooting. They, however, soon returned, not overloaded with game. By this time the cooks had done their parts, in which little art was required; and after a hearty repast on what the day had produced, we lay down to rest, but took care to rise early the next morning, in order to have the other bout among the ducks before we left the cove. Accordingly, at daylight, we prepared for the attack. Those who had reconnoitred the place before chose their stations accordingly, whilst myself and another remained in the boat and rowed to the head of the cove to start the game, which we did so effectually that, out of some scores of ducks, we only detained one to ourselves, sending all the rest down to those stationed below. About nine o'clock we all collected together, when the success of every one was known, which was by no means answerable to our expectations. The morning, indeed, was very unfavourable for shooting, being rainy the most of the time we were out. After breakfast we set out on our return to the ship, which we reached by seven o'clock in the evening, with about seven dozen of wild fowl and two seals.

On the 18th, our friends the natives paid us another visit; and the next morning the chief and his daughter were induced to come on board.

Before they came on board I showed them our goats and sheep that were on shore, which they viewed for a moment with a kind of stupid insensibility. After this I conducted them to the bow; but before the chief set his foot upon it to come into the ship, he took a small green branch in his hand, with which he struck the ship's side several times, repeating a speech or prayer. When this was over, he threw the branch into the main chains and came on board.

This custom and manner of making peace, as it were, is practised by all the nations in the South Seas that I have seen. I took them both down into the cabin, where we were to breakfast. They sat at table with us, but would not taste any of our victuals. The chief wanted to know where we slept, and indeed to pry into every corner of the cabin, every part of which he viewed with some surprise. But it was not possible to fix his attention to any one thing a single moment. The works of art appeared to him in the same light as those of nature, and were as far removed beyond his comprehension. What seemed to strike them most was the number and strength of our decks and other parts of the ship. The chief, before he came aboard, presented me with a piece of cloth and a green talc hatchet.

This custom of making presents before they receive any is common with the natives of the South Sea Isles; but I never saw it practised in New Zealand before. Of all the various articles I gave my guest, hatchets and spike-nails were the most valuable in his eyes. These he would never suffer to go out of his hands after he had once laid hold of them; whereas many other articles he would carelessly lay down anywhere, and at last leave them behind him.

At daylight on Tuesday, the 20th, I took two men in the small boat, and, with Mr. Forster, went to take a view of the flat land at the head of the bay. We landed on one side, and ordered the boat to meet us on the other side; but had not been long on the shore before we saw some ducks, which, by their creeping through the bushes, we got a shot at and killed one.

The moment we had fired, the natives, whom we had not discovered before, set up a most hideous noise in two or three places close by us. We hallooed in our turn, and at the same time returned to our boat, which was full half a mile off.

The natives kept up their clamouring noise, but did not follow us. Indeed we found afterwards that they could not, because of a branch of the river between us and them. At length two natives appeared on the banks of the river, a man and a woman, and the latter kept waving something white in her hand, as a sign of friendship.

I landed with two others unarmed, the natives standing about one hundred yards from the water side, with each a spear in his hand. When we advanced they retired.

It was some time before I could prevail on them to lay down their spears. This at last one of them did, and met me with a grass plant in his hand, one end of which he gave me to hold, while he held the other. Standing in this manner, he began a speech, not one word of which I understood, and made some long pauses, waiting, as I thought, for me to answer, for when I spoke he proceeded.

As soon as this ceremony was over, which was not long, we saluted each other. He then took his *hahou* or coat from off his own back and put it upon mine, after which peace seemed firmly established. More people joining us did not in the least alarm them. On the contrary, they saluted every one as he came up.

I gave to each a hatchet and a knife, having nothing else with me. Perhaps these were the most valuable things I could give them—at least they were the most useful. They wanted us to go to their habitation, telling us they would give us something to eat, and I was not sorry the tide and other circumstances would not permit me to accept of their invitation. When we took leave they followed us to our boat, and seeing the muskets lying across the stern, they made signs for them to be taken away, which being done, they came alongside and assisted us to launch her. At this time it was necessary for us to look well after them, for they wanted to take away everything they could lay their hands on, except the muskets. These they took care not to touch, being taught by the slaughter they had seen us make among the wild fowl to look upon them as instruments of death.

We saw no canoes or other boats with them; two or three logs of wood tied together served the same purpose, and were indeed sufficient for the navigation of the river, on the banks of which they lived.

In the afternoon of the 21st, I went with a party out to the isles on seal-hunting. The surf ran so high that we could only land in one place, where we killed ten. These animals served us for three purposes: the skins we made use of for our rigging; the fat gave oil for our lamps; and the flesh we ate, which latter is little inferior to beefsteaks.

In the morning of the 23rd, Mr. Pickersgill, Mr. Gilbert, and two others, went to Cascade Cove, in order to ascend one of the mountains, the summit of which they reached by two o'clock in the afternoon, as we could see by the fire they made. In the evening they returned on board and reported that inland nothing was to be seen but barren mountains with huge craggy precipices, disjoined by valleys, or rather chasms, frightful to behold.

Having five geese left out of those we brought from the Cape of Good Hope, I went with them next morning to Goose Cove (named so on this account), where I left them. I chose this place for two reasons—first, here are no inhabitants to disturb them, and secondly, here being the most food. I make no doubt that they will breed, and may in time spread over the whole country, and fully answer my intention in leaving them.

We spent the day shooting in and about the cove. One of the party shot a white heron, which agreed exactly with the description of the white herons that either now are or were formerly in England.

The 25th was the eighth fair day we had had successively, a circumstance, I believe, very uncommon in this place, especially at this season of the year. This fair weather gave us an opportunity to complete our wood and water, to overhaul the rigging, calk the ship, and put her in a condition for sea.

Having got the tents and every other article on board on the 28th, we only now waited for a wind to carry us out of the harbour and through New Passage, the way I proposed to go to sea. Everything being removed from the shore, I set fire to the topwood, etc., in order to dry a piece of the ground we had occupied, which next morning I dug up and sowed with several sorts of garden seeds. The soil was such as did not promise success to the planter. It was, however, the best we could find.

At two o'clock in the afternoon we weighed with a light breeze at SW., and stood up the bay for the New Passage. Soon after we had got through, between the east end of Indian Island and the west end of Long Island, it fell calm, which obliged us to anchor under the north side of the latter island.

May. At daylight on the 1st of May we got again under sail and attempted to work to windward, having a light breeze down the bay; but the breeze died away, and we were obliged to anchor.

In the night we had some very heavy squalls of wind, attended with rain, hail, and snow, and some thunder. Daylight exhibited to our view all the hills and mountains covered with snow.

In the morning of the 11th we at last got under sail, and with a light breeze at SE. we stood out to sea. It was noon before we got clear of land. We had a prodigious swell from SW., which broke with great violence on all the shores that were exposed to it.

As there are few places where I have been in New Zealand that afford the necessary refreshments in such plenty as Dusky Bay, a short description of it and of the adjacent country may prove of use to the curious reader and to some future navigators; for although this country be far remote from the present trading part of the world, we can by no means tell what use future ages may make of the discoveries made in the present.

The reader of this journal must already know that there are two entrances to this bay.

The south entrance is situated on the N. side of Cape West, in lat. 45° 48′ S. It is formed by the land of the cape to the south and Five Fingers Point to the north. To sail into the bay by this entrance is by no means difficult, as I know of no danger but what shows itself. It must be needless to enumerate all the anchoring places in this capacious bay.

The north entrance lies in the lat. of 45° 38′ S., and five leagues to the north of Five Fingers Point.

The country is exceedingly mountainous, not only about Dusky Bay, but through all the southern part of this western coast of Tavai Poenammoo. A prospect more rude and craggy is rarely to be met with, for inland appears nothing but the summits of mountains of a stupendous height, and consisting of rocks that are totally barren and naked, except where they are covered with snow. But the land bordering on the sea-coast, and all the islands, are thickly clothed with wood, almost down to the water's edge. The trees are of various kinds, such as are common to other parts of this country, and are fit for the shipwright, house-carpenter, cabinetmaker, and many other uses. Except in the river Thames, I have not seen finer timber in all New Zealand. Both here and in that river the most considerable for size is the spruce tree. Many of these trees are from six to eight and ten feet in girth, and from sixty to eighty or one hundred feet in length, large enough to make a mainmast for a fifty-gun ship.

Here are, as well as in all other parts of New Zealand, a great number of aromatic trees and shrubs, most of the myrtle kind; but amidst all this variety we met with none which bore fruit fit to eat.

The soil is a deep black mould, evidently composed of decayed vegetables, and so loose that it sinks under you at every step, and this may be the reason why we meet with so many large trees blown down by the wind, even in the thickest part of the woods. All the ground amongst the trees is covered with moss and fern, of both which there is a great variety; but except the flax or hemp plant and a few other plants, there is very little herbage of any sort, and none that was eatable, that we found, except about a handful of water-cresses and about the same quantity of celery.

What Dusky Bay most abounds with is fish. A boat with six or eight men with hooks and lines caught daily sufficient to serve the whole ship's company. Of this article the variety is almost equal to the plenty, and of such kinds as are common to the more northern coast; but some are superior, and in particular the cole fish, as we called it, which is both larger and finer flavoured than any I had seen before, and was, in the opinion of most on board, the highest luxury the sea afforded us.

The shellfish are mussels, cockles, scallops, crayfish, and many other sorts. The only amphibious animals are seals. These are to be found in great numbers about this bay, on the small rocks and isles near the sea-coast.

We found here five different kinds of ducks, some of which I do not recollect to have anywhere seen before. The largest are as big as a Muscovy duck, with a very beautiful variegated plumage, on which account we called it the painted duck; both male and female have a large white spot on each wing, but all the other feathers are of a dark variegated colour. The second sort have a brown plumage, with bright green feathers in their wings, and are about the size of an English tame duck. The third sort is the blue-grey duck before mentioned, or the whistling duck, as some called them from the whistling noise they made. The fourth sort is something bigger than teal, and all black, except the drake, which has some white feathers in his wing. There are but few of this sort, and we saw them nowhere but in the river at the head of the bay. The last sort is a good deal like a teal, and very common, I am told, in England. The other fowls, whether belonging to the sea or land, are the same that are to be found in common in other parts of this country, except the blue petrel before mentioned and the water or wood hens. These last, although they are numerous enough here, are so scarce in other parts that I saw but one. The reason may be that, as they cannot fly, they inhabit the skirts of the woods and feed on the sea beach, and are so very tame or foolish as to stand and stare at us till we knocked them down with a stick.

Amongst the small birds I must not omit to particularize the wattle-bird, poy-bird, and fantail, on account of their singularity, especially as I find they are not mentioned in the narrative of my former voyage.

The wattle-bird, so called because it has two wattles under its beak, is larger, particularly in length, than an English blackbird. Its bill is short and thick, and its feathers of a dark lead colour;

the colour of its wattles is a dull yellow, almost an orange colour.

The poy-bird is less than the wattle-bird; the feathers of a fine mazarine blue, except those of its neck, which are of a most beautiful silver-grey, and two or three short white ones, which are on the pinion joint of the wing. Under its throat hang two little tufts of curled, snow-white feathers, called its *poies*, which being the Otaheitean word for earrings, occasioned our giving that name to the bird, which is not more remarkable for the beauty of its plumage than for the sweetness of its note. The flesh is also most delicious, and was the greatest luxury the woods afforded us.

For three or four days after we arrived in Pickersgill Harbour, and as we were clearing the woods to set up our tents, etc., a four-footed animal was seen by three or four of our people; but as no two gave the same description of it, I cannot say of what kind it is. All, however, agreed that it was about the size of a cat, with short legs and of a mouse colour. One of the seamen, and he who had the best view of it, said it had a bushy tail and was the most like a jackal of any animal he knew. The most probable conjecture is that it is of a new species. Be this as it may, we are now certain that this country is not so destitute of quadrupeds as was once thought. The most mischievous animals here are the small black sand-flies, which are very numerous, and so troublesome that they exceed everything of the kind I ever met with. Wherever they bite they cause a swelling and such an intolerable itching that it is not possible to refrain from scratching.

The almost continual rains may be reckoned another evil attending this bay; though perhaps they may only happen at this season of the year. Our people, who were daily exposed to the rain, felt no ill effects from it; on the contrary, such as were sick and ailing when we came in, recovered daily, and the whole crew soon became strong and vigorous, which can only be attributed to the healthiness of the place and the fresh provisions it afforded. The beer certainly contributed not a little. We at first made it of a decoction of the spruce leaves; but finding that this alone made the beer too astringent, we afterwards mixed with it an equal quantity of the tea-plant (a name it obtained in my former voyage from our using it as tea then, as we also did now), which partly destroyed the astringency of the other, and made the beer exceedingly palatable and esteemed by every one on board.

We brewed it in the same manner as spruce beer, and the process is as follows: first, make a strong decoction of the small branches of the spruce and tea plants by boiling them three or four hours, or until the bark will strip with ease from off the branches; then take them out of the copper and put in the proper quantity of molasses, ten gallons of which are sufficient to make a tun of 240 gallons of beer. Let this mixture just boil; then put it into casks, and to it add an equal quantity of cold water; when the whole is milk-warm put in a little grounds of beer or yeast if you have it, or anything else that will cause fermentation, and in a few days the beer will be fit to drink.

Any one who is in the least acquainted with spruce pines will find the tree which I have distinguished by that name. There are three sorts of it; that which has the smallest leaves and deepest colour is the sort we brewed with, but doubtless all three might safely serve that purpose.

The tea-plant is a small tree or shrub, with five white petals or flower-leaves, shaped like those of a rose. The tree sometimes grows to a moderate height, and is generally bare on the lower part, with a number of small branches growing close together towards the top. The leaves are small and pointed, like those of the myrtle; it bears a dry roundish seed-case, and grows commonly in dry places near the shores.

The inhabitants of this bay are of the same race of people with those in other parts of this country, speak the same language, and observe nearly the same customs. These indeed seem to have a custom of making presents before they receive any, in which they come nearer to the Otaheiteans than the rest of their countrymen. What could induce three or four families to separate themselves so far from the society of the rest of their fellow-creatures is not easy to guess. By our meeting with inhabitants in this place, it seems probable that there are people scattered over all this southern island. But the many vestiges of them in different parts of this bay, compared with the number that we actually saw, indicates that they live a wandering life; and, if one may judge from appearances and circumstances, few as they are, they live not in perfect amity one family with another. For if they did, why do they not form themselves into some society? a thing not only natural to man, but observed even by the brute creation.

I shall conclude this account of Dusky Bay with some observations made and communicated to me by Mr. Wales. He found, by a great variety of observations, that the latitude of his observatory at Pickersgill Harbour was 45° 47' 26½" S., and, by the mean of several distances of the moon from the sun, that its longitude was 166° 18' E., which is about half a degree less than it is laid down in my chart constructed in my former voyage. He found the variation of the needle or compass to be 13° 49' E., and the dip of the south end 70° 5¾'. The times of high water on the full and change days he found to be at 10^h 57', and the tide to rise and fall, at the former eight feet, at the latter five feet eight inches.

CHAPTER XX.

PASSAGE FROM DUSKY BAY TO QUEEN CHARLOTTE'S SOUND, WITH AN ACCOUNT OF SOME WATER-SPOUTS, AND OF OUR JOINING THE "ADVENTURE"—CAPTAIN FURNEAUX'S NARRATIVE.

1773.
May.

AFTER leaving Dusky Bay, I directed my course along shore for Queen Charlotte's Sound, where I expected to find the *Adventure*. In this passage we met with nothing remarkable till the 17th at four o'clock in the afternoon. Being then about three leagues to the westward of Cape Stephen, having a gentle gale at west by south, and clear weather, the wind at once flattened to a calm, the sky became suddenly obscured by dark dense clouds and seemed to forebode much wind.

This occasioned us to clew up all our sails, and presently six water-spouts were seen. Four rose and spent themselves between us and the land, the fifth was without us, the sixth first appeared in the SW. at the distance of two or three miles at least from us. Its progressive motion was to the NE., not in a straight but in a crooked line, and passed within fifty yards of our stern, without our feeling any of its effects. The diameter of the base of this spout I judged to be about fifty or sixty feet; that is, the sea within this space was much agitated and foamed up to a great height. From this a tube or round body was formed, by which the water, or air, or both, were carried up to the clouds. Some of our people said they saw a bird in the one near us, which was whirled round like the fly of a jack as it was carried upwards. Some of these spouts appeared at times to be stationary; and at other times to have a quick but very unequal progressive motion, and always in a crooked line, sometimes one way and sometimes another, so that once or twice we observed them to cross one another.

From the ascending motion of the bird and several other circumstances, it was very plain to us that these spouts were caused by whirlwinds; and that the water in them was violently hurried upwards, and did not descend from the clouds, as I have heard some assert. The first appearance of them is by the violent agitation and rising up of the water, and presently after you see a round column or tube forming from the clouds above, which apparently descends till it joins the agitated water below. I say apparently, because I believe it not to be so in reality, but that the tube is already formed from the agitated water below and ascends, though at first it is either too small or too thin to be seen. When the tube is formed or becomes visible, its apparent diameter increaseth until it is pretty large; after that, it decreaseth, and at last it breaks or becomes invisible towards the lower part. Soon after, the sea below resumes its natural state, and the tube is drawn, by little and little, up to the clouds, where it is dissipated.

I am told that the firing of a gun will dissipate these waterspouts, and I am very sorry I did not try the experiment; but as soon as the danger was past, I thought no more about it, being too attentive in viewing these extraordinary meteors. At the time this happened, the barometer stood at 29, and the thermometer at 56.

In coming from Cape Farewell to Cape Stephen, I had a better view of the coast than I had when I passed in my former voyage; and observed that, about six leagues to the east of the first-mentioned cape, is a spacious bay, which is covered from the sea by a low point of land. This is, I believe, the same that Captain Tasman anchored in on the 18th of December 1642, and by him called Murderers' Bay, by reason of some of his men being killed by the natives.

The wind having returned to the west, we resumed our course to the east, and at daylight the next morning we appeared off Queen Charlotte's Sound, where we discovered our consort the *Adventure*, by the signals she made to us—an event which every one felt with an agreeable satisfaction.

With the assistance of a light breeze, our boats, and the tides, we, at six o'clock in the evening, got to an anchor in Ship Cove near the *Adventure;* when Captain Furneaux came on board and gave me the following account of his proceedings from the time we parted to my arrival here.

"On the 7th of February 1773, in the morning, the *Resolution* being then about two miles ahead, the wind, shifting then to the westward, brought on a very thick fog, so that we lost sight of her. We soon after heard a gun, the report of which we imagined to be on the larboard beam. We kept firing a four-pounder every half-hour, but had no answer, nor further sight of her; then we kept the course we steered on before the fog came on.

"In the evening it began to blow hard, and was at intervals more clear; but could see nothing of her, which gave us much uneasiness. We then tacked and stood to the westward, to cruise in the place where we last saw her, according to agreement, in case of separation; but next day came on a very heavy gale of wind and thick weather that obliged us to bring to, and thereby prevented us reaching the intended spot. However, the wind coming more moderate and the fog in some measure clearing away, we cruised as near the place as we could get for three days, when, giving over all hopes of joining company again, we bore away for winter quarters, distant 1,400 leagues, through a sea entirely unknown, and reduced the allowance of water to one quart per day.

"We directed our course toward the land laid down in the charts by the name of Van Diemen's Land, discovered by Tasman in 1642, and laid down in the latitude of 44° S. and longitude 140° E., and supposed to join to New Holland.

"On the 9th of March we saw the land, bearing NNE., about eight or nine miles distant. It appeared moderately high and uneven near the sea. A point, much like the Ramhead off Plymouth, which I take to be the same that *T*asman calls South Cape, bore north four leagues of us. *T*he land from this cape runs directly to the eastward. About four leagues along shore are three islands about two miles long. After you pass these islands the land lies E. by N. and W. by S. by the compass nearly. Here the country is hilly and full of trees, the shore rocky, and difficult landing occasioned by the wind blowing here continually from the westward, which occasions such a surf that the sand cannot lie on the shore. We saw no inhabitants here.

"Finding no place to anchor in with safety, we made sail for Frederick Henry Bay, and on the 10th of March we were abreast of the westernmost point of a very deep bay called by Tasman Stormy Bay. While crossing this bay we had very heavy squalls and thick weather. From here the land trends away about N. by E. four leagues. At half-past six we hauled round a high bluff point, the rocks whereof were like so many fluted pillars. Being abreast of a fine bay, and having little wind, we anchored, thinking this bay to be that which Tasman called Frederick Henry Bay, but afterwards found it five leagues to the northward of this.

"We lay here five days, which time was employed in wooding and watering and overhauling the rigging. We found the country very pleasant, the soil a black, rich, though thin one; the sides of the hills covered with large trees and very thick, growing to a great height before they branch off.

"While we lay here we saw several smokes and large fires about eight or ten miles inshore to the northward, but did not see any of the natives, though they frequently came into this bay, as there were several wigwams or huts, where we found some bags and nets made of grass, in which I imagine they carry their provisions and other necessaries. We never found more than three or four huts in a place, capable of containing three or four persons each only; and what is remarkable, we never saw the least marks either of canoe or boat, and it is generally thought they have none, being altogether, from what we could judge, a very ignorant and wretched set of people, though natives of a country capable of producing every necessary of life, and a climate the finest in the world.

"Having completed our wood and water, we sailed from Adventure Bay, intending to coast it up along shore till we should fall in with the land seen by Captain Cook, and discover whether Van Diemen's Land joins with New Holland.

"On the 16th we passed Maria's Islands, so named by Tasman; they appear to be the same as the mainland. On the 17th we hauled in for the mainland. The country here appears to be very thickly inhabited, as there was a continual fire along shore as we sailed. The land hereabouts is much pleasanter, low and even, but no signs of a harbour or bay where a ship might anchor with safety. On the 19th, observing breakers about half a mile within shore of us, we sounded, and finding but eight fathoms, immediately hauled off, then bore away, and kept along shore again.

"The coast from Adventure Bay to the place where we stood away for New Zealand is about seventy-five leagues, and it is my opinion that there are no straits between New Holland and Van Diemen's Land, but a very deep bay. I should have stood further to the northward; but the wind blowing strong at SSE., and looking likely to haul round to the eastward, which would have blown right on the land, I therefore thought it more proper to leave the coast and steer for New Zealand.

"After we left Van Diemen's Land we had very uncertain weather, with rain and heavy gusts of wind. On the 24th we were surprised with a very severe squall, the sea rising equally quick. We shipped many waves, one of which stove the large cutter and drove the small one from her lashing into the waist, and with much difficulty we saved her from being washed overboard. This gale lasted twelve hours, after which we had, upon the whole, good weather; but as we got near to the land it came on thick and dirty for several days, till we made the coast of New Zealand in 40° 30' S., having made twenty-four degrees of longitude from Adventure Bay after a passage of fifteen days.

"The land, when we first made it, appeared high, and formed a confused jumble of hills and mountains.

"At eight o'clock on the 3rd of April we entered the straits, and steered NE. till midnight. Standing to the eastward for Charlotte's Sound in the morning of the 5th, we were taken aback with a strong easterly gale, which obliged us to haul our wind to the SE. and work to windward up under Point Jackson. As we stood off and on we fired several guns, but saw no sign of any inhabitants. On the 6th of April we sailed up the sound, and about five o'clock on the 7th anchored in Ship Cove. In the night we heard the howling of dogs and people hallooing on the east shore.

"The following two days were employed in clearing a place on Motuara Island for erecting our tents for the sick (having then several on board much afflicted with the scurvy), the sailmakers, and coopers. On the top of the island was a post erected by the

Endeavour's people, with her name and time of departure on it. On the 9th we were visited by three canoes with about sixteen of the natives; and to induce them to bring us fish and other provisions we gave them several things, with which they seemed highly pleased. One of our young gentlemen seeing something wrapt up in a better manner than common, had the curiosity to examine what it was, and to his great surprise found it to be the head of a man lately killed. They were very apprehensive of its being forced from them, and particularly the man who seemed most interested in it, whose very flesh crept on his bones for fear of being punished by us, as Captain Cook had expressed his great abhorrence of this unnatural act. They used every method to conceal the head by shifting it from one to another, and by signs endeavouring to convince us that there was no such thing amongst them, though we had seen it but a few minutes before.

"They frequently mentioned Tupia, which was the name of the native of George's Island (or Otaheite) brought here by the *Endeavour*, and who died at Batavia; and when we told them he was dead, some of them seemed to be very much concerned, and, as well as we could understand them, wanted to know whether we killed him, or if he died a natural death. By these questions they are the same tribe Captain Cook saw. In the afternoon they returned again with fish and fern roots, which they sold for nails and other trifles. The man and woman who had the head did not come off again.

"Next morning they returned again to the number of fifty or sixty, with their chief (as we supposed) at their head in five double canoes. They gave us their implements of war, stone hatchets, and clothes, etc., for nails and old bottles, which they put a great value on. A number of the head-men came on board us, and it was with some difficulty we got them out of the ship by fair means; but on the appearance of a musket with a fixed bayonet they all went into their canoes very quickly.

"We struck our tents on the Motuara, and having removed the ship farther into the cove on the west shore, moored her for the winter.

"On the 11th of May we felt two severe shocks of an earthquake, but received no kind of damage. On the 17th we were surprised, our people firing guns from the Hippa, a small island that is joined to Motuara at low water; and having sent the boat, as soon as she opened the sound, had the pleasure of seeing the *Resolution* off the mouth of it.

"We immediately sent out the boats to her assistance to tow her in, it being calm. In the evening she anchored about a mile without us, and next morning weighed and warped within us.

"Both ships felt uncommon joy at our meeting after an absence of fourteen weeks."

CHAPTER XXI.

TRANSACTIONS IN QUEEN CHARLOTTE'S SOUND, WITH SOME REMARKS ON THE INHABITANTS—ROUTE FROM NEW ZEALAND TO OTAHEITE.

KNOWING that scurvy-grass, celery, and other vegetables were to be found in this sound, I went myself the morning after my arrival, at daybreak, to look for some, and returned on board at breakfast with a boat-load. Being now satisfied that enough was to be got for the crews of both ships, I gave orders that they should be boiled with wheat and portable broth every morning for breakfast, and with peas and broth for dinner, knowing from experience that these vegetables thus dressed are extremely beneficial in removing all manner of scorbutic complaints.

1773. May.

I have already mentioned a desire I had of visiting Van Diemen's Land in order to inform myself if it made a part of New Holland, and I certainly should have done this had the winds proved favourable. But as Captain Furneaux had now in a great measure cleared up that point, I could have no business there, and therefore came to a resolution to continue our researches to the east between the latitudes of 41° and 46°. I acquainted Captain Furneaux therewith, and ordered him to get his ship in readiness to put to sea as soon as possible.

In the morning of the 20th I sent ashore, to the watering place near the *Adventure's* tent, the only ewe and ram remaining of those which I brought from the Cape of Good Hope, with an intent to leave in the country. Soon after I visited the several gardens Captain Furneaux had caused to be made and planted with various articles, all of which were in a flourishing state, and, if attended to by the natives, may prove of great utility to them. The next day I set some men to work to make a garden on Long

Island, which I planted with garden seeds, roots, etc. On the 22nd, in the morning, the ewe and ram I had with so much care and trouble brought to this place were both found dead, occasioned, as was supposed, by eating some poisonous plant. Thus my hopes of stocking this country with a breed of sheep were blasted in a moment. About noon we were visited for the first time since I arrived by some of the natives, who dined with us, and it was not a little they devoured. In the evening they were dismissed with presents. On the morning of the 24th, accompanied by Captain Furneaux and Mr. Forster, I went in a boat to the west bay on a shooting party. In our way we met a large canoe in which were fourteen or fifteen people. One of the first questions they asked was for Tupia, the person I brought from Otaheite on my former voyage, and they seemed to express some concern when we told them he was dead.

Nothing worthy of notice happened till the 29th, when several of the natives made us a visit, and brought with them a quantity of fish, which they exchanged for nails, etc. One of these people I took over to Motuara and showed him some potatoes planted there. There seemed no doubt of their succeeding; and the man was so well pleased with them that he of his own accord began to hoe the earth up about the plants. We next took him to the other gardens and showed him the turnips, carrots, and parsnips, roots which, together with the potatoes, will be of more real use to them than all the other articles we had planted. It was easy to give them an idea of these roots by comparing them with such as they knew.

Two or three families of these people now took up their abode near us, employing themselves daily in fishing, and supplying us with the fruits of their labours—the good effects of which we soon felt; for we were by no means such expert fishers as they are, nor were any of our methods of fishing equal to theirs.

June. On the 2nd of June, the ships being nearly ready to put to sea, I sent on shore two goats, male and female. The former was something more than a year old, but the latter was much older. She had two fine kids some time before we arrived in Dusky Bay, which were killed by cold. Captain Furneaux also put on shore in Cannibal Cove a boar and two breeding sows, so that we have reason to hope this country will in time be stocked with these animals if they are not destroyed by the natives before they become wild, for afterwards they will be in no danger. But as the natives knew nothing of their being left behind, it may be some time before they are discovered.

In our excursion to the east we met with the largest seal I had ever seen. It was swimming on the surface of the water, and suffered us to come near enough to fire at it, but without effect, for, after a chase of near an hour, we were obliged to leave it. It certainly bore much resemblance to the drawing in Lord Anson's voyage. Our seeing a sea lion when we entered this sound in my former voyage increaseth the probability; and I am of opinion they have their abode on some of the rocks which lie in the strait or off Admiralty Bay.

It was very common for the natives to bring their children with them and present them to us, in expectation that we would make them presents. This happened to me the preceding morning: a man brought his son, a boy about nine or ten years of age, and presented him to me. As there was a report among our people that some of the natives had offered their children for sale, I thought at first that he wanted me to buy the boy. But at last I found that he wanted me to give him a white shirt, which I accordingly did. The boy was so fond of his new dress that he went all over the ship presenting himself before every one that came in his way. This freedom used by him offended Old Will, the ram goat, who gave him a butt with his horns, and knocked him backward on the deck. Will would have repeated his blow had not some of the people come to the boy's assistance. The misfortune, however, seemed to him irreparable. The shirt was dirtied, and he was afraid to appear in the cabin before his father, until brought in by Mr. Forster, when he told a very lamentable story against Gourey, the great dog (for so they call all the quadrupeds we had aboard); nor could he be reconciled till his shirt was washed and dried. This story, though extremely trifling in itself, will show how liable we are to mistake these people's meaning, and to ascribe to them customs they never knew even in thought.

About nine o'clock, a large double canoe, in which were twenty or thirty people, appeared in sight. Our friends on board seemed much alarmed, telling us that these were their enemies. Two of them, the one with a spear and the other with a stone hatchet in his hand, mounted the arm chests on the poop, and there in a kind of bravado bid these enemies defiance, while the others who were on board took to their canoe and went ashore, probably to secure the women and children.

All I could do, I could not prevail on the two that remained to call these strangers alongside; on the contrary, they were displeased at my doing it, and wanted me to fire upon them. The people in the canoe seemed to pay very little regard to those on board, but kept advancing slowly towards the ship, and, after performing the usual ceremonies, put alongside. After this the chief was easily prevailed upon to come on board, followed by many others, and peace was immediately established on all sides.

One of the first questions these strangers asked was for Tupia; and when I told them he was dead, one or two expressed their sorrow by a kind of lamentation which to me appeared more formal than real. A trade soon commenced between our people and them. It was not possible to hinder the former from selling the clothes off their backs for the merest trifles, things that were neither useful nor curious. This caused me to dismiss the strangers sooner than I would have done.

These natives live dispersed in small parties, knowing no head but the chief of the family or tribe, whose authority may be very little; they feel many inconveniences to which well-regulated societies, united under one head or any other form of government, are not subject. These form laws and regulations for their general good; they are not alarmed at the appearance of every stranger; and, if attacked or invaded by a public enemy, have strongholds to retire to, where they can with advantage defend themselves, their property, and their country. This seems to be the state of most of the inhabitants of Eaheinomauwe; whereas those of *T*avai Poenammoo, by living a wandering life in small parties, are destitute of most of these advantages, which subjects them to perpetual alarms. We generally found them upon their guard, travelling and working, as it were, with their arms in their hands. Even the women are not exempted from bearing arms, as appeared by the first interview I had with the family in Dusky Bay, where each of the two women was armed with a spear not less than eighteen feet in length.

I was led into these reflections by not being able to recollect the face of any one person I had seen here three years ago. Nor did it appear that any one of them had the least knowledge of me or of any person with me that was here at that time. It is therefore highly probable that the greatest part of the people who inhabited this sound in the beginning of the year 1770 have been since driven out of it, or have, of their own accord, removed somewhere else. Certain it is, that not one-third of the inhabitants were here now that were then. It may be asked, if these people had never seen the *Endeavour*, nor any of her crew, how could they become acquainted with the name of Tupia, or have in their possession such articles as they could only have got from that ship? To this it may be answered that the name of Tupia was so popular among them when the *Endeavour* was here, that it would be no wonder if, at this time, it was known over great part of New Zealand, and as familiar to those who never saw him as to those who did. Had ships of any other nation whatever arrived here, they would have equally inquired of them for Tupia. By the same way of reasoning, many of the articles left here by the *Endeavour* may be now in possession of those who never saw her. I got from one of the people now present an ear ornament, made of glass very well formed and polished. The glass they must have got from the *Endeavour*.

Both ships being now ready for sea, I gave Captain Furneaux an account in writing of the route I intended to take, which was to proceed to the east, between the latitudes of 41° and 46° S. until I arrived in the longitude of 140° or 135° W.; then, provided no land was discovered, to proceed to Otaheite; from thence back to this place by the shortest route; and after taking in wood and water, to proceed to the south and explore all the unknown parts of the sea between the meridian of New Zealand and Cape Horn. Therefore, in case of separation before we reached Otaheite, I appointed that island for the place of rendezvous, where he was to wait till the 20th of August. If not joined by me before that time, he was then to make the best of his way back to Queen Charlotte's Sound, where he was to wait until the 20th of November. After which, if not joined by me, he was to put to sea and carry into execution their lordships' instructions.

Some may think it an extraordinary step in me to proceed on discoveries as far south as 46° of latitude, in the very depth of winter. But though it must be owned that winter is by no means favourable for discoveries, it nevertheless appeared to me necessary that something should be done in it, in order to lessen the work I was upon, lest I should not be able to finish the discovery of the southern part of the South Pacific Ocean the ensuing summer. Besides, if I should discover any land in my route to the east, I should be ready to begin with the summer to explore it. Setting aside all these considerations, I had little to fear, having two good ships well provided, and healthy crews.

Where then could I spend my time better? If I did nothing more, I was at least in hopes of being able to point out to posterity that these seas may be navigated, and that it is practicable to go on discoveries even in the very depth of winter.

On the 7th of June, at four in the morning, the wind being more favourable, we unmoored, and at seven weighed and put to sea, with the *Adventure* in company. We had no sooner got out of the sound than we found the wind at south, so that we had to ply through the straits. After getting clear of the straits, I directed my course SE. by E., having a gentle gale, but variable between the north and west. The late SE. winds having caused a swell from the same quarter which did not go down for some days, we had little hopes of meeting with land in that direction. We, however, continued to steer to the SE., and on the 11th crossed the meridian of 180°, and got into the west longitude according to my way of reckoning.

We continued to stretch to the SE., with a fresh gale and fair weather, till Saturday the 26th, when we stood to the NE. At this time we were in the latitude of 42° 32', longitude 161° 15' W. The wind remained not long at west, before it veered back to the east by north, but never blew strong.

July. On July 2nd we had a calm, which brought the wind back to the west; but it was not of long continuance, for the next day it returned to the E. and SE., blew fresh at times and by squalls, with rain.

On the 7th, being in latitude 41° 22', longitude 150° 12' W., we had two hours' calm, in which Mr. Wales went on board the *Adventure* to compare the watches; and they were found to agree, allowing for the difference of their rates of going—a probable if not a certain proof that they had gone well since we had been in this sea.

The calm was succeeded by a wind from the south; between which point and the NW. it continued for the six succeeding days, but never blew strong. It was, however, attended with a great hollow swell from SW. and W., a sure indication that no large land was near in these directions. We stretched to the SE. till five o'clock in the afternoon of the 14th, at which time, being in the latitude of 43° 15', longitude 137° 39' W., we tacked and stood to the north under our courses, having a very hard gale with heavy squalls attended with rain till near noon the next day, when it ended in a calm. In the evening, the calm was succeeded by a breeze from SW., which soon after increased to a fresh gale, and with it we steered NE. ½ E.

We continued to steer NE. ½ E. before a very strong gale, which blew in squalls, attended with showers of rain and hail and a very high sea from the same quarter till the 17th. Being then in latitude 39° 44', longitude 133° 32' W., which was a degree and a half farther east than I had intended to run, nearly in the middle between my track to the north in 1769 and the return to the south in the same year, and seeing no signs of land, I steered northeasterly, with a view of exploring that part of the sea lying between the two tracks just mentioned, down as low as the latitude of 27°, a space that had not been visited by any preceding navigator that I knew of.

On Thursday the 22nd we were in the latitude of 32° 30', longitude 133° 40' W. From this situation we steered NNW. The weather was now so warm that it was necessary to put on lighter clothes; the mercury in the thermometer at noon rose to 63°. It had never been lower than 46°, and seldom higher than 54° at the same time of the day since we left New Zealand. This day was remarkable by our not seeing a single bird. Not one had passed since we left the land without our seeing some of the following birds—namely, albatrosses, sheerwaters, pintadoes, blue petrels, and Port Egmont hens. But these frequent every part of the Southern Ocean in the higher latitudes. Not a bird, nor any other thing, was seen that could induce us to think that we had ever been in the neighbourhood of any land.

The wind kept veering round from the south by the west to NNW., with which we stretched north till noon the next day, when, being in the latitude of 29° 22′, we tacked and stretched to the westward. The wind soon increased to a very hard gale, attended with rain, and blew in such heavy squalls as to split the most of our sails. In the afternoon of the 25th the sky cleared up, and the weather became fair and settled. We now met the first tropical bird we had seen in this sea.

On the 29th I sent on board the *Adventure* to inquire into the state of her crew, having heard that they were sickly; and this I now found was but too true. Her cook was dead, and about twenty of her best men were down in the scurvy and flux. At this time *we* had only three men on the sick list, and only one of them attacked with the scurvy. Several more, however, began to show symptoms of it, and were accordingly put upon the wort, marmalade of carrots, rob of lemons and oranges.

I know not how to account for the scurvy raging more in one ship than in the other, unless it was owing to the crew of the *Adventure* being more scorbutic when they arrived in New Zealand than we were, and to their eating few or no vegetables while they lay in Queen Charlotte's Sound, partly from want of knowing the right sorts and partly because it was a new diet, which alone was sufficient for seamen to reject it. To introduce any new article of food among seamen, let it be ever so much for their good, requires both the example and authority of a commander, without both of which it will be dropped before the people are sensible of the benefits resulting from it. Were it necessary, I could name fifty instances in support of this remark. Many of my people, officers as well as seamen, at first disliked celery, scurvy-grass, etc., being boiled in the peas and wheat, and some refused to eat it. But as this had no effect on my conduct, this obstinate kind of prejudice by little and little wore off; they began to like it as well as the others; and now, I believe, there was hardly a man in the ship that did not attribute our being so free from the scurvy to the beer and vegetables we made use of at New Zealand. After this, I seldom found it necessary to order any of my people to gather vegetables whenever we came where any were to be got; and if scarce, happy was he who could lay hold on them first. I appointed one of my seamen to be cook of the *Adventure*, and wrote to Captain Furneaux, desiring him to make use of every method in his power to stop the spreading of the disease amongst his people, and proposing such as I thought might tend towards it. But I afterwards found all this unnecessary, as every method had been used they could think of.

On the 1st of August, at noon, we were in the latitude of 25° 1', longitude 134° 6' W., and had a great hollow swell from NW. The situation we were now in was nearly the same that Captain Carteret assigns for Pitcairn's Island, discovered by him in 1767. We therefore looked well out for it, but saw nothing. According to the longitude in which he has placed it, we must have passed about fifteen leagues to the west of it. But as this was uncertain, I did not think it prudent, considering the situation of the *Adventure's* people, to lose any time in looking for it.

August.

As we had now got to the northward of Captain Carteret's tracks, all hopes of discovering a continent vanished. Islands were all we were to expect to find, until we returned again to the south. I had now—that is, on this and my former voyage—crossed this ocean in the latitude of 40° and upwards, without meeting anything that did in the least induce me to think I should find what I was in search after. On the contrary, everything conspired to make me believe there is no southern continent between the meridian of America and New Zealand; at least, this passage did not produce any indubitable signs of any, as will appear by the following remarks.

After leaving the coasts of New Zealand, we daily saw, floating in the sea, rock-weed, for the space of 18° of longitude. In my passage to New Zealand in 1769, we also saw of this weed, for the space of 12° or 14° of longitude before we made the land. The weed is, undoubtedly, the produce of New Zealand; because the nearer the coast, the greater quantity you see. At the greatest distance from the coast, we saw it only in small pieces, generally more rotten, and covered with barnacles, an indubitable sign that it had been long at sea. Were it not for this, one might be led to conjecture that some other large land lay in the neighbourhood; for it cannot be a small extent of coast to produce such a quantity of weed as to cover so large a space of sea.

It hath been already mentioned that we were no sooner clear of the straits than we met with a large hollow swell from the SE., which continued till we arrived in the longitude of 177° W., and latitude 46°. There we had large billows from the N. and NE. for five days successively, and until we got 5° of longitude more to the east, although the wind, great part of the time, blew from different directions. This was a strong indication that there was no land between us and my track to the west in 1769. After this we had, as is usual in all great oceans, large billows from every direction in which the wind blew 'a fresh gale, but more especially from the SW. These billows never ceased with the cause that first put them in motion; a sure indication that we were not near any large land, and that there is no continent to the south, unless in a very high latitude.

But this was too important a point to be left to opinions and conjectures. Facts were to determine it, and these could only be obtained by visiting southern parts, which was to be the work of the ensuing summer, agreeably to the plan I had laid down.

On the 6th I hoisted a boat out and sent for Captain Furneaux to dinner; from whom I learned that his people were much better, the flux having left them, and the scurvy was at a stand. Some cider which he happened to have, and which he gave to the seorbutic people, contributed not a little to this happy change.

On the 11th, at daybreak, land was seen to the south. This, upon nearer approach, we found to be an island of about two leagues in extent, clothed with wood, above which the cocoa-nut trees showed their lofty heads. I judged it to be one of those isles discovered by Mr. Bougainville. It lies in the latitude of 17° 24', longitude 141° 39' W., and I called it, after the name of the ship, Resolution Island.

The sickly state of the *Adventure's* crew made it necessary for me to make the best of my way to Otaheite, where I was sure of finding refreshments. Consequently we continued our course to the west, and at six o'clock in the evening land was seen from the mast-head bearing W. by S. Probably this was another of Bougainville's discoveries. I named it Doubtful Island.

At daybreak, the next morning, we discovered land right ahead, distant about two miles, so that daylight advised us of our danger but just in time. This proved another of these low or half-drowned islands. We ranged the south side of this isle or shoal at the distance of one or two miles from the coral bank, against which the sea broke in a dreadful surf. In the middle is a large lake or inland sea, in which was a canoe under sail. This island I named after Captain Furneaux.

On the 13th we saw another of these low islands, which obtained the name of Adventure Island. M. de Bougainville very properly calls this cluster the Dangerous Archipelago. The smoothness of the sea sufficiently convinced us that we were surrounded by them, and how necessary it was to proceed with the utmost caution, especially in the night.

CHAPTER XXII.

THE ARRIVAL OF THE SHIPS AT OTAHEITE, WITH AN ACCOUNT OF THE CRITICAL SITUATION THEY WERE IN, AND OF SEVERAL INCIDENTS THAT HAPPENED WHILE THEY LAY IN OAITI-PIHA BAY—AN ACCOUNT OF SEVERAL VISITS TO AND FROM OTOO, OF GOATS BEING LEFT ON THE ISLAND, AND MANY OTHER PARTICULARS WHICH HAPPENED WHILE THE SHIPS LAY IN MATAVAI BAY.

1773. August. ON the 15th, at five o'clock in the morning, we saw Osnaburg Island or Maitea, discovered by Captain Wallis. Soon after I brought to and waited for the *Adventure* to come up with us, to acquaint Captain Furneaux that it was my intention to put into Oaiti-piha Bay, near the SE. end of Otaheite, in order to get what refreshments we could from that part of the island before we went down to Matavai. At daybreak, on the 16th, we found ourselves not more than half a league from the reef. The breeze now began to fail us, and at last fell to a calm. This made it necessary to hoist out our boats to tow the ships off; but all their efforts were not sufficient to keep them from being carried near the reef. A number of the inhabitants came off in canoes from different parts; the most of them knew me again, and many inquired for Mr. Banks and others who were with me before, but not one asked for Tupia.

As the calm continued, our situation became still more dangerous. We were, however, not without hopes of getting round the western point of the reef and into the bay, till about two o'clock in the afternoon, when we came before an opening or break in the reef through which I hoped to get with the ships. But on sending to examine it, I found there was not a sufficient depth of water, though it caused such an indraught of the tide of flood through it as was very near proving fatal to the *Resolution*; for as soon as the ships got into this stream they were carried with great impetuosity towards the reef. The moment I perceived this I ordered one of the warping machines, which we had in readiness, to be carried out with about four hundred fathoms of rope; but it had not the least effect.

The horrors of shipwreck now stared us in the face. We were not more than two cables' length from the breakers, and yet we could find no bottom to anchor, the only probable means we had left to save the ships. We, however, dropped an anchor, but before it took hold and brought us up, the ship was in less than three fathoms water, and struck at every fall of the sea, which broke close under our stern in a dreadful surf and threatened us every moment with shipwreck. The *Adventure*, very luckily, brought up close upon our bow without striking.

We presently carried out two kedge anchors with hawsers to each. These found ground a little without the bower, but in what depth we never knew. By heaving upon them and cutting away the bower anchor we got the ship afloat, where we lay some time in the greatest anxiety, expecting every minute that either the kedges would come home, or the hawsers be cut in two by the rocks. At length the tide ceased to act in the same direction. I ordered all the boats to try to tow off the *Resolution*, and when I saw this was practicable, we hove the two kedges up. At that moment a light air came off from the land, which so much assisted the boats that we soon got clear of all danger.

Thus we were once more safe at sea, after narrowly escaping being wrecked on the very island we, but a few days before, so ardently wished to be at. The calm, after bringing us into this dangerous situation, very fortunately continued; for had the sea-breeze, as is usual, set in, the *Resolution* must inevitably have been lost, and probably the *Adventure* too.

During the time we were in this critical situation, a number of the natives were on board and about the ships. They seemed to be insensible of our danger, showing not the least surprise, joy, or fear when we were striking, and left us a little before sunset quite unconcerned.

The next morning being the 17th, we anchored in Oaiti-piha Bay. Both ships soon became crowded with natives, who brought with them cocoa-nuts, plantains, bananas, apples, yams, and other roots, which they exchanged for nails and beads. They promised to bring hogs and fowls, many of which were seen about the houses of the natives. Nothing, however, was brought to market but fruits and roots. The cry was that they belonged to Waheatoua, the *Earee de ni* or king, and him we had not yet seen. Many, however, who called themselves carees came on board, partly with a view of getting presents, and partly to pilfer whatever came in their way.

One of this sort of earees I had, most of the day, in the cabin, and made presents to him and all his friends, which were not a few. At length he was caught taking things which did not belong to him, and handing them out of the quarter gallery. Many complaints of the like nature were made to me against those on deck, which occasioned my turning them all out of the ship. My cabin guest made haste to be gone. I was so much exasperated at his behaviour that, after he had got some distance from the ship, I fired two muskets over his head, which made him quit the canoe and take to the water. It was not till the evening of this day that any one inquired after Tupia, and then but two or three. As soon as they learned the cause of his death they were quite satisfied. They were continually asking for Mr. Banks and several others who were with me in my former voyage.

The people informed us that Tootaha, the regent of the greater peninsula of Otaheite, had been killed in a battle which was fought between the two kingdoms about five months before, and that Otoo was the reigning prince. Tubourai Tamaide and several more of our principal friends about Matavai fell in this battle, as also a great number of common people; but at present a peace subsisted between the two kingdoms.

Nothing worthy of note happened till the 20th, when, in the dusk of the evening, one of the natives made off with a musket belonging to the guard on shore. I was present when this happened, and sent some of our people after him, which would have been to little purpose had not some of the natives, of their own accord, pursued the thief. They knocked him down, took from him the musket, and brought it to us. Fear, on this occasion, certainly operated more with them than principle. They, however, deserve to be applauded for this act of justice; for if they had not given their immediate assistance, it would hardly have been in my power to have recovered the musket by any gentle means whatever, and by making use of any other I was sure to lose more than ten times its value.

On the 22nd I was informed that Waheatoua was come into the neighbourhood and wanted to see me. Accordingly, early the next morning, I set out in company with Captain Furneaux, Mr. Forster, and several of the natives. We met the chief about a mile from the landing-place, toward which he was advancing to meet us; but as soon as he saw us he stopped, with his numerous train, in the open air. I found him seated upon a stool with a circle of people round him, and knew him at first sight and he me, having seen each other several times in 1769. At that time he was but a boy and went by the name of Tearee, but upon the death of his father Waheatoua, he took upon himself that name.

After the first salutation was over, having seated me on the same stool with himself, and the other gentlemen on the ground by us, he began to inquire after several by name who were with me on my former voyage. He next inquired how long I would stay, and when I told him no longer than next day, he seemed sorry, asked me to stay some months, and at last came down to five days, promising that in that time I should have hogs in plenty; but as I had been here already a week without so much as getting one, I could not put any faith in this promise. And yet, I believe, if I had stayed, we should have fared much better than at Matavai. The present I made him consisted of a shirt, a sheet, a broad axe, spike-nails, knives, looking-glasses, medals, beads, etc. In return he ordered a pretty good hog to be carried to our boat. We stayed with him all the morning, during which time he never suffered me to go from his side where he was seated. I was also seated on the same stool, which was carried from place to place by one of his attendants, whom we called stool-bearer. At length we took leave in order to return on board to dinner, after which we visited him again and made him more presents, and he in return gave Captain Furneaux and me each a hog. Some others were got by exchanges at the trading places, so that we got on the whole to-day as much fresh pork as gave the crews of both ships a meal, and this in consequence of our having this interview with the chief.

The fruits we got here greatly contributed towards the recovery of the *Adventure's* sick people. Many of them who had been so ill as not to be able to move without assistance were, in a short time, so far recovered that they could walk about of themselves. When we put in here the *Resolution* had but one scorbutic man on board, and a marine who had been long sick, and who died, the second day after our arrival, of a complication of disorders without the least mixture of the scurvy. I left Lieutenant Pickersgill with the cutter behind in the bay to purchase hogs, as several had promised to bring some down to-day and I was not willing to lose them.

On the 25th Mr. Pickersgill returned with eight pigs which he got at Oaiti-piha. He spent the night at Ohedea, and was well entertained by Ereti, the chief of that district. It was remarkable that this chief never once asked after Aotourou, nor did he take the least notice when Mr. Pickersgill mentioned his name. And yet M. de Bougainville tells us this is the very chief who presented Aotourou to him; which makes it the more extraordinary that he should neither inquire after him now, nor when he was with us at Matavai, especially as they believed that we and M. de Bougainville came from *Pretane*, for so they called our country. We told several of them that M. de Bougainville came from *France*, a name they could by no means pronounce, nor could they pronounce that of *Paris* much better, so that it is not likely that they will remember either the one or the other long, whereas *Pretane* is in every child's mouth, and will hardly ever be forgotten. It was not till the evening of this day that we arrived in Matavai Bay.

Before we got to an anchor, our decks were crowded with the natives, many of whom I knew, and almost all of them knew me. A great crowd were gotten together upon the shore, amongst whom was Otoo their king. I was just going to pay him a visit, when I was told he was "*mataow'd*" and gone to Oparree. I could not conceive the reason of his going off in a fright, as every one seemed pleased to see me.

Having given directions to pitch tents for the reception of the sick, coopers, sailmakers, and the guard, I set out on the 26th for Oparree, accompanied by Captain Furneaux, Mr. Forster, and others. As soon as we landed, we were conducted to Otoo, whom we found seated on the ground, under the shade of a tree, with an immense crowd round him. After the first compliments were over, I presented him with such articles as I guessed were most valuable in his eyes, well knowing that it was my interest to gain the friendship of this man. The king inquired for Tupia and all the gentlemen that were with me in my former voyage by name, although I do not remember that he was personally acquainted with any of us. He promised that I should have some hogs the next day, but I had much ado to obtain a promise from him to visit me on board. He said he was afraid of the guns. Indeed all his actions showed him to be a timorous prince. He was about thirty years of age, six feet high, and a fine, personable, well-made man as one can see. All his subjects appeared uncovered before him, his father not excepted. What is meant by uncovering is the making bare the head and shoulders, or wearing no sort of clothing above the breast. When I returned from Oparree, I found the tents and the astronomer's observatories set up, on the same spot where we observed the transit of Venus in 1769. In the afternoon I had the sick landed; twenty from the *Adventure*, all ill of the scurvy, and one from the *Resolution*.

On the 27th, early in the morning, Otoo, attended by a numerous train, paid me a visit. He first sent into the ship a large quantity of cloth, fruits, a hog, and two large fish; and after some persuasion, came aboard himself, with his sister, a younger brother, and several more of his attendants. To all of them I made presents, and after breakfast took the king, his sister, and as many more as I had room for, into my boat and carried them home to Oparree.

I had no sooner landed than I was met by a venerable old lady, the mother of the late Tootaha. She seized me by both hands, and burst into a flood of tears, saying, "Toutaha *T*iyo no Toutee matty Tootaha" (Tootaha, your friend or the friend of Cook, is dead). I was so much affected with her behaviour that it would have been impossible for me to have restrained mingling my tears with hers had not Otoo come and taken me from her.

Captain Furneaux, who was with me, presented the king with two fine goats, male and female, which if taken care of, or rather if no care at all is taken of them, will no doubt multiply.

A little after sunrise on the 28th I had another visit from Otoo. When he came into the cabin, Ereti and some of his friends were sitting there. The moment they saw the king enter, they stripped themselves in great haste, being covered before. Seeing that I took notice, they said, " Earee, earee," giving me to understand that it was on account of Otoo being present. This was all the respect they paid him, for they never rose from their seats, nor made him any other obedience. When the king thought proper to depart, I carried him again in my boat to Oparree, where I entertained him and his people with the bagpipes (of which music they are very fond), and dancing by the seamen.

On the evening of the 29th we were conducted to the theatre, where we were entertained with a dramatic play in which were both dancing and comedy. The performers were five men and one woman, who was no less a person than the king's sister. The music consisted of three drums only. It was not possible for us to find out the meaning of the play. Some part seemed adopted to the present time, as my name was frequently mentioned. The dancing dress of the lady was more elegant than any I saw there, by being decorated with long tassels made of feathers, hanging from the waist downwards. As soon as all was over the king himself desired me to depart.

On the 31st we paid our last visit to Otoo. When I acquainted him that I should sail from the island the next day, he seemed much moved and embraced me several times.

Sept. The sick being all pretty well recovered, our water-casks repaired and water completed, as well as the necessary repairs of the ships, I ordered everything to be got off from the shore and the ships to be unmoored. Some hours before we got under sail, a young man whose name was Poreo came and desired I would take him with me. Many more offered themselves, but I refused to take them. I consented to take the youth, thinking he might be of service to us on some occasion. Though he seemed pretty well satisfied, he could not refrain from weeping when he viewed the land astern.

DANCING WOMAN, OTAHEITE.
Page 240.

DOUBLE CANOE OF TONGATABU.
Page 256.

CHAPTER XXIII.

AN ACCOUNT OF THE RECEPTION WE MET WITH AT HUAHEINE, WITH THE INCIDENTS THAT HAPPENED WHILE THE SHIPS LAY THERE, AND OF OMAI, ONE OF THE NATIVES, COMING AWAY IN THE "ADVENTURE"—ARRIVAL AT AND DEPARTURE OF THE SHIPS FROM ULIETEA, WITH AN ACCOUNT OF WHAT HAPPENED THERE, AND OF OEDIDEE, ONE OF THE NATIVES, COMING AWAY IN THE "RESOLUTION."

AS soon as we were clear of the bay, I directed my course for the island of Huaheine. At daylight in the morning of the 3rd we made sail for the harbour of Owharre, in which the *Resolution* anchored. I landed with Captain Furneaux, and was received by the natives with the utmost cordiality. I distributed some presents among them, and presently after they brought down hogs, fowls, dogs, and fruit. Trade was soon opened on board the ships, so that we made fair prospect of being plentifully supplied with fresh pork and fowls, and, to people in our situation, this was no unwelcome thing. I learned that my old friend Oree, chief of the isle, was still living, and that he was hastening to this part to see me.

1773. Sept.

On the 4th of September, accompanied by Captain Furneaux and Mr. Forster, I went to pay my first visit to Oree. We were conducted to the place by one of the natives, but were not permitted to go out of the boat till we had gone through some part of the following ceremony. The boat, in which we were desired to remain, being landed béfore the chief's house, that stood close to the shore, five young plantain trees, which are their emblems of peace, were brought on board separately and with some ceremony. Three young pigs, with their ears ornamented with cocoa-nut fibres, accompanied the first three; and a dog the fourth. Lastly, the chief sent to me the inscription engraved on a small piece of pewter which I left with him in July 1769. It was in the same bag I had made for it, together with a piece of counterfeit English coin and a few beads, put in at the same time, which shows how well he had taken care of the whole. When they had made an end of putting into the boat the things just mentioned, our guide, who still remained with us, desired us to decorate three young plantain trees with looking-glasses, nails, etc. This being accordingly done, we landed with these in our hands, and were conducted towards the chief through the multitude, they making a lane, as it were, for us to pass through. We were made to sit down a few paces short of the chief, and our plantains were then taken from us and one by one laid before him. One was for Eatou (or God), the second for the Earee (or king), and the third for Tiyo (or friendship). This being done the king came to me, fell upon my neck, and embraced me. This was by no means ceremonious; the tears which trickled plentifully down his venerable old cheeks sufficiently bespoke the language of his heart. The whole ceremony being over, all his friends were introduced to us, to whom we made presents. Mine to the chief consisted of the most valuable articles I had, for I regarded this man as a father.

This good old chief made me a visit early in the morning on the 5th, bringing me a hog and some fruit, for which I made him a suitable return. He carried his kindness so far as not to fail to send me every day, for my table, the very best of ready-dressed fruit and roots in great plenty.

On the 7th, early in the morning, I went to pay my farewell visit to Oree, accompanied by Captain Furneaux and Mr. Forster. We took with us for a present such things as were not only valuable but useful. I also left with him the inscription plate he had before in keeping, and another small copper plate on which were engraved the words, " Anchored here, His Britannic Majesty's ships *Resolution* and *Adventure,* September 1773," together with some medals, all put up in a bag; all of which the chief promised to take care of, and to produce to the first ship or ships that should arrive at the island.

The chief came on board and stayed till we were full half a league out at sea, then took a most affectionate leave of me, and went away in a canoe conducted by one man and himself.

During our short stay at the small but fertile island of Huaheine, we procured for both ships not less than three hundred hogs, besides fowls and fruits; and had we stayed longer might have got many more: for none of these articles of refreshment were seemingly diminished, but appeared everywhere in as great abundance as ever.

Before we quitted this island Captain Furneaux agreed to receive on board his ship a young man named Omai, a native of Ulietea, where he had had some property, of which he had been dispossessed by the people of Bolabola. I at first rather wondered that Captain Furneaux would encumber himself with this man, who, in my opinion, was not a proper sample of the inhabitants of these happy islands, not having any advantage of birth or acquired rank, nor being eminent in shape, figure, or complexion; for their people of the first rank are much fairer, and usually better behaved and are more intelligent, than the middling class of people, among whom Omai is to be ranked. I have, however, since my arrival in England, been convinced of my error, for I much doubt whether any other of the natives would have given more general satisfaction by his behaviour among us. Omai has most certainly a very good understanding, quick parts, and honest principles; he has a natural good behaviour, which rendered him acceptable to the best company, and a proper degree of pride, which taught him to avoid the society of persons of inferior rank.

Soon after his arrival in London, the Earl of Sandwich, the first Lord of the Admiralty, introduced him to His Majesty at Kew, when he met with a most gracious reception, and imbibed the strongest impression of duty and gratitude to that great and amiable prince, which I am persuaded he will preserve to the latest moments of his life. During his stay among us he was caressed by many of the principal nobility, and did nothing to forfeit the esteem of any one of them; but his principal patrons were the Earl of Sandwich, Mr. Banks, and Dr. Solander. The former probably thought it a duty of his office to protect and countenance an inhabitant of that hospitable country where the wants and distresses of those in his department had been alleviated and supplied in the most ample manner; the others, as a testimony of their gratitude for the generous reception they had met with during their residence in his country.

It is to be observed that though Omai lived in the midst of

amusements during his residence in England, his return to his native country was always in his thoughts; and though he was not impatient to go, he expressed a satisfaction as the time of his return approached. He embarked with me in the *Resolution* when she was fitted out for another voyage, loaded with presents for his several friends, and full of gratitude for the kind reception and treatment he had experienced among us.

The chief was no sooner gone than we made sail for Ulietea. Arriving off the harbour of Ohamaneno at the close of the day, we spent the night making short boards. It was dark, but we were sufficiently guided by the fishers' lights on the reefs and shores of the isles. The next morning we gained the entrance of the harbour.

We were no sooner at anchor than the natives crowded round us in their canoes with hogs and fruit.

I had forgot to mention that Tupia was much inquired after at Huaheine; but at this place every one asked about him and the occasion of his death, and, like true philosophers, were perfectly satisfied with the answers we gave them. Indeed, as we had nothing but the truth to tell, the story was the same, by whomsoever told.

Next morning we paid a formal visit to Oreo, the chief of this part of the isle, carrying with us the necessary presents. We went through no sort of ceremony at landing, but were at once conducted to him. He was seated in his own house, which stood near the water-side, where he and his friend received us with great cordiality. He expressed much satisfaction at seeing me again, and desired that we might exchange names, which I accordingly agreed to. I believe this is the strongest mark of friendship they can show to a stranger. He inquired after *T*upia and all the gentlemen, by name, who were with me when I first visited the island.

The next day we were entertained by him with such a comedy or dramatic display as is generally acted in these isles. The music consisted of three drums; the actors were seven men and one woman, the chief's daughter. The only entertaining part in the drama was a theft committed by a man and his accomplice, in such a masterly manner as sufficiently displayed the genius of the people in this vice. After the play was over we returned on board to dinner; and in the cool of the evening took a walk on shore, where we learned from one of the natives that nine small islands, two of which were uninhabited, lay to the westward, at no great distance from hence.

On the 11th, early in the morning, I had a visit from Oreo and his son, a youth about twelve years of age. The latter brought me a hog and some fruit, for which I made him a present of an axe, and dressed him in a shirt and other things, which made him not a little proud of himself.

On Tuesday the 14th I acquainted the chief that I would dine with him, and desired he would order two pigs to be dressed after their manner, which he accordingly did; and about one o'clock, I and the officers and gentlemen of both ships went to partake of these. When we came to the chief's house we found the cloth laid—that is, green leaves were strewed thick on the floor. Round them we seated ourselves. Presently one of the pigs came over my head souse upon the leaves, and immediately after the other, both so hot as hardly to be touched. The table was garnished round with hot bread-fruit, and plantains, and a quantity of cocoa-nuts brought for drink. Each man being ready, with his knife in his hand, we turned to without ceremony, and it must be owned in favour of their cookery that victuals were never cleaner or better dressed. For though the pigs were served up whole, and the one weighed between 50 and 60 lbs. and the other about half as much, yet all the parts were equally done, and ate much sweeter than if dressed in any of our methods. The chief and his son and some other of his male friends ate with us, and pieces were handed to others who sat behind, for we had a vast crowd about us, so that it might be truly said we dined in public. The chief never failed to drink his glass of madeira whenever it came to his turn, not only now, but at all other times when he dined with us, without ever being once affected by it. When we rose up, many of the common people rushed in to pick up the crumbs which had fallen, and for which they searched the leaves very narrowly. This leads me to believe that, though there is plenty of pork at these isles, but little falls to their share. In the afternoon we were entertained with a play.

On the 16th I was told that my Otaheitean young man, Porco, had taken a resolution to leave me. He had contracted a friendship with a young woman. Having my powder-horn in keeping, he came and gave it to one of my people who was by me, and then went away with her, and I saw him no more.

Having now got on board a large supply of refreshments, I determined to put to sea the next morning. At four o'clock we began to unmoor, and as soon as it was light, Oreo, his son, and some of his friends, came on board. Many canoes also came off with fruit and hogs; the latter they even begged of us to take from them, calling out, "Tiyo boa atoi" (I am thy friend, take my hog and give me an axe). But our decks were already so full of them that we could hardly move, having on board both ships between three and four hundred.

The chief and his friends did not leave me till we were under sail, and before he went away, pressed me much to know if I would not return, and when?—questions which were daily put to me by many of these islanders. My Otaheitean youth's leaving me proved of no consequence, as many young men of this island voluntarily offered to come away with us. I thought proper to take one, who was about seventeen or eighteen years of age, named Oedidee, a native of Bolabola, and a near relation of the great Opoony, chief of that island.

CHAPTER XXIV.

PASSAGE FROM ULIETEA TO THE FRIENDLY ISLANDS, WITH AN ACCOUNT OF THE DISCOVERY OF HERVEY'S ISLAND AND THE INCIDENTS THAT HAPPENED AT MIDDLEBURG—THE ARRIVAL OF THE SHIPS AT AMSTERDAM; A DESCRIPTION OF A PLACE OF WORSHIP, AND AN ACCOUNT OF THE INCIDENTS WHICH HAPPENED WHILE THEY REMAINED AT THAT ISLAND—A DESCRIPTION OF THE ISLANDS, THEIR PRODUCE, ETC.

AFTER leaving Ulietea, as before mentioned, I steered to the west, inclining to the south, to get clear of the tracks of former navigators, and to get into the latitude of the islands of Middleburg and Amsterdam, for I intended to run as far west as these islands, and to touch there, if I found it convenient, before I hauled up for New Zealand. 1773. Sept.

On the 23rd, at ten o'clock in the morning, land was seen from the top-mast head. This was found to consist of two or three small islets, connected together by breakers, lying in a triangular form. We saw no people or signs of inhabitants. I named it Hervey's Island, in honour of the Hon. Captain Hervey of the navy, one of the Lords of the Admiralty and now Earl of Bristol.

At two o'clock p.m. on the 1st of October we made the island of Middleburg. We had scarcely got to an anchor before we were surrounded by a great number of canoes full of people, who had brought with them cloth and other curiosities, which they exchanged for nails, etc. Several came on board: amongst them was one whom, by the authority he seemed to have over the others, I found to be a chief, and accordingly made him a present of a hatchet, spike-nails, etc., with which he was highly pleased. Thus I obtained the friendship of this chief, whose name was Tioony. October.

Soon after, a party of us embarked in two boats, in company with Tioony, who conducted us to a little creek where landing was extremely easy. Here we found an immense crowd of people, who welcomed us on shore with loud acclamations. Not one of them had so much as a stick or any other weapon in his hand—an indubitable sign of their pacific intentions.

The chief conducted us up to his house, which was situated about three hundred yards from the sea, at the head of a fine lawn and under the shade of some shaddock trees. The situation was most delightful. In front was the sea, and the ships at anchor; behind and on each side were plantations, in which were some of the richest productions of nature. The floor was laid with mats, on which we were seated, and the people seated themselves in a circle round us on the outside. Bananas and cocoa-nuts were set before us to eat, and a bowl of liquor prepared in our presence of the juice of *eava* for us to drink. Pieces of the root were first offered to us to chew, but as we excused ourselves from assisting in the operation, this was performed by others. When sufficiently chewed, it was put into a large wooden bowl, then mixed with water in the manner already related; and as soon as it was properly strained for drinking, they made cups by folding of green leaves, which held near half a pint, and presented to each of us one of these filled with the liquor. But I was the only one who tasted it, the manner of brewing it having quenched the thirst of every one else.

After this, we signified our desire of seeing the country. Tioony very readily assented, and conducted us through several plantations, which were laid out with great judgment and enclosed with very neat fences made of reeds. Some hogs and very large fowls were the only domestic animals we saw, and these they did not seem willing to part with. Nor did any one, during the whole day, offer in exchange any fruit or roots worth mentioning, which determined me to leave this island and to visit that of Amsterdam.

We anchored in Van Diemen's Road on the 3rd of October in eighteen fathoms water, little more than a cable's length from the breakers which line the coast. We were soon crowded with people; some came off in canoes and others swam, but, like those at the other isle, brought nothing with them but cloth, matting, etc. But when the natives saw we would purchase nothing but eatables, they brought off bananas and cocoa-nuts in abundance, some fowls, and pigs.

After breakfast I landed, accompanied by Captain Furneaux, having along with us a chief, Attago, who had attached himself to me from the first moment of his coming on board. I know not how he came to discover I was the commander, but certain it is he was not long on deck before he singled me out from all the other gentlemen, making me a present of some cloth; and, as a greater testimony of friendship, we now exchanged names, a custom which is practised at Otaheite and the Society Isles. My friend Attago conducted us to a creek, and there we landed dry on the beach, in the face of a vast crowd of people, who received us in the same friendly manner that those of Middleburg had done.

On the 4th of October we signified to the chief our desire to see the country. He immediately took the hint and conducted us along a lane that led to an open green, on the one side of which was a house of worship built on a mount that had been raised by the hand of man, about 16 or 18 feet above the common level. It had an oblong figure, and was enclosed by a wall or parapet of stone about three feet in height. From this wall the mount rose with a gentle slope, and was covered with a green turf. On the top of it stood the house, which had the same figure as the mount, about 20 feet in length and 14 or 16 broad. As soon as we came before the place every one seated himself on the green, about 50 or 60 yards from the front of the house. Presently came three elderly men, who seated themselves between us and it and began a speech, which I understood to be a prayer, it being wholly directed to the house. This lasted about ten minutes, and then the priests—for such I took them to be—came and sat down along with us, when we made them presents of such things as were about us. Having then made signs that we wanted to view the premises, my friend Attago immediately got up, and going with us, gave us full liberty to examine every part of it.

In the front were two stone steps leading to the top of the wall; from this the ascent to the house was easy, round which was a fine gravel walk. The house was built in all respects like to their common dwelling-houses; that is, with posts and rafters, and covered with palm thatch. The floor of the house was laid with fine gravel. At the corner of the house stood an image rudely carved in wood, and on one side lay another, each about two feet in length.

I, who had no intention to offend either them or their gods, did not so much as touch them, but asked Attago as well as I could if they were gods. Whether he understood me or not I cannot say, but he immediately turned them over and over in as rough a manner as he would have done any other log of wood, which convinced me that they were not there as representatives of the Divinity. I was curious to know if the dead were interred there, and asked Attago several questions relative thereto; but I was not sure that he understood me—at least I did not understand the answers he made well enough to satisfy my inquiries. For the reader must know that, at our first coming among these people, we hardly could understand a word they said. Before we quitted the house we thought it necessary to make an offering at the altar. Accordingly we laid down upon the blue pebbles some medals, nails, and several other things; which we had no sooner done than my friend Attago took them up and put them in his pocket.

This mount stood in a kind of grove open only upon the side which fronted the high-road and the green on which the people were seated. At this green or open place was a junction of five roads, two or three of which appeared to be very public ones. After we had done examining this place of worship, we desired to return, but instead of conducting us to the water-side, as we expected, they struck into a road leading into the country. The road, which was about sixteen feet broad and as level as a bowling-green, seemed to be a very public one, there being many other roads from different parts leading into it, all enclosed on each side with neat fences made of reeds, and shaded from the scorching sun by fruit trees. I thought I was transplanted into the most fertile plains in Europe. There was not an inch of waste ground; the roads occupied no more space than was absolutely necessary, the fences did not take up above four inches each, and even this was not wholly lost, for in many were planted some useful trees or plants. It was everywhere the same; change of place altered not the scene. Nature, assisted by a little art, nowhere appears in more splendour than at this isle. In these delightful walks we met numbers of people. They all gave us the road by turning either to the right or left, and sitting down, or standing, with their backs to the fences, till we had passed.

On our return I happened to go down with Attago to the landing-place, and there found Mr. Wales in a laughable though distressed situation. The boats which brought us on shore not being able to get near the landing-place for want of a sufficient depth of water, he pulled off his shoes and stockings to walk through; and as soon as he got on dry land he put them down betwixt his legs to put on again, but they were instantly snatched away by a person behind him, who immediately mixed with the crowd. It was impossible for him to follow the man barefooted over the sharp coral rocks which compose the shore without having his feet cut to pieces. The boat was put back to the ship; his companions had each made his way through the crowd, and he left in this condition alone. Attago soon found out the thief, recovered his shoes and stockings, and set him at liberty.

The chief, probably thinking that we might want water on board, conducted us to a plantation hard by, and showed us a pool of fresh water, though we had not made any inquiry after any. I believe this to be the same that Tasman calls the *washing-place* for his kings and nobles.

Attago was very importunate with me to return again to this isle, and to bring with me cloth, axes, nails, etc., telling me I should have hogs, fowls, fruit, and roots in abundance. He particularly desired me, more than once, to bring him such a suit of clothes as I had on, which was my uniform. This good-natured islander was very serviceable to me on many occasions during our short stay. He was always ready, either on board or on shore, to do me all the service in his power; his fidelity was rewarded at a small expense, and I found my account in having such a friend.

At ten o'clock on the 7th we got under sail; but as our decks were much encumbered with fruit, etc., we kept plying under the land till they were cleared. The supplies we got at this isle were about 150 pigs, twice that number of fowls, as many bananas and cocoa-nuts as we could find room for, with a few yams; and had our stay been longer, we, no doubt, might have got a great deal more. This in some degree shows the fertility of the island, of which, together with the neighbouring one of Middleburg, I shall now give a more particular account.

These islands were first discovered by Captain Tasman in January 1642-3, and by him called Amsterdam and Middleburg. But the former is called by the natives Tongatabu, and the latter Ea-oo-wee. Middleburg is about ten leagues in circuit; the skirts of the isle are mostly taken up in the plantations. The interior parts are but little cultivated, though very fit for cultivation. However, the want of it added greatly to the beauty of the isle; for here are, agreeably dispersed, groves of cocoa-nuts and other trees, lawns covered with thick grass, here and there plantations, and paths leading to every part of the island, in such beautiful disorder as greatly enlivens the prospect.

This island, and also that of Amsterdam, is guarded from the sea by a reef of coral rocks extending out from the shore one hundred fathoms more or less. On this reef the force of the sea is spent before it reaches the land or shore. Indeed, this is in some measure the situation of all the tropical isles in this sea that I have seen; and thus nature has effectually secured them from the encroachments of the sea, though many of them are mere points when compared to this vast ocean.

The island of Amsterdam, or Tongatabu, is wholly laid out in plantations, in which are planted some of the richest productions of nature, such as bread-fruit, cocoa-nut trees, plantains, bananas, shaddocks, yams and some other roots, sugar-cane, and a fruit like a nectarine, called by them *fighega*, and at Otaheite *ahuya*. In short, here are most of the articles which the Society Isles produce, besides some which they have not. And I probably have added to their stock of vegetables by leaving with them an assortment of garden seeds, pulse, etc. Bread-fruit here, as well as at all the other isles, was not in season.

The produce and cultivation of Middleburg is the same as at Amsterdam, with this difference, that a part only of the former is cultivated, whereas the whole of the latter is. The lanes or roads necessary for travelling are laid out in so judicious a manner as to open a free and easy communication from one part of the island to the other. Here are no towns or villages; most of the houses are built in the plantations. They are neatly constructed, but do not exceed those in the other isles. Their household furniture consists of a few wooden platters, cocoa-nut shells, and some neat wooden pillows shaped like four-footed stools or forms. Their common clothing, with the addition of a mat, serves them for bedding.

We saw no other domestic animals amongst them but hogs and fowls. We saw no dogs, and believe they have none, as they were exceedingly desirous of these we had on board. My friend Attago was complimented with a dog and a bitch, the one from New Zealand, the other from Ulietea. The name of a dog with them is gooree, the same as at New Zealand, which shows that they are not wholly strangers to them. We saw no rats, nor any other wild quadrupeds, except small lizards. The land birds are pigeons, turtle-doves, parrots, paroquets, owls, baldcouts with a blue plumage, a variety of small birds, and large bats in abundance. The produce of the sea we know but little of. It is reasonable to suppose that the same sorts of fish are found here as at the other isles. Their fishing instruments are the same—that is, hooks made of mother of pearl, gigs with two, three, or more prongs, and nets made of a very fine thread, with the meshes wrought exactly like ours. But nothing can be a more demonstrative evidence of their ingenuity than the construction and make of their canoes, which in point of neatness and workmanship exceed everything of this kind we saw in this sea. They are built of several pieces, sewed together with bandage, in so neat a manner that on the outside it is difficult to see the joints. All the fastenings are on the inside, and pass through cants or ridges, which are wrought on the edges and ends of the several boards which compose the vessel for that purpose. They are of two kinds—namely, double and single. The single ones are from 20 to 30 feet long, and about 20 or 22 inches broad in the middle. The stern terminates in a point, and the head something like the point of a wedge. At each end is a kind of deck. In some the middle of the deck is decorated with a row of white shells stuck on little pegs, wrought out of the same piece which composes it. These canoes have all outriggers, and are sometimes navigated with sails, but more generally with paddles, the blades of which are short, and broadest in the middle.

The two vessels which compose the double canoe are each about 60 or 70 feet long and four or five broad in the middle, and each terminates nearly in a point, so that the body or hull differs a little in construction from the single canoe, but is put together exactly in the same manner; these having a rising in the middle round the open part in the form of a long trough, which is made of boards closely fitted together, and well secured to the body of the vessel. Two such vessels are fastened to and parallel to each other, about six or seven feet asunder, by strong cross beams, secured by bandages to the upper part of the risings above mentioned. Over these beams and others is laid a boarded platform. All the parts which compose the double canoe are made as strong and light as the nature of the work will admit, and may be immerged in water to the very platform without being in danger of filling. Nor is it possible, under any circumstances whatever, for them to sink, so long as they hold together. Thus they are not only made vessels of burden, but fit for distant navigation. They are rigged with one mast, which steps upon the platform, and can easily be raised or taken down. The sail is made of mats; the rope they make use of is laid exactly like ours, and some of it is four or five inch. On the platform is built a little shed or hut, which screens the crew from the sun and weather. They also carry a movable fire-hearth, which is a square but shallow trough of wood filled with stones.

Their working tools are made of stone, bone, shells, etc., as at the other islands. When we view the work which is performed with these tools, we are struck with admiration at the ingenuity and patience of the workman.

Both men and women are of a common size with Europeans, and their colour is that of a lightish copper. They are active, brisk, and lively. The women in particular are the merriest creatures I ever met with, and will keep chattering by one's side without the least invitation or consideration whether they are understood, provided one does but seem pleased with them. Their hair in general is black, but more especially that of the women. Both sexes wear it short.

How these people amuse themselves in their leisure hours I cannot say, as we are but little acquainted with their diversions.

The women frequently entertained us with songs in a manner which was agreeable enough. They accompanied the music by snapping their fingers, so as to keep time to it. Not only their voices but their music was very harmonious, and they have a considerable compass in their notes.

The common method of saluting one another is by touching or meeting noses, as is done in New Zealand; and their sign of peace to strangers is the displaying a white flag or flags—at least such were displayed to us when we first drew near the shore. But the people who came first on board brought with them some of the pepper plant, and sent it before them into the ship; a stranger sign of friendship than which one could not wish for.

They have a singular custom of putting everything you give them to their heads, by way of thanks as we conjectured. This manner of paying a compliment is taught them from their very infancy, for when we gave things to little children the mother lifted up the child's hand to its head.

A still more singular custom prevails in these isles. We observed that the greater part of the people, both men and women, had lost one or both of their little fingers. We endeavoured, but in vain, to find out the reason of this mutilation, for no one would take any pains to inform us. It was peculiar neither to rank, age, nor sex; nor is it done at any certain age, as I saw those of all ages on whom the amputation had just been made. They also burn or make incisions in their cheeks near the cheekbone. The reason of this was equally unknown to us. In some the wounds were quite fresh, in others they could only be known by the scars or colour of the skin. I saw neither sick nor lame amongst them. All appeared healthy, strong, and vigorous; a proof of the goodness of the climate in which they live.

I am of opinion that this government is much like that of Otaheite—that is, in a king or great chief, who is here called Areeke, with other chiefs under him, who are lords of certain districts, and perhaps sole proprietors, to whom the people seem to pay great obedience. I also observed a third rank, who had not a little authority over the common people; my friend Attago was one of these. I am of opinion that all the land on Tongatabu is private property, and that there are here, as at Otaheite, a set of people who are servants or slaves, and have no property in hand. It is unreasonable to suppose everything in common in a country so highly cultivated as this. Interest being the greatest spring which animates the hand of industry, few would toil in cultivating and planting the land if they did not expect to reap the fruit of their labour; were it otherwise, the industrious man would be in a worse state than the idle sluggard. Though benevolent nature has been very bountiful to these isles, it cannot be said that the inhabitants are wholly exempt from the curse of our forefathers; part of their bread must be earned with the sweat of their brows. The high state of cultivation their lands are in must have cost them immense labour. This is now amply rewarded by the great produce, of which every one seems to partake. No one wants the common necessaries of life; joy and contentment are painted in every face. Indeed, it can hardly be otherwise. An easy freedom prevails among all ranks of people; they feel no wants which they do not enjoy the means of gratifying; and they live in a clime where the painful extremes of heat and cold are equally unknown. If nature has been wanting in anything, it is in the article of fresh water, which, as it is shut up in the bowels of the earth, they are obliged to dig for. A running stream was not seen, and but one well, at Amsterdam. At Middleburg we saw no water but that the natives had in vessels; but as it was sweet and cool, I had no doubt of its being taken up upon the island.

So little do we know of their religion that I hardly dare mention it. The buildings called Asiatoncas, before mentioned, are undoubtedly set apart for this purpose. Some of our gentlemen were of opinion that they were merely burying-places. I can only say, from my own knowledge, that they are places to which particular persons directed set speeches, which I understood to be prayers, as hath been already related. Joining my opinion with that of others, I was inclined to think that they are set apart to be both temples and burying-places, as at Otaheite, or even in Europe. But I have no idea of the images being idols, not only from what I saw myself, but from Mr. Wales informing me that they set one of them up for him and others to shoot at.

It cannot be supposed that we could know much either of their civil or religious policy in so short a time as four or five days, especially as we understood but little of their language. Even the two islanders we had on board could not at first understand them; and yet as we became the more acquainted with them we found their language was nearly the same spoken at Otaheite and the Society Isles, the difference not being greater than what we find betwixt the most northern and western parts of England.

CHAPTER XXV.

PASSAGE FROM AMSTERDAM TO QUEEN CHARLOTTE'S SOUND, WITH AN ACCOUNT OF AN INTERVIEW WITH THE INHABITANTS, AND THE FINAL SEPARATION OF THE TWO SHIPS—TRANSACTIONS IN QUEEN CHARLOTTE'S SOUND, WITH AN ACCOUNT OF THE INHABITANTS BEING CANNIBALS, AND VARIOUS OTHER INCIDENTS—DEPARTURE FROM THE SOUND, AND OUR ENDEAVOURS TO FIND THE "ADVENTURE," WITH SOME DESCRIPTION OF THE COAST.

1773.
October.

ON Thursday, the 7th of October, we made sail to the southward, having a gentle gale at SE. by E., it being my intention to proceed directly to Queen Charlotte's Sound in New Zealand, there to take in wood and water, and then to go on further discoveries to the south and east. In the afternoon of the 8th we made the island of Pilstart, discovered by Tasman.

At five o'clock in the morning of the 21st we made the land of New Zealand. I was very desirous of having some intercourse with the natives of this country as far to the north as possible, that is about Poverty or Tolago Bays, where I apprehended they were more civilized than at Queen Charlotte's Sound, in order to give them some hogs, fowls, seeds, roots, etc., which I had provided for the purpose.

We continued our course along shore, past Cape Kidnappers, till nine o'clock, when being about three leagues short of Blackhead, we saw some canoes put off from the shore. Those in the first canoe were fishers, and exchanged some fish for pieces of cloth and nails. In the next were two men, whom by their dress and behaviour I took to be chiefs. These two were easily prevailed on to come on board. To the principal of them I gave pigs, fowls, seeds, and roots. He made me a promise not to kill the pigs and fowls, and if he keeps his word and proper care is taken of them, there were enough to stock the whole island in due time, being two boars, two sows, four hens, two cocks. The seeds were such as are most useful—namely, wheat, French and kidney beans, peas, cabbage, turnips, onions, carrots, parsnips, and yams. With these articles they were dismissed. It was evident these people had not forgot the *Endeavour* being on their coast, for the first words they spoke to us were, "*Matou no te pow pow*" (we are afraid of the guns). At eleven o'clock on the 23rd we were close in with Cape Turnagain, and at noon on the 24th Cape Palliser bore west, distant eight or nine leagues. This cape is the southern point of Eaheinomauwe.

On the 29th the wind shifted to SW. We were now about three leagues from the cape, and we began to reckon what time we should reach the sound the next day. But at nine the wind shifted to its old quarter, NW., and blew a fresh gale, with which we stretched to the SW., with the *Adventure* in company. She was seen until midnight, at which time she was two or three miles astern, and presently after she disappeared; nor was she to be seen at daylight. We supposed she had tacked and stood to the NE., by which manœuvre we lost sight of her.

We continued to stretch to the westward, with the wind at NNW., which increased in such a manner as to bring us under two courses, after splitting a new maintop-sail. At noon Cape Campbell bore W. by N., distant seven or eight leagues. At three in the afternoon the gale began to abate and to veer more to the north, so that we fetched in with the land, under the Snowy Mountains, about four or five leagues to windward of the Lookers-on, where there was the appearance of a large bay.

I now regretted the loss of the *Adventure*, for had she been with me I should have given up all thoughts of going to Queen Charlotte's Sound to wood and water, and have sought for a place to get these articles farther south, as the wind was now favourable for ranging along the coast. But our separation made it necessary for me to repair to the sound, that being the place of rendezvous.

On the 1st of November we passed Cape Campbell and entered the strait with a brisk gale astern, and so likely to continue that we thought of nothing less than reaching our port the next morning. Once more we were to be deceived. At six o'clock, being off Cloudy Bay, our favourable wind was succeeded by one from the north-west, which increased to a fresh gale. We spent the night plying. Our tacks proved disadvantageous, and

Nov.

we lost more on the ebb than we gained on the flood. Next morning we stretched over for the shore of Eaheinomauwe. At sunrise, the horizon being extraordinarily clear to leeward, we looked well out for the *Adventure*, but as we saw nothing of her, judged she had got into the sound.

On the 2nd of November we hauled up into the sound just at dark, after making two boards, in which most of our sails were split, and anchored in eighteen fathoms water. The next day we weighed and ran up into Ship Cove, where we did not find the *Adventure* as was expected.

The first thing we did, after mooring the ship, was to unbend all the sails, there not being one but what wanted repair. Indeed both our sails and rigging had suffered much damage in beating off the strait's mouth.

We had no sooner anchored than we were visited by the natives, several of whom I remembered to have seen when I was here in the *Endeavour*, particularly an old man named Goubiah.

Most of our bread being in casks, I ordered some to be opened, when, to our mortification, we found a good deal of it damaged. To repair this loss in the best manner we could, all the casks were opened, the bread was picked, and the copper oven set up to bake such parcels of it as, by that means, could be recovered.

Here I saw the youngest of the two sows Captain Furneaux had put on shore in Cannibal Cove when we were last here; it was lame of one of its hind-legs, otherwise in good case and very tame. If we understood these people right, the boar and the other sow were also taken away and separated, but not killed. We were likewise told that the two goats I had put on shore up the sound had been killed by that old rascal Goubiah. Thus all our endeavours to stock this country with useful animals were likely to be frustrated by the very people we meant to serve. Our gardens had fared somewhat better. Everything in them, except the potatoes, they had left entirely to nature, who had acted her part so well that we found most articles in a flourishing state, a proof that the winter must have been mild. The potatoes had most of them been dug up; some, however, still remained, and were growing, though I think it is probable they will never be got out of the ground.

Next morning I went over to the cove where the natives reside, to haul the seine, and took with me a boar and a young sow, two cocks and two hens, we had brought from the isles. These I gave to the natives, being persuaded they would take proper care of them by their keeping Captain Furneaux's sow near five months; for I am to suppose it was caught soon after we sailed. We had no good success with the seine; nevertheless we did not return on board quite empty, having purchased a large quantity from the natives.

When we were upon this traffic, they showed a great inclination to pick my pockets, and to take away the fish with one hand which they had just given me with the other. This evil one of the chiefs undertook to remove, and with fury in his eyes made a show of keeping the people at a proper distance. I applauded his conduct, but at the same time kept so good a lookout as to detect him in picking my pocket of a handkerchief, which I suffered him to put in his bosom before I seemed to know anything of the matter, and then told him what I had lost. He seemed quite ignorant and innocent, till I took it from him, and then he put it off with a laugh, acting his part with so much address that it was hardly possible for me to be angry with him, so that we remained good friends and he accompanied me on board to dinner.

The 15th being a pleasant morning, a party of us went over to East Bay and climbed one of the hills, which overlooked the eastern part of the strait, in order to look for the *Adventure*. We had a fatiguing walk to little purpose, for when we came to the summit we found the horizon so foggy that we could not see above two miles. I now began to despair of seeing the *Adventure* any more; but was totally at a loss to conceive what was become of her. Till now I thought she had put into some port in the strait, when the wind came to NW., the day we anchored in the cove, and waited to complete her water. This conjecture was reasonable enough at first, but it was now hardly probable she could be twelve days in our neighbourhood without our either hearing or seeing something of her.

The hill we now mounted is the same that I was upon in 1770, when I had the second view of the strait; we then built a tower with the stones we found there, which we now saw had been levelled to the ground, no doubt by the natives with a view of finding something hid in it.

On the 22nd I took four hogs (that is, three sows and one boar), two cocks and two hens, which I landed in the bottom of the West Bay, carrying them a little way into the woods, where we left them with as much food as would serve them ten or twelve days. We also left some cocks and hens in the woods in Ship Cove, but these will have a chance of falling into the hands of the natives, whose wandering way of life will hinder them from breeding, even suppose they should be taken proper care of. Indeed they took rather too much care of those which I had already given them, by keeping them continually confined, for fear of losing them in the woods. The sow pig we had not seen since the day they had her from me; but we were now told she was still living, as also the old boar and sow given them by Captain Furneaux, so that there is reason to hope they may succeed. It will be unfortunate, indeed, if every method I have taken to provide this country with useful animals should be frustrated. We were likewise told that the two goats were still alive and running about; but I gave more credit to the first story than this. I should have replaced them by leaving behind the other two I had left, but had the misfortune to lose the ram soon after our arrival here. After this it would have been vain to leave the she-goat. Thus the reader will see how every method I have taken to stock this country with sheep and goats has proved ineffectual.

Calm or light airs from the north all day on the 23rd hindered us from putting to sea as intended. In the afternoon some of the officers went on shore to amuse themselves among the natives, where they saw the head and bowels of a youth, who had been lately killed, lying on the beach; and the heart stuck on a forked stick, which was fixed to the head of one of the largest canoes. One of the gentlemen bought the head and brought it on board, where a piece of the flesh was broiled and eaten by one of the natives before all the officers and most of the men. I was on shore at this time, but soon after returning on board was informed of the above circumstances, and found the quarter-deck crowded with natives, and the mangled head lying on the tafferel.

The sight of the head and the relation of the above circumstance struck me with horror, and filled my mind with indignation against these cannibals. Curiosity, however, got the better of my indignation, especially when I considered that it would avail but little; and being desirous of becoming an eye-witness of a fact which many doubted, I ordered a piece of the flesh to be broiled and brought to the quarter-deck, where one of these cannibals ate it with surprising avidity. This had such an effect on some of our people as to make them sick. Oedidee (who came on board with me) was so affected with the sight as to become perfectly motionless, and seemed as if metamorphosed into the statue of horror. It is utterly impossible for art to describe that passion with half the force that it appeared in his countenance. When roused from this state by some of us, he burst into tears, continued to weep and scold by turns, told them they were evil men, and that he neither was nor would be any longer their friend. He even would not suffer them to touch him. He used the same language to one of the gentlemen who cut off the flesh, and refused to accept, or even touch, the knife with which it was done. Such was Oedidee's indignation against the vile custom; and worthy of imitation by every rational being.

That the New Zealanders are cannibals can now no longer be doubted. The account given of this in my former voyage,* being partly founded on circumstances, was, as I afterwards understood, discredited by many persons. Few consider what a savage man is in his natural state, and even after he is, in some degree, civilized. The New Zealanders are certainly in some state of civilization; their behaviour to us was manly and mild, showing on all occasions a readiness to oblige. This custom of eating their enemies slain in battle (for I firmly believe they eat the flesh of no others) has undoubtedly been handed down to them from the earliest times; and we know it is not an easy matter to wean a nation from their ancient customs, let these be ever so inhuman and savage, especially if that nation has no manner of connection or commerce with strangers. For it is by this that the greatest part of the human race has been civilized. An intercourse with foreigners would reform their manners and polish their savage minds. At present they have but little idea of treating others as

* See page 110.

themselves would *wish* to be treated, but treat them as they *expect* to be treated. If I remember right, one of the arguments they made use of to Tupia, who frequently expostulated with them against this custom, was that there could be no harm in killing and eating the man who would do the same by them if it were in his power. "For," said they, "can there be any harm in eating our enemies whom we have killed in battle? Would not these very enemies have done the same to us?" I have often seen them listen to Tupia with great attention, but I never found he could persuade any one of them that this custom was wrong. And when Oedidee and several of our people showed their abhorrence of it, they only laughed at them.

Among many reasons which I have heard assigned for the prevalence of this horrid custom, the want of animal food has been one; but how far this is deducible either from facts or circumstances, I shall leave those to find out who advanced it. In every part of New Zealand where I have been, fish was in such plenty that the natives generally caught as much as served both themselves and us. They have also plenty of dogs, nor is there any want of wild fowl; so that neither this nor the want of food of any kind can, in my opinion, be the reason.

During our stay in the sound we were plentifully supplied with fish; and besides the vegetables our own gardens afforded, we found everywhere plenty of scurvy-grass and celery, which I caused to be dressed every day for all hands. By this means they had been mostly on a fresh diet for the three preceding months, and at this time we had neither a sick nor scorbutic man on board.

The morning before we sailed I wrote a memorandum, setting forth the time we last arrived, the day we sailed, the route I intended to take, and such other information as I thought necessary for Captain Furneaux, in case he should put into the sound, and buried it in a bottle under the root of a tree in the garden, in such a manner as must be found by him or any European who might put into the cove.

I was resolved not to leave the coast without looking for her, where I thought it most likely for her to be. It was with this view that I stood over for Cape Terawite, and afterwards ran along shore, from point to point, to Cape Palliser, firing guns every half-hour; but all to no effect.

At daylight on the 26th we made sail round Cape Palliser, firing guns as usual as we ran along the shore. In this manner we proceeded till, the wind shifting to NE., we bore away for Cape Campbell on the other side of the strait, every one being unanimously of opinion that the *Adventure* could neither be stranded on the coast nor be in any of the harbours thereof. I gave up looking for her, and all thoughts of seeing her any more during the voyage, as no rendezvous was absolutely fixed upon after leaving New Zealand.

On our quitting the coast, and consequently all hopes of being joined by our consort, I had the satisfaction to find that not a man was dejected, or thought the dangers we had yet to go through were in the least increased by being alone; but as cheerfully proceeding to the south, or wherever I might think proper to lead them, as if the *Adventure* or even more ships had been in our company.

CHAPTER XXVI.

ROUTE OF THE SHIP FROM NEW ZEALAND IN SEARCH OF A CONTINENT, WITH AN ACCOUNT OF VARIOUS OBSTRUCTIONS MET WITH FROM THE ICE, AND THE METHODS PURSUED TO EXPLORE THE SOUTHERN PACIFIC OCEAN—PASSAGE TO EASTER ISLAND AND TRANSACTIONS THERE—PASSAGE FROM EASTER ISLAND TO THE MARQUESAS ISLANDS—DEPARTURE FROM THE MARQUESAS.

1773.
Nov.

Dec.

AT eight o'clock in the evening of the 26th we took our departure from Cape Palliser and steered to the south. We daily saw some rock-weeds, seals, Port Egmont hens, albatrosses, pintadoes and other petrels; and on the 2nd of December, being in the latitude of 48° 23' S., longitude 179° 16' W., we saw a number of red-billed penguins. At half an hour past eight o'clock on the 6th, we reckoned ourselves antipodes to our friends in London, consequently as far removed from them as possible.

On Saturday the 11th the mercury in the thermometer fell to 32°, consequently the weather was very cold and seemed to indicate that ice was not far off. We fell in with several large islands on the 14th, and about noon with a quantity of loose ice, through which we sailed. But as it blew strong, and the weather at times was exceedingly foggy, it was necessary for us to get clear of this loose ice. It was not such ice as is usually found in bays or rivers and near shore, but such as breaks off from islands; but before we got clear of this loose ice, we had received several knocks from the larger pieces, which with all our care we could not avoid. After clearing one danger we still had another to encounter; for many large islands lay in our way, so that we had to luff for one and bear up for another. These difficulties, together with the improbability of finding land farther south, and the impossibility of exploring it on account of the ice, determined me to get more to the north.

We continued to stand to the north till the 16th, when we stretched to the SE., having thick hazy weather, with snow showers, and all our rigging covered with ice.

Steering south again till the 20th, we came, the second time, within the antarctic or polar circle. The ice islands we now met with were very high and rugged, forming at their tops many peaks; many of them were between two and three hundred feet in height, and between two and three miles in circuit, with perpendicular cliffs or sides astonishing to behold.

The 22nd we steered ESE., with a fresh gale at north, blowing in squalls, one of which took hold of the mizzentop-sail, tore it all to rags, and rendered it for ever after useless. At four o'clock in the afternoon of the 22nd, in the latitude of 67° 20′, longitude 137° 12′, we fell in with such a quantity of field or loose ice as covered the sea, and was so thick and close as wholly to obstruct our passage. The shivers were frozen so fast in the blocks that it required our utmost efforts to get a top-sail down and up, the cold so intense as hardly to be endured, with a hard gale and a thick fog. Under all these unfavourable circumstances, it was natural for me to think of returning more to the north.

We spent Christmas day much in the same manner as we did the preceding one. We were fortunate in having continual daylight and clear weather, for had it been as foggy as on some of the preceding days, nothing less than a miracle could have saved us from being dashed to pieces.

While we were in the high latitudes, many of our people were attacked with a slight fever occasioned by colds, but it happily yielded to the simplest remedies.

On the 26th we came, the third time, within the antarctic polar circle in the longitude 109° 31′ W. About noon, seeing the appearance of land to the SE., we immediately trimmed our sails and stood towards it. Soon after it disappeared, and we were well assured that it was nothing but clouds or a fog bank.

On the 30th, at four o'clock in the morning, we perceived the clouds to be of an unusual snow-white brightness, which we knew announced our approach to field-ice. Soon after, it was seen from the topmast-head; and at eight o'clock we were close to its edge. Ninety-seven ice hills were distinctly seen within the field, many of them very large, and looking like ridges of mountains, rising one above another till they were lost in the clouds.

The outer or northern edge of this immense field was composed of loose or broken ice close packed together, so that it was not possible for anything to enter it. This was about a mile broad, within which was solid ice in one continued compact body. It was rather low and flat, but seemed to increase in height as you traced it to the south. Such mountains of ice as these were, I believe, never seen in the Greenland seas—at least not that I ever heard or read of—so that we cannot draw a comparison between the ice here and there. It must be allowed that these prodigious ice mountains must add such additional weight to the ice fields which enclose them as cannot but make a great difference between navigating this icy sea and that of Greenland.

I will not say it was impossible anywhere to get farther to the south; but the attempting it would have been a dangerous and rash enterprise, and what, I believe, no man in my situation would have thought of. It was indeed *my* opinion, as well as the opinion of most on board, that this ice extended quite to the pole, or perhaps joined to some land, to which it had been fixed from the earliest time; and that it is here—that is, to the south of this parallel—where all the ice we find scattered up and down to the north is first formed, and afterwards broken off by gales of wind and other causes and brought to the north by the currents, which we always found to set in that direction in high latitudes. As we drew near this ice some penguins were heard, but none seen; and but few other birds or any other thing that could induce us to think any land was near. And yet I think there must be some to the south behind this ice; but if there is, it can afford no better retreat for birds or any other animal than the ice itself, with which it must be wholly covered.

I, who had ambition not only to go farther than any one had been before, but as far as it was possible for man to go, was not sorry at meeting with this interruption, as it, in some measure, relieved us—at least, shortened the dangers and hardships inseparable from the navigation of the southern polar regions. Since, therefore, we could not proceed one inch farther to the south, no other reason need be assigned for my tacking and standing back to the north, being at this time in the latitude of 71° 10' S., longitude 106° 54' W.

But for me at this time to have quitted altogether this Southern Pacific Ocean, with a good ship expressly sent out on discoveries, a healthy crew, and not in want either of stores or of provisions, would have been betraying not only a want of perseverance but of judgment, in supposing the South Pacific Ocean to have been so well explored that nothing remained to be done in it. This, however, was not my opinion; for although I had proved there was no continent but what must lie far to the south, there remained room for very large islands in places wholly unexamined, and I was of opinion that my remaining in this sea some time longer would be productive of improvements in navigation and geography as well as other sciences. My intention was first to go in search of Easter Island or Davis' Land, whose situation was known with so little certainty. I next intended to get within the tropic, and then proceed to the west till we arrived at Otaheite, where it was necessary I should stop to look for the *Adventure*. I intended if possible to be the length of Cape Horn in November next, when we should have the best part of the summer before us to explore the southern part of the Atlantic Ocean.

Great as this design appeared to be, I, however, thought it possible to be executed; and when I came to communicate it to the officers, I had the satisfaction to find that they all heartily concurred in it. I should not do these gentlemen justice if I did not take some opportunity to declare that they always showed the utmost readiness to carry into execution, in the most effectual manner, every measure I thought proper to take. Under such circumstances, it is hardly necessary to say that the seamen were always obedient and alert; and on this occasion they were so far from wishing the voyage at an end, that they rejoiced at the prospect of its being prolonged another year, and of soon enjoying the benefits of a milder climate.

As we advanced to the north, we felt a most sensible change in the weather, and the mercury in the thermometer rose to 66°.

On the 25th I was taken ill of the bilious colic, which confined me to my bed; so that the management of the ship was left to Mr. Cooper, the first officer, who conducted her very much to my satisfaction. It was several days before the most dangerous symptoms of my disorder were removed, during which time Mr. Patten the surgeon was to me not only a skilful physician, but an affectionate nurse; and I should ill deserve the care he bestowed on me if I did not make this public acknowledgment. When I began to recover, a favourite dog belonging to Mr. Forster fell a sacrifice to my tender stomach. We had no other fresh meat whatever on board; and I could eat of this flesh, as well as broth made of it, when I could taste nothing else. Thus I received nourishment and strength from food which would have made most people in Europe sick; so true it is that necessity is governed by no law.

We were now meeting every day with great numbers of birds, such as men-of-war, tropic and egg birds, noddies, sheerwaters, etc.; and once we passed several pieces of sponge and a small dried leaf not unlike a bay one. We also saw plenty of fish, but were such bad fishers that we caught only four albacores, which were very acceptable, to me especially, who was just recovering from my late illness.

1774. At eight o'clock in the morning of the 11th, land was March. seen from the mast-head bearing west. I made no doubt that this was Davis' Land or Easter Island. On Monday the 14th we anchored, and I went ashore, accompanied by some of the gentlemen, to see what the island was likely to afford us. We landed at the sandy beach, where some hundreds of natives were assembled; not one of them had so much as a stick or weapon of any sort in his hand. After distributing a few trinkets amongst them, we made signs for something to eat; on which they brought down a few potatoes, plantains, and sugar-canes.

We presently discovered they were expert thieves. It was with some difficulty we could keep the hats on our heads, but hardly possible to keep anything in our pockets, for they would watch every opportunity to snatch it from us, so that we sometimes bought the same thing two or three times over, and after all did not get it.

The country appeared barren and without wood; there were nevertheless several plantations of potatoes, plantains, and sugarcanes. We also saw some fowls, and found a well of brackish water. I resolved therefore to stay a day or two. But there can be few

WOMAN OF EASTER ISLAND.

STATUES ON EASTER ISLAND.

places which offer less convenience for shipping than it does. Here is no safe anchorage, no wood for fuel, nor any fresh water worth taking on board. Nature has been exceedingly sparing of her favours to this spot.

The inhabitants do not seem to exceed 600 or 700 souls. In colour, features, and language, they bear such affinity to the people of the more western isles, that no one will doubt that they have the same origin. Their clothing is a piece or two of quilted cloth about six feet by four, or a mat; but the men for the most part are almost naked. Their hair in general is black; the women wear it long, and sometimes tied up on the crown of the head. Both men and women have very large holes or rather slits in their ears, extending to near three inches in length.

Their houses are low miserable huts, constructed by setting sticks upright in the ground, at six or eight feet distance, then bending them towards each other and tying them together at the top, forming thereby a kind of Gothic arch. The whole is thatched over with leaves of sugar-cane. The doorway is in the middle of one side, formed like a porch, and so low and narrow as just to admit a man to enter on all fours.

The east side of the island is full of gigantic statues, some placed in groups on platforms of masonry, others single, fixed only in the earth. Having measured one that had fallen down we found it very near twenty-seven feet long and upwards of eight feet over the breast or shoulders, and yet this appeared considerably short of the size of one we saw standing. The workmanship is rude, but not bad; nor are the features of the face ill formed, the nose and chin in particular; but as to the bodies there is hardly anything like a human figure about them.

We could hardly conceive how these islanders, wholly unacquainted with any mechanical power, could raise such stupendous figures, and afterwards place the large cylindric stones upon their heads.

They gave different names to them, such as Gotomoara, Marapate, Goway-too-goo, Matta Matta, etc., to which they sometimes prefix the word Moi, and sometimes annex Areekee. The latter signifies chief, and the former burying or sleeping place, as well as we could understand.

After leaving Easter Island I steered NW. by N., intending to touch at the Marquesas, if I met with nothing before I got there.

April. I continued to steer to the west till the 6th of April, when in the latitude of 9° 20', longitude 138° 14' W., we discovered an island; two hours after we saw another, and next morning a third. I was well assured these were the Marquesas, discovered by Mendana in 1595.

The first isle was a new discovery, which I named Hood's Island, after the young gentleman who first saw it; the second was that of St. Pedro, the third La Dominica, and the fourth S. Christina.

We had no sooner anchored in the entrance of a bay of S. Christina than thirty or forty of the natives came off to us in ten or twelve canoes. We observed a heap of stones in the bow of each canoe, and every man to have a sling tied round his hand.

Next morning they visited us in greater numbers, bringing with them bread-fruit, plantains, and one pig, all of which they exchanged for nails, etc. But in this traffic they would frequently keep our goods and make no return, till at last I was obliged to fire a musket ball over one man who had several times served us in this manner, after which they dealt more fairly.

But when I found this island was not likely to supply us, on any conditions, with sufficient refreshments, such as we might expect at the Society Isles, nor very convenient for taking in wood and water, nor for giving the ship the necessary repairs she wanted, I resolved forthwith to leave it and proceed to some other place where our wants might be effectually relieved. For after having been nineteen weeks at sea, and living all the time upon salt diet, we could not but want some refreshments; although I must own, and that with pleasure, that on our arrival here it could hardly be said we had one sick man.

We left the Madre de Dios, which I named Resolution Bay, at three o'clock in the afternoon of the 12th, and steered SW. for Otaheite.

On the 17th we found a string of low islets connected together by a reef of coral rocks. We ranged the NW. coast till we came to a creek or inlet that seemed to open a communication into the lake in the middle of the isle. This island, which is called by the natives Tiookea, was discovered and visited by Commodore Byron.

On the 18th we were down to another isle, which we found to be just such another as we had left. These must be the same islands to which Commodore Byron gave the name of George's Islands.

On the 19th, at seven in the morning, land was seen to the westward, and as we drew near we saw another of these low isles; soon after a second and a third appeared, and drawing near the west end we discovered a fourth. As we ranged along the coast we saw people, huts, canoes, and places built seemingly for the drying of fish. These four isles I called Palliser's Isles, in honour of my worthy friend Sir Hugh Palliser, at this time comptroller of the navy.

We made the high land of Otaheite on the 21st, and next morning anchored in Matavai Bay. This was no sooner known to the natives than many of them made us a visit, and expressed not a little joy at seeing us again. Our very good friends the natives supplied us with fruit and fish sufficient for the whole crew.

On the 24th Otoo the king and several other chiefs, with a train of attendants, paid us a visit and brought as presents ten or twelve large hogs, besides fruits, which made them exceedingly welcome. I was advertised of the king's coming, and looked upon it as a good omen. Knowing how much it was my interest to make this man my friend, I met him at the tents and conducted him and his friends on board in my boat, where they stayed to dinner; after which they were dismissed with suitable presents, and highly pleased with the reception they had met with.

Next day we had much thunder, lightning, and rain. This did not hinder the king from making me another visit and a present of a large quantity of refreshments. When we were at the island of Amsterdam we had collected some red parrot feathers. When this was known here, all the principal people of both sexes endeavoured to ingratiate themselves into our favour by bringing us hogs, fruit, and every other thing the island afforded, in order to obtain these valuable commodities. Our having these feathers was a fortunate circumstance, for as they were valuable to the natives, they became so to us, more especially as my stock of trade was by this time greatly exhausted, so that if it had not been for the feathers I should have found it difficult to have supplied the ship with the necessary refreshments.

In the morning of the 26th I went down to Oparree to pay Otoo a visit by appointment. As we drew near we observed a number of large canoes in motion, but were surprised when we arrived to see upwards of three hundred ranged in order for some distance along the shore, all completely equipped and manned, besides a vast number of armed men upon the shore.

We landed in the midst of them and were received by a vast multitude, many of them under arms and many not. The chief, we afterwards learned, was admiral or commander of the fleet and troops present.

The moment we landed I was met by a chief whose name was Tee, uncle to the king, of whom I inquired for Otoo.

Presently afterwards we were met by Towha, who received me with great courtesy. He took me by one hand and Tee by the other, and without my knowing where they intended to carry me, dragged me, as it were, through the crowd that was divided into two parties, both of which professed themselves my friends by crying out, "Tiyo no Tootee." One party wanted me to go to Otoo, and the other to remain with Towha. Coming to the usual place of audience, a mat was spread for me to sit down upon, and Tee left me to go and bring the king. Towha was unwilling I should sit down, partly insisting on my going with him, but as I knew nothing of this chief I refused to comply. Presently Tee returned and wanted to conduct me to the king, taking hold of my hand for the purpose. This Towha opposed, so that between the one party and the other I was like to have been torn in pieces, and was obliged to desire Tee to desist and to leave me to the admiral and his party, who conducted me down to the fleet. As soon as we came before the admiral's vessel, we found two lines of armed men drawn up before her to keep off the crowd, as I suppose, and to clear the way for me to go in. But as I was determined not to go, I made the water which was between me and her an excuse. This did not answer, for a man immediately squatted himself at my feet, offering to carry me; and then I declared I would not go. That very moment Towha quitted me without my seeing which way he went, nor would any one inform me. Turning myself round I saw Tee, who, I believe, had never lost sight of me. Inquiring of him for the king, he told me he was gone into the country

Mataou, and advised me to go to my boat, which we accordingly did.

When we got into our boat we took time to view this grand fleet. The vessels of war consisted of 160 large double canoes, very well equipped, manned, and armed. The chiefs and all those on the fighting stages were dressed in their war habits—that is, in a vast quantity of cloth, turbans, breastplates, and helmets. Their whole dress seemed to be ill calculated for the day of battle, and to be designed more for show than use. The vessels were decorated with flags, streamers, etc., so that the whole made a grand and noble appearance, such as we had never seen before in this sea, and what no one would have expected. Besides the vessels of war there were 170 sail of smaller double canoes, all with a little house upon them, and rigged with mast and sail, which the war canoes had not. In these 330 vessels I guessed there were no less than 7,760 men, a number which appears incredible.

After we had well viewed this fleet, I wanted much to have seen the admiral. We inquired for him as we rowed past the fleet; we also put ashore and inquired, but the noise and crowd was so great that no one attended to what we said. We accordingly proceeded to the ship. When we got to Matavai our friends there told us that this fleet was part of the armament intended to go against Eimeo, whose chief had thrown off the yoke of Otaheite and assumed an independency. We were likewise informed that Otoo neither was nor had been at Matavai. The reason of his not seeing me in the morning was that some of his people having stolen a quantity of my clothes, which were on shore washing, he was afraid I should demand restitution. He thought I was displeased when I refused to go aboard his vessel, and that I was jealous of seeing such a force in our neighbourhood without being able to know anything of its design. But matters were cleared up between us, and mutual presents soon passed between Otoo and me.

CHAPTER XXVII.

PREPARATIONS TO LEAVE THE ISLAND—THE ARRIVAL OF THE SHIP AT THE ISLAND OF HUAHEINE, WITH AN ACCOUNT OF SEVERAL INCIDENTS WHICH HAPPENED WHILE SHE LAY THERE—ARRIVAL AT ULIETEA.

1774.
April.
AS the most essential repairs of the ship were nearly finished, I resolved to leave Otaheite in a few days. Oedidee, I found, was desirous of remaining at this isle, having before told him that we should not return. I now mentioned to him that he was at liberty to remain here, or to quit us at Ulietea, or to go with us to England; frankly owning that if he chose the latter, it was very probable he would never return to his country, in which case I would take care of him, and he must afterwards look upon me as his father. He threw his arms about me and wept much, saying many people persuaded him to remain at Otaheite. He was well beloved in the ship, so that every one was persuading him to go with us, telling him what great things he would see in England, and the immense riches he would return with. But I thought proper to undeceive him, as knowing the only inducement to his going was the expectation of returning, and I could see no prospect of an opportunity of that kind happening. I thought it an act of the highest injustice to take a person from these isles under any promise which was not in my power to perform. Next morning, early, Oedidee came on board with a resolution to stay at the island, but Mr. Forster prevailed upon him to go with us to Ulietea.

May.
On the 14th of May we went with Otoo to one of his dockyards where the canoes were building, each of which was 108 feet long. They were almost ready to launch, and were intended to make one joint double canoe. The king begged of me a grappling and rope, to which I added an English jack and pendant, and desired the canoe might be called *Britannia*. This

he very readily agreed to, and she was named accordingly. After this he gave me a hog and a turtle of about sixty pounds weight, likewise a large shark they had poisoned in a creek; but the fine pork and fish we had got at this isle had spoiled our palates for such food.

The king and his prime minister Tee accompanied us on board to dinner, and after it was over took a most affectionate farewell. He hardly ever ceased soliciting me this day to return to Otaheite.

Our treatment at this isle was such as had induced one of our gunner's mates to form a plan to remain at it. He took the opportunity as soon as we were out, the boats in and sails set, to slip overboard, being a good swimmer. But he was discovered before he got clear of the ship, and we presently hoisted a boat out and took him up. When I considered this man's situation in life I did not think him so culpable, nor the resolution he had taken of staying here so extraordinary, as it may at first appear. He was an Irishman by birth, and had sailed in the Dutch service. I picked him up at Batavia, and he had been with me ever since. I never learned that he had either friends or connections to confine him to any particular part of the world. Where, then, could such a man be more happy than at one of these isles, where, in one of the finest climates in the world, he could enjoy not only the necessaries but the luxuries of life in ease and plenty? I know not if he might not have obtained my consent if he had applied for it in proper time. As soon as we had got him on board I steered for Huaheine, in order to pay a visit to our friends there.

But before we leave Otaheite it will be necessary to give some account of the present state of that island, especially as it differs very much from what it was eight months before. There were improvements in every part into which we came. It seemed to us almost incredible that so many large canoes and houses could be built in so short a space as eight months. The iron tools which they had got from the English had, no doubt, greatly accelerated the work. When I was last here I conceived but an unfavourable opinion of Otoo's talents. The improvements since made in the island convinced me of my mistake, and that he must be a man of good parts. But notwithstanding his kingly establishment, there was very little about Otoo's person or court by which a stranger could distinguish the king from the subject. He seemed to avoid all necessary pomp. All have free access to him, and speak to him wherever they see him without the least ceremony, such is the easy freedom which every individual of this happy isle enjoys.

I have occasionally mentioned the extraordinary fondness the people of Otaheite showed for red feathers. These they call *oona*, and they are as valuable here as jewels in Europe. These feathers they make up in little bunches and fix them to the end of a cord about three or four inches long, which is made of the strong outside fibres of the cocoa-nut, twisted so hard that it is like a wire and serves as a handle to the bunch. Thus prepared they are used as symbols of the *Eatuas* or divinities in all their religious ceremonies. I have often seen them hold one of these bunches and say a prayer, not one word of which could I ever understand. Whoever comes to this island will do well to provide himself with red feathers; he must also have a good stock of axes and hatchets, etc.

The two goats which Captain Furneaux gave to Otoo when we were last here seemed to promise fair for answering the end for which they were put on shore. The people seemed to be very fond of them, and they were in excellent condition. The sheep which we left died soon after, excepting one, which we understood was yet alive. We have also furnished them with a stock of cats, no less than twenty having been given away at this isle, besides what were left at Ulietea and Huaheine.

At one o'clock on the 15th of May we anchored in the entrance of Owharre Harbour in the island of Huaheine. Several of the natives soon made us a visit, amongst whom was old Oree the chief, who brought us a hog and other articles, which he presented to me with the usual ceremony. When I returned Oree's visit next morning and made my present to him, one article was red feathers. Two or three of these the chief took in his right hand, holding them up between his finger and thumb, and said a prayer, as I understood.

On the 18th, Oree came on board with a present of fruit, stayed dinner, and desired to see some great guns fired, which I complied with. The reason of his making this request was his hearing from Oedidee that we had so done at Otaheite.

Early on the morning of the 20th three of the officers set out on a shooting party, rather contrary to my inclination, as I found the natives were continually watching every opportunity to rob straggling parties, and were daily growing more daring. About three o'clock in the afternoon I got intelligence that they were seized and stripped of everything they had about them. Upon this I immediately went on shore with a boat's crew, and took possession of a large house with all its effects and two chiefs whom I found in it. In this situation I remained till I heard the officers had got back safe and had all their things restored to them. I learned from Oedidee in the evening that Oree was so much concerned at what had happened that he wept.

On the 23rd, early in the morning, we unmoored, and at eight weighed and put to sea. The good old chief was the last man who went out of the ship. At parting I told him we should see each other no more, at which he wept and said, " Let your sons come; we will treat them well." Oree is a good man in the utmost sense of the word.

As soon as we were clear of the harbour we made sail and stood over for the south end of Ulietea, dropping the anchor next day between two points of the reef which form the entrance to the harbour, each not more than two-thirds the length of a cable from us, and on which the sea broke with such height and violence as, to people less acquainted with the place, would have been terrible.

My old friend Oree the chief and several more soon came to see us. The chief came not empty. Early in the morning of the 27th, Oree, his wife, son, daughter, and several more of his friends, made us a visit and brought with them a good quantity of all manner of refreshments. They stayed dinner, after which a party of us accompanied them ashore, where a play was acted for the entertainment of such as would spend their time in looking at it. Besides these plays, which the chief caused frequently to be acted, there were a set of strolling players in the neighbourhood who performed every day. But their pieces seemed to be so much alike that we soon grew tired of them, especially as we could not collect any interesting circumstances from them. We, our ship, and our country were frequently brought on the stage, but on what account I know not.

As I could not premise, or even suppose, that more English

ships would be sent to these isles, our faithful companion, Oedidee, chose to remain in his native country. But he left us with a regret fully demonstrative of the esteem he bore to us; nor could anything but the fear of never returning have torn him from us. When the chief teased me so much about returning, I sometimes gave such answers as left them hopes. Oedidee would instantly catch at this, take me on one side, and ask me over again. In short, I have not words to describe the anguish which appeared in this young man's breast when he went away. He looked up at the ship, burst into tears, and then sank down into the canoe. The maxim that a prophet has no honour in his own country was never more fully verified than in this youth. At Otaheite he might have had anything that was in their power to bestow; whereas here he was not in the least noticed. Just as Oedidee was going out of the ship, he asked me to *tatou* some *parou* for him, in order to show the commanders of any other ships which might stop here. I complied with his request, gave him a certificate of the time he had been with us, and recommended him to the notice of those who might touch at the island after me.

June.

We did not get clear of our friends till eleven o'clock on the 4th of June, when we weighed and put to sea; but Oedidee did not leave us till we were almost out of the harbour. He stayed in order to fire some guns; for it being His Majesty's birthday, we fired the salute at going away. I had now got on board a plentiful supply of all manner of refreshments, so I directed my course to the west, taking final leave of these happy isles, on which benevolent nature has spread her luxuriant sweets with a lavish hand. The natives, copying the bounty of nature, are equally liberal, contributing plentifully and cheerfully to the wants of navigators. During the six weeks we had remained at them we had fresh pork, and all the fruits which were in season in the utmost profusion, besides fish at Otaheite and fowls at the other isles.

CHAPTER XXVIII.

PASSAGE FROM ULITEA TO NEW ZEALAND—DISCOVERY OF HOWE ISLAND, PALMERSTON ISLAND, SAVAGE ISLAND—RECEPTION AT ANNAMOOKA—THE PASSAGE FROM THE FRIENDLY ISLES TO THE NEW HEBRIDES—DISCOVERY OF TURTLE ISLAND AND THE ISLAND OF MALLICOLLO—ARRIVAL OF THE SHIP AT TANNA—RECEPTION.

ON the 6th, being the day after leaving Ulietea, at eleven o'clock a.m., we saw land, which upon a nearer approach we found to be a low reef island. It is composed of several small patches, connected together by breakers. This is Howe Island, discovered by Captain Wallis. The inhabitants of Ulietea speak of an uninhabited island about this situation, called by them Mopeha, to which they go for turtle. Perhaps this may be the same.

1774. June.

From this day to the 16th we met with nothing remarkable, and our course was west-southerly. About half an hour after sunrise this morning, land was seen from the topmast-head. We altered our course, and, steering for it, found it to be another reef island, composed of five or six woody islets connected together by sand-banks and breakers, enclosing a lake into which we could see no entrance. We found no anchorage, nor saw we any signs of inhabitants. There were plenty of various kinds of birds, and the coast seemed to abound with fish. I looked upon it as a new discovery, and named it Palmerston Island, in honour of Lord Palmerston, one of the Lords of the Admiralty.

On Monday the 20th we again saw land from the mast-head, and as we drew nearer found it to be an island. Perceiving some people on the shore, we hoisted out two boats, with which I put off to the land, accompanied by some of the officers and gentlemen. We landed with ease in a small creek, and displayed our colours. I took two men, and with them entered a kind of chasm, which opened a way into the woods. We had not gone far before we heard the natives approaching; they appeared at the entrance of a chasm not a stone's-throw from us. We began to speak, and make all the friendly signs we could think of, to them, which they answered by menaces, and one of two men who were advanced before the rest threw a stone.

Upon this two muskets were fired, without order, which made them all retire under cover of the woods, and we saw them no more. After a time more natives—I cannot say how many— rushed out of the wood upon us. The endeavours we used to bring them to a parley were to no purpose, for they came with the ferocity of wild boars, and threw their darts. Two or three muskets discharged in the air did not hinder one of them from advancing still farther and throwing another spear, which passed close over my shoulder. His courage would have cost him his life had not my musket missed fire, for I was not five paces from him when he threw his spear, and had resolved to shoot him to save myself. I was glad afterwards that it happened as it did.

Seeing no good was to be got with these people, we returned on board, and having hoisted in the boats, made sail to WSW. The conduct and aspect of these islanders occasioned my naming it Savage Island.

As we drew near Rotterdam, or Annamooka, we were met by a number of canoes laden with fruit and roots. The people in one canoe inquired for me by name, a proof that these people have an intercourse with those of Amsterdam.

Before we had got well to an anchor the natives came off from all parts in canoes, bringing with them yams and shaddocks, which they exchanged for small nails and old rags. Early in the morning I went ashore with Mr. Gilbert to look for fresh water. We were received with great courtesy by the natives. After I had distributed some presents amongst them I asked for water, and was conducted to a pond that was brackish about three-fourths of a mile from the landing-place, which I suppose to be the same that Tasman watered at. In the meantime the people in the boat had laden her with fruit and roots, which the natives had brought down and exchanged for nails and beads.

On the 29th, having got under sail with a light breeze, we stood to the north. At daybreak we stretched out for Amattafoa. Day no sooner dawned than we saw canoes coming from all parts. The summit of Amattafoa was hid in the clouds the whole day, so that we were not able to determine with certainty whether there was a volcano or not; but everything we could see concurred to make us believe there was.

Continuing our course to the west, on the 1st of July we discovered land, and upon a nearer approach found it to be a small island. At this time four or five people were seen on the reef which lies round the isle. As the boat advanced they retired, and when the boat landed they all fled to the woods. The island seems to be too small to contain many inhabitants, and probably the few whom we saw may have come from some island in the neighbourhood to fish for turtle, as many were seen near this reef, and occasioned the name Turtle Isle to be given to the island.

July.

The boats were now hoisted in, and we made sail to the west, with a brisk gale at east. The next day the weather was foggy, and the wind blew in heavy squalls attended with rain, which in this ocean, within the tropics, generally indicates the vicinity of some high land. This was verified at three in the afternoon, when high land was seen bearing SW. No one doubted that this was the Australia del Espirito Santo of Quiros.

The gale kept increasing till the 18th, when I hauled round the north end of Aurora Island, and then stretched over for the Isle of Lepers. We now saw people on the shore, and many beautiful cascades of water pouring down the neighbouring hills. Though we made all the signs of friendship, we could not bring the natives nearer than a stone's-throw.

At daybreak on the 21st we found ourselves before the channel that divides Whitsuntide Island from the south land. At this time the land to the southward extended farther than the eye could reach, and on the part nearest to us we observed two very large columns of smoke, which I judged ascended from volcanoes. As we drew nearer the shore we discovered a creek: on this a number of people were assembled, who seemed to invite us ashore, probably with no good intent, as the most of them were armed with bows and arrows. We had no sooner anchored than a good many of them came round us, some in canoes, and others swimming. I soon prevailed on one to come on board, which he no sooner did than he was followed by more than I desired, so that not only our deck, but rigging, was presently filled with them.

About nine o'clock we landed in the face of four or five hundred people who were assembled on the shore. Though they were all armed with bows and arrows, clubs and spears, they made not the least opposition. On the contrary, seeing me advance alone, with nothing but a green branch in my hand, one of them, who seemed to be a chief, giving his bow and arrows to another, met me in the water, bearing also a green branch. He then took me by the hand, and led me up to the crowd. I made signs (for we understood not a word of their language) that we wanted wood, and they made signs to us to cut down the trees. By this time a small pig was brought down and presented to me. This made us hope that we should soon have some more; but we were mistaken. The pig was not brought to be exchanged for what we had, but probably as a peace-offering; for all we could say or do did not prevail on them to bring down about half a dozen cocoa-nuts and a small quantity of fresh water.

Being unwilling to lose the benefit of the moonlight nights, which now happened, at 7 a.m. on the 23rd we weighed. When the natives saw us under sail they came off in canoes, making exchanges with more confidence than before, and giving such extraordinary proofs of their honesty as surprised us.

In general they are the most ugly, ill-proportioned people I ever saw, and in every respect different from any we had ever met with in this sea. They are a very dark-coloured and rather diminutive race, with long heads, flat faces, and monkey countenances. Their hair, mostly black or brown, is short and curly. We saw but few women, and they were not less ugly than the men. Their heads, faces, and shoulders are painted red; they wear a kind of petticoat, and some of them had something over their shoulders like a bag, in which they carry their children.

Soon after we got to sea we discovered several more islands. Continuing our course to the south, we found a large island and three or four smaller ones lying off its north side. I named these Montague and Hinchinbrook, and the large island Sandwich, in honour of my noble patron the Earl of Sandwich. This latter exhibited a most delightful prospect, being spotted with woods and lawns, agreeably diversified over the whole surface. The examining it not being so much an object with me as the getting to the south, in order to find the southern extremity of the archipelago, with this view I steered SSE.

At 4 a.m. on the 27th we discovered a new land bearing south. We were three days in gaining it, in which time we discovered an elevated land to the south of this. Reaching it on the 1st of August, natives appeared in several parts, and invited us to land.

August.

They received us with great courtesy and politeness. One man whom I took to be a chief I loaded with presents, and asked by signs for fresh water. The chief immediately sent a man for some, who ran to a house, and presently returned with a little in a bamboo. I next asked for something to eat, and they as readily brought me a yam and some cocoa-nuts. In short, I was charmed with their behaviour, and the only thing which could give the least suspicion was that most of them were armed with clubs, spears, darts, and bows and arrows. For this reason I kept my eye continually upon the chief, and watched his looks as well as his actions. He made many signs to me to haul the boat up upon the shore, and at last slipped into the crowd, where I observed him speak to several people and then return to me, repeating signs to haul the boat up, and hesitating a good deal before he would receive some spike-nails which I then offered him. This made me suspect something was intended, and immediately I stepped into the boat, telling them by signs that I should soon return. But they were not for parting so soon, and now attempted by force what they could not obtain by gentler means. As we were putting off the boat they laid hold of the gang-board, and unhooked it off the boat's stern, and attempted to haul her ashore; others at the same time snatched the oars out of the people's hands. Signs and threats having no effect, our own safety became the only consideration; and yet I was unwilling to fire on the multitude, and resolved to make the chief alone fall a victim to his own treachery, but my musket at this critical moment missed fire.

Whatever idea they might have formed of the arms we held in our hands, they must now have looked upon them as childish weapons, and began to let us see how much better theirs were by throwing stones and darts and by shooting arrows. This made it absolutely necessary for me to give orders to fire. The first discharge threw them into confusion, but a second was hardly sufficient to drive them off the beach; and after all they continued to throw stones from behind the trees and bushes, and every now and then to pop out and throw a dart. Four lay to all appearance dead on the shore, but two of them afterwards crawled into the bushes. Happy it was for these people that not half our muskets would go off, otherwise many more must have fallen.

I now ordered the anchor to be weighed. A breeze sprang up at N. of which we took the advantage, set our sails, and plied out of the bay, as it did not seem capable of supplying our wants with that conveniency I wished to have. At two o'clock in the afternoon we were clear of the bay, and bore up round the head, on the SW. side of which is a pretty deep bay. This promontory or peninsula I named Traitors' Head, from the treacherous behaviour of its inhabitants.

On the 5th, at sunrise, we discovered an island, which we had passed in the night without seeing it. We now made sail for it, and presently after discovered a small inlet, which had the appearance of being a good harbour. While we were employed in anchoring, many of the natives got together in parties, all armed with bows, spears, etc. Some swam off to us, others came in canoes. At first they were shy, and kept at the distance of a stone's-throw, but they grew insensibly bolder.

As we wanted to take in a large quantity both of wood and water, I found it practicable to lay the ship much nearer the landing-place than she now was. While we were about this we observed the natives assembling from all parts to the amount of some thousands, armed as before. Their chief design seemed to be to invite us on shore. But everything conspired to make us believe they meant to attack us as soon as we should be on shore, the consequence of which was easily supposed: many of them must have been killed and wounded, and we should hardly have escaped unhurt. Since therefore they would not give us the room we required, I thought it was better to frighten them into it. I accordingly ordered a musket to be fired over the party, but the alarm it gave them was momentary. In an instant they recovered themselves, and began to display their weapons. After this I ordered three or four more muskets to be fired. This was the signal for the ship to fire a few great guns, which presently dispersed them.

During the night the volcano, which was about four miles to the west of us, vomited up vast quantities of fire and smoke, as it had also done the night before, and the flames were seen to rise above the hill which lay between us and it. At every eruption it made a long rumbling noise like that of thunder, or the blowing up of large mines. A heavy shower of rain which fell at this time seemed to increase it, and the wind blowing from the same quarter, the air was loaded with its ashes, which fell so thick that everything was covered with the dust. It was a kind of fine sand or stone, ground or burnt to powder, and was exceedingly troublesome to the eyes.

We learned from the people that the proper name of this island is Tanna. They gave us to understand, in a manner which I thought admitted of no doubt, that they ate human flesh. They began the subject of eating human flesh of their own accord, by asking us if we did; otherwise I should never have thought of asking them such a question. I have heard people argue that no nation could be cannibals if they had other flesh to eat, or did not want food, thus deriving the custom from necessity. The people of this island can be under no such necessity; they have fine pork and fowls, and plenty of roots and fruits. But since we have not actually seen them eat human flesh, it will admit of doubt with some whether they are cannibals.

On the 9th, when the launch was on the west side of the harbour taking in ballast, one of the men employed in this work had scalded his fingers in taking a stone up out of some water. This circumstance produced the discovery of several hot springs at the foot of the cliff, and rather below high-water mark.

During the night, and also all the next day, the volcano was exceedingly troublesome, and made a terrible noise, throwing up prodigious columns of fire and smoke at each explosion, which happened every three or four minutes, and at one time great stones were seen high in the air. There were three places up the hill from whence smoke of a sulphurous smell issued through cracks or fissures in the earth. The ground about these was exceedingly hot and parched or burned, and they seemed to keep pace with the volcano, for at every explosion of the latter the quantity of smoke or steam in these was greatly increased, and forced out so as to rise in small columns, which we saw from the ship, and had taken for common fires made by the natives.

CHAPTER XXIX.

DEPARTURE FROM TANNA—SOME ACCOUNT OF ITS INHABITANTS—DISCOVERY OF NEW CALEDONIA, AND INCIDENTS THAT HAPPENED WHILE THE SHIP LAY IN BALADE—THE ISLE OF PINES—DEPARTURE FOR NEW ZEALAND.

DURING the night of the 20th the wind had veered round to SE. As this was favourable for getting out of the harbour, at four o'clock in the morning we began to unmoor and put to sea.

1774. August.

The produce of this island is bread-fruit, plantains, cocoa-nuts, a fruit like a nectarine, yams, a sort of potato, sugar-cane, wild figs. The bread-fruit, cocoa-nuts, and plantains are neither so plentiful nor so good as at Otaheite. On the other hand, sugar-canes and yams are not only in greater plenty, but of superior quality and much larger. Hogs did not seem to be scarce, but we saw not many fowls. These are the only domestic animals they have. At first we thought the people of this island were a race between the natives of the Friendly Islands and those of Mallicollo, but they had little or no affinity to either. Their hair grows to a tolerable length, and is very crisp and curly. They separate it into small locks, which they cue round with the rind of a slender plant down to about an inch of the ends. Each of these cues is somewhat thicker than common whip-cord, and they look like a parcel of small strings hanging down from the crown of their heads.

Both sexes are of a very dark colour, but not black. They make themselves blacker than they really are by painting their faces with a pigment of the colour of blacklead. They also use another sort which is red, and a third sort brown. All these they lay on with a liberal hand, not only on the face, but on the neck, shoulders, and breast.

We now stretched to the eastward to make a survey of this whole archipelago. The northern islands were discovered by that great navigator Quiros in 1606, and were considered as part of the southern continent which at that time and until very lately was supposed to exist. They were next visited by M. de Bougainville in 1768, who called the islands the Great Cyclades. But as we added to them several new ones which were not known before, and explored the whole, I think we have obtained a right to name them, and shall in future distinguish them by the name of the New Hebrides.

The next island, which lies farthest north, is that of Tierra del Espiritu Santo. It is the most western and largest of all the Hebrides. The next considerable island is that of Mallicollo. To judge of this island from what we saw of it, it must be very fertile and well inhabited. St. Bartholomew lies between the SE. end of Tierra del Espiritu Santo and the N. end of Mallicollo. The Isle of Lepers lies between Espiritu Santo and Aurora Island. Aurora, Whitsuntide, Ambrym, Paoom and its neighbour Apee, Threehills and Sandwich Islands, lie all nearly under the meridian of 167° 30' E.

Having now finished the survey of the whole archipelago, the season of the year made it necessary for me to return to the south while I had yet some time left to explore any land I might meet with between this and New Zealand, where I intended to touch, that I might refresh my people and recruit our stock of wood and water for another southern course.

September. No more land was seen till eight o'clock on the 4th, when land was discovered bearing SSW., for which we steered. We had hardly got to an anchor before we were surrounded by a great number of the natives in sixteen or eighteen canoes, the most of whom were without any sort of weapons. At first they were shy of coming near the ship, but in a short time we prevailed on the people in one boat to get close enough to receive some presents. These we lowered down to them by a rope, to which in return they tied two fish that stunk intolerably. These mutual exchanges bringing on a kind of confidence, two ventured on board the ship, and presently after she was filled with them, and we had the company of several at dinner in the cabin.

MAP OF THE NEW HEBRIDES, ETC.

Page 290.

Our pea-soup, salt beef, and pork they had no curiosity to taste, but they ate of some yams which we happened to have yet left. Like all the natives we had lately seen, the men were almost naked. They were curious in examining every part of the ship, which they viewed with uncommon attention. They had not the least knowledge of goats, hogs, dogs, or cats, and had not even a name for one of them.

We landed on a sandy beach before a vast number of people. Many of them had not a stick in their hands, consequently we were received with great courtesy, and with the surprise natural for people to express at seeing men and things so new to them as we must be. Here we found the chief, whose name we now learned was Teabooma, and we had not been on shore above ten minutes before he called for silence. Being instantly obeyed by every individual present, he made a short speech. It was pleasing to see with what attention he was heard.

Having inquired by signs for fresh water, the chief undertook to conduct us to it. We rowed about two miles up the coast to the east, where the shore was mostly covered with mangrove trees, and entering amongst them by a narrow creek or river, which brought us to a little straggling village, there we landed, and were shown fresh water. The ground near this village was finely cultivated, being laid out in plantations of sugar-canes, plantains, yams, and other roots, and watered by little rills, conducted by art from the main stream, whose source was in the hills. Here were some cocoa-nut trees, and we heard the crowing of cocks, but saw none.

The day being far spent, we now took leave of the people, and got on board a little after sunset. It was easy to see these people had little else than good nature to bestow. In this they exceeded all the natives we had yet met with, and although it did not satisfy the demands of nature, it at once pleased and left our minds at ease.

About seven o'clock in the evening of the 6th died Simon Monk, our butcher, a man much esteemed in the ship, his death being occasioned by a fall down the fore-hatchway the preceding night. On the morning of the 7th a party of us went to take a view of the country. The country in general bore great resemblance to some parts of New Holland, several of its natural productions seeming to be the same. The plain or flat land, which lies along the shore, appeared from the hills to great advantage, the winding streams which ran through it, the plantations, the little straggling villages, the variety in the woods and the shoals on the coast, so variegating the scene that the whole might afford a picture for romance. Indeed, if it were not for these fertile spots on the plains, and some few on the sides of the mountains, the whole country might be called a dreary waste. The little soil on the mountains is scorched and burnt up with the sun.

This afternoon, a fish being struck by one of the natives, my clerk purchased it and sent it to me after my return on board. It was of a new species, something like a sunfish. Having no suspicion of its being of a poisonous nature, we ordered it to be dressed for supper, but luckily the operation took so much time that it was too late, so that only the liver and roe were dressed, of which the two Mr. Forsters and myself did but taste. About three o'clock in the morning we found ourselves seized with an extraordinary weakness and numbness all over our limbs. I had almost lost the sense of feeling, nor could I distinguish between light and heavy bodies of such as I had strength to move—a quart pot full of water and a feather being the same in my hand. Medicine gave us much relief. In the morning one of the pigs which had eaten part was found dead. When the natives came on board and saw the fish hung up they immediately gave us to understand it was not wholesome food, and expressed the utmost abhorrence of it.

On the 8th I received a message acquainting me that Teabooma, the chief, was come with a present consisting of a few yams and sugar-canes. In return I sent him, amongst other articles, two dogs. One was red and white and one all red. I mention this because they may prove the Adam and Eve of their species in that country. It was some time before the chief would believe the dogs were intended for him, but as soon as he was convinced he seemed lost in an excess of joy, and sent them away immediately.

On the 11th I went on shore, and on a large tree which stood close to the shore had an inscription cut, setting forth the ship's

SCENE IN NEW CALEDONIA. *Page 292.*

name, date, etc., as a testimony of our being the first discoverers of this country. This being done, we took leave of our friends and returned on board, when I ordered all the boats to be hoisted in, to be ready to put to sea in the morning.

I shall now conclude our transactions at this place with some account of the country and its inhabitants. They are a strong, robust, active, well-made people, courteous and friendly, and not in the least addicted to pilfering, which is more than can be said of any other nation in this sea. They are nearly of the same colour as the natives of Tanna, but have better features and more agreeable countenances. Their houses are circular, something like a bee-hive, and full as close and warm. The entrance is by a small door, or long square hole, just big enough to admit a man bent double. The floor is laid with dry grass, and here and there mats are spread for the principal people to sleep or sit on. In most of them we found two fireplaces, and commonly a fire burning; and as there was no vent for the smoke but by the door, the whole house was both smoky and hot, insomuch that we who were not used to such an atmosphere could hardly endure it a moment. This may be the reason why we found these people so chilly when in the open air and without exercise. We frequently saw them make little fires anywhere, and hustle round them with no other view than to warm themselves. Smoke within doors may be a necessary evil, as it prevents the mosquitoes, which are pretty numerous here, from coming in. They subsist chiefly on roots and fish and the bark of a tree. The last they roast, and are almost continually chewing. It has a sweetish, insipid taste, and was liked by some of our people. Water is their only liquor. I never saw any other made use of.

All our endeavours to get the name of the whole island proved ineffectual. Probably it is too large for them to know by one name. Balade was the name of the district we were at, and Teabooma the chief. "Tea" seems a title prefixed to the names of all of their chiefs or great men. My friend honoured me by calling me "Tea Cook."

The canoes which these people use are somewhat like those of the Friendly Isles, but the most heavy, clumsy vessels I ever saw. Everything being in readiness to put to sea, at sunrise on the 13th of September we weighed, and with a fine gale at E. by S. stood out for the same channel we came in by.

We continued to ply along the coast, which seemed to trend to the south in a lofty promontory, which, on account of the day, received the name of Cape Coronation. At daybreak on the 23rd an elevated point appeared in sight beyond Cape Coronation. It proved to be the SE. extremity of the coast, and obtained the name of Queen Charlotte's Foreland.

On the 25th we stood to SSW. in hopes of getting round the Foreland, but as we drew near we perceived more low isles, which appeared to be connected by breakers, extending towards the Foreland, and seeming to join the shore. One island was covered with elevations, which had the appearance of tall pines, which occasioned my giving that name to the island. Having made two attempts to weather the Isle of Pines before sunset with no good success, this determined me to stretch off till midnight. This day at noon the thermometer was at 68°, which is lower than it had been since the 27th of February. The coast was strewed with sandbanks, breakers, and small low isles. We continued to range the outside of these small isles and breakers, which seemed to form a chain extending to the isles which lie off the Foreland.

I chose to spend the night in making short boards over that space we had in some measure made ourselves acquainted with in the day. And thus it was spent, but under the terrible apprehension every moment of falling on some of the many dangers which surrounded us.

Daylight showed that our fears were not ill founded, and that we had been in the most imminent danger, having had breakers continually under our lee and at a very little distance from us. We owed our safety to the interposition of Providence, a good lookout, and the very brisk manner in which the ship was managed, for as we were standing to the N. the people on the lee gangway and forecastle saw breakers under the lee-bow, which we escaped by quickly tacking the ship. I was now almost tired of a coast which I could no longer explore but at the risk of losing the ship and ruining the whole voyage.

On the 29th we landed on a little isle on which were some trees measuring 20 inches in diameter, and between 60 and 70 feet in length. These would have done very well for a foremast to the *Resolution* had one been wanting. If I except New Zealand, I at this time knew of no island in the South Pacific Ocean where a ship could supply herself with a mast or yard were she ever so much distressed for want of one. My carpenter, who was a mastmaker as well as a shipwright, was of opinion that these trees would make exceedingly good masts. The wood is white, close grained, tough, and light.

We also found on the isle a sort of scurvy-grass and a plant called by us lamb's quarters, which when boiled ate like spinach. I had now to consider what was next to be done. We had from the topmast-head taken a view of the sea around us, and observed the whole to the west to be strewed with small islets, sandbanks, and breakers to the utmost extent of our horizon. But when I considered the great risk attending a more accurate survey, and the time it would require to accomplish it, on account of the many dangers we should have to encounter, I determined not to hazard the ship down to leeward, where we might be so hemmed in as to find it difficult to return, and by that means lose the proper season for getting to the south.

Next morning at daybreak we got under sail, with a light breeze at E. by N.

On the morning of the 3rd the wind veered to SW., and blew a strong gale by squalls, attended with rain. I October. now gave over all thoughts of returning to the land we had left. Indeed, when I considered the vast ocean we had to explore to the south, the state and condition of the ship, already in want of some necessary stores, that summer was approaching fast, and that any considerable accident might detain us in this sea another year, I did not think it advisable to attempt to regain the land.

Thus I was obliged, as it were, by necessity for the first time to leave a coast I had discovered, before it was fully explored. I called it New Caledonia, and, if we except New Zealand, it is perhaps the largest island in the South Pacific Ocean.

CHAPTER XXX.

PASSAGE FROM NEW CALEDONIA TO NEW ZEALAND, WITH AN ACCOUNT OF THE DISCOVERY OF NORFOLK ISLAND, AND THE INCIDENTS THAT HAPPENED WHILE THE SHIP LAY AT QUEEN CHARLOTTE'S SOUND—FROM NEW ZEALAND TO TIERRA DEL FUEGO—TRANSACTIONS IN CHRISTMAS SOUND—RANGE FROM CHRISTMAS SOUND, ROUND CAPE HORN, THROUGH STRAIT LE MAIRE, AND ROUND STATEN LAND.

1774. October. THE wind blowing a fresh gale, and now and then squalls, with showers of rain, we steered SSE. without meeting with any remarkable occurrence till the 6th, when it fell calm. I now ordered the carpenters to calk the decks. As we had neither pitch, tar, nor resin left to pay the seams, this was done with varnish of pine, and afterwards covered with coral sand, which made a cement far exceeding my expectation.

On the 8th, Mr. Cooper having struck a porpoise with a harpoon, it was necessary to bring to and have two boats out before we could kill it and get it on board. It was six feet long; it had eighty-eight teeth in each jaw. The haslet and lean flesh were to us a feast. The latter was a little liverish, but had not the least fishy taste. It was eaten roasted, boiled, and fried, first soaking in warm water. Indeed, little art was wanting to make anything fresh palatable to those who had been living so long on salt meat.

We continued to stretch to WSW. till the 10th, when at daybreak we discovered land, which on a nearer approach we found to be an island of good height. I named it Norfolk Isle, in honour of the noble family of Howard. After dinner a party of us embarked in two boats and landed on the island without any difficulty. We found it uninhabited, and were undoubtedly the first that ever set foot on it. We observed many trees and plants common at New Zealand, and in particular the flax plant;

but the chief produce is a sort of spruce pine, which grows in great abundance.

On the isle is fresh water, and cabbage-palm, wood-sorrel, sow-thistle, and samphire abounding in some places. We brought on board as much of each sort as the time we had to gather them would admit. These are not only wholesome, but exceedingly palatable, and proved the most agreeable repast we had for some time.

Next morning at sunrise we made sail and steered for New Zealand, my intention being to touch at Queen Charlotte's Sound, to refresh my crew and put the ship in a condition to encounter the southern latitudes.

On the 17th we saw Mount Egmont, which was covered with everlasting snow. Next day we hauled round Point Jackson through a sea which looked terrible, occasioned by a rapid tide and a high wind; but as we knew the coast, it did not alarm us.

On the morning of the 19th we weighed and warped the ship into the cove, and there moored with the two bowers. We unbent the sails to repair them, several having been split and otherwise damaged in the late gale. I gave orders that vegetables (of which there were plenty) should be boiled every morning with oatmeal and portable broth for breakfast, and with peas and broth every day for dinner, for the whole crew, over and above their usual allowance of salt meat.

In the afternoon, as Mr. Wales was setting up his observatory, he discovered that several trees, which were standing when we last sailed from this place, had been cut down with saws and axes; and a few days after, the place where an observatory, clock, etc., had been set up, was also found, in a spot different to that where Mr. Wales had placed his. It was therefore now no longer to be doubted that the *Adventure* had been in this cove after we had left it.

The weather being fair, on the afternoon of the 22nd I visited our gardens on Motuara, which we found almost wholly neglected by the inhabitants. Nevertheless, many articles were in a flourishing condition, and showed how well they liked the soil in which they were planted.

Nothing remarkable happened till the 24th, when two canoes

were seen coming down the sound; but as soon as they perceived the ship, they retired behind a point on the west side. After breakfast, I went in a boat to look for them, and as we proceeded along the shore we shot several birds. The report of the muskets gave notice of our approach, and the natives discovered themselves by hallooing to us. The moment we landed they knew us. Joy then took place of fear; and the rest of the natives hurried out of the woods and embraced us over and over again, leaping and skipping about like madmen. There were only a few amongst them whose faces we could recognize; and on our asking why they were afraid of us, and inquiring for some of our old acquaintances by name, they talked much about killing, but we could gather nothing of what they meant by it.

Our good friends the natives brought us a plentiful supply of fish. They afterwards went on shore and informed our people that a ship like ours had lately been lost in the strait; that some of the people got on shore, and that the natives stole their clothes, for which several were shot; that afterwards, when they could fire no longer, the natives got the better of them, killed them with their patapatoos, and ate them. One man said it was two moons ago; but another contradicted him, and counted on his fingers about twenty or thirty days. They described by actions how the ship was beat to pieces by going up and down against the rocks, till at last it was all scattered abroad. These stories made me very uneasy about the *Adventure*. But I afterwards learned, in a manner which admitted of no doubt, that, soon after we were gone, she arrived; that she stayed between ten and twenty days, and had been gone ten months.

November. On the 8th we put two pigs—a boar and a sow—on shore, in the cove next beyond Cannibal Cove; so that it is hardly possible all the methods I have taken to stock this country with these animals should fail. We had also reason to believe that some of the cocks and hens which I left here still existed—although we had not seen any of them—for a hen's egg was, some days before, found in the woods almost new laid.

At daybreak on the 10th, with a fine breeze at WNW., we weighed and stood out of the sound, and after getting round the Two Brothers, steered for Cape Campbell. At four in the afternoon we passed the cape, and got into the latitude 54°, my intention being to cross this vast ocean nearly in these parallels, so as to pass over those parts which were left unexplored the preceding summer. We steered east till the 27th, when I gave up all hopes of finding any more land in this ocean, and came to a resolution to steer directly for the west entrance of the Straits of Magellan, with a view of coasting the south side of Tierra del Fuego, round Cape Horn, to the Strait Le Maire. As the world has but a very imperfect knowledge of this shore, I thought the coasting of it would be of more advantage, both to navigation and to geography, than anything I could expect to find in a higher latitude. In the afternoon of this day the wind blew in squalls, and carried away the main topgallant mast.

On the 17th of December we saw land, which could be no other than the west coast of Tierra del Fuego. *December.*

This was the first run that had been made directly across this ocean in a high southern latitude, and I must observe that I never made a passage anywhere of such length where so few interesting circumstances occurred. The weather had been neither unusually stormy nor cold.

I have now done with the Southern Pacific Ocean, and flatter myself that no one will think that I have left it unexplored, or that more could have been done in one voyage towards obtaining that end than has been done in this.

Continuing to range along the coast, we passed a projecting point, which I called Cape Gloucester. On the 18th we passed Cape Noir, and SE. point of the Bay of S. Barbara, which I called Cape Desolation, because near it commenced the most desolate and barren country I ever saw. It seems entirely composed of rocky mountains, without the least appearance of vegetation. These mountains terminate in horrible precipices, whose craggy summits spire up to a vast height; so that hardly anything in nature can appear with a more barren and savage aspect than the whole of this country. The inland mountains were covered with snow. There is a lofty promontory which terminated in two high towers, which obtained the name of York Minster.

Seeing a small cove ahead, we hauled up under the east side of the land, and here anchored in thirty fathoms, the bottom sand

and broken shells. I had now an opportunity to verify what we had observed at sea—that the sea-coast is composed of a number of large and small islands. On one of these low islands we found several huts, which had lately been inhabited; and near them was a good deal of celery, with which we loaded our boat.

I was now told of a melancholy accident which had befallen one of our marines. He had not been seen since eleven or twelve o'clock the preceding night. It was supposed that he had fallen overboard and was drowned.

On the 24th we made up two shooting parties and went over to a large island opposite our station, which obtained the name of Goose Island. As soon as we got under the island, we found plenty of shags in the cliffs; but without staying to spend our time and shot upon these, we proceeded on, and presently found sport enough, for in the south side of the island were abundance of geese. It happened to be the moulting season, and most of them were on shore for that purpose, and could not fly. There being a great surf, we found great difficulty in landing, and very bad climbing over the rocks when we were landed; so that hundreds of the geese escaped us, some into the sea, and others up into the island. We, however, by one means or other, got sixty-two, with which we returned on board, all heartily tired; but the acquisition we had made overbalanced every other consideration, and we sat down with a good appetite to supper on part of what the preceding day had produced. I was able to make distribution to the whole crew, which was the more acceptable on account of the approaching festival; for, had not Providence thus singularly provided for us, our Christmas cheer must have been salt beef and pork.

I now learned that a number of the natives in nine canoes had been alongside the ship. They seemed to be well enough acquainted with Europeans, and had amongst them some of their knives.

On the 25th they made us another visit. They are a little, ugly, half-starved, beardless race. I saw not a tall person amongst them. They were almost naked. Their clothing was a seal-skin; some had two or three sewed together, so as to make a cloak which reached to the knees. The women and children remained in their canoes. These were made of bark; and in each was a fire, over which the poor creatures huddled themselves. I cannot suppose that they carry a fire in their canoes for this purpose only, but rather that it may be always ready to remove ashore wherever they land. They likewise carry in their canoes large sealhides, which, I judged, were to shelter them when at sea, and to serve as covering to their huts on shore; and occasionally to be used for sails.

They all retired before dinner, and did not wait to partake of our Christmas cheer. Indeed, I believe no one invited them, and for good reasons; for their dirty persons and the stench they carried about them were enough to spoil the appetite of any European, and that would have been a real disappointment, as we had not experienced such fare for some time. Roast and boiled geese, goose-pie, etc., was a treat little known to us; and we had yet some Madeira wine left, which was the only article of our provision that was mended by keeping. So that our friends in England did not, perhaps, celebrate Christmas more cheerfully than we did.

In the evening of the 26th, when it was cold, the natives made us another visit; and it being distressing to see them stand trembling and naked on the deck, I could do no less than give them some baize and old canvas to cover themselves.

Having already completed our water, I ordered the wood, tent, and observatory to be got on board; and as this was work for the day, a party of us went in two boats to shoot geese, the weather being fine and pleasant. We proceeded round by the south side of Goose Island, and picked up in all thirty-one.

When I returned on board, I found everything got off the shore and the launch in; so that we now only waited for a wind to put to sea. The festival which we celebrated at this place occasioned my giving it the name of Christmas Sound.

The refreshments to be got here are precarious, as they consist chiefly of wild fowl, and may probably never be found in such plenty as to supply the crew of a ship; and fish, so far as we can judge, are scarce. The wild fowl are geese, ducks, sea-pies, shags, and that kind of gull known as Port Egmont hen. Here is a kind of duck, called by our people race-horses, on account of the great swiftness with which they run on the water; for they cannot fly, the wings being too short to support the body in the air.

From the knowledge which the inhabitants seem to have of Europeans, we may suppose that they do not live here continually, but retire to the north during the winter. I have often wondered that these people do not clothe themselves better, since nature has certainly provided materials. They might line their seal-skin cloaks with the skins and feathers of aquatic birds; they might make their cloaks larger, and employ the same skins for other parts of clothing. In short, of all the nations I have seen, these Pecheras are the most wretched. They are doomed to live in one of the most inhospitable climates in the world, without having sagacity enough to provide themselves with such conveniences as may render life in some measure more comfortable.

At eight o'clock in the morning of the 28th, we weighed and stood out to sea, with a light breeze at NW. At half-past seven next day we passed the famous Cape Horn and entered the Southern Atlantic Ocean. It is the very same point of land I took for the cape, when I passed it in 1769, which at that time I was doubtful of. It is the most southern extremity on a group of islands of unequal extent, lying before Nassau Bay, known by the name of Hermite Islands.

From Cape Horn we steered NE. for Strait Le Maire, with a view of looking into Success Bay, to see if there were any traces of the *Adventure* having been there. I had inscribed our ship's name on a card, which we nailed to a tree at the place where the *Endeavour* watered. This was done with a view of giving Captain Furneaux some information in case he should be behind us and put in here. Next morning we bore up for the east end of Staten Land. The land was obscured in a thick haze, and we were obliged to make way, as it were, in the dark; for it was but now and then we got a sight of the coast. In hauling round the east end of one of the islands we saw an abundance of seals and birds. This was a temptation too great for people in our situation to withstand, to whom fresh provisions of any kind were acceptable, and determined me to anchor in order that we might taste of what we now only saw at a distance. After dinner we hoisted out three boats, and landed with a large party of men;

some to kill seals, others to catch birds, fish, or what came in our way. To find the former, it mattered not where we landed; for the whole shore was covered with them, and by the noise they made, one would have thought the island was stocked with cows and calves. On landing, we found they were a different animal from seals, but in shape and motion exactly resembling them. We called them lions, on account of the great resemblance the male has to that beast. Here were also the same kind of seals which we found in New Zealand, generally known by the name of sea-bears—at least we gave them that name. They were in general so tame, or rather stupid, as to suffer us to come near enough to knock them down with sticks; but the large ones we shot, not thinking it safe to approach them. We also found on the islands abundance of penguins and shags; here were geese and ducks, but not many. In the evening we returned on board, our boats well laden with one thing or other.

Next day being January 1, 1775, finding that nothing was wanting but a good harbour to make this a tolerable place for ships to refresh at, I sent Mr. Gilbert over to Staten Land in the cutter to look for one. Appearances promised success in a place opposite the ship. About ten o'clock, Mr. Gilbert returned from Staten Land, where he found a good port, situated three leagues to the westward of Cape St. John. It may be known by some small islands lying in the entrance. The harbour is nearly two miles in length; in some places near a mile broad. Its shores are covered with wood fit for fuel, and in it are several streams of fresh water. The day on which this port was discovered occasioned my calling it New-Year's Harbour.

On the 3rd we weighed, with a fresh gale, and stood for Cape St. John. This cape, being the eastern point of Staten Land, a description of it is unnecessary. In sailing round the cape, we met with a very strong current from the south. It made a race which looked like breakers, and it was as much as we could do, with a strong gale, to make head against it.

After getting round the cape, I hauled up along the south coast till eight o'clock on the 3rd, and steered SE., with a resolution to leave the land, judging it to be sufficiently explored to answer the most general purposes of navigation and geography.

CHAPTER XXXI.

DISCOVERY OF THE ISLE OF GEORGIA—PROCEEDINGS AFTER LEAVING THE ISLE OF GEORGIA, AND AN ACCOUNT OF THE DISCOVERY OF SANDWICH LAND; WITH SOME REASONS FOR THERE BEING LAND ABOUT THE SOUTH POLE—AN ACCOUNT OF OUR PROCEEDINGS TILL OUR ARRIVAL AT THE CAPE OF GOOD HOPE.

1775. January. WE stood to the south till the 13th, when we saw several penguins and a snow petrel, which we looked on to be signs of the vicinity of ice. The air, too, was much colder than we had felt it since we left New Zealand.

At eight o'clock the next morning we saw an island of ice, as we then thought, but at noon we were doubtful whether it was ice or land. It was wholly covered with snow. It proved to be an island, which obtained the name of Willis's Island, after the person who first saw it.

At this time we had a great swell from the south, an indication that no land was near us in that direction; nevertheless the vast quantity of snow on that in sight induced us to think it was extensive, and I chose to begin with exploring the northern coast. With this view we bore up for Willis's Island, all sails set, having a fine gale at SSW. As we advanced to the north, we perceived another isle lying east of Willis's, and between it and the main. Seeing there was a clear passage between the two isles we steered for it.

Willis's Isle is a high rock of no great extent; the other isle, which obtained the name of Bird Isle, on account of the vast number of birds that were upon it, is not so high, but of greater extent, and is close to the NE. point of the mainland, which I called Cape North.

After getting through the passage, we found the north coast trended E. by N. for about nine miles, and then E. to Cape Buller.

We now steered along shore at the distance of four or five miles, when, seeing the appearance of an inlet, we hauled in for it. As soon as we drew near the shore, having hoisted out a boat, I embarked in it, with a view to reconnoitring the bay before we ventured in with the ship. But as I came to a resolution not to bring the ship in, I did not think it worth my while to go and examine these places; for it did not seem probable that any one would ever be benefited by the discovery. I landed in three different places, displayed our colours, and took possession of the country in His Majesty's name, under a discharge of small arms.

The head of the bay, as well as two places on each side, was terminated by perpendicular ice-cliffs of considerable height. The inner parts of the country were not less savage and horrible. The wild rocks raised their lofty summits till they were lost in the clouds, and the valleys lay covered with everlasting snow. Not a tree was to be seen, nor a shrub even big enough to make a toothpick.

All the land birds we saw consisted of a few small larks, nor did we meet with any quadrupeds.

Having made the above observations, we set out for the ship and got aboard a little after twelve o'clock with a quantity of seals and penguins, an acceptable present to the crew.

It must not, however, be understood that we were in want of provisions. We had yet plenty of every kind, and since we had been on this coast, I had ordered, in addition to the common allowance, wheat to be boiled every morning for breakfast; but any kind of fresh meat was preferred by most on board to salt. For my own part, I was now for the first time heartily tired of salt meat of every kind, and though the flesh of the penguins could scarcely vie with bullock's liver, its being fresh was sufficient to make it go down. I called the bay we had been in Possession Bay, and a pretty large bay beyond, Cumberland Bay. We now hauled off the coast, from which we were distant about four miles. The nearest land to us, being a projecting point which terminated in a round hillock, was, on account of the day, named Cape Charlotte. On the west side of Cape Charlotte lies a bay which obtained the name of Royal Bay, and the west point of it was named Cape George. An isle lying distant eight leagues from

Cape Charlotte was called Cooper's Isle, after my first lieutenant. The coast between them forms a large bay, to which I gave the name of Sandwich Bay.

At sunrise on the 19th, a new land was seen; its first appearance in a single hill like a sugar-loaf. Some time after other detached pieces appeared above the horizon near the hill. In the afternoon we had a prospect of a ridge of mountains behind Sandwich Bay, whose lofty and icy summits were elevated high above the clouds. This proved to be an island quite detached from the main, and obtained the name of Pickersgill Island, after my third officer. It was no more than seventy leagues in circuit.

Who would have thought that an island of no greater extent than this, situated between the latitude of 54° and 55°, should, in the very height of summer, be in a manner wholly covered, many fathoms deep, with frozen snow? The very sides and craggy summits of the lofty mountains were cased with snow and ice; but the quantity which lay in the valleys is incredible, and at the bottom of the bays the coast was terminated by a wall of ice of considerable height. It can hardly be doubted that a great deal of ice is formed here in the winter, which, in the spring, is broken off and dispersed over the sea; but the island cannot produce the ten-thousandth part of what we saw; so that either there must be more land or the ice is formed without it.

I called this land the Isle of Georgia, in honour of His Majesty. It is remarkable that we did not see a river or stream of fresh water on the whole coast. I think it highly probable there are no perennial springs in the country, and that the interior parts never enjoy heat enough to melt the snow in such quantities as to produce a river or stream of water.

On the 25th we steered ESE., with a fresh gale at NNE., attended with foggy weather.

I now reckoned we were in lat. 60° S., and farther I did not intend to go, unless I observed certain signs of soon meeting with land; for it would not have been prudent in me to have spent my time in penetrating to the south, when it was at least as probable that a large tract of land might be found near Cape Circumcision. Besides, I was tired of these high southern latitudes, where nothing was to be found but ice and thick fogs.

At seven o'clock in the evening, the fog receding from us a little gave us a sight of an ice island, several penguins, and some snow petrels. We continued to stand to the east till half-past two o'clock p.m., when we fell in, all at once, with a vast number of large ice islands and a sea strewed with loose ice. The ice-islands which at this time surrounded us were nearly all of equal height, and showed a flat, even surface; but they were of various extent, some being two or three miles in circuit.

At half an hour past six in the morning of the 31st we discovered land ahead; this proved to be three rocky islets of considerable height. The outermost terminated in a lofty peak like a sugar-loaf, and obtained the name of Freezeland Rock, after the man who first discovered it. Behind this rock appeared an elevated coast, whose lofty, snow-clad summits were seen above the clouds. It extended N. by E., and I called it Cape Bristol in honour of the noble family of Hervey. At the same time another elevated coast appeared in sight. I called this land Southern Thule, because it is the most southern land that has ever yet been discovered. It shows a surface of vast height, and is everywhere covered with snow. Some thought they saw land in the space between Thule and Cape Bristol. It is more than probable that these two lands are connected, and that this space is a deep bay which I called Forster's Bay.

At one o'clock, finding that we could not weather Thule, we tacked and stood to the north. Soon after it fell little wind, and we were left to the mercy of a great westerly swell, which set right upon the shore. The weather clearing up, we saw Cape Bristol terminating in a point to the north, beyond which we could see no land. This discovery relieved us from the fear of being carried by the swell on the most horrible coast in the world.

On the 1st we got signs of a new coast. It proved a high promontory, which I named Cape Montagu, seven *February.* or eight leagues to the north of Cape Bristol. We saw land from space to space between them, which made me conclude that the whole was connected. I was sorry I could not determine this with greater certainty; but prudence would not permit me to venture near a coast subject to thick fogs, on which there was no anchorage, where every port was blocked or filled up with ice, and the whole country covered many fathoms thick with everlasting snow.

Continuing to steer to the north all night, at six o'clock next morning a new land was seen. It appeared in two hummocks just peeping above the horizon; but the weather was now become very hazy, which made it unsafe to stand for the shore. Thus we were obliged to leave it on the supposition of its being an island, which I named Saunders, after my honourable friend Sir Charles.

On the 3rd we found two isles, and the day on which they were discovered was the occasion of calling them Candlemas Isles.

We continued to steer to the south. Seeing neither land nor signs of any, I concluded that what we had seen, which I named Sandwich Land, was either a group of islands or else a point of the continent; for I firmly believe that there is a track of land near the Pole which is the source of most of the ice that is spread over this vast southern ocean. It is true, however, that the greatest part of this southern continent must be within the polar circle, where the sea is so pestered with ice that the land is thereby inaccessible. The risk one runs in exploring a coast in these unknown and icy seas is so very great that I can be bold enough to say that no man will ever venture farther than I have done, and that the lands which may lie to the south will never be explored. Thick snows, snow-storms, intense cold, and every other thing that can render navigation dangerous, must be encountered; and these difficulties are greatly heightened by the inexpressibly horrid aspect of the country—a country doomed by nature never once to feel the warmth of the sun's rays, but to lie buried in everlasting snow and ice.

The ports which may be on the coast are, in a manner, wholly filled up with frozen snow of vast thickness; but if any should be so far open as to invite a ship into it, she would run a risk of being fixed there for ever, or coming out in an ice island. The islands and floes on the coast, the great falls from the ice cliffs in the port, or a heavy snow-storm attended with a sharp frost, would be equally fatal. After such an explanation as this, the reader must not expect to find me much farther to the south.

These reasons induced me to alter the course to east, with a very strong gale at north attended with an exceedingly heavy fall of snow. The quantity which lodged in our sails was so great, that we were frequently obliged to throw the ship up in the wind to shake it out of them, otherwise neither they nor the ship could have supported the weight.

On the 18th we were in the latitude 54° 25'. I thought this a good latitude to keep in to look for Cape Circumcision; because, if the land had ever so little extent in the direction of north and south, we could not miss seeing it, as the northern point is said to lie in 54°. We had yet a great swell from the south, so that I was now well assured it could only be an island.

By the 22nd we had run down 13° of longitude, in the very latitude assigned for Bouvet's Land. I was therefore well assured that what he had seen could be nothing but an island of ice; for if it had been land it is hardly possible we could have missed it, though it were ever so small.

As we were now no more than two degrees of longitude from our route to the south when we left the Cape of Good Hope, it was to no purpose to proceed any farther to the east under this parallel, knowing that no land could be there. But an opportunity now offering of clearing up some doubts of our having seen land farther to the south, I steered to the SE.

I had now made the circuit of the southern ocean in a high latitude, and traversed it in such a manner as to leave not the least room for the possibility of there being a continent, unless near the Pole and out of the reach of navigation. By twice visiting the tropical sea I had not only settled the situation of some old discoveries, but made there many new ones, and left very little more to be done even in that part. Thus I flatter myself that the intention of the voyage has in every respect been fully answered; the southern hemisphere sufficiently explored; and a final end put to the searching after a southern continent, which has at times engrossed the attention of some of the maritime powers for near two centuries past, and been a favourite theory amongst the geographers of all ages.

That there may be a continent near the Pole I will not deny; on the contrary, I am of opinion there is, and that we have seen part of it. If any one should have resolution and perseverance to clear up this point by proceeding farther than I have done, I shall not envy him the honour of the discovery, but I will be bold to say that the world will not be benefited by it.

Our sails and rigging were now so much worn that something was giving way every hour, and we had nothing left either to repair or to replace them. Our provisions were in a state of decay, and consequently afforded little nourishment, and we had been a long time without refreshments. My people, indeed, were yet healthy, and would have cheerfully gone wherever I had thought proper to lead them; but I dreaded the scurvy laying hold of them at a time when we had nothing left to remove it. I must say further that it would have been cruel in me to have continued the fatigues and hardships they were continually exposed to longer than was absolutely necessary. Their behaviour throughout the whole voyage merited every indulgence which it was in my power to give them. Animated by the conduct of the officers, they showed themselves capable of surmounting every difficulty and danger which came in their way, and never once looked either upon the one or the other as being at all heightened by our separation from our consort, the *Adventure.*

All these considerations induced me to steer for the Cape of Good Hope. I now, in pursuance of my instructions, demanded of the officers and petty officers the logbooks and journals they had kept, which were delivered to me accordingly, and sealed up for the inspection of the Admiralty. I also enjoined them and the whole crew not to divulge where we had been till they had their lordships' permission so to do.

At daybreak on the 16th we saw two sail standing to the westward, and one of them showing Dutch colours. Having little or no wind we hoisted out a boat, and sent on board one of the two ships before mentioned, which were about two leagues from us; but we were too impatient after news to regard the distance. Our people were told by some English seamen on board this ship that the *Adventure* had arrived at the Cape of Good Hope twelve months ago, and that the crew of one of her boats had been murdered and eaten by the people of New Zealand; so that the story we heard in Queen Charlotte's Sound was now no longer a mystery.

On the 19th we had light airs next to a calm till next morning, when a breeze sprung up at west, and the English ship, which was to windward, bore down to us. She proved to be the *True Briton*, Captain Broadly, from China. As he did not intend to touch at the Cape, I put a letter on board him for the secretary of the Admiralty. The account which we had heard of the *Adventure* was now confirmed to us by this ship. We also got from on board her a parcel of old newspapers, which were new to us, and gave us some amusement; but these were the least favours we received from Captain Broadly. With a generosity peculiar to the commanders of the India Company's ships, he sent us fresh provisions, tea, and other articles, which were very acceptable, and deserve from me this public acknowledgment. In the afternoon we parted company. The *True Briton* stood out to sea and we in for the land, having a very fresh gale at west, which split our fore-topsail in such a manner that we were obliged to bring another to the yard.

The next morning, being with us Wednesday the 22nd, but with the people here Tuesday the 21st, we anchored in Table Bay. Before we had got well to an anchor I despatched an officer to acquaint the governor with our arrival, and to request the necessary stores and refreshments, which were readily granted. As soon as the officer came back we saluted the garrison with thirteen guns, which compliment was immediately returned with an equal number.

I now learned that the *Adventure* had called here on her return, and I found a letter from Captain Furneaux acquainting me with the loss of his boat, and of ten of his best men, in Queen Charlotte's Sound. The captain afterwards, on my arrival in England, put into my hands a complete narrative of his proceedings from the time of our second and final separation, which I now lay before the public in the following chapter.

CHAPTER XXXII.

CAPTAIN FURNEAUX'S NARRATIVE OF HIS PROCEEDINGS IN THE "ADVENTURE," INCLUDING LIEUTENANT BURNEY'S REPORT CONCERNING THE BOAT'S CREW WHO WERE MURDERED BY THE INHABITANTS OF QUEEN CHARLOTTE'S SOUND.

1773.
October.

AFTER a passage of fourteen days from Amsterdam, we made the coast of New Zealand near the Table Cape, and stood along shore till we came as far as Cape Turnagain. The wind then began to blow strong at west, with heavy squalls and rain, which split many of our sails, and blew us off the coast for three days; in which time we parted company with the *Resolution*, and never saw her afterwards.

On the 4th of November we again got inshore near Cape Palliser, and were visited by a number of the natives in their canoes, bringing a great quantity of crayfish, which we bought of them for nails and Otaheite cloth. The next day it blew hard from WNW., which again drove us off the coast, and obliged us to bring to for two days, during which time it blew one continual gale of wind, with heavy falls of sleet. By this time our decks were very leaky, our beds and bedding wet, and several of our people complaining of colds, so that we began to despair of ever getting into Charlotte Sound or joining the *Resolution*. On the 6th, the wind being at SW. and blowing strong, we bore away for some bay to complete our water and wood, being in great want of both, having been at the allowance of one quart of water for some days past.

We anchored in Tolaga Bay on the 9th. The natives here are the same as those at Charlotte Sound, but more numerous, and seemed settled, having regular plantations of sweet potatoes and other roots which are very good; and they have plenty of cray and other fish, which we bought of them for nails, beads, and other trifles, at an easy rate. Having got about ten tons of water and some wood, we sailed for Charlotte Sound on the 12th. We were no sooner out than the wind began to blow hard, dead on the shore, so that we could not clear the land on either tack. This obliged us to bear away again for the bay, where we anchored the next morning, and rode out a very heavy gale of wind at E. by S., which threw in a very great sea. We now began to fear we should never join the *Resolution*, having reason to believe she was in Charlotte Sound, and by this time ready for sea. We soon found it was with great difficulty we could get any water, owing to the swell setting in so strong. At last, however, we were able to go on shore, and got both wood and water.

Whilst we lay here we were employed about the rigging, which was much damaged by the constant gales of wind we had met with since we made the coast. Having made the ship as snug as possible, we sailed again on the 16th. After this we met with several gales of wind off the mouth of the strait, and continned beating backwards and forwards till the 30th, when we were so fortunate as to get a favourable wind, which we took every advantage of, and at last got safe into our desired port. We saw nothing of the *Resolution*, and began to doubt her safety; but on going ashore we discerned the place where she had erected her tents, and on an old stump of a tree in the garden observed these words cut out, " Look underneath." There we dug, and soon found a bottle corked and waxed down, with a letter in it from Captain Cook, signifying their arrival on the 3rd instant and departure on the 24th; and that they intended spending a few days in the entrance of the straits to look for us.

We immediately set about getting the ship ready for sea as fast as possible, erected our tents, sent the cooper on shore to repair the casks, and began to unstow the hold to get at the bread that was in butts; but on opening them found a great quantity of it entirely spoiled, and most part so damaged that we were obliged to fix our copper oven on shore to bake it over again, which undoubtedly delayed us a considerable time.

Whilst we lay here, the inhabitants came on board as before, supplying us with fish and other things, which we bought of them for nails, etc., and appeared very friendly, though twice in the middle of the night they came to the tent with an intention to steal, but were discovered before they could get anything into their possession.

On the 17th of December, having refitted the ship, completed our wood and water, and got everything ready for sea, we sent our large cutter, with Mr. Rowe, a midshipman, and the boat's crew, to gather wild greens for the ship's company, with orders to return that evening, as I intended to sail the next morning. But on the boat's not returning the same evening nor the next morning, being under great uneasiness about her, I hoisted out the launch, and sent her, with the second lieutenant, Mr. Burney, manned with the boat's crew and ten marines, in search of her. My orders to Mr. Burney were, first to look well into East Bay, and then to proceed to Grass Cove, the place to which Mr. Rowe had been sent; and if he heard nothing of the boat there, to go farther up the sound and come back along the west shore. As Mr. Rowe had left the ship an hour before the time proposed, and in a great hurry, I was strongly persuaded that his curiosity had carried him into East Bay, none in our ship having ever been there, or else that some accident had happened to the boat, either by going adrift through the boat-keeper's negligence, or by being stove among the rocks. This was almost everybody's opinion; and on this supposition the carpenter's mate was sent in the launch with some sheets of tin. I had not the least suspicion that our people had received any injury from the natives, our boats having frequently been higher up and worse provided. How much I was mistaken too soon appeared, for Mr. Burney, having returned about eleven o'clock the same night, made his report of a horrible scene indeed, which cannot be better described than in his own words, which now follow :—

"On the 18th we left the ship; we soon got round Long Island and within Long Point. I examined every cove as we went along, looking well all around with a spyglass which I took for that purpose. At half-past one we stopped at a beach on the left-hand side going up East Bay to boil some victuals, as we brought nothing but raw meat with us. Whilst we were cooking I saw an Indian on the opposite shore running along a beach to the head of the bay. Our meat being dressed, we got into the boat and put off, and in a short time arrived at the head of this reach, where we saw an Indian settlement. As we drew near some of the Indians came down on the rocks and waved for us to be gone; but seeing we disregarded them, they altered their notes. Here we found six large canoes hauled up on the beach, most of them double ones, and a great many people, though not so many as one might expect from the number of houses and size of the canoes. Leaving the boat's crew to guard the boat, I stepped ashore with the marines (the corporal and five men) and searched a good many of their houses, but found nothing to give me any suspicion. Three or four well-beaten paths led farther into the woods, where were many more houses; but the people continuing friendly, I thought it unnecessary to continue our search. Coming down to the beach, one of the Indians had brought a bundle of hepatoos (long spears), but seeing I looked very earnestly at him, he put them on the ground and walked about with seeming unconcern. Some of the people appearing to be frightened, I gave a looking-glass to one and a large nail to another. From this place the bay ran, as nearly as I could guess, a good mile. I looked all around with the glass, but saw no boat, canoe, or sign of inhabitants. I therefore contented myself with firing some guns, which I had done in every cove as I went along.

"I now kept close to the east shore, and came to another settlement, where the Indians invited us ashore. I inquired of them about the boat, but they pretended ignorance. They appeared very friendly here, and sold us some fish. Within an hour after we left this place, on a small beach adjoining Grass Cove, we saw a very large double canoe just hauled up, with two men and a dog. The men, on seeing us, left their canoe and ran up into the woods. This gave me reason to suspect I should here get tidings of the cutter. We went ashore, searched the canoe, and found one of the rowlock-ports of the cutter and some shoes, one of which was known to belong to Mr. Woodhouse, one of our midshipmen. One of the people at the same time brought me a piece of meat, which he took to be some of the salt meat belonging to the cutter's crew. On examining this, and smelling it, I found it to be fresh. Mr. Fannin (the master), who was with me, supposed it was dog's flesh, and I was of the same opinion, for I still doubted their being cannibals. But we were soon convinced by the most horrid and undeniable proof.

"A great many baskets (about twenty) lying on the beach tied up, we cut them open. Some were full of roasted flesh, and some of fern-root, which serves them for bread. On further search were found more shoes and a hand, which we immediately knew to have belonged to Thomas Hill, one of our forecastle-men, it being marked "*T. H.*" with an Otaheitean tattoo instrument. I went with some of the people a little way into the woods, but saw nothing else. Coming down again there was a round spot covered with fresh earth about four feet in diameter, where something had been buried. Having no spade, we began to dig with a cutlass, and in the meantime I launched the canoe with intent to destroy her; but seeing a great smoke ascending over the nearest hill, I got all the people into the boat, and made all the haste I could to be with them before sunset.

"On opening the next bay, which was Grass Cove, we saw four canoes and a great many people on the breach, who, on our approach, retreated to a small hill about a ship's length from the waterside, where they stood talking to us. A large fire was on the top of the high land beyond the woods, whence, all the way down the hill, the place was thronged like a fair. The savages on the hill still kept hallooing and making signs for us to land. However, as soon as we got close in we all fired. The first volley did not seem to affect them much, but on the second they began to scramble away as fast as they could, some of them howling. We continued firing as long as we could see the glimpse of any of them through the bushes. Among the Indians were two very stout men, who never offered to move till they found themselves forsaken by their companions, and then marched away with great composure and deliberation, their pride not suffering them to run. One of them, however, got a fall, and either lay there or crawled on all-fours. The other got clear, without any apparent hurt. I then landed with the marines, and Mr. Fannin stayed to guard the boat.

"On the beach were two bundles of celery which had been gathered for loading the cutter. A broken oar was stuck upright in the ground, to which the natives had tied their canoes, a proof that the attack had been made here. I then searched all along at the back of the beach to see if the cutter was there. We found no boat, but instead of her we saw such a shocking scene of carnage and barbarity as never can be mentioned or thought of but with horror; for the heads, hearts, and lungs of several of our people were seen lying on the beach, and at a little distance the dogs gnawing their entrails.

"Whilst we remained almost stupefied on the spot, Mr. Fannin called to us that he heard the savages gathering together in the woods; on which I returned to the boat, and, hauling alongside the canoes, we demolished three of them. While this was transacting the fire on the top of the hill disappeared, and we could hear the Indians in the woods at high words—I suppose quarrelling whether they should attack us and try to save their canoes. It now grew dark. I therefore just stepped out and looked once more behind the beach to see if the cutter had been hauled up in the bushes; but, seeing nothing of her, returned and put off. Our whole force would have been barely sufficient to have gone up the hill, and to have ventured with half (for half must have been left to guard the boat) would have been foolhardiness. As we opened the upper part of the sound, we saw a very large fire about three or four miles higher up, which formed a complete oval, reaching from the top of the hill down almost to the waterside, the middle space being enclosed all round by the fire like a hedge. I consulted with Mr. Fannin, and we were both of opinion that we could expect to reap no other advantage than the poor satisfaction of killing some more of the savages.

"At leaving Grass Cove we had fired a general volley towards where we heard the Indians talking; but by going in and out of the boat the arms had got wet, and four pieces missed fire. What was still worse, it began to rain, our ammunition was more than half expended, and we left six large canoes behind us in one place. With so many disadvantages, I did not think it worth while to proceed, where nothing could be hoped for but revenge.

"Coming between two round islands situated to the southward of East Bay, we imagined we heard somebody calling. We lay on our oars and listened, but heard no more of it. We hallooed several times, but to little purpose—the poor souls were far enough out of hearing; and, indeed, I think it some comfort to reflect that, in all probability, every man of them must have been killed on the spot."

Thus far Mr. Burney's report; and to complete the account of this tragical transaction, it may not be unnecessary to mention that the people in the cutter were: Mr. Rowe, Mr. Woodhouse; Francis Murphy, quartermaster; William Facey, Thomas Hill, Michael Bell, and Edward Jones, forecastle-men; John Cavenaugh and Thomas Miller, belonging to the afterguard; and James Savilly, the captain's man—being ten in all. Most of these were the *Adventure's* very best seamen, the stoutest and most healthy men in the ship. Mr. Burney's party brought on board two hands, one belonging to Mr. Rowe, known by a hurt he had received on it, and the other to Thomas Hill, as before mentioned; also the head of the captain's servant. These, with more of the remains, were tied in a hammock and thrown overboard, with ballast and shot sufficient to sink it.

None of their arms or clothes were found, except part of a pair of trousers and six shoes, no two of them being fellows.

I am not inclined to think this was any premeditated plan of these savages; for the morning Mr. Rowe left the ship he met two canoes, which came down and stayed all the forenoon in Ship Cove. It might probably happen from some quarrel which was decided on the spot, or the fairness of the opportunity might tempt them, our people being so incautious and thinking themselves too secure. Another thing which encouraged the New Zealanders was, they were sensible that a gun was not infallible, that they sometimes missed, and that when discharged they must be loaded before they could be used again, which time they knew how to take advantage of. After their success, I imagine there was a general meeting on the east side of the sound. The Indians of Shag Cove were there (this we knew by a cock which was in one of the canoes, and by a long single canoe), which some of our people had seen four days before in Shag Cove, where they had been with Mr. Rowe in the cutter.

We were detained in the sound by contrary winds four days after this melancholy affair happened, during which time we saw none of the inhabitants. What is very remarkable, I had been several times up in the same cove with Captain Cook, and never saw the least sign of an inhabitant, except some deserted towns which appeared as if they had not been occupied for several years; and yet when Mr. Burney entered the cove he was of opinion there could not be less than fifteen hundred or two thousand people. I doubt not, had they been apprised of his coming, they would have attacked him. From these considerations I thought it imprudent to send a boat up again, as we were convinced there was not the least probability of any of our people being alive.

On the 23rd we weighed and made sail out of the sound, and stood to the eastward to get clear of the straits, which we accomplished the same evening, but were baffled for two or three days with light winds before we could clear the coast. We then stood to the SSE. till we got into the latitude of 56° S., without anything remarkable happening, having a great swell from the southward. At this time the winds began to blow strong from the SW. and the weather to be very cold; and as the ship was low and deep laden, the sea made a continual breach over her, which kept us always wet; and by her straining, very few of the people were dry in bed or on deck, having no shelter to keep the sea from them.

The birds were the only companions we had in this vast ocean, except now and then we saw a whale or porpoise. We found a very strong current setting to the eastward. We were very little more than a month from Cape Palliser in New Zealand to Cape Horn, which is one hundred and twenty-one degrees of longitude, and had continual westerly winds from SW. to NW., with a great sea following.

On opening some casks of pease and flour that had been stowed on the coals, we found them very much damaged and not eatable, so thought it most prudent to make for the Cape of Good Hope.

On the 17th made the land of the Cape of Good Hope, and on the 18th anchored in Table Bay. Here I remained, refitting the ship and refreshing my people till the 16th of April, when I sailed for England, and on the 14th of July anchored at Spithead.

CHAPTER XXXIII.

TRANSACTIONS AT THE CAPE OF GOOD HOPE—ARRIVAL OF THE SHIP AT ST. HELENA—PASSAGE FROM ST. HELENA TO THE WESTERN ISLANDS, WITH AN ACCOUNT OF THE ISLAND OF ASCENSION AND FERNANDO NORONHA—ARRIVAL AT THE ISLAND OF FAYAL—THE RETURN OF THE "RESOLUTION" TO ENGLAND.

1775.
March.

I NOW resume my own journal, which Captain Furneaux's interesting narrative in the preceding chapter had obliged me to suspend.

The day after my arrival at the Cape of Good Hope I went on shore and waited on the governor, Baron Plettenberg, and other principal officers, who received and treated us with the greatest politeness, contributing all in their power to make it agreeable. And as there are few people more obliging to strangers than the Dutch in general at this place, and refreshments of all kinds are nowhere to be got in such abundance, we enjoyed some real repose after the fatigues of a long voyage.

The good treatment which strangers meet with at the Cape of Good Hope, and the necessity of breathing a little fresh air, has introduced a custom not common anywhere else, which is for all the officers who can be spared out of the ships to reside on shore. We followed this custom. Myself, the two Mr. Forsters, and Mr. Sparrman took up our abode with Mr. Brandt, a gentleman well known to the English by his obliging readiness to serve them. My first care after my arrival was to procure fresh-baked bread, fresh meat, greens, and wine for those who remained on board, and, being provided every day during our stay with these articles, they were soon restored to their usual strength. We had only three men on board whom it was thought necessary to send on shore for the recovery of their health, and for these I procured quarters at the rate of half a crown per day, for which they were provided with victuals, drink, and lodging.

We now went to work to supply all our defects. For this purpose we erected a tent on shore, to which we sent our casks and sails to be repaired. That our rigging, sails, etc., should be worn out will not be wondered at when it is known that during this circumnavigation of the globe—that is, from our leaving this place to our return to it again, we had sailed no less than twenty thousand leagues, an extent of voyage nearly equal to three times the equatorial circumference of the earth, and which, I apprehend, was never sailed by any ship in the same space of time before. And yet, in all this great run, we sprung neither low-masts, topmast, lower nor topsail yard, nor so much as broke a lower or topmast shroud, which, with the great care and abilities of my officers, must be owing to the good properties of our ship.

By the 26th of April our work was finished, and having got on board all necessary stores and a fresh supply of provisions and water, we took leave of the governor and other principal officers, and the next morning repaired on board. Soon after, the wind coming fair, we weighed and put to sea. As soon as we were under sail we saluted the garrison with thirteen guns, which compliment was immediately returned with the same number.

At daybreak in the morning of the 15th of May we saw the island of St. Helena, and at midnight anchored in the road before the town, on the north-west side of the island.

Governor Sheltowe and the principal gentlemen of the island received me, and treated me during my stay with the greatest politeness by showing me every kind of civility in their power. Within these three years * a new church has been built, some other new buildings were in hand, a commodious landing-place for boats has been made, and several other improvements which add strength and beauty to the place.

During our stay here we finished some necessary repairs of the ship which we had not time to do at the Cape. We also filled all our empty water-casks, and the crew were served with fresh beef purchased at fivepence per pound. Their beef is exceedingly good, and is the only refreshment to be had worth mentioning.

On the 21st I took leave of the governor, and repaired on board. Upon my leaving the shore I was saluted with thirteen

* See page 191, first Voyage.

guns, and upon my getting under sail I was saluted with thirteen more. In the morning of the 28th I made the island of Ascension, and the same evening anchored in Cross Bay.

The island of Ascension is about ten miles in length and about five or six in breadth. It shows a surface composed of barren hills and valleys, on the most of which not a shrub or plant is to be seen for several miles, and where we found nothing but stones and sand, or rather slags and ashes—an indubitable sign that the isle, at some remote time, has been destroyed by a volcano which has thrown up vast heaps of stones and even hills. A high mountain at the south-east end of the isle seems to be left in its original state and to have escaped the general destruction.

I was told that about some part of the isle is very good land on which might be raised many necessary articles, and some have been at the trouble of sowing turnips and other useful vegetables. Turtle, I am told, are to be found at this isle from January to June. The method of catching them is to have people upon the several sandy bays to watch their coming on shore to lay their eggs, which is always in the night, and then to turn them on their backs till there be an opportunity to take them off the next day.

On the 31st of May we left Ascension, and steered to the northward with a fine gale at SE. by E. I had a great desire to visit the island of St. Matthew to settle its situation; but as I found the winds would not let me fetch it, I steered for the island of Fernando de Noronha on the coast of Brazil. Perhaps I should have performed a more acceptable service to navigation if I had gone in search of the island of St. Paul. The truth is, I was unwilling to prolong the passage in searching for what I was not sure to find, nor was I willing to give up every object which might tend to the improvement of navigation or geography for the sake of getting home a week or a fortnight sooner. It is but seldom that opportunities of this kind offer, and when they do they are too often neglected.

On the 9th of June at noon we made the island of Fernando de Noronha. It appeared in detached and peaked hills, the largest of which looked like a church tower or steeple. As we drew near the south-east part of the isle, we perceived several unconnected sunken rocks lying nearly a league from the

June.

shore, on which the sea broke in a great surf. After standing very near these rocks, we hoisted our colours, and then bore up round the north end of the isle, for we could see that the land was divided by narrow channels. We continued to steer round the northern point till the sandy beaches began to appear. At this time, on a gun being fired from one of the forts, the Portuguese colours were displayed, and the example was followed by all the other forts. As the purpose for which I made the island was now answered, I had no intention to anchor, and therefore we made sail and stood away to the northward, with a fine fresh gale at ESE.

On the 11th, at three o'clock in the afternoon, we crossed the equator. At five o'clock in the evening of the 13th we made the island of Fayal, one of the Azores, and at eight o'clock next morning we anchored in twenty fathoms water, something more than half a mile from the shore.

As my sole design in stopping here was to give Mr. Wales an opportunity of fixing with some degree of certainty the longitude of these islands, the moment we anchored I sent an officer to wait on the English consul and to notify our arrival to the governor. Mr. Dent, who was acting as consul, not only procured permission for Mr. Wales to make observations on shore, but accommodated him with a convenient place in his garden to set up his instruments.

We were not more obliged to Mr. Dent for the very friendly readiness he showed in procuring us this and every other thing we wanted than for the very liberal and hospitable entertainment we met with at his house, which was open to accommodate us both night and day. During our stay the ship's company was served with fresh beef, and we took on board about fifteen tons of water, which we brought off in the country's boats at the rate of about three shillings per ton.

Fresh provisions for present use may be got—such as beef, vegetables, and fruit, and hogs, sheep, and poultry for sea-stock— all at a pretty reasonable price; but I do not know that any sea-provisions are to be had, except wine. The bullocks and hogs are very good, but the sheep are small and wretchedly poor. The principal produce of Fayal is wheat and Indian corn.

The little city of Villa de Horta, like all others belonging to the Portuguese, is crowded with religious buildings—there being no less than three convents of men and two of women, and eight churches.

Having left the bar at four in the morning of the 19th, I steered for the west end of St. George's Island. As soon as we had passed it, I steered for the island of Terceira. I now edged away for the north side of the island, with a view to ranging the coast to the eastern point in order to ascertain the length of the island; but the weather coming on very thick and hazy, and night approaching, I gave up the design and proceeded with all expedition for England.

On the 29th we made the land near Plymouth. The next morning we anchored at Spithead, and the same day I landed at Portsmouth and set out for London.

Having been absent from England three years and eighteen days, in which time and under all changes of climate I lost but four men, and only one of them by sickness, it may not be amiss at the conclusion of this journal to enumerate the several causes to which, under the care of Providence, I conceive this uncommon good state of health experienced by my people was owing.

Mention has been made of the extraordinary attention paid by the Admiralty in causing such articles to be put on board as, either from experience or suggestion, it was judged would tend to preserve the health of the seamen. I shall not trespass upon the reader's time in mentioning them all, but confine myself to such as were found the most useful.

We were furnished with a quantity of malt, of which was made sweet wort. To such of the men as showed the least symptoms of the scurvy this was given, from two to three pints a day to each man. This is, without doubt, one of the best antiscorbutic sea medicines yet discovered.

Sour krout, of which we had a large quantity, is not only a wholesome vegetable food, but, in my judgment, highly anti-scorbutic, and it spoils not by keeping. A pound of this was served to each man when at sea twice a week or oftener, as was thought necessary. Portable broth was another great article of which we had a large supply. An ounce of this to each man was boiled in their pease three days in the week; and when we were in places where vegetables were to be got, it was boiled with them and wheat or oatmeal every morning for breakfast, and also with pease and vegetables for dinner. It enabled us to make several nourishing and wholesome messes, and was the means of making the people eat a greater quantity of vegetables than they would otherwise have done.

Rob of lemon and orange is an anti-scorbutic we were not without. The surgeon made use of it in many cases with great success.

But the introduction of the most salutary articles, either as provisions or medicines, will generally prove unsuccessful unless supported by certain regulations. On this principle many years' experience, together with some hints I had from Sir Hugh Palliser, Captains Campbell, Wallis, and other intelligent officers, enabled me to lay a plan whereby all was to be governed.

The crew were at three watches, except upon some extraordinary occasions. By this means they were not so much exposed to the weather as if they had been at watch and watch, and had generally dry clothes to shift themselves when they happened to get wet. Care was also taken to expose them as little to wet weather as possible. Proper methods were used to keep their persons, hammocks, bedding, and clothes constantly clean and dry. Equal care was taken to keep the ship clean and dry between decks. Once or twice a week she was aired with fires, and when this could not be done, she was smoked with gunpowder mixed with vinegar or water. I also frequently had a fire made in an iron pot at the bottom of the well, which was of great use in purifying the air in the lower parts of the ship. To this and to cleanliness, as well in the ship as amongst the people, too great attention cannot be paid. The least neglect occasions a disagreeable smell below, which nothing but fires will remove. Proper attention was paid to the ship's coppers, so that they were kept constantly clean.

The fat which boiled out of the salt beef and pork I never suffered to be given to the people, being of opinion that it promotes the scurvy.

I was careful to take in water wherever it was to be got, even though we did not want it; because I look upon fresh water from the shore to be more wholesome than that which has been kept some time on board a ship. Of this essential article we were never at an allowance, but had always plenty for every necessary purpose. Navigators in general cannot, indeed, expect, nor would they wish to meet with such advantages in this respect as fell to my lot. The nature of our voyage carried us into very high latitudes; but the hardships and dangers inseparable from that situation were in some degree compensated by the singular felicity we enjoyed of extracting inexhaustible supplies of fresh water from an ocean strewed with ice.

We came to few places where either the art of man or the bounty of nature had not provided some sort of refreshment or other, either in the animal or vegetable way. It was my first care to procure whatever of any kind could be met with by every means in my power, and to oblige our people to make use thereof, both by my example and authority; but the benefit arising from refreshments of any kind soon become so obvious that I had little occasion to recommend the one or to exert the other.

It doth not become me to say how far the principal objects of our voyage have been obtained. Though it hath not abounded with remarkable events, nor been diversified by sudden transitions of fortune; though my relation of it has been more employed in tracing our course by sea than in recording our operations on shore—this, perhaps, is a circumstance from which the curious reader may infer that the purposes for which we were sent into the southern hemisphere, were diligently and effectually pursued. Had we found out a continent there, we might have been better enabled to gratify curiosity; but we hope our not having found it, after all our persevering researches, will leave less room for future speculations about unknown worlds remaining to be explored.

But, whatever may be the public judgment about other matters, it is with real satisfaction, and without claiming any merit but that of attention to my duty, that I can conclude this account with an observation which facts enable me to make, that our having discovered the possibility of preserving health among a numerous ship's company for such a length of time, in such varieties of climate, and amidst such continued hardships and fatigues, will make this voyage remarkable in the opinion of every benevolent person, when the dispute about a southern continent shall have ceased to occupy the attention and to divide the judgment of philosophers.

Third Voyage.

CHAPTER XXXIV.

PREPARATION FOR THE VOYAGE—OMAI'S BEHAVIOUR ON EMBARKING—INSTRUCTIONS TO CAPTAIN COOK—DEPARTURE OF THE "RESOLUTION."

HAVING on the 9th day of February 1776 received a commission to command His Majesty's sloop the *Resolution*, I went on board the next day, hoisted the pendant, and began to enter men. At the same time, the *Discovery*, of three hundred tons burden, was purchased into the service, and the command of her given to Captain Clerke, who had been my second lieutenant on board the *Resolution* in my second voyage round the world, from which we had lately returned. **1776. February.**

On the 9th of March, the *Resolution* was hauled out of dock into the river; where we completed her rigging and took on board the stores and provisions requisite for a voyage of such duration. Both ships, indeed, were supplied with as much of every necessary article as we could conveniently stow, and with the best of every kind that could be procured. And, besides this, everything that had been found by the experience acquired during our former extensive voyages to be of any utility in preserving the health of seamen was supplied in abundance. While we lay in Long Reach, the Earl of Sandwich, Sir Hugh Palliser, and others of the Board of Admiralty, as the last mark of the very great attention they had all along shown to this equipment, paid us a visit on the 8th of June, to examine whether everything had been completed conformably to their intentions and orders and to the satisfaction of all who were to embark in the voyage.

With the benevolent view of conveying some permanent

benefit to the inhabitants of Otaheite, and of the other islands in the Pacific Ocean whom we might happen to visit, His Majesty having commanded some useful animals to be carried out, we took on board, on the 10th, a bull, two cows with their calves and some sheep, with hay and corn for their subsistence. I was also, from the same laudable motives, furnished with a sufficient quantity of such of our European garden seeds as could not fail to be a valuable present to our newly-discovered islands, by adding fresh supplies of food to their own vegetable productions.

The same humane attention was extended to our own wants. Some additional clothing, adapted to a cold climate, was ordered for our crews. Nor did the extraordinary care of those at the head of the naval department stop here. They were equally solicitous to afford us every assistance towards rendering our voyage of public utility. Accordingly we received on board several astronomical and nautical instruments which the Board of Longitude entrusted to me; we having engaged to that board to make all the necessary observations, during the voyage, for the improvement of astronomy and navigation.

On the 15th, the *Resolution* sailed from Long Reach, with the *Discovery* in company. As we were to touch at Otaheite and the Society Islands on our way to the intended scene of our fresh operations, it had been determined not to omit this opportunity of carrying Omai back to his native country. Omai left London with a mixture of regret and satisfaction. When we talked about England, and about those who, during his stay, had honoured him with their protection or friendship, I could observe that his spirits were visibly affected, and that it was with difficulty he could refrain from tears. But the instant the conversation turned to his own islands, his eyes began to sparkle with joy. He was furnished by His Majesty with an ample provision of every article which, during our intercourse with his country, we had observed to be in any estimation there, either as useful or as ornamental. In short every method had been employed, both during his abode in England and at his departure, to make him the instrument of conveying to the inhabitants of the islands of the Pacific Ocean the most exalted opinion of the greatness and generosity of the British nation.

On the 8th of July I received, by express, my instructions for the voyage :—

SECRET INSTRUCTIONS FOR CAPTAIN JAMES COOK, COMMANDER OF HIS MAJESTY'S SLOOP THE "RESOLUTION."

"Whereas the Earl of Sandwich has signified to us His Majesty's pleasure that an attempt should be made to find out a northern passage by sea from the Pacific to the Atlantic Ocean; and whereas we have, in pursuance thereof, caused His Majesty's sloops *Resolution* and *Discovery* to be fitted, in all respects proper, to proceed upon a voyage for the purpose above mentioned; and from the experience we have had of your abilities and good conduct in your late voyages, have thought fit to entrust you with the conduct of the present intended voyage, and with that view appointed you to command the first-mentioned sloop, and directed Captain Clerke, who commands the other, to follow your orders for his further proceedings : You are hereby required and directed to proceed with the said two sloops directly to the Cape of Good Hope, unless you shall judge it necessary to stop at Madeira, the Cape de Verd, or Canary Islands, to take in wine for the use of their companies; in which case you are at liberty so to do, taking care to remain there no longer than may be necessary for that purpose. On your arrival at the Cape of Good Hope, you are to refresh the sloops' companies with as much provision and water as can be conveniently stowed.

"You are, if possible, to leave the Cape of Good Hope by the end of October or beginning of November next, and proceed to the southward in search of some islands, said to have been lately seen by the French, in the latitude 48° south, and about the meridian of Mauritius. In case you find those islands, you are to examine them thoroughly for a good harbour; and upon discovering one, make the necessary observations to facilitate the finding it again; as a good port in that situation may hereafter prove very useful, although it should afford nothing more than shelter, wood, and water. You are not, however, to spend too much time in looking out for those islands, or in the examination of them if found, but to proceed to Otaheite, or the Society Isles (touching at New Zealand in your way thither if you should judge it necessary and convenient), and taking care to arrive there time enough to admit of your giving the sloops' companies the refreshment they may stand in need of, before you prosecute the further object of these instructions.

"Upon your arrival at Otaheite, or the Society Isles, you are to land Omai at such of them as he may choose, and to leave him there.

"You are to distribute among the chiefs of those islands such part of the presents with which you have been supplied as you shall judge proper, reserving the remainder to distribute among the natives of the country you may discover in the Northern Hemisphere; and having refreshed the people belonging to the sloops under your command, and taken on board such wood and water as they may respectively stand in need of, you are to leave those islands in the beginning of February, or sooner if you shall judge it necessary, and then to proceed in as direct a course as you can to the coast of New Albion, endeavouring to fall in with it in the latitude of 45° north; and taking care in your way thither not to lose any time in search of new lands, or to stop at any you may fall in with, unless you find it necessary to recruit your wood and water.

"You are also, in your way thither, strictly enjoined not to touch upon any part of the Spanish dominions on the western continent of America, unless driven thither by some unavoidable accident, in which case you are to stay no longer there than shall be absolutely necessary, and to be very careful not to give any umbrage or offence to any of the inhabitants or subjects of His Catholic Majesty. And, if, in your further progress to the northward, as hereafter directed, you find any subjects of any European prince or state upon any part of the coast you may think proper to visit, you are not to disturb them, or give them any just cause of offence, but, on the contrary, to treat them with civility and friendship.

"Upon your arrival on the coast of New Albion, you are to put into the first convenient port to recruit your wood and water, and procure refreshments, and then to proceed northward along the coast, as far as the latitude of 65°, or farther, if you are not obstructed by lands or ice; taking care not to lose any time in exploring rivers or inlets, or upon any other account, until you get in the before-mentioned latitude of 65°, where we could wish you to arrive in the month of June next. When you get that length, you are very carefully to search for, and explore, such rivers or inlets as may appear to be of a considerable extent, and pointing towards Hudson or Baffin Bays; and if, from your own observations, or from information from the natives (who, there is reason to believe, are the same race of people, and speak the same language—of which you are furnished with a vocabulary—as the Esquimaux), there shall appear to be a certainty, or even a probability, of a water passage into the afore-mentioned bays, or either of them, you are, in such case, to use your utmost endeavours to pass through with one or both of the sloops, unless you shall be of opinion that the passage may be effected with more certainty, or with greater probability, by smaller vessels; in which case you are to set up the frames of one or both of the small vessels with which you are provided, and, when they are put together, and are properly fitted, stored, and victualled, you are to despatch one or both of them, under the care of proper officers, with a sufficient number of petty officers, men, and boats, in order to attempt the said passage; with such instructions for their rejoining you, if they should fail, or for their further proceedings, if they should succeed in the attempt, as you shall judge most proper. But, nevertheless, if you shall find it more eligible to pursue any other measures than those above pointed out, in order to make a discovery of the before-mentioned passage (if any such there be), you are at liberty; and we leave it to your discretion to pursue such measures accordingly.

"In case you shall be satisfied that there is no passage through to the above-mentioned bays, sufficient for the purposes of navigation, you are, at the proper season of the year, to repair to the port of St. Peter and St. Paul, in Kamtchatka, or wherever else you shall judge more proper, in order to refresh your people and pass the winter; and, in the spring of the ensuing year, 1778, to proceed from thence to the northward, as far as in your prudence you may think proper, in further search of a north-east or northwest passage from the Pacific Ocean into the Atlantic Ocean or the North Sea; and if, from your own observation, or any information you may receive, there shall appear to be a probability of such a passage, you are to proceed as above directed; and, having discovered such a passage, or failed in the attempt, make the best of your way back to England, by such route as you may think best for the improvement of geography and navigation; repairing to Spithead with both sloops, where they are to remain till further orders.

"At whatever places you may touch in the course of your voyage, where accurate observations of the nature hereafter mentioned have not already been made, you are, as far as your time will allow, very carefully to observe the true situation of such places, both in latitude and longitude; the variation of the needle; bearings of headlands; height, direction, and course of the tides and currents; depths and soundings of the sea; shoals, rocks, etc.; and also to survey, make charts, and take views of such bays, harbours, and different parts of the coast, and to make such notations thereon as may be useful either to navigation or commerce. You are also carefully to observe the nature of the soil and the produce thereof; the animals and fowls that inhabit or frequent it; the fishes that are to be found in the rivers or upon the coast, and in what plenty; and, in case there are any peculiar to such places, to describe them as minutely and to make as accurate drawings of them as you can; and, if you find any metals, minerals, or valuable stones, or any extraneous fossils, you are to bring home specimens of each; as also of the seeds of such trees, shrubs, plants, fruits, and grains peculiar to those places as you may be able to collect, and to transmit them to our secretary, that proper experiments and examination may be made of them. You are likewise to examine the genius, temper, disposition, and number of the natives and inhabitants, where you find any; and to endeavour, by all proper means, to cultivate a friendship with them; making them presents of such trinkets as you may have on board, and they may like best; inviting them to traffic, and showing them every kind of civility and regard; but taking care, nevertheless, not to suffer yourselves to be surprised by them, but to be always on your guard against any accidents.

"You are also, with the consent of the natives, to take possession, in the name of the King of Great Britain, of convenient situations in such countries as you may discover, that have not already been discovered or visited by any other European power; and to distribute among the inhabitants such things as will remain as traces and testimonies of your having been there; but if you find the countries so discovered are uninhabited, you are to take possession of them for His Majesty, by setting up proper marks and inscriptions as first discoverers and possessors.

"But forasmuch as, in undertakings of this nature, several emergencies may arise not to be foreseen, and therefore not particularly to be provided for by instructions beforehand, you are, in such cases, to proceed as you shall judge most advantageous to the service on which you are employed. You are, by all opportunities, to send to our secretary, for our information, accounts of your proceedings, and copies of the surveys and drawings you shall have made; and upon your arrival in England, you are immediately to repair to this office, in order to lay before us a full account of your proceedings in the whole course of your voyage; taking care, before you leave the sloop, to demand from the officers and petty officers the logbooks and journals they may have kept, and to seal them up for our inspection; and enjoining them and the whole crew not to divulge where they have been, until they shall have permission so to do; and you are to direct Captain Clerke to do the same with respect to the officers, petty officers, and crew of the *Discovery*.

"If any accident should happen to the *Resolution* in the course of the voyage, so as to disable her from proceeding any further, you are, in such case, to remove yourself and her crew into the *Discovery*, and to prosecute your voyage in her, her commander being hereby strictly required to receive you on board, and to obey your orders, the same in every respect as when you were actually on board the *Resolution*. And, in case of your inability by sickness, or otherwise, to carry these instructions into execution, you are to be careful to leave them with the next officer in command, who is hereby required to execute them in the best manner he can.

"Given under our hands the 6th day of July 1776.

"SANDWICH.
"By command of their Lordships,   "C. SPENCER.
    "PH. STEPHENS."   "H. PALLISER.

The *Resolution* was fitted out with the same complement of officers and men she had before. The petty officers and seamen had two months' wages in advance, and the officers and crew were paid up to the 30th of last month. Such indulgence to the former is no more than what is customary in the navy. But the payment of what was due to the superior officers was humanely ordered by the Admiralty, in consideration of our peculiar situation, that we might be better able to defray the very great expense of furnishing ourselves with a stock of necessaries for a voyage which probably would be of unusual duration, and to regions where no supply could be expected.

CHAPTER XXXV.

ARRIVAL OF THE "RESOLUTION" AT TENERIFFE—DEPARTURE FROM TENERIFFE—DANGER OF THE SHIP NEAR BONAVISTA—ARRIVAL AT THE CAPE OF GOOD HOPE—THE TWO SHIPS LEAVE THE CAPE OF GOOD HOPE—ARRIVAL IN CHRISTMAS HARBOUR—PASSAGE TO VAN DIEMEN'S LAND—FROM VAN DIEMEN'S LAND TO NEW ZEALAND—TRANSACTIONS WITH THE NATIVES.

FINDING that we had not hay and corn sufficient for the subsistence of the stock of animals on board till our arrival at the Cape of Good Hope, I determined to touch at Teneriffe to get a supply of these, and of the usual refreshments for ourselves.

At eight o'clock on the morning of the 1st of August we anchored in the road of Santa Cruz. The ample supplies which we received here convinced us that they had enough and to spare. Besides wine, beef may be obtained at a moderate price. Hogs, sheep, goats, and poultry are to be bought, and fruits in great plenty.

August.

Having completed our water, and got on board every other thing we wanted at Teneriffe, we weighed anchor on the 4th of August, and proceeded on our voyage with a fine gale at NE.

At nine o'clock in the evening of the 10th we saw the island of Bonavista distant little more than a league, though at this time we thought ourselves much farther off, but this proved a mistake, for at twelve o'clock we found ourselves close upon them, and did but just weather the breakers. Our situation for a few minutes was very alarming. As soon as we were clear of the rocks we steered SSW. From this time till the 30th we had frequent rains, and the weather was dark and gloomy. These rains, and the close, sultry weather accompanying them, too often bring on sickness in this passage, and commanders of ships cannot be too much upon their guard by purifying the air between decks with fires and smoke, and by obliging the people to dry their clothes at every opportunity. These precautions were constantly observed on board the *Resolution* and *Discovery*, and we certainly profited by them, for we had now fewer sick than on either of my former voyages. We had, however, the mortification to find our ship exceedingly leaky in all her upper works. The hot and sultry weather we had just passed through had opened her seams so wide that they admitted the rain-water through as it fell. There was hardly a man that could lie dry in his bed. The sails in the sail-room got wet, and before we had weather to dry them many of them were much damaged.

September. On the 1st of September we crossed the equator, and proceeded on our voyage without meeting anything of note till the 6th of October. We had for some days before seen albatrosses, pintadoes, and other petrels, and now we saw three penguins. On the 8th one of those birds which the sailors call noddies settled on our rigging, and was caught.

On the 17th we had sight of the Cape of Good Hope, and the next day anchored in Table Bay. As soon as we had saluted I went on shore, accompanied by some of my officers, and waited on the governor and other officials. These gentlemen received me with the greatest civility, and the governor in particular promised me every assistance that the place afforded. At the same time I obtained his leave to set up our observatory, to pitch tents for the sailmakers and coopers, and to bring the cattle on shore to graze near our encampment. Before I returned on board I ordered soft bread, fresh meat, and greens to be provided every day for the ship's company.

Nothing remarkable happened till the evening of the 31st, when it came on to blow excessively hard at south-east, and continued for three days, during which time there was no communication between the ship and the shore. *The Resolution* was the only ship in the bay that rode out the gale without dragging her anchors. We felt its effects as sensibly on shore. Our tents and observatory were torn to pieces, and the astronomical quadrant narrowly escaped irreparable damage. On the 3rd of November.
November the storm ceased. I added to my original stock by purchasing two young bulls, two heifers, two young stone horses, two mares, two rams, several ewes and goats, and some rabbits and poultry. All of them were intended for New Zealand,

Otaheite, and the neighbouring islands, or any other place in the course of our voyage where there might be a prospect of their proving useful to posterity.

Having given Captain Clerke a copy of my instructions, and an order directing him how to proceed in case of separation, we repaired on board, and on the 30th we weighed and stood out of the bay. We continued our course to the SE., with a very strong gale from the westward, followed by a mountainous sea, which made the ship roll and tumble exceedingly, and gave us a great deal of trouble to preserve the cattle we had on board. Notwithstanding all our care several goats, especially the males, died, and some sheep. This misfortune was in a great measure owing to the cold, which we now began most sensibly to feel. On the 12th of December we found two islands, which we now called Prince Edward's Islands, after His Majesty's fourth son.

On the 24th we saw land, which upon a nearer approach we found to be an island of considerable height. Soon after we saw another of the same magnitude, and between these two some smaller ones. Here we anchored, and the people having wrought the two preceding days, and nearly completed our water, I allowed them the 27th as a day of rest, to celebrate Christmas. In the evening one of them brought to me a quart bottle, which he had found fastened with some wire to a projecting rock on the north side of the harbour. The bottle contained a piece of parchment, on which was written the following inscription :—

> "*Ludovico XV. Galliarum*
> *rege, et d. de Boynes*
> *regi a Secretis ad res*
> *Maritimas annis 1772 et 1773.*"

From this inscription it is clear that we are not the first Europeans who have been in this harbour. As a memorial of our having been here, I wrote on the other side of the parchment :—

> "*Naves Resolution*
> *et Discovery*
> *de Rege Magnæ Britanniæ.*
> *Decembris 1776.*"

I then put it again into a bottle, together with a silver twopenny piece of 1772, and having covered the mouth of the bottle with a leaden cap, I placed it the next morning in a pile of stones erected for the purpose, near to the place where it was first found. Here I displayed the British flag, and named the place Christmas Harbour, from our having arrived in it on that festival. From the sterility of this island I should, with great propriety, call it the Island of Desolation, but that I would not rob M. de Kerguelen of the honour of its bearing his name. After leaving Kerguelen's Land I steered E. by N., intending to touch next at New Zealand to recruit our water, to take in wood, and to make hay for the cattle.

On the 24th of January, at three o'clock in the morning, we discovered the coast of Van Diemen's Land, and on the 26th we carried the ships into Adventure Bay, where I might expect a supply of wood, and of grass for the cattle. Of both articles we should, as I now found, have been in great want if I had waited till our arrival in New Zealand. As soon as we had anchored I ordered the boats to be hoisted out. In one of them I went myself to look for the most commodious place for furnishing ourselves with the necessary supplies. Wood and water we found in plenty, but grass, of which we stood most in need, was scarce, and also very coarse. In the evening we drew the seine at the head of the bay, and at one haul caught a great quantity of fish. We should have got many more had not the net broken in drawing it ashore. Most of them were known to seamen by the name of elephant-fish.

In the afternoon next day we were agreeably surprised, at the place where we were cutting wood, with a visit from some of the natives, eight men and a boy. They approached us from the woods without betraying any marks of fear, or rather with the greatest confidence imaginable; for none of them had any weapons, except one, who held in his hand a stick about two feet long, and pointed at one end.

They were quite naked, and wore no ornaments. They were of the common stature, but rather slender. Their skin was black, and also their hair, which was as woolly as that of any native of Guinea, but they were not distinguished by remarkably thick lips, nor flat noses. On the contrary, their features were far from

COAST OF VAN DIEMEN'S LAND.

being disagreeable. They had pretty good eyes, and their teeth were tolerably even, but very dirty. Most of them had their hair and beards smeared with a red ointment, and some had their faces also painted with the same composition.

They received every present we made to them without the least appearance of satisfaction. I had brought two pigs ashore, with a view to leave them in the woods. The instant these came within their reach they seized them, as a dog would have done, by the ears, and were for carrying them off immediately, with no other intention, as we could perceive, but to kill them.

Immediately after their retreat I ordered the two pigs, being a boar and a sow, to be carried about a mile within the woods at the head of the bay. I saw them left there, by the side of a freshwater brook. A young bull and a cow, and some sheep and goats, were also at first intended to have been left by me as an additional present to Van Diemen's Land. But I soon laid aside all thought of this, from a persuasion that the natives, incapable of entering into my views of improving their country, would destroy them. If ever they should meet with the pigs, I have no doubt this will be their fate.

Van Diemen's Land has been twice visited before. It was so named by Tasman, who discovered it in November 1642. From that time it had escaped all further notice by European navigators, till Captain Furneaux touched at it in March 1773. I hardly need say that it is the southern point of New Holland, which, if it doth not deserve the name of a continent, is by far the largest island in the world.

The only animal of the quadruped kind we got was a sort of opossum, about twice the size of a large rat. It is of a dusky colour above, tinged with a brown or rusty cast, and whitish below. About a third of the tail towards its tip is white, and bare underneath, by which it probably hangs on the branches of trees, as it lives on berries. The kangaroo, without all doubt, also inhabits here, as the natives we met with had some pieces of their skins; and we several times saw animals, though indistinctly, in the woods which, from the size, could be no other.

At eight o'clock in the morning of the 30th, a light breeze springing up at west, we weighed anchor, and put to sea from Adventure Bay. On the 10th of February, at four in the afternoon, we discovered the land of New Zealand, and at ten o'clock on the 12th anchored in our old station in Queen Charlotte's Sound.

We had not been long at anchor before several canoes filled with natives came alongside of the ships, but very few of them would venture on board, which appeared the more extraordinary, as I was well known to them all. There was one man in particular among them whom I had treated with remarkable kindness during the whole of my stay when I was last there. Yet now neither professions of friendship nor presents could prevail upon him to come into the ship. This shyness was to be accounted for only upon the supposition that they were apprehensive we had revisited their country in order to revenge the death of Captain Furneaux's people.

Seeing Omai on board my ship now, whom they must have remembered to have seen on board the *Adventure* when the melancholy affair happened, and whose first conversation with them as they approached generally turned on that subject, they must be well assured that I was no longer a stranger to it. I thought it necessary, therefore, to use every endeavour to assure them of the continuance of my friendship, and that I should not disturb them on that account. I do not know whether this had any weight with them, but certain it is, that they very soon laid aside all manner of restraint and distrust.

On the 13th we set up two tents, one from each ship, on the same spot where we had pitched them formerly. The remainder of the water-casks were also sent on shore, with the cooper to trim and a sufficient number of sailors to fill them. Two men were appointed to brew spruce beer, and the carpenter and his crew were ordered to cut wood. A boat with a party of men, under the direction of one of the mates, was sent to collect grass for our cattle, and the people that remained on board were employed in refitting the ship. In this manner we were all profitably busied during our stay.

If the natives entertained any suspicion of our revenging these acts of barbarity, they very soon laid it aside. For during the course of the day a great number of families came from different

DISAPPEARANCE OF ENGLISH SEEDS.

parts of the coast, and took up their residence close to us. The advantage we received from the natives coming to live with us was not inconsiderable; for every day some of them went out to catch fish. Nor was there any deficiency of other refreshments. Celery, scurvy-grass, and portable soup were boiled with the pease and wheat for both ship's companies every day during our whole stay; so that, if any of our people had contracted the seeds of the scurvy, such a regimen soon removed them. But the truth is, when we arrived here there were only two invalids upon the sick lists in both ships.

Amongst our occasional visitors was a chief named Kahoora, who, as I was informed, headed the party that cut off Captain Furneaux's people, and himself killed Mr. Rowe, the officer who commanded. To judge of the character of Kahoora by what I have heard from many of his countrymen, he seemed to be more feared than beloved among them. Not satisfied with telling me that he was a very bad man, some of them even importuned me to kill him; and I believe they were not a little surprised that I did not listen to them, for, according to their ideas of equity, this ought to have been done. If I had followed the advice of all our pretended friends, I might have extirpated the whole race, for the people of each hamlet or village by turns applied to me to destroy the other.

When the *Adventure* first arrived at Queen Charlotte's Sound in 1773, Mr. Bayly and the people with him, at their leisure hours, planted several spots with English garden seeds. Not the least vestige of these now remained. It is probable they had all been rooted out to make room for buildings when the village was reinhabited, for at all the other gardens then planted by Captain Furneaux we found cabbages, onions, leeks, and a few potatoes. These potatoes, which were first brought from the Cape of Good Hope, had been greatly improved by change of soil.

At daybreak on the 16th I set out with a party of men in five boats to collect food for our cattle. We proceeded about three leagues up the sound, and then landed on the east side, at a place where I had formerly been. Here we cut as much grass as loaded the two launches.

As we returned down the sound we visited Grass Cove, memorable as the scene of the massacre of Captain Furneaux's people. Whilst we were at this place our curiosity prompted us to inquire into the circumstances attending the melancholy fate of our countrymen, and Omai was made use of as interpreter for this purpose. The natives present answered all the questions that were put to them on the subject without reserve, and like men who are under no dread of punishment for a crime of which they are not guilty; for we already knew that none of them had been concerned in the unhappy transaction. They told us that while our people were sitting at dinner, surrounded by several of the natives, some of the latter stole, or snatched from them, some bread and fish, for which they were beaten. This being resented, a quarrel ensued, and two New Zealanders were shot dead by the only two muskets that were fired; for, before our people had time to discharge a third, or to load again those that had been fired, the natives rushed in upon them, overpowered them with their numbers, and put them all to death.

Besides relating the history of the massacre, they made us acquainted with the very spot that was the scene of it. They pointed to the place of the sun to mark to us at what hour of the day it happened, and according to this it must have been late in the afternoon. They also showed us the place where the boat lay. One of their number—a black servant of Captain Furneaux—was left in the boat to take care of her. This black was the cause of the quarrel, which was said to have happened thus: One of the natives stealing something out of the boat, the negro gave him a severe blow with a stick. The cries of the fellow being heard by his countrymen at a distance, they imagined he was killed, and immediately began the attack on our people, who, before they had time to reach the boat, or to arm themselves against the unexpected impending danger, fell a sacrifice to the fury of their savage assailants.

We stayed here till the evening, when, having loaded the rest of the boats with grass, celery, and scurvy-grass, we embarked to return to the ships, where some of the boats did not arrive till one o'clock the next morning; and it was fortunate that they got on board then, for it afterwards blew a perfect storm, with abundance of rain.

These storms are very frequent here, and sometimes violent and troublesome. The neighbouring mountains, which at these times are always loaded with vapours, not only increase the force of the wind, but alter its direction in such a manner that no two blasts follow each other from the same quarter and the nearer the shore, the more their effects are felt.

By this time more than two-thirds of the inhabitants of the sound had settled themselves about us. Great numbers of them daily frequented the ships and the encampment on the shore, but the latter became by far the most favourite place of resort.

They were specially delighted while our people melted some seal blubber. No Greenlander was ever fonder of train-oil than our friends here seemed to be. They relished the very skimmings of the kettle and dregs of the casks; but a little of the pure stinking oil was a delicious feast, so eagerly desired that I suppose it is seldom enjoyed.

On the 24th of February we were visited by Kahoora, the leader of the party who cut off the crew of the *Adventure's* boat. This was the third time he had visited us, without betraying the smallest appearance of fear. I was ashore when he now arrived, but had got on board just as he was going away. Omai, who had returned with me, presently pointed him out, and solicited me to shoot him. Not satisfied with this, he addressed himself to Kahoora, threatening to be his executioner if ever he presumed to visit us again. The New Zealander paid so little regard to these threats that he returned the next morning with his whole family —men, women, and children to the number of twenty and upwards. Omai was the first who acquainted me with his being alongside the ship, and desired to know if he should ask him to come on board. I told him he might, and accordingly he introduced the chief into the cabin, saying, "There is Kahoora; kill him!" He afterwards expostulated with me very earnestly. "Why do you not kill him? You tell me if a man kills another in England that he is hanged for it. This man has killed ten, and yet you will not kill him, though many of his countrymen desire it, and it would be very good."

Omai's arguments, though specious enough, having no weight with me, I desired him to ask the chief why he had killed

Captain Furneaux's people. At this question Kahoora folded his arms, hung down his head, and looked like one caught in a trap, and I firmly believe he expected instant death. But no sooner was he assured of his safety than he became cheerful. He did not, however, seem willing to give me an answer to the question that had been put to him till I had again and again repeated my promise that he should not be hurt. Then he ventured to tell us that one of his countrymen having brought a stone hatchet to barter, the man to whom it was offered took it, and would neither return it nor give up anything for it, on which the owner of it snatched up the bread as an equivalent, and then the quarrel began.

The remainder of Kahoora's account of this unhappy affair differed very little from what we had before learned from the rest of his countrymen. He mentioned the narrow escape he had during the fray, a musket being levelled at him, which he avoided by skulking behind the boat, and another man who stood close to him was shot dead.

It was evident that most of the natives we had met with since our arrival, as they knew I was fully acquainted with the history of the massacre, expected I should avenge it with the death of Kahoora; and many of them seemed not only to wish it, but expressed their surprise at my forbearance.

For some time before we arrived at New Zealand, Omai had expressed a desire to take one of the natives with him to his own country. We had not been there many days before a youth, about seventeen or eighteen years of age, named Tiarooa, offered to accompany him, and took up his residence on board. I paid little attention to this at first, imagining that he would leave us when we were about to depart, and after he had got what he could from Omai.

At length, finding that he was fixed in his resolution to go with us, and having learned that he was the only son of a deceased chief, and that his mother, still living, was a woman much respected here, I caused it to be made known to them all that if the young man went away with us he would never return. But this declaration seemed to make no sort of impression. Tiarooa parted from his mother with all the marks of tender affection that might be expected between a parent and a child who were never to meet again.

That Tiarooa might be sent away in a manner becoming his birth, a boy about nine or ten years old, named Kokoa, was to go with him as his servant. He was presented to me by his own father, who, I believe, would have parted with his dog with far less indifference. The very clothing the boy had he stripped him of, and left him as naked as he was born. It was to no purpose that I endeavoured to convince these people of the impossibility of these youths ever returning home. Not one, not even their nearest relations, seemed to trouble themselves about their future fate.

From my own observations, and from the information of Taweiharooa and others, it appears to me that the New Zealanders must live under perpetual apprehension of being destroyed by each other; there being few of their tribes that have not, as they think, sustained wrongs from some other tribe, which they are continually upon the watch to revenge. And perhaps the desire of a good meal may be no small incitement. I am told that many years will sometimes elapse before a favourable opportunity happens, and that the son never loses sight of an injury that has been done to his father. Their method of executing their horrible designs is by stealing upon the adverse party in the night, and if they find them unguarded, they kill every one indiscriminately, not even sparing the women and children. When the massacre is completed, they either feast and gorge themselves on the spot, or carry off as many of the bodies as they can, and devour them at home with acts of brutality too shocking to be described.

This perpetual state of war operates so strongly in producing habitual circumspection that one hardly ever finds a New Zealander off his guard, either by night or by day. Indeed, no other man can have such powerful motives to be vigilant, as the preservation both of body and soul depends upon it. For according to their system of belief, the soul of the man whose flesh is devoured by the enemy is doomed to perpetual fire, while the soul of the man whose body has been rescued from those who killed him ascends to the habitations of the gods.

CHAPTER XXXVI.

PROSECUTION OF THE VOYAGE—AN ISLAND CALLED MANGEEA DISCOVERED—THE DISCOVERY OF AN ISLAND CALLED WATEEOO—MR. ANDERSON'S NARRATIVE —OTAKOOTAIA VISITED—HERVEY'S ISLAND FOUND TO BE INHABITED— PALMERSTON'S ISLAND TOUCHED AT—REFRESHMENTS OBTAINED—ARRIVAL AT THE FRIENDLY ISLANDS.

ON the 25th, at ten o'clock in the morning, a light breeze springing up at NW. by W., we weighed, stood out of the sound, and made sail through the strait, with the *Discovery* in company.

We had no sooner lost sight of the land than the two New Zealand boys who had wished to accompany our ship repented heartily of the step they had taken, partly due to the sea-sickness they now experienced. All the soothing encouragement we could think of availed but little. They wept both in public and in private, and made their lamentations in a kind of song, which, as far as we could comprehend the meaning of the words, was expressive of their praises of their country and people, from which they were to be separated for ever. Thus they continued for many days, till their sea-sickness wore off, and the tumult of their minds began to subside. Then these fits of lamentation became less and less frequent, and at length entirely ceased. *T*heir native country and their friends were by degrees forgotten, and they appeared to be as firmly attached to us as if they had been born among us.

On the 29th of March, at ten in the morning, as we were standing to the NE., the *Discovery* made the signal of seeing land. We soon discovered it to be an island of no great extent, and stood for it till sunset. At daybreak next morning I bore up for the lee or west side of the island, as neither anchorage nor landing appeared to be practicable on the south side, on account of a great surf, which broke everywhere with violence against the shore.

March.

We presently found that the island was inhabited, and being near the shore, we could perceive with our glasses that several of the natives, who appeared upon a sandy beach, were all armed with long spears and clubs, which they brandished in the air with signs of threatening, or as some on board interpreted their attitudes, with invitations to land. Most of them appeared naked, but some of them had pieces of cloth of different colours, which they wore as a garment thrown about their shoulders. And almost all of them had a white wrapper about their heads, not much unlike a turban or high conical cap. We could also perceive that they were of a tawny colour, and in general of a middling stature, but robust, and inclining to corpulence.

At this time a small canoe was launched in a great hurry from the farther end of the beach, and putting off with two men, paddled towards us, when I brought to. They stopped short, however, as if afraid to approach, until Omai, who addressed them in the Otaheite language, in some measure quieted their apprehensions. They then came near enough to take some beads and nails, which were tied to a piece of wood and thrown into the canoe. Omai, perhaps improperly, put the question to them, whether they ever ate human flesh, which they answered in the negative with a mixture of indignation and abhorrence. One of them, whose name was Mourooa, being asked how he came by a scar on his forehead, told us that it was the consequence of a wound he had got in fighting with the people of an island which lies to the north-eastward, who sometimes came to invade them. They afterwards took hold of a rope, but still would not venture on board.

Omai inquired where we could land, and we were directed to two different places. But I saw with regret that the attempt could not be made at either place, unless at the risk of having our boats filled with water, or even staved to pieces. Nor were we more fortunate in our search for anchorage, for we could find no bottom till within a cable's length of the breakers. There we met with from forty to twenty fathoms depth, over sharp coral rocks, so that anchoring would have been attended with much more danger than landing.

Thus we were obliged to leave unvisited this fine island, which seemed capable of supplying all our wants. The name of the island they called Mangeea. The natives seemed to resemble those of Otaheite and the Marquesas in the beauty of their persons. They salute strangers much after the manner of the New Zealanders, by joining noses; adding, however, the additional ceremony of taking the hand of the person to whom they are paying civilities, and rubbing it with a degree of force upon their nose and mouth.

After leaving Mangeea, on the afternoon of the 30th, we continued our course northward all that night and till noon on the 31st, when we again saw land in the direction of NE. by N., distant eight or ten leagues. Next morning we got abreast of its north end. Soon after I sent three armed boats to look for anchoring ground and a landing-place. In the meantime we worked up under the island with the ships. Just as the boats were putting off, we observed several single canoes coming from the shore. They first went to the *Discovery*, she being the nearest ship; and soon after, three of the canoes came alongside the *Resolution*, each conducted by one man. They are long and narrow, and supported by outriggers. Some knives, beads, and other trifles were conveyed to our visitors, and they gave us a few cocoa-nuts upon our asking for them. But they did not part with them by way of exchange for what they had received from us, for they seemed to have no idea of bartering, nor did they appear to estimate any of our presents at a high rate. With a little persuasion one of them came on board, and the other two, encouraged by his example, soon followed him. Their whole behaviour denoted that they were quite at ease, and felt no sort of apprehension of our detaining or using them ill.

After their departure another canoe arrived, conducted by a man who brought a bunch of plantains specially as a present to me, for whom he asked by name, which he had learned from Omai, who was sent before us in a boat with Mr. Gore. In return for this civility I gave him an axe and a piece of red cloth, when he paddled back to the shore well satisfied. I afterwards understood from Omai that this present was sent from the king or principal chief of the island. Not long after, a double canoe, in which were twelve men, came towards us. As they drew near the ship they recited some words in concert, by way of chorus, one of their number first standing up and giving the word before each repetition. When they had finished their solemn chant they came alongside and asked for the chief. As soon as I showed myself, a pig and a few cocoa-nuts were conveyed up into the ship, and the principal person in the canoe made me an additional present of a piece of matting. Our visitors were conducted into the cabin and to other parts of the ship. Some objects seemed to strike them with a degree of surprise; but nothing fixed their attention for a moment. They were afraid to come near the cows and horses, nor did they form the least conception of their nature. But the sheep and goats did not surpass the limits of their ideas, for they gave us to understand that they knew them to be birds. I made a present to my new friend of what I thought would be most acceptable to him, but on his going away he seemed rather disappointed than pleased. I afterwards understood that he was very desirous of obtaining a dog, of which animal this island could not boast.

On the 3rd of April some of the officers landed safely upon the reef, and I shall give Mr. Anderson's account in his own words. "An islander took hold of each of us, obviously with an intention to support us in walking over the rugged rocks to the beach. We were conducted from the beach by our guides, amidst a great crowd of people, who flocked with very eager curiosity to look at us. We were led up an avenue of cocoa-palms, and soon came to a number of men, arranged in two rows, armed with clubs, which they held on their shoulders. After walking a little way amongst these, we found a person, who seemed a chief, sitting on the ground cross-legged, cooling himself with a sort of triangular fan made from a leaf of the cocoa-palm, with a polished handle of black wood fixed to one corner.

"We proceeded still amongst the men armed with clubs, and came to a second chief, who sat fanning himself. In the same manner we were conducted to a third chief; he also was sitting, and adorned with red feathers, and after saluting him as we had done the others, he desired us to sit down, which we were very willing to do, being pretty well fatigued with walking up, and with the excessive heat we felt amongst the vast crowd that surrounded us.

"After this, making use of Omai as interpreter, we informed

the chiefs, whose names were Otteroo, Taroa, and Fatouweera, with what intention we had come on shore, but were given to understand that we must wait till the next day, and then we should have what was wanted.

"They now seemed to take some pains to separate us from each other, and every one of us had his circle to surround and gaze at him. For my own part, I was at one time above an hour apart from my friends, and when I told the chief that I wanted to speak to Omai, he peremptorily refused my request. At the same time, I found the people began to steal several trifling things which I had in my pocket. From these circumstances I now entertained apprehensions that they might have formed the design of detaining us amongst them. They did not, indeed, seem to be of a disposition so savage as to make us anxious for the safety of our persons; but it was, nevertheless, vexing to think we had hazarded being detained by their curiosity. In this situation I asked for something to eat and they readily brought to me some cocoa-nuts, bread-fruit, and a sort of sour pudding; and on my complaining much of the heat occasioned by the crowd, the chief himself condescended to fan me, and gave me a small piece of cloth which he had round his waist.

"Mr. Burney happening to come to the place where I was, I mentioned my suspicions to him, and to put it to the test whether they were well founded, we attempted to get to the beach. But we were stopped when about half way by some men, who told us that we must go back to the place which we had left. On coming up, we found Omai entertaining the same apprehensions. But he had, as he fancied, an additional reason for being afraid, for he had observed that they had dug a hole in the ground for an oven, which they were now heating, and he could assign no other reason for this than that they meant to roast and eat us, as is practised by the inhabitants of New Zealand. Nay, he went so far as to ask them the question, at which they were greatly surprised, asking in return whether that was a custom with us.

" In the afternoon, the second chief, directing the multitude to make a pretty large ring, made us sit down by him. A considerable number of cocoa-nuts were now brought, and shortly after a long green basket, with a sufficient quantity of baked plantains to have served a dozen persons. A piece of the young hog that had been dressed was then set before each of us, of which we were desired to eat. Our appetites, however, had failed, from the fatigues of the day; and though we did eat a little to please them, it was without satisfaction to ourselves.

"It being now near sunset, they allowed us to go on board, and we rowed to the ship, very well pleased that we had at last got out of the hands of our troublesome masters."

It has been mentioned that Omai was sent on this expedition. He was asked by the natives a great many questions concerning us, our country, and the sort of arms we used; and according to the account he gave me, his answers were not a little upon the marvellous. As, for instance, he told them that our country had ships as large as their island, on board which were instruments of war of such dimensions that several people might sit within them, and that one of these was sufficient to crush the whole island at one shot. This led them to inquire what sort of guns we actually had in our two ships. He said, that though they were but small in comparison with those he had just described, yet, with such as they were, we could, with the greatest ease, and at the distance the ships were from the shore, destroy the island, and kill every soul in it. They persevered in their inquiries regarding the means by which this could be done, and Omai explained the matter as well as he could. He happened, luckily, to have a few cartridges in his pocket. These he produced, and the balls and the gunpowder were submitted to inspection. In the centre of a circle formed by the natives, the inconsiderable quantity of gunpowder collected from his cartridges was properly disposed upon the ground, and by means of a bit of burning wood from the oven where the dinner was dressing, set on fire. The sudden blast and loud report, the mingled flame and smoke that instantly succeeded, now filled the whole assembly with astonishment. They no longer doubted the tremendous power of our weapons, and gave full credit to all Omai had said.

This island is called Wateeoo by the natives; but from the circumstances already mentioned, it appears that Wateeoo can be of little use to any ship that wants refreshment, unless in a case of the most absolute necessity.

I quitted Wateeoo without regret on the 4th of April, and

steered for the neighbouring island, called by the natives Otakootaia or Wenooaette. There was a reef here surrounding the land, and a considerable surf breaking against the rocks; notwithstanding which, our boats no sooner reached the west side of the island than they ventured in, and the party got safe on shore. The supply obtained here consisted of about a hundred cocoa-nuts for each ship, and besides this refreshment for ourselves, we got for our cattle some grass and a quantity of the leaves and branches of young cocoa trees.

As soon as the boats were hoisted in I made sail again, intending to try our fortune at Hervey's Island, which was discovered in 1773, during my last voyage. As we drew near the island, six or seven canoes soon came near us. There were three to six men in each of them. They stopped at the distance of about a stone's throw from the ship, and it was some time before Omai could prevail upon them to come alongside; but no entreaties could induce any of them to venture on board. Indeed, their disorderly and clamorous behaviour by no means indicated a disposition to trust us or treat us well. We afterwards learned that they had attempted to take some oars out of the *Discovery's* boat that lay alongside, and struck a man who endeavoured to prevent them. They also cut away with a shell a net with meat which hung over the ship's stern, and absolutely refused to restore it, though we afterwards purchased it of them.

These people seemed to differ as much in person as in disposition from the natives of Wateeoo, though the distance between the two islands is not very great. Their colour was of a deeper cast, and several had a fierce, rugged aspect, resembling the natives of New Zealand. The shell of a pearl oyster polished, hung about the neck, was the only ornamental fashion that we observed amongst them; for not one of them had adopted that mode of ornament so generally prevalent amongst the natives of this ocean of puncturing or tattooing their bodies. Though singular in this, we had the most unequivocal proofs of their being of the same common race. Their language approached still nearer to the dialect of Otaheite than that of Wateeoo or Mangeea.

Like the inhabitants of these two islands, they inquired from whence our ships came, and whither bound; who was our chief;

the number of our men on board; and even the ship's name. And they very readily answered such questions as we proposed to them. Amongst other things, they told us they had seen two great ships like ours before, but that they had not spoken with them as they sailed past. There can be no doubt that these were the *Resolution* and *Adventure*. According to the account that they gave, their articles of food are cocoa-nuts, fish, and turtle, the island not producing plantains or bread-fruit, and being destitute of hogs and dogs.

Having but very little wind, it was one o'clock before we drew near the north-west part of the island. I sent Lieutenant King, with two armed boats, to sound and reconnoitre the coast, while we stood off and on with the ships. At three o'clock the boats returned, and Mr. King informed me that there was no anchorage for the ships, and that the boats could only land on the outer edge of the reef, which lay about a quarter of a mile from the dry land. He said that a number of the natives came down upon the reef, armed with long pikes and clubs, as if they intended to oppose his landing. But as he had no motive to land, he did not give them an opportunity to use them.

Having received this report, I considered that, as the ships could not be brought to an anchor, we should find the attempt to procure grass here would occasion much delay, as well as be attended with some danger. Besides, we were equally in want of water, and though the inhabitants had told us that there was water on their island, yet we knew neither in what quantity nor from what distance we might be obliged to fetch it.

Being thus disappointed at all the islands we had met with since our leaving New Zealand, and the unfavourable winds and other unforeseen circumstances having unavoidably retarded our progress so much, it was now impossible to think of doing anything this year in the high latitudes of the northern hemisphere, from which we were still at so great a distance, though the season for our operations there was already begun. In this situation it was absolutely necessary to pursue such measures as were most likely to preserve the cattle we had on board in the first place, and in the next place to save the stores and provisions of the ships, that we might be better able to prosecute our northern discoveries, which could not now commence till a year later than was originally intended.

If I had been so fortunate as to have procured a supply of water and of grass at any of the islands we had lately visited, it was my purpose to have stood back to the south till I had met with a westerly wind. But the certain consequence of doing this without such a supply would have been the loss of all the cattle before we could possibly reach Otaheite, without gaining any one advantage with regard to the great object of our voyage. I therefore determined to bear away for the Friendly Islands, where I was sure of meeting with abundance of everything I wanted.

On the 7th of April I steered west by south, with a fine breeze easterly. I preposed to proceed first to Middleburgh, or Eooa, thinking, if the wind continued favourable, that we had food enough on board for the cattle to last till we should reach that island. But about noon next day those faint breezes that had attended and retarded us so long again returned, and I found it necessary to haul more to the north to get into the latitude of Palmerston and Savage Islands, discovered in 1774, during my last voyage, so that, if necessity required it, we might have recourse to them. At length, at daybreak on the 13th, we saw Palmerston Island, distant about five leagues. However, we did not get up with it till eight o'clock the next morning. I then sent four boats, with an officer in each, to search the coast for the most convenient landing-place. For now we were under an absolute necessity of procuring from this island some food for the cattle, otherwise we must have lost them.

What is comprehended under the name of Palmerston Island is a group of small islets. The boats first examined the south-easternmost of the islets which compose this group, and failing there, ran down to the second, where we had the satisfaction to see them land. About one o'clock one of the boats came on board, laden with scurvy-grass and young cocoa-nut trees, which at this time was a feast for the cattle. This determined me to get a good supply of these articles before I quitted this station.

The island is scarcely a mile in circuit, and not above three feet higher than the level of the sea. There were no traces of inhabitants having ever been here. Having got a sufficient supply of food for the cattle by sunset, I ordered everybody on board.

The nine or ten low islets comprehended under the name of Palmerston Island, may be reckoned the heads or summits of the reef of coral rock that connects them together, covered only with a thin coat of sand, yet clothed, as already observed, with trees and plants.

After leaving Palmerston Island, I steered west, with a view to make the best of my way to Annamooka. We still continued to have variable winds, frequently between the north and west, with squalls, some thunder, and much rain. The heat, which had been great for about a month, became now much more disagreeable in this close, rainy weather, and, from the moisture attending it, threatened soon to be noxious. However, it is remarkable enough, that though the only refreshment we had received since leaving the Cape of Good Hope was that at New Zealand, there was not as yet a single person on board sick from the constant use of salt food or vicissitude of climate.

In the night between the 24th and 25th we passed Savage Island, which I had discovered in 1774,* and on the 28th I hauled up for Annamooka. The weather being squally, with rain, I anchored at the approach of night in fifteen fathoms deep water over a bottom of coral-sand and shells.

* See page 281.

CHAPTER XXXVII.

ARRIVAL AT ANNAMOOKA—TRANSACTIONS THERE—ARRIVAL OF THE SHIPS AT HAPAEE, AND FRIENDLY RECEPTION—ENTERTAINMENTS—POULAHO, KING OF THE FRIENDLY ISLES—RETURN TO ANNAMOOKA—ARRIVAL AT TONGATABOO.

1777.
May.
SOON after we had anchored, two canoes, one with four and the other with three men, paddled toward us and came alongside without the least hesitation. They brought some cocoa-nuts, bread-fruit, plantains, and sugar-cane, which they bartered with us for nails. The following day I went ashore to fix on a place where the observatories might be set up and a guard be stationed, the natives having readily given us leave. Toobou, the chief of the island, conducted me and Omai to his house. We found it situated on a pleasant spot in the centre of his plantation. A fine grass plot surrounded it, which, he gave us to understand, was for the purpose of cleaning their feet before they went within doors. I had not before observed such an instance of attention to cleanliness at any of the places I had visited in this ocean, but afterwards found that it was very common at the Friendly Islands. The floor of Toobou's house was covered with mats, and no carpet in the most elegant English drawing-room could be kept neater.

While we were on shore we procured a few hogs and some fruit by bartering, and before we got on board again, the ships were crowded with the natives. Few of them coming empty-handed, every necessary refreshment was now in the greatest plenty.

In the afternoon the horses and such of the cattle as were in a weakly state were sent on shore. On the 6th we were visited by a great chief from Tongataboo, whose name was Feenou, and who was introduced to us as king of all the Friendly Isles. In the afternoon I went to pay this great man a visit, having first received a present of two fish from him, brought on board by one of his servants. As soon as I landed he came up to me. He appeared to be about thirty years of age, tall, but thin, and had more of the European features than any I had yet seen here. When the first salutation was over I asked if he was the king. For, notwithstanding what I had been told, finding he was not the man whom I remembered to have seen under that character during my former voyage, I began to entertain doubts. Taipa, the chief, officiously answered for him, and enumerated no less than one hundred and fifty-three islands of which he said Feenou was the sovereign. After a short stay, our new visitor accompanied me on board. I gave suitable presents to them all, and entertained them in such a manner as I thought would be most agreeable. Feenou was so fond of associating with us that he dined on board every day, though sometimes he did not partake of our fare. One day some of his servants brought a mess which had been dressed for him on shore. It consisted of fish, soup, and yams. I tasted of the mess, and found it so good that I afterwards had some food dressed in the same way. Though my cook succeeded tolerably well, he could produce nothing equal to the dish he imitated.

Finding we had quite exhausted the island of almost every article of food that it afforded, I moved off from the shore the horses, observatories, and other things that we had landed. Feenou warmly recommended an island, or rather group of islands, called Hapaee, lying to the NE. There, he assured us, in the easiest manner we could be supplied plentifully with every refreshment, and, to add weight to his advice, he engaged to attend us thither in person.

To the N. and NE. of Annamooka, in the direct track to Hapaee, the sea is sprinkled with a great number of small isles, and I could not be assured that there was a safe passage for such large ships as ours, though the natives sailed through the intervals in their canoes. In the afternoon of the 14th we were within two leagues of Toofoa. The Friendly islanders have some superstitious notions about the volcano upon it, which they say is an Oteoa or divinity. In the course of the night we could plainly see flames issuing from the volcano, though to no great height.

We reached Hapaee on the 17th, and lay before a creek in the reef, which made it convenient landing at all times. By the time we had anchored, the ships were filled with the natives. They brought from the shore hogs, fowls, fruit, and roots, which they exchanged for hatchets, knives, nails, beads, and cloth.

Early next morning I accompanied Feenou and Omai on shore. The chief conducted me to a hut, situated close to the sea-beach, which I had seen brought thither, but a few moments before, for our reception. In this Feenou, Omai, and myself were seated. The other chiefs and the multitude formed a circle on the outside, and they also sat down. I was then asked how long I intended to stay. On my saying five days, *T*aipa was ordered to come and sit by me, and proclaim this to the people. He then harangued them in a speech mostly dictated by Feenou. *T*he purport of it, as I learned from Omai, was that they were all, both old and young, to look upon me as a friend who intended to remain with them a few days; that during my stay they must not steal anything, or molest me in any other way; and that it was expected they should bring hogs, fowls, fruit, etc., to the ships, where they would receive in exchange for them such and such things which he enumerated. *T*aipa then took occasion to signify to me that it was necessary I should make a present to the chief of the island, whose name was Earoupa. I was not unprepared for this, and gave him some articles as far exceeded his expectation. My liberality brought on me demands of the same kind from two chiefs of other isles who were present, and from *T*aipa himself.

On the 18th Feenou and Omai, who scarcely ever quitted the chief, came on board. The object of this visit was to require my presence upon the island. Upon landing I was conducted to the same place where I had been seated the day before, and where I saw a large concourse of people already assembled. I guessed that something more than ordinary was in agitation, but could not tell what.

. I had not been long seated before near a hundred of the natives appeared in sight, and advanced, laden with yams, bread-fruit, plantains, cocoa-nuts, and sugar-canes. *T*hey deposited their burdens in two heaps or piles upon our left. Soon after arrived a number of others bearing the same kind of articles, which were collected into two piles upon that side. To these were tied two pigs and six fowls, and those upon the left six pigs and two turtles. Earoupa seated himself before the several articles upon the left, and another chief before those upon the right—they being, as I judged, the two chiefs who had collected them by order of Feenou, who seemed to be as implicitly obeyed here as he had been at Annamooka, and, in consequence of his commanding superiority over the chiefs of Hapaee, had laid this tax upon them for the present occasion.

As soon as this munificent collection of provisions was laid down in order and disposed to the best advantage, the bearers of it joined the multitude, who formed a large circle round the whole. Presently after, a number of men entered this circle or area before us, armed with clubs made of the green branches of the cocoa-nut tree. These paraded about for a few minutes, and then retired, one half to one side and the other half to the other side, seating themselves before the spectators. Soon after, they successively entered the lists, and entertained us with single combats. One champion, rising up and stepping forward from one side, challenged those of the other side, by expressive gestures more than by words, to send one of their body to oppose him. If the challenge was accepted, which was generally the case, the two combatants put themselves in proper attitudes, and then began the engagement, which continued till one or other owned himself conquered or till their weapons were broken. As soon as each combat was over, the victor squatted himself down, facing the chief, and then rose up and retired. At the same time some old men, who seemed to sit as judges, gave their plaudit in a few words, and the multitude, especially those on the side to which the victor belonged, celebrated the glory he had acquired in two or three huzzas.

As soon as these diversions were ended, the chief told me that the heaps of provisions on our right hand were a present to Omai, and that those on our left hand, being about two-thirds of the whole quantity, were given to me. There was as much as four loaded boats, and I could not but be struck with the munificence of Feenou; for this present far exceeded any I had ever received from any of the sovereigns of the various islands I had visited in the Pacific Ocean.

Feenou had expressed a desire to see the marines go through the military exercise. As I was desirous of gratifying his curiosity, I ordered them all ashore from both ships in the morning of the 20th. After they had performed various evolutions, and fired several volleys, with which the numerous body of spectators seemed well pleased, the chief entertained us in his turn with an exhibition which, as was acknowledged by us all, was performed with a dexterity and exactness far surpassing the specimen we had given of our military manœuvres. It was a kind of dance, so entirely different from anything I had ever seen that I can give no description that will convey any tolerable idea of it to my readers. It was performed by men, and one hundred and five persons bore their parts in it. Each of them had in his hand an instrument neatly made, shaped somewhat like a paddle, two feet and a half in length, with a small handle and a thin blade, so that they were very light. With these instruments they made many and various flourishes, each of which was accompanied with a different movement. At first the performers ranged themselves in three lines, and by various evolutions each man changed his station in such a manner that those who had been in the rear came into the front. Nor did they remain long in the same position. At one time they extended themselves in one line, they then formed into a semicircle, and lastly in two square columns. While this last movement was executing, one of them advanced and performed an antic dance, with which the whole ended.

The musical instruments consisted of two drums, or rather two hollow logs of wood, from which some varied notes were produced by beating on them with two sticks. Their song was not destitute of pleasing melody, and all their corresponding motions were executed with so much skill that the numerous body of dancers seemed to act as if they were one great machine. It was the opinion of every one of us that such a performance would have met with universal applause in a European theatre, and it so far exceeded any attempt we had made to entertain them that they seemed to pique themselves upon the superiority they had over us. As to our musical instruments, they held none of them in the least esteem except the drum, and even that they did not think equal to their own. Our French horns in particular seemed to be held in great contempt, for neither here nor at any other of the islands would they pay the smallest attention to them.

In order to give them a more favourable opinion of English amusements, and to leave their minds fully impressed with the deepest sense of our superior attainments, I directed some fireworks to be got ready, and after it was dark played them off in the presence of Feenou, the other chiefs, and a vast concourse of their people. Our water and sky rockets, in particular, pleased and astonished them beyond all conception, and the scale was now turned in our favour. This, however, seemed only to furnish them with an additional motive to proceed to fresh exertions of their very singular dexterity, and our fireworks were no sooner ended than a succession of dances began. As a prelude to them a band of music or chorus of eighteen men seated themselves before us in the centre of the circle. Four or five of this band had pieces of large bamboo, from three to five or six feet long, the upper end open, but the other end closed by one of the joints. With this closed end the performers kept constantly striking the ground, though slowly, thus producing different notes, according to the different lengths of the instruments, but all of them of the hollow or bass sort, to counteract which, a person kept striking quickly and with two sticks a piece of the same substance split and laid along the ground, and by that means furnishing a tone as acute as those produced by the others were grave. The rest of the band, as well as those who performed upon the bamboo, sang a slow and soft air, which so tempered the harsher notes of the above instruments that no bystander, however accustomed to hear the most perfect and varied modulation of sweet sounds, could avoid confessing the vast power and pleasing effect of this simple harmony.

The concert having continued about a quarter of an hour, twenty women entered the circle. Most of them had upon their heads garlands of the crimson flowers of the China rose or others, and many of them had ornamented their persons with leaves of trees cut with a great deal of nicety about the edges. They made a circle round the chorus, turning their faces toward it, and began by singing a soft air, to which responses were made by the chorus in the same tune, and these were repeated alternately. All this while the women accompanied their song with several very graceful motions of their hands toward their faces, making constantly a step forward and then back again with one foot while the other was fixed. Their manner of dancing was soon changed to a quicker measure, in which they made a kind of half turn by leaping, and clapped their hands in conjunction with the chorus.

The entertainments of this memorable night concluded with a dance in which the principal people present exhibited. It resembled the preceding one in some respects, but they increased their motions to a prodigious quickness, shaking their heads from shoulder to shoulder with such force that a spectator, unaccustomed to the sight, would suppose that they ran a risk of dislocating their necks. This was attended by a smart clapping of the hands and a kind of savage holla, or shriek. The last dances were performed with so much spirit and so great exactness that they met with universal approbation.

The place where the dances were performed was an open space amongst the trees, just by the sea, with lights at small intervals placed round the inside of the circle.

On the morning of the 23rd, as we were going to unmoor in order to leave the island, Feenou and his prime minister, Taipa, came alongside in a sailing canoe, and informed me that they were setting out for Vavaoo, an island which, they said, was about two days' sail to the northward of Hapaee. The object of their voyage, they would have me believe, was to get for me an additional supply of hogs and some red-feathered caps for Omai to carry to Otaheite, where they are in high esteem. Feenou assured me that he should be back in four or five days, and desired me not to sail till his return, when he promised he would accompany me to Tongatabu. I thought this a good opportunity to acquire some knowledge of Vavaoo, and proposed to him to go thither with the ships; but he seemed not to approve of the plan, and, by way of diverting me from it, told me that there was neither harbour nor anchorage about it. I therefore consented to wait in my present station for his return, and he immediately set out.

In my walk on the 25th I happened to step into a house, where I found a woman shaving a child's head with a shark's tooth stuck into the end of a piece of stick. I observed that she first wetted the hair with a rag dipped in water, applying her instrument to that part which she had previously soaked. The operation seemed to give no pain to the child, although the hair was taken off as close as if one of our razors had been employed. Encouraged by what I now saw, I soon after tried one of those singular instruments upon myself, and found it to be an excellent substitute. However, the men of these islands have recourse to another contrivance when they shave their beards. The operation is performed with two shells, one of which they place under a part of the beard; and with the other, applied above, they scrape that part off. In this manner they are able to shave very close. The process is indeed rather tedious, but not painful; and there are men amongst them who seem to profess the trade. It was as common, while we were here, to see our sailors go ashore to have their beards scraped off after the fashion of Hapaee, as it was to see their chiefs come on board to be shaved by our barbers.

Finding that little or nothing of the produce of the island was now brought to the ships, I resolved to change our station; and in the forenoon of the 26th I hauled into a bay that lies between the south end of Lafooga and the north end of Hoolaiva, and there anchored.

About noon a large sailing canoe came under our stern, in which was a person named Futtafaihe, or Poulaho, or both, who, as the natives then on board told us, was king of Tongataboo and all the neighbouring islands. It being my interest, as well as my inclination, to pay court to all the great men without making inquiry into the validity of their assumed titles, I invited Poulaho on board. He brought with him, as a present, two fat hogs, though not so fat as himself. If weight of body could give weight in rank or power, he was certainly the most eminent man in that respect we had seen; for though not very tall, he was very unwieldy, and almost shapeless with corpulence. He seemed to be about forty years of age, had straight hair, and his features differed a good deal from those of the bulk of his people.

I found him to be a sedate, sensible man. He viewed the ship and the several new objects with uncommon attention, and asked many pertinent questions, one of which was, What could induce us to visit these islands? After he had satisfied his curiosity in looking at the cattle and other novelties which he met with on deck, I desired him to walk down into the cabin. To this his attendants objected, saying that if he were to accept of the invitation, it must happen that people would walk over his head; but the chief himself, less scrupulous in this respect than his attendants, waived all ceremony and walked down.

Poulaho sat down with us to dinner, but he ate little and drank less. When he rose from the table he desired me to accompany him ashore. I attended him in my own boat, having first made presents to him of such articles as I observed he valued most, and were even beyond his expectation to receive. I was not disappointed in my view of thus securing his friendship; for the moment the boat reached the beach, he ordered two more hogs to be brought and delivered to my people. He was then carried out of the boat by some of his own people upon a board resembling a hand-barrow, and went and seated himself in a small house near the shore, which seemed to have been erected there for his accommodation. He placed me at his side, and his attendants seated themselves in a semicircle before us outside the house. Behind the chief, or rather on one side, sat an old woman with a sort of fan in her hand, whose office it was to prevent his being pestered with the flies. I stayed till several of his attendants left him, first making him obeisance by bowing the head down to the sole of his foot, and touching or tapping the same with the upper and under side of the fingers of both hands. Others, who were not in the circle, came as it seemed on purpose, and paid him this mark of respect, and then retired without speaking a word. I was charmed with the decorum that was observed, and had nowhere seen the like, not even among more civilized nations.

On Wednesday the 28th, Poulaho, the king, as I shall now call him, came on board betimes, and brought as a present to me one of their caps, or rather bonnets, composed of the tail feathers of the tropic-bird, with the red feathers of the paroquets wrought upon them or jointly with them. They are made so as to tie upon the forehead, without any crown, and have the form of a semicircle whose radius is eighteen or twenty inches. The chief stayed on board till the evening, when he left us; but his brother and one or two of his attendants continued in the ship all night.

At daybreak the next morning I weighed with a fine breeze, and stood to the westward with a view to return to Annamooka. We were followed by several sailing canoes, in one of which was the king. He quitted us in a short time, but left his brother and five of his attendants on board. We had also the company of a chief just then arrived from Tongatabu, whose name was Tooboueitoa. The moment he arrived he sent his canoe away, and declared that he and five more who came with him would sleep on board, so that I had now my cabin filled with visitors. They brought plenty of provisions with them, for which they always had suitable returns.

At daybreak on the 31st I stood for the channel which is between Kotoo and a reef of rocks; but on drawing near, I found the wind too scant to lead us through. Toward night the wind blew fresh and by squalls, with rain, and we were not without apprehensions of danger. I kept the deck till midnight, when I left it to the master, with such directions as I thought would keep the ships clear of the shoals and rocks that lay around us. At one time the *Resolution* was very near running upon a low sandy isle surrounded with breakers. It happened, very fortunately, that the people had just been ordered upon the deck to put the ship about, and the most of them were at their stations, so that the necessary movements were not only executed with judgment, but also with alertness; and this alone saved us from destruction. This circumstance frightened our passengers so much that they expressed a strong desire to get ashore.

On the 5th we anchored at Annamooka, nearly in the same station which we had so lately occupied. June.

About noon next day, Feenou arrived from Vavaoo. He told us that several canoes, laden with hogs and other provisions, which had sailed with him from that island, had been lost owing to the late stormy weather, and that everybody on board perished. This melancholy tale did not seem to affect any of his countrymen that heard it; and as to ourselves, we were by this time too well acquainted with his character to give much credit to such a story. The following morning, Poulaho and the other chiefs who had been wind-bound with him, arrived. I happened at this time to be ashore in company with Feenou, who now seemed to be sensible of the impropriety of his conduct in assuming a character that did not belong to him; for he not only acknowledged Poulaho to be king of Tongatabu and the other isles, but affected to insist much on it, which, no doubt, was with a view to make amends for his former presumption.

I left him to visit this greater man, whom I found sitting with a few people before him; but as every one hastened to pay court to him, the circle increased pretty fast. I was very desirous of observing Fcenou's behaviour on this occasion, and had the most convincing proof of his inferiority; for he placed himself amongst the rest that sat before Poulaho as attendants on his majesty. He seemed at first rather abashed, but he soon recovered himself.

Both he and Poulaho went on board with me to dinner, but only the latter sat at table. Feenou, having made his obeisance in the usual way, saluting his sovereign's foot with his head and hands, retired out of the cabin. *T*he king had before told us that this would happen, and it now appeared that Feenou could not eat or drink in his royal presence.

At eight o'clock next morning we steered for Tongataboo. Feenou was to have taken his passage in the *Resolution*, but preferred his own canoe; and put two men on board to conduct us to the best anchorage. By the direction of our pilots, we steered for the widest space between two isles which we were to pass, having our boats ahead employed in sounding. We were insensibly drawn upon a large flat, upon which lay innumerable coral rocks, at different depths below the surface of the water. Notwithstanding all our care and attention to keep the ship clear of them, we could not prevent her from striking on one of these rocks. But fortunately neither of the ships stuck fast nor received any damage. We could not get back without increasing the danger, as we had come in almost before the wind, nor could we cast anchor but with the certainty of having our cables instantly cut in two by the rocks. We had no other resource but to proceed.

While we were plying up to the harbour to which the natives directed us, the king kept sailing round us in his canoe. There were, at the same time, a great many small canoes about the ships. Two of these, which could not get out of the way of his royal vessel, he ran quite over, with as little concern as if they had been bits of wood.

Amongst many others who came on board the *Resolution* was Attago,* who had been so useful to me when I visited Tongatabu during my last voyage. He brought a hog and some yams as a testimony of his friendship, and I was not wanting on my part in making a suitable return.

* See page 249.

CHAPTER XXXVIII.

FRIENDLY RECEPTION AT TONGATABU—ENTERTAINMENT GIVEN BY MAREEWAGEE—ECLIPSE OF THE SUN—ACCOUNT OF THE ISLAND—DEPARTURE FROM TONGATABU—ARRIVAL AT EOOA—ACCOUNT OF THAT ISLAND—ACCOUNT OF THE FRIENDLY ISLES.

SOON after we had anchored I landed, accompanied by Omai and some of the officers. We found the king waiting for us upon the beach. He immediately conducted us to a small neat house, situated a little within the skirts of the woods, with a fine large area before it. This house, he told me, was at my service during our stay at the island; and a better situation we could not wish for.

As I intended to make some stay at Tongatabu we pitched a tent, landed our horses, cattle, and sheep, and appointed a party to cut wood for fuel and planks for the ships. The gunners were ordered to remain upon the spot to conduct traffic with the natives, who thronged from every part of the island with hogs, yams, etc. In a short time our land post was like a fair, and the ships were so crowded with visitors that we had hardly room to sit upon the decks.

Feenou had taken up his residence in our neighbourhood, but he was no longer the leading man. However, we still found him to be a person of consequence, and we had daily proofs of his opulence and liberality by the continuance of his valuable presents. We now heard that there were other great men of the island whom we had not yet seen. In particular they mentioned a person, considerably over sixty, named Mareewagee, superior even to Poulaho, to whom he was related. Being old, he lived in retirement, and therefore would not visit us. Some of the natives even hinted that he was too great a man to confer that honour upon us. I was desirous of waiting upon Mareewagee, and accordingly set out with Omai pretty early on the 12th. But we could receive no satisfactory information; and suspecting that the old chief was purposely concealed from us, we went back to our boats, much piqued at our disappointment. About noon next day, I was informed that Mareewagee was in the neighbourhood. Accompanied by Feenou, I landed to pay him a visit. We found not only Mareewagee, but another chief called Toobou. Both chiefs had a venerable appearance; and we afterwards discovered they were brothers, and that Feenou was one of Mareewagee's sons. Both were men of great property in the island, and seemed to be in high estimation with the people, Mareewagee in particular having the honourable appellation given to him of father of Tonga, or of his country.

The 17th was fixed upon by Mareewagee for giving a grand haiva, or entertainment, to which we were all invited. For this purpose a large space had been cleared before the temporary hut of the chief near our post, as an area where the performances were to be exhibited. In the morning great multitudes of the natives came in from the country, every one carrying upon his shoulders a pole about six feet long, with a yam suspended at each end. These yams and poles were deposited on each side of the area so as to form two large heaps, decorated with different sorts of small fish, and piled up to the greatest advantage. They were Mareewagee's present to Captain Clerke and me, and it was hard to say whether the wood for fuel or the yams for food were of the most value to us. As for the fish, they might serve to please the sight, but were very offensive to the smell, part of them having been kept two or three days to be presented to us on this occasion. Everything being thus prepared, about eleven o'clock they began to exhibit various dances which they call "mai." The music consisted, at first, of seventy men as a chorus, who sat down; and amidst them were placed three instruments which we called drums, though very unlike them, and the natives "naffa." These instruments produce a rude though loud and powerful sound.

The first dance consisted of four ranks of twenty-four men each, holding in their hands a little thin light wooden instrument about two feet long, and in shape not unlike a small oblong paddle.

With these, which are called "pagge," they made a great many different motions, all which were accompanied by corresponding attitudes of the body. Their motions were at first slow, but quickened as the drums beat faster; and the whole time they recited sentences in a musical tone, which were answered by the chorus. At the end of a short space they all joined, and finished with a shout. Then the rear rank, dividing, shifted themselves very slowly round each end, and meeting in the front, formed the first rank, the whole number continuing to recite the sentences as before. The other ranks did the same successively, till that which at first was the front became the rear; and the evolution continued in the same manner, till the last rank regained its first situation. They then began a much quicker dance, though slow at first, and sung for about ten minutes, when the whole body divided into two parts, retreated a little, and then approached, forming a sort of circular figure, which finished the dance.

In a short time seventy men sat down as a chorus to another dance. This consisted of two ranks, of sixteen persons each, with young Toobou at their head, who was richly ornamented with a garment covered with red feathers. These danced, sung, and twirled the "pagge" as before, but in general much quicker. A motion that met with particular approbation was one in which they held the face aside, as if ashamed. The back rank closed before the front one, and that again resumed its place, as in the two former dances. At that instant two men entered very hastily, and exercised the clubs which they use in battle. They did this by first twirling them in their hands, and making circular strokes before them with great force and quickness, but so skilfully managed that, though standing quite close, they never interfered. They shifted their clubs from hand to hand with great dexterity, and after continuing a little time, kneeled, tossing the clubs up in the air, which they caught as they fell. A person with a spear then came in the same hasty manner, looking about eagerly as if in search of somebody to throw it at. He then ran hastily to one side of the crowd in the front, and put himself in a threatening attitude, as if he meant to strike with his spear at one of them, bending the knee a little, and trembling as it were with rage. He continued in this manner only a few seconds, when he moved to the other side, and having stood in the same posture there for the same short time, retreated from the ground as fast as when he made his appearance.

These dances, if they can properly be called so, lasted from eleven till near three o'clock; and though they were doubtless intended particularly either in honour of us or to show a specimen of their dexterity, vast numbers of their own people attended as spectators.

On the evening of the 18th I assembled all the chiefs before our house, and my intended presents to them were marched out. To Poulaho, the king, I gave a young English bull and cow, to Mareewagee a Cape ram and two ewes, and to Feenou a horse and a mare. As most of the people in the neighbourhood were then present, I instructed Omai to tell them that there were no such animals within many months' sail of their island; that we had brought them for their use from that immense distance at a vast trouble and expense; that therefore they must be careful not to kill any of them till they had multiplied to a numerous race; and lastly, that they and their children ought to remember that they had received them from the men of Britain.

It soon appeared that some were dissatisfied with this allotment of our animals; for early next morning one of our kids and two turkey cocks were missing, and it was not till four o'clock they were brought back. We still, however, had thieves about us, and, encouraged by the negligence of our people, we had continual instances of their depredations. Some of the officers belonging to both ships, who had made an excursion into the interior of the island without my leave or knowledge, returned this evening, after an absence of two days. They had taken with them their muskets, with the necessary ammunition, and several small articles of the favourite commodities, all of which the natives had the dexterity to steal from them in the course of their expedition. Feenou and Poulaho upon this occasion very justly observed that if any of my people at any time wanted to go into the country they ought to be acquainted with it, in which case they would send proper persons along with them, and then they would be answerable for their safety. Though I gave myself no trouble about the recovery of the things stolen upon this occasion, most of them, through Feenou's interposition, were recovered, except one musket and a few other articles of inferior value.

I had prolonged my stay at this island on account of the approaching eclipse. Having therefore some days of leisure before me, a party of us, accompanied by Poulaho, set out early next morning in a boat for Mooa, the village where he and the other great men usually reside. As we rowed up the inlet we met fourteen canoes fishing in company, in one of which was Poulaho's son. In each canoe was a triangular net, extended between two poles, at the lower end of which was a cod to receive and secure the fish. They had already caught some fine mullet, and they put about a dozen into our boat. I desired to see their method of fishing, which they readily complied with. A shoal of fish was supposed to be in one of the banks, which they instantly enclosed in a large net like a seine, or set-net. This the fishers, one getting into the water out of each boat, surrounded with the triangular nets in their hands, with which they scooped the fish out of the seine, or caught them as they attempted to leap over it.

Leaving the prince and fishing party, we proceeded to the bottom of the bay. Here we observed a fiatooka, or burying-place, which was much more extensive, and seemingly of more consequence, than any we had seen at the other islands. We were told that it belonged to the king. It consisted of three pretty large houses, situated upon a rising ground, with a small one at a distance, all ranged longitudinally. The floors were covered and paved with fine pebbles, and the whole was enclosed by large flat stones of hard coral rock, properly hewn, placed on their edges; one of the stones measured twelve feet in length, two in breadth, and above one in thickness. Within one of these houses were two rude wooden busts of men. On inquiring what these images were intended for, we were told they were merely memorials of some chiefs who had been buried there, and not the representations of any deity. In one of them was a carved head of an Otaheitean canoe, which had been driven ashore on their coast and deposited here.

After we had refreshed ourselves we made an excursion into the country, attended by one of the king's ministers. Our train was not great, as he would not suffer the rabble to follow us. He also obliged all those whom we met upon our progress to sit down till we had passed, which is a mark of respect due only to their sovereigns.

By far the greater part of the country was cultivated, and planted with various sorts of productions. There were many public and well-beaten roads, and abundance of footpaths leading to every part of the island. It is remarkable that when we were on the most elevated parts, at least a hundred feet above the level of the sea, we often met with the same coral rock which is found at the shore, and yet these very spots, with hardly any soil upon them, were covered with luxuriant vegetation. We were conducted to several little pools and some springs, but in general they were either stinking or brackish.

When we returned from our walk, which was not till the dusk of the evening, our supper was ready. It consisted of a baked hog, some fish, and yams, all excellently well cooked after the method of these islands. As there was nothing to amuse us after supper, we followed the custom of the country and lay down to sleep, our beds being mats spread upon the floor, and cloth to cover us. The king, who had made himself very happy with some wine and brandy which we had brought, slept in the same house, as well as several others of the natives.

In the morning of the 5th, the day of the eclipse, the weather was dark and cloudy, with showers of rain, so that we had little hopes of an observation. About nine o'clock the sun broke out at intervals for about half an hour, after which it was totally obscured, till within a minute or two of the beginning of the eclipse. We were all at our telescopes, but I lost the observation by not having a dark glass at hand suitable to the clouds that were continually passing over the sun. The sun appeared at intervals till about the middle of the eclipse, after which it was seen no more during the day, so that the end could not be observed.

July.

As soon as we knew the eclipse to be over we packed up the instruments, took down the observatories, and sent everything on board. As none of the sheep allotted to Mareewagee had been taken the least notice of, I ordered them to be carried back to the ships. I was apprehensive that if I had left them here they ran great risk of being destroyed by dogs. That animal did not exist upon this island when I first visited it in 1773, but I now found they had got a good many, partly from the breed then left by myself, and partly from some imported since from an island not very remote, called Feejee.

Preparing now for our departure, I got on board all the cattle, poultry, and other animals, except such as were destined to remain, and on the following day we unmoored, that we might be ready to take advantage of the first favourable wind. The king, who was one of our company this day at dinner, took particular notice of the plates, which induced me to make him an offer of one, either of pewter or of earthenware. He chose the first, and then began to tell us the several uses to which he intended to apply it, two being of so extraordinary a nature that I cannot omit mentioning them. He said that whenever he should have occasion to visit any of the other islands he would leave this plate behind him at Tongatabu as a sort of representative in his absence, that the people might pay it the same obeisance as they did to himself in person. He was asked what had been usually employed for that purpose before he got this plate, and we had the satisfaction of learning from him that this singular honour had been hitherto conferred on a wooden bowl in which he washed his hands. The other extraordinary use to which he meant to apply this plate, in the place of the wooden bowl, was to discover a thief. He said that when anything was stolen, and the thief could not be found out, the people were all assembled together before him, when he washed his hands in water in this vessel, after which it was cleaned, and then the whole multitude advanced one after another and touched it in the same manner that they touch his foot when they pay him obeisance. If the guilty person touched it he died immediately upon the spot, not by violence, but by the hand of Providence; and if any one refused to touch it, his refusal was a clear proof that he was the man.

Being now on the eve of our departure from this island, I shall add some particulars about it and its productions.

Amsterdam, Tongatabu, or Tonga, is about twenty leagues in circuit, and somewhat oblong. The general appearance of the country does not afford that beautiful kind of landscape that is produced from a variety of hills and valleys, lawns, rivulets, and cascades, but at the same time it conveys to the spectator an idea of the most exuberant fertility. Of cultivated fruits the principal are plantains, of which they have fifteen different sorts, breadfruit, a kind of plum, and vast numbers of shaddocks. Besides vast numbers of cocoa-nut trees, they have three other sort of palms, two of which are very scarce.

The only quadrupeds, besides hogs, are a few rats and some dogs. Amongst the birds are parrots, owls, cuckoos, kingfishers, and a bird of the thrush kind, which is the only singing one we observed here, but it compensates a good deal for the want of others by the strength and melody of its notes, which fill the woods at dawn, in the evening, and at the breaking up of bad weather.

The sea abounds with fish. The most frequent sorts are mullets, several sorts of parrot fish, some beautifully spotted soles, eels, sharks, a sort of pike, and some curious devil-fish.

We were now ready to sail, but the wind being easterly, we were under a necessity of waiting two or three days. July 6.

On the 10th, at eight o'clock in the morning, we weighed anchor, and with a steady gale at SE. turned through the channel, and anchored on the 12th off Middleburgh, or Eooa, being nearly the same place where I had my station in 1773, then named by me "English Road." We had no sooner anchored than Taoofa, the chief, and several other natives visited us on board, and seemed to rejoice much at our arrival. This Taoofa knew me when I was here during my last voyage, and I now went ashore with him in search of fresh water, which was the chief object that brought me to Eooa. I was first conducted to a brackish spring, between low and high water mark, in the cove where we landed. Finding that we did not like this, our friends took us a little inland, where, in a deep chasm, we found very good water; but rather than undertake the tedious task of bringing it down to the shore, I resolved to rest content with the supply that the ships had got at Tongatabu. I put ashore the ram and the two ewes of the Cape of Good Hope breed, entrusting them to the care of Taoofa, who seemed proud of his charge.

As we lay at anchor this island bore a very different aspect from any we had lately seen, and formed a most beautiful landscape. It is higher than any we had passed since leaving New Zealand, and from its top, which is almost flat, declines very gently towards the sea.

The 13th, in the afternoon, a party of us made an excursion to the highest part of the island, in order to have a full view of the country. On the most elevated part of the whole island we found a mound of earth, supported by a wall of coral stones, to bring which to such a height must have cost much labour. Our guides told us that this mound had been erected by order of their chief. Not many paces from it was a spring of excellent water.

While I was surveying this delightful prospect, I could not help flattering myself with the pleasing idea that some future navigator may, from the same station, behold these meadows stocked with cattle, brought to these islands by the ships of England; and that the completion of this single benevolent purpose, independently of all other considerations, would sufficiently mark to posterity that our voyages had not been useless to the general interests of humanity. Our guides informed us that all or most of the land on this island belonged to the great chiefs of Tongatabu, and that the inhabitants were only tenants or vassals to them. Omai, who was a great favourite with Feenou and these people in general, was tempted with the offer of being made chief of this island if he would have stayed amongst them.

The next morning I planted a pine-apple, and sowed the seeds of melons and other vegetables in the chief's plantation. I had some encouragement, indeed, to flatter myself that my endeavours of this kind would not be fruitless, for this day there was served up at my dinner a dish of turnips, being the produce of the seeds I had left during my last voyage. I had fixed on the 15th for sailing, till Taoofa pressed me to stay a day or two longer, to receive a present he had prepared for me, consisting of two small heaps of yams and some fruit, which seemed to be collected by a kind of contribution, as at the other isles.

On the 17th we weighed, and with a light breeze at SE. stood out to sea. We thus took leave of the Friendly Islands after a stay of nearly two months, during which time we lived with the natives in the most cordial friendship. Some accidental differences, it is true, now and then happened, owing to their great propensity for thieving, which was too often encouraged by the negligence of our own people. The time employed amongst them was not thrown away. We expended very little of our sea provisions, subsisting in general upon the produce of the islands while we stayed, and carrying away with us a quantity of refreshments sufficient to last till we arrived at another station where we could depend upon a fresh supply. I was not sorry, besides, to have had an opportunity of bettering the condition of these good people by leaving the useful animals before mentioned among them; and at the same time those designed for Otaheite received fresh strength in the pastures of Tongatabu. Upon the whole, therefore, the advantages we received by touching here were very great, and I had the additional satisfaction to reflect that they were received without retarding one moment the prosecution of the great object of our voyage, the season for proceeding to the north being, as has been already observed, lost before I took the resolution of bearing away for these islands.

But besides the immediate advantages which both the natives of the Friendly Islands and ourselves received by this visit, future navigators from Europe, if any such ever tread in our steps, will profit by the knowledge acquired of the geography of this part of the Pacific Ocean; and the more philosophical reader, who loves to view human nature in new situations, will perhaps find matter of amusement, if not of instruction, in the information which I have been enabled to convey to him concerning the inhabitants of this archipelago.

We found by experience that the best articles for traffic at these islands are iron tools in general. Axes and hatchets, nails, rasps, files, and knives are much sought after. A string of large blue beads would purchase a hog. In return for the favourite commodities all the refreshments may be procured that the islands produce. These are hogs, fowls, fish, yams, bread-fruit, plantains, cocoa-nuts, sugar-cane, and in general every such supply as can be met with at Otaheite or any of the Society Islands. Good water, which ships on long voyages stand so much in need of, is scarce at these islands.

According to the information that we received there, this

archipelago is very extensive. About one hundred and fifty islands were reckoned up to us by the natives, who made use of bits of leaves to ascertain their number. I have not the least doubt that Prince William's Islands, discovered and so named by Tasman, are included in the foregoing list.

The natives of the Friendly Islands seldom exceed the common stature, but are very strong and well made. They are generally broad about the shoulders, and though the muscular disposition of the men rather conveys the appearance of strength than of beauty, there are some to be seen who are really handsome. Their eyes and teeth are good. The general colour is a cast deeper than the copper brown, but several of the men and women have a fine olive complexion. Their countenances very remarkably express the abundant mildness or good nature which they possess, and are entirely free from that savage keenness which marks nations in a barbarous state. Their peaceable disposition is sufficiently evinced by the friendly reception all strangers have met with who have visited them. Perhaps no nation in the world traffic with more honesty and less distrust. The only defect sullying their character that we know of is a propensity to thieving, to which we found those of all ages and both sexes addicted, and to an uncommon degree. Great allowances should be made for the foibles of these poor natives of the Pacific Ocean, whose minds we overpowered with the glare of objects, equally new to them as they were captivating. Their hair is in general straight, thick, and strong. When I first visited these islands I thought it had been a universal custom for both men and women to wear the hair short, but during our present stay we found they were so whimsical in their fashions of wearing it, that it is hard to tell which is most in vogue.

Nothing appears to give them greater pleasure than personal cleanliness, to produce which they frequently bathe in the ponds, which seem to serve no other purpose.

Their domestic life is of that middle kind, neither so laborious as to be disagreeable, nor so vacant as to be indolent. The employment of the women is of the easy kind; they manufacture their cloth, their mats, combs, little baskets made from fibrous cocoa-nut husk and interwoven with small beads. The province allotted to the men is agriculture, architecture, boat-building, and fishing.

I think I may venture to assert that they do not worship anything that is the work of their own hands, or any visible part of the creation; but that they offer real human sacrifices is with me beyond a doubt. The chiefs are, by the people, styled not only lords of the earth, but of the sun and sky.

The language of the Friendly Islands has the greatest affinity imaginable to that of New Zealand, of Wateeoo and Mangeea, and consequently to that of Otaheite and the Society Islands.

CHAPTER XXXIX.

THE ISLAND TOOBOUAI DISCOVERED—ARRIVAL IN OHEITEPEHA BAY AT OTAHEITE
—OMAI'S RECEPTION—INTERVIEW WITH OTOO, KING OF THE ISLAND—
HUMAN SACRIFICE—OTOO'S PRESENT TO THE KING OF GREAT BRITAIN—
DEPARTURE FROM OTAHEITE.

IN the evening of the 17th, the island of Eooa was distant some three or four leagues. The wind was at east, and blew a fresh gale. With it I stood to the south till half an hour past six o'clock the next morning, when a sudden squall took our ship aback, and before she could be trimmed on the other tack, the mainsail and the topgallant sails were much torn. The night between the 20th and 21st an eclipse of the moon was observed.

July.

At eleven o'clock in the morning of the 8th, land was seen, which, as we drew nearer, we found to be an island guarded by a reef of coral rock with a high surf breaking upon it. We saw several people on the coast running along shore, and after we had reached the lee side of the island we saw them launch two canoes. Omai was employed to use all his eloquence to prevail upon the men to come nearer, but no entreaties would induce them to trust themselves within our reach. They kept eagerly pointing to the shore with their paddles, and calling us to go thither. We could very well have done this, as there was good anchorage without the reef; but I did not think it proper to risk losing the advantage of a fair wind for the sake of examining an island that appeared to be of little consequence. After making several unsuccessful attempts to induce these people to come alongside, I made sail to the north and left them, but not without getting from them the name of their island, which they called Toobouai.

August.

At daybreak on the morning of the 12th, we saw the island of Maitea, and soon after Otaheite made its appearance. When we first drew near the island several canoes came off to the ship, each conducted by two or three men. But as they were common fellows Omai took no particular notice of them, nor they of him. At length a chief, whom I had known before, named Ootee, and Omai's brother-in-law, and three or four more persons, all of whom knew Omai, came on board. There was nothing either tender or striking in their meeting. On the contrary, there seemed to be a perfect indifference on both sides, till Omai, having taken his brother-in-law down into the cabin, opened the drawer where he kept his red feathers and gave him a few. This being presently known among the rest of the natives upon deck, the face of affairs was entirely changed, and Ootee, who would hardly speak to Omai before, now begged that they might be friends, and exchanged names. Omai accepted the honour, and confirmed it with a present of red feathers; and Ootee, by way of return, sent ashore for a hog. But it was evident to every one of us that it was not the man but his property they were in love with. Such was Omai's first reception among his countrymen.

I own I never expected it would be otherwise, but still I was in hopes that the valuable cargo of presents with which the liberality of his friends in England had loaded him would be the means of raising him into consequence, and of making him respected by the first persons throughout the extent of the Society Islands. This would have happened had he conducted himself with any degree of prudence. But instead, I am sorry to say that he paid too little regard to the repeated advice of those who wished him well, and suffered himself to be duped by every designing knave.

The important news of red feathers being on board our ships having been conveyed on shore by Omai's friends, day had no sooner begun to break next morning than we were surrounded by a multitude of canoes, crowded with people bringing hogs and fruit to market. At first a quantity of feathers not greater than what might be got from a tomtit would purchase a hog of forty or fifty pounds weight, but as almost everybody in the ships was possessed of some of this precious article of trade, it fell in its value above five hundred per cent. before night.

Soon after we had anchored, Omai's sister came on board to see him. I was happy to observe that, much to the honour of them both, their meeting was marked with expressions of the tenderest affection, easier to be conceived than described. This moving scene having closed, and the ship being properly moored, Omai and I went on shore. My first object was to pay a visit to a man whom my friend represented as a very extraordinary personage indeed, for he said that he was the god of Bolabola. We found him seated under one of those small awnings which they usually carry in their larger canoes. He was an elderly man, and had lost the use of his limbs, so that he was carried from place to place upon a hand-barrow. From Omai's account of this person I expected to have seen some religious adoration paid to him. But I could observe nothing by which he might be distinguished from other chiefs. Omai presented to him a tuft of red feathers tied to the end of a small stick; but after a little conversation on indifferent matters with this Bolabola man, his attention was drawn to an old woman, the sister of his mother. She was already at his feet, and had bedewed them plentifully with tears of joy. I left him with the old lady in the midst of a number of people who had gathered round him, and went to view a house said to be built by strangers since I was here before. When I returned I found Omai holding forth to a large company, and it was with some difficulty that he could be got away to accompany me on board, where I had an important affair to settle.

As I knew that Otaheite and the neighbouring islands could furnish us with a plentiful supply of cocoa-nuts, I was desirous of prevailing upon my people to be content to be abridged, during our stay here, of their stated allowance of spirits to mix with water. But as this stopping of a favourite article without assigning some reason might have occasioned a general murmur, I thought it most prudent to assemble the ship's company, and to make known to them the intent of the voyage and the extent of our future operations. To induce them to undertake which with cheerfulness and perseverance, I took notice of the rewards offered by Parliament to such of His Majesty's subjects as shall first discover a communication between the Atlantic and Pacific Oceans, in any direction whatever, in the northern hemisphere, and also to such as shall first penetrate beyond the eighty-ninth degree of northern latitude. I made no doubt, I told them, that I should find them willing to co-operate with me in attempting, as far as might be possible, to become entitled to one or both these rewards, but that to give us the best chance of succeeding it would be necessary to observe the utmost economy in the expenditure of our stores and provisions, as there was no probability of getting a supply anywhere after leaving these islands. I begged them to consider the various obstructions and difficulties we might still meet with, and the hardships they would labour under, if it should be found necessary to put them on short allowances in a cold climate. Therefore I submitted to them, Would they not consent to be without their grog now, when we had so excellent a liquid as that of cocoa-nut to substitute in its place?—but I left the determination entirely to their own choice. I had the satisfaction to find that this proposal did not remain a single moment under consideration. Accordingly we stopped serving grog, except on Saturday nights, when the companies of both ships had full allowance of it that they might drink the healths of their friends in England.

The next day we began some necessary operations. The calkers were set to work to calk the ship, which she stood in great need of, having at times made much water on our passage from the Friendly Islands. I also put on shore the bull, cows, horses, and sheep, and appointed two men to look after them.

During the two following days it hardly ceased raining, but the natives nevertheless came to us from every quarter, the news of our arrival having rapidly spread. On the 17th, Omai and I went on shore to pay a formal visit to a young chief named Waheiadooa, who had come down to the beach. On this occasion Omai, assisted by some of his friends, dressed himself, not after the English fashion, nor that of Otaheite, nor that of Tongatabu, nor in the dress of any country upon earth, but in a strange medley of all that he was possessed of.

On our landing, Etary, or the god of Bolabola, carried on a hand-barrow, attended us to a large house, where he was set down, and we seated ourselves on each side of him. I caused a piece of Tongatabu cloth to be spread out before us, on which I laid the presents I intended to make. Presently the young chief came, attended by his mother and several principal men, who all seated themselves at the other end of the cloth facing us. Then a man who sat by me made a speech, consisting of short and separate sentences, part of which was dictated by those about him. He was answered by one from the opposite side near the chief; Etary spoke next, then Omai, both of them being answered from the same quarter. These orations were entirely about my arrival and connections with them. The person who spoke last told me, among other things, that he was authorized to make a formal surrender of the province of Tiaraboo to me, and of everything in it, which marks very plainly that these people are no strangers to the policy of accommodating themselves to present circumstances. At length the young chief was directed by his attendants to come and embrace me; and, by way of confirming this treaty of friendship, we exchanged names. The ceremony being closed, he and his friends accompanied me on board to dinner.

Having taken in a fresh supply of water, and finished all other necessary operations, on the 22nd I brought off the cattle and sheep, and made ready for sea. On the 23rd we got under sail, and steered for Matavai Bay, where the *Resolution* anchored the same evening, the *Discovery* not arriving till the next day.

About nine o'clock in the morning, Otoo, the king of the whole island, attended by a great number of canoes full of people, came from Oparre, his place of residence, and sent a message on board expressing his desire to see me. Accordingly I landed, accompanied by Omai and some of the officers. We found a prodigious number of people assembled on this occasion, and in the midst of them was the king, attended by his father, his two brothers, and three sisters. I went up first and saluted them, followed by Omai, who kneeled and embraced his legs. Omai had prepared himself for this ceremony by dressing in his very best suit of clothes, and behaved with a great deal of respect and modesty; nevertheless, very little notice was taken of him. Perhaps envy had some share in producing this cold reception. He made the chief a present of a large bunch of red feathers and about two or three yards of gold cloth, and I gave him a suit of fine linen, a gold-laced hat, some tools, and, what was of more value than all the other articles, a quantity of red feathers and one of the bonnets in use at the Friendly Islands.

After the hurry of this visit was over, the king and the whole royal family accompanied me on board, followed by several canoes laden with all kinds of provisions, in quantity sufficient to have served the companies of both ships for a week. Soon after the king's mother, who had not been present at the first interview, came on board, bringing with her a quantity of provisions and cloth, which she divided between me and Omai. For although he was but little noticed at first by his countrymen, they no sooner gained a knowledge of his riches than they began to court his friendship. I encouraged this as much as I could, for it was my wish to leave him with Otoo. As I intended to land all my European animals at this island, I thought he would be able to give some instructions about the management of them and their use. Besides, I knew and saw that the farther he was from his native island the more he would be respected; unfortunately, however, poor Omai rejected my advice, and conducted himself in so imprudent a manner that he soon lost the friendship of Otoo, and of every other person of note in Otaheite.

As soon as we had dined, a party of us accompanied Otoo to Oparre, taking with us the poultry with which we were to stock the island. They consisted of a peacock and hen, a turkey cock and hen, one gander and three geese, a drake and four ducks. These I left at Oparre in the possession of Otoo, and the geese and ducks began to breed before we sailed. We found there a gander, which the natives told us was the same that Captain Wallis had given to Oberea ten years before, several goats, and the Spanish bull, which they kept tied to a tree near Otoe's house. I never saw a finer animal of this kind. He was now the property of Etary, and had been brought from Oheitepeha to this place in order to be shipped for Bolabola. But it passes my comprehension how they can contrive to carry him in one of their canoes. Next day I put ashore three cows, a horse and mare, and sheep.

Having thus disposed of these passengers, I found myself lightened of a very heavy burden. The trouble and vexation that attended the bringing this living cargo thus far is hardly to be conceived; but the satisfaction I felt in having been so fortunate as to fulfil His Majesty's humane design, in sending such valuable animals to supply the wants of two worthy nations, sufficiently recompensed me for the many anxious hours I had passed before this subordinate object of my voyage could be carried into execution.

As I intended to make some stay here, we set up the two observatories on Matavai Point. Adjoining to them two tents were pitched, for the reception of a guard and of such people as it might be necessary to leave on shore in different departments. I entrusted the command to Mr. King, who at the same time attended the observations for ascertaining the correctness of the timekeeper, and other purposes.

On the 26th, I had a piece of ground cleared for a garden, and planted in it several articles. Some melons, potatoes, and two pine-apple plants were in a fair way of succeeding before we left the place. I had brought from the Friendly Islands several shaddock trees, which I also planted here; and they can hardly fail of success, unless their growth should be checked by the same premature curiosity which destroyed a vine planted by the Spaniards at Oheitepeha. A number of the natives got together to taste the first fruit it bore, but, as the grapes were still sour, they considered it as little better than poison, and it was unanimously determined to tread it under foot. In that state Omai found it by chance, and was overjoyed at the discovery, for he had full confidence that, if he had but grapes, he could make wine. Accordingly he had several slips cut off from the tree to carry with him, and we pruned and put in order the remains of it.

We had not been long at anchor in Matavai Bay, before we were visited by all our old friends. We found there the young man whom we called Oedidee, but whose real name is Hecte-heete. I had carried him from Ulietea in 1773, and brought him back in 1774, after he had visited the Friendly Islands, New Zealand, Easter Island, and the Marquesas, and been on board my ship about seven months. He was tenacious of his good breeding, and " Yes, sir," or " If you please, sir," were frequently repeated by him. Heete-heete, who is a native of Bolabola, had arrived in Otaheite three months before. It was evident, however, that he preferred the mode, and even the garb, of his own countrymen to ours, for though I gave him some clothes which our Admiralty Board had been pleased to send for his use, to which I added a chest of tools and a few other articles as a present from myself, he declined wearing them after a few days. This instance may be urged as a proof of the strong propensity natural to man, of returning to habits acquired at an early age, and only interrupted by accident. And perhaps it may be concluded that even Omai, who had imbibed almost the whole English manners, will in a very short time after our leaving him, return to his native garments.

Hitherto the attention of Otoo and his people was confined to us; but, next morning, messengers arrived from Eimeo, with the intelligence that the people in the island were in arms, and that Otoo's partisans there had been worsted, and obliged to retreat to the mountains. The quarrel between the two islands, which commenced in 1774, had, it seems, partly subsisted ever since. The formidable armament which I saw at that time had sailed soon after I left Otaheite, but the malcontents of Eimeo had made so stout a resistance, that the fleet had returned without effecting much; and now another expedition was necessary.

On the arrival of the messengers, all the chiefs who happened to be at Matavai assembled at Otoe's house, where I actually was at the time, and had the honour to be admitted into their council. One of the messengers opened the business in a speech of considerable length, in order to excite the assembled chiefs of Otaheite to arm on this occasion. This opinion was combated by others who were against commencing hostilities, but at length the party for war prevailed; Otoo, during the whole debate, remained silent. Those of the council who were for prosecuting the war applied to me for assistance, and all of them wanted to know what part I would take. Omai was sent to be my interpreter, but, as he could not be found, I was obliged to speak for myself, and told them, as well as I could, that as the people of Eimeo had never offended me, I could not think myself at liberty to engage in hostilities against them. With this declaration they seemed satisfied.

It is certain that human sacrifices are not the only barbarous custom we find still prevailing amongst this benevolent, humane people. For, besides cutting out the jawbones of their enemies slain in battle, which they carry about as trophies, they in some measure offer their bodies as a sacrifice to the Eatooa. Soon after the battle in which they have been victors, they collect all the dead that have fallen into their hands, and bring them to the "morai," where, with a great deal of ceremony, they dig a hole and bury them all in it as so many offerings to the gods; but their skulls are never after taken up. We made no scruple in freely expressing our sentiments about their horrid ceremonies to Otoo and those who attended him, and I could not conceal my detestation of them in a subsequent conversation with Towha. Omai was made use of as our interpreter; and he entered into our arguments with so much spirit that the chief seemed to be in great wrath, especially when he was told that if he had put a man to death in England as he did here, his rank would not protect him from being hanged for it. Upon this he exclaimed, "Maeno! maeno!" ("Vile! vile!") and would not hear another word.

September. In the evening of the 7th, we played off some fireworks before a great concourse of people. Some were highly entertained with the exhibition, but by far the greater number of the spectators were terribly frightened: insomuch that it was with difficulty we could prevail upon them to keep together to see the end of the show. A table-rocket was the last. It flew off the table and dispersed the whole crowd in a moment; even the most resolute among them fled with precipitation.

Otoo was not more attentive to supply our wants by a succession of presents than he was to contribute to our amusement by a succession of diversions. A party of us having gone down to Oparre on the 10th, he treated us with what may be called a play. His three sisters were the actresses, and the dresses they appeared in were new and elegant—that is, more so than we had usually met with at any of these islands. In the evening we returned from Oparre, where we left Otoo and all the royal family, and I saw none of them till the 12th, when all but the chief himself paid me a visit; he, as they told me, was gone to Attahooroo, to assist this day at another human sacrifice, which the chief of Tiaraboo had sent thither to be offered up at the "morai."

The following evening Otoo returned from exercising this most disagreeable of all his duties as sovereign; and the next day, being now honoured with his company, Captain Clerke and I, mounted on horseback, took a ride round the plain of Matavai, to the very great surprise of a great train of people, who attended on the occasion, gazing upon us with as much astonishment as if we had been centaurs; Omai, indeed, had once or twice before this attempted to get on horseback, but he had been as often thrown off before he could contrive to seat himself, so that this was the first time they had seen anybody ride a horse. Though this performance was repeated every day while we stayed, by one or other of our people, the curiosity of the natives continued still unabated. They were exceedingly delighted with these animals, after they had seen the use that was made of them; and, as far as I could judge, they conveyed to them a better idea of the greatness of other nations than all other European novelties put together.

On the morning of the 18th, Mr. Anderson, myself, and Omai, went again with Otoo to Oparre, and took with us the sheep which I intended to leave upon the island, consisting of an English ram and ewe and three Cape ewes, all of which I gave to Otoo.

After dining with Otoo we returned to Matavai, leaving him at Oparre. This day, and also the 19th, we were very sparingly supplied with fruit. Otoo hearing of this, he and his brother, who had attached himself to Captain Clerke, came from Oparre between nine and ten o'clock in the evening, with a large supply for both ships. The next day all the royal family came with presents, so that our wants were not only relieved, but we had more provisions than we could consume.

Having got all our water on board, the ships being calked, the rigging overhauled, and everything put in order, I began to think of leaving the island that I might have sufficient time for visiting the others in this neighbourhood. With this view we removed from the shore our observatories and instruments and bent our sails.

Early in the morning of the 22nd, Otoo and his father came on board to know when I proposed sailing; for, having been informed that there was a good harbour at Eimeo, I told them that I should visit that island on my way to Huaheine, and they were desirous of taking a passage with me, and of their fleet sailing at the same time to reinforce Towha. As I was ready to take my departure, I left it to them to name the day, and the Wednesday following was fixed upon, when I was to take on board Otoo, his father, mother, and, in short, the whole family. These points being settled, I proposed setting out immediately for Oparre, where all the fleet fitted out for the expedition was to assemble that day, and to be reviewed. I had just time to get into my boat when news was brought that Towha had concluded a treaty with Maheine, and returned with his fleet to Attahooroo. This unexpected event made all further proceedings in a military way quite unnecessary; and the war canoes, instead of rendezvousing at Oparre, were ordered home to their respective districts. I now returned on board my ship, attended by Otoo's mother, his three sisters, and eight more women. At first I thought this numerous train of females came into my boat with no other intention than to get a passage to Matavai; but when we arrived at the ship they told me that they intended to pass the night on board for the express purpose of undertaking the cure of a disorder I had complained of, which was a pain of the rheumatic kind. I accepted the friendly offer, had a bed spread for them on the cabin floor, and submitted myself to their directions. They began to squeeze me with both hands from head to foot, but particularly on the parts where the pain was lodged, till they made my bones crack, and my flesh became a perfect mummy. In short, after undergoing this discipline for about a quarter of an hour, I was glad to get away from them. However, the operation gave me immediate relief, which encouraged me to submit to another rubbing down before I went to bed; and it was so effectual that I found myself pretty easy all the night after. My female physicians repeated their prescription the next morning before they went ashore, and again in the evening, when they returned on board, after which I found the pains entirely removed, and the cure being perfected, they took their leave of me the following morning. This operation is universally practised amongst these islanders, being sometimes performed by the men, but more generally by the women.

The war with Eimeo being finally closed, all our friends paid us a visit on the 26th; and as they knew that we were on the point of sailing, brought with them more hogs than we could take off their hands; for, having no salt left to preserve any, we wanted no more than for present use.

The next day I accompanied Otoo to Oparre; and before I left it I looked at the cattle and poultry. Everything was in a promising way, and properly attended unto. Two of the geese and two of the ducks were sitting.

On the 28th, Otoo came on board and informed me that he had got a canoe, which he desired I would take with me, and carry home as a present from him to the "Earee rabie no Pretane" (His Majesty the King of Great Britain); it being the only thing, he said, that he could send worth his acceptance. I was not a little pleased with Otoo for this mark of his gratitude. It was a thought entirely his own, not one of us having given him the least hint about it, and it showed that he fully understood to whom he was indebted for the most valuable presents he had received. As it was too large for me to take on board, I could only thank him for his good intention; but it would have pleased him much better if his present could have been accepted.

We were detained here some days longer than I expected by light breezes from the west. At length, at three o'clock in the evening of the 29th, the wind came east, and we weighed anchor. As soon as the ships were under sail, at the request of Otoo and to gratify the curiosity of his people, I fired seven guns loaded with shot, after which all our friends, except him and two or three more, left us with such marks of affection and grief as sufficiently showed how much they regretted our departure. If I could have prevailed upon Omai to fix himself at Otaheite, I should not have left it so soon as I did. For there was not a probability of our being better or cheaper supplied with refreshments at any other place. Besides such a cordial friendship and confidence subsisted between us and the inhabitants, as could hardly be expected anywhere else; and this friendly intercourse had never once been suspended by any untoward accident.

CHAPTER XL.

ARRIVAL AT EIMEO—ARRIVAL AT HUAHEINE—COUNCIL OF CHIEFS—OMAI'S ESTABLISHMENT IN THE ISLAND AGREED TO—A HOUSE BUILT FOR HIM—ARRIVAL AT ULIETEA—ARRIVAL AT BOLABOLA.

1777.
September.

AS I did not give up my design of touching at Eimeo, at daybreak on the morning of the 30th, after leaving Otaheite, I stood for the north end of the island.

We had no sooner anchored than the ships were crowded with the inhabitants, whom curiosity alone brought on board, for they had nothing with them for the purpose of barter; but the next morning several canoes arrived from more distant parts, bringing with them abundance of bread-fruit, cocoa-nuts, and a few hogs. These they exchanged for hatchets, nails, and beads; for red feathers were not so much sought for here as at Otaheite.

In the morning of the 2nd of October, Maheine, the chief of the island, paid me a visit. He approached the ship with great caution, and it required some persuasion to get him on board. This chief, who, with a few followers, had made himself independent of Otaheite, is between forty and fifty years old. He is bald-headed, which is rather uncommon in these islands at that age, and wore a kind of turban, as he seemed ashamed to show his head. In the evening, Omai and I mounted on horseback and took a ride along the shore to the eastward. On the 6th, we prepared to put to sea, but an accident happened that prevented it and gave me a good deal of trouble. We had sent our goats ashore to graze, with two men to look after them; but, notwithstanding this precaution, the natives had contrived to steal one of them in the evening. The loss of this goat would have been of little consequence if it had not interfered with my views of stocking other islands with these animals; but this being the case, it became necessary to recover it if possible. The next morning we got intelligence that it had been carried to the chief. Accordingly I dispatched a threatening message to Maheine, and the goat was returned next morning.

At Eimeo we abundantly supplied the ships with firewood. We had not taken any in at Otaheite, there not being a tree at Matavai but what is useful to the inhabitants. We also got here good store of refreshments, both in hogs and vegetables, that is, bread-fruit and cocoa-nuts, little else being in season. I do not know that there is any difference between the produce of this island and of Otaheite; but there is a very striking difference in their women, that I can by no means account for. Those of Eimeo are of low stature, have a dark hue, and, in general, forbidding features. If we met with a fine woman among them, we were sure to find, upon inquiry, that she had come from some other island. The general appearance of Eimeo is very different from that of Otaheite. The latter, rising in one steep hilly body, has little low land, except some deep valleys; Eimeo, on the contrary, has hills running in different directions, which are very steep and rugged.

Having left Eimeo with fine weather at daybreak on the 12th, we saw Huaheine the next morning, and at noon we anchored at the north entrance of Owharre harbour.

While I was at Otaheite, I had learned that my old friend Oree was no longer the chief of Huaheine, and that at this time he resided at Ulietea. His two sons, Opoony and Towha, were the first who paid me a visit, coming on board before the ship was well in the harbour, and bringing a present with them.

Our arrival brought all the principal people to our ships, which was what I wished, as it was high time to think of settling Omai, and the presence of these chiefs, I thought, would enable me to do it in the most satisfactory manner. He now seemed to have an inclination to establish himself at Ulietea; and if he and I could have agreed about the mode of bringing that plan to bear, I should have had no objection to it. But it was impossible to fix him at Ulietea, and Huaheine seemed the proper place. I therefore resolved to avail myself of the presence of the chief men of the island and to make this proposal to them.

After the hurry of the morning was over, we got ready to pay a formal visit to Taireetareea, the sovereign, meaning then to introduce this business. Omai dressed himself very properly on this occasion, and prepared a handsome present for the chief himself, and another for his Eatooa; indeed, after he got clear of the gang that surrounded him at Otaheite, he behaved with such prudence as to gain respect. We waited some time for Taireetareea, but when he appeared, I found that his presence might have been dispensed with, as he was not above eight or ten years of age. Omai, who stood at a little distance from this circle of great men, began with making his offerings to the gods, consisting of red feathers, cloth, etc. Each article was laid before one of the company, who, I understood, was a priest, and delivered with a set speech or prayer, spoken by one of Omai's friends who sat by him, but mostly dictated by himself. In these prayers he did not forget his friends in England, nor those who had brought him safe back; the "Earee rahie no Pretane," Lord Sandwich, Toote, and Tatee (Cook and Clerke), were mentioned in every one of them. When Omai's offerings and prayers were finished, the priest took each article, in the same order in which it had been laid before him, and, after repeating a prayer, sent it to the "morai," which as Omai told us was at a great distance, otherwise the offerings would have been made there. These religious ceremonies having been performed, Omai sat down by me and we entered upon business.

Omai's establishment was then proposed to the assembled chiefs; he acquainted them "that he had been carried by us into our country, where he was well received by the great king and his Earees, and treated with every mark of regard and affection while he stayed amongst us; that he had been brought back again, enriched by our liberality with a number of articles, which would prove very useful to his countrymen; and that, besides the two horses, which were to remain with him, several new and valuable animals had been left at Otaheite, which would soon multiply, and furnish a sufficient number for the use of all the islands in the neighbourhood. He then signified to them that it was my earnest request, in return for all my friendly offices, that they would give him a piece of land to build a house upon, and to raise provisions for himself and servants; adding that, if this could not be obtained for him in Huaheine, either by gift or by purchase, I was determined to carry him to Ulietea, and fix him there."

One of the chiefs immediately expressed himself to this effect; "That the whole island of Huaheine, and everything in it, were mine, and that therefore I might give what portion of it I pleased to my friend." Omai was greatly pleased to hear this; thinking, no doubt, that I should be very liberal, and give him enough. But to offer what it would have been improper to accept, I considered as offering nothing at all, and therefore I now desired that they would not only assign the particular spot, but also the exact quantity of land which they would allot for the settlement. After a short consultation among themselves my request was granted, and the ground immediately pitched upon, adjoining to the house where our meeting was held. The extent along the shore of the harbour was about two hundred yards, and its depth, to the foot of the hill, somewhat more, but a proportional part of the hill was included in the grant.

This business being settled to the satisfaction of all parties, I set up a tent ashore, established a post, and erected the observatories. The carpenters of both ships were also set to work to build a small house for Omai, in which he might secure the European commodities that were his property. At the same time some hands were employed in making a garden for his use, planting shaddocks, vines, pine-apples, melons, and other vegetable articles; all of which I had the satisfaction of observing to be in a flourishing state before I left the island.

While we lay in this harbour, we carried ashore the bread remaining in the bread-room, to clear it of vermin. The number of cockroaches that infested the ship at this time is incredible. The damage they did us was very considerable, and every method devised by us to destroy them proved ineffectual. These animals, which at first were a nuisance, had now become a real pest, and so destructive that few things were free from their ravages. If food of any kind was exposed only for a few minutes it was covered with them, and they soon pierced it full of holes, resembling a honeycomb. They were particularly destructive to birds we had stuffed and preserved as curiosities, and, what was worse, they were uncommonly fond of ink, so that the writing on the labels was quite eaten out. According to Mr. Anderson's observations, they were of two sorts, the *Blatta orientalis* and *germanica*. The first of these had been carried home in the ship from her former voyage, where they withstood the severity of the hard winter in 1766, though she was in dock all the time. The others had only made their appearance since our leaving New Zealand, but had increased so fast that when a sail was loosened thousands of them fell upon the decks. The *orientalis*, though in infinite numbers, scarcely came out but in the night, when they made everything in the cabin seem as if in motion, from the particular noise in crawling about.

The intercourse of trade and friendly offices was carried on between us and the natives, without being disturbed by any one accident, till the evening of the 22nd, when a man found means to get into Mr. Bayley's observatory, and to carry off the sextant unobserved. As soon as I was made acquainted with this, I went ashore, and got Omai to apply to the chiefs to procure restitution. He did so, but they took no steps towards it, being more attentive to a heeva that was then acting, till I ordered the performers of the exhibition to desist. They were now convinced that I was in earnest, and began to make some inquiry after the thief, who was sitting in the midst of them, quite unconcerned, insomuch that I was in great doubt of his being the guilty person, especially as he denied it. Omai, however, assuring me that he was the man, I sent him on board the ship and there confined him. This raised a general ferment amongst the assembled natives, and the whole body fled, in spite of all my endeavours to stop them. Having employed Omai to examine the prisoner, with some difficulty he was brought to confess where he had hid the sextant; but, as it was now dark, we could not find it till daylight the next morning, when it was brought back uninjured. After this, the natives recovered from their fright, and began to gather about us as usual, and as to the thief, he appearing to be a hardened scoundrel, I punished him more severely than I had ever done any one culprit before. Besides having his head and beard shaved, I ordered both his ears to be cut off and then dismissed him. This, however, did not deter him, for in the night of the 24th, a general alarm was spread, occasioned, as was said, by one of our goats being stolen by this very man. On examination, we found that all was safe in that quarter; probably the goats were so well guarded that he could not put his design into execution, but it appeared that he had destroyed and carried off several vines and cabbage plants in Omai's grounds, and he publicly threatened to kill him and to burn his house as soon as we should leave the island. To prevent the fellow's doing me and Omai any more mischief, I had him seized and confined again on board the ship, with a view of carrying him off the island; and it seemed to give general satisfaction to the chiefs that I meant thus to dispose of him.

Omai's house being nearly finished, many of his movables were carried ashore on the 26th. Amongst a variety of other useless articles was a box of toys, which, when exposed to public view, seemed greatly to please the gazing multitude. But as to his pots, kettles, dishes, plates, drinking mugs, glasses, and the whole train of our domestic accommodation, hardly any one of his countrymen would so much as look at them. Omai himself now began to think that they were of no manner of use to him; that a baked hog was more savoury food than a boiled one; that a plantain-leaf made as good a dish or plate as pewter; and that a cocoa-nut shell was as convenient a goblet as a black jack, and therefore he very wisely disposed of as many of these articles of English furniture for the kitchen and pantry as he could find purchasers for amongst the people of the ships, receiving from them in return hatchets and other iron tools, which had a more intrinsic value in this part of the world, and added more to his distinguishing superiority over those with whom he was to pass the remainder of his days.

In the long list of the presents bestowed upon him in England, fireworks had not been forgot. Some of these we exhibited in the evening of the 28th before a great concourse of people, who beheld them with a mixture of pleasure and fear.

As soon as Omai was settled in his new habitation, I began to think of leaving the island, and got everything off from the shore this evening, except the horse and mare, which were left in the possession of our friend, with whom we were now finally to part. I also gave him a boar and two sows of the English breed, and he had got a sow or two of his own. After he had got on shore everything that belonged to him and was settled in his house, he had most of the officers of both ships two or three times to dinner, and his table was always well supplied with the very best provisions that the island produced.

Before I sailed I had the following inscription cut upon the outside of his house :—

> Georgius Tertius, Rex, 2 Novembris 1777.
> Naves { *Resolution*, Jac. Cook, Pr.
> { *Discovery*, Car. Clerke, Pr.

On the 2nd of November, at four in the afternoon, I took advantage of a breeze which then sprung up at east, and sailed out of the harbour. Most of our friends remained on board till the ships were under sail, when, to gratify their curiosity, I ordered five guns to be fired. They then took their leave, except Omai, who remained till we were at sea; an hour or two later he went ashore, taking a very affectionate farewell of all the officers. He sustained himself with a manly resolution till he came to me; then his utmost efforts to conceal his tears failed, and Mr. King, who went in the boat, told me that he wept all the time in going ashore.

Omai's return, and the substantial proofs he brought back with him of our liberality, encouraged many to offer themselves as volunteers to attend me to Pretane. I took every opportunity of expressing my determination to reject all such applications. If there had been the most distant probability of any ship being again sent to New Zealand, I would have brought home with me two youths of that country, who were very desirous of continuing with us. Tiarooa, the elder, was an exceedingly well-disposed young man, with strong natural sense, and capable of receiving any instruction. He seemed to be fully sensible of the inferiority of his own country to these islands, and resigned himself, though perhaps with reluctance, to end his days in ease and plenty in Huaheine. But the other was so strongly attached to us that he was taken out of the ship and carried ashore by force. He was a witty, smart boy, and on that account much noticed on board. But notwithstanding this, Omai, who was very ambitious of remaining the only great traveller, frequently reminded me that

Lord Sandwich had told him no others of his countrymen were to come to England.

On the return of the boat which carried Omai ashore, never to join us again, I immediately stood over for Ulietea, where I intended to touch next. At ten o'clock at night we brought to, till four the next morning, when we made sail round the south end of the island for the harbour of Ohamaneno. We met with calms and light airs of wind from different directions by turns, so that at noon we were still a league from the entrance of the harbour. While we were thus detained, my old friend Oreo, chief of the island, with his son, and Pootoe, his son-in-law, came off to visit us.

Being resolved to make for the harbour, I ordered all the boats to be hoisted out, and sent them ahead to tow, but we were obliged to come to an anchor at its entrance at two o'clock, and to warp in, which employed us till night set in. As soon as we were within the harbour the ships were surrounded with canoes filled with people, who brought hogs and fruit to barter with us for our commodities. Next morning, being the 4th, I moored the ship, head and stern, close to the north shore at the head of the harbour, hauled up the cables on deck, and opened one of the ballast ports. From this a slight stage was made to the land, about twenty feet distant, with a view to get clear of some of the rats that continued to infest us. While this work was going forward I returned Oreo's visit. The present I made him on the occasion consisted of a linen gown, a shirt, a red-feathered cap from Tongatabu, and other things of less value. I then brought him and some friends on board to dinner. On the 6th we set up the observatories, and got the necessary instruments on shore.

Nothing worthy of note happened till the night of the 12th, when John Harrison, a marine, who was sentinel at the observatory, deserted, carrying with him his musket and accoutrements. Having in the morning got intelligence which way he had moved off, a party was sent after him, but they returned in the evening, after an ineffectual inquiry and search. The next day I applied to the chief to interest himself in the matter. He promised to send a party of his men after him, but I had reason to suspect that no steps had been taken by him. We had at this time a great number of natives about the ships, and some thefts were committed; dreading the consequences, very few visitors came near us the next morning. The chief himself with his whole family fled. I thought this a good opportunity to oblige them to deliver up the deserter, and having heard that he was at a place called Hamoa, on the other side of the island, I went thither with two armed boats, accompanied by one of the natives and the chief. I landed about a mile and a half from the place, with a few people, and marched briskly up to it, lest the sight of the boats should give the alarm and allow the man time to escape to the mountains. But this precaution was unnecessary, for the natives there had got information of my coming, and were prepared to deliver him up.

Paha, the chief of the district, came with a plantain tree and a sucking pig as a peace-offering. I rejected it and ordered him out of my sight, and having embarked, with the deserter Harrison, on board the first boat that arrived, returned to the ships. The fellow had nothing to say in his defence but that the natives had enticed him away. As it appeared that he had remained upon his post till within a few minutes of the time when he was to have been relieved, the punishment that I inflicted upon him was not very severe.

Though we had separated from Omai, we were still near enough to have intelligence of his proceedings; and I had desired to hear from him. Accordingly, about a fortnight after our arrival at Ulietea, he sent two of his people in a canoe; who brought me the satisfactory intelligence that he remained undisturbed by the people of the island, and that everything went well with him, except that his goat had died. He accompanied this intelligence with a request that I would send him another goat and two axes. Being happy to have this additional opportunity of serving him, the messengers were sent back to Huaheine with the axes and two kids.

On the morning of the 24th, I was informed that a midshipman and a seaman, both belonging to the *Discovery*, were missing. Soon after, we learned from the natives that they went away in a canoe the preceding evening, and were at this time at the other end of the island. As the midshipman was known to have expressed a desire to remain at these islands, it seemed pretty certain that he and his companion had gone off with this intention; and Captain Clerke set out in quest of them with two armed boats and a party of marines. His expedition proved fruitless, for he returned in the evening without having got any certain intelligence where they were. From the conduct of the natives, Captain Clerke seemed to think that they intended to conceal the deserters, and with that view had given him false information the whole day, which turned out to be correct, for the next morning we were told that our runaways were at Otaha. As these two were not the only persons in the ships who wished to end their days at these favourite islands, in order to put a stop to any further desertion, it was necessary to get them back at all hazards; and that the natives might be convinced that I was in earnest, I resolved to go after them myself, having observed, from repeated instances, that they seldom offered to deceive me with false information.

Accordingly, I set out the next morning with two armed boats, being accompanied by the chief himself. I proceeded as he directed, without stopping anywhere, till we came to the middle of the east side of Otaha. Then we put ashore, and Oreo dispatched a man before us with orders to seize the deserters, and keep them till we should arrive with the boats. But when we got to the place where we expected to find them, we were told that they had quitted this island, and gone over to Bolabola the day before. I did not think proper to follow them thither, but returned to the ships, fully determined, however, to have recourse to a measure which I guessed would oblige the natives to bring them back.

Soon after daybreak the chief, his son, daughter, and son-in-law, came on board the *Resolution*. The last three I resolved to detain till the two deserters should be brought back. With this view Captain Clerke invited them to go on board his ship, and, as soon as they arrived there, confined them in his cabin. The chief was with me when the news reached him. He immediately acquainted me with it, supposing that this step had been taken without my knowledge, and consequently without my approbation. I instantly undeceived him, when he began to have apprehensions as to his own situation, and his looks expressed the utmost perturbation of mind. But I soon made him easy as to this, by telling him that he was at liberty to leave the ship whenever be pleased, and to take such measures as he should judge best calculated to get our two men back; that if he succeeded, his friends on board the *Discovery* should be delivered up; if not, that I was determined to carry them with me. I added, that his own conduct, as well as that of many of his people, in not only assisting these two men to escape, but in being, even at this time, assiduous in enticing others to follow them, would justify any step I could take to put a stop to such proceedings.

This explanation of the motives upon which I acted, and which we found means to make Oreo and those of his people who were present fully comprehend, seemed to reassure them in great measure. But, if relieved from apprehension about their own safety, they continued under the deepest concern for those who were prisoners. Many of them went under the *Discovery's* stern in canoes to bewail their captivity, which they did with long and loud exclamations. "Poedooa!" (for so the chief's daughter was called) resounded from every quarter; and the women seemed to vie with each other in mourning her fate with more significant expressions of their grief than tears and cries, for there were many bloody heads upon the occasion.

Oreo himself did not give way to unavailing lamentations, but instantly began his exertions to recover our deserters by dispatching a canoe to Bolabola, with a message to Opoony, the sovereign of that island, acquainting him with what had happened, and requesting him to seize the two fugitives and send them back. The messenger, who was no less a man than the father of Pootoe, Oreo's son-in-law, before he set out, came to receive my commands. I strictly enjoined him not to return without the deserters, and to tell Opoony from me, that if they had left Bolabola he must send canoes to bring them back, for I suspected that they would not long remain in one place. The consequence, however, of the prisoners was so great, that the natives did not think proper to trust to the return of our people for their release; or at least their impatience was so great, that it hurried them to meditate an attempt which might have involved them in still greater distress, had it not been fortunately prevented. Between five and six o'clock in the evening I observed that all their canoes, in and about the harbour, began to move off, as if some sudden panic had seized them. I was ashore, abreast of the ship at the time, and inquired in vain to find out the cause, till our people called to us from the *Discovery*, and told us that a party of the natives had seized Captain Clerke and Mr. Gore, who had walked out a little way from the ships. Struck with the boldness of this plan of retaliation, which seemed to counteract me so effectually in my own way, there was no time to deliberate; I instantly ordered the people to arm, and in less than five minutes a strong party, under the command of Mr. King, was sent to rescue our two gentlemen. At the same time two armed boats, and a party under Mr. Williamson, went after the flying canoes, to cut off their retreat to the shore. These several detachments were hardly out of sight before an account arrived that we had been misinformed, upon which I sent and called them all in.

It was evident, however, from several corroborating circumstances, that the design of seizing Captain Clerke had really been in agitation amongst the natives. Nay, they made no secret in speaking of it the next day; but their first and great plan of operation was to have laid hold of me. It was my custom, every evening, to bathe in the fresh water. Very often I went alone, and always without arms. Expecting me to go as usual this evening, they had determined to seize me, and Captain Clerke, too, if he had accompanied me; but I had, after confining Oreo's family, thought it prudent to avoid putting myself in their power, and had cautioned Captain Clerke and the officers not to go far from the ships. In the course of the afternoon the chief asked me three several times if I would not go to the bathing-place, and when he found, at last, that I could not be prevailed upon to do so, he went off, with the rest of his people, in spite of all that I could do or say to stop him. But as I had no suspicion at this time of their design, I imagined that some sudden fright had seized them, which would, as usual, soon be over. Finding themselves disappointed as to me, they fixed on those who were more in their power. It was fortunate for all parties that they did not succeed, and not less fortunate that no mischief was done on the occasion. For not a musket was fired, except two or three to stop the canoes. To that firing, perhaps, Messrs.

Clerke and Gore owed their safety, for, at that very instant a party of the natives, armed with clubs, were advancing towards them, and on hearing the reports of the muskets they dispersed.

On the 27th our observatories were taken down, and everything we had ashore carried on board; the moorings of the ship were cast off, and we transported them a little way down the harbour, where they were brought to an anchor again. Towards the afternoon, the natives began to shake off their fears, gathering round and on board the ships as usual, and the awkward transactions of the day before seemed to be forgotten on both sides.

The following night the wind blew in hard squalls from south to east, attended with heavy showers of rain. In one of the squalls, the cable by which the *Resolution* was riding, parted just beyond the hawse. We had another ready to let go, so that the ship was presently brought up again. In the afternoon, the wind became moderate, and we hooked the end of the best small bower cable, and got it again into the hawse.

Oreo, the chief, being uneasy as well as myself that no account had been received from Bolabola, set out this evening for that island, and desired me to follow him the next day with the ships. This was my intention, but the wind would not admit of our getting to sea, though the same wind which kept us in the harbour brought Oreo back from Bolabola with the two deserters. They had reached Otaha the same night they deserted, but finding it impossible to get to any of the islands to the eastward, for want of wind, they had proceeded to Bolabola, and from thence to the small island Toobaee, where they were taken by the father of Pootoe, in consequence of the first message sent to Opoony. As soon as they were on board, the three prisoners were released. Thus ended the affair, which had given me much trouble and vexation; nor would I have exerted myself so resolutely on the occasion, but for the reasons before mentioned, and to save the son of a brother officer from being lost to his country.

December. The wind continued between the north and west, and confined us in the harbour till eight o'clock in the morning of the 7th, when we took advantage of a light breeze which then sprang at north-east, and, with the assistance of all the boats, got out to sea, with the *Discovery* in company.

During the last week we had been visited by people from all parts of the island, who furnished us with a large stock of hogs and green plantains; so that the time we lay wind-bound in the harbour was not entirely lost, green plantains being an excellent substitute for bread, as they will keep for a fortnight or three weeks.

The inhabitants of Ulietea seemed smaller and blacker than those of the neighbouring islands, and appeared also less orderly. Oreo, their chief, is only a sort of deputy of the sovereign of that island. Ulietea, though now reduced to this humiliating state, was formerly, we were told, the most important of this cluster of islands, and probably the first seat of government, for they say that the present royal family of Otaheite is descended from that which reigned here before the late revolution. Ooroe, the dethroned monarch of Ulietea, was still alive when we were at Huaheine, where he resides, preserving all the ensigns which they appropriate to majesty, though he has lost his dominions.

As soon as we got clear of the harbour, we took our leave of Ulietea, and steered for Bolabola. The chief, if not the sole object I had in view in visiting that island, was to procure from its monarch, Opoony, one of the anchors which Monsieur de Bougainville had lost at Otaheite. This, having afterwards been taken up by the natives there, had, as they informed me, been sent by them as a present to that chief. My desire to get possession of it did not arise from our being in want of anchors, but, having expended all the hatchets and other iron tools which we had brought from England in purchasing fresh provisions, we were now reduced to the necessity of creating a fresh assortment of trading articles by fabricating them out of the spare iron we had on board; and in such conversions, and in the occasional uses of the ships, great part of that had been already expended. I thought that M. de Bougainville's anchor would supply our want of this useful material, and I made no doubt that I should be able to tempt Opoony to part with it.

Oreo, and six or eight men from Ulietea, took a passage with us to Bolabola; indeed, most of the natives, except the chief himself, would have gladly taken a passage with us to England. At sunset, being near the south point of Bolabola, we shortened sail, and spent the night making short boards. At daybreak on the 8th we made sail for the harbour, which is on the west side of the island; but the tide and wind being against us, I gave up the design of carrying the ships into the harbour; and having ordered the boats to be got ready, I embarked in one of them, accompanied by Oreo and his companions, and was rowed in for the island.

We landed where the natives directed us, and soon after I was introduced to Opoony, in the midst of a great concourse of people. Having no time to lose, as soon as the necessary formalities were over, I asked the chief to give me the anchor, and produced the present I had prepared for him, consisting of a linen night-gown, a shirt, some gauze handkerchiefs, a looking-glass, some beads and other toys, and six axes. At the sight of these last there was a general outcry, but I could only guess the cause by Opoony's absolutely refusing to receive my present till I should get the anchor. He ordered three men to go and deliver it to me; and as I understood, I was to send by them what I thought proper in return. With these messengers we set out in our boat for an island, lying at the north side of the entrance into the harbour, where the anchor had been deposited. I found it to be neither so large nor so perfect as I expected. It had originally weighed seven hundred pounds, according to the mark that was upon it; but the ring, with part of the shank and two palms, were wanting. I was no longer at a loss to guess the reason of Opoony's refusing my present. Having thus completed my negotiation, I returned on board, and having hauled in the boats, made sail from the island to the north.

While the boats were hoisting in, some of the natives came off in three or four canoes to see the ship, as they said. They brought with them a few cocoa-nuts and one pig, which was the only one we got at the island. I make no doubt, however, that if we had stayed till the next day, we should have been plentifully supplied with provisions. But as we had already a very good stock, both of hogs and of fruit, on board, and very little of anything left to purchase more, I could have no inducement to defer any longer the prosecution of our voyage.

CHAPTER XLI.

PROGRESS OF THE VOYAGE AFTER LEAVING THE SOCIETY ISLANDS—CHRISTMAS ISLAND DISCOVERED—ACCOUNT OF THE ISLAND—DISCOVERY OF THE SANDWICH ISLANDS—SOME ACCOUNT OF ATOOI.

AFTER leaving Bolabola, I steered to the northward, close-hauled, with the wind between north-east and east, hardly ever having it to the southward of east till after we had crossed the line, and had got into north latitudes.

1777. Dec.

Though seventeen months had now elapsed since our departure from England, during which we had not, upon the whole, been unprofitably employed, I was sensible that, with regard to the principal object of my instructions, our voyage was at this time only beginning; and therefore my attention to every circumstance that might contribute towards our safety and our ultimate success was now to be called forth anew. With this view I had examined into the state of our provisions at the last islands; and as soon as I had left them, and got beyond the extent of my former discoveries, I ordered a survey to be taken of all the boatswain's and carpenter's stores that were in the ships, that I might be fully informed of the quantity, state, and condition of every article, and by that means know how to use them to the greatest advantage.

In the night of the 22nd, we crossed the line in the longitude of 203° 15′ E., and on the 24th, about half an hour after daybreak, land was discovered bearing north-east. Upon a nearer approach, it was found to be one of those low islands so common in this ocean—that is, a narrow bank of land enclosing the sea within. A few cocoa-nut trees were seen in two or three places, but in general the land had a very barren appearance. Having dropped anchor in thirty fathoms, a boat was dispatched to examine whether it was practicable to land, of which I had some doubt, as the sea broke in a dreadful surf all along the shore. When the boat returned, the officer whom I had entrusted with this examination reported to me that he could see no place where a boat could land, but that there was a great abundance of fish in the shoal water without the breakers.

At daybreak the next morning I sent two boats, one from each ship, to search more accurately for a landing-place, and at the same time two others to fish near the shore. These last returned about eight o'clock with upwards of two hundredweight of fish. Encouraged by this success, they were dispatched again after breakfast, and I then went in another boat to take a view of the coast and attempt landing, which, however, I found to be wholly impracticable. Towards noon the two boats sent on the same search returned. The master reported to me that about a league and a half to the north was a creek in the land and a channel into the "lagoon;" consequently, the ships weighed anchor and came to in twenty fathoms water, before a small island that lies at the entrance of the lagoon.

On the 28th I landed, in company with Mr. Bayley, to prepare the telescopes for observing an approaching eclipse of the sun, which was one great inducement to my anchoring here.

On the morning of the 30th, the day when the eclipse was to happen, Mr. King, Mr. Bayley, and myself went ashore on the small island above mentioned, to attend the observation. The sky was overcast till past nine o'clock, when the clouds about the sun dispersed long enough to take its altitude to rectify the time by the watch we made use of. After this, it was again obscured till about thirty minutes past nine, and then we found that the eclipse had begun. We now fixed the micrometers to the telescopes, and observed or measured the uneclipsed part of the sun's disc. At these observations I continued about three-quarters of an hour before the end, when I left off, being, in fact, unable to continue them any longer, on account of the great heat of the sun, increased by the reflection from the sand.

In the afternoon, the boats and turtling party at the south-east part of the island all returned on board, except a seaman belonging to the *Discovery*, who had been missing two days.

There were two of them at first who had lost their way, but disagreeing about the most probable track to bring them back to their companions, they had separated; one of them joined the party after having been absent twenty-four hours and been in great distress. Not a drop of fresh water could be had, for there is none upon the whole island, nor was there a single cocoa-nut tree on that part of it. In order to allay his thirst he had recourse to a singular expedient of killing turtles and drinking their blood. His mode of refreshing himself when weary, of which he said he felt the good effects, was equally whimsical: he undressed himself and lay down for some time in the shallow water upon the beach.

It was a matter of surprise to every one how these men could contrive to lose themselves. The land over which they had to travel, from the sea-coast to the lagoon, where the boats lay, was not more than three miles across, nor was there anything to obstruct their view, for the country was flat, with a few shrubs scattered upon it, and from many parts of it the masts of the vessels could easily be seen.

As soon as Captain Clerke knew that one of the stragglers was still in this awkward situation, he sent a party in search of him; but neither the man nor the party having come back the next morning, I ordered two boats into the lagoon, to go different ways, in prosecution of the search. Not long after, Captain Clerke's party returned with their lost companion, and my boats having now no object left, I called them back by signal. This poor fellow must have suffered far greater distress than the other straggler, not only as having been lost a longer time, but because he had been too squeamish to drink turtle's blood.

Having some cocoa-nuts and yams on board in a state of vegetation, I ordered them to be planted on the spot where we had observed the eclipse, and some melon seeds were sown in another place. I also left on the little island a bottle, containing the following inscription:—

Georgius Tertius, Rex, 31 Decembris 1777.
Naves { *Resolution*, Jac. Cook, Pr.
{ *Discovery*, Car. Clerke, Pr.

On the 1st of January 1778, I sent boats to bring on board

1778.
January.
all our parties from the island, and the turtles they had caught. Before this was completed it was too late in the afternoon, so that I did not think proper to sail till the next morning. We got at this island, for both ships, about three hundred turtles, weighing, one with another, about ninety or a hundred pounds. This island has been produced by accessions from the sea, and is in a state of increase, for not only the broken pieces of coral, but many of the shells, are too heavy and large to have been brought by any birds from the beach to the places where they now lie. Not a drop of fresh water was anywhere found, though frequently dug for.

There were not the smallest traces of any human being having ever been here before us. On the few cocoa-trees upon the island, the number of which did not exceed thirty, very little fruit was found, and, in general, what was found was either not fully grown or had the juice salt or brackish. So that a ship touching here must expect nothing but fish and turtle; but of these an abundant supply may be depended upon.

As we kept our Christmas here, I called this discovery Christmas Island. I judge it to be about fifteen or twenty leagues in circumference. Like most others in this ocean, it is bounded by a reef of coral rocks, which extends but a little way from the shore.

On the 2nd of January, at daybreak, we weighed anchor and resumed our course to the north. At daybreak in the morning of the 18th, an island made its appearance,* and soon after we saw more land bearing north, and entirely detached from the former. Both had the appearance of being high land. We were in some doubt whether or no the island was inhabited; but this doubt was soon cleared up by seeing some canoes coming off from the shore toward the ships. They had from three to six men each, and on their approach we were agreeably surprised to find that they spoke the language of Otaheite and of the other islands we had lately visited. These people were of a brown colour, and though of the common size, were stoutly made. Some of them ventured on board next morning. In the course of my several voyages, I never met before with the natives of any place so

* Sandwich Islands.

SCENE IN ATOOI, SANDWICH ISLANDS.
Page 411.

much astonished as these people were upon entering a ship. Their eyes were continually flying from object to object, the wildness of their looks and gestures fully expressing their entire ignorance about everything they saw, and strongly marking to us that till now they had never been visited by Europeans, nor been acquainted with any of our commodities. When we shewed them some beads they asked first what they were, and then whether they should eat them.

At first, on their entering the ship, they endeavoured to steal everything they came near, or rather to take it openly as what we either should not resent or hinder; but we soon convinced them of their mistake.

At nine o'clock, being pretty near the shore, I sent three armed boats, under the command of Lieutenant Williamson, to look for a landing-place and for fresh water. I ordered him that, if he should find it necessary to land in search of the latter, he was not to suffer more than one man to go with him out of the boats. Just as they were pulling off from the ship one of the natives, having stolen the butcher's cleaver, leaped overboard, and got into his canoe, the boats pursuing him in vain.

While the boats were occupied in examining the coast we stood on and off with the ships, waiting for their return. About noon Mr. Williamson came back, and reported that he had seen a large pond behind a beach, near one of the villages, which the natives told him contained fresh water, and that there was anchoring ground before it. He also reported that he had attempted to land in another place, but was prevented by the natives, who, coming down to the boats in great numbers, attempted to take away the oars, muskets, and in short everything that they could lay hold of, and pressed so thick upon him that he was obliged to fire, by which one man was killed. This unhappy circumstance I did not know till after we had left the island, so that all my measures were directed as if nothing of the kind had happened. Mr. Williamson told me that after the man fell, his countrymen took him up, carried him off, and then retired from the boat, but still made signals for our people to land, which he declined.

The ships being stationed, between three and four o'clock I went ashore with three armed boats and twelve marines, to examine the water, and to try the disposition of the inhabitants, several hundreds of whom were assembled on a sandy beach before the villages, behind which was a narrow valley, the bottom of which was occupied by the piece of water.

The very instant I leaped on shore the natives all fell flat upon their faces, and remained in that very humble posture till, by expressive signs, I prevailed upon them to rise. They then brought a great many small pigs, which they presented to me, with plantain trees, using much the same ceremonies that we had seen practised on such occasions at the Society and other islands, a long prayer being also spoken by a single person, in which others of the assembly sometimes joined. I expressed my acceptance of their proffered friendship by giving them in return such presents as I had brought with me from the ship for that purpose. When this introductory business was finished, I stationed a guard upon the beach, and got some of the natives to conduct me to the water, which proved to be very good, and in a proper situation for our purpose. It was so considerable that it may be called a lake, and it extended farther up the country than we could see. Having satisfied myself about this point, and about the peaceable disposition of the natives, I returned on board; and having given orders that everything should be in readiness for landing and filling our water-casks in the morning, I returned with the people employed in that service, and a guard of marines, who were stationed on the beach.

As soon as we landed, a trade was set on foot for hogs and potatoes, which the people of this island gave us in exchange for nails and pieces of iron formed into something like chisels. We met with no obstruction in watering; on the contrary, the natives assisted our men in rolling the casks to and from the pool, and readily performed whatever we required.

Everything going on thus to my satisfaction, and considering my presence on the spot as unnecessary, I left the command to Mr. Williamson, who had landed with me, and made an excursion into the country, up the valley, accompanied by Mr. Anderson and Mr. Webber, the former of whom was as well qualified to describe with the pen as the latter was to represent with his pencil everything we might meet with worthy of observation. A numerous train of natives followed us, and one of them, whom I had distinguished for his activity in keeping the rest in order, I made choice of as our guide. This man from time to time proclaimed our approach, when every one we met fell prostrate on the ground, and remained in that position till we had passed. This, as I afterwards understood, is the mode of paying their respect to their own great chiefs. As we ranged down the coast in the ships we had observed at every village one or more elevated white objects, like pyramids, or rather obelisks; and one of these, which I guessed to be at least fifty feet high, was very conspicuous from the ships' anchoring station, and seemed to be at no great distance up this valley. To have a nearer inspection of it was the principal object of my walk. Our guide perfectly understood what we wished; but as it was separated from us by the pool of water, and another of the same kind lay within our reach about half a mile off, we set out to visit that. We saw that it stood in a burying-ground, or morai, the resemblance of which, in many respects, to those we were so well acquainted with at other islands in this ocean, and particularly Otaheite, could not but strike us, and we also soon found that the several parts that compose it were called by the same names. It was an oblong space, of considerable extent, surrounded by a wall of stone about four feet high. The space enclosed was loosely paved with smaller stones, and at one end of it stood what I call the pyramid, which appeared to be an exact model of the larger one observed by us from the ships. It was about four feet square at the base, and about twenty feet high; the four sides were composed of small poles, interwoven with twigs and branches, thus forming an indifferent wicker-work, hollow or open within, from bottom to top. It seemed to be in a rather ruinous state, but there were sufficient remaining marks to show that it had originally been covered with a thin, light grey cloth, which these people appear to consecrate to religious purposes. On each side of the pyramid were long pieces of wicker-work, in the same ruinous condition, with two slender poles inclining to each other, at one corner, where some plantains were laid upon a board, fixed at a height of five or six feet; this fruit was an offering to their god. Before the pyramid were a few pieces of wood, carved into something like human figures, which, with a stone near two feet high, covered with pieces of cloth called "hoho," and consecrated to Tongarooa, who is the god of these people, still more and more reminded us of what we used to meet with in the islands we had lately left.

On the farther side of the area of the morai stood a house or shed about forty feet long, ten broad in the middle, each end being narrower, and about ten feet high. On the farther side of this house, opposite the entrance, stood two wooden images cut out of one piece, with pedestals, in all about three feet high, neither very indifferently designed nor executed. These were said to be representations of goddesses. On the head of one of them was a carved helmet, not unlike those worn by the ancient warriors, and on that of the other a cylindrical cap, resembling the head-dress at Otaheite, called tomou; and both of them had pieces of cloth tied about the loins, and hanging a considerable way down. At the side of each was also a piece of carved wood, with bits of the cloth hung on them in the same manner, and between or before the pedestals lay a quantity of fern in a heap. It was obvious it had been deposited there piece by piece, and at different times.

In the middle of the house, and before the two images, was an oblong space, enclosed by a low edging of stone, and covered with shreds of the cloth so often mentioned. This, on inquiry, we found was the grave of seven chiefs, whose names were enumerated.

Before them was an oblong space, and our conductor told us explicitly that three human sacrifices had been buried there. It was with most sincere concern that I could trace on such undoubted evidence the prevalence of these bloody rites throughout this immense ocean.

After we had examined carefully everything that was to be seen about the morai, and Mr. Webber had taken drawings of it and of the adjoining country, we returned by a different route. I found a great crowd assembled at the beach, and a brisk trade for pigs, fowls, and roots going on there with the greatest good order, though I did not observe any particular person who took the lead amongst the rest of his countrymen.

These people merited our best commendations in their commercial intercourse, never once attempting to cheat us, either ashore or alongside the ships.

Among the articles which they brought to barter this day we noticed a particular sort of cloak and cap, which, even in countries where dress is more particularly attended to, might be reckoned elegant. The first are nearly of the size and shape of the short cloaks worn by the women in England and by the men in Spain, reaching to the middle of the back and tied loosely before. The ground is a network, upon which the most beautiful red and yellow feathers are so closely fixed that the surface might be compared to the thickest and richest velvet, which they resemble both as to feel and glossy appearance. The manner of varying the mixture is very different, some having triangular spaces of red and yellow alternately, others a kind of crescent, and some that were entirely red had a broad yellow border, which made them appear at some distance exactly like a scarlet cloak edged with gold lace. The brilliant colours of the feathers in those that happened to be new added not a little to their fine appearance, and we found that they were in high estimation with their owners; for they would not at first part with one of them for anything that we offered, asking no less a price than a musket. However, some were afterwards purchased for very large nails.

The cap is made almost exactly like a helmet, with the middle part or crest sometimes of a handbreadth, and it sits very close upon the head, having notches to admit the ears. It is a frame of twigs and osiers covered with a network, into which are wrought feathers in the same manner as upon the cloaks, though rather closer and less diversified, the greater part being red, with some black, yellow, or green stripes on the side, following in a curve the direction of the crest. These probably complete the dress with the cloaks, for the natives sometimes appeared in both together.*

In the night and all the morning on the 22nd it rained almost continually. The wind was at SE., which brought in a short, chopping sea, and as there were breakers little more than two cables' length from the stern of our ship, her situation was none of the safest. The surf broke so high upon the shore that we could not land in our boats, but the natives ventured in their canoes, and bartered some hogs and roots. One of our visitors on this occasion, who offered some fish-hooks for sale, was observed

* These articles may be seen in the British Museum.

to have a very small parcel tied to the string of one of them, which he separated with great care, and reserved for himself when he parted with the hook. On seeing him so anxious to conceal the contents of this parcel, he was requested to open it, which he did with great reluctance and some difficulty, as it was wrapped up in many folds of cloth. We found that it contained a thin bit of flesh, which to appearance had been dried. It struck us that it might be human flesh, and that these people might perhaps eat their enemies, as we knew that this was the practice of some of the natives of the South Sea Islands. The question being put to the person who produced it, he answered that the flesh was part of a man. Another of his countrymen, who stood by, was then asked whether it was their custom to eat those killed in battle, and he immediately answered in the affirmative and laughed, seemingly at the simplicity of such a question. He also said it was excellent food, or, as he expressed it, "savoury eating."

We had light airs and calms by turns, with showers of rain, all night, and at daybreak in the morning of the 24th, we found that the current had carried the ships to the NW., so that the west end of the island upon which we had been, called Ateoi by the natives, was one league distant, another island called Oreehoua W. by S., and the high land of a third island called Oneeheow from SW. by W. to WSW.

I now came to the resolution of trying whether we could not procure what we wanted at Oneeheow, and sent the master in a boat to look out for a landing-place. Six or seven canoes came off to us before we anchored, bringing some small pigs and potatoes and many yams and mats. The people in them resembled those of Atooi, and seemed to be equally well acquainted with the use of iron, which they asked for by the names of "hamaite" and "toe," parting eagerly with all their commodities for pieces of this precious metal. Several more canoes soon reached the ships after they had anchored; but the natives in these seemed to have no other object than to pay us a formal visit. Many of them came readily on board, crouching down upon the deck, and not quitting that humble posture till they were desired to get up. They had brought several females with them, who remained alongside in the canoes, behaving with less modesty than their countrywomen of

Atoei, and at times all joining in a song not remarkable for its melody, though performed in very exact concert by beating time upon their breasts with their hands. The men who had come on board did not stay long, and they laid down on the deck locks of their hair.

On the 30th, I sent Mr. Gore ashore with a guard of marines and a party to trade with the natives for provisions. I intended to have followed soon after, and went from the ship with that design; but the surf had increased so much by this time that I was fearful if I got ashore I should not be able to get off again. This really happened to our people who had landed with Mr. Gore, the communication between them and the ships to our own boats being stopped. In the evening they made a signal for the boats, which were sent accordingly, and, not long after, they returned with a few yams and some salt.

The violence of the surf, which our own boats could not act against, did not hinder the natives from coming off to the ships in their canoes with provisions, which were purchased in exchange for nails and pieces of iron hoops, and I distributed many pieces of ribbon and some buttons as bracelets among the women in their canoes.

About ten or eleven o'clock at night the wind veered to the south, and the sky seemed to forebode a storm. With such appearances, thinking we were rather too near the shore, I ordered the anchors to be hove up, and having moved the ships into forty-two fathoms, came to again in this safer station. The precaution, however, proved to be unnecessary, for the wind soon after veered to north-east, from which quarter it blew a fresh gale with squalls, attended with heavy showers of rain.

This weather continued all the next day, and the sea ran so high that we had no communication with our party on shore, and even the natives themselves durst not venture out to the ships in their canoes. In the evening I sent the master in a boat up to the south-east head or point of the island to try if he could land under it. He returned with a favourable report; but it was too late now to send for our party till the next morning, and thus they had another night to improve their intercourse with the natives. Encouraged by the master's report, I sent a boat to the

south-east point as soon as daylight returned, with an order to
Mr. Gore that, if he could not embark his people from
February. the spot where they now were, he was to march them up
to the point. As the boat could not get to the beach, one of the
crew swam ashore and carried the order. On the return of the
boat, I went myself with the pinnace and launch up to the point
to bring the party on board; and being very desirous of benefiting
these poor people by furnishing them with additional articles of
food, took with me a ram goat and two ewes, a boar and a sow
of the English breed, and the seeds of melons, pumpkins, and
onions. I landed with the greatest ease under the west side of
the point, and found my party already there, with some of the
natives in company. To one of them, whom Mr. Gore had
observed assuming some command over the rest, I gave the goats,
pigs, and seeds.

While the people were engaged in filling the water-casks from
a small stream occasioned by the late rain, I walked a little way
up the country, attended by the man above mentioned, and followed by two others, carrying the two pigs.

As soon as we got on a rising ground, I stopped to look round
me, and observed a woman on the opposite side of the valley where
I landed calling to her countrymen who attended me. Upon this
the chief began to mutter something, which I supposed was a
prayer, and the two men who carried the pigs continued to walk
round me all the time, making at least a dozen circuits before the
other had finished his oration.

This ceremony being performed we proceeded, and presently
met people coming from all parts, who, on being called by my
attendants, threw themselves prostrate on their faces till I was
out of sight. The ground through which I passed was in a state
of nature, very stony, and the soil seemed poor. It was, however,
covered with shrubs and plants, which perfumed the air with
a more delicious fragrance than I had ever met with at any of the
other islands visited by us in this ocean. The habitations of the
natives were thinly scattered about, and it was supposed there
could not be more than five hundred people upon the island, as
the greater part were seen at the marketing-place of our party,
and few found about the houses by those who walked up the

SURF-SWIMMING, SANDWICH ISLANDS. *Page 419.*

country. Our people who had been obliged to remain on shore had an opportunity of observing the method of living amongst the natives, and it appeared to be decent and cleanly. They did not, however, see any instances of the men and women eating together, and the latter seemed generally associated together in companies. It was found that they used the oily nuts of the "dooe dooe," which are stuck upon a kind of skewer and burned as candles, and that they baked their hogs in ovens, as at Otaheite.

About noon on the 2nd, we stood away to the northward in prosecution of our voyage, our ships supplied with provisions sufficient for three weeks at least.

It is worthy of observation that the islands in the Pacific Ocean which these voyages have added to the geography of the globe have been generally found in groups or clusters, the single intermediate islands as yet discovered being few in proportion to the others, though probably there are many more of them still unknown, which serve as steps between the several clusters. Of what number this newly-discovered archipelago consists must be left to future investigation. We saw five of them, whose names, as given to us by the natives, are Woahoo, Ateei, Oneeheow, Oreehoua, and Taboora. I named the group the Sandwich Islands, in honour of the Earl of Sandwich.

Ateoi, which is the largest, is at least ten leagues in length. The land, as to its general appearance, does not in the least resemble any of the islands we have hitherto visited within the tropic on the south side of the equator. Though it be destitute of the delightful borders of Otaheite and of the luxuriant plains of Tongatabu, covered with trees, which at once afford a friendly shelter from the scorching sun, and an enchanting prospect to the eye, and food for the natives which may truly be said to drop from the trees into their mouths; though Ateei be destitute of these advantages, its possessing a greater quantity of gently-rising land renders it in some measure superior to the above favourite islands as being more capable of improvement.

The inhabitants are vigorous, active, and most expert swimmers, leaving their canoes upon the most trifling occasion, diving under them, and swimming to others, though at a great distance. It was very amusing to see women with infants at the breast, when the surf was so high that they could not land in the canoes, leap overboard and, without endangering their little ones, swim to the shore through a sea that looked dreadful.

They seem to be blessed with a frank, cheerful disposition, and to live very sociably in their intercourse with one another, and, except the propensity to thieving, which seems innate in most of the people we have visited in this ocean, they were exceedingly friendly to us, and on all occasions appeared deeply impressed with a consciousness of their own inferiority. It was a pleasure to see with how much affection the women managed their infants, and how readily the men lent their assistance to such a tender office, thus sufficiently distinguishing themselves from those savages who esteem a wife and child as things rather necessary than desirable or worthy of their notice.

The hair in both sexes is cut in different forms, and the general fashion, especially among the women, is to have it long before and short behind. The men often had it cut or shaved on each side in such a manner that the remaining part in some measure resembled the crest of their caps or helmets formerly described. Both sexes, however, seem very careless about their hair, and have nothing like combs to dress it with. Instances of wearing it in a singular manner were sometimes met with among the men, who twist it into a number of separate parcels like the tails of a wig, each about the thickness of a finger, though the greater part of these, which are so long that they reach far down the back, were artificially fixed upon the head over their own hair.

Both sexes adorn themselves with necklaces made of bunches of small black cord or many strings of very small shells, or of the dried flowers of the Indian mallow, and sometimes a small human image of bone about three inches long, neatly polished, is hung round the neck. The women also wear bracelets of a single shell, pieces of black wood, with bits of ivory interspersed, well polished, and fixed by a string drawn very closely through them; or others, of hogs' teeth laid parallel to each other, with the concave side outward and the points cut off, fastened together as the former, some of them, made only of large boars' tusks, being very elegant. The men sometimes wear plumes of the tropic-bird's feathers stuck in their heads, or those of cocks fastened round neat polished sticks two feet long, commonly decorated at the lower part with oora, and for the same purpose the skin of a white dog's tail is sewed over a stick with its tuft at the end. They also frequently wear on the head a kind of ornament of a finger's thickness or more, covered with red and yellow feathers curiously varied and tied behind, and on the arm above the elbow a kind of broad shellwork grounded upon network.

Though they seem to have adopted the mode of living in villages, there is no proportion as to the size of their houses, some being large and commodious—from forty to fifty feet long and from twenty to thirty broad—while others of them are mere hovels. The entrance is made indifferently at the end or side, and is an oblong hole so low that one must rather creep than walk in, and is often shut up by a board of planks fastened together, which serves as a door. No light enters the house but at this opening, and though such close habitations may afford a comfortable retreat in bad weather, they seem but ill adapted to the warmth of the climate. They are, however, kept remarkably clean, and their floors are covered with a large quantity of dried grass, over which they spread mats to sit and sleep upon. At one end stands a bench about three feet high, on which their household utensils are placed. These consist of gourd-shells, which they convert into vessels that serve as bottles to hold water and as baskets to contain their victuals and other things, with covers of the same, and a few wooden bowls and trenchers of different sizes.

Of animal food they can be in no want, as they have abundance of hogs, which run without restraint about the houses, and if they eat dogs, which is not improbable, their stock of these seemed to be very considerable.

They bake their vegetable food with heated stones, as at the Southern Islands. The only artificial dish we met with was a "faro" pudding, which, though a disagreeable mess from its sourness, was greedily devoured by the natives.

Their amusements seem pretty various, for during our short stay several were discovered. The dances, at which they use the feathered cloaks and caps, were not seen. The only two musical instruments which we observed were of an exceedingly rude kind. One of them does not produce melody exceeding that of a child's rattle.

In everything manufactured by these people there appears to be an uncommon degree of neatness and ingenuity. They fabricate a great many white mats, which are strong, with many red stripes, rhombuses, and other figures interwoven on one side. These probably make a part of their dress occasionally, but they make others coarser, which they spread over their floors to sleep upon.

Their canoes in general are about twenty-four feet long, and have the bottom, for the most part, formed of a single piece or log of wood hollowed out to the thickness of an inch or an inch and a half, and brought to a point at each end. The sides consist of three boards, each about an inch thick, and neatly fitted and lashed to the bottom part. The extremities, both at head and stern, are a little raised, and both are made sharp, somewhat like a wedge, but they flatten more abruptly, so that the two sideboards join each other, side by side, for more than a foot. As they are not more than fifteen or eighteen inches broad, those that go single (for they sometimes join them as at the other islands) have outriggers, which are shaped and fitted with more judgment than any I had before seen. They are rowed by paddles, such as we had generally met with, and some of them have a light triangular sail, like those of the Friendly Islands, extended to a mast and boom. The ropes used for their boats and the smaller cord for their fishing-tackle are strong and well made.

What we saw of their agriculture furnished sufficient proofs that they are not novices in that art. The potato fields and spots of sugar-cane or plantains are planted with regularity, and always in some determinate figure. But notwithstanding their skill in agriculture, the general appearance of the island showed that it was capable of much more extensive improvement, and of maintaining at least three times the number of the inhabitants that are at present upon it.

Besides their spears or lances, made of a fine chestnut-coloured wood beautifully polished, some of which are barbed at one end and flattened to a point at the other, they had a sort of weapon which we had never seen before, and not mentioned by any navigator as used by the natives of the South Sea. It is somewhat like a dagger, in general about a foot and a half long, sharpened at one or both ends, and secured to the hand by a string. Its use is to stab in close fight, and it seems well adapted to the purpose. Some of these may be called double daggers, having a handle in the middle, with which they are better enabled to strike different ways. The knife or saw with which they dissect the dead bodies may also be ranked amongst their weapons, as they both strike and cut with it when closely engaged. It is a small flat wooden instrument, of an oblong shape, about a foot long, rounded at the corners, with a handle almost like one sort of the patoos of New Zealand, but its edges are entirely surrounded with sharks' teeth, strongly fixed to it, and pointing outward, having commonly a hole in the handle, through which passes a long string, which is wrapped several times round the wrist.

The language at Atooi is almost word for word the same as Otaheite. How shall we account for this nation's having spread itself in so many detached islands, so widely disjoined from each other, in every quarter of the Pacific Ocean? We find it from New Zealand in the south as far as the Sandwich Islands to the north; and in another direction from Easter Island to the Hebrides.

Had the Sandwich Islands been discovered at an early period by the Spaniards, there is little doubt that they would have taken advantage of so excellent a situation, and have made use of Ateoi, or some other of the islands, as a refreshing place to the ships that sail annually from Acapulco to Manilla. They lie almost midway between the first place and Guam, one of the Ladrones, which is at present their only port in traversing this vast ocean. An acquaintance with the Sandwich Islands would have been equally favourable to our buccaneers, who used sometimes to pass from the coast of America to the Ladrones with a stock of food and water scarcely sufficient to preserve life. Here they might have found plenty, and have been within a month's sail of the very port of California which the Manilla ship is obliged to make, or else have returned to the coast of America, thoroughly refitted, after an absence of two months. How happy would Lord Anson have been, and what hardships would he have avoided, had he known that there was a group of islands half-way between America and Tinian, where all his wants could have been effectually supplied!

CHAPTER XLII.

PROSECUTION OF THE VOYAGE—ARRIVAL ON THE COAST OF AMERICA—THE SHIPS ENTER ST. GEORGE'S SOUND, OR NOOTKA—TRANSACTIONS WITH THE NATIVES —SOME ACCOUNT OF NOOTKA AND ITS INHABITANTS.

1778. February. ON the 2nd we stood away to the northward, close-hauled, with a gentle gale from the east. On the 7th of March the longed-for coast of New Albion was seen, distant ten or twelve leagues. The land appeared to be of moderate height, diversified with hills and valleys, and almost everywhere covered with wood. At the northern extreme the land formed a point, which I called Cape Foul Weather, from the very bad weather that we soon after met with.

At length, at nine o'clock in the morning of the 28th, we anchored in a large bay which I called Hope Bay. We no sooner drew near the inlet than we found the coast to be inhabited, and three canoes came off to the ship. In one of these were two men, in another six, and in the third ten. Having come pretty near us, a person in one of the last two stood up and made a long harangue, inviting us to land, as we guessed by his gestures; at the same time he kept strewing handfuls of feathers towards us, and some of his companions threw handfuls of a red dust powder in the same manner. The person who played the orator wore the skin of some animal, and held in each hand something which rattled as he kept shaking it. After tiring himself with his repeated exhortations, of which we did not understand a word, he was quiet; and then others took it up by turns to say something, though they acted their part neither so long nor with so much vehemence as the other. We observed that two or three had their hair quite strewed over with small white feathers, and others had large ones stuck in different parts of the head. After the tumultuons noise had ceased, they lay at a little distance from the ship, and conversed with each other in a very easy manner; nor did they seem to show the least surprise or distrust. Some of them now and then got up and said something after the manner of their first harangues, and one sang a very agreeable air with a degree of softness and melody that we could not have expected. The breeze which soon after sprang up bringing us nearer the shore, the canoes began to come off in greater numbers, and we had at one time thirty-two of them near the ship, carrying from three to seven or eight persons each, both men and women. Several of these stood up in their canoes, haranguing and making gestures after the manner of our first visitors. One canoe was remarkable for a singular head, which had a bird's eye and bill of an enormous size painted on it; and a person in it, who seemed to be a chief, was no less remarkable for his uncommon appearance, having many feathers hanging from his head, and being painted in an extraordinary manner. He held in his hand a carved bird of wood as large as a pigeon, with which he rattled, as the person first mentioned had done, and was no less vociferous in his harangue, which was attended with some expressive gestures.

Though our visitors behaved very peaceably, and could not be suspected of any hostile intention, we could not prevail upon any of them to come on board. They showed great readiness, however, to part with anything they had, and took from us whatever we offered them in exchange, but were more desirous of iron than of any other of our articles of commerce, appearing to be perfectly acquainted with the use of that metal. Many of the canoes followed us to our anchoring place, and a group of ten or a dozen of them remained alongside the *Resolution* most part of the night.

These circumstances gave us a reasonable ground of hope that we should find this a comfortable station to supply all our wants, and to make us forget the hardships and delays experienced during a constant succession of adverse winds and boisterous weather, almost ever since our arrival on the coast of America.

A trade was soon commenced between us and the natives, which was carried on with the strictest honesty on both sides. The articles which they offered for sale were skins of various animals, such as bears, wolves, foxes, deer, polecats, martens, sea otters, also garments made of skins, and another sort of clothing made of the bark of a tree, weapons such as bows, arrows, and spears, fish-hooks and instruments of various kinds, beads, little ornaments of thin brass and iron shaped like a horse-shoe, which they hang at their noses. But the most extraordinary of all articles for sale were human skulls, and hands not quite stripped of the flesh, which they made our people plainly understand they had eaten. We had but too much reason to suspect from this circumstance that the horrid practice of feeding on their enemies is as prevalent here as we had found it at New Zealand and other South Sea Islands.

The fame of our arrival brought a great concourse of the natives to our ships in the course of this day. We counted above a hundred canoes at one time, which might be supposed to contain on an average five persons in each, for few of them had less than three on board, great numbers had seven, eight, or nine, and one was manned with no less than seventeen. Among these visitors many now favoured us with their company for the first time, which we could guess from their approaching the ships with their orations and other ceremonies. If they had any distrust or fear of us at first, they now appeared to have laid it aside, for they came on board and mixed with our people with the greatest freedom. We soon discovered by this nearer intercourse that they were as light-fingered as any of our friends in the islands we had visited in the course of the voyage. And they were far more dangerous thieves, for, possessing sharp iron instruments, they could cut a hook from a tackle, or any other piece of iron from a rope, as soon as our backs were turned. As to our boats, they stripped them of every bit of iron that was worth carrying away, though we had always men left in them as a guard. They were dexterous enough in effecting their purpose, for one fellow would contrive to amuse the boat-keeper at one end of a boat while another was pulling out the ironwork at the other. If we missed a thing immediately after it had been stolen, we found little difficulty in detecting the thief, as they were ready enough to impeach one another. But the guilty person generally relinquished his prize with reluctance, and sometimes we found it necessary to have recourse to force.

A considerable number of the natives visited us daily, and

every now and then we saw new faces. On their first coming they generally went through a singular mode of introducing themselves. They would paddle with all their strength quite round both ships, a chief, or other principal person in the canoe, standing up with a spear or some other weapon in his hand, and speaking or hallooing all the time. Sometimes the orator of the canoe would have his face covered with a mask, representing either a human visage or that of some animal, and instead of a weapon would hold a rattle in his hand, as before described. After making this circuit round the ships, they would come alongside and begin to trade without further ceremony. Very often, indeed, they would first give us a song, in which all in the canoes joined with a very pleasing harmony.

During these visits they gave us no other trouble than to guard against their thievish tricks. In the morning of the 4th we had a serious alarm. Our party on shore, who were employed in cutting wood and getting water, observed that the natives all around them were arming themselves in the best manner they could, those who were not possessed of proper weapons preparing sticks and collecting stones. On hearing this I thought it prudent to arm also, but, being determined to act upon the defensive, I ordered our workmen to retreat to the rock upon which we had placed our observatories, leaving the natives in quiet possession of the ground. Our fears were ill-grounded. These hostile preparations were not directed against us, but against a body of their own countrymen, who were coming to fight them; and our friends of the sound, on observing our apprehensions, used their best endeavours to convince us that this was the case. We could see that they had people looking out on each point of the cove, and canoes frequently passed between them and the main body assembled near the ships. At length the adverse party, in about a dozen large canoes, appeared off the south point of the cove, when they stopped, and lay drawn up in a line of battle, a negotiation having commenced. Some people in canoes, in conducting the treaty, passed between the two parties, and there was some speaking on both sides. At length the difference, whatever it was, seemed to be compromised, but the strangers were not allowed to come alongside the ships, nor to have any trade or intercourse with us.

From the time of our putting into the sound till now the weather had been exceedingly fine, without either wind or rain, but on the morning of the 8th, the wind freshened at south-east, attended with thick hazy weather and rain; and, according to the old proverb, misfortunes seldom come singly. The mizzen was now the only mast on board the *Resolution* that remained rigged, with its topmast up. The former was so defective that it could not support the latter during the violence of the squalls, but gave way at the head under the rigging. About eight o'clock the gale abated, but the rain continued, with very little intermission, for several days; and that the carpenters might be enabled to proceed in their labours while it prevailed, a tent was erected over the foremast, where they could work with some degree of convenience.

The bad weather which now came on did not, however, hinder the natives from visiting us daily; and they frequently brought us a tolerable supply of fish—either sardines, or what resembled them much, a small kind of bream, and sometimes small cod.

In the afternoon of the next day I went into the woods with a party of our men, and cut down a tree for a mizzenmast, which on the day following was brought to the place where the carpenters were employed upon the foremast. In the evening the wind increased to a very hard gale, with rain, which continued till eight o'clock the next morning, when it abated.

The foremast being by this time finished, we hauled it alongside, but the bad weather prevented our fitting it in till the afternoon. We set about rigging it with the greatest expedition, while the carpenters were going on with the mizzenmast on shore. They had made very considerable progress in it on the 16th, when they discovered that it was sprung, or wounded, owing probably to some accident in cutting it down, so that all their labour was thrown away, and it became necessary to get another tree out of the woods, which employed all hands above half a day. During these various operations several of the natives, who were about the ship, looked on with an expressive silent surprise, which we did not expect from their general indifference and inattention.

On the 18th, a party of strangers, in six or eight canoes, came into the cove, where they remained looking at us for some time, and then retired without coming alongside either ship. We supposed that our old friends, who were more numerous at this time about us than these new visitors, would not permit them to have any intercourse with us.

After a fortnight's bad weather, the 19th proving a fair day, we availed ourselves of it to get up the topmasts and yards, and to fix the rigging. Having now finished most of our heavy work, I set out the next morning to take a view of the sound. I first went to the west point, where I found a large village, and before it a very snug harbour, in which was from four to nine fathoms of water over a bottom of fine sand. The people of this village, who were numerous, and to most of whom I was well known, received me very courteously, every one pressing me to go into his house, or rather his apartment, for several families live under the same roof. I did not decline the invitations; and my hospitable friends whom I visited spread a mat for me to sit down upon, and showed me every other mark of civility. In most of the houses were women at work, making dresses of the plant or bark before mentioned, which they executed exactly in the same manner that the New Zealanders manufacture their cloth. Others were occupied in opening sardines, a large quantity of which I had seen brought on shore from canoes, and divided, by measure, amongst several people, who carried them up to their houses, where the operation of curing by smoke-drying is performed. They hang them on small rods, at first about a foot from the fire; afterwards they remove them higher and higher, to make room for others, till the rods on which the fish hang reach the top of the house. When they are completely dried they are taken down and packed close in bales, which they cover with mats. Thus they are kept till wanted, and are not a disagreeable article of food. Cod and other large fish are also cured in the same manner by them, though they sometimes dry them in the open air without fire.

From this place I crossed over to the other or east side of the sound, and found, what I had before conjectured, that the land under which the ships lay was an island, and that there were many smaller ones lying scattered in the sound, on the west side of it. Opposite the north end of our large island, upon the mainland, I observed a village, and there I landed. The inhabitants of it were not so polite as those of the other I had just visited, especially one surly chief, who would not let me enter their houses, following me wherever I went; and several times, by expressive signs, marking his impatience that I should be gone. I attempted in vain to soothe him by presents, but though he did not refuse them, they did not alter his behaviour. Some of the young women, better pleased with us than our inhospitable chief, dressed themselves expeditiously in their best apparel, and assembling in a body, welcomed us to their village by joining in a song, which was far from harsh or disagreeable.

The day being now far spent, I proceeded to the ships, and on my arrival was informed that, while I was absent, the ships had been visited by some strangers in two or three large canoes, who, by signs, made our people to understand that they came from the south-east, beyond the bay. They brought several skins, garments, and other articles, which they bartered; but what was most singular, two silver tablespoons were purchased from them, which, from their peculiar shape, were judged to be of Spanish manufacture. One of these strangers wore them round his neck, by way of ornament. These visitors also appeared to be more plentifully supplied with iron than the inhabitants of the sound.

On the 22nd, about eight o'clock, we were visited by a number of strangers in twelve or fourteen canoes. They drew up in a body about two or three hundred yards from the ships. At first we thought that they were afraid to come nearer; but we were mistaken in this. On advancing toward the ships they all stood up in their canoes and began to sing. Some of the songs, in which the whole body joined, were in a slow, and others in quicker time, and they accompanied their notes with the most regular motions of their hands, or beating in concert with their paddles on the sides of the canoes, and making other very expressive gestures. At the end of each song they remained silent a few seconds, and then began again, and at length, after entertaining us with this specimen of their music, which we listened to with admiration for above half an hour, they came alongside the ships, and bartered what they had to dispose of. Some of our old friends of the sound were now found to be amongst them; and they took the whole management of the traffic between us and the strangers, much to the advantage of the latter.

When I was at the village at the west point of the sound, I had observed that plenty of grass grew near it; and it was necessary to lay in a quantity of this as food for the few goats and sheep which were still left on board. I ordered some of my people to begin their operation of cutting. I had not the least imagination that the natives could make any objection to our furnishing ourselves with what seemed to be of no use to them, but was necessary for us. However, I was mistaken; for the moment that our men began to cut, some of the inhabitants interposed and would not permit them to proceed, saying they must first buy it. I bargained with them for it, and finally they permitted us to cut wherever we pleased, and carry away as much as we chose.

Everything being now ready, at noon of the 26th we cast off the moorings, and with our boats towed the ships out of the cove. After this we had variable light airs and calms till four in the afternoon, when a breeze sprung up northerly with very thick, hazy weather. The mercury in the barometer fell unusually low, and we had every other forerunner of an approaching storm, which we had reason to expect would be from the southward. This made me hesitate a little, as night was at hand, whether I should venture to sail, or wait till the next morning. But my anxious impatience to proceed upon the voyage, and the fear of losing this opportunity of getting out of the sound, making a greater impression on my mind than any apprehension of immediate danger, I determined to put to sea at all events.

Our friends the natives attended us till we were almost out of the sound, some on board the ships, and others in their canoes. One of the chiefs, who had some time before attached himself to me, was among the last who left us. Having bestowed upon him a small present, I received in return a beaver skin of much greater value. This called upon me to make some addition to my present, which pleased him so much that he insisted upon my acceptance of the beaver-skin cloak which he then wore, and of which he was particularly fond. Struck with this instance of generosity, and desirous that he should be no sufferer by his friendship to me, I presented to him a new broadsword with a brass hilt, the possession of which made him completely happy.

On my arrival in this inlet, I had honoured it with the name of King George's Sound, but I afterwards found that it is called Nootka by the natives. The climate, so far as we had any experience of it, is infinitely milder than that on the east coast of America under the same parallel of latitude. The mercury in the thermometer never, even in the night, fell lower than 42°; and very often, in the day, it rose to 60°. No such thing as frost was perceived in any of the low ground; on the contrary, vegetation had made a considerable progress, for I met with grass that was already above a foot long. The trees, chiefly Canadian pine and white cypress, grow with great vigour, and are all of a large size.

There is little variety of other vegetable productions. About the verge of the woods we found strawberry plants, some raspberry, currant, and gooseberry bushes, which were all in a most flourishing state. We also found some wild rose bushes, a great quantity of young leeks, and some watercresses.

As excursions inland were never attempted, the account of the quadrupeds is taken from the skins which the natives brought to sell. Of these the most common were bears, deer, foxes, and wolves. Hogs, dogs, and goats have not as yet found their way to this place. The sea animals seen off the coast were whales, porpoises, and seals. Birds in general are not only rare as to the different species, but very scarce as to numbers. Those which frequent the woods are crows and ravens, a bluish jay or magpie, common wrens (which are the only singing birds that we heard), the Canadian thrush, and a considerable number of brown eagles.

The persons of the natives are in general under the common stature; the visage of most of them is round and full, and sometimes also broad, with high, prominent cheeks. The forehead rather low, the eyes small and black, the mouth round, with thickish lips. The hair of the head is in great abundance, very coarse and strong, and without a single exception black, straight and lank, or hanging down over the shoulders. Their colour we could never positively determine, as their bodies were incrusted with paint and dirt; though when these were well rubbed off, the whiteness of the skin appeared almost to equal that of Europeans.

Their common dress is a flaxen garment or mantle, ornamented on the upper edge by a narrow strip of fur, and at the lower edge by fringes or tassels. It passes under the left arm, and is tied

MAN OF NOOTKA SOUND.
Page 432.

WOMAN OF NOOTKA SOUND.
Page 433.

over the right shoulder by a string before and one behind near its middle, by which means both arms are left free; and it hangs evenly, covering the left side, but leaving the right open, unless when the mantle is fastened by a girdle of coarse matting or wool round the waist, which is often done. Over this, which reaches below the knees, is worn a small cloak of the same substance, likewise fringed at the lower part. In shape this resembles a round dish-cover, being quite close, except in the middle, where there is a hole just large enough to admit the head; and then, resting upon the shoulders, it covers the arms to the elbows, and the body as far as the waist. Their head is covered with a cap, of the figure of a truncated cone, or like a flower-pot, made of fine matting, having the top frequently ornamented with a round or pointed knob, or bunch of leathern tassels; and there is a string that passes under the chin, to prevent its blowing off. Besides the above dress, which is common to both sexes, the men frequently throw over their other garments the skin of a bear, wolf, or sea-otter, with the hair outward, and tie it as a cloak near the upper part, wearing it sometimes before and sometimes behind. In rainy weather they throw a coarse mat about their shoulders. They have also woollen garments, which, however, are little in use. The hair is commonly worn hanging down loose; but some, when they have no cap, tie it in a bunch on the crown of the head. Their dress, upon the whole, is convenient, and would not be inelegant were it kept clean. But as they rub their bodies constantly over with a red paint, mixed with oil, their garments by this means contract a rancid, offensive smell and a greasy nastiness, so that they make a very wretched, dirty appearance. Though their bodies are always covered with red paint, their faces are often stained with a black, a lighter red, or a white colour. The last of these gives them a ghastly, disgusting aspect.

The ears of many of them are perforated in the lobe, where they make a pretty large hole, and two others higher up on the outer edge. In these holes they hang bits of bone, quills fixed upon a leathern thong, small shells, bunches of woollen tassels, or pieces of thin copper, which our beads could never supplant. The septum of the nose on many is also perforated, through which they draw a piece of soft cord; and some wear at the same place small, thin pieces of iron, brass, or copper, shaped almost like a horse-shoe, the narrow opening of which receives the septum, so that the two points may gently pinch it and the ornament that hangs over the upper lip. The rings of our brass buttons, which they eagerly purchased, were appropriated to this use. About their wrists they wear bracelets or bunches of white bugle beads, made of a conic shelly substance, bunches of thongs, with tassels, or a black, shiny, horny substance, of one piece; and about their ankles they frequently wear many folds of leathern thongs, or the sinews of animals twisted to a considerable thickness. On extraordinary occasions they wear carved wooden masks or visors, applied on the face or on the upper part of the head or forehead. Some of these resemble human faces furnished with hair, beards, and eyebrows; the others the heads of birds, particularly of eagles; and many the heads of land and sea animals, such as deer, wolves, porpoises, and others. But, in general, these representations much exceed the natural size, and they are painted and often strewed with pieces of the foliaceous mica, which makes them glitter, and serves to augment their enormous deformity. They even fix in the same part of the head large pieces of carved work, resembling the prow of a canoe, painted in the same manner, and projecting to a considerable distance. So fond are they of these disguises, that I have seen one of them put his head into a tin kettle he had got from us, for want of another sort of mask. Whether they use these extravagant masquerade ornaments on any particular religious occasion or diversion, or whether they are put on to intimidate their enemies when they go to battle, by their monstrous appearance, or as decoys when they go to hunt animals, is uncertain.

Though there be but too much reason, from their bringing for sale human skulls and bones, to infer that they treat their enemies with a degree of brutal cruelty, this circumstance makes a general agreement of character of almost every tribe of uncivilized man, in every age and in every part of the globe. We had no reason to judge unfavourably of their disposition in this respect. They seemed to be a docile, courteous, good-natured people.

In trafficking with us, some of them would betray a knavish disposition, and carry off our goods without making any return.

But, in general, it was otherwise; and we had abundant reason to commend the fairness of their conduct.

The village at the entrance of the sound stands on the side of a rising ground, which has a pretty steep ascent from the beach to the verge of the wood.

The houses are built of very long and broad planks, resting upon the edges of each other, fastened or tied with withes of pine-bark here and there, and have only slender posts, or rather poles, at considerable distances, on the outside, to which they are also tied, but within are some larger poles placed aslant. The height of the sides and ends of these habitations is seven or eight feet, but the back part is a little higher, by which means the planks that compose the roof slant forward, and are laid on loose, so as to be moved about either to let in the light or carry out the smoke. They are, however, upon the whole, miserable dwellings, and constructed with little care or ingenuity.

Their furniture consists chiefly of a great number of chests and boxes of all sizes, which are generally piled upon each other, close to the sides or ends of the house, and contain their spare garments, skins, masks, and other things which they set a value upon. Their domestic utensils are mostly square and oblong pails or baskets to hold water or other things, round wooden cups or bowls, small shallow wooden troughs about two feet long out of which they eat their food, baskets of twigs, and bags of matting. Their fishing implements and other things also lie or hang up in different parts of the house, but without the least order, so that the whole is a complete scene of confusion; and the only places that do not partake of this confusion are the sleeping benches, which have nothing on them but the mats. The nastiness and stench of their houses are, however, at least equal to the confusion. For as they dry their fish within doors, they also gut them there, which, with their bones and fragments thrown down at meals, and the addition of other sorts of filth, lie everywhere in heaps, and are, I believe, never carried away, till it becomes troublesome, from their size, to walk over them. Their houses are as filthy as hog-sties, everything in and about them stinking of fish, train-oil, and smoke. But, amidst all the filth and confusion, many of them are decorated with images. These are nothing more than the trunks of very large trees, four or five feet high, set up singly or by pairs, at the upper end of the apartment, with the front carved into a human face, and the arms and hands cut out upon the sides, and variously painted, so that the whole is a truly monstrous figure. The general name of these images is Klumma, and the names of two particular ones, which stood abreast of each other, three or four feet asunder in one of the houses, were Natchkoa and Matseeta. A mat, by way of curtain, for the most part hung before them, which the natives were not willing at all times to remove, and when they did unveil them, they seemed to speak of them in a very mysterious manner.

Naturally we thought they were representatives of their gods, or symbols of some religious or superstitious object, and yet we had proofs of the little estimation they were held in, for with a small quantity of iron or brass I could have purchased all the gods (if their images were such) in the place. I did not see one that was not offered to me, and I actually got two or three of the very smallest sort.

The chief employment of the men seems to be that of fishing and killing land or sea animals for the sustenance of their families, for we saw few of them doing anything in the houses; whereas the women were occupied in manufacturing their flaxen or woollen garments, and in preparing the sardines for drying. The women are also sent in the small canoes to gather mussels and other shell-fish, and they manage these with as much dexterity as the men.

Their weapons are bows and arrows, slings, spears, short truncheons of bone, something like the patoo-patoo of New Zealand, and a small pickaxe, not unlike the common American tomahawk. The spear has generally a long point made of bone; some of the arrows are pointed with iron, but most commonly these points were of indented bone. The tomahawk is a stone, six or eight inches long, pointed at one end, and the other end fixed into a handle of wood. This handle resembles the head and neck of the human figure, and the stone is fixed in the mouth, so as to represent an enormously large tongue. To make the resemblance still stronger, human hair is also fixed to it. They have another stone weapon, nine inches or a foot long, with a square point. From the number of these and other weapons we might almost conclude that it is their custom to engage in close fight; and we had, too, convincing proofs that their wars were both frequent and bloody, from the vast number of human skulls which they brought to sell.

Their canoes are of a simple structure, but to appearance well calculated for every useful purpose. Even the largest, which carry twenty people or more, are formed of one tree. Many of them are forty feet long, seven broad, and three deep. From the middle, towards each end, they become gradually narrower, the after-part or stern ending abruptly or perpendicularly, with a small knob on the top; but the fore-part is lengthened out, stretching forward and upward, ending in a notched point or prow considerably higher than the sides of the canoe, which run nearly in a straight line. For the most part they are without any ornament; but some have a little carving, and are decorated by setting seals' teeth on the surface like studs, as is the practice on their masks and weapons. They have no seats, but only several round sticks, little thicker than a cane, placed across at mid-depth. They are very light, and their breadth and flatness enable them to swim firmly, without an outrigger—a remarkable distinction between the craft of all the American nations and that of the Southern Pacific Ocean. Their paddles are small and light, the shape in some measure resembling that of a large leaf, pointed at the bottom, broadest in the middle, and gradually losing itself in the shaft; the whole being about five feet long.

Their implements for fishing and hunting, which are both ingeniously contrived and well made, are nets, hooks, lines, harpoons, and an instrument like an oar. This last is about twenty feet long, four or five inches broad, and about half an inch thick. Each edge, for about two-thirds of its length—the other third being its handle—is set with sharp bone teeth about two inches long. Herrings and sardines, and such other small fish as come in shoals, are attacked with this instrument, which is struck into the shoal, and the fish are caught either upon or between the teeth. Their hooks are made of bone and wood, and rather inartificially; but the harpoon with which they strike the whales and lesser sea animals shows much contrivance. It is composed of a piece of bone, cut into two barbs, in which is fixed the oval blade of a large mussel-shell, having the point of the instrument, to which is fastened about two or three fathoms of repe. To throw this harpoon they use a shaft of about twelve or fifteen feet long, to which the harpoon is fixed, so as to separate from the shaft and leave it floating on the water as a buoy when the animal darts away with the harpoon.

They sometimes decoy animals by covering themselves with a skin, and running about on all-fours, which they do very nimbly, as appeared from the specimens of their skill which they exhibited to us, making a kind of noise or neighing at the same time; and on these occasions the masks, or carved heads, as well as the real dried heads of the different animals, are put on. As to the materials of which they make their various articles, it is to be observed that everything of the rope kind is formed either from thongs of skins and sinews of animals, or from the same flaxen substance of which their mantles are manufactured. The sinews often appeared to be of such a length that it might be presumed they could be of no other animal than the whale; and the same may be said of the bones of which they made their weapons, already mentioned, such as their bark-beating instruments, the points of their spears, and barbs of their harpoons.

They expressed no marks of surprise at seeing our ships; nor were they even startled at the report of a musket, till one day, upon their endeavouring to make us sensible that their arrows and spears could not penetrate the hide-dresses, one of our gentlemen shot a musket-ball through one of them, folded six times. At this they were so much staggered that they plainly discovered their ignorance of the effect of firearms.

CHAPTER XLIII.

THE SHIPS LEAVE NOOTKA SOUND—TRANSACTIONS IN PRINCE WILLIAM'S SOUND—
PROGRESS ALONG THE COAST—DISCOVERY OF COOK'S RIVER.

HAVING put to sea, on the evening of the 26th, with strong signs of an approaching storm, these signs did not deceive us. We were hardly out of the sound before the wind suddenly shifted, and increased to a strong gale, with squalls and rain, and so dark a sky that we could not see the length of the ship. Being apprehensive, from the experience I had since our arrival on this coast, of the wind veering more to the south, which would put us in danger of a lee-shore, we got the tacks on board, and stretched off to the south-west under all the sail the ships would bear. At daylight the next morning we were quite clear of the coast, and the *Discovery* being at some distance astern, I brought to till she came up, and then bore away, steering north-west, in which direction I supposed the coast to lie. At half-past one in the afternoon it blew a perfect hurricane; so that I judged it highly dangerous to run any longer before it, and therefore brought the ships to, with their heads to the southward, under the foresails and mizzen-staysails. At this time the *Resolution* sprung a leak, which at first alarmed us not a little, as from the bread-room we could both hear and see the water rush in, and, as we then thought, it was two feet under water. But in this we were happily mistaken, for it was afterwards found to be even with the water-line, if not above it, when the ship was upright. It was no sooner discovered than the fish-room was found to be full of water, and the casks in it afloat, but this was in a great measure owing to the water not finding its ways to the pumps through the coals that lay in the bottom of the room. For, after the water was baled out, which employed us

1778.
April.

till midnight, and had found its way directly from the leaks to the pumps, it appeared that one pump kept it under, which gave us no small satisfaction. In the evening the wind veered to the south, and its fury in some degree ceased; on this we set the mainsail and two topsails, close-reefed, and stretched to the westward. But at eleven o'clock the gale again increased, and obliged us to take in the topsails till five o'clock the next morning, when the storm began to abate, so that we could bear to set them again.

At seven in the evening of the 1st, being in the latitude of 55° 20', we got sight of the land. Between eleven and twelve o'clock we passed a group of small islands off the south point of a large bay. An arm of this bay seemed to extend in toward the north, behind a round elevated mountain that lies between it and the sea. This mountain I called Mount Edgecumbe. At half an hour past four in the morning of the 3rd we passed a very high peaked mountain, which obtained the name of Mount Fair Weather. This mountain is the highest of a chain of mountains wholly covered with snow, from the highest summit down to the sea-coast. At five in the afternoon the summit of an elevated mountain appeared above the horizon. We supposed it to be Behring's Mount St. Elias, and it stands by that name in our chart. There was also the appearance of a bay, which I shall distinguish by the name of Behring's Bay, in honour of its discoverer.

May.

On the 10th, we were no more than three leagues from the coast of the continent, which extended as far as the eye could reach. To the westward of this last direction was an island that extended from north to south, distant six leagues. A point shoots out from the main toward the north-east end of the island, about five or six leagues distant; this point I named Cape Suckling.

On the 11th, I bore up for the island. At ten o'clock in the morning I went in a boat and landed upon it, with a view of seeing what lay on the other side, but finding it farther to the hills than I expected, and the way being steep and woody, I was obliged to drop the design. At the foot of a tree, on a little eminence not far from the shore, I left a bottle with a paper in it, on which were inscribed the names of the ships and the date of our discovery; and along with it I enclosed two silver twopenny pieces of His

Majesty's coin of the date of 1772. These, with many others, were furnished me by the Rev. Dr. Kaye (now Dean of Lincoln), and as a mark of my esteem and regard for that gentleman, I named the island after him, Kaye's Island. It is eleven or twelve leagues in length, but its breadth is not above a league and a half in any part of it. On this island there are a considerable number of pines, and the whole seems covered with a broad girdle of wood.

On the NW. side of Kaye's Island lies another island; and the bay between this island and the coast is distinguished by the name of Comptroller's Bay. From Comptroller's Bay to a point I named Cape Hinchingbroke, the direction of the coast is nearly east and west. Beyond this it seemed to incline to the southward, a direction so contrary to the modern charts founded upon the late Russian discoveries, that we had reason to expect we should find a passage to the north by the inlet before us. Add to this, that the wind was now at SE., and we were threatened with a fog and a storm, and I wanted to get into some place to stop the leak before we encountered another gale. These reasons induced me to steer for the inlet, which we had no sooner reached than the weather became so foggy that we could not see a mile before us.

We continued to sail about the bay, for I had thought of laying the ship ashore, if a convenient place could be found where we might begin our operations to stop the leak. For this purpose I sent a boat to sound the head of the bay.

Just as we were going to weigh the anchor to proceed farther up the bay, it began to blow and to rain as hard as before. Toward evening, finding the gale did not moderate, and that it might be some time before an opportunity offered to get higher up, I came to a resolution to heel the ship where we were, and with this view moored her.

In heaving the anchor out of the boat, one of the seamen, either through ignorance or carelessness, or both, was carried overboard by the buoy-rope, and followed the anchor to the bottom. It is remarkable that in this very critical situation he had presence of mind to disengage himself, and come up to the surface of the water, where he was taken up with one of his legs fractured in a dangerous manner.

Early next morning we gave the ship a good heel to port, in

order to come at and stop the leak. On ripping off the sheathing, we found the leak to be in one of the seams. While the carpenters were making good these defects, we filled all our empty water-casks at a stream hard by the ship.

In the evening of the 16th, the weather cleared up, and we then found ourselves surrounded on every side by land. Our station was on the east side of the sound, in a place which in the chart is distinguished by the name of Snug Corner Bay. And a very snug place it is.

The leak being stopped, and the sheathing made good over it, at four o'clock on the morning of the 17th we sailed to the northwestward, thinking, if there should be any passage to the north, that it must be in that direction.

We met with a good deal of foul ground, and many sunken rocks, even out in the middle of the channel. The wind too failed us, and was succeeded by calms and light airs from every direction, so that we had some trouble to extricate ourselves from the threatening danger.

In the morning the weather had been very hazy, but it afterward cleared up, so as to give us a distinct view of all the land round us, particularly to the northward where it seemed to close. This left us but little hopes of finding a passage that way; or indeed in any other direction, without putting out again to sea.

As soon as the wind next morning had become favourable for getting out to sea, I resolved to spend no more time in searching for a passage in a place that promised so little success. Having thus taken my resolution, we proceeded to the southward. To the inlet, which we now left, I gave the name of Prince William's Sound. The natives, who came to make us several visits, were mostly dressed in long skins reaching to the ankles, with a hole for the head and sleeves that reach to the wrist. They were made of sea-otter, grey fox, raccoon, and real seal-skin. Some had frocks made of the skins of fowls with only the down remaining, which they glue on to other substances. They all have their ears and noses perforated, and bunches of beads hung on; but the most uncommon and unsightly ornamental fashion is their having the under lip slit quite through in the direction of the mouth, giving the appearance of a second mouth. And, indeed, when the first

MAN OF PRINCE WILLIAM'S SOUND.
Page 442.

WOMAN OF PRINCE WILLIAM'S SOUND.
Page 442.

native made his appearance with this incision, one of our seamen called out that the man had two mouths.

After leaving Prince William's Sound I steered to the south-west, and on the 21st passed a lofty promontory. As the discovery of it was connected with the Princess Elizabeth's birthday, I called it Cape Elizabeth. Beyond it we could see no land, so that at first we were in hopes that it was the western extremity of the continent; but not long after we saw our mistake, for fresh land appeared in sight bearing WSW. On it was seen a ridge of mountains covered with snow. By what I can gather from the account of Behring's voyage, I conclude that this must be called Cape St. Hermogenes. We were detained off the cape by variable light airs, but a breeze springing up we steered along the coast, and soon found the land of Cape St. Hermogenes to be an island, separated from the adjacent coast by a channel one league broad.

At noon the island bore south, and the land to the NW. of it ended in a low point, which was called Point Banks. Off this point I found a group of high islands, which obtained the name of Barren Isles from their very naked appearance. I intended going through one of the channels that divide these islands; but meeting with a strong current setting against us, I went to the leeward of them all. Toward the evening we got sight of a very lofty promontory which I named Cape Douglas, in honour of my very good friend Dr. Douglas, Canon of Windsor. Between Point Banks and Cape Douglas the coast seemed to form a large and deep bay, which, from some smoke that had been seen, obtained the name of Smoky Bay.

The weather being fair and tolerably clear, we saw land on each side, with a ridge of mountains rising one behind another without the least separation. On the eastern shore we now saw two columns of smoke, a sure sign that there were inhabitants. Between one and two in the morning of the 30th we weighed, and worked up till near seven o'clock, when, the tide being done, we anchored in nineteen fathoms, under the same shore as before. About noon two canoes, with a man in each, came off to the ship from near the place where we had seen the smoke the preceding day. They laboured very hard in paddling across the stormy tide, and hesitated a little before they would come quite close; but upon signs being made to them they approached. One of them talked a great deal, but we did not understand a word he said. He kept pointing to the shore, which we interpreted to be an invitation to go thither. They accepted a few trifles from me, which I conveyed to them from the quarter gallery. These men in every respect resembled the people we had met with in Prince William's Sound as to their person and dress. Their canoes were also of the same construction. One of our visitors had his face painted jet black, and seemed to have no beard; but the other, who was more elderly, had no paint and a considerable beard.

When the flood made we weighed, and then the canoes left us. I stood over to the western shore, with a fresh gale at north-north-east, and fetched under the point above mentioned; this, with the other on the opposite shore, contracted the channel to the breadth of four leagues. Through this channel ran a prodigious tide.

At eight in the evening we anchored under a point of land which bore north-east three leagues distant, in fifteen fathoms of water. Here we lay during the ebb, which ran near five knots to the hour. Until we had got thus far the water had retained the same degree of saltness at low as at high water, and was as salt as that in the ocean. But now the marks of a river displayed themselves. We weighed with the next flood in the morning of the 31st, and about eight o'clock were visited by several of the natives in one large and several small canoes. The latter carried only one person each, and some had a paddle with a blade at each end, after the manner of the Esquimaux; in the large canoes were men, women, and children. Before they reached the ship they displayed a leathern frock upon a long pole, as a sign apparently of their peaceable intentions. This frock they conveyed into the ship in return for some trifles which I gave them. We procured from them some of their fur dresses made of the skins of sea-otters, martens, hares, and other animals, a few of their darts, and a small supply of salmon and halibut. In exchange for these they took old clothes, beads, and pieces of iron. We found that they were in possession of large iron knives and sky-blue glass beads, which they seemed to value much, and consequently those which we now gave them. After spending about two hours between the one ship and the other they all retired to the western shore.

At nine o'clock we came to an anchor in sixteen fathoms of water, about two leagues from the west shore : the weather was misty, with drizzling rain, and clear by turns. At the clear intervals we saw an opening between the mountains on the eastern shore, bearing east from the station of the ships, with low land, which we supposed to be islands lying between us and the mainland. Low land was also seen to the northward, which seemed to extend from the foot of the mountains on the one side to those on the other; and at low water we perceived large shoals stretching out from this low land, some of which were at no great distance from us. From these appearances we were in some doubt whether the inlet did not take an easterly direction through the above opening, or whether that opening was only a branch of it, and the main channel continued its northern direction through the low land now in sight.

To determine this point and to examine the shoals I despatched the boats, under the command of the master, and, as soon as the flood-tide made, followed with the ships; but as it was a dead calm, and the tide strong, I anchored, after driving about ten miles in an east direction. At the lowest of the preceding ebb the water at the surface, and for near a foot below it, was found to be perfectly fresh. Besides this, we had now many other and but too evident proofs of being in a great river; such as low shores, very thick and muddy water, large trees and all manner of dirt and rubbish floating up and down with the tide.

June.
At two o'clock on the following morning, the 1st of June, the master returned, and reported that he found the inlet, or rather river, contracted to the breadth of one league by low land on each side, through which it took a northerly direction. He proceeded three leagues through this narrow part, which he found navigable for the largest ships, being from seventeen to twenty fathoms deep. While the ebb or stream ran down, the water was perfectly fresh, but after the flood made it was brackish.

All hopes of finding a passage were now given up; but, as the ebb was almost spent, and we could not return against the flood, I thought I might as well take advantage of the latter to get a nearer view of the eastern branch, and by that means finally to determine whether the low land on the east side of the river was an island, as we had supposed, or not. With this purpose in view we weighed with the first of the flood, and stood over for the eastern shore, with boats ahead sounding; but a contrary wind springing up, I despatched two boats, under the command of Lieutenant King, to examine the tides and to make such other observations as might give us some insight into the nature of the river.

At ten o'clock, finding the ebb begun, I anchored in nine fathoms of water, but observing the tide to be too strong for the boats to make head against it, I made a signal for them to return on board before they had got half-way to the entrance of the river they were sent to examine, which was three leagues distant. The principal information gained by this tide's work was the determining that all the low land, which we had supposed to be an island or islands, was one track, from the banks of the great river to the foot of the mountains, which it joined, and that it terminated at the south entrance of this eastern branch, which I shall distinguish by the name of River *T*urnagain. On the north side of this river the low land again begins, and stretches out from the foot of the mountains down to the banks of the great river, so that before the river *T*urnagain it forms a large bay, on the south side of which we were now at anchor.

We had traced this river seventy leagues or more from its entrance without seeing the least appearance of its source.

If the discovery of this great river,* which promises to vie with the most considerable ones already known to be capable of extensive inland navigation, should prove of use either to the present or to any future age, the time we spent in it ought to be the less regretted. But to us, who had a much greater object in view, the delay thus occasioned was an essential loss. The season was advancing apace. We knew not how far we might have to proceed to the south, and we were now convinced that the continent of North America extended farther to the west than from the modern most reputable charts we had reason to expect. This made the existence of a passage into Baffin's or Hudson's Bay less

---

* Captain Cook having here left a blank, which he had not filled up with any particular name, Lord Sandwich directed, with the greatest propriety, that it should be called Cook's River. This arm of the sea is now known as Cook's Inlet, and was further explored, in 1794, by Captain Vancouver.

probable, or at least showed it to be of greater extent. It was a satisfaction to me, however, to reflect that if I had not examined this very considerable inlet it would have been assumed by speenlative fabricators of geography as a fact that it communicated with the sea to the north, or with Baffin's or Hudson's Bay to the east.

In the afternoon I sent Mr. King again with two armed boats, with orders to land on the northern point of the low land on the south-east side of the river; thence to display the flag and take possession of the country and river in His Majesty's name; and also to bury in the ground a bottle containing some pieces of English coin of the year 1772, and a paper on which was inscribed the names of our ships and the date of our discovery. In the meantime the ships were got under sail in order to proceed down the river. The wind blew fresh easterly, but a calm ensued not long after we were under way, and the floed-tide meeting us off the point where Mr. King landed (and which thence got the name of Point Possession), we were obliged to drop anchor in six fathoms of water, with the point bearing south two miles distant.

When Mr. King returned, he informed me that, as he approached the shore, about twenty of the natives made their appearance with their arms extended, probably to express their peaceable disposition and to show that they were without weapons. On Mr. King and the gentlemen with him landing with muskets in their hands, they seemed alarmed, and made signs expressive of their request to lay them down; this was accordingly done, and then they suffered the gentlemen to walk up to them, and appeared to be cheerful and sociable. They had with them a few pieces of fresh salmon and several dogs. Mr. Law, surgeon of the *Discovery*, who was one of the party, having bought one of the latter, took it down towards the boat and shot it dead in their sight. This seemed to surprise them exceedingly, and, as if they did not think themselves safe in such company, they walked away; but it was soon after discovered that their spears and other weapons were hid in the bushes close behind them.

We weighed anchor as soon as it was high water, and stood over to the west shore, where the return of the flood obliged us to anchor early next morning. Soon after several large and some small canoes with natives came off, who first bartered their skins, and then sold their garments, till many of them were quite naked; amongst others they brought a number of white hare or rabbit skins, and very beautiful reddish ones of foxes; but there were only two or three skins of otters. They also sold us some pieces of salmon and halibut, and preferred iron to everything else offered to them in exchange.

At half-past ten we weighed with the first of the ebb, and while plying down the river, owing to the inattention and neglect of the man at the lead, the *Resolution* struck and stuck fast on a bank that lies nearly in the middle of the river, and about two miles above the two projecting bluff points before mentioned. As soon as the ship got aground I made a signal for the *Discovery* to anchor; she, as I afterwards understood, had been near ashore on the west side of the bank. As the flood-tide came in, the ship floated off soon after five o'clock in the afternoon, without receiving the least damage or giving us any trouble, and after standing over to the west shore into deep water, we anchored to wait for the ebb, as the wind was still contrary.

We weighed again with the ebb, at ten o'clock at night, and between four and five the next morning, when the tide was finished, we once more cast anchor about two miles below the bluff point on the west shore. Many of the natives came off, and attended upon us all the morning. Their company was very acceptable, for they brought with them a quantity of fine salmon, which they exchanged for such trifles as we had to give them. Most of it was split ready for drying, and several hundredweight of it was procured for the two ships.

The wind remaining southerly, we continued to tide it down the river, and on the morning of the 5th, coming to the place where we had lost our kedge-anchor, made an attempt to recover it, but without success. Before we left this place six canoes came off from the east shore, some conducted by one and others by two men. They remained at a little distance from the ships, viewing them with a kind of silent surprise, at least half an hour, without exchanging a single word with us or with one another. At length they took courage and came alongside, when they began to barter with our people, and did not leave us till they had parted with everything they brought with them, consisting of a few skins and some salmon.

As soon as the ebb tide made in our favour, we weighed and plied down the river. On the 6th, we passed the Barren Islands and stretched away for Cape St. Hermogenes. To the westward lay a promontory which was named after the day, Cape Whitsunday, and a large bay to the west of it obtained the name of Whitsuntide Bay. The following days we had almost constant misty weather with drizzling rain, so that we seldom had a sight of the coast. I continued to ply to the SW. as the coast trended, and on the 14th we found an island which was named Trinity Island. The country here is more broken and rugged than any part we had yet seen; the coast seemed full of creeks or small inlets, none of which appeared to be of any great depth. Every part had a very barren aspect, and was covered with snow from the summits of the highest hills down to a very small distance from the sea-coast.

On the 19th of June, the *Discovery*, now two miles astern, suddenly fired three guns and made the signal to speak with us. This alarmed me not a little; and as no apparent danger had been remarked in the passage through the channel, it was apprehended that some accident must have happened. A boat was immediately sent to her, and in a short time returned with Captain Clerke on board. I now learned from him that some natives in canoes, who had been following the ship for some time, at length got under his stern. One of them made many signs, taking off his cap and bowing, after the manner of Europeans. A rope being handed down from the ship, to this he fastened a small wooden box, made some signs, and left the ship. No one on board had any suspicion that the box contained anything till after the departure of the canoes, when it was accidentally opened, and a piece of paper was found, folded up carefully, upon which something was written in the Russian language, as was supposed. The date 1778 was prefixed to it, and in the body of the note there was a reference to the year 1776. Not learned enough to decipher the alphabet of the writer, his numerals marked sufficiently that others had preceded us in visiting this dreary part of the globe; and the hopes of soon meeting with some of the Russian traders could not but give a sensible satisfaction to those who had, for such a length of time, been conversant with the savages of the Pacific Ocean and of the continent of North America.

Early on the morning of the 20th, some breakers were seen two miles distant, which forced us so far from the continent that we had but a distant view of the coast. Over some adjoining islands we could see the mainland covered with snow, but particularly some hills, whose elevated tops were seen towering above the clouds to a most stupendous height. The most south-westerly of these hills was discovered to have a volcano, which continually threw up vast columns of black smoke. It stands not far from the coast, and is also remarkable from its figure, which is a complete cone, having the volcano at the very summit.

In the afternoon, having three hours' calm, our people caught upwards of a hundred halibuts, some of which weighed a hundred pounds; this was a very seasonable refreshment to us. While thus engaged, a small canoe, conducted by one man, came to us from the large island; on approaching the ship, he took off his cap and bowed. It was evident that the Russians must have communication and traffic with these people, not only from their acquired politeness, but from their possessing certain articles only used among civilized nations; thus our present visitor wore a pair of green cloth breeches, and a jacket of black cloth or stuff, under the gut-shirt of his own country. He had nothing to barter except a grey fox-skin and some fishing implements or harpoons, the heads of the shafts of which were neatly made of bone.

The weather was cloudy and hazy, with now and then sunshine, till the afternoon of the 22nd, when the wind came round to the south-east, and, as usual, brought thick rainy weather. Before the fog came on, no part of the mainland was in sight, except the volcano and another mountain close by it. We made but little progress for some days, having the wind variable, and but little of it.

On the morning of the 25th, we got an easterly breeze and, what was uncommon with this wind, clear weather, so that we not only saw the volcano, but other mountains, both to the east and west of it, and all the coast of the mainland under them, much plainer than at any time before. The weather in the afternoon became gloomy, and at length turned to a mist, so thick that we could not see a hundred yards before us. We were now alarmed at hearing the sound of breakers on our larboard bow, and on heaving the lead found twenty-eight fathoms of water. I immediately brought the ship to, and a few hours after, the fog having cleared a little, it appeared that we had escaped very imminent danger. We found ourselves three-quarters of a mile from the north-east side of an island, and two elevated rocks were about half a league each from us, and about the same distance from each other. There were several breakers about them, and yet Providence had, in the dark, guided the ships between these rocks, which I should not have ventured on a clear day, and to such an anchoring-place that I could not have chosen a better.

Finding ourselves so near land, I sent a boat to examine what it produced. The officer reported that it produced some tolerably good grass and several other small plants, one of which was like purslane, and ate very well either in soups or as a salad.

On the 27th, we steered to the northward. We had now land in every direction: that to the south extended to the south-west in a ridge of mountains, but our sight could not determine whether it composed one or more islands. We afterwards found it to be only one, known by the name of Oonalashka. Between it and the land to the north there seemed to be a channel in the direction of north-west.

On a point which bore west from the ship three-quarters of a mile distant, were several natives and their habitations. In this place we saw them tow in two whales, which we supposed they had just killed. A few of them now and then came off to the ships and bartered a few trifling things with our people, but never remained above a quarter of an hour at a time; they rather seemed shy, and yet we could judge that they were no strangers to vessels something like ours. They behaved with a degree of politeness uncommon to savage tribes.

At daybreak on the 28th, we weighed with a light breeze at south, which was succeeded by variable light airs from all directions. But as there ran a rapid tide in our favour, we got through before the ebb made, and came to an anchor in twenty-eight fathoms of water near the southern shore.

While we lay here, several of the natives came off to us and bartered a few fishing implements for tobacco. One of them, a young man, having upset his canoe while alongside one of our boats, our people caught hold of him, but the canoe went adrift. The youth, by this accident, was obliged to come into the ship, and he went down into my cabin upon the first invitation, without expressing the least reluctance or uneasiness. His own clothes being wet, I gave him others, in which he dressed himself with as much case as I could have done. From his behaviour, and that of some others, we were convinced that these people were no strangers to Europeans and to some of their customs. But there was something in our ships that greatly excited their curiosity, for such as could not come off in their canoes assembled on the neighbouring hills to look at them.

Soon after we anchored, a native of the island brought on board a note, which he presented to me; but it was written in the Russian language, which none of us could read. As it could be of no use to me, and might be of consequence to others, I returned it to the bearer, and dismissed him with a few presents, for which he expressed his thanks by making several low bows as he retired. In walking next day along the shore, I met a group of natives of both sexes, seated on the grass at a repast consisting of raw fish, which they seemed to eat with as much relish as we should a turbot served up with the richest sauce. By the evening we had completed our water, and made such observations as the time and weather would permit.

Thick fogs and a contrary wind detained us till the 2nd of July, which afforded an opportunity of acquiring some knowledge of the country and of its inhabitants.

CHAPTER XLIV.

PROGRESS NORTHWARD AFTER LEAVING OONALASHKA—DEATH OF MR. ANDERSON, THE SURGEON—THE COUNTRY OF THE TSCHUTSKI—THE SHIPS CROSS THE STRAIT TO THE COAST OF AMERICA—SITUATION OF ICY CAPE—SEA-HORSES—THE SEA BLOCKED UP WITH ICE—CAPE NORTH.

HAVING put to sea with a light breeze, we steered to the north, meeting with nothing to obstruct us in this course. As we advanced we found the depth of water gradually decreasing and the coast trending more and more northerly.

1778. July.

On the morning of the 16th, we found ourselves nearer the land than we expected. Here, between two points, the coast forms a bay, in some parts of which the land was hardly visible from the mast-head. I sent Lieutenant Williamson with orders to land, and see what direction the coast took, and what the country produced, for it had but a barren appearance. Soon after, Mr. Williamson returned and reported that he had landed on the point, and having climbed the highest hill, found that the farthest part of the coast in sight bore nearly north. He took possession of the country in His Majesty's name, and left on the hill a bottle in which was inscribed on a piece of paper the names of the ships, and the date of the discovery. The promontory, to which he gave the name of Cape Newenham, is a rocky point of tolerable height; the hills are naked, but on the lower grounds grew grass and other plants. He saw no other animal but a doe and her fawn, and a dead sea horse or cow upon the beach.

On the 21st we were obliged to anchor, to avoid running upon a shoal which had only a depth of five feet. While we lay here, twenty-seven men of the country, each in a canoe, came off to the ship, which they approached with great caution, hallooing and opening their arms as they advanced, which we understood was to express their pacific intentions. At length some approached near enough to receive a few trifles that were thrown to them. This encouraged the rest to venture alongside, and traffic presently commenced between them and our people, who got dresses of skins, bows, arrows, darts, and wooden vessels, our visitors taking in exchange whatever was offered them. They seemed to be the same sort of people that we had of late met with all along this coast, and wore the same kind of ornaments in their lips and noses, but were far more dirty and not so well clothed. They appeared to be wholly unacquainted with people like us, knew not the use of tobacco, nor was any foreign article seen in their possession, unless a knife made of a piece of common iron fitted in a wooden handle may be looked upon as such. Most of them had their hair shaved; for a covering for the head they wore a hood of skins and a bonnet which appeared to be of wood. Our boats returning from sounding seemed to alarm them, so that they all left us sooner than probably they would otherwise have done.

On 3rd August, Mr. Anderson, my surgeon, who had been lingering under a consumption for more than twelve months, expired between three and four in the afternoon. He was a sensible young man, an agreeable companion, well skilled in his own profession, and had it pleased God to have spared his life, the public, I make no doubt, might have received from him such communications on various parts of the natural history of the several places we visited, as would have abundantly shown that he was not unworthy of this commendation.

August.

Soon after he had breathed his last, land was seen to the westward. It was supposed to be an island, and to perpetuate the memory of the deceased, for whom I had a very great regard, I named it Anderson's Island. The next day I removed Mr. Law, the surgeon of the *Discovery*, into the *Resolution*, and appointed Mr. Samuel, the surgeon's first mate of the *Resolution*, to be surgeon of the *Discovery*.

At three o'clock in the afternoon of the 4th, land was seen, which we supposed to be the continent of America. It appeared low next the sea; but inland, it swelled into hills which rise, one behind another, to a considerable height.

At ten in the morning of the 5th, with the wind at south-west, we ran down and anchored between the continent and an island four leagues in extent, which was named Sledge Island. I landed here, but saw neither shrub nor tree either upon the island or on the continent. That people had lately been on the island was evident from the marks of feet. We found, near where we landed, a sledge, which occasioned this name being given by me to the island. It seemed to be such an one as the Russians in Kamtchatka make use of over the ice or snow, and was ten feet long, twenty inches broad, and had a kind of rail-work on each side, and was shod with bone. The construction of it was admirable, and all the parts neatly put together. After several observations, from the 6th to the 9th, I was satisfied that the whole was a continued coast. I tacked and stood away for its north-west part, and came to anchor near a point of land, which I named Cape Prince of Wales. It is the western extremity of all America hitherto known.

At daybreak in the morning of the 10th, we resumed our course to the west, and about ten o'clock anchored in a large bay two miles from the shore. As we were standing into this bay we perceived on the north shore a village, and some people whom the sight of the ships seemed to have thrown into confusion or fear. We could plainly see persons running up the country with burdens upon their backs. At these habitations I proposed to land, and accordingly went with three armed boats, accompanied by some of the officers. About thirty or forty men, each armed with a spontoon and bow and arrows, stood drawn up on a rising ground close by the village. As we drew near, three of them came down towards the shore, and were so polite as to take off their caps and to make us low bows. We returned the civility; but this did not inspire them with sufficient confidence to wait for our landing, for the moment we put the boats ashore they retired. I followed them alone, without anything in my hand, and by signs and gestures prevailed on them to stop and receive some trifling presents. In return for these they gave me two fox-skins and a couple of sea-horse teeth.

They seemed very fearful and cautious, expressing their desire by signs that no more of our people should be permitted to come up. On my laying my hand on the shoulder of one of them, he started back several paces. In proportion as I advanced, they retreated, always in the attitude of being ready to make use of their spears, while those on the rising ground stood ready to support them with their arrows. Insensibly, myself and two or three of my companions got in amongst them. A few beads distributed to those about us soon caused a kind of confidence, so that they were not alarmed when a few more of our people joined us, and by degrees a sort of traffic between us commenced. In exchange for knives, beads, tobacco, and other articles, they gave us some of their clothing and a few arrows. But nothing that we had to offer could induce them to part with a spear or a bow. These they held in constant readiness, never once quitting them, except at one time when four or five persons laid theirs down while they gave us a song and a dance. And even then they placed them in such a manner that they could lay hold of them in an instant, and, for their security, they desired us to sit down.

The arrows were pointed either with bone or stone, but very few of them had barbs, and some had a round blunt point. What use these may be applied to I cannot say, unless it be to kill small animals without damaging the skin. The bows were such as we had seen on the American coast, and like those used by the Esquimaux. The spears or spontoons were of iron or steel, and of European or Asiatic workmanship, in which no little pains had been taken to ornament them with carving and inlayings of brass, and of a white metal. Those who stood ready with bows and arrows in their hands, had the spear slung over their right shoulder by a leathern strap; a leathern quiver, slung over their left shoulder, contained arrows, and some of the quivers were extremely beautiful, being made of red leather, on which was very neat embroidery and other ornaments.

Several other things, and in particular their clothing, showed that they were possessed of a degree of ingenuity far surpassing what one could expect to find among so northern a people. All the Americans we had seen, since our arrival on that coast, were rather low of stature, with round chubby faces and high cheekbones. The people we now were amongst were far from resembling them; in short, they appeared to be quite a different nation. We saw neither women nor children of either sex, nor any aged, except one man, who was bald-headed, and he was the only one who carried no arms; the others seemed to be picked men, and rather under than above the middle age.

Their clothing consisted of a cap, a frock, a pair of breeches, a pair of boots, and a pair of gloves, all made of leather, or of the skins of deer, dogs, or seals, etc., and extremely well dressed, some with the hair or fur on. The caps were made to fit the head very close, and they also had hoods, made of the skin of dogs, that were large enough to cover both head and shoulders. Their hair seemed to be black, but their heads were either shaved or the hair cut close off, and none of them wore any beard.

We found the village composed both of their summer and their winter habitations. The latter are exactly like a vault, the floor of which is sunk a little below the surface of the earth. One of them which I examined was of an oval form, about twenty feet long and twelve or more high; the framing was of wood and the ribs of whales, disposed in a judicious manner, and bound together with smaller materials of the same sort; over this framing is laid a covering of strong, coarse grass; and that again is covered with earth, so that on the outside the house looks like a little hillock supported by a wall of stone, three or four feet high, which is built round the two sides and one end. At the other end the earth is raised and sloping, to form a walk up to the entrance, which is by a hole in the top of the roof over that end. The floor was boarded, and under it a kind of cellar, in which I saw nothing but water, and at the end of each house was a vaulted room, which I took to be a store-room. These store-rooms communicated with the house by a dark passage and with the open air by a hole in the roof, which was even with the ground one walked upon; but they cannot be said to be wholly underground, for one end leads to the edge of the hill along which they were made, and which was built up with stone. Over it stood a kind of sentry-box, or tower, composed of the bones of large fish.

The summer huts were pretty large and circular, being brought to a point at the top; the framing was of slight poles and bones, covered with the skins of sea animals. I examined the inside of one; there was a fireplace just within the door, where lay a few wooden vessels, all very dirty. Their bed-places were close to the side, and took up about half the circuit; some privacy seemed to be observed, for there were several partitions made with skins; the bed and bedding were of deer-skins, and most of them were dry and clean.

Above the habitations were erected several stages, ten or twelve feet high, such as we had observed in some parts of the American coast. They were wholly composed of bones, and seemed intended for drying their fish and skins, which were thus placed beyond the reach of their dogs, of which they had a great many. These dogs are of the fox kind, rather large and of different colours, with long soft hair like wool. They are probably used in drawing their sledges in winter, of which I saw a great many laid up in one of the winter huts. It is also not improbable that dogs may constitute a part of their food, as several lay dead that had been killed that morning.

The canoes of these people are of the same sort as those of the North Americans, some, both of the large and small sizes, being seen lying in a creek under the village.

By the large bones of fish and of other sea animals it appeared that the sea supplied them with the greater part of their subsistence. The country appeared to be exceedingly barren, yielding neither tree nor shrub that we could see. At some distance westward we observed a ridge of mountains covered with snow that had lately fallen.

At first we supposed this land to be a part of the island of Alaschka, laid down in Mr. Stæhlin's map; but, from the figure of the coast, the situation of the opposite shore of America, and from the longitude, we soon began to think that it was more probably the country of the Tschutski, or the eastern extremity of Asia explored by Behring in 1728. But to have admitted this, without further examination, I must have pronounced Mr. Stæhlin's map and his account of the New Northern Archipelago to be either exceedingly erroneous, even in latitude, or else to be a mere fiction—a judgment which I had no right to pass upon a publication so respectably vouched, without producing the clearest proofs.

After a stay of between two and three hours with these people, we returned to our ships; and soon after, the wind veering to the south, we weighed anchor, stood out of the bay, and steered to the north-east, between the coast and the two islands. From this station we steered east, in order to get nearer the American coast. In this course the water shoaled gradually, and, there being but little wind, and all our endeavours to increase our depth failing, I was obliged at last to drop anchor in six fathoms, the only remedy we had left to prevent the ships driving into less.

A breeze of wind springing up at the north, we weighed at nine in the evening, and stood to the westward, which course soon brought us into deep water; and during the 12th we worked up to the north, both coasts being in sight, but we kept nearest to that of America.

On the 15th of August a strong gale blew, and this was followed by a thick fog. Some time before noon we perceived a brightness in the northern horizon, like that reflected from ice, commonly called the blink. It was little noticed from a supposition that it was improbable we should meet with ice so soon. And yet the sharpness of the air and gloominess of the weather for two or three days past seemed to indicate some sudden change. About an hour after, the sight of a large field of ice left us no longer in doubt about the cause of the brightness of the horizon. We tacked close to the edge of the ice, not being able to go on any farther; for the ice was quite impenetrable, and extended as far as the eye could reach. It was as compact as a wall, and seemed to be ten or twelve feet high at least. Its surface was extremely rugged, and here and there we saw upon it pools of water. At this time the weather, which had been hazy, clearing up a little, we saw land about three or four miles distant. The eastern extremity forms a point, which was much encumbered with ice; for which reason it obtained the name of Icy Cape. The other extreme of the land was lost in the horizon, so that there can be no doubt of its being a continuation of the American continent.

Our situation was now more and more critical. It was evident that if we remained much longer between the ice and the land, it would force us ashore, and it was in too large pieces to attempt forcing the ships through it. On the ice there lay a prodigious number of sea-horses; and as we were in want of fresh provisions, the boats were sent to get some. By seven in the evening we had received nine of these animals on board, which, till now, we had supposed to be sea-cows; so that we were not a little disappointed, especially some of the seamen, who, for the novelty of the thing, had been feasting their eyes for some days past. Nor would they have known the difference now if we had not happened to have one or two on board who had been in Greenland, and declared no one ever ate of these animals. But, notwithstanding this, we lived upon them as long as they lasted, and there were few on board who did not prefer them to our salt meat. The fat, at first, is as sweet as marrow; but in a few days it grows rancid, unless it be salted. The lean flesh is coarse, black, and has rather a strong taste; and the heart is nearly as well tasted as that of a bullock. The fat, when melted, yields a good deal of oil, which burns very well in lamps; and their hides, which are very thick, were very useful about our rigging.

These animals lie in herds of many hundreds upon the ice, huddling one over the other like swine, and roar or bray very loud; so that in the night or in foggy weather they gave us notice of the vicinity of the ice before we could see it. We never found the whole herd asleep; some being always upon the watch. These, on the approach of the boat, would wake those next to them, and the alarm being thus gradually communicated, the whole herd would be awoke presently. But they were seldom in a hurry to get away till after they had been once fired at; then they would tumble one over the other into the sea in the utmost confusion.

By the time we had got our sea-horses on board we were, in a manner, surrounded with ice. At two in the afternoon we fell in with the main ice, along the edge of which we kept, being partly directed by the roaring of the sea-horses, for we had a very thick fog. Thus we continued sailing till near midnight, when we got in amongst the loose ice, and heard the surge of the sea upon the main ice.

I now hauled to the southward, and at ten o'clock the next morning, the fog clearing away, we saw the continent of America. I continued to steer in for the American land until eight o'clock, in order to get a nearer view of it, and to look for a harbour, but seeing nothing like one, I stood again to the north, with a light breeze westerly. The southern extremity of the coast seemed to form a point, which was named Cape Lisburne, and appeared to be high land, even down to the sea.

Everywhere else, as we advanced northward, we had a low coast from which the land rises to a middle height. The coast now before us was without snow, except in one or two places, and had a greenish hue. But we could not perceive any wood upon it.

On the 22nd the weather was foggy, with some intervals of sunshine. In the evening it fell calm, and at midnight we heard the surge of the sea against the ice, and had several loose pieces about us.

In the evening of the 27th we were close with the edge of the ice, which lay ENE. and WSW. as far each way as the eye could reach. Having but little wind, I went with the boats to examine the state of the ice. I found it consisting of loose pieces of various extent, and so close together that I could hardly enter the outer edge with a boat, and it was as impossible for the ships to enter it as if it had been so many rocks. It appeared to be entirely composed of frozen snow, and to have been all formed at sea. It seems very improbable that this ice could have been the production of the preceding winter alone. I should suppose it rather to have been the production of a great many winters. The sun contributes very little toward reducing these great masses; for, although that luminary is a considerable while above the horizon, it seldom shines out for more than a few hours at a time, and often is not seen for several days in succession. It is the wind, or rather the waves raised by the wind, that brings down the bulk of these enormous masses, by grinding one piece against another, and by undermining and washing away those parts that lie exposed to the surge of the sea.

A thick fog, which came on while I was thus employed with the boats, hastened me aboard rather sooner than I could have wished, with one sea-horse to each ship. We had killed more, but could not wait to bring them with us. The number of these animals on all the ice we had seen is almost incredible. We spent the night standing off and on amongst the drift-ice, and at nine o'clock the next morning, the fog having partly dispersed, boats from each ship were sent for sea-horses, for by this time our people began to relish them, and those we had procured before were all consumed.

On the morning of the 29th we saw the main ice to the northward, and, not long after, land bearing south-west by west. Presently after this more land showed itself, bearing west, in two hills like islands, but afterwards the whole appeared connected. As we approached the coast, it appeared to lie low next the sea, with elevated land farther back. It was perfectly destitute of wood, and even snow. In the low ground, lying between the high land and the sea, was a lake extending to the south-east farther than we could see. As we stood off, the westernmost of the two hills before mentioned came open off the bluff point in the direction of north-west. This point, which is steep and rocky, was named Cape North. Its situation is nearly in the latitude of 68° 56', and in the longitude of 180° 51'.

Being desirous of seeing more of the coast to the westward, we tacked again at two o'clock in the afternoon, thinking we could weather Cape North. But finding we could not, the wind freshening, a thick fog coming on, with much snow, and being fearful of the ice coming down upon us, I gave up the design I had formed of plying to the westward, and stood off shore again.

The season was now so far advanced, and the time when the frost is expected to set in so near at hand, that I did not think it consistent with prudence to make any farther attempts to find a passage into the Atlantic this year in any direction, so little prospect was there of succeeding. My attention was now directed towards finding out some place where we might supply ourselves with wood and water, and the object uppermost in my thoughts was how I should spend the winter, so as to make some improvements in geography and navigation, and at the same time be in a condition to return to the north in farther search of a passage the ensuing summer.

CHAPTER XLV.

RETURN FROM CAPE NORTH ALONG THE COAST OF ASIA—THE TSCHUTSKÍ—BAY OF ST. LAWRENCE—NORTON SOUND—ACCOUNT OF THE SETTLEMENT AT OONALASHKA—DEPARTURE FROM OONALASHKA—ARRIVAL AT OWHYHEE, ONE OF THE SANDWICH ISLANDS.

1778. August.

AFTER having stood off till we got into eighteen fathoms water, I bore to the eastward along the coast, which by this time it was pretty certain could only be the continent of Asia. As the wind blew fresh, with a very heavy fall of snow and a thick mist, it was necessary to proceed with great caution.

At daybreak on the 30th we made sail, and steered such a course as I thought would bring us in with the land, for the weather was as thick as ever, and it snowed incessantly. At ten we got sight of the coast, bearing south-west four miles distant. The inland country hereabout is full of hills, some of which are of a considerable height, and the land was covered with snow.

For the two preceding days the mean height of the mercury in the thermometer had been very little above the freezing-point and often below it, so that the water in the vessels upon the deck was frequently covered with a sheet of ice.

The coast seemed to form several rocky points, connected by a low shore, without the least appearance of a harbour, and I was now well assured of what I had believed before—that this was the country of the Tschutski, or the north-east coast of Asia, and that thus far Behring proceeded in 1728.

On the 2nd of September we had fair weather and sunshine, and as we ranged along the coast at the distance of four miles saw several of the inhabitants and some of their habitations, which looked like little hillocks of earth.

In the evening we passed the Eastern Cape, from which the coast changes its direction and trends SW. It is the same point of land we had passed on the 11th of August. I conclude, as Behring did before me, that this is the most eastern point of Asia. It is a peninsula of considerable height, joined to the continent by a very low, narrow neck of land.

After passing the cape, I steered for the northern point of St. Lawrence Bay, in which we had anchored on the 10th of last month. We reached it by eight o'clock next morning, and saw some of the inhabitants at the place where I had seen them before. None of them, however, attempted to come off to us, which seemed a little extraordinary, as the weather was favourable enough. These people must be the Tschutski.

This Bay of St. Lawrence* is at least five leagues broad at the entrance. It appeared to be tolerably well sheltered from the sea winds, provided there be sufficient depth of water for ships. I did not wait to examine it, although I was very desirous of finding a harbour in these parts to which I might resort next spring.

In justice to the memory of Behring, I must say that he has delineated the coast very well. I was now convinced we were upon the coast of Asia, but I had no way of accounting for the great difference but by supposing that I had mistaken some part of what he calls the island of Alaschka for the American continent. It was with me a matter of some consequence to clear up this point the present season, that I might have but one object in view the next. And as these northern isles are represented by him as abounding with wood, I was in hopes of getting a supply of that article, which we now began to be in great want of on board. With these views I steered for the American coast, and on the 6th we got sight of it near Sledge Island.

September.

Pursuing our course, on the 9th we found ourselves upon a coast covered with wood, an agreeable sight to which of late we had not been accustomed. Next morning, being about a league from the west shore, I took two boats and landed, attended by Mr. King, to seek wood and water. We observed tracks of deer and foxes on the beach, on which also lay a great quantity of driftwood, and there was no want of fresh water. I returned on board

---

* Captain Cook gives it this name, having anchored in it on St. Lawrence's Day, August 10. It is remarkable that Behring sailed past this very place on the 10th of August 1728, on which account the neighbouring island was named by him after the same saint.

with an intention to bring the ships to an anchor here, but, the wind veering to north-east, I stretched over to the opposite shore, in hopes of finding wood there also, and anchored at eight o'clock in the evening under the south end of the island. So we then supposed it to be; but next morning we found it to be a peninsula, united to the continent by a low neck of land, on each side of which the coast forms a bay, which obtained the name of Cape Denbigh.

Several people were seen upon the peninsula, and one man came off in a small canoe. I gave him a knife and a few beads, with which he seemed well pleased. Having made signs to bring us something to eat, he immediately left us, and paddled towards the shore; but meeting another man coming off who happened to have two dried salmon, he got them, and would give them to nobody but me.

Lieutenant Gore being now sent to the peninsula, reported that there was but little fresh water, and that wood was difficult to be got at, by reason of the boats grounding at some distance from the beach. This being the case, I stood back to the other shore, and at eight o'clock the next morning I sent all the boats and a party of men with an officer to get wood from the place where I had landed two days before.

Next day a family of the natives came near to our wooding party. I know not how many there were at first, but I saw only the husband, the wife, and their child, and a fourth person who bore the human shape, and that was all, for he was the most deformed cripple I had ever seen.

Iron was their favourite article. For four knives which we had made out of an old iron hoop I got from them near 400 lbs. of fish, which they had caught on this or the preceding day. Some were trout, and the rest were something between a mullet and a herring. I gave the child, who was a girl, a few beads, on which the mother burst into tears, then the father, then the cripple, and at last, to complete the concert, the girl herself.

Before night we had the ship amply supplied with wood, and had carried on board above twelve tons of water to each. Some doubts being still entertained whether the coast we were now upon belonged to an island or the American continent, and the shallowness of the water putting it out of our power to determine this with our ships, I sent Lieutenant King with two boats under his command to make such searches as might leave no room for a variety of opinions on the subject. This officer returned from his expedition on the 16th, and reported that he proceeded with the boats about three or four leagues farther than the ships had been able to go; that he then landed on the west side; that from the heights he could see the two coasts join, and the inlet terminate in a small river or creek, before which were banks of sand or mud, and everywhere shoal water. From the elevated spot on which Mr. King surveyed the sound he could distinguish many extensive valleys, with rivers running through them, well wooded and bounded by hills of a gentle ascent and moderate height. In honour of Sir Fletcher Norton, Speaker of the House of Commons, and Mr. King's near relative, I named this inlet Norton's Sound.

Having now fully satisfied myself that Mr. Stæhlin's map must be erroneous, and having restored the American continent to that space which he had occupied with his imaginary island of Alaschka, it was high time to think of leaving these northern regions, and to retire to some place during the winter, where I might procure some refreshments for my people and a small supply of provisions. Petropaulowska, or the harbour of St. Peter and St. Paul, in Kamtchatka, did not appear likely to furnish the one or the other for so large a number of men.

I had besides other reasons for not repairing thither at this time. The first, and on which all the others depended, was the great dislike I had to lie inactive for six or seven months, which would have been the necessary consequence of wintering in any of these northern parts. No place was so conveniently within our reach, where we could expect to have our wants relieved, as the Sandwich Islands. To them therefore I determined to proceed.

But before this could be carried into execution a supply of water was necessary. With this view I resolved to search the American coast for a harbour. If I failed, my plan was then to proceed to Samganoodha, which was fixed upon as our place of rendezvous in case of separation.

October.   On the 2nd of October, at daybreak, we saw the island of Oonalashka, bearing south east, and as all harbours were alike to me, provided they were equally safe and convenient, I hauled into a bay, but finding very deep water, we were glad to get out again. The natives, many of whom lived here, visited us at different times, bringing with them dried salmon and other fish, which they exchanged with the seamen for tobacco. A few days before every ounce of tobacco that was in the ships had been distributed among them, and the quantity was not half sufficient to answer their demands. Notwithstanding this, so improvident a creature is an English sailor, that they were as profuse in making their bargains as if they were in a port of Virginia, so that in less than eight-and-forty hours the value of this article of barter was lowered above one thousand per cent.

Next morning the carpenters of both ships were set to work. Many of the seams were found quite open, so that it was no wonder that much water had found its way into the ship. While we lay here we cleared the fish and spirit rooms, and besides this work, and completing our water, we cleared the forehold to the very bottom, and took in a quantity of ballast. In order to avail ourselves as much as possible of refreshments, one-third of the people by turns had leave to go and pick berries, so that if there were any seeds of the scurvy those berries, and the use of spruce beer, which they had to drink every other day, effectually eradicated them. We also got plenty of fish, chiefly salmon-trout and halibut.

On the 14th, in the evening, while Mr. Webber and I were at a village a small distance from Samganoodha, a Russian landed there, who I found was the principal person among his countrymen in this and the neighbouring islands. Ismyloff, as he was called, arrived in a canoe carrying three persons, attended by twenty or thirty other canoes, each conducted by one man. I took notice that the first thing they did after landing was to make a small tent for Ismyloff of materials which they brought with them, and then they made others for themselves of their canoes and paddles, which they covered with grass, so that the people of the village were at no trouble to find them lodging. Ismyloff, having invited us into his tent, set before us some dried salmon and berries, which I was satisfied was the best cheer he had. He appeared to be a sensible, intelligent man, and I felt no small mortification in not being able to converse with him unless by signs, assisted by figures and other characters, which, however, were a very great help. I desired to see him on board the next day, and accordingly he came, with all his attendants. Indeed, he had moved into our neighbourhood for the express purpose of waiting upon us.

I found that he was very well acquainted with the geography of these parts, and with all the recent discoveries of the Russians. On seeing the modern maps, he at once pointed out their errors.

Both Ismyloff and the others affirmed that they knew nothing of the continent of America to the northward, and they called it by the same name which Mr. Stæhlin gives to his great island— that is, Alaschka. From what we could gather from Ismyloff and his countrymen, the Russians have made several attempts to get a footing upon that part of this continent that lies contiguous to Oonalashka and the adjoining islands, but have always been repelled by the natives, whom they describe as a very treacherous people. They mentioned two or three captains or chief men who had been murdered by them, and some of the Russians showed us wounds which they said they had received there.

In the following afternoon M. Ismyloff, after dining with Captain Clerke, left us with all his retinue, promising to return in a few days. Accordingly, on the 19th, he paid us another visit, and brought with him the charts, which he allowed me to copy. He remained with us till the evening of the 21st, when he took his final leave. To his care I entrusted a letter* to the Lords Commissioners of the Admiralty, in which was enclosed a chart of all the northern coasts I had visited. He said there would be an opportunity of sending it to Kamtchatka or to Okotsk the ensuing spring, and that it would be at St. Petersburg the following winter. He gave me a letter to Major Behm, governor of Kamtchatka, and another to the commanding officer at Petropaulowska.

As we became acquainted with these Russians, some of our gentlemen at different times visited their settlement on the island, where they always met with a hearty welcome. This settlement consisted of a dwelling-house and two store-houses.

The island supplies them with food, and in a great measure with clothing. This consists chiefly of skins; the upper garment

* This letter reached its destination in safety, and may be found in the Admiralty archives among the other papers of the great navigator.

is made like our waggoner's frock, and reaches as low as the knee. Besides this they wear a waistcoat or two, a pair of breeches, a fur cap, and a pair of boots, the soles and upper leathers of which are of Russian leather; but the legs are made of some kind of strong gut. Their two chiefs, Ismyloff and Ivanovitch, wore each a calico frock, and they, as well as some others had shirts which were of silk.

There are Russians settled upon all the principal islands between Oonalashka and Kamtchatka, for the sole purpose of collecting furs. Their great object is the sea-beaver or otter. I never heard them inquire after any other animal, though those whose skins are of superior value also form part of their cargoes.

To all appearance the natives are the most peaceable, inoffensive people I ever met with; and as to honesty, they might serve as a pattern to the most civilized nation upon earth. The natives have their own chiefs in each island, and seem to enjoy liberty and property unmolested, but whether or not they are tributaries to the Russians we could never find out.

These people are rather low of stature, but plump and well shaped, with rather short necks, swarthy, chubby faces, black eyes, small beards, and long straight black hair, which the men wear loose behind and cut before, but the women tie up in a bunch. Both sexes wear the same dresses in fashion; the only difference is in the materials. The women's frock is made of seal-skin, and that of the men of the skins of birds, both reaching below the knee. This is the whole dress of the women, but the men wear over the frock another made of gut, which resists water, and has a hood to it, which draws over the head. Some of them wear boots, and all of them have a kind of cap made of wood, with a rim to admit the head. These caps are dyed with green and other colours, and round the upper part of the rim are stuck the long bristles of some sea animal, on which are strung glass beads, and on the front is a small image or two made of bone.

They make use of no paint, but the women puncture their faces slightly, and both men and women bore the under lip, to which they fix pieces of bone. Their food consists of flesh, sea animals, birds, roots, and berries, and even of seaweed. They dry large quantities of fish in summer, which they lay up in small huts for winter use. They eat everything raw. Boiling and broiling were the only methods of cookery that I saw them make use of, and the first was probably learned from the Russians. Some have got little brass kettles, and those who have not make one of a flat stone, with sides of clay.

I was once present when the chief of Oonalashka made his dinner of the raw head of a large halibut, just caught. Before any was given to the chief, two of his servants ate the gills, without any other dressing than squeezing out the slime. This done, one of them cut off the head of the fish, took it to the sea and washed it, then came with it and sat down by the chief, first pulling up some grass, upon a part of which the head was laid, and the rest was strewed before the chief. He then cut large pieces off the cheeks, and laid them within the reach of the great man, who swallowed them with as much satisfaction as we should do raw oysters. When he had done, the remains of the head were cut in pieces and given to the attendants, who tore off the meat with their teeth, gnawing the bones like so many dogs.

There are few, if any of them, that do not both smoke and chew tobacco and take snuff. They did not seem to wish for much iron, or to want any instrument except sewing needles, their own being made of bone. I saw not a fireplace in any of their houses. They are lighted, as well as heated, by lamps, which are simple, and yet answer the purpose very well. They produce fire both by collision and by attrition, the former by striking two stones one against another, on one of which a good deal of brimstone is first rubbed; the latter method is with two pieces of wood, one of which is a stick about eighteen inches in length, and the other a flat piece. The pointed end of the stick they press upon the other, whirling it nimbly round as a drill, thus producing fire in a few minutes. This method is common in many parts of the world. It is practised by the Kamtchadales, by these people, by the Greenlanders, by the Brazilians, by the Otaheiteans, by the New Hollanders, and probably by many other nations.

The canoes made use of by the natives are the smallest we had anywhere seen upon the American coast, though built after the same manner, with some little difference in the construction. The stern of these terminates a little abruptly, the head is forked, the upper point of the fork projecting beyond the under one, which is even with the surface of the water; the framing is of slender laths, and the covering of seal-skins. They are about twelve feet long, a foot and a half broad in the middle, and twelve or fourteen inches deep. Upon occasion they can carry two persons, one of whom is stretched at full length in the canoe, and the other sits in the seat or round hole, which is nearly in the middle. Round this hole is a rim or hoop of wood, about which is sewed gut-skin, that can be drawn together or opened like a purse with leathern thongs fitted to the outer edge. The man seats himself in this place, draws the skin tight round his body over his gut-pouch, and brings the end of the thongs or purse-string over the shoulder to keep it in its place. The sleeves of his frock are tied tight round his wrists, and it being close round his neck, and the hood drawn over his head, where it is confined by his cap, water can scarcely penetrate either to his body or into the canoe. If any should, however, insinuate itself, the boatman carries a piece of sponge, with which he dries it up. He uses the double-bladed paddle, which is held by both hands in the middle, striking the water with a quick regular motion, first on one side and then on the other. By this means the canoe is impelled at a great rate, and in a direction as straight as a line can be drawn.

The fishing and hunting implements lie ready upon the canoes, under straps fixed for the purpose. They are all made in great perfection of wood and bone, and differ very little from those used by the Greenlanders, as they are described by Crantz. These people are very expert in striking fish both in the sea and in rivers. They also make use of hooks and lines, nets, and weirs; the hooks are composed of bone, and the lines of sinews.

The people of Oonalashka bury their dead on summits of hills, and raise a little hillock over the grave. In a walk into the country, one of the natives who attended me pointed out several of these receptacles of the dead. There was one of them by the side of the road leading from the harbour to the village, over which was raised a heap of stones. It was observed that every one who passed it added one to it. I saw in the country several stone hillocks that seemed to have been raised by art. Many of them were apparently of great antiquity.

They are remarkably cheerful and friendly amongst each other, and always behaved with great civility to us.

In the morning of Monday, the 26th of October, we put to sea from Samganoodha harbour. My intention was now to proceed to the Sandwich Islands, there to spend a few of the winter months, in case we should meet with the necessary supplies, and then to direct our course to Kamtchatka, so as to endeavour to be there by the middle of May in the ensuing summer. In consequence of this resolution, I gave Captain Clerke orders how to proceed in case of separation, appointing the Sandwich Islands for the first place of rendezvous, and the harbour of Petropaulowska, in Kamtchatka, for the second.

November. At daybreak on the 26th, land was seen extending from SSE. to W. We made sail and stood for it. We were now satisfied that the group of the Sandwich Islands had only been imperfectly discovered, as those of them which we had visited in our progress northward all lie to the leeward of our present station.

In the country was an elevated saddle hill, whose summit appeared above the clouds. From this hill the land fell in a gentle slope, and terminated in a steep rocky coast, against which the sea broke in a dreadful surf. The country seemed to be both well wooded and watered, and running streams were seen falling into the sea in various places. It was not long before we saw people on several parts of the shore, and some houses and plantations.

As soon as they got alongside, many of the people came into the ship without the least hesitation. We found them to be of the same nation with the inhabitants of the islands more to leeward, which we had already visited.

We got from our visitors a quantity of cuttle-fish in exchange for nails and pieces of iron. They brought very little fruit and roots, but told us that they had plenty of them on their island, as also hogs and fowls. In the evening, the horizon being clear to the westward, we judged the westernmost land in sight to be an island, separated from that off which we now were. Having no

MOWEE, SANDWICH ISLANDS. *Page 472.*

doubt that the people would return to the ships next day with the produce of their country, I kept plying all night, and in the morning stood close inshore. At first only a few of the natives visited us, but towards noon we had the company of a good many, who brought bread-fruit, potatoes, tarro or eddy-roots, a few plantains, and small pigs, all of which they exchanged for nails and iron tools; indeed we had nothing else to give them. We continned trading with them till four o'clock in the afternoon, when, having disposed of all their cargoes, and not seeming inclined to fetch more, we made sail and stood off shore. While we were lying-to the wind blew fresh.

In the afternoon of the 30th, being off the north-east end of the island, several canoes came off to the ships. Most of these belonged to a chief named Terreeoboo, who came in one of them. He made me a present of two or three small pigs, and we got by barter from the people a little fruit. After a stay of about two hours they all left us, except six or eight of their company, who chose to remain on board; a double-sailing canoe came soon after to attend upon them, which we towed astern all night. In the evening we discovered another island to windward, which the natives call Owhyhee.* The name of that off which we had been for some days, we were also told, is Mowee.

On the 1st of December, at eight in the morning, finding that we could fetch Owhyhee, I stood for it, and our visitors from Mowee, not choosing to accompany us, embarked in their canoe and went ashore. At seven in the evening we were close up with the north side of Owhyhee, where we spent the night, standing off and on.

December.

In the morning of the 2nd, we were surprised to see the summits of the mountains on Owhyhee covered with snow. As we drew near the shore some of the natives came off to us; they were a little shy at first, but we soon enticed some of them on board, and at last prevailed upon them to return to the island and bring off what we wanted. Soon after they had reached the

---

* The Sandwich Islands, of which Owhyhee or Hawaii is the chief, consists of eight inhabited islands, and two or three rocky and desolate islets. The former are called Woahoo or Oahu, Mowee, Kawai or Atooi, which Cook had already visited; Molokai, Lanai, Niihaw, and Kahoolawe. The whole superficial area is 6,000 square miles, 4,000 of which are comprised in Owhyhee alone.

shore we had company enough, and few coming empty-handed, we got a tolerable supply of small pigs, fruit, and roots. We continued trading with them till the evening, when we made sail and stood off. We resumed trading with the natives on the 6th and 7th, and procured pork, fruit, and roots sufficient for four or five days. We then made sail, and continued to work up to windward.

Having procured a quantity of sugar-cane, and finding that a strong decoction of it produced a very palatable beer, I ordered some more to be brewed for our general use; but when the cask was now broached, not one of my crew would even so much as taste it. As I had no motive in preparing this beverage but to save our spirits for a colder climate, I gave myself no further trouble, either by exerting authority or by having recourse to persuasion to prevail upon them to drink it, knowing that there was no danger of the scurvy so long as we could get a plentiful supply of other vegetables. But, that I might not be thwarted in my views, I gave orders that no grog should be served in either ship. I myself and the officers continued to make use of the sugar-cane beer whenever we could get materials for brewing it. A few hops, of which we had some on board, improved it much. It has the taste of new malt beer, and I believe no one will doubt of its being very wholesome, yet my inconsiderate crew alleged that it was injurious to their health.

They had no better reason to support a resolution which they took on our first arrival in King George's Sound, not to drink the spruce beer made there. But, whether from consideration that it was not the first time of their being required to use that liquor, or from some other reason, they did not attempt to carry their purpose into actual execution, and I had never heard of it until now, when they renewed their ignorant opposition to my best endeavours to serve them. Every innovation whatever on board a ship, though ever so much to the advantage of seamen, is sure to meet with their highest disapprobation. Both portable soup and sour krout were at first condemned as stuff unfit for human beings. Few commanders have introduced into their ships more novelties, as useful varieties of food and drink, than I have done; indeed, few commanders have had the same opportunities of trying such experiments. It has, however, been in a great measure owing to various little deviations from established practice that I have been able to preserve my people, generally speaking, from that dreadful distemper the scurvy, which has perhaps destroyed more of our sailors in their peaceful voyages than have fallen by the enemy in military expeditions.

I kept at some distance from the coast till the 13th, when I stood in again six leagues farther to windward than we had as yet reached, and after having some trade with the natives who visited us, stood out to sea. I now determined to get round, or at least to get a sight of the south-east end of the island, but the wind was variable between the 14th and 18th, blowing sometimes in hard squalls, and at other times calm, with thunder, lightning, and rain.

In the evening it shifted to east by south, and we stood to the southward, close-hauled under easy sail, as the *Discovery* was at some distance astern. At this time the south-east point of the island bore south-west by south about five leagues distant, and I made no doubt that I should be able to weather it. But at one o'clock next morning it fell calm, and we were left to the mercy of a north-easterly swell, which impelled us fast towards the land, so that, long before daybreak, we saw lights and the shore, which was not more than a league distant. The night was dark, with thunder, lightning, and rain.

At three o'clock the calm was succeeded by a breeze, blowing in squalls, with rain, and at daybreak the coast was seen extending from north to south-west, a dreadful surf breaking upon the shore, which was not more than half a league distant. It was evident that we had been in the most imminent danger; nor were we yet in safety, the wind veering more easterly, so that for some time we did but just keep our distance from the coast. What made our situation more alarming was the leech-rope* of the maintopsail giving way, which was the occasion of the sail being rent in two; and the two topgallant sails gave way in the same manner, though not half worn out. By taking a favourable opportunity we soon bent others, and then we left the land astern.

* The leech-rope is that vertical part of the bolt-rope to which the edge of the sail is sewed.

The *Discovery*, by being at some distance to the north, was never near the land, nor did we see her till eight o'clock.

As soon as daylight appeared, the natives ashore displayed a white flag, which we conceived to be a signal of peace and friendship. Some of them ventured out after us, but the wind freshening, and it not being safe to wait, they were soon left astern. In the afternoon, after making an attempt to weather the eastern extreme, which failed, I gave it up, and ran down to the *Discovery*. Indeed, it was of no consequence to get round the island, for we had seen its extent to the south-east, which was the thing I aimed at; and according to the information we had gained from the natives, there is no other island to the windward of this. However, as we were so near the south-east end of it, and as the least shift of wind in our favour would serve to carry us round, I did not wholly give up the idea of weathering it, and therefore continned to ply.

On the 20th, in the afternoon, some of the natives came off in their canoes, bringing with them a few pigs and plantains; but the supply being barely sufficient for one day, I stood in again the next morning, till within three or four miles of the land, where we were met by a number of canoes laden with provisions. We brought to, and continued trading with the people till four in the afternoon, when, having got a pretty good supply, we made sail, and stretched off to the northward.

I had never met with a behaviour so free from reserve and suspicion in my intercourse with any tribes of savages as we experienced in the people of this island. It was very common for them to send up into the ship the several articles they brought off for barter, after which they would come in themselves and make their bargains on the quarter-deck. The people of Otaheite, even after our repeated visits, do not care to put so much confidence in us, whence I infer that those of Owhyhee must be more faithful in their dealings with one another than the inhabitants at Otaheite are; for, if little faith were observed amongst themselves, they would not be so ready to trust strangers. It is also to be observed, to their honour, that they had never once attempted to cheat us in exchanges, nor to commit a theft.

On the 22nd, at four in the afternoon, after purchasing everything that the natives had brought off, we made sail and stretched to the north; and at midnight we tacked and stood to the south-east. Supposing that the *Discovery* would see us tack, the signal was omitted, but she did not see us, as we afterwards found, and continued standing to the north, so that at daylight next morning she was not in sight. At this time, the weather being hazy, we could not see far, so that it was possible the *Discovery* might be following us; and being past the north-east part of the island, I was tempted to stand on, till, by the wind veering to north-east, we could not weather the land upon the other tack. Consequently we could not stand to the north to join or look for the *Discovery*. At six in the evening we had succeeded in getting to windward of the island, which we had aimed at with so much perseverance. The *Discovery*, however, was not yet to be seen; but the wind, as we had it, being very favourable for her to follow us, I concluded that it would not be long before she joined us; I therefore kept cruising off this south-east point of the island till I was satisfied that Captain Clerke would not join me here. I now conjectured that he had not been able to weather the north-east part of the island, and had gone to leeward, in order to meet me that way.

As I generally kept from five to ten leagues from the land, no canoes except one came off to us till the 28th, when we were visited by a dozen or fourteen.

On the morning of the 5th of January 1779, we passed the south point of the island, on which stands a pretty large village, the inhabitants of which thronged off to the ship with hogs. As I had now got a quantity of salt I purchased no hogs but such as were fit for salting, refusing all that were under size; however, we could seldom get any above fifty or sixty pounds weight. It was happy for us that we had still some vegetables on board, for we now received few such productions; indeed, this part of the country, from its appearance, did not seem capable of affording them. Marks of its having been laid waste by the explosion of a volcano everywhere presented themselves, and though we had as yet seen nothing like one upon the island, the devastation that it had made in this neighbourhood was visible to the naked eye.

The next morning the natives visited us again, bringing with them the same articles of commerce as before. Being now near the shore, I sent Mr. Bligh, the master, in a boat to sound the coast, with orders to land and to look for fresh water. Upon his return he reported that he found no running stream, but only rain water deposited in holes upon the rocks, and even that was brackish from the spray of the sea, and that the surface of the country was ·entirely composed of slags and ashes, with a few plants interspersed. Between ten and eleven we saw with pleasure the *Discovery* coming round the south point of the island, and at one in the afternoon she joined us. Captain Clerke coming on board, informed me that he had cruised four or five days where we were separated, and then worked round the east side of the island, but that, meeting with unfavourable winds, he had been carried to some distance from the coast. He had one of the islanders on board all the time, who had remained there from choice, and had refused to quit the ship, though opportunities offered.

Having spent the night standing off and on, we stood in again the next morning, and when we were about a league from the shore, many of the natives visited us. At daybreak on the 8th, we found that the currents had carried us back considerably to windward, so that we were now off the south-west point of the island. There we brought to, in order to give the natives an opportunity of trading with us. We spent the night as usual, standing off and on, and, at four in the morning of the 11th, the wind being at west, I stood in for the land, in order to get some supplies. We lay to or stood on and off during the next few days, trading with the natives, but got a very scanty supply.

At daybreak on the 16th, seeing the appearance of a bay, I sent Mr. Bligh with a boat from each ship to examine it, being at this time three leagues off. Canoes now began to arrive from all parts, so that before ten o'clock there were not fewer than a thousand about the two ships, most of them crowded with people, and well laden with hogs and other productions of the island. We had the most satisfying proof of their friendly intentions, for we did not see a single person who had with him a weapon of any sort. Trade and curiosity alone had brought them off. Among such numbers as we had at that time on board, it is no wonder that some should betray a thievish disposition. One of our visitors took out of the ship a boat's rudder. He was discovered, but too late to recover it. I thought this a good opportunity to show these people the use of firearms, and two or three muskets, and as many four-pounders, were fired over the canoe which carried off the rudder. As it was not intended that any of the shot should take effect, the surrounding multitude of natives seemed rather more surprised than frightened. In the evening Mr. Bligh returned, and reported that he had found a bay in which was good anchorage and fresh water in a situation tolerably easy of access. Into this bay I resolved to carry the ships, there to refit and supply ourselves with every refreshment that the place could afford. As night approached, the greater part of our visitors retired to the shore, but numbers of them requested our permission to sleep on board. Curiosity was not the only motive, at least with some, for the next morning several things were missing, which determined me not to entertain so many another night.

At eleven o'clock in the forenoon we anchored in a bay which is called by the natives **Karakakooa**, in thirteen fathoms of water, and about a quarter of a mile from the north-east shore. The ships continued to be much crowded with natives, and were surrounded by a multitude of canoes. I had nowhere in the course of my voyages seen so numerous a body of people assembled at one place, for, besides those who had come off to us in canoes, all the shore of the bay was covered with spectators, and many hundreds were swimming round the ships like shoals of fish. We could not but be struck with the singularity of this scene, and perhaps there were few on board who now lamented our having failed in our endeavours to find a northern passage homeward last summer. To this disappointment we owed our having it in our power to revisit the Sandwich Islands, and to enrich our voyage with a discovery which, though the last, seemed in many respects to be the most important that had hitherto been made by Europeans throughout the extent of the Pacific Ocean.

(Here Captain Cook's journal ends. The remaining transactions of the voyage are related by Captain King.)

CHAPTER XLVI.

DESCRIPTION OF KARAKAKOOA BAY—VAST CONCOURSE OF NATIVES—VISIT FROM KOAH—THE MORAI AT KAKOOA DESCRIBED—CEREMONIES AT THE LANDING OF CAPTAIN COOK—RECEPTION OF CAPTAIN COOK—ARRIVAL OF TERREEOBOO, KING OF THE ISLAND—VISIT FROM THE KING—RETURNED BY CAPTAIN COOK.

KARAKAKOOA BAY is situated on the west side of the island of Owhyhee, in a district called Akona. It is about a mile in depth, and bounded by the low points of land distant half a league from each other. On the north point, which is flat and barren, stands the village of Kowrowa; and in the bottom of the bay, near a grove of tall cocoa-nut trees, there is another village of a more considerable size, called Kakooa; between them runs a high rocky cliff, inaccessible from the sea-shore. On the south side the coast, for about a mile inland, has a rugged appearance, beyond which the country rises with a gradual ascent, and is overspread with cultivated enclosures and groves of cocoa-nut trees, where the habitations of the natives are scattered in great numbers. The shore all round the bay is covered with a black coral rock, which makes the landing very dangerous in rough weather, except at the village of Kakooa, where there is a fine sandy beach with a morai, or burying-place, at one extremity, and a small well of fresh water at the other. This bay appearing to Captain Cook a proper place to refit the ships and lay in an additional supply of water and provisions, we moored on the north side, about a quarter of a mile from the shore.

As soon as the inhabitants perceived our intention of anchoring in the bay they came off from the shore in astonishing numbers, and expressed their joy by singing and shouting, and exhibiting a variety of wild and extravagant gestures. The sides, the decks, and rigging of both ships were soon completely covered with them, and a multitude of women and boys, who had not been able to get canoes, came swimming round us in shoals; many of them not finding room on board, remained the whole day playing in the water.

Among the chiefs who came on board the *Resolution* was a young man called Pareea, whom we soon perceived to be a person of great authority. On presenting himself to Captain Cook, he told him that he was a "Jakanee" to the king of the island, who was at that time engaged in a military expedition at Mowee, and was expected to return within three or four days. A few presents from Captain Cook attached him entirely to our interests, and he became exceedingly useful to us in the management of his countrymen, as we had soon occasion to experience. For we had not been long at anchor when it was observed that the *Discovery* had such a number of people hanging on one side, as occasioned her to heel considerably, and that the men were unable to keep off the crowds which continued pressing into her. Captain Cook being apprehensive that she might suffer some injury, pointed out the danger to Pareea, who immediately went to their assistance, cleared the ship of its encumbrances, and drove away the canoes that surrounded her.

The authority of the chief over the inferior people appeared from this incident to be of the most despotic kind. A similar instance of it happened the same day on board the *Resolution*, when the crowd being so great as to impede the necessary business of the ship, we were obliged to have recourse to the assistance of Kaneena, another of their chiefs, who had likewise attached himself to Captain Cook. The inconvenience we laboured under being made known, he immediately ordered his countrymen to quit the vessel, and we were not a little surprised to see them jump overboard, without a moment's hesitation, all except one man, who, loitering behind and showing some unwillingness to obey, Kaneena took him up in his arms and threw him into the sea.

Both these chiefs were men of strong and well-proportioned bodies, and of countenances remarkably pleasing. Kaneena especially, whose portrait was drawn by Mr. Webber, was one of the finest men I ever saw. He was about six feet high, had regular and expressive features, with lively, dark eyes, and his carriage was easy, firm, and graceful.

It has been already mentioned, that during our long cruise near this island the inhabitants had always behaved with fairness and honesty in their dealings, and had not shown the slightest propensity to theft, which appeared to us the more extraordinary because those with whom we had hitherto held any intercourse were of the lowest rank, either servants or fishermen. We now found the case exceedingly altered: the immense crowd of islanders which blocked up every part of the ships not only afforded frequent opportunity of pilfering without risk of discovery, but our inferiority in numbers held forth a prospect of escaping with impunity, in case of detection. Another circumstance, to which we attributed this alteration in their behaviour, was the presence and encouragement of their chiefs; for, generally tracing the booty into the possession of some men of consequence, we had the strongest reason to suspect that these depredations were committed at their instigation.

Soon after the *Resolution* had got into her station, our two friends, Pareea and Kaneena, brought on board a third chief, named Koah, who, we were told, was a priest, and had been in his youth a distinguished warrior. He was a little old man, of an emaciated figure, his eyes exceedingly sore and red, and his body covered with a white leprous scurf, the effects of an immoderate use of the ava. Being led into the cabin, he approached Captain Cook with great veneration, and threw over his shoulders a piece of red cloth, which he had brought along with him; then, stepping a few paces back, he made an offering of a small pig, which he held in his hand whilst he pronounced a discourse that lasted for a considerable time. This ceremony was frequently repeated during our stay at Owhyhee, and appeared to us, from many circumstances, to be a sort of religious adoration. Their idols we found always arrayed with red cloth, in the same manner as was done to Captain Cook, and a small pig was their usual offering to the Eatooas. Their speeches, or prayers, were muttered, too, with a readiness and volubility that indicated them to be according to some formulary.

When this ceremony was over, Koah dined with Captain Cook, eating plentifully of what was set before him, but, like the rest of the inhabitants in these seas, could scarcely be prevailed upon to taste, a second time, our wine or spirits. In the evening, Captain Cook, attended by Mr. Bayley and myself, accompanied him on shore. We landed at the beach, and were received by four men, who carried wands tipped with dogs' hair, and marched before us, pronouncing, with a loud voice, a short sentence, in which we could only distinguish the word "Orono." * Captain Cook generally went by this name amongst the natives of Owhyhee, but we could never learn its precise meaning; sometimes they applied it to an invisible being, who, they said, lived in the heavens; and we also found that it was a title belonging to a personage of great rank or power in the island. The crowd which had been collected on the shore retired at our approach, and not a person was to be seen, except a few lying prostrate on the ground, near the huts of the adjoining village.

Before I proceed to relate the adoration that was paid to Captain Cook, and the peculiar ceremonies with which he was received on this fatal island, it will be necessary to describe the morai, situated as I have already mentioned, at the south side of the beach at Kakooa. It was a square, solid pile of stones, about forty yards long, twenty broad, and fourteen in height; the top was flat and well paved, and surrounded by a wooden rail, on which were fixed the skulls of the captives sacrificed on the death of their chiefs. In the centre of the area stood a ruinous old building of wood, connected with the rail on each side by a stone wall, which divided the whole space into two parts. On the side next the country were five poles, upwards of twenty feet high, supporting an irregular kind of scaffold; on the opposite side, towards the sea, stood two small houses with a covered communication.

We were conducted by Koah to the top of this pile by an easy ascent leading from the beach to the north-west corner of the area. At the entrance we saw two large wooden images, with

---

* Mr. S. S. Hill, in his "Travels in the Sandwich and Society Islands," says that the natives call Captain Cook "Lono," and entertain the greatest veneration for his memory. It appears that, at the time of Cook's visit, there were traditions among the people concerning the life and actions of some wonderful person named Lono, who had long since suddenly disappeared—supposed to be blown off the coast in his canoe—but who, it was believed, would one day reappear. Though several generations had passed away, Captain Cook was supposed to be this Lono; and, though their god or hero was transformed to a white man, accompanied by men of another race as his subjects, and without any recollection of his former language, yet the supernatural resuscitation and return of their hero gave rise to no inquiry or surprise.

features violently distorted, and a long piece of carved wood, of a conical form inverted, rising from the top of their heads; the rest was without form, and wrapped round with red cloth. We were here met by a tall young man with a long beard, who presented Captain Cook to the images, and, after chanting a kind of hymn, in which he was joined by Koah, they led us to that end of the morai where the five poles were fixed. At the foot of them were twelve images ranged in a semicircular form, and before the middle figure stood a high stand or table, exactly resembling the "whatta" of Otaheite, on which lay a putrid hog, and under it pieces of sugar-cane, cocoa-nuts, bread-fruit, plantains, and sweet potatoes. Koah having placed the captain under this stand, took down the hog, and held it toward him; and after having a second time addressed him in a long speech, pronounced with much vehemence and rapidity, he let it fall to the ground, and led him to the scaffolding, which they began to climb together, not without great risk of falling. At this time we saw coming in solemn procession, at the entrance of the top of the morai, ten men carrying a live hog and a large piece of red cloth. Having advanced a few paces, they stopped and prostrated themselves, and Kaireekeea, the young man above mentioned, went to them and receiving the cloth, carried it to Koah, who wrapped it round the captain, and afterwards offered him the hog which was brought by Kaireekeea with the same ceremony.

Whilst Captain Cook was aloft in this awkward situation, swathed round with red cloth, and with difficulty keeping his hold amongst the pieces of rotten scaffolding, Kaireekeea and Koah began their office, chanting sometimes in concert, and sometimes alternately. This lasted a considerable time; at length Koah let the hog drop, when he and the captain descended together. He then led him to the images before mentioned, and having said something to each in a sneering tone, snapping his fingers at them as he passed, he brought him to that in the centre, which, from its being covered with red cloth, appeared to be in greater estimation than the rest. Before this figure he prostrated himself and kissed it, desiring Captain Cook to do the same, who suffered himself to be directed by Koah throughout the whole of this ceremony.

We were now led back into the other division of the morai, where there was a space ten or twelve feet square, sunk about three feet below the level of the area. Into this we descended, and Captain Cook was seated between two wooden idols, Koah supporting one of his arms, whilst I was desired to support the other. At this time arrived a second procession of natives, carrying a baked hog and a pudding, some bread-fruit, cocoa-nuts, and other vegetables. When they approached us, Kaireekeea put himself at their head, and presenting the pig to Captain Cook in the usual manner, began the kind of chant as before, his companions making regular responses. We observed that, after every response, their parts became gradually shorter, till, toward the close, Kaireekeea's consisted of only two or three words, which the rest answered by the word Orono.

When this offering was concluded, which lasted a quarter of an hour, the natives sat down fronting us, and began to cut up the baked hog, to peel the vegetables, and break the cocoa-nuts; whilst others employed themselves in brewing the ava, which is done by chewing it in the same manner as at the Friendly Islands. Kaireekeea then took part of the kernel of a cocoa-nut, which he chewed, and wrapping it in a piece of cloth, rubbed with it the captain's face, head, hands, arms, and shoulders. The ava was then handed round, and after we had tasted it, Koah and Pareea began to pull the flesh of the hog in pieces, and to put it into our mouths. I had no great objection to being fed by Pareea, who was very cleanly in his person; but Captain Cook, who was served by Koah, recollecting the putrid hog, could not swallow a morsel, and his reluctance, as may be supposed, was not diminished, when the old man, according to his own mode of civility, had chewed it for him.

When this last ceremony was finished, which Captain Cook put an end to as soon as he decently could, we quitted the morai, after distributing amongst the people some pieces of iron and other trifles, with which they seemed highly gratified. The men with wands conducted us to the boats, repeating the same words as before. The people again retired, and the few that remained prostrated themselves as we passed along the shore. We immediately went on board, our minds full of what we had seen, and extremely well satisfied with the good disposition of our new friends. The meaning of the various ceremonies with which we had been received, and which, on account of their novelty and singularity, have been related at length, can only be the subject of conjectures, and those uncertain and partial; they were, however, without doubt, expressive of high respect on the part of the natives, and, as far as related to the person of Captain Cook, they seemed approaching to adoration.

The next morning I went on shore, with a guard of eight marines, including the corporal and lieutenant, having orders to erect the observatory on the most suitable spot for superintending and protecting the waterers and the other working parties that were to be on shore. As we were viewing a spot conveniently situated for this purpose in the middle of the village, Pareea, who was always ready to show his power and his goodwill, offered to pull down some houses that would have obstructed our observations. However, we thought it proper to decline this offer, and fixed on a field of sweet potatoes, adjoining the morai, which was readily granted to us; and the priests, to prevent the intrusion of the natives, immediately consecrated the place by fixing their wands round the wall by which it was enclosed.

This sort of religious interdiction they call "taboo,"* a word we heard often repeated during our stay amongst these islanders, and found to be of very powerful and extensive operation, and it procured us even more privacy than we desired. No canoes ever presumed to land near us; the natives sat on the wall, but none offered to come within the tabooed space till he had obtained our permission.

But though the men, at our request, would come across the field with provisions, yet not all our endeavours could prevail on the women to approach us. Presents were tried, but without effect. Pareea and Koah were tempted to bring them, but in vain. We were invariably answered that the Eatooa and Terreeoboo (which was the name of their king) would kill them. This circumstance afforded no small matter of amusement to our friends on board, where the crowds of people, and particularly of

* This word "taboo," which, as we have seen, is in use both in the Friendly and Sandwich Islands, has been Anglicized; and to taboo a thing is to forbid or interdict it.

women, that continued to flock thither obliged them almost every hour to clear the vessel, in order to have room to do the necessary duties of the ship. On these occasions two or three hundred women were frequently made to jump into the water at once, where they continued swimming and playing about till they could again procure admittance.

From the 19th to the 24th, when Farcea and Koah left us to attend Terreeoboo, who had landed on some other part of the island, nothing very material happened on board. The calkers were set to work on the sides of the ships, and the rigging was carefully overhauled and repaired. The salting of hogs for sea store was also one of the principal objects of Captain Cook's attention, and met with complete success.

We had not long been settled on shore at the observatory before we discovered, in our neighbourhood, the habitations of a society of priests, whose regular attendance at this morai had excited our curiosity. Their huts stood round a pond of water, and were surrounded by a grove of cocoa-nut trees, which separated them from the beach and the rest of the village, and gave the place an air of religious retirement. On my acquainting Captain Cook with these circumstances, he resolved to pay them a visit, and as he expected to be received in the same manner as before, he brought Mr. Webber with him to make a drawing of the ceremony.

On his arrival at the beach he was conducted to a sacred building called Harre-no-Orono, or the house of Orono, and seated before the entrance at the foot of a wooden idol, of the same kind with those in the morai. I was here again made to support one of his arms, and, after wrapping him in red cloth, Kaireekeea, accompanied by twelve priests, made an offering of a pig with the usual solemnities. The pig was then strangled, and a fire being kindled, it was thrown into the embers, and after the hair was singed off, it was again presented, with a repetition of the chanting, in the manner before described. The dead pig was then held for a short time under the captain's nose, after which it was laid with a cocoa-nut at his feet, and the performers sat down. The ava was then brewed and handed round; a fat hog, ready dressed, was brought in, and we were fed as before.

During the rest of the time we remained in the bay, whenever Captain Cook came on shore he was attended by one of these priests, who went before him, giving notice that the Orono had landed, and ordering the people to prostrate themselves. The same person also constantly accompanied him on the water, standing in the bow of the boat, with a wand in his hand, and giving notice of his approach to the natives, who were in canoes, on which they immediately left off paddling, and lay down on their faces till he had passed. Whenever he stopped at the observatory, Kaireekeca. and his brethren immediately made their appearance with hogs, cocoa-nuts, bread-fruit, etc., and presented them with the usual solemnities. It was on these occasions that some of the inferior chiefs frequently requested to be permitted to make an offering to the Orono. When this was granted, they presented the hog themselves, generally with evident marks of fear in their countenances, whilst Kaireekeea and the priests chanted their accustomed hymns.

The civilities of this society were not, however, confined to mere ceremony and parade. Our party on shore received from them every day a constant supply of hogs and vegetables, more than sufficient for our subsistence; and several canoes, loaded with provisions, were sent to the ships with the same punctuality. No return was ever demanded or even hinted at in the most distant manner. Their presents were made with a regularity more like the discharge of a religious duty than the effort of mere liberality; and when we inquired at whose charge all this munificence was displayed, we were told it was at the expense of a great man called Kaoo, the chief of the priests, and grandfather of Kaireekeea, who was at that time absent, attending the king of the island.

As everything relating to the character and behaviour of this people must be interesting to the reader, on account of the tragedy that was afterwards acted here, it will be proper to acquaint him that we had not always so much reason to be satisfied with the conduct of the warrior chiefs, or Earees, as with that of the priests. In all our dealings with the former we found them sufficiently attentive to their own interests; and besides their habit of stealing, which may admit of some excuse from the universality of the practice amongst the islanders of these seas, they made use of other artifices equally dishonourable.

I shall only mention one instance in which we discovered, with regret, our friend Koah to be a party principally concerned. As the chiefs who brought us presents of hogs were always sent back handsomely rewarded, we had generally a greater supply than we could make use of. On these occasions Koah, who never failed in his attendance on us, used to beg such as we did not want, and they were always given to him. It one day happened that a pig was presented to us by a man whom Koah himself introduced as a chief who was desirous of paying his respects, and we recollected the pig to be the same that had been given to Koah just before. This leading us to suspect some trick, we found, on further inquiry, the pretended chief to be an ordinary person; and on connecting this with other circumstances, we had reason to suspect that it was not the first time we had been the dupes of the like imposition.

Things continued in this state till the 24th, when we were a good deal surprised to find that no canoes were suffered to put off from the shore, and that the natives kept close to their houses. After several hours' suspense, we learned that the bay was tabooed, and all intercourse with us interdicted on account of the arrival of Terreeoboo. As we had not foreseen an accident of this sort, the crews of both ships were obliged to pass the day without their usual supply of vegetables. The next morning, therefore, they endeavoured, both by threats and promises, to induce the natives to come alongside, and, as some of them were at last venturing to put off, a chief was observed attempting to-drive them away. A musket was immediately fired over his head to make him desist, which had the desired effect, and supplies were soon after purchased as usual. In the afternoon Terreeoboo arrived, and visited the ships in a private manner, attended only by one canoe, in which were his wife and children. He stayed on board till near ten o'clock, when he returned to the village of Kowrowa.

The next day, about noon, the king, in a large canoe attended by two others, set out from the village, and paddled towards the ships in great state. Their appearance was grand and magnificent. In the first canoe was Terreeoboo and chiefs, dressed in their rich feathered cloaks and helmets, and armed with long spears and daggers; in the second canoe the venerable Kaoo, the chief of the priests, and his brethren, with their idols displayed on red cloth. These idols were busts of a gigantic size, made of wickerwork, and curiously covered with small feathers of various colours, wrought in the same manner as their cloaks. Their eyes were made of large pearl oysters, with a black nut fixed in the centre; their mouths were set with a double row of the fangs of dogs, and, together with the rest of their features, were strangely distorted. The third canoe was filled with hogs and various sorts of vegetables. As they went along, the priests in the centre canoe sung their hymns with great solemnity, and, after paddling round the ships, instead of going on board, as was expected, they made towards the shore at the beach where we were stationed. As soon as I saw them approaching, I ordered out our little guard to receive the king; and Captain Cook, perceiving that he was going on shore, followed him and arrived nearly at the same time. We conducted them into the tent, where they had scarcely been seated, when the king rose up, and, in a very graceful manner, threw over the captain's shoulders the cloak he himself wore, put a feathered helmet upon his head and a curious fan into his hand. He also spread at his feet five or six other cloaks, all exceedingly beautiful, and of the greatest value. His attendants then brought four very large hogs, with sugar-canes, cocoa-nuts, and bread-fruit; and this part of the ceremony was concluded by the king exchanging names with Captain Cook, which, amongst all the islanders of the Pacific Ocean, is esteemed the strongest pledge of friendship. A procession of priests, with a venerable old personage at their head, now appeared, followed by a long train of men leading large hogs, and others carrying plantains, sweet potatoes, and other articles of food. By the looks and gestures of Kiareekeea, I immediately knew the old man to be the chief of the priests before mentioned, on whose bounty we had so long subsisted. He had a piece of red cloth in his hands, which he wrapped round Captain Cook's shoulders, and afterward presented him with a small pig in the usual form. A seat was then made for him next to the king, after which Kaireekeea and his followers began their ceremonies, Kaoo and the chiefs joining in the responses.

I was surprised to see, in the person of this king, the same infirm and emaciated old man that came on board the *Resolution* when we were off the north-east side of the island of Mowee, and we soon discovered amongst his attendants most of the persons who at that time had remained with us all night. Of this number were the two younger sons of the king, the eldest of whom was sixteen years of age, and his nephew, Maiha-Maiha, whom at first we had some difficulty in recollecting, his hair being plastered over with a dirty brown paste and powder, which was no mean heightening to the most savage face I ever beheld. As soon as the formalities of the meeting were over, Captain Cook carried Terreeoboo, and as many chiefs as the pinnace would hold, on board the *Resolution*. They were received with every mark of respect that could be shown them; and Captain Cook, in return for the feathered cloak, put a linen shirt on the king, and girt his own hanger round him. The ancient Kaoo and about half a dozen old chiefs remained on shore and took up their abode at the priests' houses. During all this time not a canoe was seen in the bay, and the natives either kept within their huts, or lay prostrate on the ground. Before the king left the *Resolution*, Captain Cook obtained leave for the natives to come and trade with the ships as usual; but the women, for what reason we could not learn, still continued under the effects of the taboo.

CHAPTER XLVII.

FURTHER TRANSACTIONS WITH THE NATIVES—THEIR HOSPITALITY—DEATH OF ONE OF OUR SEAMEN—THE WOODWORK AND IMAGES ON THE MORAI PURCHASED—MAGNIFICENT PRESENTS OF TERREEOBOO TO CAPTAIN COOK—THE SHIPS LEAVE THE ISLAND—THE "RESOLUTION" DAMAGED IN A GALE AND OBLIGED TO RETURN.

THE quiet and inoffensive behaviour of the natives having taken away every apprehension of danger, we did not hesitate to trust ourselves amongst them at all times and in all situations. The officers of both ships went daily up the country in small parties, or even singly, and frequently remained out the whole night. It would be endless to recount all the instances of kindness and civility which we received upon these occasions. Wherever we went the people flocked about us, eager to offer every assistance in their power, and highly gratified if their services were accepted. Various little arts were practised to attract our notice, or to delay our departure. The boys and girls ran before us as we walked through the villages, and stopped us at every opening where there was room to form a group for dancing. At one time we were invited to accept a draught of cocoa-nut milk, or some other refreshment, under the shade of their huts; at another we were seated within a circle of young women, who exerted all their skill and agility to amuse us with songs and dances.

The satisfaction we derived from their gentleness and hospitality was, however, frequently interrupted by the propensity to stealing which they have in common with all the other islanders of these seas. This circumstance was the more distressing as it sometimes obliged us to have recourse to acts of severity, which we would willingly have avoided if the necessity of the case had not absolutely called for them. Some of their most expert swimmers were one day discovered under the ships, drawing out the filling-nails of the sheathing, which they performed very dexterously, by means of a short stick with a flint stone fixed in the end of it. To put a stop to this practice, which endangered the very existence of the vessels, we at first fired small shot at the offenders, but they easily got out of our reach by diving under the ship's bottom. It was therefore found necessary to make an example by flogging one of them on board the *Discovery*.

About this time a large party of gentlemen, from both ships, set out on an excursion into the interior of the country, with a view of examining its natural productions. It afforded Kaoo a fresh opportunity of showing his attention and generosity; for as soon as he was informed of their departure he sent a large supply of provisions after them, together with orders that the inhabitants of the country through which they were to pass should give them every assistance in their power; and, to complete the delicacy and disinterestedness of his conduct, even the people he employed could not be prevailed on to accept the smallest present. After remaining out six days our officers returned, without having been able to penetrate above twenty miles into the island, partly from want of proper guides, and partly from the impracticability of the country.

The head of the *Resolution's* rudder being found exceedingly shaken, and most of the pintles either loose or broken, it was unhung, and taken on shore on the 27th to undergo a thorough repair. At the same time, the carpenters were sent into the country, under conduct of some of Kaoo's people, to cut planks for the head-rail work, which was also entirely decayed and rotten.

On the 28th Captain Clerke, whose ill health confined him for the most part on board, paid Terreeoboo his first visit at his hut on shore. He was received with the same formalities as were observed towards Captain Cook; and on his coming away, though the visit was quite unexpected, he received a present of thirty large hogs, and as much fruit and roots as his crew could consume in a week.

As we had not seen anything of their sports or athletic exercises, the natives, at the request of some of our officers, entertained us this evening with a boxing match. Though these games were much inferior, as well in point of solemnity and magnificence as in the skill and prowess of the combatants, to what we had seen exhibited at the Friendly Islands, yet, as they differed in some particulars, it may not be improper to give a short account of them. We found a vast concourse of people assembled on a level spot of ground, at a little distance from our tents. A long space was left vacant in the midst of them, at the upper end of which sat the judges, under three standards, from which hung slips of cloth of various colours, the skins of wild geese, a few small birds, and bunches of feathers. When the sports were ready to begin, the signal was given by the judges, and immediately two combatants appeared. They came forward slowly, lifting up their feet very high behind, and drawing their hands along the soles. As they approached they frequently eyed each other from head to foot in a contemptuous manner, casting several arch looks at the spectators, straining their muscles, and using a variety of affected gestures. Being advanced within reach of each other, they stood with both arms held out straight before their faces, at which part all their blows were aimed. They struck, in what appeared to our eyes an awkward manner, with a full swing of the arm; made no attempt to parry, but eluded their adversary's attack by an inclination of the body, or by retreating. The battle was quickly decided; for if either of them was knocked down, or even fell by accident, he was considered as vanquished, and the victor expressed his triumph by a variety of gestures, which usually excited, as was intended, a loud laugh among the spectators. He then waited for a second antagonist, and if again victorious, for a third, till he was at last in his turn defeated. A singular rule observed in these combats is, that whilst any two are preparing to fight, a third person may step in, and choose either of them for his antagonist, when the other is obliged to withdraw. Sometimes three or four followed each other in this manner before the match was settled. When the combat proved longer than usual, or appeared too unequal, one of the chiefs generally stepped in, and ended it by putting a stick between the combatants. The same good humour was preserved throughout which we before so much admired in the Friendly islanders. As these games were given at our desire, we found it universally expected that we should have borne our part in them; but our people, though much pressed by the natives, turned a deaf ear to their challenge, remembering full well the blows they got at the Friendly Islands.

This day died William Watman, a seaman of the gunner's crew, an event which I mention the more particularly, as death had hitherto been very rare amongst us. He was an old man, and much respected on account of his attachment to Captain Cook. He had formerly served as a marine twenty-one years; after which he entered as a seaman on board the *Resolution* in 1772, and served with Captain Cook in his voyage towards the South Pole. On their return he was admitted into Greenwich Hospital through the captain's interest, at the same time with himself; and being resolved to follow throughout the fortunes of his benefactor, he also quitted it along with him on his being appointed to the command of the present expedition.

At the request of the king of the island he was buried on the morai, and the ceremony was performed with as much solemnity as our situation permitted. Old Kaoo and his brethren were spectators, and preserved the most profound silence and attention whilst the service was reading. When we began to fill up the grave, they approached it with great reverence, threw in a dead pig, some cocoa-nuts, and plantains; and for three nights afterwards they surrounded it, sacrificing hogs, and performing their usual ceremonies of hymns and prayers, which continued till daybreak. At the head of the grave we erected a post, and nailed upon it a square piece of board, on which was inscribed the name of the deceased, his age, and the day of his death. This they promised not to remove; and we have no doubt that it will be suffered to remain as long as the frail materials of which it is made will permit.

The ships being in great want of fuel, Captain Cook desired me, on the 2nd of February, to treat with the priests for the purchase of the rail that surrounded the top of the morai. I must confess I had at first some doubt about the decency of this proposal, and was apprehensive that even the bare mention of it might be considered by them as a piece of shocking impiety.

In this, however, I found myself mistaken; not the smallest surprise was expressed at the application, and the wood was readily given, even without stipulating for anything in return. Whilst the sailors were taking it away, I observed one of them carrying off a carved image, and on further inquiry I found that they had conveyed to the boats the whole semicircle. Though this was done in the presence of the natives, who had not shown any mark of resentment at it, but had even assisted them in the removal, I thought it proper to speak to Kaoo on the subject, who appeared very indifferent about the matter, and only desired that we would restore the centre image I have mentioned before, which he carried into one of the priests' houses.

Terreeoboo and his chiefs had for some days past been very inquisitive about the time of our departure. This circumstance had excited in me a great curiosity to know what opinion this people had formed of us, and what were their ideas respecting the cause and objects of our voyage. I took some pains to satisfy myself on these points, but could never learn anything further than that they imagined we came from some country where provisions had failed, and that our visit to them was merely for the purpose of filling our bellies. Indeed, the meagre appearance of some of our crew, the hearty appetites with which we sat down to their fresh provisions, and our great anxiety to purchase as much as we were able, led them naturally enough to such a conclusion.

We had now been sixteen days in the bay, and if our enormous consumption of hogs and vegetables be considered, it need not be wondered that they should wish to see us take our leave. It is very probable, however, that Terreeoboo had no other view in his inquiries at present than a desire of making sufficient preparation for dismissing us with presents suitable to the respect and kindness with which he had received us. For, on our telling him we should leave the island on the next day but one, we observed that a sort of proclamation was immediately made through the villages to require the people to bring in their hogs and vegetables, for the king to present to the Orono on his departure.

We were this day much diverted on the beach by the buffooneries of one of the natives. His style of dancing was entirely burlesque, and accompanied with strange grimaces and pantomimical distortions of the face, which, though at times inexpressibly ridiculous, yet on the whole was without much meaning or expression.

In the evening we were again entertained with wrestling and boxing matches, and we displayed in return the few fireworks we had left. Nothing could be better calculated to excite the admiration of these islanders, and to impress them with an idea of our great superiority, than an exhibition of this kind.

Captain Cook has already described the extraordinary effects of that which was made at Hepaee, and though the present was, in every respect, infinitely inferior, yet the astonishment of the natives was not less.

I have before mentioned that the carpenters from both ships had been sent up the country to cut planks for the head-rail work of the *Resolution*. This was the third day since their departure, and having received no intelligence from them, we began to be very anxious for their safety. We were communicating our apprehensions to old Kaoo, who appeared as much concerned as ourselves, and were concerting measures with him for sending after them, when they arrived in safety. They had been obliged to go farther into the country than was expected before they met with trees fit for their purpose; and it was this circumstance, together with the badness of the roads and the difficulty of bringing back the timber, which had detained them so long. They spoke in high terms of their guides, who both supplied them with provisions and guarded their tools with the utmost fidelity.

The next day being fixed for our departure, Terreeoboo invited Captain Cook and myself to attend him on the 3rd to the place where Kaoo resided. On our arrival we found the ground covered with parcels of cloth, a vast quantity of red and yellow feathers tied to the fibres of cocoa-nut husks, and a great number of hatchets and other pieces of ironware that had been got in barter from us. At a little distance from these lay an immense quantity of vegetables of every kind, and near them was a large herd of hogs. At first we imagined the whole to be intended as a present for us, till Kaireekeea informed me that it was a gift or tribute from the people of that district to the king; and accordingly, as we were seated, they brought all the bundles and laid them severally at Terreeoboo's feet, spreading out the cloth and displaying the feathers and ironware before him. The king seemed much pleased with this mark of their duty; and having selected about a third part of the ironware, the same proportion of feathers, and a few pieces of cloth, these were set aside by themselves, and the remainder of the cloth, together with all the hogs and vegetables, were afterwards presented to Captain Cook and myself. We were astonished at the value and magnitude of this present, which exceeded everything of the kind we had seen either at the Friendly or Society Islands. Boats were immediately sent to carry them on board; the large hogs were picked out to be salted for sea store, and upwards of thirty smaller pigs and the vegetables were divided between the two crews.

The same day we quitted the morai, and got the tents and astronomical instruments on board. The charm of the taboo was now removed, and we had no sooner left the place than the natives rushed in and searched eagerly about in expectation of finding something of value that we might have left behind. As I happened to remain the last on shore, and waited for the return of the boat, several came crowding round me, and having made me sit down by them, began to lament our separation.

It was, indeed, not without difficulty I was able to quit them. Having had the command of the party on shore during the whole time we were in the bay, I had an opportunity of becoming better acquainted with the natives, and of being better known to them, than those whose duty required them to be generally on board. As I had every reason to be satisfied with their kindness in general, so I cannot too often nor too particularly mention the unbounded and constant friendship of their priests.

On my part I spared no endeavours to conciliate their affections and gain their esteem, and I had the good fortune to succeed so far that, when the time of our departure was made known, I was strongly solicited to remain behind, not without offers of the most flattering kind. When I excused myself by saying that Captain Cook would not give his consent, they proposed that I should retire into the mountains, where they said they would conceal me till after the departure of the ships, and on my further assuring them that the captain would not leave the bay without me, Terreeoboo and Kaoo waited upon Captain Cook, whose son they supposed I was, with a formal request that I might be left behind. The captain, to avoid giving a positive refusal to an offer so kindly intended, told them that he could not part with me at that time, but that he should return to the island next year, and would then endeavour to settle the matter to their satisfaction.

Early in the morning of the 4th, we unmoored and sailed out of the bay, with the *Discovery* in company, and were followed by a great number of canoes. Captain Cook's design was to finish the survey of Owhyhee before we visited the other islands, in hopes of meeting with a road better sheltered than the bay we had just left; and in case of not succeeding here, he proposed to take a view of the south-east part of Mowee, where the natives informed us we should find an excellent harbour.

We had calm weather all this and the following day, which made our progress to the northward very slow. We were accompanied by a great number of the natives in their canoes, and Terreeoboo gave a fresh proof of his friendship to Captain Cook by a large present of hogs and vegetables that was sent after him.

In the night of the 5th, having a light breeze off the land, we made some way to the northward, and in the morning of the 6th, having passed the westernmost point of the island, we found ourselves abreast of a deep bay called by the natives Toe-yah-yah. We had great hopes that this bay would furnish us with a commodious harbour, as we saw several fine streams of water, and the whole had the appearance of being well sheltered. These observations agreeing with the accounts given us by Koah, who accompanied Captain Cook, and had changed his name out of compliment to us into Britannee, the pinnace was hoisted out, and the master, with Britannee for his guide, was sent to examine the bay whilst the ships worked up after them.

In the afternoon the weather became gloomy, and the gusts of wind that blew off the land were so violent as to make it necessary to take in all the sails and bring to under the mizzen-staysail. All the canoes left us at the beginning of the gale; and Mr. Bligh, on his return, had the satisfaction of saving an old woman and two men whose canoe had been upset by the violence of the wind, as they were endeavouring to gain the shore. Besides these distressed people, we had a great many women on board whom the natives had left behind in their hurry to shift for themselves.

The master reported to Captain Cook that he had landed at

the only village he saw, where he was directed to some wells of water, but found they would by no means answer our purpose; that he afterwards proceeded farther into the bay, which runs inland to a great depth, and stretches toward the foot of a very conspicuous high mountain, but that instead of meeting with safe anchorage, as Britannee had taught him to expect, he found the shores low and rocky, and a flat bed of coral rocks running along the coast, and extending upwards of a mile from the land; and that in the meantime Britannee had contrived to slip away, being afraid of returning, as we imagined, because his information had not proved true and successful.

In the evening, the weather being more moderate, we again made sail; but about midnight it blew so violently as to split both the fore and main topsails. On the morning of the 7th we bent fresh sails, and had fair weather and a light breeze. We were four or five leagues from the shore, and as the weather was very unsettled none of the canoes would venture out, so that our guests were obliged to remain with us, much indeed to their dissatisfaction, for they were all sea-sick, and many of them had left young children behind them.

In the afternoon, though the weather was still squally, we stood in for the land, and being about three leagues from it, we saw a canoe with two men paddling toward us, which we immediately conjectured had been driven off the shore by the late boisterous weather, and therefore stopped the ship's way in order to take them in. These poor wretches were so exhausted with fatigue that, had not one of the natives on board, observing their weakness, jumped into the canoe to their assistance, they would scarcely have been able to fasten it to the rope we had thrown out for that purpose. It was with difficulty we got them up the ship's side, together with a child about four years old, which they had lashed under the thwarts of the canoe, where it had lain with only its head above water. They told us they had left the shore the morning before, and had been from that time without food or water. The usual precautions were taken in giving them victuals, and the child being committed to the care of the women, soon perfectly recovered.

At midnight a gale of wind came on, which obliged us to

double-reef the topsails and send down the topgallant yards. On the 8th, at daybreak, we found that the foremast had given way, the fishes,* which were put on the head in King George's or Nootka Sound, on the coast of America, being sprung, and the parts so very defective as to make it absolutely necessary to replace them, and of course to unstep the mast. In this difficulty Captain Cook was for some time in doubt whether he should run the chance of meeting with a harbour in the islands to leeward or return to Karakakooa. That bay was not so remarkably commodious in any respect, but that a better might probably be expected, both for the purpose of repairing the masts and for securing supplies, of which it was imagined the neighbourhood of Karakakooa had been already pretty well drained. On the other hand, it was considered as too great a risk to leave a place that was tolerably sheltered, and which once left could not be regained, for the mere hope of meeting with a better, the failure of which might perhaps have left us without resource.

We therefore continued standing on towards the land, in order to give the natives an opportunity of releasing their friends on board from their confinement; and at noon, being within a mile of the shore, a few canoes came off to us, but so crowded with people that there was not room in them for any of our guests. We therefore hoisted out the pinnace to carry them on shore, and the master, who went with them, had directions to examine the south coasts of the bay for water, but returned without finding any.

The winds being variable, and a current setting to the northward, we made but little progress in our return, and at eight o'clock in the evening of the 9th, it began to blow very hard from the south-east, which obliged us to close-reef the topsails. At two in the morning of the 10th, in a heavy squall, we found ourselves close in with the breakers that lie to the northward of the west point of Owhyhee, and we had just room to haul off and avoid them, and fired several guns to apprise the *Discovery* of the danger.

* A fish, or fish-piece, is a long piece of hard wood, convex on one side and concave on the other; two are bound opposite to each other to strengthen the lower masts or the yards when they are sprung, to effect which they are well secured by bolts and hoops, or stout rope called woolding.

In the forenoon the weather was more moderate, and a few canoes came off to us, from which we learned that the late storms had done much mischief, and that several large canoes had been lost. During the remainder of the day we kept beating about to windward, and before night we were within a mile of the bay; but not choosing to run in while it was dark, we stood off and on till daylight next morning, when we dropped anchor nearly in the same place as before.

CHAPTER XLVIII.

SUSPICIOUS BEHAVIOUR OF THE NATIVES ON OUR RETURN TO KARAKAKOOA BAY —THEFT ON BOARD THE "DISCOVERY"—THE PINNACE ATTACKED—THE CUTTER OF THE "DISCOVERY" STOLEN—MEASURES TAKEN BY CAPTAIN COOK FOR ITS RECOVERY—NEWS ARRIVES OF ONE OF THE CHIEFS BEING KILLED BY OUR PEOPLE—FERMENT ON THIS OCCASION—ONE OF THE NATIVES THREATENS CAPTAIN COOK, AND IS SHOT BY HIM—GENERAL ATTACK BY THE NATIVES—DEATH OF CAPTAIN COOK.

UPON coming to anchor we were surprised to find our reception very different from what it had been on our first arrival—no shouts, no bustle, no confusion, but a solitary bay, with only here and there a canoe stealing close along the shore. The hospitable treatment we had invariably met with, and the friendly footing on which we parted, gave us some reason to expect that they would again have flocked about us with great joy on our return.

We were forming various conjectures when our anxiety was relieved by the return of a boat which had been sent on shore, and brought us word that the king was absent, and had left the bay under taboo. However, next morning the king, on his supposed arrival, came immediately to visit Captain Cook, and the consequent return of the natives to their former friendly intercourse with us are strong proofs that they neither meant nor apprehended any change of conduct. Things went on in their usual quiet course till the afternoon of the 13th.

Towards the evening of the 13th, the officer who commanded the watering-party of the *Discovery* came to inform me that several chiefs had assembled at the well near the beach, driving away the natives whom he had hired to assist the sailors in rolling down the casks to the shore. He told me at the same time that he thought their behaviour extremely suspicious, and that they meant to cause a disturbance. At his request, therefore, I sent a marine along with him, but suffered him to take only his side-arms. In a short time the officer returned, and on his acquainting me that the islanders had armed themselves with stones, and were grown very tumultuous, I went myself to the spot, attended by a marine with his musket. Seeing us approach, they threw away their stones, and on my speaking to some of the chiefs, the mob were driven away, and those who chose it were suffered to assist in filling the casks. Having left things quiet here, I went to meet Captain Cook, whom I saw coming on shore in the pinnace. I related to him what had just passed, and he ordered me, in case of their beginning to throw stones or behave insolently, immediately to fire a ball at the offenders. I accordingly gave orders to the corporal to have the pieces of the sentinels loaded with ball instead of small shot.

Soon after our return to the tents we were alarmed by a continued fire of muskets from the *Discovery*, which we observed to be directed at a canoe that we saw paddling towards the shore in great haste, pursued by one of our small boats. We immediately concluded that the firing was in consequence of some theft, and Captain Cook ordered me to follow him with an armed marine, and to endeavour to seize the people as they came on shore. Accordingly we ran towards the place where we supposed the canoe would land, but were too late, the people having quitted it and made their escape into the country before our arrival.

We were at this time ignorant that the goods had been already restored, and as we thought it probable, from the circumstance we had at first observed, that they might be of importance, were unwilling to relinquish our hopes of recovering them. Having therefore inquired of the natives which way the people had fled, we followed them till it was near dark, when, judging ourselves to be about three miles from the tents, and suspecting that the natives, who frequently encouraged us in the pursuit, were amusing themselves by giving us false information, we thought it in vain to continue our search, and returned to the beach.

During our absence a difference of a more serious and unpleasant nature had happened. The officer who had been sent in the small boat, and was returning on board with the goods which had been restored, observing Captain Cook and me engaged in the pursuit of the offenders, thought it his duty to seize the canoe which was left drawn up on the shore. Unfortunately this canoe belonged to Pareea, who, arriving at the same moment from on board the *Discovery*, claimed his property, with many protestations of his innocence. The officer refusing to give it up, and being joined by the crew of the pinnace, which was waiting for Captain Cook, a scuffle ensued, in which Pareea was knocked down by a violent blow on the head with an oar. The natives who were collected about the spot, and had hitherto been peaceable spectators, immediately attacked our people with such a shower of stones, as forced them to retreat with great precipitation and swim off to a rock at some distance from the shore. The pinnace was immediately ransacked by the islanders, and but for the timely interposition of Pareea, who seemed to have recovered from the blow and forgotten it at the same instant, would soon have been entirely demolished. Having driven away the crowd, he made signs to our people that they might come and take possession of the pinnace, and that he would endeavour to get back the things which had been taken out of it. After their departure he followed them in his canoe, with a midshipman's cap and some other trifling articles of the plunder, and with much apparent concern at what had happened, asked if the Orono would kill him, and whether he would permit him to come on board the next day. On being assured that he would be well received, he joined noses (as their custom is) with the officers, in token of friendship, and paddled over to the village of Kowrowa.

When Captain Cook was informed of what had passed, he expressed much uneasiness at it, and as we were returning on board, "I am afraid," said he, " that these people will oblige me to use some violent measures; for," he added, "they must not be left to imagine that they have gained an advantage over us." However, as it was too late to take any steps this evening, he contented himself with giving orders that every man and woman on board should be immediately turned out of the ship. As soon as this order was executed I returned on shore; and our former confidence in the natives being now much abated by the events of the day, I posted a double guard on the morai, with orders to call me if they saw any men lurking about the beach. At about eleven o'clock five islanders were observed creeping round the bottom of the morai; they seemed very cautious in approaching us, and at last, finding themselves discovered, retired out of sight. About midnight one of them venturing up close to the observatory, the sentinel fired over him, on which the men fled, and we passed the remainder of the night without further disturbance.

Next morning at daylight I went on board the *Resolution* for the timekeeper, and in my way was hailed by the *Discovery*, and informed that their cutter had been stolen during the night from the buoy where it was moored.

When I arrived on board I found the marines arming, and Captain Cook loading his double-barrelled gun. Whilst I was relating to him what had happened to us in the night he interrupted me with some eagerness, and acquainted me with the loss of the *Discovery's* cutter, and with the preparations he was making for its recovery. It had been his usual practice, whenever anything of consequence was lost at any of the islands in this ocean, to get the king or some of the principal Erces on board, and to keep them as hostages till it was restored. This method, which had been always attended with success, he meant to pursue on the present occasion, and at the same time had given orders to stop all the canoes that should attempt to leave the bay, with an intention of seizing and destroying them if he could not recover the cutter by peaceable means. Accordingly the boats of both ships, well manned and armed, were stationed across the bay, and before I left the ship some great guns had been fired at two large canoes that were attempting to make their escape. It was between seven and eight o'clock when we quitted the ship together; Captain Cook in the pinnace, having Mr. Phillips and nine marines with him, and myself in the small boat. The last orders I received from him were to quiet the minds of the natives on our side of the bay by assuring them they should not be hurt, to keep my people together, and to be on my guard. We then parted; the captain went towards Kowrowa, where the king resided, and I proceeded to the beach. My first care on going ashore was to give strict orders to the marines to remain within the tent, to load their pieces with ball, and not to quit their arms. Afterwards I took a walk to the huts of old Kaoo and the priests, and explained to them as well as I could the hostile preparations, which had exceedingly alarmed them. I found that they had already heard of the cutter being stolen, and I assured them that, though Captain Cook was resolved to recover it, and to punish the authors of the theft, yet that they, and the people of the village on our side, need not be under the smallest apprehension of suffering any evil from us.

I desired the priests to explain this to the people, and to tell them not to be alarmed, but to continue peaceable and quiet. Kaoo asked me with great earnestness if Terreeoboo was to be hurt? I assured him he was not, and both he and the rest of his brethren seemed much satisfied with this assurance.

In the meantime Captain Cook, having called off the launch, which was stationed at the north point of the bay, and taken it along with him, proceeded to Kowrowa, and landed with the lieutenant and nine marines. He immediately marched into the village, where he was received with the usual marks of respect, the people prostrating themselves before him, and bringing their accustomed offerings of small hogs. Finding that there was no suspicion of his design, his next step was to inquire for Terreeoboo and the two boys, his sons, who had been his constant guests on board the *Resolution*. In a short time the boys returned along with the natives who had been in search of them, and immediately led Captain Cook to the house where the king had slept. After a short conversation with him about the loss of his cutter, from which Captain Cook was convinced that he was in nowise privy to it, he invited him to return in the boat and spend the day on board the *Resolution*. To this proposal the king readily assented, and immediately got up to accompany him.

Things were in this prosperous train, the two boys being already in the pinnace, and the rest of the party having advanced near the water-side, when an elderly woman called Kanee-Kabareea, the mother of the boys and one of the king's favourite wives, came after him, and with many tears and entreaties besought him not to go on board. At the same time, two chiefs, who came along with her, laid hold of him and forced him to sit down. The natives, who were collecting in prodigious numbers along the shore, and had probably been alarmed by the firing of the great guns and the appearance of hostility in the bay, began to throng round Captain Cook and their king. In this situation, the lieutenant of marines, observing that his men were huddled close together in the crowd, and thus incapable of using their arms if any occasion should require it, proposed to the captain to draw them up along the rocks close to the water's edge, and the crowd readily making way for them to pass, they were drawn up in a line, at a distance of about thirty yards from the place where the king was sitting. All this time the old king remained on the ground, with the strongest marks of terror and dejection in his countenance. Captain Cook, not willing to abandon the object for which he had come on shore, continued to urge him in the most pressing manner to proceed; whilst on the other hand, whenever the king appeared inclined to follow him, the chiefs who stood round him interposed, at first with prayers and entreaties, but afterward with force and violence, insisting on his staying where he was. Captain Cook therefore, finding that the alarm had spread too generally, and that it was in vain to think any longer of getting the king off without bloodshed, at last gave up the point, observing to Mr. Phillips that it would be impossible to compel him to go on board without the risk of killing a great number of the inhabitants.

Though the enterprise which had carried Captain Cook on shore had now failed, and was abandoned, yet his person did not appear to have been in the least danger till an accident happened which gave a fatal turn to the affair. The boats which had been stationed across the bay having fired at some canoes that were attempting to get out, unfortunately had killed a chief of the first rank. The news of his death arrived at the village where Captain Cook was just as he had left the king and was walking slowly towards the shore. The ferment it made was very conspicuous; the women and children were immediately sent off, and the men put on their war-mats and armed themselves with spears and stones. One of the natives having in his hands a stone and a large iron spike, which they call a pahooa, came up to the captain, flourishing his weapon by way of defiance, and threatening to throw the stone. The captain desired him to desist, but the man persisting in his insolence, he was at length provoked to fire a load of small shot. The man having his mat on, which the shot were

DEATH OF CAPTAIN COOK.

unable to penetrate; this had no other effect than to irritate and encourage them. Several stones were thrown at the marines, and one of the Earees attempted to stab Mr. Phillips with his pahooa, but failed in the attempt, and received from him a blow with the butt-end of his musket. Captain Cook now fired his second barrel loaded with ball, and killed one of the foremost of the natives. A general attack with stones immediately followed, which was answered by a discharge of musketry from the marines and the people in the boats. The islanders, contrary to the expectations of every one, stood the fire with great firmness, and before the marines had time to reload, they broke in upon them with dreadful shouts and yells. What followed was a scene of the utmost horror and confusion.

Four of the marines were cut off amongst the rocks in their retreat, and fell a sacrifice to the fury of the enemy; three more were dangerously wounded, and the lieutenant, who had received a stab between the shoulders with a pahooa, having fortunately reserved his fire, shot the man who had wounded him just as he was going to repeat his blow. Our unfortunate commander, the last time he was seen distinctly, was standing at the water's edge, and calling out to the boats to cease firing and to pull in.

If it be true, as some of those who were present have imagined, that the marines and boatmen had fired without his orders, and that he was desirous of preventing any further bloodshed, it is not improbable that his humanity on this occasion proved fatal to him. For it was remarked that whilst he faced the natives none of them had offered him any violence, but having turned about to give his orders to the boats he was stabbed in the back, and fell on his face into the water. On seeing him fall the islanders set up a great shout, and his body was immediately dragged on shore and surrounded by the enemy, who, snatching the dagger out of each other's hands, showed a savage eagerness to have a share in his destruction.

Thus fell our great and excellent commander! After a life of so much distinguished and successful enterprise, his death, as far as regards himself, cannot be reckoned premature, since he lived to finish the great work for which he seemed to have been designed, and was rather removed from the enjoyment than cut off from the acquisition of glory. How sincerely his loss was felt and lamented by those who had so long found their general security in his skill and conduct, and every consolation under their hardships in his tenderness and humanity, it is neither necessary nor possible for me to describe. Much less shall I attempt to paint the horror with which we were struck, and the universal dejection and dismay which followed so dreadful and unexpected a calamity.

Nothing now remained but to perform the last offices to our great and unfortunate commander. The bones were put in a coffin, the service read over them, and they were committed to the deep with the usual military honours. What our feelings were on this occasion I leave the world to conceive.

During the 22nd, not a canoe was to be seen paddling in the bay, but later we requested that the "taboo" might be taken off, and that the people might bring presents as usual. We assured them that as "Orono" was buried, all remembrance of what had passed was buried with him. The ships were soon surrounded with canoes, and many of the chiefs came on board, expressing great sorrow at what had happened, and their satisfaction at our reconciliation. Several of our friends sent presents of large hogs. Amongst the rest came the treacherous old Koah, but he was refused admittance. Everything now being ready for sea, Captain Clerke gave orders to sail, and the voyage was continued.

INDEX.

"ADVENTURE," the ship, 193, 217, 259, 311.
Alaschka, island of, 464, 468.
Albatrosses, 26, 73.
Amsterdam, island of, 252, 256.
Anderson Island, 454.
Annamooko, reception at, 282.
Anson, Lord, 423.
Ascension, island of, 322.
Attago, a chief, 249.

BATAVIA, 186, 190.
Bay of Islands, 104.
Bird Island, 29.
Bolabola, island of, 64, 70, 401.
Bonavista, island of, 13.
Botany Bay, 128, 166.
Bream Bay, 101.
Bream Head, 101.
Butterflies, thousands of, 17.

CAPE BRET, 102, 107.
Cape Capricorn, 134.
Cape Colville, 100.
Cape Flattery, 153.
Cape Foul Weather, 424.
Cape Horn, 26, 73, 118.
Cape Kidnapper, 84.
Cape Maria Van Diemen, 105, 107.
Cape of Good Hope, 188, 196, 310.
Cape Runaway, 92.
Cape Table, 82, 86.
Cape Turnagain, 85, 94, 114, 259.
Christmas Harbour, 338.
Christmas Island, discovery of, 410.
Christmas Sound, 301.
Cobras, island of, 14.
Cook, Captain, death of, 509.

DAVIS' LAND OR EASTER ISLAND, 270, 272.
Discovery, the ship, 327, 402, 476, 501.
Dolphin, the ship, 27, 33, 40.
Doubtless Bay, 105.
Dusky Bay, 202, 210, 215.

EAST CAPE, 91.
East Island, 91.
Eatuas, inferior deities in Otaheite, 62.
E'midho, branches of a tree, 31.
Endeavour, the ship, 33, 66, 119, 180.
Esquimaux, 444, 456.

FAIR WEATHER, MOUNT, 440.
Falkland's Islands, 18.
Fayal, island of, 323.
Feenou, king of the Friendly Isles, 356, 360, 366.
First Voyage, 11-192.
Friendly Islands, 356, 376.
Funchal, 195.

GABLE-END FORELAND, 86, 89.
Great Canoe Harbour, 34.
Guanaco skin, clothing of natives, 19.

HAWKE'S BAY, 85.
Howe Island, discovery of, 281.
Huaheine, island of, 64, 69, 241.

ISLE OF GEORGIA, discovery of the, 306.

KAMTCHATKA, 466, 469, 472.
Kaneena, a chief, 481.
Kaoo, a priest, 491, 497, 506.
Karakakooa, bay of, 479, 480, 501.
Kaye's Island, 441.
Kihiargo, nearest native imitation of King George, 45.
King George III.'s Island, 31, 66, 90.
King George's Sound, 427, 432, 474.
Klumma, images of that name, 436.

LAGOON ISLAND, 28, 29.
Le Maire, strait of, 18, 26.
Lizard Island, 155.

MADEIRA, island of, 11.
Magellan, strait of, 27.
Magellanic jacket, 18.
Malama, name given to the moon in Otaheite, 63.
Mangrove River, 97
Manioe, name of the only image of its kind in Otaheite, 51.
Mareewagee, 368.
Matavai Bay, 32, 51, 238.
Matseeta, an image, 436.
Maurua, island of, 67, 69.
Mauwe, one of the eatuas, or gods of the second class, 51.
Mercury Bay, 97.
Middleburg, island of, 252, 256.
Monoe, oil for the head, 58.

INDEX.

Mories, places of worship in Otaheite, 62.
Motuara, island of, 220, 297.
Mount Camel, 105.
Mount Dromedary, 124.
Mount Edgecumbe, 93.
Moutou, island of, 72.
Mowtohora, island of, 93.

NATCHROA, an image, 436.
New Albion, 424.
New Holland, 163, 170.
New Zealand, 119, 258, 426, 436.
Norfolk Island, discovery of, 296.
North Cape, 106, 463.

OBEREA, 37, 43, 47, 52.
Oedidee, 276, 280.
Ohitepepa, 50.
Omai, a chief, 400.
Omoe, 50.
Opoony, sovereign of Bolabola, 68, 402, 406.
Oree, king of Huaheine, 64, 241, 279.
Oreo, a chief, 244, 401, 406.
Osnaburgh Island (*Maitea*), 30.
Otaba, island of, 64, 67, 68, 401.
Otaheite, 41, 54, 79, 273, 423, 484.
Otoo, a king, 238, 273, 387.
Owhaa, 33, 38.
Owharre, harbour of, 64.
Owhyhee, one of the Sandwich Islands, 473, 482, 502.
Oyster River, 97.

PAHA, a chief, 400.
Pahies, or canoes, 70.
Palmerston Island, discovery of, 281.
Pareea, a chief, 481, 505.
Peak of Bolabola, 67.
Peak of Teneriffe, 12.
Plymouth Sound, 11.
Point Rodney, 100.
Point Venus, 64.
Portland Island, native name Teahowray, 82, 85.
Port Royal, 49.
Port Royal Bay—Indian name Matavai, 50.
Poverty Bay, 80, 86.
Pyramids in burial ground, 413.

QUEEN CHARLOTTE'S SOUND, 112, 115, 119, 258, 297.

"RESOLUTION," the ship, 195, 218, 222, 235, 327, 401, 425, 448, 506.
Rio de Janeiro, 13, 14, 17.
Royal Bay, 50.

SANDWICH ISLANDS, discovered and named, 419.
Sandwich Land, discovery of, 308.
Santo Espirito, 14.
Savage Island, discovery of, 282.
Second Voyage, 193-326.
Sledge Island, 455, 464.
Society Islands—Ulietea, Otaha, Bolabola, Huaheine, Tubia, Maurua, 69, 498.
Sour krout, 32, 324.
South Sea dog, 56.
South Sea Islands, 426.
Southern Islands, 421, 423.
Staten Land, 303.
St. Elias, Mount, 440.
St. Helena, island of, 321.
Strait Le Maire, 302.
Success, bay of, 19.
Sun, eclipse of the, 373, 408.

TANE, the god of the island Otaheite, 62.
Tanna Island, reception at, 287.
Tate ete—little men, 51.
"Taboo," a word used in the Sandwich Islands, 486.
Teneriffe, 335.
Tethuroa, island of, 64.
Thames, river, 99.
Third Voyage, 327-510.
Tiarrabou, 50.
Tiata, Tupia's servant, 84.
Tierra del Fuego, 18, 25, 299.
Tituboalo, 49.
Toahoutu, island of, 67.
Tomio, 38, 45, 52.
Tomow, head-dress of natives of the island of Ulietea, 68.
Tolago, bay of, 89, 91.
Tongatabu, 368.
Tootaha, 38, 43, 49, 53, 239.
Transit of Venus, 15, 45.
Tubia, island of, 67, 69.
Tubourai Tamaide, 36, 39, 45.
Tupia, 53, 64, 70, 75, 81, 92, 105, 126, 142, 178, 183.
Turtle Island, discovery of, 283.

ULIETEA, island of, 64, 90, 244, 281, 400, 405.

VAN DIEMEN'S LAND, 124, 338.
Vincent's Bay, 19.

WHENNUAIA, island of, 67.
White Island, 92.
Wort, 32.

YORK ISLAND, 45.

THE END.

G Cook, James
420 Voyages round the world
C62S85
1897

PLEASE DO NOT REMOVE
CARDS OR SLIPS FROM THIS POCKET

UNIVERSITY OF TORONTO LIBRARY

Lightning Source UK Ltd.
Milton Keynes UK
UKHW011358181218
334174UK00009B/705/P